UNIVERSAL MESSAGE OF THE
Bhagavad Gītā

An Exposition of the Gītā in the Light of Modern Thought and Modern Needs

VOLUME 1

by

SWAMI RANGANATHANANDA

Advaita Ashrama
(PUBLICATION DEPARTMENT)
5 DEHI ENTALLY ROAD • KOLKATA 700 014

Published by
Swami Bodhasarananda
Adhyaksha, Advaita Ashrama
Mayavati, Champawat, Uttarakhand, Himalayas
from its Publication Department, Kolkata
Email: mail@advaitaashrama.org
Website: www.advaitaashrama.org

First Edition, July 2000
Seventh Reprint, October 2012
3M3C

ISBN 978-81-7505-213-0

Printed in India at
Trio Process
Kolkata 700 014

Publisher's Preface

We are happy to present before our readers the first volume of a three-volume work, *Universal Message of the Bhagavad Gītā*—a verse by verse exposition of the *Gītā* by Swami Ranganathanandaji, President of Ramakrishna Math and Ramakrishna Mission. This commentary was originally given as a series of Sunday discourses, from 1988 to 1990, at the 1200-capacity Vivekananda Hall of the Ramakrishna Math, Hyderabad, and it regularly drew an overflow audience consisting of a cross-section of the city population, including many youths.

These lectures, delivered extempore, were recorded, and the audio and video cassettes have reached many homes in various parts of India and abroad. The nature of the subject as well as its treatment by the speaker and his method of delivery, invariably held the attention and sustained the interest and enthusiasm of a large and varied audience. Packed with many stimulating and delightfully refreshing ideas, and drawing upon the works of eminent national and international poets, scientists, authors, and historians, this commentary explains the universal and humanistic teachings of *The Song Celestial*, as Edwin Arnold called the *Gītā*, in the context of modern thought and modern needs. Thus it is bound to keep the readers absorbed from beginning to end. This three-volume work on the *Gītā* also makes a wonderful companion to the Swami's *Message of the Upaniṣads*, published by Bharatiya Vidya Bhavan, Mumbai, now in its seventh edition, which contains an appendix of the Swami's correspondence with the biologist, the late Sir Julian Huxley, on the book.

In transcribing the lectures from the audio cassettes, we have received substantial help from Swami Satyapriyananda of the Ramakrishna Mission, as well as Sanskrit scholar and Vedanta Student, Miss Dana Sugu of Romania whose translations of several Upaniṣads into Romanian have been published in Bucharest. These lectures on the *Gītā* were thoroughly edited by Swami Ranganathanandaji with the help of Swami Satyapriyananda, Brahmachari Saswatachaitanya, and Swami Nischalananda. As Swami Ranganathanandaji is 91 and is in frail health, without their devoted help, the author says, this work could not have come out.

Volume one presents the first four chapters of the *Gītā*. Every effort will be made by Swami Ranganathanandaji and the Publishers, to bring out the second and third volumes expounding the remaining fourteen chapters, in due course.

Guru Purnima
16 July 2000

Publisher

CONTENTS

Publisher's Preface 3
Hints on Transliteration and Pronunciation 6
Introduction: 9

Prefatory Remarks: India's Erstwhile Misunderstanding of the *Gītā*—First English Translation of the *Gītā*—Greatness of the *Gītā* Revealed through Ādi Śaṅkara—*Gītā Dhyāna Ślokas*—Significance of *Jñānamudrā*—Meaning and Significance of *Tapas*—Ādi Śaṅkara's Introduction to his *Gītā* Commentary—Two Paths of Human Life: *Pravṛtti* and *Nivṛtti*—Two Fruits of these Paths: *Abhyudaya* and *Niḥśreyasa*—Evils Arising from the Predominance of Sensate Values—*Brāhmaṇatva*: The Goal of Human Evolution—Bhagavān Buddha on the *Brāhmaṇatva* Ideal—Vivekananda on the Divinity of Sri Ramakrishna—Indian Concept of *Śruti* and *Smṛti*—Role of a Divine Incarnation in Advancing Human Evolution—Is America on Decline and How it can be Avoided—How India has Experienced Many a Decay but Avoided Death—Cultural Decay Avoided by Cross-fertilization of Cultures—Conclusion

Chapter One 69
Chapter Two 85
Chapter Three 255
Chapter Four 355
Index 491

Hints on Transliteration and Pronunciation

In the book, Devanāgarī characters are transliterated according to the scheme adopted by the International Congress of Orientalists at Athens in 1912 and since then generally acknowledged to be the only rational and satisfactory one. In it the inconsistency, irregularity, and redundancy of English spelling are ruled out: f, q, w, x, and z are not called to use; one fixed value is given to each letter. According to this scheme

	sounds like		*sounds like*
अ	a o in son	ड	ḍ d
आ	ā in master	ढ	ḍh dh in godhood
इ	i in if	ण	ṇ n in under
ई	ī ee in feel	त	t French t
उ	u u in full	थ	th th in thumb
ऊ	ū oo in boot	द	d th in then
ऋ	ṛ somewhat between r and ri	ध	dh theh in breathe here
ए	e a in evade	न	n n
ऐ	ai y in my	प	p p
ओ	o oh	फ	ph ph in loop hole
औ	au ow in now	ब	b b
क	k k	भ	bh bh in abhor
ख	kh ckh in blockhead	म	m m
ग	g g (hard)	य	y
घ	gh gh in log-hut	र	r r
ङ	ṅ ng	ल	l l
च	c ch in chuckle	व	v in avert
छ	ch chh in catch him	श	ś sh
ज	j j	ष	ṣ sh in show
झ	jh dgeh in hedgehog	स	s s
ञ	ñ n (somewhat)	ह	h h
ट	ṭ t	ं	m ng
ठ	ṭh th in ant-hill	ः	ḥ half h

The following points may also be noted:

(1) All Sanskrit words, except when they are proper nouns, or have come into common use in English, or represent a class of literature, cult, sect, or school of thought, are italicized.

(2) Anglicized Sanskrit words like 'kārmic', 'sāmsāric', 'Arhathood', etc., are romanized.

(3) Current geographical names, except in cases where their Sanskrit forms are given, or in special cases where the context requires it, and all modern names from the commencement of the nineteenth century are given in their usual spelling and without diacritical marks.

INTRODUCTION

The Charm And Power Of The Gītā

We shall begin with a *Śāntipāṭha* or Peace Chant of the Upaniṣads:

Om Sahanāvavatu; sahanaubhunaktu;
Sahavīryam karavāvahai;
Tejasvināvadhitamastu;
Mā vidviṣāvahai;
Om śāntiḥ, śāntiḥ, śāntiḥ —

'Om, May God protect us (teacher and students) together. May we be nourished together. May we attain vigour together. May we become illumined by this study. May we not hate each other. Om, peace, peace, peace.'

Prefatory Remarks: India's Erstwhile Misunderstanding of the Gītā

We shall commence the study of the *Bhagavad Gītā* this evening. The first three chapters convey the central theme of the philosophy and spirituality of Yoga, which Śrī Kṛṣṇa refers to at the beginning of the fourth chapter. That philosophy is enriched in the remaining fourteen chapters. But the core of his original message has been expounded in chapters two and three. It is a book that is meant to be a help to realize the eternal spiritual reality within all men and women, along with the humanistic objectives which we have in our Constitution and also those which humanity is seeking in the modern age. That is why this *Gītā* message is spreading now in various parts of the world. So far as we are concerned, we have to approach this study in this modern period from a point of view different from our traditional way. In the past, people mostly read the *Gītā* as a pious act, and for a little peace of mind. We never realized that this is a book of intense practicality, that this is the greatest book of practical Vedanta capable of helping us to create a society of fully developed human beings. We never understood the practical application of the *Gītā* teachings. If we had done so, we would not have had the thousand years of foreign invasions, internal caste conflicts, feudal oppressions, and mass poverty. We never took the *Gītā* seriously; but now we have to. We need a philosophy that can help us to build a new welfare society, based on human dignity, freedom, and equality. That is what we have set before ourselves in modern India, and that is also what is inspiring all the people of the world; and here in the *Gītā* is a philosophy that will train people's minds and hearts in that direction. This orientation, a practical orientation, was given to the *Gītā* for the first time in the modern age by Swami Vivekananda. Śrī Kṛṣṇa gave it several thousand years ago as a practical philosophy, but we converted it into a mere book of piety. When we read the *Gītā Dhyāna Ślokas*—those remarkable verses on '*The Meditation Verses on the Gītā,*' we will find this idea there. The *Gītā* is compared to the milk taken out of the cow, meaning the Vedas, by Śrī Kṛṣṇa, the milkman. What is the milk for? It is not meant for worship, but it is meant to be drunk for our nourishment. Then alone can one get strength. But all these hundreds of years, we took that glass of milk, worshipped it with flowers, and saluted it, but never drank it. That is why we are feeble, physically, mentally, and socially. That will change if we now start drinking this milk and assimilate it. That will help us to develop character strength, work efficiency, and a spirit of service, and to forge a new national destiny.

Travelling in various parts of India, I noticed this widespread misunderstanding among our people. But it was forcibly brought to my mind when I was in Hyderabad for a five-day programme of lectures, just after the Police Action in 1949, during my extensive tour of Andhra Pradesh enroute to New

Delhi to take charge of the Ramakrishna Mission there. A friend suggested that I pay a visit to General J.N. Chowdhury, the Military Governor of the State. So, I went to meet him along with my friend who was my host there. General Chowdhury received us and did all the talking for the first half-an-hour and I listened. There was Communist insurrection in some parts of the state and he had to attend to the telephone quite often; but the conversation was going on. Then I noticed on his table a copy of the *Gītā*. That gave me an opportunity to do the talking. 'General Chowdhury, do you read the *Gītā?* I see the book on your table,' I asked. In a very tired way he replied, 'Of course, when I feel tired and want to find some peace of mind, I read a few lines from the *Gītā*.' I said firmly, 'That is not its purpose.' That remark took him by surprise and he asked, 'Do you mean to say that this book has other values than merely giving us a little peace of mind?' 'Yes, that book is not meant merely to give peace of mind; it is meant to give you strength to serve the people, to make you a responsible citizen. It contains a comprehensive philosophy of life and work.' He was amazed and asked me again and again, 'Do you mean to say that this book has a relevance to me as a Military Governor of this State?' I said, 'Exactly so. We must realize that men and women of action, of responsibility, have the need for a philosophy of life and action. The *Gītā* provides that philosophy calling it by the simple word, "Yoga". We never understood it till now. Take the opening verse of the fourth chapter of the *Gītā*. Śrī Kṛṣṇa tells us there: "I gave this philosophy of Yoga to men of responsibility, so that, through this philosophy, they will become strong to serve and protect the people, to nourish the people." This is the purpose of this great book.' I stressed this again and again, and he asked repeatedly, 'Can I, the Governor of this State, learn any lesson from this book to become a more efficient person?' 'Yes, that is the purpose of this book, to inspire all men and women of responsibility to work for the good of all. That is the nature of this book. It is not meant for putting you to sleep. It is meant to wake you up. It is not merely to give you peace of mind. It is to give you that tremendous humanistic impulse and resolve, to work for the good of all in society.'

He was very happy. An hour passed and I asked him, 'Have you read any book of Swami Vivekananda?' 'Yes, I have read some small books of his sayings.' I said, 'That won't do! I want you to read one particular book, his lectures in India known as *Lectures from Colombo to Almora.* These lectures awakened our nation and threw up great patriots who fought for the freedom of our nation. Man-making and nation-building is its theme. I shall send to you from Delhi a copy of it with my autograph, provided you promise to read it. I do not want to waste a book.' 'Yes, I shall read it,' he said. Then I took leave of him. The next day, I went to Delhi and from there I sent him that book, and he wrote to me a nice letter of thanks. Later on, when he was our High Commissioner in Canada, he took my permission to publish, in French, the first lecture *Essence of Indian Culture* from the first volume of my book *Eternal Values for a Changing Society,* for spreading among the French citizens of Canada, a knowledge of Indian culture.

From this experience I understood that millions of people in India treat the *Gītā* like any of the *stotras* or hymns which we read every morning as a pious act. Today we need a philosophy to guide our footsteps, so that we can meet the challenges of developing the immense manhood and womanhood of India. It is that philosophy and spirituality that we get in the *Gītā.* The message of the *Gītā* was given on the tumultuous battlefield of Kurukṣetra a few thousand years ago. The *Gītā* alone represents such a philosophy. All other teachings were given in a temple, or a cave, or a forest. Here the student and teacher, Arjuna and Śrī Kṛṣṇa, were remarkable personalities; they were warriors. And the teacher, Śrī Kṛṣṇa, was a man full of compassion, and endowed with universal vision. The *Gītā* is thus a heroic message from a heroic teacher to a heroic pupil. Its universality makes it applicable to any human being anywhere in the world, to make him or her realize one's fullest human possibilities. The

Upaniṣads or the Vedanta expounded the science of human possibilities a thousand years earlier, and the *Gītā* expounds the practical application of that science. Hence, Swami Vivekananda considered the *Gītā* as the best book of practical Vedanta.

THE FIRST ENGLISH TRANSLATION OF THE GĪTĀ

The *Gītā* was first translated into English by Sir Charles Wilkins and published by the British East India Company with an Introduction by Warren Hastings, the first British Governor-general of India, in which we find the following prophetic sentence:

'The writers of the Indian philosophies will survive when the British Dominion in India shall long have ceased to exist, and when the sources which it yielded of wealth and power are lost to remembrance.'

A century later, another beautiful rendering of the *Gītā* in English appeared, namely, *The Song Celestial* by Sir Edwin Arnold (1832–1904). He had learnt the Sanskrit language while he was working in India; in Pune and other places. He developed a great love for Indian culture, and after he went to England, he produced this outstanding book and another equally outstanding book about Buddha, namely, *The Light of Asia.* Both have gone through more than fifty to sixty editions. Both go straight to the heart of the reader.

The *Bhagavad Gītā* deals with human problems in a human way. That is why it has a tremendous appeal. It has inspired the human mind in India for centuries and centuries, and today, it is inspiring millions of people in various parts of the world. It is interesting to see that in all these countries, after reading the *Gītā,* people find their whole outlook changed. Thinkers and writers like Emerson, Walt Whitman, and Thoreau in U.S.A, and Carlyle in England, experienced this broadening and deepening of their outlook after studying the *Gītā,* and their writings also began to convey a new message.

GREATNESS OF THE GĪTĀ REVEALED THROUGH ĀDI ŚAṄKARA

In the modern period, the *Gītā* has the whole world as its empire. In the beginning, it was known only in India, not even in the whole of India, but known only to a few Sanskrit scholars. For the first time, in the 8th century AD, this book was taken out of that mighty epic, *The Mahābhārata,* by Śaṅkarācārya, who wrote a great commentary in Sanskrit on it and placed it before the people. Till then it had been lost in the *Bhīṣma Parva* of the mighty epic. Swami Vivekananda expressed great appreciation for this great work of Śaṅkarācārya. To quote his own words from his lecture on 'Vedanta in All Its Phases' (*The Complete Works of Swami Vivekananda,* vol. III, p. 328):

'The great glory of Śaṅkarācārya was his preaching of the *Gītā*. It is one of the greatest works that this great man did among the many noble works of his noble life—the preaching of the *Gītā*, and writing the most beautiful commentary upon it. And he has been followed by all founders of the orthodox sects in India, each of whom has written a commentary on the *Gītā*.'

Even then, it was still limited to a few scholars and saints. Later, others wrote commentaries and slowly the book entered into our national languages; *Jñāneśvarī* in Marathi, by the saint Jñāneśvar, a few centuries after Śaṅkarācārya. In the modern period, Lokamanya Tilak wrote his great book, *The Gītā Rahasya,* in two volumes. He wrote it when the British Government had imprisoned him for a few years in Mandalay jail in Burma. He had no books to consult with, but wrote from his memory. That is a remarkable book; many other books have come out since then, and the *Gītā* today is very popular all over India and in many parts of the world. Many editions in world languages are also coming out; and, as soon as the books are out, they are sold out. So, we are living in an age that indeed is being shaped gently by this great book. Its message is universal, practical, strengthening, and purifying. The great Upaniṣads, which expound a science of human resources, a great science of human possibilities, have found their practical orientation in the *Gītā*. We have to study this book from that point of view, as a science of human development and fulfilment. The metre of the 700 verses is also very simple, the usual metre of eight letters in one line, called *anuṣṭup,* though occasionally we come across longer metres also.

GĪTĀ DHYĀNA ŚLOKAS

The *Gītā* is extremely simple, and many of its ideas are found in the rest of the *Mahābhārata* also. When we had its *Śānti Parva* lectures here in Hyderabad two or three years ago, you may have noticed how many ideas are common between the *Śānti Parva* and the *Gītā*. This is a development that took place after the Vedic period; it is an attempt to work out the practical implications of the philosophy of the Upaniṣads to human problems. For that, this great teacher, Śrī Kṛṣṇa, came, who was himself very practical. He lived a life of intense activity, had a universal heart and mind, and gave this philosophy of Vedanta in that practical form through the *Bhagavad Gītā.* We shall study this book verse by verse. There are 700 verses in its 18 chapters, full of beautiful ideas, so relevant to the times in which we are living. It does not give you a few dogmas, which you are not allowed to question. It invites all to question its teachings and then only follow them. Śrī Kṛṣṇa expounds his original philosophy of life for all people who are at work. Generally, before commencing the study of the text, we study what are called *Gītā Dhyāna Ślokas,* 'the nine Meditation Verses on the *Gītā*.' They are current all over India, and now, in foreign countries also. We don't know who composed them. Some people believe it was Śrīdhara Swami, a commentator on the *Gītā* and on the *Śrīmad Bhāgavatam,* who lived about three or four centuries ago. The *Gītā Dhyāna Ślokas* refer to the *Gītā,* to Vyāsa, the author of the *Mahābhārata,* and to Śrī Kṛṣṇa.

So, today I shall share with you these wonderful verses giving the English meaning of the original text. They begin with a statement about the *Gītā*:

Om Pārthāya pratibodhitām bhagavatā nārāyaṇena svayam
vyāsena grathitām purāṇa muninā madhye mahābhāratam;
Advaitāmṛtavarṣiṇīm bhagavatīm aṣṭādaśādhyāyinīm
amba tvām anusandadhāmi bhagavadgīte bhavadveṣiṇīm — 1.

'Om! O *Bhagavad Gītā,* with which Pārtha (Arjuna) was enlightened by the Lord Nārāyaṇa Himself and which was incorporated in the *Mahābhārata* by the ancient sage Vyāsa,— the Blessed Mother, the destroyer of rebirth, showering down the nectar of Advaita (philosophy of non-duality), and consisting of eighteen chapters—upon Thee, O *Bhagavad Gītā!* O loving Mother! I constantly meditate.'

That is the first verse, which addresses the *Gītā* as Mother. Mahatma Gandhi has said '*Gītā* has been my mother. I lost my mother when I was young, but I never felt the absence of a mother because I had the *Gītā* with me.' Here is the second verse:

Namo'stu te vyāsa viśāla-buddheḥ
phullāravindāyata-patra-netra;
Yena tvayā bhārata-taila-pūrṇaḥ
prajvālito jñānamayaḥ pradīpaḥ — 2.

'Salutation to Thee, O Vyāsa, of mighty intellect and with eyes large like the petals of full-blown lotus, by whom was lit the lamp of wisdom, full of the *Mahābhārata* oil.'

Prapanna pārijātāya totra-vetraika-pāṇaye;
Jñāna-mudrāya kṛṣṇāya gītāmṛta-duhe namaḥ — 3.

'Salutation to Kṛṣṇa, with (the right hand held in) *Jñāna mudrā,* the granter of desires of those who take refuge in Him, the milker of the *Gītā* nectar, in whose one hand is the cane for driving the cows.'

SIGNIFICANCE OF JÑĀNA-MUDRĀ

The verse describes Śrī Kṛṣṇa with his right hand held in *Jñāna mudrā.* This is a remarkable concept in Indian Vedantic philosophy and spirituality. It holds that there is a deep significance for this particular *Jñāna mudrā,* knowledge pose, when the thumb is opposed to the forefinger and all the three fingers are stretched out. Our body postures have psychological counterparts; as the mind is, so is the body. You are lying down in a particular way; that will show a certain state of your mind. You sit in a particular way; you will find your psyche manifesting in that posture in a particular way. Suppose one constantly shakes one's legs while sitting, that shows a scattered mental state. In all these matters, the body shows the effect of the psyche. So, from that point of view, *Jñāna mudrā* is a remarkable sign of some profound psychic expression. The very name shows that, that *mudrā* represents *Jñāna,* knowledge—knowledge of every type; from the ordinary or secular knowledge to the highest spiritual knowledge. We, in India, never made any wide distinction between secular knowledge and sacred knowledge. To us all knowledge is sacred. Remember that there is only one Goddess, Sarasvatī, who represents all knowledge and techniques. Unity of all knowledge is a profound idea in our Indian tradition. We may create different departments of knowledge for purposes of study; but we should not break up the unity of knowledge. That is our teaching in India. So we have this idea that knowledge is the greatest thing to be sought after—*Vidyā dhanam sarvadhana pradhānam,* 'the wealth of knowledge is supreme among all forms of wealth'. There is nothing in this world so purifying as knowledge, says the *Gītā* (4: 38): *'Nahi jñānena sadṛśam pavitram iha vidyate'*. That is the motto of one of our universities, namely, the Mysore University.

A human being is human because he has the organic capacity to seek knowledge; no animal can seek knowledge. Animals have only an instinctual apparatus within, and are completely controlled by the genetic system. The human being, however, has been put on the road of making research into the world of knowledge. That world of knowledge may be secular or spiritual, but all knowledge is sacred to us in India. We start with the secular, and continue the search to the spiritual.

Now, how to represent this search for knowledge through a particular posture? Our ancient sages discovered this wonderful *mudrā* which can describe the entire gamut of this search for knowledge; that is something extraordinary. I used to wonder about it. Later on, some years ago, when I studied biology, neurology, and allied subjects, I found one wonderful truth and that is, no animal, not even a chimpanzee, can oppose the thumb to the forefinger, but only the human child can do this. While in Holland, I saw in a film on chimpanzee's behaviour; a chimpanzee holding a branch from a tree with his palm enclosing all the fingers, and beating it on the ground to drive an enemy. When you hold a branch like that, the grip has no strength, and one cannot impart energy to the use of that branch until the thumb comes prominently into operation. In all animals, the thumb does not know how to co-operate with the other fingers, particularly with the forefinger.

However, at the human level of evolution, for the first time, the human being learned to oppose the thumb to the forefinger. That is the beginning of humanity's technical efficiency, his or her capacity to handle tools, his capacity to manipulate the world around him, and acquire knowledge. The human being entered into the world of *jñāna* or knowledge, with this initial physical capacity. That is why this opposing of the thumb to the forefinger is highly symbolic of man's search for knowledge from the most ordinary to the most extraordinary levels. I found this perfectly valid from the scientific point of view. Then I also found that the number of brain cells needed to manipulate these two fingers is the largest compared to all other fingers. If the thumb is cut off, the manipulating efficiency of the hand will suffer automatically. In the *Mahābhārata,* we read of Droṇa, the teacher of archery, asking Ekalavya to cut off his thumb and offer it to him as his guru-dakśiṇa or offering to the guru, so that he does not successfully compete with his favourite student, Arjuna; and Ekalavya obeyed that command of Droṇa whom he respected as his own teacher. The British rulers of India are said to have cut off the thumbs of our Dacca weavers, who wove fine Dacca muslin, so that they may not compete with their own Lancashire weavers.

The importance of the thumb and the capacity to oppose it to the forefinger, is the beginning of man's march to knowledge, secular and spiritual. There is no distinction between secular and spiritual so far as knowledge is concerned; all knowledge is sacred. On the Sarasvatī Pūjā day, you find all instruments of knowledge placed before Sarasvatī. In my childhood, every year, I used to join the worship of Sarasvatī in my home. I saw carpenters' tools, doctors' medical instruments, and all types of holy books being kept before Sarasvatī, also called *Vāṇī*, 'speech'. She represents the unity of all knowledge. She is a wonderful, austere goddess, so inspiring to the human mind. So long as we worshipped Sarasvatī in the true spirit, our land was devoted to knowledge. But when we left Sarasvatī, and ran after Lakṣmī, the goddess of wealth, both Lakṣmī and Sarasvatī, both wealth and knowledge, vanished from India. Today we have to bring both of them back to our country, first Sarasvatī, then Lakṣmī. Lakṣmī is the product of Sarasvatī.

The more knowledge you have, the more wealth you can create; except through efficient work inspired by knowledge, there is no other way to gain wealth. You cannot create wealth by magic and mystery. That lesson we have to learn today. Sarasvatī is primary, and Lakṣmī is a by-product of Sarasvatī. This knowledge must come so that poverty will be eliminated in India. Pure science is Sarasvatī, and applied science is Lakṣmī. Knowledge applied to agriculture improves the wealth of the nation; so also industry. Everywhere these two austere goddesses reign, but we in India have to re-learn how to truly worship them. Merely making *ārati*, waving of light, before their picture is not the way to worship them. Go to the university, study various books, think for yourself—that is how you become students of Sarasvatī. And, hard work, teamwork, trying to improve efficiency—that is how we have to worship Lakṣmī. *Ārati* we can do once a year, but everyday we have to worship Lakṣmī only through this kind of hard work. Then alone Lakṣmī *kaṭākṣa* or grace will come to us.

Therefore, in this modern age, the ideal is *jñāna,* and everyone is to be on the road to knowledge. Nature has given human being the capacity to oppose the thumb to the forefinger, and thus manipulate the world around him or her, and acquire knowledge and power. This is the beginning of human evolution. In the description of Śrī Kṛṣṇa, this wonderful expression is there; *jñāna mudrāya kṛṣṇāya.* In all the iconography of India, of great saints, sages, incarnations, and of the Divine Mother, you will find this particular pose of *jñāna mudrā.* It is especially seen in depicting Śiva as Dakṣiṇāmūrti. By this *jñāna mudrā,* he is able to remove the doubts of students around him. This is the tradition coming down to us from very ancient times and we should apply the essence of this tradition to deal with our own present-day problems. The whole land must become dedicated to knowledge and knowledge-seeking.

MEANING AND SIGNIFICANCE OF TAPAS

The Western people showed tremendous love for knowledge by which they created modern civilization. Hours and hours of research, no time for going to clubs, no time even for regular eating and drinking, that is the type of work people did for two centuries out of which have come the great modern scientific knowledge, technique, and wealth. We had the same tendency in India ages ago, tremendous love for knowledge. A man in the south hears that there is a teacher in far away Benares; and he starts walking to Benares—'I must study under that teacher'. Students walked from other parts of India to Taxila in West Punjab (now in Pakistan) to study medicine and surgery from reputed teachers like Caraka and Ṣuṣruta. Wherever there is real love for knowledge, nobody will mind a little inconvenience on the way. Knowledge-seeking is a *tapas,* austerity. Without *tapas* there is no knowledge. *Tapas* and knowledge go together. *Bahavo jñāna-tapasā pūtā,* Śrī Kṛṣṇa will say later on in the *Gītā* (4. 10), 'many purified in the *tapas* of *jñāna*'. If our whole nation becomes inspired by the concept of *jñāna-tapas,* there will be tremendous advances in our national life. Without *tapas,* merely sitting in an easy chair, you are not going to get any knowledge. You have to pay for it by effort and struggle, that is called *tapas. Tapas* is a great word in our culture. It occurs often in the Upaniṣads and the *Gītā*. Quoting a verse from the *Yājñavalkya Smṛti,* Śaṅkarācārya defines this wonderful word in his commentary on the *Taittirīya Upaniṣad* statement: *tapasā brahma vijijñāsasva,* 'realize Brahman through *tapas*'; *manasaśca indriyāṇām ca aikāgryam tapa ucyate,* 'the concentration of the energies of the mind and the sense organs is called *tapas*', and that definition you can give to any and every search for knowledge in this world. That is what the scientists do—they train their minds in scientific methods and attitudes; with that they are able to penetrate into the heart of nature and lay bare the truths zealously guarded by nature for ages and ages. So also, the Atman is hidden in this world of *Māyā*. Our Vedic sages penetrated this *Māyā* and discovered the infinite and immortal reality, the Atman, behind this ever-changing world of *Māyā*.

All our students must keep before themselves this definition of *tapas* before they enter a school or college. At a school or college or university, one cannot get knowledge without a good deal of serious effort. If you take away *tapas,* knowledge-seeking becomes cheap and that is what has happened to our education today; when you go to knowledge-seeking centres like universities, you do not find the *tapas* attitude and atmosphere; everything is easy-going, except for a few, who still keep the fire of *tapas* burning all the time. *Tapas* and *svādhyāya* go together in our culture. *Svādhyāya* means study. The *Rāmāyaṇa* of Vālmiki begins with the words: *tapaḥ svādhyāya niratam nāradam,* 'Nārada who was constantly engaged in *tapas* and *svādhyāya.*' So, this is the concept of *jñānamudrā* behind which lie *tapas* and *svādhyāya.* So, the verse says *jñānamudrāya kṛṣṇāya,* '(we salute) Kṛṣṇa who has this *jñāna-mudrā'*; and the verse further says *Gītāmṛta duhe,* 'who has milked the nectar of the *Gītā* (from the cow of the Upaniṣads).' That latter description will come fully in the next verse. *Duhe* in Sanskrit means one who milks a cow; *dugdham* means milk; *duhitā* means daughter who used to milk the cows in ancient *Āryan* households. From that Sanskrit word comes the Russian or Slav word 'doch' for daughter, 'tochter' in German and daughter in English.

> *Sarvopaniṣado gāvo dogdhā gopālanandanaḥ;*
> *Pārtho vatsaḥ sudhīḥ bhoktā dugdham gītāmṛtam mahat*—4.

'All the Upaniṣads are the cow; the milkman is the cowherd boy (Śrī Kṛṣṇa); Pārtha, or Arjuna, is the calf; men and women of purified intellect are the drinkers; and the supreme nectar, *Gītā,* is the milk.'

This is a famous verse popular all over India. The *Gītā* is described as the essence of the Upaniṣads. Then comes a tribute to Śrī Kṛṣṇa in the next verse:

> *Vasudeva sutam devam kamsa-cāṇūra-mardanam;*
> *Devakī-paramānandam kṛṣṇam vande jagad-gurum* — 5.

'The divine son of Vasudeva, the destroyer of (the evil doers) Kamsa and Cāṇūra, the supreme bliss of (mother) Devakī — I salute that Kṛṣṇa, the guru of the world.'

Śrī Kṛṣṇa did not come to the earth to teach an ethnic group or nation or race. He came for all humanity, and that is what the verse says *Kṛṣṇam vande jagad-gurum*. The next verse is a big one, full of imageries:

> *Bhīṣmadroṇa-taṭā jayadrathajalā gāndhāranīlotpalā*
> *śalyagrāhavatī kṛpeṇa vahanī karṇena velākulā;*
> *Aśvatthāma-vikarṇa-ghoramakarā duryodhanāvartinī*
> *sottīrṇā khalu pāṇḍavai raṇanadī kaivartakaḥ keśavaḥ* — 6.

'The battle river, with Bhīṣma and Droṇa as its banks, Jayadratha as its waters, the king of Gāndhāra as the blue water lilies, Śalya as the shark, Kṛpa as its current, Karṇa as its breakers, Aśvatthāmā and Vikarṇa as its terrible crocodiles, and

Duryodhana as the whirlpool in it — was indeed crossed over by the Pāṇḍavas, with Keśava (Śrī Kṛṣṇa) as the ferry-man.'

Then comes the next verse:

Pārāśaryavacaḥsarojamamalam gītārthagandhotkaṭam
nānākhyānakakesaram harikathāsambodhanābodhitam;
Loke sajjanaṣaṭpadaiḥ aharahaḥ pepīyamānam mudā
bhūyāt bhāratapaṅkajam kalimalapradhvamsi naḥ śreyase—7.

'May the taintless lotus of the *Mahābhārata,* growing on the waters of the words of Parāśara's son (Vyāsa), having the *Gītā* as its strong sweet fragrance, with many a narrative as its stamens, fully opened by the discourses on Hari (the Supreme Divinity), and drunk joyously day after day by the bees of the good and the pure in the world—be productive of the supreme good to him or her who is eager to destroy the taint of *Kali Yuga* (evil age).'

The next verse is about Śrī Kṛṣṇa's grace. It is also a very famous verse:

Mūkam karoti vācālam paṅgum laṅghayate girim;
Yatkṛpā tamaham vande paramānandamādhavam — 8.

'I salute that all-blissful Mādhava (Śrī Kṛṣṇa) whose grace makes the dumb eloquent and the cripple cross mountains.'

Many saints and sages in India have used this verse again and again to express the power of Divine Grace. Sri Ramakrishna tells us that divine grace is like the wind that is blowing all the time, only your boat is not going onward because you have not unfurled your sails. Unfurl your sails, then you will catch the wind and move forward. That much work we have to do to experience grace.

Next comes the last verse, often recited by our people:

Yam brahmā varuṇendrarudramarutaḥ stunvanti divyai stavaiḥ
vedaiḥ sāṅgapadakramopaniṣadaiḥ gāyanti yam sāmagāḥ;
Dhyānāvasthitatadgatena manasā paśyanti yam yogino
yasyāntam na viduḥ surāsuraganā devāya tasmai namaḥ—9.

'Salutation to that Divine Being whom Brahma, Varuṇa, Indra, Rudra, and the Maruts praise with divine hymns,

Whom the singers of *Sāma* sing by the Vedas, with their full complement of parts, consecutive sections, and Upaniṣads, Whom the yogīs see with their minds absorbed in Him through perfection in meditation, and Whose limit the hosts of *Devas* and *Asuras* know not.'

ĀDI ŚAṄKARĀCĀRYA'S INTRODUCTION TO HIS GĪTĀ COMMENTARY

It was Śaṅkarācārya, as I have said earlier, who discovered the importance of the Gītā and preached it to the people by writing a commentary on it. He lived between 788 and 820 AD. He was an extraordinary creative personality who embodied in his person the full spirit of Indian Culture and philosophy and spirituality. He travelled on foot from south to north and from west to east of India, and wrote many scholarly and popular Vedantic books, and put his stamp on the spiritual and cultural unity of India. And, all this he did in his brief life of 32 years.

We shall study the major part of his two-page Introduction to his *Gītā* commentary, which expounds a comprehensive view of human development. I wish every reader who loves the *Gītā* studies this two-page Introduction and appreciates it, impressed by its universality. The *Gītā* does not cut up life into the secular and the sacred, but takes a unified view of human life and human destiny. We shall therefore study the more important portion of this Introduction today.

In his Introduction, Śaṅkara first quotes a *Paurāṇic* verse, whose echo is found in modern western cosmology in part, dealing with the nature of the Divine:

Nārāyaṇaḥ paro avyaktāt aṇḍamavyaktasambhavam;
Aṇḍasyāntastvime lokāḥ saptadvīpā ca medinī —

'Nārāyaṇa (the Supreme Divine Being) is beyond the *avyakta* (undifferentiated Nature), the Cosmic Egg has come out of the *avyakta;* within the Cosmic Egg are these universes including the earth with its seven island-continents.'

India's cosmology, not only very similar in some respects to modern Western astronomy, but also richer than it, finds expression in this verse; except that India treats the sacred source of the universe as spiritual whereas modern Western astronomy treats it as material, though some Western cosmologists like Fred Hoyle of England are trying to transform it into the spiritual. Fred Hoyle had written a book on cosmology over forty years ago which was fully materialistic. Now he has written a new book where the very title has a spiritual orientation: *The Intelligent Universe.* The universe is intelligent; it is the same as what Vedanta calls it—Infinite, non-dual Consciousness.

So here we have in this first verse, Nārāyaṇa, which has no corresponding concept in Western astronomy; but the next stage, *avyakta,* the undifferentiated state, can find its equivalent in modern Western astronomy as the state of singularity. Nārāyaṇa, that supreme Divine Personality, is invoked as beyond the undifferentiated nature. Nature, Vedanta says, has two dimensions, the differentiated and the undifferentiated. Differentiated is what you see as this manifested universe; and behind it, there is the *avyakta,* i.e., Nature in its undifferentiated state, the state just before the Big Bang of Western astronomy. From the *avyakta* comes the *vyakta,* the manifested, what the verse calls the *Brahmāṇḍa,* the Cosmic Egg, containing these millions of universes, including the earth with its seven continents. God, the Supreme Primordial Reality, is called *ananta koṭi brahmāṇḍa nāyaka,* 'the Master of millions of universes' by Vedanta. India had the vision of infinite time and space, unlike the very limited view of time and space of Semitic thought, but similar to modern Western astronomical views. Vedanta says that the whole *Brahmāṇḍa* has come from Brahman, exists in Brahman, and gets dissolved into Brahman at the end of a cosmic cycle; and it has come from Brahman in a particularly orderly fashion, from an undifferentiated state to a differentiated state; and this differentiation follows a certain evolutionary sequence; cosmic evolution, organic evolution, human—ethical, moral, and spiritual—evolution. That is the language used in Vedantic cosmology. As the *Viṣṇusahasranāma* sings (*Mahābhārata, Anuśāsana Parva*):

Yataḥ sarvāṇi bhūtāni bhavanti ādi yugāgame;
Yasminśca pralayam yānti punareva yugakṣaye —

'From where all the beings come out at the beginning of a Yuga, or Cosmic Cycle, and in which all are dissolved at the end of a Yuga'—that is Nārāyaṇa.

The Divine Nārāyaṇa is the personal aspect of the Impersonal-Personal Brahman, which is of the nature of Infinite Pure Consciousness, one and non-dual.

TWO PATHS OF HUMAN LIFE: *PRAVṚTTI AND NIVṚTTI*

Having said this, Śaṅkara gives a comprehensive philosophy of life at the human stage of evolution with a view to making human society move on an even keel:

Sa bhagavān sṛṣṭvedam jagat, tasya ca sthitim cikīrṣuḥ, marīcyādīn agre śṛṣṭvā prajāpatīn, pravṛttilakṣaṇam dharmam grāhayāmāsa vedoktam—

'That Blessed Lord, having projected this universe (from within Himself), desirous of its maintenance in good order, projecting *Prajāpatis* like Marīci and others, in the beginning, imparted to them the Vedic message of *pravṛtti* or action.'

Tataḥ anyān ca sanaksanandanādīn utpādya, nivṛttilakṣaṇam dharmam jñānavairāgyalakṣaṇam grāhayāmāsa—

'And, projecting also others like Sanaka, Sanandana, and (Sanātana and Sanatkumār), imparted to them the philosophy characterized by *nivṛtti* or inward meditation, characterized by spiritual knowledge and renunciation.'

Sanaka, Sanandana, Sanātana, and Sanatkumāra are called the four *Kumāras,* Eternal Children of the Spirit, who are honoured in Indian literature as children of the Supreme Divine, untouched by worldliness.

Dvividho hi vedokto dharmaḥ—pravṛttilakṣaṇo, nivṛttilakṣaṇaśca, jagataḥ sthitikāraṇam. Prāṇinām sākṣāt-abhyudaya-niḥśreyasa-hetuḥ —

'The *dharma* or philosophy taught in the Vedas is of a two-fold nature, characterized by *pravṛtti,* outward action, and *nivṛtti,* inward contemplation, meant for the even stability of the world, which are meant to ensure the true *abhyudaya,* socio-economic welfare, and *niḥśreyasa,* spiritual freedom, of all beings.'

Both action and meditation are needed for human well-being; if only one or the other is there, there will be no health, individual or social. See the wonderful insight, the comprehensive wisdom of the ancient Indian sages! Through *pravṛtti* you establish a welfare society through the improvement of your economy and the political system. Through *nivṛtti* you achieve, what we call today, a value-oriented life that comes from humanity's inner spiritual dimension. Otherwise, plenty of wealth, power, and everything else you may have through *pravṛtti,* but with only *pravṛtti* and no *nivṛtti,* society will be all right in the short run, but in the long run, it will be in trouble. The whole of modern Western civilization today is in trouble because there is no emphasis on *nivṛtti,* there is emphasis only on *pravṛtti*—work, work, and work; earn more and more money, but remain inwardly poorer and poorer, until one becomes a nervous wreck. Many people are suffering thus in the modern world. I often quote the German philosopher Schopenhauer from his book, *The World as Will and Idea;* mind you, he told this about 130 years ago and what he said then is absolutely true today. He said: 'When men achieve security and welfare, now that they have solved all other problems, they become a problem to themselves.'

How literally true is this for men and women in this modern age! Even in our own country, there is the endless pursuit of money, power, and pleasure; and the result is the creation of widespread value erosion and increasing violence. That is not the way to maintain a healthy human society. The second element, *nivṛtti,* is lacking. So Śaṅkara says *Prāṇinām sākṣāt abhyudaya-niḥśreyasa-hetuḥ,* 'a philosophy of life which integrates social welfare and spiritual freedom', through action and meditation. There is one point to be mentioned in this context. *Udaya* after *abhi* means welfare; *abhi* means together, not alone; it is an important prefix added to this particular expression; that means, that no socio-economic development can come without co-operative endeavour; there is need for co-ordination, team spirit, to create a healthy society. If each one fights against the other, there will be no prosperity. Social peace is absolutely essential, co-operation is essential, teamwork is essential; all that is emphasized by that one word *abhi*. That is the one value which we have not assimilated enough in our society in India in recent centuries. Today we have to learn that lesson; we have to develop public spirit. All our villages can become heavens tomorrow, if our people know how to work together. We have not learnt it yet, and so our co-operative societies often fail. If there is no co-operative spirit, how can we make a success of our co-operative movement?

TWO FRUITS OF THESE PATHS: *ABHYUDAYA AND NIḤŚREYASA*

Thus the word *abhi* added to *udaya* is very important; it emphasizes togetherness. We have to learn how to deal with our neighbours in our villages; let me make peace with them and we shall together improve our villages: improvement of sanitation, good roads, better housing, and all people properly fed and educated—all these we can achieve only by working together. That is the way to make our Pañcāyats and municipalities healthy. That is the way we can bring a new healthy India to life. So, this philosophy of *abhyudaya* is important; the West has achieved it to a large extent; and we can learn from the West how to work it out in our country. Three values we have to bring into our life and work: hard work, efficient work, and co-operative work. Śaṅkarācārya says that this Vedic philosophy, with its twofold ideology of *pravṛtti* and *nivṛtti*, makes for the *abhyudaya* of men and women on the one side, and *niḥśreyasa* on the other. This is what we speak of concerning a full welfare state today; there is nothing utopian about it; many societies have achieved *abhyudaya* today; and we also can achieve it in India, provided we develop what is called character efficiency. As Jesus said, 'if you cannot love Me whom you have seen, how can you love God whom you have not seen?' Our people must learn that one great lesson. We have been most interested in relating ourselves to a far away God, or to an image of God in a temple, than to the man in our neighbourhood, with whom we more often pick up a quarrel. This has to change, and that change is what brings about *abhyudaya.* Then comes *niḥśreyasa.* You may achieve all the comforts of life—house, education, clean surroundings, economic strength, and varieties of pleasures. Yet there will be no peace of mind; life will be full of tension. Why? Because you have missed one thing; you have not known your true Self, the spark of innate divinity; your centre of gravity is always outside. You miss your true dignity and have become a slave of things. Out of that comes inner tensions; crime and delinquency increase in society and slowly decay sets in.

This can be avoided when we add that second value to human life, namely, *nivṛtti,* meditation, through which one comes in touch with the ever-present Divine within. This is not a dogma or mere belief, but a truth realized through the science of spirituality by the sages of the Upaniṣads; a truth to be realized by every one and not just believed in. And the more inward you go, the more you become capable of penetrating into other human beings, establishing happy relations with them. When you go deeper into your inner nature, you go beyond the tiny ego controlled by the genetic system, and come in contact with the larger Self which is the Self of all.

Thus, this combination of *pravṛtti* and *nivṛtti,* of *abhyudaya* and *niḥśreyasa,* is the great teaching of the *Gītā.* It contains a philosophy to make for total human development. That is the speciality of this great book. So, Śaṅkarācārya said, '*Prāṇinām sākṣāt abhyudaya niḥśreyasa hetuḥ*'. He did not say that it is only for Hindus, or only for the people of India, but *prāṇinām,* 'for all human beings'. That is its universality. By adding *niḥśreyasa* to *abhyudaya,* the *Gītā* prevents human beings from becoming reduced to mere machines. In modern Western civilization there is that tendency. Bertrand Russell says in his book *Impact of Science on Society,* that if this mechanization of men and women goes too far, the time will come when a workman will go to the factory, with a flower in his hand and placing it before a huge machine, will pray: 'O machine, make me a good nut and bolt in your system!' That is called mechanization of man. If the second value emphasized by Śaṅkarācārya, namely, *niḥśreyasa,* is given due attention, spiritual values will manifest and then such a problem will never arise. *Abhyudaya* and *niḥśreyasa* together constitute the means for the maintenance of this world on an even keel. Stress one and neglect the other, it will tilt to one side or the other, like a boat. India in recent centuries tilted to *niḥśreyasa* side, and that too not properly, and neglected *abhyudaya* side and suffered stagnation from which it is being rescued in the modern period by teachers like Swami Vivekananda; while the modern West tilted to *abhyudaya* side from which it is now hankering to be rescued. The West had experience of *nivṛtti* in the Christian ideas of meditation which had produced great mystics and saints, but which has become obsolete in the modern age; modern Western civilization is based entirely on *pravṛtti* till now. But today there is a reaction in the West against this one-sided approach to life; that is amazing as it comes from some thinkers, psychologists, and nuclear scientists, when they see that this one-sided attitude is producing one-sided people and a one-sided civilization. Something else is needed; that feeling has begun to make its appearance after all these 200 years of cultural experiment in America; some thinkers have come now to the conclusion that there must be a stress on *nivṛtti* also. How does it express itself in American thought?

Vedanta recognizes a super-conscious level of cognition, besides the conscious, the pre-conscious, the sub-conscious, and the unconscious. *Nivṛtti* refers to that super-conscious level with respect to human creativity. This is also hinted at in the recent studies of cognition with reference to human creativity by several Western psychologists.

When I was in Washington D.C., during my eight-month lecture tour of America in 1971–72, I came across a book, a very bulky book: *American Handbook of Psychiatry,* vol. III, by several authors. To enhance creativity, American youth at one time resorted to various forms of drug abuse; this book protests against it and provides a healthy procedure. In his studies of *Creativity and Its Cultivation,* Sylvano Ariety says (pp. 737–40):

'Instead of resorting to toxic procedures, we must consider, and possibly recommend, special attitudes, habits, and environmental conditions. The first condition to be considered is *aloneness.* Aloneness may be viewed as a partial sensory deprivation. ... He has more possibility of listening to his inner self, to come in contact with his inner resources and with some manifestations of the primary process. (Modern Western psychology speaks of the knowledge derived from the pre-conscious state, or the non-logical type of knowledge, as primary cognition, and that derived from the conscious state or the logical type of knowledge, as secondary cognition.) Unfortunately, aloneness is not advocated in our modern forms of educating adolescents. On the contrary, gregariousness and popularity are held in high esteem.

'Aloneness should not be confused with painful loneliness or with withdrawal or constant solitude. ...

'A second characteristic, which seems to promote creativity, is one which is contrary to the present spirit of American culture: *Inactivity*...

'The third characteristic is *daydreaming*.... It is in daydream life that the individual permits himself to diverge from the usual ways, and to make little excursions into irrational worlds.

'Another requirement for the creative person is even more difficult to accept: *gullibility.* This word is used here to mean the willingness to accept, at least temporarily or until proved wrong, that there are certain underlying orderly arrangements in everything outside us and inside us. Creativity often implies the discovery of these underlying arrangements, more than the inventing of new things....

'*Alertness and discipline* are other requirements. Although they are necessary pre-requisites for productivity in general, they acquire a particular aspect in creativity.'

These are some prescriptions by Sylvano Arieti; and one of the prescriptions is most revolutionary: you must develop the capacity for gullibility; believe what people say, don't disbelieve. Today, there is a tendency to disbelieve everything, which has gone too far, say the authors. You must have a certain capacity to believe until a thing is proved false. Little children are creative because they believe, but grown-ups have lost the power to believe. When the capacity to believe disappears, and generally it happens due to one-sided development, you slowly develop a cynical attitude. Disbelieving everything is the prevailing disease of many human minds all over the world. One extreme is cynicism, which is to be tackled with the other extreme of gullibility. Then a balanced attitude will develop, says that book.

All creativity is destroyed by the cynical attitude. I think it was Byron, the British poet, who said that there was not a single chaste woman in the whole of England except two, namely, Queen Victoria and his own mother. Then he added that he included Queen Victoria because, otherwise, he would be punished, and he included his mother because he would be a bastard otherwise!

That kind of judgement comes from a deep-rooted negativity of mind. We find in many intellectuals in present-day India such a cynical attitude. We find a good deal of it also in some of our journalists and other media people. That basic faith in truth, in man, in his or her destiny, has been eroded. When the science of spirituality asks you to sit quiet and meditate, it is asking you to be alone and not to rub shoulders all the time with others. Rubbing shoulders will also rub the nerves. Learn to enjoy being alone occasionally. All these come under this ancient Vedantic teaching of *nivṛtti*. *Pravṛtti* need not be taught, because we are naturally *pravṛtti*-prone. A child jumps up, runs about, engages in pushing and pulling things; so *pravṛtti* is natural. But *nivṛtti* needs training. That is what humanity is seeking today. What a psychological depth-knowledge it reveals!

This message, the blessing of *nivṛtti,* is slowly percolating into the Western mind, through not only influences going from India, but also from China and Japan, and from their own writers, thinkers, and psychologists, reacting wisely to their one-sided cultural situation. By *pravṛtti,* you achieve social welfare—good houses, plenty to eat and drink, good dress, education, lighted streets, and good roads; but too much of it is called consumerism today. For being peaceful, harmonious, fulfilled, and for the development of capacity to love people and to live in peace with them, we need the blessing of *nivṛtti,* which helps to manifest the spiritual energy that is within all in the form of the inherent divine spark. And, that *nivṛtti* can inspire all our *pravṛtti* also. That is what is taught in the *Gītā; nivṛtti* inspiring *pravṛtti.* We have plenty of *pravṛtti* in India; just now we have had our elections, and what an amount of *pravṛtti* we witnessed—full of violent thinking, violent actions, somebody snatching away the ballot boxes and many such things. Why do we do so? Because there is so little *nivṛtti* to stabilize and purify our thinking today. We should think and ask ourselves, 'Why should we do this? Is it good for our democracy?' We have to give our people the freedom to vote as *they* like; why should any political party control or interfere with it? We have all these distractions in our politics, and much corruption along with it. But a touch of *nivṛtti* can change all this.

The *Gītā* is going to tell us about that kind of life where there will be tremendous efficiency, great productivity, and better inter-human relations. Mark the comprehensiveness of this approach of the *Gītā* to human life and destiny! Śaṅkarācārya is giving us in a nutshell this comprehensive spirituality of the *Gītā*. It says that every human being is spiritual, even when he or she is in the *pravṛtti* field of life; one is never outside spirituality. That is a wonderful idea. Spirituality is life encompassing, you are never outside of spirituality. That is the attitude of the *Gītā* and the Vedanta. That is why I like this second sentence of his commentary, beginning with '*Dvividho hi vedokto dharmaḥ*'. We never understood this truth these several centuries; we had diluted our religion and philosophy until in the last century our religion became like the milk in our erstwhile market—90% water and 10% milk!

We have to build up our whole nation on this profound unifying philosophy. That is why Swami Vivekananda is remembered as one who raised the banner of this comprehensive philosophy and spirituality of Vedanta very high in the modern period. It is rational, practical, universal, and humanism-oriented. Raise that banner once again. He exhorted the nation in his Lahore lecture on Vedanta in 1897 (*Complete Works of Swami Vivekananda,* vol. III, 1960 edition, pp. 430–31):

'Therefore, young men of Lahore, raise once more that mighty banner of Advaita, for on no other ground can you have that wonderful love, until "you see that the same Lord is present everywhere." Unfurl that banner of love! "Arise, awake, and stop not till the goal is reached." Arise, arise once more, for nothing can be done without renunciation. If you want to help others, your little self must go. The nation is sinking; the curse of unnumbered millions is on our heads—those to whom we have been giving ditch-water to drink when they have been dying of thirst and while the perennial river of water was flowing past, the unnumbered millions whom we have allowed to starve in sight of plenty, the unnumbered millions to whom we have talked of Advaita and whom we have hated with all our strength. Wipe off this blot. Arise and awake and be perfectly sincere. Our insincerity in India is awful. What we want is character, that steadiness and character that make a man cling on to a thing like grim death.'

Today we get that lion roar of Vedanta with a tremendous modern relevance in the teachings of Sri Ramakrishna and Swami Vivekananda as Practical Vedanta.

By saying *'Prāṇinām sākṣāt-abhyudaya-niḥśreyasa-hetuḥ'*, Śaṅkara stresses that Vedanta or *Sanātana Dharma* works for the happiness and welfare of all beings, including animals, unlike some religions and some political systems which will look after only one's own followers.

Then Śaṅkara continues:

Yaḥ sa dharmaḥ brāhmaṇādyaiḥ varṇibhiḥ āśramibhiḥ ca śreyo'rthibhiḥ anuṣṭhīyamānaḥ dīrgheṇa kālena—

'this twofold dharma was practised for long ages by all sections of people, desirous of spiritual welfare, like brāhmaṇas and members of other three varṇas and members of the four āśramas'.

EVILS ARISING FROM THE PREDOMINANCE OF SENSATE VALUES

Things were going on well for long years; and then what happened? Śaṅkara continues:

anuṣṭhātṛṇām kāmodbhavāt hīyamāna vivekavijñānahetukena adharmeṇa abhibhūyamāne dharme pravardhamāne ca adharme—

'those who practised this dharma, due to becoming bereft of discrimination and wisdom, developed excessive sensory desires, with the result that dharma or value awareness was overthrown, and adharma or social evils multiplied.'

When such a situation comes, the society concerned reaches a state of decay with increasing lust, greed, violence, and self-centredness and devoid of the virtues and graces that integrated human being with human being in its healthy state earlier. The first thing that happens when overcome by *kāma* and *krodha,* lust and anger, is that *viveka,* capacity for discrimination, and *vijñāna,* wisdom, desert the people. The understanding regarding right and wrong gets dimmer and dimmer. Discrimination as to the stage at which one has to restrain oneself from the pursuit of sensate pleasures is lost. Then what happens? *Dharma* is overpowered by *adharma;* ethical restraints get completely eliminated. Everyone does whatever he or she likes, just what we find in many fields of life in India today. When *dharma* is overcome, it is a negative state giving birth to another positive state—increase of *adharma.* There are more and more of evil deeds and less and less of good deeds. We study in history the birth and growth, and decay and death of several civilizations. The best example is the once powerful Roman civilization well documented by Edward Gibbon's

Decline and Fall of the Roman Empire. It well illustrates what Śaṅkarācārya says here. Gibbon describes vividly the steady decay of moral and humanist values in the Roman Empire, century after century, and its final fall from a barbarian invasion.

India also, in her five-thousand-year history, has experienced such decay; but she did not experience the last step, namely, death. Every decay was followed by a dynamic regeneration. That is expressed by Śaṅkarācārya in the next passage of his introduction:

> *Jagataḥ sthitim paripipālayiṣuḥ, sa ādikartā nārāyaṇākhyaḥ viṣṇuḥ bhaumasya brahmaṇaḥ brāhmaṇatvasya rakṣaṇārtham devakyām vasudevāt amśena kṛṣṇaḥ kila sambabhūva. Brāḥmaṇtvasya hi rakṣaṇena rakṣitaḥ syāt vaidiko dharmaḥ, tadadhīnatvāt varṇāśramabhedānām.*

'Therefore, with a view to ensuring the wellbeing of the world, the primal world-projecting Lord, celebrated as Viṣṇu, known as Nārāyaṇa, was born of Vasudeva (father) through Devakī (mother) as Kṛṣṇa, in order to protect the spirituality, the brāhmaṇahood, of the earth.

'When *brāhmaṇatva* is protected, the Vedic law of righteousness is also protected, for, on it depends the organization of society into four-fold working groups and four-fold āśramas.' Vedanta does not speak of creation of the world, like potter creating pots out of clay, but it speaks of projection of the world, like the sparks coming out of a blazing fire or the cobweb issuing out of a spider. The many coming out of the One, and later merging back into the One.

BRĀHMAṆATVA: THE GOAL OF HUMAN EVOLUTION

No politician or intellectual or priest can do this work of social regeneration; only a person of God realization can do it. Such divine souls have appeared again and again in India's long history, and we are dealing in this passage with one such episode that happened over 3000 years ago, namely, the birth of Śrī Kṛṣṇa. In India, we have a fundamental idea:

there is such a thing as human evolution, and that evolution is human development from *tamas* to *rajas,* and from *rajas* to *sattva.* The man or woman who is all *sattva* is a remarkable type of person, who is highly evolved and manifesting the divine within. We in India found that, that is the goal of human evolution. How to produce more and more of such people in a society? Every member of society is given this goal, and he or she should try to reach it, or at least direct one's life in that direction. Move on at your own pace, but do go towards that direction, says Vedanta. What you call in modern thought 'social theory' is only social statistics; that won't do. But Vedanta points out that, in sociology there is a need to provide social direction and humanity must adopt that line of human evolutionary advance. That direction is to be a *sāttvika* person, without any hatred or violence, and ever loving and kind. When such persons are there in a society, there will be no need for even the police, not even for a political state, and much less need for laws and regulations, because here are persons who are self-disciplined and have realized their spiritual oneness with all others. India holds that, that society is most advanced which has the largest number of such people, who are *sāttvika* and spiritual and evolved, and who have manifested the divine within. Such a person is called a *brāhmaṇa,* according to the original Vedantic understanding of that word, and not in the evil casteism context.

The earliest definition of the word *brāhmaṇa* occurs in the four-thousand-year-old *Bṛhadāraṇyaka Upaniṣad* (3. 8. 10):

Yo vā etadakṣaram gārgī aviditvā asmāt lokāt praiti, sa kṛpaṇaḥ; atha ya etadakṣaram gārgī viditvā asmāt lokāt praiti, sa brāhmaṇaḥ —

'One, O Gārgī, who departs from this world without knowing this Imperishable (Reality), is miserable, a *kṛpaṇaḥ.* But one, O Gārgī, who departs from this world after knowing this Imperishable (Reality) is a *brāhmaṇa.*'

In his commentary on the above, Śaṅkarācārya defines *kṛpaṇaḥ* as 'miserable like a slave bought for a price.'

BHAGAVĀN BUDDHA ON THE *BRĀHMAṆTVA* IDEAL

In the seventh century before Christ, Bhagavān Buddha appeared in India and preached his great message of love and compassion, and instituted a monastic Order which ignored all caste and class distinctions and admitted people of all castes and classes. But he expressed great respect and admiration to the *brāhmaṇatva* ideal. In the great Buddhist book, *The Dhammapada,* which is a part of the *Khuddaka Nikāya* of the *Sūtta Piṭaka,* there is a whole chapter, the last chapter, chapter 26, named *Brāhmaṇa Vaggo,* in praise and appreciation of the *brāhmaṇa* ideal. I give below a few selected verses from that chapter (*The Dhammapada,* English translation by Dr. S. Radhakrishnan, Oxford University Press, Tenth Impression, Ch. XXVI):

Yassa pāram apāram vā pārāpāram na vijjati;
Vītaddaram visannuttam tam aham brūmi brāhmaṇam — 3.

'Him I call a brāhmaṇa, for whom there is neither this shore nor that shore, nor both, who is free from fear and free from shackles.'

Jhāyim virajam āsīnam, katakiccam anāsavam;
Uttamattam anuppattam tam aham brūmi brāhmaṇam — 4.

'Him I call a brāhmaṇa, who is meditative, free from passions, settled, whose work is done, free from taints, and who has attained the highest end (of sainthood).'

Bāhitapāpo hi brāhmaṇo samacariyā samaṇo ti vuccati;
Pabbājayam āttano malam tasmā pabbajito ti vuccati — 6.

'Because he has put aside evil, he is called a *brāhmaṇa;* because he lives in serenity, he is called a *samaṇa;* because he puts away his impurities, he is called a *pabbajita.*

Yassa kāyena vācāya manasā natthi dukhatam;
Samyutam tihi thānehi tam aham brūmi brāhmaṇam — 9.

'Him I call a brāhmaṇa, who does not hurt by body, speech, or mind, who is controlled in these three things.'

Na jātāhi na gottena na jaccā hoti brāhmaṇo;
Yam hi saccam ca dhammo ca so sukhi so ca brāhmaṇo — 11.

'Not by matted hair, not by lineage, not by caste, does one become a brāhmaṇa; he is a brāhmaṇa in whom there are truth and righteousness.'

Gambhīrapaññam medhāvim maggāmaggassa kovidam;
Uttamattham anuppattham tam aham brūmi brāhmaṇam—21.

'Him I call a brāhmaṇa, whose wisdom is deep, who possesses knowledge, who discerns the right way and the wrong, and who has attained the highest end.'

And in this modern age, Swami Vivekananda, who has severely criticized all casteism and untouchability, has upheld this *brāhmaṇatva* ideal of human evolution. He says in his lecture on *The Future of India* (*The Complete Works of Swami Vivekananda,* vol. III, pp. 293–94):

'The Brāhminhood is the ideal of humanity in India, as wonderfully put forward by Śaṅkarācārya at the beginning of his commentary on the *Gītā,* where he speaks about the reason for Kṛṣṇa's coming as a preacher for the preservation of Brāhminhood, or Brāhmaṇtva. That was the great end. This Brāhmin, the man of God, he who has known Brahman, the ideal man, the perfect man, must remain, he must not go.'

And referring to the evils of casteism, especially to the claim of special privileges by the higher castes, he said (*ibid,* p. 297):

'The day for these privileges and exclusive claims is gone. *The duty of every aristocracy is to dig its own grave, and the sooner it does so, the better. The more it delays, the more it will fester and the worse death it will die.*'

In recent centuries, we have spoilt that great word *brāhmaṇa,* and it has come to mean a caste-bound superiority-minded person, full of *rajas* and *tamas,* and no touch of *sattva,* and who looks down upon the members of all other castes. This degradation of such a great word has been going on for the last thousand years by the brāhmin caste claiming special privileges for itself among masses of less privileged and unprivileged people. The conscience of modern India has revolted against it and is taking energetic steps to rid Indian society of this evil.

From the Upaniṣads, through Buddha and Śaṅkarācārya, we were taught that this word means one who has realized Brahman, and has become a person full of love and compassion. And the word used in this introductory passage is the abstract form of brāhmaṇa, namely, *brāhmaṇatva,* that is brāhminness, indicating a human type. *Brāhmaṇatva* does not mean any particular individual or group, but it means a high level of human evolution, which is not confined to any special caste or class or nation. There are *brāhmaṇa* types in Russia, America, China, and everywhere else. We have a wonderful idea that a divine incarnation appears in the world; he or she does not initiate any social reforms, for that is a very superficial treatment of social problems, like treating the symptom and not the disease. The incarnation introduces a new value system, which slowly inspires the heart and mind of the people, out of which will come ethical and humanistic awakening, giving rise to all the necessary social reforms. He comes to establish two things: one is the glory and universality of *Sanātana Dharma* or Eternal Religion, and the other is the protection of the ideal type of person who is the embodiment of moral and spiritual values and who has achieved *brāhmaṇatva,* the goal of human evolution.

All people must grow in that direction. Śrī Kṛṣṇa's incarnation is related to *bhaumasya brahmaṇo brāhmaṇatvasya rakṣaṇārtham. Bhaumasya brahmaṇaḥ*—Brahman of the world, that is, the Vedas, the tremendous philosophy and spirituality of the Vedas, where these universal ideas are found. Nobody need be afraid of questioning this philosophy. It welcomes questioning, for it is very rational, and experiential. Secondly, it is very universal, dealing with humanity as a unit, not as cut up into caste, creed, nation, and race. That is the importance of this Vedic tradition. So, he calls it *bhaumasya brahmaṇo* and *brāhmaṇatvasya rakṣaṇārtham.* The Vedas or the *Śruti* or the Upaniṣads contain only universal principles about

God and humanity. Śrī Kṛṣṇa came to protect it and to protect that person who embodies that *Śruti* in his or her own life, the *brāhmaṇa* type. These two have been constantly emphasized in our tradition and literature. In order to achieve this, that very Nārāyaṇa, who promulgated this twofold *dharma*, and created those *prajāpatis* and *kumāras*, exemplars of *pravṛtti* and *nivṛtti*, to stabilize this world, when he saw that the world was going in the wrong direction, came as Kṛṣṇa, the son of Devakī and Vasudeva, with a view to strengthening the great message of the *Śruti;* the spiritual quality of life, and the human type who embodies the *Śruti*, the *brāhmaṇatva*; that is the focus of the divine incarnation.

We often hear that Buddhism is anti-brāhministic. Western writers have been misrepresenting many such things, not knowing that a *brāhmaṇa* as a priest is different from the *brāhmaṇa* as expounded in the great books. There have been many such great *brāhmaṇas* who were really holy and pure. All what we see now is only the priest *brāhmaṇa*, who is a great source of trouble to the society, no doubt. But, never forget what exactly it means, and therefore, in the Buddha incarnation, you find this very idea expressed by Bhagavān Buddha. He had great respect for the *brāhmaṇas*. Buddha knew that they are dedicated to the highest spiritual and intellectual endeavours, and that their life is extremely simple. There have been, of course, people failing to measure up to the ideal, but the ideal should not be forgotten. The terms *brāhmaṇa* and *śramaṇa* occur again and again in Buddha's discourses. Respect both of them, the *brāhmaṇa* and the *śramaṇa*, says Buddha. *Brāhmaṇas* are generally householders, and *śramaṇas* are monastic. Even householders are highly respected because they live a *sāttvika* life.

From very ancient times, we understood that every human being has the potentiality to evolve into a *brāhmaṇa* of this type, without any enemity or hatred, and with a heart full of love and compassion. We had Mahatma Gandhi in the modern period. In one sense, caste-wise he was a *vaiśya;* but, by his character, he was a *brāhmaṇa*. He showed no hatred to anyone, even to the police who struck him down in South Africa; and he refused to go and give witness against them in the court. Even today we have such people, and a man like Gandhiji once again reassures us that it is not an impossible thing to achieve this state. So, what do we do?

Modern biology says that, with the appearance of the human being on the evolutionary scene, organic evolution has ceased to have any relevance; the higher brain in humans can do wonders; we have to seek evolution continuing at a higher level, and Sir Julian Huxley calls it *psycho-social* evolution while Vedanta calls it *spiritual evolution*. Biology itself has not yet found the goal of human evolution. It has, however, concluded that, that goal will be governed by quality and not quantity. It is that quality that India sees in its fullness in the *brāhmaṇa* ideal. Here is the ideal and here are a few examples; make your movements in that direction. You may be an ordinary man, full of *tamas*. It does not matter, but there is a progress in life and that progress is in this direction. The whole of India will be completely transformed when this ideal is placed before the people. Proceed in that direction according to your strength. One step, two steps, three steps, and what a change will come into your life. This is applicable to America, Russia, Germany, China, and everywhere—this *brāhmaṇa* concept of human excellence. *Today we need to understand that that is the goal of social evolution.* Much of current sociology is only social statistics, but real sociology is that which stresses human spiritual growth and social evolution. What is the nature of a society, which evolves in that direction? We call it spiritual direction. The spiritual direction is the goal of evolution at the human stage. That is being slowly promulgated by 20th century biology: go beyond this bodily limitation, sensory limitation; this higher brain is meant for that. They are also speaking of psychosocial evolution. The psyche that can feel one with all people and society. Then there will be no exploitation, and that is the *brāhmaṇa* spirit.

So, the whole direction of evolution as given by 20th century biology is towards the *brāhmaṇa* type in every society.

That is the importance of this statement in Śaṅkara's commentary.

This is the path and goal of human evolution, according to Vedanta. To put people on the road of this evolution, to give them a little push, a little stimulus, an incarnation of God comes. When that stimulus is given, many evils disappear in course of time, because your attitude is changed, your value system is changed, and you have yoked your life to some high purpose. Whatever little mistakes you commit are not harmful. This is the idea of human growth and development, and only an incarnation of God, who is a *yuga-pravartaka* or a history-maker and divinity in one, can do this kind of work. The power that is needed to set in motion this tremendous current of spiritual energy comes only from that type of person whom we call an incarnation. You may use any other term. It is an extraordinary power, not what you find even in an ordinary saint, but something extraordinary, which can create a new historical epoch. Such people, very few only, are world-moving personalities. We treat Śrī Rāma, Śrī Kṛṣṇa and Buddha as world-moving personalities; a Jesus, and now, in this modern period, we have Sri Ramakrishna. It is a wonderful study against the background of our whole tradition. When things go bad, that same power has to come once again, and he comes. Śrī Kṛṣṇa will say later on in the fourth chapter of the *Gītā*, many will not recognize him, because he comes as an ordinary human being. However, in course of time, he will be recognized by millions. Since we are too near a great man, we cannot recognize him. This concept of *avatāra,* which Śrī Kṛṣṇa will describe in the fourth chapter of the *Gītā*, is central to *Sanātana Dharma* and Christianity. No other religion has this concept of *avatāra.* In this modern age, a similar adjustment became necessary, and a great person, Sri Ramakrishna, was born. The teaching is with us in the books, but we are not able to understand it, or how to follow it. Somebody must come and give us a new insight. Who will do that? Not a pundit, nor a priest, nor a professor. What do they know? There must be a tremendous spiritual personality, and he comes silently, quietly, and sets in motion a new current of spirituality. That spirituality slowly envelopes people little by little, and slowly changes the world.

VIVEKANANDA ON THE DIVINITY OF SRI RAMAKRISHNA

How does the *avatāra* change the ratio of forces in the society? Śaṅkara will answer this in the course of his commentary, but at this particular stage of our subject, I wish to share with you what Swami Vivekananda said about the importance of the *avatāra,* who comes to set right things in society when they go wrong. He was speaking in New York in America, on the important subject of *My Master*. He never spoke on Sri Ramakrishna in America or Europe, during his four years there; he only spoke of Vedanta. When people heard he had a teacher by name Ramakrishna, and that he was a wonderful personality, they pressed him to talk about his Master. So, in New York and in London, he gave this one lecture on 'My Master'. That lecture, in the beginning, contains this statement of Śaṅkara: When circumstances go beyond control and society becomes corrupt, in order to restore the moral values, a great power becomes manifest. That is how he begins his lecture. It is a wonderful lecture in beautiful English and a beautiful characterization of a great teacher. As a student at home, and as a *brahmacāri* of the Ramakrishna Order, I must have read this lecture about twenty-five times. So wonderful it is, from every point of view. He begins (*Complete Works of Swami Vivekananda,* Vol. IV, pp. 154–56):

'"Whenever virtue subsides and vice prevails, I come down to help mankind", declares Kṛṣṇa in the *Bhagavad Gītā.* Whenever this world of ours, on account of growth, on account of added circumstances, requires a new adjustment, a wave of power comes, and as a man acts on two planes, the spiritual and the material, the waves of adjustment come on both the planes. On the one side, of the adjustment on the material plane, Europe has mainly been the basis during modern times; and of the adjustment on the other, the spiritual plane, Asia has been the basis throughout the history of the world. Today, man requires one more adjustment on the spiritual plane; today, when material ideas are at the height of their glory and power; today, when man is likely to forget his divine nature, through his growing dependence on matter, and is likely to be reduced to a mere money-making machine, an adjustment is necessary; the voice has spoken, and the power is coming to drive away the clouds of gathering materialism. The power has been set in motion, which, at no distant date, will bring unto mankind once more the memory of its real nature; and again the place from which this power will start will be Asia.

'This world of ours is organized on the plan of division of labour. It is vain to say that one man shall possess everything. It is still more vain to say that one nation shall possess everything. Yet how childish we are! The baby in its ignorance thinks that its doll is the only possession that is to be coveted in this whole universe. So a nation which is great in the possession of material power thinks that that is all that is to be coveted, and that that is all that is meant by progress, that that is all that is meant by civilization, and if there are other nations which do not care for possession and do not possess that power, they are not fit to live, their whole existence is useless!

'On the other hand, another nation may think that mere material civilization is utterly useless. From the Orient came the voice, which once told the world that if a man possesses everything that is under the sun, and does not possess spirituality, of what avail is it? This is the Oriental type; the other is the Occidental type.

'Each of these types has its grandeur, each has its glory. The present adjustment will be the harmonizing, the mingling, of these two ideals. To the Oriental, the world of spirit is as real as to the Occidental is the world of the senses. In the spiritual, the Oriental finds everything what he wants or hopes for; in it he finds all that makes life real to him. To the Occidental, he is a dreamer; to the Oriental, the Occidental is a dreamer, playing with ephemeral toys, and he laughs to think that grown-up men and women should make so much of a handful of matter which they will have to leave sooner or later. Each calls the other a dreamer.

'But the Oriental ideal is as necessary for the progress of the human race as is the Occidental, and I think, it is more necessary. Machines never made mankind happy and never will make. He who is trying to make us believe this, will claim that happiness is in the machine; but it is always in the mind. That man alone who is the lord of his mind can become happy, and none else. And what, after all, is this power of machinery? Why should a man who can send a current of electricity through a wire be called a very great man and a very intelligent man? Does not nature do a million times more than that every moment? Then why not fall down and worship nature? What avails it if you have power over the whole world, if you have mastered every atom in the universe? That will not make you happy unless you have the power of happiness in yourself, until you have conquered yourself. Man is born to conquer nature, it is true, but the Occidental means by 'nature' only physical or external nature. It is true that external nature is majestic, with its mountains and oceans, and rivers, and with its infinite powers and varieties. Yet there is a more majestic internal nature of man, higher than the sun, moon, and stars, higher than the earth of ours, higher than the physical universe, transcending these little lives of ours. And it affords another field of study. There the Orientals excel, like the Occidentals excel in the other. Therefore, it is fitting that, whenever there is a spiritual adjustment, it should come from the Orient. It is also fitting that when the Oriental wants to learn about machine-making, he should sit at the feet of the Occidental and learn from him. When the Occidental wants to learn about the spirit, about God, about the soul, about the meaning and mystery of this universe, he must sit at the feet of the Orient to learn.

'I am going to present before you the life of one man who has put in motion such a wave in India.

Then, after narrating the wonderful story of Sri Ramakrishna's life, he concludes in these words (*ibid.*, p. 187):

'This is the message of Sri Ramakrishna to the modern world: "Do not care for doctrines, do not care for dogmas, or sects, or churches, or temples; they count for little compared with the essence of existence in each man, which is spirituality; and the more this is developed in a man, the more powerful is he for good. Earn that first, acquire that, and criticize no one, for all doctrines and creeds have some good in them. Show by your lives that religion does not mean words, or names, or sects, but that it means spiritual realization. Only those can understand who have felt. Only those who have attained to spirituality can communicate it to others, can be great teachers of mankind. They alone are the powers of light."

'The more such men are produced in a country, the more that country will be raised; and that country where such men absolutely do not exist is simply doomed, nothing can save it. Therefore, my Master's message to mankind is: "Be spiritual and realize truth for yourself." He would have you give up for the sake of your fellow-beings. He would have you cease talking about love for your brother, and set to work to prove your words. The time has come for renunciation, for realization, and then you will see the harmony in all the religions of the world. You will know that there is no need of any quarrel, and then only will you be ready to help humanity.

'To proclaim and make clear the fundamental unity underlying all religions was the mission of my Master. Other teachers have taught special religions, which bear their names, but this great teacher of the nineteenth century made no claim for himself. He left every religion undisturbed because he had realized that, in reality, they are all part and parcel of the one eternal religion.'

INDIAN CONCEPT OF *ŚRUTI* AND *SMṚTI*

When you study these old books like the Upaniṣads, you will find how much they harmonize with the thinking of the great souls, which we produced in the modern period. There is a historical continuity. This new adjustment is the same ancient adjustment, but in terms of modern conditions. This is what India has been taught again and again. Circumstances change, we need a new formulation of the ancient truth. Truth remains the same, only the dressing is changed. This is what we understand from our very ancient and continuing tradition. There are two words, *Śruti* and *Smṛti*. *Śruti* means the Vedas, especially in its Upaniṣad portions, which deal with the eternal verities, whereas, *Smṛtis* deal with contemporary social rules and regulations. *Smṛti* is secondary to *Śruti*. Indian tradition emphasizes this point: *Śruti smṛti virodhe tu śrutireva garīyasī*, 'when there is a conflict between the *Śruti* and the *Smṛti*, the *Śruti* shall prevail as greater authority.' *Śruti* is eternal. What you call *Sanātana Dharma* refers to the *Śruti*, the nature of man, nature of God, how we achieve spiritual realization, these are eternal truths. They are truths for us, for Americans, for every one; they are universal. Just as scientific truths are universal, so also *Śruti* truths are universal, because they are products of a science of human being in depth, a science of human possibilities. That is why we call it *Sanātana Dharma*, that *Dharma* which is *Sanātana*, eternal. Bhagawān Buddha constantly refers to this in his teachings: *eṣa dharmaḥ sanātanaḥ*, 'this *dharma* is *sanātana* or eternal'. Along with it comes *Yuga Dharma*, a *dharma* for a particular *Yuga* or period, for a particular age of history, a particular group of people. That is called *Smṛti*.

The *Smṛtis* come and go. How many *Smṛtis* were promulgated and set aside in India? Today all the old *Smṛtis* are abrogated, if they go against our national democratic Constitution. We have the courage to change our *Smṛtis* and develop a new *Smṛti* in tune with contemporary thinking. This is the great idea in India—social change. And the teachings, which are eternal, are reformulated according to the changed circumstances. For that you need great teachers, for they have the spiritual knowledge and authority to do this. That authority does not come from a status like that of a bishop, or a pope, or a priest or any traditional religious authority. It comes from spiritual realization; it comes from infinite compassion in the heart of a spiritual teacher. That is how new *Smṛtis* come into being. India held fast to this ideal. And the result is that from the Vedic age up to this modern age, many changes have taken place in religion, in society, in our country, and yet we are the same. *We are eternal and yet changing all the time.* That is the gist of the very term *Sanātana Dharma.* Professor Brajendranath Seal was a college mate of Vivekananda and Vice-Chancellor of the Mysore University; he had a brilliant intellect. He has said, 'India is ever ageing, but never old'; it is because of this adjustment that takes place at particular periods. This is the India that is taking shape today in a new setting, the same ancient India but adopting necessary changes. Much dead wood is being cut and removed. *This courage to change a Smṛti, and that too peacefully, is purely a Hindu heritage.* No other religion has shown that courage. In all other religions, *Smṛtis* are all in all; they cannot be touched, and if any reformer attempts to change them, he is persecuted and killed. But we say, 'Change the out-dated *Smṛti* and form a new *Smṛti,* if it does not fit us now.' Sri Ramakrishna himself has said, 'Mughal coins have no currency under the East India Company rule.' That means old *Smṛtis* have no current value. A new currency was needed in the period of the East India Company, and another in the Republic of India. About a hundred years ago, a person was ex-communicated by Indian society if one went to a foreign country. But who cares for it now?

Many changes have taken place and they have purified our religion and made our society healthy. But do not forget the *Śruti,* the eternal truth, the spiritual nature of man, and the life's journey to realize this truth. That is the *Sanātana Dharma.* The great contribution of an *avatāra* is to stress this. A mere social leader will come and advocate and effect some social reforms. But an *avatāra* does not disturb society at all. He puts a new value system into the society; with that we know what is good and what is bad, reforms are effected, and we change accordingly silently. That is the gentle, silent way in which this great spiritual method works on society. It is a great idea. We do not know that the great teacher has come and gone. But a wonderful energy has been left behind. I had a letter from far away Sofia, Bulgaria, just a few days ago. One letter from one Mr. Alexander; a wonderful letter, it says: 'My wife and I read *The Gospel of Sri Ramakrishna.* I am thirty years old, and she is twenty-three. Tanthia is her name; my name is Alexander. A wonderful book. But we do not know anything more about Ramakrishna and Vivekananda. We want you to give us some information. I wrote to somebody in Bangalore, Mrs. Devika Rani, the famous film-actress. She replied to me to write to the Swami in Hyderabad.' The man writes that he wants to know more about Sri Ramakrishna, more about Vivekananda. They are so eager to get all this inspiration. So I wrote, 'I will send you some books', and I asked somebody in West Berlin to send them. These great teachers like Sri Ramakrishna enter your life silently, without any noise, and changes take place within the reader. That is what happens when an incarnation comes. Śaṅkarācārya explains the idea of how an *avatāra* functions in society and gently transforms the society, putting people on the road of their own spiritual development. How is it done? Śaṅkara will explain it in a few sentences, and we shall study it.

During our study of Śaṅkarācārya's introduction to the *Gītā*, we came across two great ideas. One, society deteriorates in course of time due to attitudinal changes in people. Excessive lust, anger, and such other traits manifest, and disturb the ethical equilibrium in society. Therefore *dharma* declines and *adharma* increases, as Śaṅkarācārya said. Then decline begins due to excessive sensory attractions and uncontrollable desires, and the result is that *viveka* and *vijñāna* are destroyed. *Viveka* means discrimination—the ability to judge what one should do and what one should not do. Wherever there is excessive attachment to something, our discrimination suffers. Along with this, *vijñāna,* wisdom, gets disturbed. When a human being is not able to control his or her sensory appetites, something happens to the mind. The senses run away, as the *Kaṭha Upaniṣad* puts it, like the horses dragging away the carriage, making the passenger a helpless victim. That is the state of men and society when on the decline. When *dharma* declines, *adharma* automatically increases. When morality is low, immorality increases in human society.

ROLE OF A DIVINE INCARNATION IN ADVANCING HUMAN EVOLUTION

In India, we have the tremendous faith that whenever such a situation arises, when ordinary human wisdom cannot restore the balance, a divine manifestation appears on the earth, and through his teachings, society begins to achieve a new balance, a fresh understanding of values; *dharma* rises and *adharma* declines. It is only because of this, that despite problems every now and then, we have been living for the past 5000 years. Before the birth of Buddha, there was much intellectualism, meaningless asceticism, and the masses of people lived with all sorts of superstitions and mental weakness. Then Buddha came in the 7th or 6th century BC. He did not initiate any social reform movement. He merely stimulated the spiritual impulses in human beings. As a result, people once again developed honesty, integrity, compassion and the spirit of service. These are consequences of the spiritual awareness of human beings. That is how great teachers work and great reform movements are born as a result of the inspiration derived from such great people. It is like watering the roots of the tree and not merely the branches and leaves.

These great people do not initiate any reform movements, for such movements do not deal with the fundamental malady of society or of human beings. Take Sri Ramakrishna, for example. He did not start any reform movement, but by his inspiration many reform movements will be born, many saints, artists, etc., will come. A basic spiritual stimulus is given to human society. This is what has happened, time and again, in our country. It has seen decline, but it has also seen resurrection, regeneration. When a nation lives very long, often such physical and mental maladies arise, but the nation becomes young once again. This experience is unique to India and has been referred to by many historians.

Many other civilizations arose in this world, played their part for a few centuries, and then decline started and they died. We now only study about them in books and museums, whereas our civilization has a continuity. Every now and then it gets refreshed, a new youthfulness comes to it, tremendous energy comes, and things begin to improve. A new *Yuga* begins and the people develop high moral awareness, humanistic impulse, and spirit of service.

When we read Edward Gibbon's *The Decline and Fall of the Roman Empire,* we come to know how powerful that empire was. The Eastern Mediterranean region, Southern Europe, and North Africa were under the Romans, including Palestine and Israel. Slowly, decline set in and what was its nature? How did it come about? The race was the same, they were intelligent, but love of pleasure increased and they did not want to do hard work and live a hard life. Everyone wanted profit and pleasure, but very few cared to contribute to the good of the society. So, the Romans became lazy; they wanted only pleasure while they had slaves to do physical labour. With pleasure and comfort, man's aesthetic taste suffered; they indulged in violence and orgies. In their amphitheatres, slaves were made to fight with wild animals; and thousands of people, including the top hierarchy of the Government, would watch, and when a lion tore a man to pieces, they would applaud. In such situations, you can see a decline of taste and of human values. People living at that time, amazingly, did not realize that they were on the decline, because it was a slow decline. Civilization grows slowly and declines slowly. It is only after a century or so that one realizes that something is wrong with society. Gibbon also refers to the state of religion in the Roman Empire in a wonderful sentence. All the cults and religions of the Roman Empire were believed to be equally true by the people, equally false by the philosophers, and equally useful by the magistrates! The title of the book, *The Decline and Fall of the Roman Empire,* is very suggestive. People led a corrupt life. When foreign invaders came, the young people did not want to fight and defend the Empire. They had mercenaries to fight for them.

We want comfort, pleasure. One does not want to give up night-clubs, one is reluctant to go to the war front. When this decline affects the important people of society, the whole structure collapses. With a single foreign invasion, the whole Roman society was shattered, never to rise again. This is the story of the Roman Empire. Many other empires passed through similar phases—Egypt, Babylonia, Assyria.

After the First World War, many thinkers in Europe began to wonder whether Europe too was passing through such a phase. The first book that was published in Europe in this century, regarding European Civilization, was by Oswal Spengler [1880-1936], the German scholar and philosopher, entitled *The Decline of the West*. It was very powerfully written, wherein he said that Western society has finished its task and was on the decline. But some conservatives, such as Henri Massau of France who wrote *In Defence of the West,* did not agree; they felt they were still strong, for they had many colonies under them. Then came the Second World War, more serious, and there is much thinking in the West about a deficiency in their culture. Too much of crude materialism, multiplication of wants, signifies something terribly wrong with society. Therefore, more books are being written on the decline of the modern Western Civilization.

IS AMERICA ON DECLINE AND HOW IT CAN BE AVOIDED

During my extensive tour of America in 1971–72, I came across the weekly U.S. News Magazine, *Time,* of 19 July 1971, which, under its 'American Notes' section and under the title 'Of the U.S. and Rome', had published the following despatch: 'Odd how Rome continues to spook the American imagination of Interventionists and Cold War warriors invoke the ancient empire as an example of world order that the U.S. must help to impose. On the other hand, Rome is also invoked by those who see the decline of the West in every long-haired head and every puff of pot.' Speaking to Northwest news editors in Kansas City, President Nixon referred to Federal buildings in Washington and said:

"Sometimes when I see those pillars, I think of seeing them on the Acropolis in Greece. I think of seeing them also in the Forum in Rome—great stark pillars—and I have walked in both at night. I think of what happened to Greece and Rome, and you see what is left—only the pillars. What has happened, of course, is that, great civilizations of the past, as they have become wealthy, as they have lost their will to live, to improve, they have become subject to the decadence that eventually destroys the civilization. The United States is now reaching that period."

To be sure, Nixon quickly went on to express his confidence that the nation has the "vitality, courage, and strength" to remain morally and spiritually healthy. Despite this upbeat note, the overall effect was one of instant spenglerism.

During my 1968–69 tour of the U.S.A., I had come across a book by the well-known doodle writer of America, Roger Price, bearing the catching title, *Decline and Fall by Gibbon and Roger Price.* The name of the author of the famous book, *The Decline and Fall of Roman Empire,* was added by Price to his own, not only because of his seeing a common trait, namely, decline, between ancient Rome and his own America, but also because he quotes an appropriate passage from Gibbon relating to Roman decline, on the left page of his book to illustrate the same on the right page with an appropriate picture relating to current American life, chosen by himself.

Present day Western Civilization, European in general and American in particular, has an intrinsic greatness. Any decay of this civilization will be a great loss to humanity. I am sure it will be prevented by the process of cross-fertilization of cultures such as what is taking place in India today, and what Vivekananda wanted Modern India to be. In America itself, in the 19th century, we had the Transcendentalist movement, which intended to give a spiritual orientation, to

American culture. That found a more prominent expression in Ralph Waldo Emerson, Henry David Thoreau and Walt Whitman. While leaving London back for America, Emerson received a copy of the *Gītā,* which we are studying in this series of lectures, from the British intellectual, Carlyle. With the receipt of the book, Emerson began to write his famous essays in a different style with the *Gītā*'s ideas prominently expressed.

In his *Life of Vivekananda,* Romain Rolland gives the following note (2nd edition, 1944, pp. 52-53):

'In July 1846 Emerson notes that Thoreau had been reading to him extracts from his *A Week on the Concord and Merrimack Rivers*. Now this work (Section, Monday) is an enthusiastic eulogy of the *Gītā,* and of the great poems and philosophies of India.'

The emotion produced in Emerson by Indian thought, must have been very strong for him to write in 1856 such a deeply *Vedantic* poem as his beautiful *Brahma* (*Ibid.* p. 54):

If the red slayer think he slays,
Or if the slain think he is slain,
They know not well the subtle ways
I keep, and pass, and turn again.

Far or forgot to me is near;
Shadow and sunlight are the same;
The vanished gods to me appear;
And one to me are shame and fame.

They reckon ill who leave me out;
When me they fly, I am the wings;
I am the doubter and the doubt,
And I the hymn the Brahmin sings.

The strong gods pine for my abode,
And pine in vain the sacred Seven;
But thou, meek lover of the good!

Find me and turn thy back on heaven.'

In his book *Walden*, American transcendentalist Thoreau refers to the *Gītā* in these words (*Walden*, p. 266, S.Chand & Co., New Delhi):

'In the morning I bathe my intellect in the stupendous and cosmogonal philosophy of the *Bhagavad-Gītā*, since whose composition years of the gods have elapsed, and in comparison with which our modern world and its literature seem puny and trivial.'

But America continued to develop only materialism based on physical science. Then came, at the end of the 19th century, Vivekananda's exposition of the *science of human possibilities*, which is Vedanta, proclaiming the divinity and immortality of every human being, in the Chicago Parliament of Religions, and thereafter for four years in various parts of America and England.

Swami Vivekananda has given a compressed statement of Vedanta in these words (*Complete Works*, Vol. 1, p. 124):

'Each soul is potentially divine. The goal is to manifest this divine within by controlling nature, external and internal. Do this either by work, or worship, or psychic control, or philosophy—by one, or more, or all of these—and be free. This is the whole of religion. Doctrines, or dogmas, or rituals, or books, or temples, or forms, are but secondary details.'

That message is slowly spreading in the West in various forms. And I am sure that the spiritual orientation of the European and American civilizations is bound to progress from the first century of the third millennium onwards.

The process of decay of civilizations is what Śaṅkarācārya depicts exactly in his psychological study: '*anuṣṭhātṛṇāṁ kāmodbhavāt hīyamāna viveka-vijñāna hetukena*'—He has put it in very simple Sanskrit. 'When there is *anuṣṭhātṛṇām*, the citizens develop excessive *kāma*, sensory urges;' when *kāma* goes beyond a certain level, many evils begin to appear in society, and, '*viveka* and *vijñāna* begin to decline'. '*Dharma* is overwhelmed'—*abhibhūyamāne dharme*, and 'when *adharma* increases'—

pravarddhamāne ca adharme. This is the sort of situation that obtains in almost all societies in a later stage, although they all begin well. One idea runs through the books written by various thinkers in the West: Spengler whom I mentioned earlier, even Arnold Toynbee; the concept is that, culture is the dynamic aspect of human society, and when it weakens, there will be a decline in civilization. According to Spengler, civilization itself is a sign of decline whereas culture is a sign of development. When people want greater comforts, more pleasure, more gadgets, the sensory system gets stimulated, wants increase, and civilization begins to decline. When we work hard and struggle to build the nation, we are, as referred to in philosophical language, at the stage of 'becoming'; that is culture. When one has 'become', that is civilization, that is the beginning of decline. A poor man works very hard and builds up an economic empire. His son, having not struggled, merely lives off the wealth and within a generation or two there sets in decline. With all comforts and pleasure, the need for struggle is no more there, and the heroic element in man is stifled. Fortune never stays in the same family for more than three or four generations. Thus, culture and civilization pass through the stages of 'becoming' and 'become'; that is the analysis given by Spengler and others.

HOW INDIA HAS EXPERIENCED MANY A DECAY BUT AVOIDED DEATH

Our Indian culture has passed through all these phases. Take the Vedic period, great culture. What struggles and hardships people endured to build it up. The mind was active and energetic and had great vigour. This continued till the Epic period. There was a tremendous setback; the *Mahābhārata* war at Kurukṣetra, more than three thousand years ago, was a great setback! The best of the race died in the war, thousands of them. That is considered to be a watershed in our history. Sometime later, new strength came but again it declined. It went on, like waves rising and falling, but the uniqueness, as

I mentioned before, is that we decay but we never die. Some new power comes and we are refreshed once again. What a depth we had gone to in the last century! When we read the literature of the time, we can see to what low level the human mind in India had degenerated. All the original strength, vigour, and creativity disappeared, and we were a half-dead people. Out of that state came a tremendous awakening and new developments. How did it come about? Here comes the great idea. Not only does a great spiritual teacher arrive on the scene and raise the people, but sometimes a cultural cross-fertilization also takes place. Western culture helped destroy many of our foolish notions. It showed us new paths and made us more energetic. This was not the intention of the Westerners, but that was the result; infusion of Western ideas into India resulted in a new awakening and a new strength and youthfulness.

CULTURAL DECAY AVOIDED BY CROSS-FERTILIZATION OF CULTURES

A cultural cross-fertilization may take place, but to utilize it fully, to make it a creative movement, we need great thinkers, far-sighted leaders. India produced in the last century many such, beginning with Raja Rāmmohan Roy, and finally flowering into a powerful, creative and unifying movement by Swami Vivekananda. When we study the history of the 19th century, beginning from Swami Vivekananda, we find that this awakening achieved great maturity and a tremendous scope, not merely national, but also international. Therefore, cross-fertilization alone is not enough. One must be able to utilize that energy and give it a proper direction. The greatest achievement of Swami Vivekananda was the combining of the best elements of our own heritage, after removing all that was weakening and superstitious in it, with that which was good in what was taken from the West. He told us that soon a new India would be created, an India much greater than what she has been in the past, by combining all the energies of the Western culture with our own energies. That is what is slowly and silently taking place in the modern period, and in course of time, it will astound the world. This is the way Swami Vivekananda channelled the energy of the tremendous awakening that took place in the last century, through our coming in touch with the dynamic culture of the West. Although India was then under foreign political domination, there was also the impact of the tremendous thought-processes of the West, which made us think in new ways. Till then we were in a groove, as it were, narrow and sectarian in outlook. Vivekananda gave expression to the then state of affairs in his *Lectures from Colombo to Almora,* a book every citizen of India must read to understand his or her country and its pulse, and how to integrate Indian and Western cultural values.

'Give up all those old discussions, old fights, about things that are meaningless, which are nonsensical in their very nature. Think of the last six hundred or seven hundred years of degradation when grown-up men by hundreds have been discussing for years whether we should drink a glass of water with the right hand or the left, whether the hand should be washed three times or four times, whether we should gargle five or six times. What can we expect from men who pass their lives in discussing such momentous questions as these and writing most learned philosophies on them!'

All this received a blow when India got in contact with the British. It made people think once again. The child of that very old pundit could later become a Nobel laureate C.V. Raman, studying and contributing to modern physical science, a new line of development. That is what is called renaissance, a new life coming to the people. That was in the last century and today we are reaping the fruits of that tremendous development. A new youthfulness, a fresh energy, has come but we are not out of the woods yet. There is so much trouble now, widespread corruption and violence; but it also shows that there is energy in the people, and that is an asset. Things can be changed and these great teachers have come to transform this energy into a better form. They are not worried about the violence and crime. From *tamas* to *rajas* is a real progress and when in *rajas,* you become a problem to yourself and to society; but still it is a progress from a state of lifelessness called *tamas* to *rajas*. The next step has to be taken, namely, *sattva*, a tremendous state of disciplined and constructive energy, humanized energy. What a wonderful state that would be! India received such teachings not only from spiritual teachers, but even from her political leaders. Lokamanya Bal Gangadhar Tilak, Subhas Chandra Bose, Motilal Nehru, and others lived noble lives, sacrificing money and material comfort for the sake of the nation. Such high minds were there in the last century and beginning of this century, apart from spiritual giants like Ramakrishna and Vivekananda. Gandhi was a tremendous spiritual force. There was the national Congress leader, Chittaranjan Das, who died in 1925, and it is reported that Gandhiji himself carried his dead body for cremation. Das was a poor man. He studied law and earned well from his practice. His father had declared himself insolvent and died in poverty. The first thing Chittaranjan Das did with his earnings was to clear all the debts and had his dead father's name struck off from the insolvency list. Here we can see the nobility of the human mind. He could have easily ignored the debts since his father was already dead, but to him honour was more important than money. Today we have lost that character. Today money is everything and honour is of no importance, and such a difference within a span of eighty years! Such great people guided our national energies to give a new life to India; and above all of them was Swami Vivekananda, whose impact had been on all these great political leaders also. We will understand the nature of this impact when we read Romain Rolland's biography of Vivekananda. When Gandhiji went to Calcutta to attend the 1921 Congress Session, he also visited the Ramakrishna Math at Belur. Addressing an informal group of people assembled on the lawns below, Gandhiji said that he had not come to Belur Math to preach *satyāgraha* but to receive inspiration from the place where Vivekananda lived, so that he could love his nation better. 'By reading Vivekananda, my love for India has increased a thousand-fold', was Gandhiji's tribute to Swamiji; and he asked the people to take some of that inspiration with them when they leave for home.

In his brief life of 39 years, Swamiji brought a fresh youthfulness to this wonderful ancient culture, which had become almost decrepit. Many Imperialist British writers had predicted that this culture would decay and die, by the touch of the dynamic Western culture. Macaulay, who introduced English education in India, wrote that it was bound to die within a short time. However, the exact opposite happened. India once again became vigorous, with a new vital energy pushing her forward. If Ramakrishna and Vivekananda had not come, we would still have been energetic and active. Modern Western culture would have made us energetic no doubt, but we would have lost our soul, the continuity with our hoary past would have been lost. That did not happen because of such great teachers.

We find these ideas in Śaṅkara's *Gītā* Introduction. Some of the then Indian leaders, taking a reactionary attitude, had said that we should have no contact with the West, we should not accept ideas from foreign countries, we should stick to our own. But the country did not listen to them. But Swamiji said we have a great culture, but added that others also have great ideas and we should accept them with humility. He asked us to learn from the West, politics, economics, public affairs, science and technology. In a letter from America to India, Swami Vivekananda wrote (*Complete Works,* vol. V, p. 29):

'Can you become an occidental of occidentals in your spirit of equality, freedom, work, and energy, and at the same time a Hindu to the very backbone in religious culture and instincts?'

This idea of learning from others is not something new. In the *Manu Smṛti* (2. 238) we find this statement:

Śraddhadānaḥ śubhām vidyām ādadīt avarādapi;
Antyādapi param dharmam, strīratnam duṣkulādapi —

'Acquire pure knowledge with great faith from even the inferiors; learn great *dharma* even from low-caste people, take a gem of a woman as wife even from a bad family.'

What a broad social attitude we find in that statement! Swami Vivekananda said that new India should be a good mingling of the East and the West; today the ancient Greek is meeting the ancient Hindu on the soil of India. These are his own words from his Madras lecture of February 1897 on the *Work before us*. Our education in ancient India used to be a unified one. We retained our culture, yet we took and assimilated what others had to give. Such mingling now, again, will create a new India. This idea has to spread slowly and steadily. We have many foibles, weaknesses, and evils today. These, however, are part of the growing process of a nation coming to life. A deprived people, getting some opportunity in life, commit mistakes and blunders, but they can correct themselves because great teachers have shown us the method, the way.

The idea of cross-fertilization of cultures is great. In fact, the modern European civilization is a product of cultural cross-fertilization. Greek thought entered Europe in the 15th–16th centuries AD. Greece by then was a dead nation. It was conquered by the Roman Empire around the second century. In the third century, it had accepted Christianity, which was entirely foreign to the ancient Greek culture. Generally we find that wherever Christianity or Islam went, they destroyed everything ancient. So, ancient Greek thought got confined to only books. Western Europeans were barbarians and were totally ignorant of the ancient Greek thought. Right across the river Danube and beyond the Roman Empire, the Scandinavian countries and Germany were all barbarian countries. Later, Romans took to Christianity, but that religion had a narrow outlook on life. It could not appreciate the great achievements of the Greeks and Romans, and called them pagans. These cultures were annihilated. This period in European history, the medieval period up to 1250 AD was called the dark ages.

Then, Roman Constantinople, the very heart of Europe connecting the East and the West, was conquered by the Turks.

The Turks, Muslims, got stronger and stronger and conquered all the nearby Christian countries. Constantinople fell in 1453 AD, and many Greek scholars started migrating to Western Europe, carrying with them their books. Europeans were not allowed to travel east through Turkey, with the result Europe lost all contact with the East, even India. That was what made the West seek new routes to India via the Cape of Good Hope and others proceeded to India westward and reached America and took it to be India. That is modern history. But around 1453 AD, with the fall of Constantinople, Greek thought entered West Europe and gave it a new vision of humanism, secularism, and broad attitudes. That brought about what is known in European history as the 'Renaissance'. All subsequent development, from the 16th century onwards, is the product of this fertilization of the European mind by Greco-Roman culture.

Later, there was the Reformation; Christianity got broken up and some people, including those like Voltaire and the Enlightened groups in Germany and other countries, turned atheists. However, this gave rise to a new Europe, full of youthfulness and vigour, which could not be contained within itself, just as in the case of ancient Greece. A tiny Athenian town with a population of only 250 thousand, exercised tremendous power covering the whole of Greece. It became an empire, and under Alexander, conquered many countries, right up to India. Now the European nations were also like that. They got tremendous energy, and not knowing how to contain it, they went out conquering, colonizing, and exploiting and destroying other nations. They however gave some new ideas also. New life came to Europe then, but that is declining now. At this very period, Indian spiritual ideas, rational and broad, have started going to Europe and America to rejuvenate their culture.

When imperial domination of India by Britain took place, it was an unpleasant confrontation between the East and the West. Now it has developed into a happy confrontation. There is an exchange of ideas between the East and the West, and people welcome many of the ideas from the West. Modern Western

Civilization will not die like Rome. Roman civilization had to die and it was taken over by Christianity. Only the Church and its power were present, everything else faded out. Historian Prof. Arnold Toynbee has referred to a confrontation between Roman paganism represented by Roman Senator Symmachus, and Catholic Christianity as represented by Bishop Ambrose of Rome. The Bishop expressed the view that his Christianity, now gathering strength in the Roman Empire, was the only way to God. The Roman Pagan Senator Symmachus upheld the pagan view that there were many paths to God. But the Christian Church silenced the senator. But, Toynbee adds that, that Senator was silenced, but the point of view he held is upheld by millions of Hindus even today.

However, now, with the renaissance of India, new ideas will enter all the Western nations and they will once again get new youthfulness and vigour. Today you find many people in the West who do not want the present type of living with its philosophy of consumerism—eating, drinking, and pleasure-seeking. The first manifestation of this was the Hippy movement, especially in America, and later in France; a boy or a girl born in a rich family but not wanting to identify himself or herself with it. They preferred to wear simple, ordinary dresses—a sign of renunciation. That is the beginning of a new energy coming to the people. It has faded for the time being, but may erupt again.

When you read these words of Śaṅkarācārya, you read the truth about human society, about collective human endeavour. Culture has a wave-like motion, going down and again coming up. This coming up, in our country, as I said earlier, was always initiated by a great spiritual teacher. No politician or military general, not even a physical scientist, can initiate such a movement. Only a man of God, who has deep insight into the Truth in the heart of man, can set in motion such a current. In that context, I had quoted earlier, Swami Vivekananda's beautiful presentation in his New York lecture on 'My Master', of how, in the modern period, a new adjustment is taking place between India and the West. By mutual give and take, a new culture and a global awareness will come into being, there will be a new global harmony in society.

I mentioned previously that in the ancient period a great incarnation had come in India in the form of Śrī Kṛṣṇa. Dealing with the *Mahābhārata* period, Śaṅkara said, and I have already quoted it, when *dharma* was overcome by *adharma,* by too much sensual desire and decline of discrimination and wisdom, in order to protect the great Vedic philosophy and spirituality of *Sanātana Dharma,* the Divine Nārāyaṇa incarnated as Kṛṣṇa, the son of Devakī and Vasudeva.

I also discussed then this aspect, the *brāhmaṇa* ideal, of Indian sociology, quoting from *The Dhammapada*, and expounding Bhagavān Buddha's great respect for this human ideal. It is an ideal, not a person, not a *jāti* or caste, and every society must keep this as its goal. Self-control, simplicity, compassion, a spirit of service, all these constitute the *brāhmaṇa* type where *sattva* is predominant. He or she is never aggressive, is full of peace and blesses everyone. We saw this expression in our time in Mahatma Gandhi, who, though a *vaiśya* from the caste point of view, was a *brāhmaṇa* from the quality point of view.

This book, the *Bhagavad-Gītā,* discusses this quality as well as the *kṣatriya* quality. Not every person sitting on a throne or wearing a crown is a *kṣatriya*. A *kṣatriya* never flees from battle, says the *Gītā: yuddhe cāpyapalāyanam;* he is courageous, generous, never petty or mean. These qualities have to be assimilated today by our politicians and administrators. The goal for everyone, however, is the *brāhmaṇa* type, a society that evolves from a lower to a higher level. Human evolution is not organic; it is essentially ethical, moral, and spiritual evolution. Human beings do not need better organs. We have the best organ, the brain. We have to make use of the energy of the organic system to take evolution to a higher level. This is where *sattva* comes in. Today we have plenty of energy and we kill people, burn houses, because that energy has not been purified by *sattva.* The challenge therefore is to purify this energy, to humanize it, and achieve the ideal, *brāhmaṇatva. Brāhmaṇatvasya rakṣaṇārtham*—'for the protection of the *brāhmaṇa* ideal', an *avatāra* comes. An *avatāra* comes to protect the Vedas and the *brāhmaṇa* ideal. Vedic *dharma,*

Sanātana Dharma, is universal in nature, very pure and rational. At one time it had spread over vast areas of the world, then it got contracted, but now it is once again spreading. Vedic *dharma* includes all *dharmas,* accepts all religions and nowhere else can we see that type of universal vision. To protect the Vedic *dharma* and uphold the *brāhmaṇa* ideal, Śrī Kṛṣṇa was born as the son of Vasudeva and Devakī. 'He had no particular purpose to fulfil, as far as He Himself was concerned', *svaprayojana abhāve api.* By His own *māyā,* He assumed the human form, and, *vaidikam dharma dvayam arjunāya upadideśa,* 'He imparted the two-fold Vedic *dharma,* namely, *pravṛtti lakṣaṇa* and *nivṛtti lakṣaṇa,* to Arjuna'. What was Arjuna's state then—*śoka moha mahodadhau nimagnāya,* 'immersed in the ocean of *śoka,* sorrow, and *moha,* delusion'. These two emotions can distort every aspect of life. An ocean as it were of sorrow and delusion overcame Arjuna, as we shall see from the description of Arjuna's grief in the first chapter of the *Gītā.*

Śrī Kṛṣṇa conveyed a profound message to Arjuna and through him to all of us. Being full of compassion, he came to this world, assuming a human form and underwent many difficulties. His life was full of troubles. We may think that a person of such an exalted state has an easy life; but it is not at all so, for it was a very tough life. Mahatma Gandhi is said to have remarked, that only a mahatma can know another mahatma's woes. There was character assassination of Śrī Kṛṣṇa, just as we see today in our political life. Some one alleged that Kṛṣṇa had stolen his precious gem, the Syāmantaka, and called Him a thief. Poor Kṛṣṇa had to prove His innocence! He searched for it, and ultimately found two poor children playing with it, and restored it to its owner. There are many such incidents of false defamation. Śrī Kṛṣṇa could have ignored them, for He had nothing to gain or lose. However, when in a human body, the incarnation has to suffer pain and insult. Whatever joys there may be, are lessened by many sorrows. Any being with a human body has to pass through this. However, an incarnation is aware that, though with a human body, deep inside there is the fullness of divinity. The greatest moment in Śrī Kṛṣṇa's life came in the war-field of Kurukṣetra where he gave the message of the *Gītā* to humanity through Arjuna, and for which we remember him for these thousands of years.

CONCLUSION

What was Śrī Kṛṣṇa's intention in imparting this message to Arjuna? That will be the subject to deal with now. Why was Śrī Kṛṣṇa talking to Arjuna on a battlefield? Can He save the world? There is a single phrase in Śaṅkara's commentary—*guṇādhikaiḥ hi gṛhītaḥ anuṣṭhīyamānaśca dharmaḥ pracayam gamiṣyati iti,* 'spiritual ideas spread when they are understood and practised by men and women of more than ordinary good qualities'; like lighting one lamp from another already lighted lamp, it slowly improves the moral and spiritual health of the community. Jesus says, 'a little leaven leavens the whole bread'. These ideas enter society slowly and ultimately change the society. How this happens we shall discuss now.

Śaṅkara continues:

> *Sa ca bhagavān jñāna aiśvarya-śakti-bala-vīrya-tejobhiḥ sadā sampannaḥ triguṇātmikām vaiṣṇavīm svām māyām mūlaprakṛtim vaśikṛtya, ajaḥ, avyayaḥ, bhūtānām īśvaraḥ, nitya-śuddha-buddha-mukta-svabhāvo'api san, svamāyayā dehavān iva, jāta iva ca, lokānugraham kurvan lakṣyate. Svaprayojanābhāve'api bhūtānujighṛkṣayā vaidikam dharmadvayam arjunāya, śoka-moha-mahodadhau nimagnāya, upadideśa, guṇādhikaiḥ hi gṛhītaḥ anuṣṭhīyamānaśca dharmaḥ pracayam gamiṣyati iti. Tam dharmam bhagavatā yathopadiṣṭam vedavyāsaḥ sarvajñaḥ bhagavān gītākhyaiḥ saptabhiḥ ślokaśataiḥ upanibabandha —*

'That *Bhagavān,* who is ever in possession of knowledge, lordliness, power, strength, energy, and splendour, controlling his all-pervading Māyā or primordial nature with its three *guṇas* (*sattva, rajas,* and *tamas*), though Himself is unborn and immutable Lord of beings, and in essence eternally pure, awakened, and free, appearing through His *Māyā,* as if with a body and as if born, is seen as working for the welfare of the world. Though He has nothing to gain for Himself, in order to ensure welfare of beings, He imparted to Arjuna, who was submerged in an ocean of grief and delusion, the two-fold Vedic spiritual message (of action and contemplation) with the conviction that when it is received and understood and practised by people of more than ordinary virtues, it is bound to spread (like one lamp being lit from another lighted lamp). That *dharma* as expounded by Bhagavān Śrī Kṛṣṇa was converted into the celebrated *Gītā* by the omniscient Bhagavān Vedavyāsa in seven hundred verses.

Having said this about the genesis of the *Gītā*, Śaṅkara continues:

> *Tat idam gītā-śāstram samasta-vedārtha-sāra-saṃgrahabhūtam durvijñeyārtham. Tadarthāviṣkaraṇāya anekaiḥ vivṛta-pada-padārtha-vākyārtha-nyāyam api atyanta viruddha anekārthatvena laukikaiḥ gṛhyamāṇam upalabhya, aham vivekataḥ artha-nirdhāraṇārtham saṃkṣepataḥ vivaraṇam kariṣyāmi —*

'The science of the *Gītā* is the collection of the essence of all the teachings of the Vedas, but its meaning is difficult to grasp. Many have attempted to explain its words, their meanings, and also their wholeness in a reasoned treatise. Men in general have got it as a mass of self-conflicting thoughts. Noting this predicament, I shall set forth its contents, briefly explaining the text with due discrimination.' ...

Śaṅkara concludes his thoughtful Introduction with these words:

> *Imam dviprakāram dharmam niḥśreyasaprayojanam paramārtha-tattvam ca vāsudevākhyam param brahmābhidheyabhūtam viśeṣataḥ abhivyañjayat viśiṣṭaprayojana-sambandhābhidheyavat gītā-śāstram. Yataḥ tadartha-vijñāne samasta-puruṣārtha-siddhiḥ ataḥ tadvivaraṇe yatnaḥ kriyate mayā —*

'The science of the *Gītā*, thus elucidating specially the two-fold *dharma* (*pravṛtti* and *nivṛtti*) of the Vedas, is aimed at spiritual freedom; it also sets forth the ultimate Truth that is known as Supreme Brahman, also as Vāsudeva (Śrī Kṛṣṇa); hence it is equipped with a specific objective, relation and content. Since knowing its meaning results in achieving all the values of life, I am making an effort to elucidate it.'

BHAGAVAD GĪTĀ

CHAPTER 1

ARJUNA-VIṢĀDA-YOGA
THE YOGA OF ARJUNA'S GRIEF

From today we begin the study of the text of the *Bhagavad Gītā,* beginning from chapter 1. This is a dialogue between Śrī Kṛṣṇa and Arjuna. How did we get it? There is a third character, Sañjaya, who was a minister of the Kauravas, of Dhṛtarāṣṭra, the blind emperor. Bhagavān Vyāsa gave a special blessing to Sañjaya that, though he will be sitting in the palace with the emperor, he will be able to see and hear what was going on in the battlefield of Kurukṣetra. On account of this blessing, Sañjaya is reporting what all were happening in Kurukṣetra to the emperor Dhṛtarāṣṭra, who is anxious to know what was going on. And so, you find the first chapter beginning with a question by Dhṛtarāṣṭra.

धृतराष्ट्र उवाच –
Dhṛtarāṣṭra uvāca —
'Dhṛtarāṣṭra said:'

धर्मक्षेत्रे कुरुक्षेत्रे समवेता युयुत्सवः ।
मामकाः पाण्डवाश्चैव किमकुर्वत सञ्जय ॥१॥

Dharmakṣetre kurukṣetre samavetā yuyutsavaḥ;
Māmakāḥ pāṇḍavāścaiva kimakurvata sañjaya — 1. 1

'Tell me, O Sañjaya! Assembled in Kurukṣetra, the centre of religious activity, desirous to fight, what indeed did my people and the Pāṇḍavas do?'

Oh, Sañjaya, what did those people do in the *dharmakṣetra kurukṣetra*? Who are 'those people'? *Samavetā yuyutsavaḥ*, 'people gathered there with a view to fight a battle'; *māmakāḥ pāṇḍavāścaiva*, 'my people, Duryodhana and others, and those on the other side, Yudhiṣṭhira and the other Pāṇḍavas'. What did they do there?

Kurukṣetra is a town about 105 miles from Delhi, a very ancient place even at the time of the *Gītā*, and considered to be holy, *dharmakṣetra*. Even today millions of people gather there on very special occasions, and take bath in the lakes there. Today there is a university developing in that big city. That is Kurukṣetra, which is a *dharmakṣetra*—a place of *dharma*, a very holy place. In that Kurukṣetra, these two sides—my children and their people as well as Yudhiṣṭhira and his people—gathered there to fight this battle of Kurukṣetra. So, what did they do, is the question Dhṛtarāṣṭra is asking his minister, Sañjaya.

सञ्जय उवाच –

Sañjaya uvāca —

'Sañjaya said:'

दृष्ट्वा तु पाण्डवानीकं व्यूढं दुर्योधनः तदा ।
आचार्यमुपसङ्गम्य राजा वचनमब्रवीत् ॥ २ ॥

Dṛṣṭvā tu pāṇḍavānīkam vyūḍham duryodhanaḥ tadā;
Ācāryamupasaṅgamya rājā vacanamabravīt — 1. 2

'Then King Duryodhana, having seen the Pāṇḍava forces in battle-array, approached his teacher Droṇa, and spoke these words:'

King Duryodhana, i.e., Dhṛtarāṣṭra's son, having seen the Pāṇḍava forces in battle-array, approached his teacher Droṇa, who was a teacher of archery for both the Kauravas and the Pāṇḍavas, and spoke these words to him. Droṇa was highly respected like Bhiṣma; these are the two highly respected people in the Mahābhārata war.

पश्यैतां पाण्डुपुत्राणामाचार्य महतीं चमूम् ।
व्यूढां द्रुपदपुत्रेण तव शिष्येण धीमता ॥ ३ ॥

Paśyaitām pāṇḍuputrāṇām ācārya mahatīm camūm;
Vyūḍhām drupada-putreṇa tava śiṣyeṇa dhīmatā — 1. 3

'Behold, O Teacher! This mighty army of the sons of Pāṇḍu arrayed by the son of Drupada, thy gifted pupil.'

The son of Drupada referred to, is Dhṛṣṭadyumna, who was a gifted disciple of Droṇa himself. Details are then given.

अत्र शूरा महेष्वासा भीमार्जुनसमा युधि ।
युयुधानो विराटश्च द्रुपदश्च महारथः ॥४॥

Atra śūrā maheṣvāsā bhīmārjunasamā yudhi;
Yuyudhāno virāṭaśca drupadaśca mahārathaḥ — 1. 4

धृष्टकेतुश्चेकितानः काशिराजश्च वीर्यवान् ।
पुरुजित् कुन्तिभोजश्च शैब्यश्च नरपुङ्गवः ॥५॥

Dhṛṣṭaketuścekitānaḥ kāśirājaśca vīryavān;
Purujit kuntibhojaśca śaibyaśca narapuṅgavaḥ — 1. 5

युधामन्युश्च विक्रान्त उत्तमौजाश्च वीर्यवान् ।
सौभद्रो द्रौपदेयाश्च सर्व एव महारथाः ॥६॥

Yudhāmanyuśca vikrānta uttamaujāśca vīryavān;
Saubhadro draupadeyāśca sarva eva mahārathāḥ —1. 6

'Here are heroes, mighty archers, equal in battle to Bhīma and Arjuna—the great warriors Yuyudhāna, Virāṭa, Drupada; the valiant Dhṛṣṭaketu, Cekitāna, the heroic king of Kāśī; the best of men, Purujit, Kuntibhoja and Śaibya; the powerful Yudhāmanyu, and the brave Uttamaujas, the son of Subhadrā and the sons of Draupadī—lords of great chariots.'

King Duryodhana points out his own army to his teacher, Droṇa.

अस्माकं तु विशिष्टा ये तान्निबोध द्विजोत्तम ।
नायका मम सैन्यस्य संज्ञार्थं तान् ब्रवीमि ते ॥७॥

Asmākam tu viśiṣṭā ye tānnibodha dvijottama;
Nāyakā mama sainyasya samjñārtham tān bravīmi te —1. 7

'Now let me tell you about our own army, O best among the twice-born. I shall tell you by their names, some of the outstanding heroes on our side.'

भवान् भीष्मश्च कर्णश्च कृपश्च समितिञ्जयः ।
अश्वत्थामा विकर्णश्च सौमदत्तिः जयद्रथः ॥८॥

Bhavān bhīṣmaśca karṇaśca kṛpaśca samitiñjayaḥ;
Aśvatthāmā vikarṇaśca saumadattiḥ jayadrathaḥ —1. 8

'First of all, you yourself, then, Bhīṣma, Karṇa, next, Kṛpa, victorious in war, Aśvatthāmā, Vikarṇa, Jayadratha, and the son of Somadatta.'

Karṇa is the eldest son of Kuntī, the elder brother of Yudhiṣṭhira and the other Pāṇḍavas, but they did not then know this truth. That was a mystery. So, Karṇa joined the Kaurava party.

अन्ये च बहवः शूरा मदर्थे त्यक्तजीविताः ।
नानाशस्त्रप्रहरणाः सर्वे युद्धविशारदाः ॥९॥

Anye ca bahavaḥ śūrā madarthe tyaktajīvitāḥ;
Nānāśastra-praharaṇāḥ sarve yuddhaviśāradāḥ — 1. 9

'And many other heroes also, well-skilled in fight, armed with many weapons, are here, determined to lay down their lives for my sake.'

अपर्याप्तं तदस्माकं बलं भीष्माभिरक्षितम् ।
पर्याप्तं त्विदमेतेषां बलं भीमाभिरक्षितम् ॥१०॥

Aparyāptam tadasmākam balam bhīṣmābhirakṣitam;
Paryāptam tvidameteṣām balam bhīmābhirakṣitam — 1. 10

'This, our army, defended by Bhīṣma, is innumerable, but that army of theirs, defended by Bhīma, is easy to number, i.e., is much less.'

अयनेषु च सर्वेषु यथाभागमवस्थिताः ।
भीष्ममेवाभिरक्षन्तु भवन्तः सर्व एव हि ॥११॥

Ayaneṣu ca sarveṣu yathābhāgamavasthitāḥ;
Bhīṣmamevābhirakṣantu bhavantaḥ sarva eva hi — 1. 11

'Now, do this, be stationed in your proper places in the divisions of the army, and support and protect Bhīṣma alone.'

Bhīṣma is the most important person. Anything adverse happening to him, will hurt us. So, it is to be seen that he is properly protected.

तस्य संजनयन् हर्षं कुरुवृद्धः पितामहः ।
सिंहनादं विनद्योच्चैः शङ्खं दध्मौ प्रतापवान् ॥१२॥

Tasya samjanayan harṣam kuruvṛddhaḥ pitāmahaḥ;
Simhanādam vinadyoccaiḥ śaṅkham dadhmau pratāpavān—1. 12

'That oldest of the Kurus, Bhīṣma, the grand-sire, now sounded aloud a lion-roar and blew his conch, just to cheer up Duryodhana.'

Bhīṣma had taken a vow not to claim the throne for himself, though he was meant to become the king at that time, in order to please Satyavatī, who was a fisher woman on the river Yamuna and the mother of sage Vyāsa, and allow her son to become the prince. So, Bhīṣma remained a celibate throughout his life; he is a man who keeps his word; so many times he was told in difficult situations to take up the throne. But he said, 'no, I don't want power.' So, Bhīṣma is considered to be a man of tremendous willpower, tremendous courage and tremendous wisdom. In the *Mahābhārata,* at the end of the war, he was lying wounded, as desired by him, on a bed of arrows. For several days he was in that condition, because he would not die till the sun started going northwards; that was January 14 or so. Śrī Kṛṣṇa and all the Pāṇḍavas went to him. Śrī Kṛṣṇa asked him to instruct the Pāṇḍavas, and that wonderful instruction is to be found in the *Śānti parva* of the *Mahābhārata*—a series of discourses on politics and spirituality. It is a wonderful teaching. It is this Bhīṣma who is now facing the battle. After some days he will die in the battle, but as I said, he won't die, he will live on till the *uttarāyaṇa* (when the sun goes northwards) begins. Then his cremation takes place. That is described in a big way in the *Mahābhārata,* and in that you will find exactly what we do today. When our Prime Minister Indira Gandhi died, she had a wonderful cremation in Delhi, a repetition of what happened in the *Mahābhārata* war time.

ततः शङ्खाश्च भेर्यश्च पणवानकगोमुखाः ।
सहसैवाभ्यहन्यन्त स शब्दस्तुमुलोऽभवत् ।।१३।।

Tataḥ śaṅkhāśca bheryaśca paṇavānakagomukhāḥ;
Sahasaivābhyahanyanta sa śabdastumulo'bhavat — 1. 13

'As soon as Bhīṣma blew his conch, all others started: all the various instruments sounded just to create a kind of atmosphere for energizing the army; conches, kettle-drums, tabors, trumpets, cow-horns blared forth suddenly from the Kaurava side, and the noise was tremendous.'

ततः श्वेतैर्हयैर्युक्ते महति स्यन्दने स्थितौ ।
माधवः पाण्डवश्चैव दिव्यौ शङ्खौ प्रदध्मतुः ॥१४॥

Tataḥ śvetairhayairyukte mahati syandane sthitau;
Mādhavaḥ pāṇḍavaścaiva divyau śaṅkhau pradadhmatuḥ—1. 14

'Then, Mādhava, i.e., Śrī Kṛṣṇa, and Pāṇḍava, i.e., Arjuna, stationed in their magnificent chariot yoked with white horses, blew their divine conches.'

पाञ्चजन्यं हृषीकेशो देवदत्तं धनञ्जयः ।
पौण्ड्रं दध्मौ महाशङ्खं भीमकर्मा वृकोदरः ॥१५॥

Pāñcajanyam hṛṣīkeśo devadattam dhanañjayaḥ;
Pauṇḍram dadhmau mahāśaṅkham bhīmakarmā vṛkodaraḥ—1. 15

'Hṛṣīkeśa, i.e., Śrī Kṛṣṇa, blew the *Pāñcajanya;* Dhanañjaya, i.e., Arjuna, blew the conch called *Devadatta;* and Vṛkodara, the doer of terrific deeds, i.e., Bhīma, blew his large conch *Pauṇḍra.*'

अनन्तविजयं राजा कुन्तीपुत्रो युधिष्ठिरः ।
नकुलः सहदेवश्च सुघोषमणिपुष्पकौ ॥१६॥

Anantavijayam rājā kuntīputro yudhiṣṭhiraḥ;
Nakulaḥ sahadevaśca sughoṣamaṇipuṣpakau — 1. 16

'King Yudhiṣṭhira, son of Kunti, blew the conch named *Anantavijaya;* and Nakula and Sahadeva blew their *Sughoṣa* and *Maṇipuṣpaka* conches.'

काश्यश्च परमेष्वासः शिखण्डी च महारथः ।
धृष्टद्युम्नो विराटश्च सात्यकिश्चापराजितः ॥१७॥

Kāśyaśca parameṣvāsaḥ śikhaṇḍī ca mahārathaḥ;
Dhṛṣṭadyumno virāṭaśca sātyakiścāparājitaḥ — 1. 17

'The expert bow-man, the king of Kāśi, and the great chariot warrior Śikhaṇḍī, Dhṛṣṭadyumna and Virāṭa, and the unconquered Sātyaki.'

द्रुपदो द्रौपदेयाश्च सर्वशः पृथिवीपते ।
सौभद्रश्च महाबाहुः शङ्खान् दध्मुः पृथक्पृथक् ॥१८॥

Drupado draupadeyāśca sarvaśaḥ pṛthivīpate;
*Saubhadraśca mahābāhuḥ śaṅkhān dadhmuḥ pṛthak pṛthak—*1. 18

'O Lord of the earth (meaning Dhṛtarāṣṭra)! Drupada and the sons of Draupadī, and the mighty-armed son of Subhadrā, each, blew his own conch.'

स घोषो धार्तराष्ट्राणां हृदयानि व्यदारयत् ।
नभश्च पृथिवीञ्चैव तुमुलोऽभ्यनुनादयन् ॥१९॥

Sa ghoṣo dhārtarāṣṭrāṇām hṛdayāni vyadārayat;
*Nabhaśca pṛthivīñcaiva tumulo'bhyanunādayan —*1. 19

'That terrific noise, resounding throughout the heaven and earth, rent the hearts of Dhṛtarāṣṭra's party because of its tremendous efficacy.'

अथ व्यवस्थितान् दृष्ट्वा धार्तराष्ट्रान् कपिध्वजः ।
प्रवृत्ते शस्त्रसंपाते धनुरुद्यम्य पाण्डवः ॥२०॥
हृषीकेशं तदा वाक्यमिदमाह महीपते ।

Atha vyavasthitān dṛṣṭvā dhārtarāṣṭrān kapidhvajaḥ;
*Pravṛtte śastrasampāte dhanurudyamya pāṇḍavaḥ—*1. 20
Hṛṣīkeśam tadā vākyamidamāha mahīpate ;

'Then, O Lord of the earth! Seeing Dhṛtarāṣṭra's party, standing marshalled and the shooting about to begin, that Pāṇḍava (Arjuna), whose ensign was the monkey, i.e., Hanuman on his flag, raising his bow, said the following words to Kṛṣṇa.'

Śrī Kṛṣṇa's part in the war was merely as a charioteer; He never took part in the battle. Now, Śrī Kṛṣṇa and Arjuna are coming into the picture.

अर्जुन उवाच –

Arjuna uvāca —

'Arjuna said.'

सेनयोरुभयोर्मध्ये रथं स्थापय मेऽच्युत ॥२१॥
यावदेतान्निरीक्षेऽहं योद्धुकामान् अवस्थितान् ।
कैर्मया सह योद्धव्यमस्मिन्रणसमुद्यमे ॥२२॥

Senayorubhayormadhye ratham sthāpaya me'cyuta —1. 21
Yāvadetānnirīkṣe'ham yoddhukāmān avasthitān;
Kairmayā saha yoddhavyamasminraṇasamudyame—1. 22

'Please place my chariot, O Acyuta, i.e., Śrī Kṛṣṇa, between the two armies, that I may see those who stand here prepared for war. On the eve of this battle, let me know with whom I am to fight.'

योत्स्यमानान् अवेक्षेऽहं य एतेऽत्र समागताः ।
धार्तराष्ट्रस्य दुर्बुद्धेर्युद्धे प्रियचिकीर्षवः ॥२३॥

Yotsyamānān avekṣe'ham ya ete'tra samāgatāḥ;
Dhārtarāṣṭrasya durbuddheryuddhe priyacikīrṣavaḥ—1. 23

'For, I desire to observe those who are assembled here for fight, wishing to please the evil-minded Duryodhana by taking his side on this battle-field.'

सञ्जय उवाच –

Sañjaya uvāca —

Sañjaya said:

एवमुक्तो हृषीकेशो गुडाकेशेन भारत ।
सेनयोरुभयोर्मध्ये स्थापयित्वा रथोत्तमम् ॥२४॥

Evamukto hṛṣīkeśo guḍākeśena bhārata;
Senayorubhayormadhye sthāpayitvā rathottamam—1. 24

भीष्मद्रोणप्रमुखतः सर्वेषां च महीक्षिताम् ।
उवाच पार्थ पश्यैतान्समवेतान् कुरूनिति ॥ २५॥

Bhīṣmadroṇapramukhataḥ sarveṣām ca mahīkṣitām;
Uvāca pārtha paśyaitānsamavetān kurūniti— 1. 25

'O Bhārata i.e., Dhṛtarāṣṭra, commanded thus by Guḍākeśa i.e., Arjuna, Hṛṣikeśa, i.e., Śrī Kṛṣṇa, drove that grandest of chariots to a place between the two armies facing Bhiṣma, Droṇa, and all the rulers of the earth, and then spoke thus to Arjuna: "Behold Arjuna, all the Kurus gathered together."'

तत्रापश्यत् स्थितान् पार्थ पितॄनथ पितामहान् ।
आचार्यान् मातुलान् भ्रातॄन् पुत्रान् पौत्रान् सखीन् तथा ॥ २६॥
श्वशुरान् सुहृदश्चैव सेनयोरुभयोरपि ।

Tatrāpaśyat sthitān pārtha pitṝnatha pitāmahān;
Ācāryān mātulān bhrātṝn putrān pautrān sakhīn tathā—1. 26
Śvaśurān suhṛdaścaiva senayorubhayorapi ;

'Then Arjuna saw, stationed in front of him, in both the armies, his own relatives, grandfathers, fathers-in-law, uncles, brothers, cousins, his own, and their sons and grandsons, and comrades and teachers, and other friends as well.'

That is the critical moment of the whole war situation.

तान् समीक्ष्य स कौन्तेयः सर्वान् बन्धून् अवस्थितान् ॥ २७॥
कृपया परयाविष्टो विषीदन् इदमब्रवीत् ।

Tān samīkṣya sa kaunteyaḥ sarvān bandhūn avasthitān—1. 27
Kṛpayā parayāviṣṭo viṣīdan idamabravīt;

'Then he, the son of Kuntī, i.e., Arjuna, seeing all those kinsmen stationed in their ranks, spoke thus with sorrow, filled with deep pity.'

In many battles, especially in civil wars, you are fighting with your own people. In the American civil war, how many people fought against their own kinsmen! Our friends are there on the other side, that is the nature of all civil wars. And this was more than a civil war. It was a family war—the same family, Kauravas on one side and the Pāṇḍavas on the other. All their comrades joined together. And Arjuna's own teachers were there. Now comes the very tragic situation facing Arjuna, and Arjuna is giving expression to his great grief. This chapter is called the Yoga of the Grief of Arjuna, *Arjuna-viśāda-yoga*. *Viśāda* is grief. That also is a *yoga*, because of that grief comes great development. We begin to think; we begin to discriminate. You ask for advice, you want some philosophy to guide you. So, this is also called a *yoga—Arjuna-viśāda-yoga*.

अर्जुन उवाच –

Arjuna uvāca —

'Arjuna said.'

दृष्ट्वेमं स्वजनं कृष्ण युयुत्सुं समुपस्थितम् ॥२८॥
सीदन्ति मम गात्राणि मुखं च परिशुष्यति ।
वेपथुश्च शरीरे मे रोमहर्षश्च जायते ॥२९॥
गाण्डीवं स्रंसते हस्तात् त्वक् चैव परिदह्यते ।

Dṛṣṭvemam svajanam kṛṣṇa yuyutsum samupasthitam—1. 28
Sīdanti mama gātrāṇi mukham ca pariśuṣyati;
Vepathuśca śarīre me romaharṣaśca jāyate — 1. 29
Gāṇḍīvam sramsate hastāt tvak caiva paridahyate;

'Seeing, O Kṛṣṇa, these my kinsmen, gathered here eager for fight, my limbs fail me, my mouth is parched up, I shiver all over my body; my hair stands on end; the bow, Gāṇḍīva, slips from my hands; and my skin burns.'

Arjuna is in a very difficult situation, he is highly worked up in his nerves.

न च शक्नोमि अवस्थातुं भ्रमतीव च मे मनः ॥३०॥
निमित्तानि च पश्यामि विपरीतानि केशव ।

Na ca śaknomi avasthātum bhramatīva ca me manaḥ—1. 30
Nimittāni ca paśyāmi viparītāni keśava;

'Neither, O Keśava (another name for Śrī Kṛṣṇa), can I stand upright. My mind is in a whirl. And I see adverse omens as well.'

A very picturesque description of a very serious nervous condition—when you are confused, when you are full of fear, full of tension—is very beautifully pictured in these verses.

न च श्रेयोऽनुपश्यामि हत्वा स्वजनमाहवे ॥३१॥
न कांक्षे विजयं कृष्ण न च राज्यं सुखानि च ।

Na ca śreyo'nupaśyāmi hatvā svajanamāhave — 1. 31
Na kāmkṣe vijayam kṛṣṇa na ca rājyam sukhāni ca;

'Neither do I see any good, O Krsna, in killing these, my own people, in battle. I desire neither victory, nor empire, nor even pleasure.'

किं नो राज्येन गोविन्द किं भोगैर्जीवितेन वा ॥३२॥
येषामर्थे कांक्षितं नो राज्यं भोगाः सुखानि च ।
त इमेऽवस्थिता युद्धे प्राणान् त्यक्त्वा धनानि च ॥३३॥
आचार्याः पितरः पुत्रास्तथैव च पितामहाः ।
मातुलाः श्वशुराः पौत्राः श्यालाः संबन्धिनस्तथा ॥३४॥

Kim no rājyena govinda kim bhogairjīvitena vā — 1. 32
Yeṣāmarthe kāmkṣitam no rājyam bhogāḥ sukhāni ca;
*Ta ime'vasthitā yuddhe prāṇān tyaktvā dhanāni ca —*1. 33
Ācāryāḥ pitaraḥ putrāstathaiva ca pitāmahāḥ;
*Mātulāḥ śvaśurāḥ pautrāḥ śyālāḥ sambandhinastathā —*1. 34

'Of what avail is dominion to us, of what avail are pleasures and even life, if these, O Govinda! for whose sake it is desired that empire, enjoyment, and pleasure should be ours, themselves stand here in battle, having renounced life and wealth: who are they?, teachers, uncles, sons, grandfathers, maternal uncles, fathers-in-law, grandsons, brothers-in-law, besides other kinsmen.'

All these are mentioned in the three verses, 32 to 34. So, Arjuna is in a very difficult situation. The remaining verses are going to tell us the deeper crises into which Arjuna entered at that time.

एतान्न हन्तुमिच्छामि घ्नतोऽपि मधुसूदन ।
अपि त्रैलोक्यराज्यस्य हेतोः किं नु महीकृते ॥३५॥

Etānna hantumicchāmi ghnato'pi madhusūdana;
Api trailokyarājyasya hetoḥ kim nu mahīkṛte — 1. 35

'Even though these were to kill me, O Slayer of Madhu i.e., Śrī Kṛṣṇa, I could not wish to kill them—not even for the sake of dominion over the three worlds, how much less for the sake of this earth!'

Arjuna is now in a definite mood to withdraw from battle, because of these emotional considerations.

निहत्य धार्तराष्ट्रान् नः का प्रीतिःस्यात् जनार्दन ।
पापमेवाश्रयेदस्मान् हत्वैतान् आततायिनः ॥ ३६ ॥

Nihatya dhārtarāṣṭrān naḥ kā prītiḥ syājjanārdana;
Pāpamevāśrayedasmān hatvaitān ātatāyinaḥ — 1. 36

'What pleasure, indeed, could be ours, O Kṛṣṇa, from killing these sons of Dhṛtarāṣṭra? Sin only would take hold of us by the slaying of these felons.'

They are certainly felons. They have done so many evils. They have tried to burn away all the Pāṇḍavas at one time. In spite of that, I find no fun in engaging in this war.

तस्मान्नार्हा वयं हन्तुं धार्तराष्ट्रान् स्वबान्धवान् ।
स्वजनं हि कथं हत्वा सुखिनः स्याम माधव ॥ ३७ ॥

Tasmānnārhā vayam hantum dhārtarāṣṭrān svabāndhavān;
Svajanam hi katham hatvā sukhinaḥ syāma mādhava—1. 37

'Therefore, we are not fit to kill our kindred, the sons of Dhṛtarāṣtra. How could we, O Kṛṣṇa, gain happiness by the slaying of our own kinsmen?'

यद्यप्येते न पश्यन्ति लोभोपहतचेतसः ।
कुलक्षयकृतं दोषं मित्रद्रोहे च पातकम् ॥ ३८ ॥
कथं न ज्ञेयमस्माभिः पापादस्मान्निवर्तितुम् ।
कुलक्षयकृतं दोषं प्रपश्यद्भिः जनार्दन ॥ ३९ ॥

Yadyapyete na paśyanti lobhopahatacetasaḥ;
Kulakṣayakṛtam doṣam mitradrohe ca pātakam — 1. 38
Katham na jñeyamasmābhiḥ pāpādasmānnivartitum;
Kulakṣayakṛtam doṣam prapaśyadbhiḥ janārdana —1. 39

'Though these Kauravas assembled in front of me do not understand this truth because of their overpowering greed, there is sin in hostility to friends. Why should not we, Oh Janārdana, who clearly see this evil leading to the decay of families and societies, turn away from this sin?'

This war will lead to the decay of society, break-up of family, resulting in so many widows, so many orphans. All these evils come from war. These Kauravas do not know these consequences, but *we* know it. Since, we know it, why should we proceed in this matter?

कुलक्षये प्रणश्यन्ति कुलधर्माः सनातनाः ।
धर्मे नष्टे कुलं कृत्स्नमधर्मोऽभिभवत्युत ॥४०॥

Kulakṣaye praṇaśyanti kuladharmāḥ sanātanāḥ;
Dharme naṣṭe kulam kṛtsnamadharmo'bhibhavatyuta—1. 40

'On the decay of the family, the memorial religious rites of the family die out. The culture enshrined in the family dies out. On the destruction of social values, impiety further overwhelms the whole family.'

Evils come in from war. We are able to realize it today. How many evils lurk in battles, in conflicts, in tension? Arjuna is giving reasons for his desire to withdraw from the battle ahead of him. And so he again says:

अधर्माभिभवात् कृष्ण प्रदुष्यन्ति कुलस्त्रियः ।
स्त्रीषु दुष्टासु वार्ष्णेय जायते वर्णसङ्करः ॥४१॥

Adharmābhibhavāt kṛṣṇa praduṣyanti kulastriyaḥ;
Strīṣu duṣṭāsu vārṣṇeya jāyate varṇasaṅkaraḥ — 1. 41

'Whenever there is a big war, how many widows and orphans are created thereby! On the prevalence of impiety, when social values go away, the women of the family become corrupt because of this terrible situation. And when anything adverse happens to our women, the whole society suffers. There will be lot of corruption in society.'

सङ्करो नरकायैव कुलघ्नानां कुलस्य च ।
पतन्ति पितरो ह्येषां लुप्तपिण्डोदकक्रियाः ॥४२॥

Saṅkaro narakāyaiva kulaghnānām kulasya ca;
Patanti pitaro hyeṣām luptapiṇḍodakakriyāḥ — 1. 42

'Social disintegration will land in hell the family and the destroyers of the family. Their ancestors will become deprived of the ritual offerings of rice-balls and water.'

That is what we do in a funeral—those who are dead, parents and others, we honour them with such offerings. That is called the funeral ceremony. In every society, there is some form of this ceremony; we call it *śrāddhā,* in the Indian tradition. All this becomes difficult to perform, and so there is a thorough confusion in society.

दोषैरेतैः कुलघ्नानां वर्णसङ्करकारकैः ।
उत्साद्यन्ते जातिधर्माः कुलधर्माश्च शाश्वताः ॥४३॥

doṣairetaiḥ kulaghnānām varṇasaṅkarakārakaiḥ;
Utsādyante jātidharmāḥ kuladharmāśca śāśvatāḥ —1. 43

'By these misdeeds of destroying the families, bringing about confusion in society, class, and caste, the memorial rites of the class and the family get destroyed.'

उत्सन्नकुलधर्माणां मनुष्याणां जनार्दन ।
नरके नियतं वासो भवतीत्यनुशुश्रुम ॥४४॥

Utsannakuladharmāṇām manuṣyāṇām janārdana;
Narake niyatam vāso bhavatītyanuśuśruma — 1. 44

'We have heard, O Kṛṣṇa, that inevitable is the dwelling in hell of those men and women in whose families religious practices have become destroyed.'

अहो बत महत्पापं कर्तुं व्यवसिता वयम् ।
यद्राज्यसुखलोभेन हन्तुं स्वजनमुद्यताः ॥४५॥

Aho bata mahatpāpam kartum vyavasitā vayam;
Yadrājyasukhalobhena hantum svajanamudyatāḥ—1. 45

'Alas! We are preparing to involve ourselves in a great sin, in that we are prepared to slay our kinsmen out of the greed of the pleasures of a kingdom.'

यदि मामप्रतीकारमशस्त्रं शस्त्रपाणयः ।
धार्तराष्ट्रा रणे हन्युस्तन्मे क्षेमतरं भवेत् ॥४६॥

Yadi māmapratīkāramaśastram śastrapāṇayaḥ;
Dhartarāṣṭrā raṇe hanyustanme kṣemataram bhavet—1. 46

'If the sons of Dhṛtarāṣṭra, i.e., the Kauravas, with weapons in hand, were to kill me, un-resistant, unarmed, in the battle, that would be better for me.'

Arjuna is now definitely giving his final verdict on the situation to Śrī Kṛṣṇa. He wants to adopt perfect unqualified non-violence. A critical situation indeed; war is about to begin, Arjuna had prepared himself for it, he wanted it, and yet at this critical moment Arjuna withdraws, giving ultimatum of that withdrawal to Śrī Kṛṣṇa, because he is so overwhelmed by sorrow, by dejection. What did Śrī Kṛṣṇa say? Śrī Kṛṣṇa gave—we will see it in the second chapter of the *Gītā*—answers to all these utterances of Arjuna. But here Sañjaya reports what happened at this point of time:

सञ्जय उवाच –
Sañjaya uvāca —

'Sañjaya said.'

एवमुक्त्वाऽर्जुनः संख्ये रथोपस्थ उपाविशत् ।
विसृज्य सशरं चापं शोकसंविग्नमानसः ॥४७॥

Evamuktvārjunaḥ samkhye rathopastha upāviśat;
Visṛjya saśaram cāpam śokasamvignamānasaḥ— 1. 47

'Speaking thus in the midst of the battle-field, Arjuna, casting away his bow and arrows, sank down on the seat of his chariot with his mind distressed with sorrow.'

Delusion, grief, sorrow. This is how the first chapter ends. Here is a picture of Arjuna in this critical situation, in the midst of the battle when it is just about to begin. He withdraws, saying 'I don't want to fight', and he gives very good arguments of kindness, of compassion, and non-violence—far superior to what we understand by non-violence. Several people ask this question: 'Was not Arjuna superior to all the other people in that battle-field? He spoke of non-violence. Non-violence is a great virtue.' This we shall discuss when we begin the second chapter. But Śrī Kṛṣṇa will say that non-violence is not a virtue in every case. Non-violence must be of a strong variety, a bold variety, a positive variety. This kind of teaching will come from Śrī Kṛṣṇa to Arjuna later on in the *Gītā*. Śrī Kṛṣṇa asks: 'Wherefrom has this dejection come upon you at this difficult situation?' It is a nervous breakdown, as it were, in the case of Arjuna. The body is shivering, mind is whirling. What is all this? A real virtue is a virtue based on strength, based on fearlessness. This is not virtue. Something has happened to the human mind. It has become unnerved as it were. A bold, courageous man, like Arjuna, behaves like a coward here on the battlefield. This is how Śrī Kṛṣṇa viewed Arjuna's situation: full of sympathy for him, but not accepting his arguments. That is how the first chapter ends.

इति अर्जुन विषादयोगो नाम प्रथमोऽध्यायः।

Iti arjuna-viṣāda-yogo nāma prathamo'dhyāyaḥ —

Thus, ends the first chapter entitled *arjuna-viṣāda-yoga,* the *yoga* of Arjuna's grief, well portrayed in this chapter.

BHAGAVAD GĪTĀ

CHAPTER 2

SĀṄKHYA-YOGA
SĀṄKHYA AND YOGA

We left Arjuna, in the last verse of the first chapter, sunk in the chariot, completely depressed. The language used in the last verse is very very expressive of this situation. The chapter itself is called Arjuna's grief or depression, *Arjuna-viṣāda-yoga*. In the last śloka of chapter 1, Sañjaya had said, *Evamuktvārjunaḥ samkhye rathopastha upāviśat,* 'having said so in the midst of the battlefield, Arjuna sat down in the chariot; he sank into the chariot'. Generally, when they fight, they stand up; that was the custom in those days. Standing up and fighting; sitting down means no more fighting. *Visṛjya saśaraṁ cāpam,* throwing away his bow and arrows. That is complete negation of the purpose for which he had come there. *Śoka samvigna mānasaḥ,* 'with the mind immersed in *śoka,* or, grief or dejection'. That was the state of Arjuna as described in the last verse.

Now we begin the second chapter. How did Śrī Kṛṣṇa react to this state of Arjuna's mind, and the various arguments Arjuna gave for wanting to run away from the field of battle? Some of the arguments appeal to us also. All over the world today nobody likes war. So, in Australia, America and Europe, people ask me this question: 'Arjuna seems to be better than Śrī Kṛṣṇa. He wants to have peace, he does not want war. Śrī Kṛṣṇa is egging him on to war. How can we accept this situation?'

I said that is correct. Arjuna is speaking of peace, non-violence, compassion, and Śrī Kṛṣṇa is asking Arjuna to give up these values and fight. But, what does that mean? What is the state of Arjuna's mind? Is there any virtue in Arjuna's state of mind? Is virtue weakness? Is virtue nervous breakdown? We have to ask these questions. Virtue is strong. It is made of 'stern stuff', in the language of Shakespeare. That stern stuff you do not find in Arjuna in that condition. He is only invoking these wonderful ideas of love, compassion, non-violence, etc. But his own condition was very pitiable, what you call these days, a psychic breakdown. Śrī Kṛṣṇa looked at him, and as the book says, with a smile, and began to speak to him. How to restore this man to his own true state of mind? He was not like this, but this state of depression, this weakness, has come upon him just now. Virtue must be made of sterner stuff. Character must be made of sterner stuff. Non-violence must also be made of sterner stuff. Even Mahatma Gandhi would say, 'I don't like the non-violence of the coward. Non-violence of the brave alone is non-violence.'

Śrī Kṛṣṇa looked at Arjuna, and in two famous verses debunked him; Śrī Kṛṣṇa showed to Arjuna that whatever he thought was right, was not right. One cannot judge oneself rightly with a sick, grief-stricken mind. A grief-stricken mind loses discrimination. One must be calm and steady. Then one will understand one's situation better. And so, this part of the second chapter is very vital in the study of the *Gītā*. Śrī Kṛṣṇa is teaching us not to run away from the battle of life. It is easy to run away. We can produce various arguments, and many do this. Suppose one has trouble at home; he simply runs away to Benares. Some people then say of him, you are wonderful, so full of renunciation. But, Śrī Kṛṣṇa won't say so. You are a weakling, you are not doing your own duty. You are escaping from all this. There is a spirit of manliness in human beings; that should not be forgotten. So, all these various life situations come to us, and Śrī Kṛṣṇa, and today Swami Vivekananda, asks us to face up to these problems. Bring up new energies from within. In this way, a positive attitude develops in us, and the mind is made stable and steady to see things clearly. What is your duty at a particular time?, you must be able to find out this. Arjuna was confused. He was dejected; in that condition his judgement had no value at all. And so, Sañjaya begins the second chapter with this statement.

सञ्जय उवाच –
Sañjaya uvāca —

'Sañjaya said:'

तं तथा कृपयाविष्टमश्रुपूर्णाकुलेक्षणम् ।
विषीदन्तमिदं वाक्यमुवाच मधुसूदनः ॥१॥

Tam tathā kṛpayāviṣṭamaśrupūrṇākulekṣaṇam;
Viṣīdantamidam vākyamuvāca madhusūdanaḥ — 2. 1

Madhusūdanaḥ *uvāca*, 'Madhusūdana said', that means Śrī Kṛṣṇa said; *Idam vākyam*, 'this utterance' Śrī Kṛṣṇa made. What Śrī Kṛṣṇa said is found in the next two verses. But He said this to whom?, to Arjuna. What kind of Arjuna?, *viṣīdantam*, 'deeply grieving'; *kṛpayāviṣṭam*, 'overwhelmed with pity'; Arjuna was in a pitiable condition. Further, *aśrupūrṇākulekṣaṇam*, 'tears were streaming from the eyes of Arjuna'. These are not the signs of stability or courage or strength.

To that kind of Arjuna, Śrī Kṛṣṇa spoke these words. You can see the abnormal state of Arjuna's mind. It was highly pathological, not healthy. A healthy mind won't be like this. That is what we have to learn first. Weeping and wailing on facing some problem is not a healthy condition. Certainly, if the problems are too much beyond our control, then we shall have to weep and wail. But if you can, you must try to face up to these problems. There are occasions when you cannot face a problem. And Vivekananda says in one place, 'I shall either fight the problem or take recourse to flight'. There is no harm in flying away, provided you have done your best to face up to it. This is the positive attitude. Śrī Kṛṣṇa is going to convey this attitude to Arjuna, and then, in the context of this, he will be expounding a wonderful philosophy of life for all people. Some of our own people would have said to Arjuna, what you said is correct, go home, wear some poor dress, and take *bhikṣā* from house to house and live an ascetic's life. But running away from problems will not be a solution, for problems will be chasing you. You have to face up to them some time or the other. That wonderful idea is coming in Śrī Kṛṣṇa's two verses in reply.

श्रीभगवानुवाच –
Śrī Bhagavān uvāca —

'Śrī Kṛṣṇa said:'

कुतस्त्वा कश्मलमिदं विषमे समुपस्थितम् ।
अनार्यजुष्टमस्वर्ग्यमकीर्तिकरमर्जुन ॥ २ ॥

Kutastvā kaśmalamidam viṣame samupasthitam;
Anāryajuṣṭamasvargyamakīrtikaramarjuna — 2. 2

This is simple Sanskrit, full of meaning: *kutastvā, kutaḥ* means wherefrom, *tvā* means, to you, wherefrom has come to you; *kaśmalam,* 'this very low attitude', *kaśmala* is the Sanskrit word signifying all that is bad. *Viṣame samupasthitam,* 'in this most difficult situation' you have brought up this kind of argument and developed this attitude. In the midst of the two armies, the battle is about to begin; at this moment you say, 'no, I cannot. I am going away. I am going to Hṛiṣīkeśa. *Anāryajuṣṭam,* 'a noble-minded person will never take to this attitude.'

Ārya is not a race; *Ārya* means a noble-minded person. The word *Ārya* is often confused with a race. In the beginning, Western historians propounded this theory of the *Āryan* race. That developed into Hitler's *Āryan* superiority. And when Hitler died, the *Āryan* race theory also died! But the word *Ārya* is used in Sanskrit always for the noble-minded person. Take any Sanskrit drama. The person will address another character as 'My dear *Ārya,* noble-minded person'. And Buddha spoke of his teachings as *Ārya-satyāni,* Noble Truths. Noble is the word for *Ārya* there. The four Noble Truths, *Ārya Satyāni.* So, the word *Ārya* was used by Buddha, as also by earlier Vedic literature. And this word *Ārya* is, therefore, a very great word in Ṣanskrit. Be an *Āryan* means, be noble-minded. Don't be petty, don't be small. So, Śrī Kṛṣṇa calls it, *anāryajuṣṭam,* the attitude you have adopted 'is not adopted by *Āryas'*. Only ignoble people, those who are not *Ārya,* have your attitude. *Asvargyam,* 'it won't give you any glory either in heaven or on earth'; you won't have any glory thereby. *Akīrtikaram,* 'also it brings you bad name', ill fame. Arjuna was a great warrior; he has fallen a prey to weakness. His name will suffer in the world. These three words, *Anāryajuṣṭam, asvargyam, akīrtikaram* acted as shock treatment to Arjuna. In cases of mental breakdown, the patient is given shock treatment. So, here is Śrī Kṛṣṇa's shock treatment to Arjuna. Arjuna never expected that. He expected that Śrī Kṛṣṇa would pat on his back: Arjuna, you have done well. You are *such* a noble soul, having compassion on everybody, you don't want to kill anybody. You would rather be a mendicant than be a fighter. All this that was expected by Arjuna did not come from Śrī Kṛṣṇa. He scolds him, gives him this kind of shock treatment. This verse gives the negative approach. Now comes the positive approach. Śrī Kṛṣṇa is telling him in the next verse:

क्लैब्यं मा स्म गमः पार्थ नैतत् त्वयि उपपद्यते ।
क्षुद्रं हृदयदौर्बल्यं त्यक्त्वोत्तिष्ठ परन्तप ॥३॥

Klaibyam māsma gamaḥ pārtha naïtat tvayi upapadyate;
Kṣudram hṛdayadaurbalyam tyaktvottiṣṭha parantapa —2. 3

This is a powerful verse. *Klaibyam,* means chicken-heartedness, you can say, weakness, absolutely no strength, no manliness in it. *Mā sma gamaḥ pārtha,* 'don't fall a prey O Arjuna' to this meanness, this chicken-heartedness. Why?, *naitattvayyupapadyate,* 'this does not befit you'. You are so heroic, you are so noble, you are so great. This behaviour does not befit you. What a wonderful idea! Whenever I read this part of the verse, I like this wonderful sentiment fit for telling children, it does not befit you, you are so good, you are so noble. The way you behave does not befit you. *That will bring the best out of a person.* So, this approach of *naitattvayyupapadyate,* 'it does not befit you', can be an educational maxim for parents and teachers with respect to children, and generally also for men and women when they deal with each other: 'this behaviour does not befit you'. That means, you respect the person, he or she has forgotten his or her true nature, and is doing something below his or her dignity. So, this appeal is a positive appeal. It has the power to evoke the best in you, the best in the listener. Śrī Kṛṣṇa is telling Arjuna, this is not your true form. Some *Māyā* has come upon your mind. This weakness, this dejection, what is called nervous breakdown, that is not your true form. When we have a nervous breakdown, how weak we become, like a baby.

I had to deal with a very close friend, a Principal of an Engineering College, a noble-minded person, highly respected by all the students and teachers, when I was in Karachi. He got a nervous breakdown. His condition was like that of a baby, absolutely no strength, no energy, no courage. Can't meet anybody. He won't go to college, he will live at home. I took him in the car, took him to the Engineering College, made him sit on the Principal's chair; you run this college, you are such a great soul, so noble. As soon as I left, he also left and came and sat in his house. He couldn't meet anybody. But after six months everything changed. All strength came back. That was just like a cloud coming over the sun, a temporary cloud. The real man came out again. The same wonderful work went on. He built and developed two more Engineering Colleges in India. Later on, he passed away very peacefully.

With nervous breakdown you become a nobody, your old self is dead. Actually it is not dead; it is there, it is clouded by this weakness that has come. And so we go to a psychiatrist; he deals with us and somehow he puts us into a good condition. We see this happening everyday. This concept that man is essentially Divine, all this weakness that you experience is not your true form, there is something profound about you—that is the basic Vedantic teaching. That is why when Vivekananda was asked in America during the question hour: Swami, are you not preaching some kind of hypnotism in the name of Vedanta—just hypnotising people, Swamiji immediately replied with a smile, 'No, sir, I am de-hypnotising people.

They are already hypnotised. They say, 'I am white', 'I am black', 'I am this', 'I am that', all that is false. You are the infinite Atman, one with all; that is your true dimension. *Tattvamasi, tattvamasi,* 'You are That, You are That', not this tiny organic system—there is something profound about you.

So, all education has this quality: it de-hypnotises you. Some weakness has come and it has obstructed your true form. You are essentially strong. How do you know, how many varieties of energies and strengths are within you! You don't know. Therefore, don't despair. You can get out of this difficulty. There is strength hidden within you. That is the positive attitude Vedanta proclaims to everyone. Here Śrī Kṛṣṇa stands on that pedestal, and then addresses Arjuna. He says, *naitattvayyupadyate* 'it does not befit you'. It is just a temporary aberration, a little cloud has come there and the sun has become dark. The sun is still there; the cloud will go away and the sun will shine once again. That is how you have to deal with human weaknesses. We are not essentially weak. We are essentially strong. But when we don't realize this truth, we weep repeatedly over every problem, like children for example. The child's only language is weeping; nothing else is there. Even grownups become like children. Swami Vivekananda's diagnosis of India during the last several centuries is a nation constantly weeping, weeping, weeping. Then he said (*Complete Works of Swami Vivekananda,* vol. 3, p. 224):

'We have wept long enough. No more weeping, but stand on your feet and be men.'

This is a famous passage in Vivekananda's teaching. The whole nation has been weeping for centuries with a sense of inadequacy with respect to our environment. We did not know our own strength. Slowly that is changing. Yes, problems are there; but we shall find the way to deal with all these. In this way, that weeping state of India is changing now. No more weeping. We shall have to manifest our strength, face up to these problems.

I went to Jakarta in 1963–64, at the time of Vivekananda's Birth Centenary, and at that time Doctor Sukarno, President, wrote a foreword to a book on Vivekananda in the Indonesian language, *Svara Vivekananda. Svara* in Sanskrit means sound; in Indonesian language it means words, words of Vivekananda or sayings of Vivekananda. Sukarno wrote the introduction and he was having a one-hour T.V session to release that book. Indian Ambassador, Appa Pant , was there as my host. In that introduction occurs this wonderful passage. Sukarno was deeply influenced by Swamiji's ideas from his young days. He always kept the *Complete Works of Swami Vivekananda* in his bed room. And he told me, you can go to the bed room, you will find all the volumes are there. I read a page or two everyday, he said. So, in that passage in the foreword, he says:

'Swami Vivekananda, ah! What a name! He was the one who taught me how to love my people, how to love my country, how to love the whole world. He was the one who said, "We have wept long enough. No more weeping now, but stand on your feet and be men". Yours, Sukarno.' That is the introduction. That book was in English as well as in the Indonesian language.

So, this attitude, which Śrī Kṛṣṇa expressed then, found a new expression in our time in Swami Vivekananda, and Swamiji loved these two verses very much. In his discourse on the *Gītā*, he says, if you can understand the spirit of these two verses, you understand the spirit of the whole *Gītā*. This presents a strong philosophy meant to make heroes out of clay. This spirit must be captured by us. We could do so, we all read the *Gītā*, but we did not catch the spirit of this powerful message. Now Swamiji has come and given us the same message of strength, facing up to the problems. And in his lectures in England and America on *Jñāna Yoga*, he referred to this particular truth in terms of his own experience.

During his *parivrājaka* (wandering) days in India, somewhere in Benares or so, he was chased by a number of monkeys. He had been moving about as a wandering monk, going all through India. A number of monkeys—monkeys in Benares are fierce—chased him, and he was running. From a distance, an old *sādhu* (monk) shouted at him, 'Bābāji, don't run away. Face the brutes, face the brutes.' Swamiji thought,

'This is a wonderful teaching'. Immediately he turned back and turned towards these monkeys with a fierce look. And the monkeys fled away. He referred to this story in his London lecture and said, 'face the brute', 'face the brute'; otherwise, you run away, and the brute will be chasing you all through your life. That is not manliness. Man has much better capacity hidden within him or her. So, this Śrī Kṛṣṇa's tonic to Arjuna, is a tonic we all need. The whole nation and the world itself will need it.

So, in the third *śloka* of this second chapter, Śrī Kṛṣṇa said: *Klaibyam mā sma gamaḥ pārtha,* 'Don't give in to *klaibyam,* actually it means a person of neuter gender, what you call a *napumsaka liṅga,* neither man nor woman, that is called *klaibya;* it suggests weakness, chicken-heartedness—all these meanings attach to this word *klaibya. Naitattvayyupapadyate,* 'it doesn't befit you'. You have such a noble nature, heroism, courage, everything you have. *Kṣudram hṛdaya-daurbalyam tyaktvā uttiṣṭha parantapa.* He was sitting down, broken, sunk in the chariot. In that condition, Śrī Kṛṣṇa says, *uttiṣṭa,* 'stand up'. The first sign that strength has come to you is when you stand up. When you are still lying down, that old weakness is there. So, 'stand up', 'stand up'; it is a powerful word in dealing with the awakening of a human being. Stand on your feet and be men. So, this *klaibyam,* give it up. *Kṣudram hṛdayadaurbalyam,* 'this weakness of the heart', which is *kṣudram,* i.e., mean, give it up. Arjuna, stand up, face up to your problems. This is what Śrī Kṛṣṇa tells to Arjuna and to all of us when we are in difficulties and we do not know our inner strength; we think we cannot proceed any more, or we break down. Then, somebody has to come and give us new strength. That strength is there. But somebody must give the touch; then only will it manifest. We all need it. In fact, in your life you can see, if one is weak, you go and strengthen him or her by a few words. Then he or she really feels stronger. Even appreciating a person increases his or her strength. It is said in the *Rāmāyaṇa,* when people were sent to search for Sītā here and there, Hanumān was asked, 'Go south. You will succeed.' Hanumān took up the job. Then Aṅgada or somebody else praised Hanumān, 'You are such a great soul. You have such great achievements in your life.' All that made Hanumān feel greater and greater confidence in himself in finding Sītā, and he succeeded.

In social relations, you can do two things to each other: either destroy one's confidence, or increase that self-confidence. Mostly we have done the negative thing in India. We have destroyed each other's self-confidence. Speak of his or her great achievements; that will immediately make him or her feel, 'I can. Yes, I can.' This is how Śrī Kṛṣṇa is dealing with Arjuna, 'Stand up. Face up to your problems. Don't become weak. Any type of weakness has no virtue about it. One great lesson Vedanta tells us: Weakness and virtue can never go together. Virtue is strength; weakness is no virtue at all. Where there is no courage, there is no virtue; *virāḥ* is a great word in Sanskrit meaning heroic persons. In that person only you find virtue. In weak people, where is virtue? So, the concept of *dharma* and virtue, even goodness, all these must be associated with strength and fearlessness. Then only they become positive. We somehow did not do so; we often call a good-for-nothing person as good, because he or she doesn't harm anybody. He or she has not the power to harm anybody; where is goodness in it? Where is virtue in it? So, this is how our judgement had been wrong for centuries. That is why I sometimes tell of parents coming to the Ashrama and saying, if there is a good-for-nothing boy in one's house, 'Swamiji, here is a boy, take him as a sannyasin in your Ashrama. He will be very good for you.' It means that what is not good for the world is good for spiritual life. The truth is just the opposite. So, our whole thinking has been defective in this matter. That heroic attitude was not there. Strength and fearlessness were not there. And today Vivekananda comes and preaches only this one great message: strength and fearlessness, *śakti* and *abhīḥ*.

Jawaharlal Nehru writes about this message of Swamiji in his *Discovery of India:* 'He gave a spirit of courage to our people.' A strength, a spirit of manliness, is the biggest contribution from any great teacher. And so, we need this kind of teaching in a big way. In olden days, Śrī Kṛṣṇa gave it. He was the very embodiment of strength and fearlessness; and the whole of Vedanta is a message of strength and fearlessness. Never will you find any stress on weakness in Vedanta. Always *abhīḥ, abhīḥ, abhīḥ. Abhīḥ* means fearless; be fearless, be fearless. Brahman, the ultimate source of the universe and human beings, is *abhayam.* What is the name of God?, fearlessness. And when you attain God, you become fearless. So, *abhayam vai prāpto'si janakaḥ—Bṛhadāraṇyaka Upaniṣad* says that Sage Yājñavalkya tells King Janaka: 'Janaka, you have achieved the state of fearlessness.' That is your fullest spiritual development. Through fearlessness, you develop spiritually; and never through weakness. Animals are all weak; they are creatures. A human being can become fearless by realizing one's own inherent divine nature. Vivekananda says that every page of the Upaniṣads preach only one message: fearlessness and strength. Are you strong? The human heart asks this question: are there no human weaknesses? Vedanta says, yes, there are. But can you remove weakness through weakness? Weakness can be removed only through strength. Dirt cannot wash dirt. Only pure water can wash dirt. So, another weakness cannot remove existing weakness. Strength alone is the remedy for the world's disease. That is the message of Vedanta. The more spiritual you become, the more fearless and strong you become, and the more compassionate also. You combine two great virtues: fearlessness and compassion. In all Indian literature, you find this confluence of two difficult virtues, difficult to co-exist: intense fearlessness, intense compassion. You can be fearful, so that others are frightened. Or, you can be so weak, anybody can frighten you. These extremes we have seen. But this rare combination is highlighted in the whole of our literature. And in this very *Gītā,* when you come to its twelfth chapter, Śrī Kṛṣṇa will tell 'he or she is my true devotee'—the one who is strong and fearless, and yet is compassionate to all beings. He doesn't fear anybody; but nobody need fear him also, because he is so gentle. *Yasmāt na udvijate lokaḥ lokāt na udvijate ca yaḥ* (12. 15), that is the sign of spiritual growth and spiritual realization. So that the whole subject of every human being is growth, development and fulfilment. This is what Śrī Kṛṣṇa is handling in *Gītā's* eighteen chapters. As I told the Australian, American and other friends, war is only in the first chapter. Afterwards you don't hear about the word 'war' at all. It is only the big problem of total human development that Śrī Kṛṣṇa handles throughout. And, therefore, this is not a book on war. This is a book of human development and fulfilment. No one will say that the second World War and the complete defeat of Hitler and his political and racialist ideology was wrong. That is the philosophy that will help a human being to develop high character which contains these two elements—strength and gentleness—in a confluence. The *Gītā* also conveys the message of combining great broad-mindedness and intensity of faith and conviction—these two cannot often coexist. I am a cosmopolitan, people say. When you examine, you will find that he has no particular conviction. He is all things to all men, because he is nobody himself. That kind of cheap cosmopolitan attitude, some people adopt, because there is no depth; the width is there, but not depth. There are people full of depth, but they are fanatical. They hold to their own, criticize everybody else. That kind of depth, you have seen. But Swamiji says Vedanta wants you to have depth plus breadth: broad attitude and deep conviction. If you can combine these two, then you have the best of character. We shall be 'deep as the ocean, and broad as the sky'; these are the words he has used. Vedanta wants to instil that kind of a character in all people all over the world. So, here you have a profound philosophy of human growth, development, and fulfilment. That cannot come to you when you are in a depressed state of mind, when you are nervous and mentally broken. Until you become somewhat normal, this message cannot come to you.

So, Śrī Kṛṣṇa is giving the first initial tonic to Arjuna's broken mind through these two verses. And the tonic had the effect. When Śrī Kṛṣṇa spoke these words, Arjuna became somewhat strengthened, somewhat composed in mind. He could speak a little more coherently thereafter. That is what you will see hereafter in the coming verses. In Arjuna's words a little coherence begins to appear and that depression is no more there. Śrī Kṛṣṇa removed it by these powerful words. And with a little more calmness, a little more of rationality, he is putting forth his arguments in his reply to Śrī Kṛṣṇa's exhortations.

That is the subject of verses 4 to 9 in this second chapter. This is what the *Kaṭha Upaniṣad* said in a few powerful words (I. iii. 14), *uttiṣṭhata jāgrata prāpya varān nibodhata*, 'arise, awake, and stop not till the goal is reached', as freely translated by Swami Vivekananda. What a beautiful concept! Our human life marching onwards. Flowing water is clean and pure; a stagnant pool is a source of trouble. So also, is a stagnant life, stagnant mind. Arjuna can now control his feelings and emotions. That is the beginning of human development. No animal can control feelings. Whenever feelings come, they express automatically their feelings in action. But man can control feelings, then try to understand the environment, then adapt oneself to that situation. So, controlling feelings is the first step in thinking, followed by effective action. Whenever you have strong feelings, you find that the mind is clouded. When your feelings are slightly calmed, then clear thinking begins. This is the dictate of neurology: animals cannot control their feelings. The first step to get control of the environment, is controlling our feelings. You see something, you jump at it, or run away from it. But, human being alone can control his or her feelings, watch, study, think, roll in one's mind the consequences of things, and express oneself in action. That is how man controls the environment, which no animal can do. Even the chimpanzee cannot have a fraction of that capacity which you see in a human being, says neurologist Gray Walter in his book: *The Living Brain*.

And therefore, Arjuna is now in a more equable frame of mind. Later on, in the middle of the second chapter, when Śrī Kṛṣṇa begins expounding his own philosophy of life, he will say, this equable mind, this balanced mind, is essential. The word is *samatva.* Keep these emotions and feelings inside, just calm them down a little. Then you can see things clearly; otherwise, it will be like life in Delhi when there is a dust storm. They call it *āndhi;* you can't see anything. The whole sky is full of dust. Similarly, emotions and feelings without any control, become like *āndhi* for the mind. When they settle down, you can see things clearly. So, in the burst of emotion, in the burst of feeling, don't do anything; don't say anything. Whatever you do at that time will not be correct. Feeling should be controlled by thinking. All aspects of the subject should be studied before you enter into the stage of action. As Swami Brahmananda, a disciple of Sri Ramakrishna, used to tell people: when you write a strong letter to somebody in reply to his or her letter, put your letter under the pillow for a day or two. Afterwards you send it. You yourself will modify it. That time you were in a flame, and that flame is slowly dying out. If you had posted the letter in the beginning itself, you yourself will feel, why did I do like that? It has spoiled the whole situation. So, human beings have that capacity. If you don't exercise it, you are behaving like an animal. We call a human being a *thinking* animal. But when thinking is removed, the animal only remains. Therefore, Arjuna is now in a more chastened mood. The tonic has acted. So, he is telling Śrī Kṛṣṇa now in a calm, collected mood, and more coherently.

अर्जुन उवाच –
Arjuna uvāca —

'Arjuna said.'

कथं भीष्ममहं संख्ये द्रोणं च मधुसूदन ।
इषुभिः प्रतियोत्स्यामि पूजार्हौ अरिसूदन ॥४॥

Katham bhīṣmamaham saṁkhye droṇam ca madhusūdana;
Iṣubhiḥ pratiyotsyāmi pūjārhau arisūdana — 2. 4

'Kṛṣṇa, how can I, in battle, shoot arrows at men like Bhīṣma and Droṇa? They are worthy to be worshipped by me.'

More coherent language you will find here. *Samkhye* means 'in war'. In a war, how can I, *iṣubhiḥ pratiyotsyāmi,* 'fight with my sharp arrows' men like Bhīṣma and Droṇa? They are *Pūjārhau,* means, people who deserve worship. They are our elders. Droṇa is a teacher. Bhīṣma is like a great-grandfather. So, that is the first question Arjuna is asking Śrī Kṛṣṇa. Secondly:

गुरूनहत्वा हि महानुभावान्
श्रेयो भोक्तुं भैक्ष्यमपीह लोके ।
हत्वार्थकामांस्तु गुरूनिहैव
भुञ्जीय भोगान् रुधिरप्रदिग्धान् ॥५॥

Gurūnahatvā hi mahānubhāvān
śreyo bhoktum bhaikṣyamapīha loke;
Hatvārthakāmāmstu gurūnihaiva
bhuñjīya bhogān rudhirapradigdhān — 2. 5

'Indeed, it were better for me to live on alms in the world and avoid slaying my honoured elders; killing these people who seek their own purposes, I should be tasting blood-stained pleasures.'

Gurūnahatva, 'without killing these gurus'; guru does not mean here the teacher; it means respected elders. *Hi mahānubhāvān,* 'also honoured people'. *Śreyo bhoktum bhaikṣyamapīha loke,* 'I would much prefer to take *bhikṣa,* begging food from several houses'. *Hatvā arthakāmān tu gurūnihaiva, bhuñjīya bhogān rudhirapradigdhān.* 'If I kill these people who run after material wealth, whatever food I eat will be smeared with their blood'. *Artha-kāma* means, *kāma,* desire, for *artha,* wealth. Why are they called *arthakāmas*?

That refers to an incident in the *Mahābhārata* in the beginning itself. Actually, that idea comes now, through the mouth of Yudhiṣṭhira. Just before the battle began, Yudhiṣṭhira, the eldest of the Pāṇḍavas, was not in a mood to fight his opponents; he walked towards the opposite side unarmed—and warriors on both sides were wondering what he was meaning to do—and touched the feet of Bhīṣma, Droṇa and Śalya—three very senior people whom he respected, and requested them to come to his side or remain neutral. And Bhīṣma, Droṇa and Śalya, all the three, replied to Yudhiṣṭhira in the same language, that we are fighting against you. Why?, because we are beholden to the Kauravas, to Duryodhana. He is giving us salary, he is giving us our food, we are bound down by these obligations. So, we are not in a position to help you. We have to fight against you. That is the statement given by all the three to Yudhiṣṭhira at that time (*Mahābhārata, Bhīṣma Parva*, 35):

Arthasya dāso puruṣo
dāsastvartho na kasyacit;
Iti satyam mahārāja
baddho'styarthena kauravaiḥ —

This is related to the early period, when Bhīṣma was the guest of Kauravas; Droṇa was also the same, he was given salary, a free house, and allowances, everything by the Kauravas. What you speak of today: an officer being appointed with all the perquisites. Droṇa also got it; Śalya also got it. All of them thus became bound to the Kauravas. The *Bhīṣma Parva* contains the *Gītā* also. This verse says, 'man is the servant of wealth, wealth is never the servant of anybody'. See the language. *Iti satyam mahārāja baddho'styarthena kauravaiḥ*, 'We have been bound down through wealth by the Kauravas; they give us our salary, our allowances, etc.' What a truth it is even today! We are bound down by the salary we get; the people whom we serve, we have our loyalty towards them; we can't do anything else. Why is it so? Because we want our sensory satisfaction, food, drink, house, all these things. And they all involve money. And so, since we need all these, we need money; most people are subject to the pressure of money. Arjuna is referring to that particular situation. They are *arthakāmas*, by killing them, what do I get? I get food smeared with their blood, which I don't like to eat. I prefer to eat *bhikṣa* taken from some houses. That is far better, says Arjuna. Then,

न चैतद्विद्मः कतरन्नो गरीयो
यद्वा जयेम यदि वा नो जयेयुः ।
यानेव हत्वा न जिजीविषामः
तेऽवस्थिताः प्रमुखे धार्तराष्ट्राः ॥६॥

Na caitadvidmaḥ kataranno garīyo
yadvā jayema yadi vā no jayeyuḥ;
Yāneva hatvā na jijīviṣāmaḥ
te'vasthitāḥ pramukhe dhārtarāṣṭrāḥ — 2. 6

In front of us are the Kauravas, the children of Dhṛtarāṣṭra, all of them ready for battle. We do not understand what is really beneficial to us in this situation. *Na caitadvidmaḥ kataranno garīyo*, 'what is supremely significant and beneficial to us, I am not able to understand'. What is that? *Yadvā jayema, yadi vā no jayeyuḥ*, 'shall we conquer or shall we allow ourselves to be conquered;—between these two questions I am unable to decide. I don't know what is good for us. *Yāneva hatvā na jijīviṣāmaḥ*, 'by killing whom we have no desire to live'; *te'vasthitāḥ pramukhe dhārtarāṣṭrāḥ*, 'those Kauravas, children of the blind Dhṛtarāṣṭra, are in front of us, by killing all of whom life will have no meaning at all. That is how he is putting his problem more cogently before Śrī Kṛṣṇa. Then *the next śloka brings what you call the precise beginnings of the Gītā teaching*. Arjuna is telling, 'I am confused, I take recourse to Your superior wisdom. My wisdom fails here. I am Your student, Your disciple. Please teach me what is really good for me.' It is only when a student says this will a teacher begin to teach. Unsought advice is not allowed in Vedanta. Unless you seek something, what is given to you has no value. Therefore, here all the commentators will say, the *Gītā* really begins from verse 7 of chapter 2, this particular verse where Arjuna says, 'I seek wisdom from You. What is really good for me, I am not able to understand myself. Please instruct me'.

कार्पण्यदोषोपहतस्वभावः
पृच्छामि त्वां धर्मसम्मूढचेताः ।
यच्छ्रेयः स्यात् निश्चितं ब्रूहि तन्मे
शिष्यस्तेऽहं शाधि मां त्वां प्रपन्नम् ॥७॥

Kārpaṇyadoṣopahatasvabhāvaḥ
pṛcchāmi tvām dharmasammūḍhacetāḥ;
Yacchreyaḥ syāt niścitam brūhi tanme
śiṣyaste'ham śādhi mām tvām prapannam —2. 7

'My inborn nature has been overwhelmed by the bane of faint-heartedness and I am confused as regards my *dharma* or duty; so I am asking you: tell me definitely what will prove beneficial to me. I am your disciple; teach me, who has surrendered to you'.

Kārpaṇyadoṣopahatasvabhāvaḥ, 'My inborn nature has been overwhelmed by the bane of faintheartedness'; *dharma-sammūḍhacetāḥ,* 'I am confused as regards my *dharma* or duty'; *pṛcchāmi tvām,* 'I am asking you'; *Yacchreyaḥ syāt niścitam brūhi tanme,* 'tell me definitely what will prove beneficial'; *śiṣyaste'ham,* 'I am your disciple'; *śādhi mām tvām prapannam,* 'teach me who has surrendered to you'.

In this verse Arjuna is explaining his position more soberly than what we heard towards the end of the first chapter. There he was completely broken down, he had lost his balance of mind. So grief-stricken he had become. After the tonic administered by Śrī Kṛṣṇa in verses 2 and 3 of this chapter as I said before, Arjuna became somewhat calm. He could explain his difficulties more cogently. We all pass through this kind of situation in our own lives. Arjuna is not unique, except in one sense. All of us have no battle to wage, or fight a war. Arjuna had to fight a war; but all of us have the battle of life, facing problems, overcoming them, trying to achieve life-fulfilment. That challenge is there before all of us. So, we are not going to become Arjunas, going to fight with everybody. That is not the meaning of the *Gītā*. One particular situation: something in it has a universal value. Take out that universal value from that situation. That is why, after the first half of the second chapter, you don't hear of war at all. It is all about character, purity, love, compassion. The whole teaching, when you come to the twelfth chapter, gets reflected in the question, 'who is My true devotee?' Śrī Kṛṣṇa will tell, 'he is My true devotee, who is strong and fearless, and makes others also strong and fearless. He doesn't use his strength to destroy other people': *Yasmānnodvijate loko lokānnodvijate ca yaḥ,* 'he who does not frighten the world, and he who is not frightened *by* the world' (*Gītā*, 12. 15), that is high character. A timid person doesn't frighten the world. But he is timid, there is no virtue in it. But a very strong person can frighten the world. That is also not a high virtue. But have strength and fearlessness and inspire the same thing in others as well—that is ideal humanity. *That is the main teaching, not only in this book but all through our Sanātana Dharma literature.* In the Upaniṣads, the *Gītā*, the *Mahābhārata*, *Śrīmad Bhāgavatam,* everywhere you will find that word which has been coined in Sanskrit, typifying the *Sanātana Dharma* mind of the best human being. That word is *ajāta śatru*, one whose enemy is not yet born. You have an enemy, you love him, you forgive him, that is one thing. You have no enemy at all, you don't recognize any enemy, that is the highest state of mind. That term is a very meaningful term: *ajāta śatru,* whose *śatru*, 'enemy', is *ajāta,* 'not yet born'—considered to be the highest level of human development. Probably only a handful of persons can achieve that highest state. But it is the highest state. To reach that highest state, we have to proceed in that direction, by becoming less and less aggressive, more and more loving and peaceful, and the whole thing will be a natural development of any human being from what he or she *is* under all conditions, to what he or she *can be* in that high level. It is this journey of man from ordinary conditions to the highest level that is being expounded in this *Gītā* as a philosophy of human development. In the course of that you will have occasion, sometimes to resist evil by fight, by war, as things are in the world. If you don't do so, you will not be able to achieve your own development or the development of society as a whole. Evil will multiply, if you don't resist the evil that is there. That message meant for a mendicant or a *sādhu* is different from the message meant for a householder. The latter has a family, he or she has to look after one's people, keep them, protect them. If somebody comes and steals from the house, he or she cannot honour the thief and say, 'take this also'. He or she will have to starve one's own children thereby. But some great *sādhus* have done it, like Pavahāri Bābā of Ghazipur, of whom we read in Vivekananda's life. When a thief stole away some things, he ran behind the thief saying, 'you have forgotten some things. I am giving this, take this also.' This he said. That is a beautiful idea. And the thief inspired by the touch of Pavahāri Bāba, later renounced the world, became a sādhu, and Vivekananda met him in Rishikesh and heard the story of his transformation by the touch of Pavahāri Bābā. But, an average citizen cannot do it. What he or she has lost, is lost, and will suffer from that loss. He or she cannot afford to lose it. One must learn to protect what one has by peaceful means and, if necessary, by violent means as well.

Now the greatest user of non-violence in the world was Mahatma Gandhi. And in his life you find a wonderful example: Some policemen went and attacked a village in U.P. Probably, Ballia may be one of those villages. And they did a lot of havoc during the *satyāgraha* days. They mishandled the women of the village. No one even protested. When Gandhiji sent an investigation team, this is the reply they gave: 'Gandhiji taught us non-violence. So, we kept quiet. We didn't resist.' Gandhiji said, 'I was ashamed to hear that statement. You couldn't protect the honour of your women! In the name of non-violence, you behaved like a coward! Is that non-violence? I preach a non-violence of the courageous person, not of a coward.' There are situations in life, therefore, where you will have to resist evil, if you want to survive. That is why, in the whole of the Hindu *Sanātana Dharma* tradition, there is no place for *pacifism,* as we call it in modern times: under any circumstance, I shall not resist. That pacifism has no place in our thinking. It is meant for a handful of persons who can stand it. To all others, there are occasions when you have to resist either peacefully or using some force—there is no aggression in it, it is a sheer need of human life.

When I was in the United States during my lecture tour, I heard the young American people there strongly protesting against the Vietnam War: 'It was a wicked war. America has no business there.' Thus, they protested, and they made America withdraw from Vietnam. That is wonderful! But not a single American protested when America joined the war against Hitler under Nazi ideology. That was a dangerous ideology; it will destroy the human spirit. If it had succeeded in the last war, humanity would have been dwarfed a good deal. So, nobody objected to that kind of a war to destroy that wicked philosophy which was gaining strength.

So, go back to the *Mahābhārata* period. How many evil deeds were done by the Kauravas, including insulting Draupadi in public by taking away her clothes. Many such insults these people suffered due to the constraints of the moral values they had upheld, until they could not suffer any more. Again and again you will find the *Mahābhārata* speaking: Peace is the greatest objective. Every state must choose peace and not war. Unless you are driven to it, avoid war by every means, was the teaching throughout the *Mahābhārata* as well as in the *Gītā*. So, when that critical situation came, when the Pāṇḍavas claimed their right to half the kingdom, after returning from exile in the forest—that was the arrangement originally—and when they were refused even that, then only they took recourse to war, to take what was due to them. You will have to take recourse to war. Even then Śrī Kṛṣṇa said, 'Wait. Let me try once again. I shall go as an ambassador on your behalf to the court of the Kauravas and plead for a peaceful settlement.' And everybody agreed, and the speech he delivered in the Kaurava court is masterly. Today, in the United Nations, you can hear echoes of some of the speeches in the Mahābhārata. You will find ideas there, almost verbatim: human values, the greatness of peace and harmony, peaceful settlement of disputes, all these you will find. And so, what did Śrī Kṛṣṇa do there? He said, 'These Pāṇḍavas, to whom the country belongs, you have usurped it by tricky means; doesn't matter. Give them half the kingdom, and the other half, you keep. They will build a new capital.' The Kauravas said, 'no.' Then Śrī Kṛṣṇa argues coming down and down. 'Give them five villages.' 'No', 'give them just one village, and they can have their own place to live and be happy there.' 'Nothing doing. Not one *sūci-mukha,* point of a needle, we will give to the Pāṇḍavas.' It was at this stage, that the situation went beyond human control. If you allow it even then to continue, it will be dangerous, as in the case of Hitler's war, if he had won. So, there was need to resist that evil, and it became very serious. So much destruction took place. This is a big civil war event in ancient Indian history: the *Mahābhārata* war. Things were not the same after that. But it was beyond control. A similar thing happened when Śrī Kṛṣṇa's own people killed each other in a tantrum state in Western India's city of Dvāraka.

Humanity has this weakness. Sometimes they can be excellent people, very peaceful; sometimes they become aggressive, wicked, violent. That is humanity. The teaching in the *Gītā* is to make humanity curb that aggressive spirit, to make people more peaceful, to live in peace with each other. That is why, throughout the book, you hear Śrī Kṛṣṇa expounding a philosophy of life based upon one particular situation centred in Arjuna. When you take a particular event, and universalize it, you get philosophy. A particular event is not philosophy. From that particular, you develop a universal concept. That is called the philosophy of life. So, Śrī Kṛṣṇa will tell to everyone, Arjuna had an actual battle to wage. You have no such battle to wage. But you have the battle of your own life to wage. So many difficulties will come, challenges will come. You like to run away like Arjuna? No; face them. That is the message He conveys to all humanity in India as well as abroad. While doing so, don't increase the evil that is already there. Do it in such a way that you will make the world a little better.

Sri Ramakrishna, in one of his beautiful parables, refers to this particular subject. A poisonous snake lived in a forest. Children used to play near about, but they were terribly afraid of the snake. One day, a holy man came by that way. He went towards the place where the snake was. And a boy told him, 'Sir, don't go that way. There is a poisonous snake.' He said, 'I am not afraid of this.' He went straight. The snake came towards him in an aggressive manner. But he uttered some mantra and the snake became very quiet in front of him. Then occurred a conversation between the sage and the snake: 'Why do you harm people? It is not proper to harm people. Live a non-violent life. Live for yourself. Allow others also to live for themselves. Hereafter don't do any harm to anybody. I give you a mantra. You keep it in mind. You will achieve something great in this very life. I will come back again.' Saying this, he went away. From that day, the snake changed its ways. It became quiet, peaceful, non-aggressive, and the children also, watching from a distance, found the snake had become less aggressive. They went closer and closer. The snake was not reacting. They did not know how all these changes had taken place, but at least they could see that the snake was not dangerous, they can play with it. So, the time came, when the boys could come near the snake; they took the snake by its tail, whirled it round and round, and dashed it on the ground. Half dead, it remained. At nightfall, it felt a little better and went into its own hole. It was slowly reduced to bone and skin. After a few days, the holy man returned. And the boys said, 'That snake is gone. No need of going there.' He said, 'That cannot be. I have given him instruction. Without realizing life's purpose, he cannot die.' So, he quietly went to the hole; he had given it a name; he called it by that name. After some time, the snake crawled out of its hole and saluted the teacher. And his teacher asked him, 'What has happened to you? You have become skin and bone.' He said, 'Probably, it is because you had asked me not to harm anybody; I have stopped eating any insects, any kind of living things, I live on dry leaves, may be that.' Because of the *sāttvika* mind, he had forgotten that the boys had done harm to him.

He could not even remember those events. So much goodness had come to him. When he said this, the teacher said, 'What a fool you are! Remember, something must have happened. This could not have happened by merely taking dry leaves.' Then the snake said, 'Yes, I remember. One day, the boys who were playing here, finding me peaceful, they came closer and closer. They became very bold, they took me by the tail, whirled me and dashed me against the ground. I vomited blood and I somehow went into my hole. That may be the reason for this condition. You have taught me not to harm, so I did not harm anyone. So, I have come to this condition and I don't mind it.' And the teacher said, 'What a fool you are! I certainly told you not to harm anybody, not to bite anybody. But you could have hissed at them. Then they would have gone away. Learn to hiss; otherwise, they will destroy you. You cannot live in the midst of the world with this kind of attitude. Certainly don't put poison into others. But don't be made an object of pity by others and destroy your own life.' Saying this Sri Ramakrishna told the audience, 'Hiss, but don't bite.'

You have this capacity to stand on your own feet, but don't increase the evil in the world by your non-resistance to the evil in the world. That is the method we have to evolve. That is what the *Gītā* teaches throughout. Never increase the evil, reduce it. But it is not on the side of unqualified pacifism, which enveloped the European mind after the first World War. We don't have that pacifism, we want peace, we want humanism, we want love and concern; while living in this imperfect world, you must learn how to protect your interests. All are not going to become mendicants. Protect your own interests. If somebody comes and snatches away your son or daughter, you are not going to keep quiet, or hand over your second child also to the person who has snatched away the first child. You won't do that. If you do so, you won't be human at all. Something has gone wrong with you. That is what the *Gītā* is going to tell you. You must be able to protect your interests, protect other people's interests, the national interest, without endangering the welfare of humanity as a whole. It is a very difficult subject, but it must be pursued as best one can. Śrī Kṛṣṇa will always say (*Gītā*, 2. 40), 'This is a high ideal, but do as much as you can. *Svalpamapyasya dharmasya trāyate mahato bhayāt.*' It will come in the course of this chapter: 'Even a little of this *Dharma* will save us from great fear'.

And so Śrī Kṛṣṇa had to tell Arjuna in the midst of the battlefield, at the end of a long course of negotiation where evil was not going to surrender to any good thought, there was nothing else to do, and a very critical situation had arisen. When Arjuna said, I don't want to fight, Śrī Kṛṣṇa had to tell him, 'No. That is unmanly. You have to. Your very bones will make you do so. Face the brute. Something has happened to you; you have become weak. You have become distressed, you have become broken down as it were.' That is why the second and third verses of this chapter made this exhortation to Arjuna: *Kutastvā kaśmalam idam viṣame samupasthitam; Anāryajuṣṭham asvargyam akīrtikaram arjuna. Klaibyam mā sma gamaḥ pārtha na etat tvayi upapadyate; Kṣudram hṛdayadaurbalyam tyaktvā uttiṣṭha parantapa.* This was exactly what Gandhiji said in our time: 'You allowed your women to be dishonoured by the police; you must use even your teeth to protect your honour.' These are the words of Gandhiji, who was a votary of non-violence from every point of view; but he knew that cowardice, and non-violence cannot go together.

That is why, in this great book, the first part of the *Gītā* teaches you how to develop yourself, gain self-confidence, capacity to face difficulties and obstacles, achieve what is called 'manliness', without any gender bias; a wonderful word in English. Towards the end of the *Gītā*, Śrī Kṛṣṇa will give you a higher dimension, 'Surrender everything to the Divine'. It is all His. You are only an instrument. That is called complete surrender. This is the *Carama śloka*, 'last verse' towards the end of the book, the last Testament of the *Gītā: Tameva śaraṇam gaccha*, 'surrender everything to the Divine'. Everybody cannot surrender. Unless you are very strong, you cannot surrender. A person who has nothing in his pocket, no bank account, he will say, 'I want to renounce'. What will you renounce? You have no money, no intelligence, nothing. What will you renounce? Have something to renounce. Work hard, earn money, gain the confidence of other people. That is called the first stage of human education. Then comes the final stage which will come in the *Gītā* later on. Have a greater strength to surrender your ego entirely to the Divine. That needs greater strength. As I say very often, to earn money needs strength and hard work, but to donate money needs greater strength. Isn't it? How difficult it is to donate what you have earned!

न हि प्रपश्यामि ममापनुद्याद्
यत् शोकमुच्छोषणमिन्द्रियाणाम् ।
अवाप्य भूमौ असपत्नमृद्धं
राज्यं सुराणामपि चाधिपत्यम् ॥८॥

Na hi prapaśyāmi mamāpanudyāt
Yat śokamucchoṣaṇamindriyāṇām;
Avāpya bhūmau asapatnamṛddham
rājyam surāṇāmapi cādhipatyam — 2. 8

Arjuna says: 'I do not see any kind of prosperous kingdom on earth or overlordship over the denizens of heaven which will remove the grief that has scorched my senses'.

Na hi prapaśyāmi, 'I do not see'; *avāpya bhūmau asapatnamṛddham rājyam,* 'that, obtaining an unrivalled prosperous kingdom on earth'; *surāṇām api cādhipatyam,* 'and overlordship over even the denizens of heaven'; *mamāpanudyāt yat śokam ucchoṣaṇam indriyāṇām,* 'will dispel the grief that has scorched my senses'.

Śoka or grief can burn away our sensory system. Some of you may have had this experience. 'I am in such a difficult situation just now'. This is Arjuna's statement; and then Sañjaya says what happened next. That leads to the beginning of Śrī Kṛṣṇa's discourse.

सञ्जय उवाच –

Sañjaya uvāca —

'Sañjaya said.'

एवमुक्त्वा हृषीकेशं गुडाकेशः परन्तपः ।
न योत्स्य इति गोविन्दमुक्त्वा तूष्णीं बभूव ह ॥९॥

Evamuktvā hṛṣīkeśam guḍākeśaḥ parantapaḥ;
Na yotsya iti govindamuktvā tūṣṇīm babhūva ha — 2. 9

'Having said this to Śrī Kṛṣṇa, Arjuna said, I am not going to fight. And he remained quiet in the chariot.'

Now what did Śrī Kṛṣṇa do?

तमुवाच हृषीकेशः प्रहसन्निव भारत ।
सेनयोरुभयोर्मध्ये विषीदन्तमिदं वचः ॥१०॥

Tamuvāca hṛṣīkeśaḥ prahasanniva bhārata;
Senayorubhayormadhye viṣīdantamidam vacaḥ — 2. 10

Śrī Kṛṣṇa had a tremendous control over the situation. He was not confused like Arjuna. Wherever there is that tremendous self-control and self-restraint, you will find that the mind is spontaneous and natural. A smile appears; Arjuna could not smile in that condition. That smile on Śrī Kṛṣṇa's face is a sign of the tremendous control He had over the situation around. When you are in a distressed state of mind, you cannot smile. Even if you smile, that would be a contorted smile, not a natural smile. Look at a baby's smile, how beautiful, how natural; we lose that power as we grow older and older. But still we can have some sort of natural, spontaneous smile. But if you are in distress, no smile can come. In the case of Śrī Kṛṣṇa, this smile was a constant feature of His mind. A tremendous mind with great control over the environment around Him. So, He confronts the problems and tensions of the world with a gentle smile, and through that He administers that calmness, that tranquillity, to the human mind. In the *Mahābhārata* epic, you will find many instances of how Śrī Kṛṣṇa faces very difficult situations and brings about calmness around Him. The expression *prahasanniva* means 'as if with a smile'. From here onwards you find Śrī Kṛṣṇa's exposition in the second chapter; from verses 11 to 38, trying His best through various arguments to prod Arjuna to face the battle. Arjuna is a *kṣatriya.* His very nature is such that he has to face this difficult situation. Everybody depends upon him for the winning of the battle. So, Śrī Kṛṣṇa wants Arjuna to recognize his duty at this time through various arguments, some of them highly metaphysical, some of them very worldly. And the metaphysical arguments are based upon the philosophy of ascetic thought, *jñāna-mārga,* which denies this world, which believes in a transcendental experience, where the Atman is ever free, without any attachment. That is everyone's true nature. Birthless, deathless is the Self of all. Based on that metaphysics and vision, Śrī Kṛṣṇa is inducing Arjuna to face up to this battle. But those arguments do not convince Arjuna. Śrī Kṛṣṇa had to give his own philosophy thereafter, under which we all can fight the battle of life and face up to its challenges.

All these are possible under that philosophy of *practical Vedanta* which Śrī Kṛṣṇa is going to expound from 39th verse onwards for all people. *That is Śrī Kṛṣṇa's original contribution to the philosophy of human life and development*. The first one will not allow you to work, face up to the problems, etc. The first one can as well encourage Arjuna to run away from battle. Let me become a mendicant; that also can be the conclusion based on that philosophy. It is valid but only for a few. Śrī Kṛṣṇa calls it *Sāṅkhya* here. *Sāṅkhya* does not refer to the metaphysical school of that name, but to the *jñāna-mārga*, the path of *neti, neti,* not this, not this. This world is unreal. The Atman is supreme, deathless. Realize that; why get into all this mess here? That can be the conclusion from that philosophy. On the basis of that philosophy, you can't work, you can't face up to problems, you can't fight a war. So, that doesn't impress Arjuna with the need for war. Therefore, Śrī Kṛṣṇa finds the need for a new philosophy of practical Vedanta, which he develops himself, *based upon a man or woman at work*, seeking also spiritual realization while continuing to work. For millions of people, that is the basis of a life of action, a life of endeavour, a positive attitude to life; all that will come from verse 39 onwards. Sañjaya now says:

श्रीभगवानुवाच –
Śrī bhagavānuvāca —

'The Blessed Lord said.'

After all this discussion with Śrī Kṛṣṇa, when Arjuna said, 'I am not going to fight', and sat in the chariot, Śrī Kṛṣṇa has to say what will inspire this warrior to face up to the problems that are there; 'it was a very critical situation', *viṣame samupasthitam.* That is the situation, which Śrī Kṛṣṇa is facing now with respect to His own friend and disciple, Arjuna. Śrī Kṛṣṇa said:

अशोच्यान् अन्वशोचस्त्वं प्रज्ञावादांश्च भाषसे ।
गतासून् अगतासूंश्च नानुशोचन्ति पण्डिताः ॥११॥

Aśocyān anvaśocastvam prajñāvādāmśca bhāṣase;
Gatāsūn agatāsūmśca nānuśocanti paṇḍitāḥ — 2. 11

The verse says that, based upon the philosophy which Arjuna had invoked in his mind, Bhiṣma and Droṇa were not to be mourned for. They are great people, what is the virtue in showing pity for them? *Aśocyān,* they are 'not to be grieved over'. They are great people themselves. *Anvaśocastvam,* 'you are feeling so much of grief'. *Prajñāvādāmśca bhāṣase,* 'and yet you are speaking wise words'. *Gatāsūn agatāsūmśca nānuśocanti paṇḍitāḥ,* under that philosophy, '*paṇḍitāḥ,* wise persons, will not grieve for the dead or the living.' So, *paṇḍita* is a great word in Sanskrit, though today it means very ordinary in North India. The Sanskrit word *paṇḍita* comes from the word *paṇḍā.* What is *paṇḍā? Ātmaviṣayā-buddhi* is called *paṇḍā,* 'the *buddhi* which is turned towards the Atman', the Infinite Divine within; that is called *paṇḍā,* and those who have this *paṇḍā* are *paṇḍitaḥ.* That is the original meaning. But, today it means also a cook. In Delhi, in many houses the cook is called the *paṇḍit.* But in the *Gītā* another definition comes, *paṇḍitāḥ samadarśinaḥ* (5.18): 'those who have an even-minded attitude towards things, they are called *paṇḍitāḥ*'.

न त्वेवाहं जातु नासं न त्वं नेमे जनाधिपाः।
न चैव न भविष्यामः सर्वे वयमतः परम् ॥१२॥

Na tvevāham jātu nāsam na tvam neme janādhipāḥ;
Na caiva na bhaviṣyāmaḥ sarve vayamataḥ param —2. 12

So far as man is concerned, there is an eternal element in everyone of us. Our philosophy tells: bodies come and go, the soul remains. That is why we say at death, we threw the body away. *Śarīr choḍ diyā.* I am the Atman, I am the soul, I have a body, I threw it away. That is our normal understanding. So, these people who are here, yourself, myself, we are always there. There is no time when we were not. There is no time when we shall not be. We are the immortal Atman. That is the truth about man as taught by India's *Sanātana Dharma:* The human beings are essentially divine; we have a body, subject to change, subject to death; but, our Self is essentially divine and deathless. We are all *amṛtasya putrāḥ,* as the *Śvetāśvatara Upaniṣad* proclaims (2. 5). *Na tvevāham jātu nāsam na tvam neme janādhipāḥ,* 'neither myself, nor yourself, nor these kings have been not; and never shall we all cease to be'. *Na caiva na bhaviṣyāmaḥ sarve vayam ataḥ param,* 'we are always there even after the death of the body'. This subject comes through several verses in this section. An example is given; this is a famous verse in the *Gītā*.

देहिनोऽस्मिन् यथा देहे कौमारं यौवनं जरा ।
तथा देहान्तरप्राप्तिः धीरस्तत्र न मुह्यति ॥१३॥

Dehino'smin yathā dehe kaumāram yauvanam jarā;
Tathā dehāntaraprāptiḥ dhīrastatra na muhyati — 2. 13

Every embodied human being passes through different states: *kaumāram,*—a child below twelve years is called a boy, *kumāra,* or, a girl, *kumārī. Kaumāram* means child stage. Then *yauvanam,* youthfulness; then, *jarā,* old age. 'Every embodied person passes through the states of childhood, youth, and old age in the body; similarly also death and rebirth; a courageous person is not deluded thereby.' We continue this human evolution through new bodies, believing in the idea of rebirth—a very important teaching in *Sanātana Dharma.* The human being passes through birth after birth until he or she realizes the truth of the immortal Self within. This process goes on until one burns away one's *karmas,* our fruits of actions, in the fire of spiritual knowledge. So, we are asked to accelerate our spiritual development with the help of this body; realize the truth, then the body's work is over. Until then, the body will remain in one form or other; for, a human body is meant not for pleasure and comfort only; for that, animal bodies are better fitted. This human body is meant for knowledge, both secular and spiritual. Realize the highest truth, burn away all your *karmas;* then you have no birth, you have no death, you are free. So says the verse. A subtle soul is within us; Vedanta calls it a subtle body, *sūkṣma śarīra.* When our sages, through scientific enquiry into the depth dimension of human nature beyond the sensory level, discovered the *sūkṣma śarīra* in human beings, behind this *sthūla śarīra*—that is, a subtle body behind a gross body, they understood that death is only the death of the *sthūla śarīra; sūkṣma śarīra* doesn't die. That is always there. The *sūkṣma śarīra* manufactures another gross body for itself to continue its search for his or her true Self, forgetting what happened in the previous life. That is why rebirth is one of the great ideas that was developed in India, *tathā dehāntaraprāptiḥ;* therefore, *dhīrastatra na muhyati,* 'there the wise one, the heroic one, will not be deluded', by this kind of changes taking place in human evolution. Śri Kṛṣṇa gives another beautiful idea now, and that is meant for all of us.

मात्रास्पर्शास्तु कौन्तेय शीतोष्णसुखदुःखदाः।
आगमापायिनोऽनित्याः तांस्तितिक्षस्व भारत ॥१४॥

Mātrāsparśāstu kaunteya śītoṣṇasukhaduḥkhadāḥ;
Āgamāpāyino'nityāḥ tāmstitikṣasva bhārata — 2. 14

The first phrase is, '*mātrāsparśāḥ*'; *sparśa* means touch; *mātrā* means sensory objects. When we touch the sensory object, then our sensory system comes in touch with the sensory object. The word *mātrā* is associated with the word measure, *mā* means to measure, this is a wonderful word. That day our nuclear scientist Raja Ramanna spoke on the subject of mind and matter, nature and mind. There he used the word *mā,* measure. And this concerns the science of measurement; here mathematics comes in. All material or physical sciences are subject to measurement. But when you go beyond the physical dimensions of nature in the human being, no measurement is possible. Up to the sensory level, we can have measurement. So, the word *mātrā* comes from this idea of measurement; this sensory system measures that object that is there. That is how we come in touch with the world. *Mātrāsparśāstu kaunteya,* 'contact with sense objects, O Arjuna'; what happens to you thereby? Sometimes 'it will give you sensation of cold, sometimes of heat; sometimes of pleasure, sometimes of pain'. That is the nature of such contact: *śīta-uṣṇa-sukha-duḥkha-dāḥ.* But, they are, *āgama-apāyino,* 'they come and they go'; they 'don't persist', *anityāḥ.* If that is so, how shall we react to them properly? *Tān titikṣasva bhārata,* 'bear with them, O Arjuna'.

That is a wonderful statement. 'What cannot be cured must be endured', we say in English. You fall ill, you go to the doctor. Doctor will treat you; there is a science about it, but, so far as *you* are concerned, co-operate with the doctor by that tremendous determination to bear with it so long as it is there. So, *tān titikṣasva,* 'bear with them'; it develops strength of mind. Try to remove them as far as you can by treatment; what you cannot cure, bear with them. The capacity to bear with these things is a tremendous capacity. We can see that the capacity to bear pain and other experiences is very relative to human beings. Somebody has more of it, somebody has less of it.

The threshold of pain, as we call it in neural language, is different in different people. Some people can stand a good deal of it; some people cannot stand even a little bit of it. When I was in charge of a hostel for students in Mysore, we had to give the Malaria injection to our students; young boys of ages 10, 11, 12; some of them came, took the injection, and went away; one or two students, as soon as they saw the needle, became unconscious and fell down! Their threshold of pain was very low. So, we have to develop that strength: say, 'I can stand it, I can stand it'. The capacity to withstand the nonsense of life is an important capacity. Therefore, Śrī Kṛṣṇa said, *tān titikṣasva bhārata,* 'bear with them'. If you don't bear, you fall down, get destroyed. If you had developed a little more strength, you could have stood it well. So, don't be so weak. Everyone must develop a little strength of mind to withstand the changes and chances of life. Life is not all fun, all pleasure; often, difficulties come. So, this kind of strengthening of the human organism against the environment is very important for human life. If your body is strong, no disease germs can enter into it and multiply there. If it is weak, any number of germs can enter and create trouble. So, keep the organism strong. Your mind also must be strong.

In fact, Śrī Kṛṣṇa will repeat this idea throughout this book. Strength of mind and control of the sensory system are very important for any decent human being. Virtue and morality cannot thrive without this kind of self-discipline. In normal life, difficulties come. If you can bear a little, probably things would be better a little later. When you swim in the ocean, the waves come and buffet you, dash against you. So, when the waves come, duck underneath; and, as it goes away, you come up again. That is the way to deal with the waves. They come and they go. They are not always there. So, you can always have the capacity developed to swim against the waves by this method. So, this concept of *tān titikṣasva* 'bear with them', because they are *anityāḥ,* 'they are not always there'. A little patience can bring about great changes. When we are weak-minded, the first onslaught of an unhappy situation makes us broken down. The very first onslaught. That shows weakness. If a little strength is there, one can say: I shall withstand it, I shall overcome it. That is called tremendous faith in oneself, *ātma-śraddhā.* Śrī Kṛṣṇa wants all of us to develop that *ātma-śraddhā,* I shall overcome. One of the national songs of the American people is: 'We shall overcome, we shall overcome'. That spirit must be there in all people. So, He said, *tān titikṣasva. Titikṣā* is a great word in Sanskrit. It is defined by Śaṅkarācārya in the *Vivekacūḍāmaṇi* in one verse (24). It is one of the virtues to be developed by a student of Vedanta: *Sahanam sarvaduḥkhānām apratikārapūrvakam; Cintāvilāparahitam sā titikṣā nigadyate.* 'The bearing of all suffering without anxiety and weeping and without the intention to react is called *titikṣā*.'

The next *śloka* says:

यं हि न व्यथयन्त्येते पुरुषं पुरुषर्षभ ।
समदुःखसुखं धीरं सोऽमृतत्वाय कल्पते ॥१५॥

Yam hi na vyathayantyete puruṣam puruṣarṣabha;
Samaduḥkhasukham dhīram so'mṛtatvāya kalpate—2. 15

'He or she, who is not thrown down by any of these experiences (happiness or misery, cold or heat), *samaduḥkhasukham dhīram,* 'the courageous one who is even-minded in *duḥkha,* grief, and *sukha,* happiness', *so'mṛtatvāya kalpate,* 'that person alone can achieve immortality'; he or she can realize the Atman which is immortal. This is a tremendous capacity; even in our political struggle for independence, we have seen that some of the leaders had the capacity to withstand pressures from outside. They didn't break down. They stood it; it is sad that we are losing it; now we have to regain it once again. I remember reading it in the papers, when Sardar Vallabhai Patel was arguing a case in the court, a man delivered a telegram to him. He just read it, put it in his pocket, continued his arguments, and then went home, to see his dead wife. That was the telegram. How many of us can withstand that shock calmly? It is not for want of love; love was there. But something more was there: the capacity to withstand the ups and downs of life. A good deal of courage is needed to go beyond the pulls of the physical system, nervous system, psychic system, and realize the Atman that is behind all this. That strength we have to develop from now onwards. That is why high character-strength is necessary for spiritual development. One has to cultivate that strength which one has, by oneself. No one can purchase it for money. You have regularly to build it up in yourself by yourself; other people can help you, guide you; but the work is your own. This human life, this packet of psycho-physical energy, I must learn to cultivate in the right way so that the best harvest will come out of it. And the highest harvest is realizing one's own true nature as the immortal

Self, the Atman. Sri Ramakrishna used to sing a Bengali song composed by Ramprasad and beginning with 'O mind! You do not know the art of farming': *Re man, tumi kṛṣi kāj jāno nā. Emon mānav jami roilo patit, Ābād korile phalto sona,* 'such rich field of human life is lying fallow, which, if cultivated, would have given the harvest of gold.'

The next *śloka* is a highly metaphysical one.

नासतो विद्यते भावो नाभावो विद्यते सतः।
उभयोरपि दृष्टोऽन्तः त्वनयोस्तत्त्वदर्शिभिः ॥१६॥

Nāsato vidyate bhāvo nābhāvo vidyate sataḥ;
Ubhayorapi dṛṣṭo'ntaḥ tvanayoḥ tattvadarśibhiḥ —2. 16

Asat and *sat,* these words are used. They have got different meanings in different contexts. In a purely philosophical context they mean the unreal and the real. But in Sāṅkhya terminology, it has got another meaning: one is called the cause, the other is called the effect. The *Sat* is the effect, the *asat* is the cause, because *sat* you can see. And cause and effect are non-different, according to the Sāṅkhyas. As the cause, so the effect. As much energy you put into your machine, that much of work that machine can do, nothing more. That is called cause and effect being non-different. But in this context, the word *sat* means the real. The word *asat* means the unreal. So, the *śloka* says, *na asato vidyate bhāvo,* 'the unreal never is'; similarly, *nābhāvo vidyate sataḥ,* 'the word "non-existent" cannot be applied to what is real'. The *sat* is the real; it can never be the non-existent. Our thinkers, when they studied the world, found two aspects to the world: one is a changeable aspect, another an unchangeable aspect. Everything in this world is changeable; every second it is changing. Says *Śaṅkarācārya* in his commentary on the *Kaṭha Upaniṣad: Pratikṣaṇam anyathā svabhāvo,* 'every moment it is becoming something else'. Change is the characteristic of this external and much of the internal world. And anything that changes, moment to moment, Vedanta calls it unreal. That is how we use the word unreal; it exists, but it is unreal. It appears, but it is unreal.

This is one great conclusion of the philosophers of India, China, as well as Greece, in ancient times. The nature of this manifested universe, a universe which one experiences with the five senses, is that, it is constantly changing, and is therefore unreal. Whatever changes, is unreal. Then where is the reality? Vedanta says, yes, there is the changeless reality beyond the sensory level, you come to the world of reality, which is unchanging, infinite, eternal. This distinction was made very early in our philosophy; in Greek philosophy also there are two schools: one holding on to the eternal, changeless reality, the other holding on to the world of change. That world of change is expressed beautifully by the Greek philosophers in the saying, 'you do not step into the same river twice'. The world is like that, constantly changing. This becomes more and more confirmed when you study modern physics dealing with matter, and modern biology dealing with living systems. For example, your body changes within a few years; everything in the body has changed. Yet, you say, 'I am'. I feel I am the same person. Some sort of unity, somewhere, is there in this world of change. Man alone can discover it. Animals change, but they do not find that unity behind the change. But man feels there is a unity where all this change is really centred. Just like all the changes of pictures in a film, making for the unity of the film. That is due to the curtain behind the film. That makes for unity. Similarly, we search for the unity behind the multiplicity in the universe. The first truth is change, and we see that whatever changes is unreal.

We have, therefore, a fine definition of what is real, given in the *Māṇḍūkya Upaniṣad Kārikā* by Gauḍapāda (II. 6): *Ādau ante ca yannāsti vartamāne'pi tat tathā; Vitataiḥ sadṛśāḥ santo avitathā iva lakṣitāḥ*, 'what is not in the beginning and in the end, is not in the present also; though it seems to be real, it is characterized as unreal.' The *śloka* says that what does not exist in the beginning and in the end, and appears only in the middle, is called unreal. Then what is real? That which exists in the past, present and future, that is called the real. Always it is there. Is there such a real? Yes, says Vedanta, and that search is the search of philosophy everywhere in the world. Even physical science is in search for that one reality behind this changing universe. In Vedanta, we undertook this task with a seriousness and thoroughness which has no comparison anywhere else in the world. Here the words *sat* and *asat* have been used. *Nāsato vidyate bhāvo, nābhāvo vidyate sataḥ*; if this external world is unreal, then what is the real? The imperishable infinite Atman, of the nature of pure Consciousness, one and non-dual, 'from Whom the whole universe has come, in Whom it rests, and unto Whom it returns at the end of a cosmic cycle'. That will be the theme of another verse immediately after.

So, we use the word *sat* for that infinite imperishable reality; *asat,* for this perishable universe. The belief that this sensory world alone is true, is called materialism, and that materialism is a strong philosophy today. The world had it earlier also. It will always be there till penetrating thinking comes. Some of today's scientists are now trying to remove materialism from modern science. Even in the last century, Thomas Huxley, a very acute thinker and collaborator of Darwin, termed materialism as an intruder into science. Matter is a useful concept. Nobody has seen matter, but it is a useful concept, like *x, y, z* in solving algebraic problems. But, those who forget that this is only a symbol, and think that it is the real thing, they are doing great injustice to human beings. They will destroy the beauty of human life. That was a warning given by Thomas Huxley in the last century. In this century also, Millikan, the astro-physicist, has said: 'to me a philosophy of materialism is the height of un-intelligence'. And many more are realizing this truth in modern times. So, matter is just a symbol. Nobody has seen matter. We are seeing, from the Indian point of view, one infinite reality, which appears as matter in the world outside, and as the Self within us. There is only one reality in this world. And we call it Brahman or Atman, of the nature of pure Consciousness. That is the language that Vedanta uses, which some Western scientists are now appreciating, that matter itself is only a condensation of Consciousness, visible to the sensory system of man. How wonderful an idea! That you can have various levels of matter: gross matter, subtle matter, still more subtle matter; we see that even in the human body. You have got matter in various levels of subtlety, from the hard bone to the transparent eyeball. In a tree, simple sap becomes hard wood, leaves, flowers, and fruits; thus, matter appears in many levels, gross, subtle, more subtle, and we do not know what that matter is.

Vedanta says that it is Consciousness in various levels of manifestation that manifests as objects and subjects. As the *Muṇḍaka Upaniṣad* expresses this truth (II. ii. 11): *Brahmaivedam viśvamidaṁ variṣṭham,* 'This manifested universe with its subjects and objects is the adorable Brahman'. Now this philosophy was developed ages ago in India, and modern Western science is going in the direction of Brahman of the Upaniṣads. This is a profound datum, says our Professor Capra in his book *Tao of Physics.* He quotes from *Chāndogya Upaniṣad* a very enigmatic passage: *Prāṇo vai brahma, 'Prāṇa* is Brahman.' *Prāṇa* is energy; here it means psychic and biological energy. But, it also includes all energies. So, all energy is Brahman. *Prāṇo vai brahma. 'Prāṇa* is verily Brahman'; then why do we mistake it for these dull, dead physical energies in the world? The next line says: *Kam brahma. Kham brahma.* A very enigmatic statement. *Ka* and *Kha* are the first two consonants in Sanskrit. Brahman is *ka;* Brahman is *kha.* Then the student says, 'I cannot understand this *ka* and *kha.* I can understand *Prāṇa* is Brahman. Please explain to me.' And the teacher explains in Sanskrit: *Kha* means the sky or space which has no limit. That means Brahman is infinite, expansive; that is quite alright. Is it then like the dull physical cosmos that you have in physics and cosmology today. No, it is also *kam*: *'kam brahma'*. *Kam* in Sanskrit means happiness, bliss. That means, its true nature is Consciousness. So, that Brahman is infinite, and yet of the nature of pure Consciousness. And the whole manifested universe is that Brahman only. With much approval this physicist quotes this particular sentence in the *Chāndogya Upaniṣad:*

Prāno vai brahma. Kam brahma. Kham brahma. And so, change is only a pulsation of that changeless infinite reality. Just like water in the ocean whose pulsation is the wave. Wave has no existence apart from the ocean. It just appears and disappears constantly. So also in today's physics, this language is used, that it is only a wave of that infinite reality behind. The whole universe is just in the wave form. It is a wave of that infinite background reality. Now these are all common terminology, concepts coming from modern physics and cosmology, which obtained earlier in Vedanta or the Upaniṣads.

So, Śrī Kṛṣṇa says here, *ubhayorapi dṛṣṭo'ntaḥ tvanayoḥ tattvadarśibhiḥ*. This *anta*, 'this conclusion', *nirṇaya*, has been arrived at by whom?, *tattvadarśibhiḥ*, 'by those who have realized the *tattvam*'. *Tattvam* also is a great scientifically precise word in Sanskrit. *Tasya bhāvaḥ tattvam*, 'the nature of a particular thing is called *tattvam*'. Not what it appears to be. Just like 'the earth is flat', is not *tattvam* but *matam*, opinion. Our senses tell us that the earth is flat. But what is the *tattvam?* It is round, the earth is a globe. That is called *tattvam*. Those who know the *tattvam* of things, by scientific investigation, they have come to this conclusion: that this *sat*, reality, is always, *is*. And what is *asat*, that which doesn't exist, has no reality. Whatever reality the *asat* possesses, comes from the *sat* itself. So, the sages, who have discriminated and investigated this subject, have come to this conclusion. How thought processes repeat, we find happening in modern physics. In the language of Einstein, 'We have in today's physics,' I am quoting his words, 'two realities. One matter, the other the field. Both cannot be true, for the field alone is true. Matter is only a condensation of that field.' Just see the language, the same language, which Vedanta used ages ago, physicists are compelled to use today, because those sages were in search of truth, not of an opinion. This is the *tattva*; not what appears, not what is pleasing; these are called beliefs and dogmas. Have plenty of them, but *tattvam* is different. This is a great word. I wish our people try to understand the meaning of this word and apply it in day-to-day life.

What is the *tattvam* of a thing? Suppose I have an opinion. I can hold on to an opinion; but, it must be based on truth. It must be a true opinion. Then only it gets the status of a *tattvam.* Otherwise, it is called *matam.* The word opinion in English is called *matam* in Sanskrit. *Tad-asmākam matam,* 'It is our opinion,' or, 'it is my religion'. It is not the truth. I have not investigated it. But when you investigate and find it to be true, then that opinion becomes a *true* opinion. It can stand challenge. So, ordinarily, our religions in the world are always a plural. They are *matams.* What pleases *me,* what attracts *me,* what is relevant to *my* needs, that is called *matam.* I choose to be a Vaiṣṇava, a Śaiva, a Hindu, a Muslim, a Christian, all this constitutes *matam.* That is one aspect of it. The second aspect is: if you scientifically investigate, what is all this *matam?* What is behind this plurality of *matams?* Is there a truth behind all this? That discovery will lead you to the *tattvam* of religion. When the *tattvam* is discovered, there will be no conflict in religions. Scientific truths do not conflict; only dogmas conflict. We know that all these are forms of the same single reality. There will be no conflict thereafter. Harmony and peace alone can come. And respect for each other: your opinion I respect, you also respect my opinion. You take some food, I respect it. I take some food, you respect that also. Don't say, my food alone is food, your food is poison. That is what we have done in the name of religion, mistaking it to be *tattvam.* *Tattvam* is quite different. Any food you may take—that is *matam.* But see that you take so many calories, so much of nourishment needed for health; that is *tattvam.*

So, you can see in religion as well as in food the distinction between *matam* and *tattvam.* Only when you investigate, you will come to this truth. In our country today, when more people begin to ask this question, why so many religions? What is the truth about all of them? Every religion says I am true; yes, you are true. But you can't take a copyright of all truth. Others also say they are true. When such questions come, very impartial objective investigation is needed, and that is what our ancient and modern sages did, and raised *matam* to the level of *tattvam*. And *tattvam* is one. *Tattvam* can never be plural. *Matam* can be plural. So, one *tattvam*, and *matams* are but different expressions of that one *tattvam*. That is how our Indian sages discovered that wonderful unity behind the diversity of religions, established harmony and peace, with so little of intolerance in the name of religion on the soil of India which found expression in the *Ṛg-Veda*, the oldest book of the human race (I. 164. 46): *Ekam sat, viprāḥ bahudhā vadanti*, 'Truth is one, sages call it by various names'; and, centuries later, in the *Śrīmad Bhāgavatam: Vadanti tat tattvavidaḥ tattvam yat jñānamadvayam, brahmeti, paramātmeti, bhagavāniti, śabdyate*. That *tattvam* idea comes here. It says, *vadanti tat tattvavidaḥ*, 'the Knowers of truth, *tattva*, declare this'. What do they say? *Tattvam yat jñānamadvayam*, 'there is one *tattvam* which is pure, non-dual Consciousness', which we call Brahman in the Upaniṣads, of the nature of pure, non-dual Consciousness. That is the *tattvam*. But 'that *tattvam* is spoken of differently in language and style by different people'. What are these? *Brahmeti Paramātmeti Bhagavāniti śabdyate. Śabda*, or sound or speech, makes that One appear as many. 'Some call It Brahman, some call It the *Paramātmā*, the supreme Self, and some call It *Bhagavān*, the all-loving God.

In this way, this investigation of *matam* versus *tattvam* has done immense good to this country. In no other country it has been attempted even, not even once. It has never been attempted, except as politically convenient arrangements. And today we have to inaugurate that kind of investigation, to find harmony behind these diverse manifestations. As in the case of philosophy, so in the case of religion. We have to consider *matam* as a plural and *tattvam* as a singular, and the plural must pay homage to the singular.

In the next verse the *Gītā* says:

अविनाशि तु तद्विद्धि येन सर्वमिदं ततम् ।
विनाशमव्ययस्यास्य न कश्चित्कर्तुमर्हति ॥१७॥

Avināśi tu tadviddhi yena sarvamidam tatam;
Vināśamavyayasyāsya na kaścitkartumarhati — 2. 17

'Consider that which pervades the whole universe as indestructible; nothing can destroy that inexhaustible reality.'

This infinite truth, of the nature of pure, non-dual, Consciousness, pervades the whole universe. Things are created and destroyed, but that out of which all this universe comes cannot be destroyed at all. *Vināśam avyayasya asya na kaścit kartum arhati,* 'none has the power to destroy that indestructible reality behind the universe'. *Avināśi tu tadviddhi,* 'know That to be indestructible'; that is also in this body as the Self, the Atman; what is 'there' is also 'here'. But, only in the human body, it can be realized; that is the supreme uniqueness of the human being. It is there in the animal body also, but that body will not help it to understand this truth. So,

अन्तवन्त इमे देहा नित्यस्योक्ताः शरीरिणः ।
अनाशिनोऽप्रमेयस्य तस्मात् युध्यस्व भारत ॥१८॥

Antavanta ime dehā nityasyoktāḥ śarīriṇaḥ;
Anāśino'prameyasya tasmāt yudhyasva bhārata — 2. 18

'These bodies—of the eternal embodied one which is indestructible and indeterminable—have an end, it is said; therefore fight, O Arjuna.'

'Therefore, fight on, *tasmāt yuddhyasva.*' Why? Because of this truth: these bodies are *antavantaḥ,* 'they have an end'; end means death. Bodies die; you can never keep them for all time. Whose bodies are they? *Nityasyoktāḥ śarīrinaḥ,* 'of that *śarīri,* the one that is embodied, who is *nitya,* eternal'; of the eternal Self these are perishable bodies. Know this truth. *Anāśino aprameyasya,* that Atman that is there in all these bodies, is *anāśi,* 'without any destruction', *aprameya,* 'which cannot be measured', which cannot be brought within the purview of speech and thought. That is called *aprameya.* Everything in the world can be brought within the limit of thought and speech, not the Atman, because it is eternally the subject, is eternally of the nature of pure Consciousness. As the *Kaṭha Upaniṣad* says (1. ii. 9): *Naiṣā tarkeṇa matirāpaneyā*—'This Atman cannot be grasped through *tarka,* logical reasoning.'

य एनं वेत्ति हन्तारं यश्चैनं मन्यते हतम् ।
उभौ तौ न विजानीतो नायं हन्ति न हन्यते ॥१९॥

Ya enam vetti hantāram yaścainam manyate hatam;
Ubhau tau na vijānīto nāyam hanti na hanyate — 2. 19

'Who considers the Atman as the slayer and who considers this Atman as the slain, both of them do not know that It does not kill nor is It killed.'

This verse 19 has attracted the attention of the American thinker, Ralph Waldo Emerson. Emerson has put this verse into a little versified form in one of his essays, as I have mentioned in the introduction. It is a wonderful book that influenced the then Transcendentalist movement of America in the last century. So, *nāyam hanti na hanyate,* 'the Atman neither kills, nor is it the object of somebody's killing'. That is the true nature of the Self. The next *śloka* expands it further:

न जायते म्रियते वा कदाचित्
नायं भूत्वाऽभविता वा न भूयः ।
अजो नित्यः शाश्वतोऽयं पुराणो
न हन्यते हन्यमाने शरीरे ॥२०॥

Na jāyate mriyate vā kadācit
nāyam bhūtvā'bhavitā vā na bhūyaḥ ;
Ajo nityaḥ śāśvato'yam purāṇo
na hanyate hanyamāne śarire — 2. 20

'This Self is never born nor does It ever die; it is not something that having been born, It again ceases to be; unborn, eternal, and everlasting, this ancient One is not killed when the body is killed.'

This verse is similar to the one in the *Kaṭha Upaniṣad,* almost verbatim. *Na jāyate,* 'the Atman has no birth'. Naturally, *na mriyate,* 'it has no death'. *Kadācit,* 'ever'. *Nāyam bhūtvā abhavitā vā na bhūyaḥ,* 'it is not that, having been, it again cease to be'; *ajo,* 'it is unborn'. *Jo,* means 'to be born'; from this the word genetic comes in the English language. So, *ajo,* without birth; *nityaḥ,* 'eternal'; *śāśvataḥ,* 'everlasting'; *purāṇo,* 'the very ancient One and yet ever fresh', that is the meaning of *purāṇaḥ* according to Ādi Śaṅkarācārya, *purā api nava eveti purāṇaḥ,* 'ancient and yet ever fresh'. In the modern period, after about 5000 years of existence, a youthfulness has come to India. So, India has the quality which we find in the Atman. It is always *purāṇa*—though old, it is always fresh. *Na hanyate hanyamāne śarīre,* 'when the body is destroyed, the Atman is not touched'. The Atman remains absolutely untouched. Nobody can destroy the Atman, the true Self of the human being. That is the truth which is emphasized in the Upaniṣads as well as in the *Gītā,* again and again—the immortal nature of the human being. The *Śvetāsvatara Upaniṣad* proclaimed all human beings as *amṛtasya putrāḥ* (2. 5). Even a bit of this awareness can give us tremendous strength, tremendous fearlessness and tremendous compassion. The same Atman is in every being. That makes us friendly to all, and brings out the spirit of love and service in inter-human relations. This knowledge is behind all ethical sense: a sense of oneness. Ethics always involves a sense of oneness between people and people. Then only ethical sense can operate. So, behind this ethical sense is the truth of fundamental unity. We are essentially one.

Behind this changing body-mind complex, there is something eternal, something infinite in man. That is the basic teaching of the sages of the Upaniṣads regarding the human being. We do not know it, but knowing or not knowing, doesn't make any difference to the truth. For, it is truth which was discovered and rediscovered, and placed before us for our own rediscovery, for our own redemption. We do not need someone from heaven coming to redeem us. Our redemption is built into us, our eternal nature as the ever-free Atman. This is constantly emphasized in the Vedantic literature. So, in this first part of the second chapter, Śrī Kṛṣṇa is speaking to all of us through Arjuna, *na jāyate mriyate vā kadācit,* 'this Atman has not got any birth, nor death', it is immortal, when the body goes it is always there. In his commentary in this section, Śaṅkarācārya says, 'even God has not the power to destroy the Self of human being'. Therefore, this Atman, in everyone of us, even in animals, insects, everywhere, is the innermost

Self. The only difference is, animals cannot realize this truth. Only the human being has the organic capacity to realize this truth. That is the highest human uniqueness. Evolution has risen to that level in man, where from he can know the truth of the world around and the truth of one's own immortal Self as well. And when one discovers this truth, he or she becomes fulfilled; for, the whole journey of evolution at the human stage is towards this discovery—ultimately, the human being discovering one's own true nature as the immortal and infinite Atman in which the whole course of evolution finds its fulfilment.

This is the message of ancient Greece also through its great oracle of Delphi: 'Man know thyself'. You may know about the stars, the earth, about this and that; they are all welcome. But the greatest knowledge you can get is about yourself. When you know your true nature, that you are deathless, ever pure, unborn, etc., what a big change will come in your life and in your dealings with others. All crime, delinquency, all pettiness and meanness, will vanish from human life.

So, a little attention to this subject is absolutely essential for every human being. Fortunately, today this modern civilization, after two hundred years of study of the external world, completely relegating man to the backyard—you simply abolish yourself, you study only physical science—after these two hundred years of such study, it is slowly turning to this profoundest of all mystery—the Self in human being. What is my true nature? I see, I understand, even I understand the world, what is the nature of this 'I' which can have this power? This is a remarkable thing. So, various hints and suggestions have been put forth by many distinguished scientists to pinpoint the significance of this new area of study. The human being—*let us study him or her in depth.* All the troubles today in the world, all the distortions of the human psyche, come from neglecting this study. Why am I petty? Why do I commit crime? If you ask this question, the answer is, I do not know my true nature. I think I am only this body, I am only the sensory-limited individual, this petty ego which is tied down within this genetic system. I don't know my true dimension.

Therefore, these verses deal with this central theme of Vedanta. First, we study the world outside; then we study the *human being* who studies that world: the human being, the *observer*; a wonderful word in modern science; what is the nature and status of this observer who experiences this world? We are now compelled to turn our searchlight on to the observer in physical science in its nuclear dimensions, where observation changes the nuclear phenomenon. Even the name of psychology is changing. One of the psychologists has called psychology 'psychology of being'. We have behavioural psychology, we have depth psychology of Freud—psycho-analysis, all these were there. But Abraham Maslow, the American psychologist, called this psychology in his book, 'psychology of being'. What is this Self of human being from which alone all knowledge comes? Let us not neglect it. If you want to live the intensest life, you must have a touch of the infinite Atman anew. This represents a new dimension coming in Western psychology. So, these verses carry a profound message to all of us. We may not realize its full significance immediately, but even a little bit of this truth will be of tremendous significance to us. Greater fulfilment, greater peace, will come out of that study. That is the importance of these verses. And so, in the next verse Śrī Kṛṣṇa says:

वेदाविनाशिनं नित्यं य एनमजमव्ययम् ।
कथं स पुरुषः पार्थ कं घातयति हन्ति कम् ॥२१॥

Vedāvināśinam nityam ya enamajamavyayam;
Katham sa puruṣaḥ pārtha kam ghātayati hanti kam—2. 21

'Know This as indestructible, eternal, unborn, and undecaying; how can a person (who knows this truth), O Arjuna, cause anyone to be killed and whom can that person kill?'

One that knows this Atman, the Self in all, to be indestructible, *avināśi,* and changeless, without birth, and immutable. There is nothing in this manifested universe which answers to this description, except in this world of the Self. Outside, everything is destructible, changeable, etc., etc. This is one point where you will find the value of changelessness, indestructibility, etc., that is in the Self—the *pratyak* dimension of reality. Vedanta recognizes two dimensions for reality: one is called *parāk* dimension, the other is called *pratyak* dimension. Mind you, these are all scientific terms, coined by great sages of Vedanta, so precise and of international significance. *Parāk* means what is out there, which the senses reveal, we call it 'object' in English. That is an object, which you can touch and feel and see. That is called *parāk*, your finger points out to something outside. Then comes a wonderful new dimension, your finger turning to yourself. That is called *pratyak*, inward. After the study of the *parāk* dimension of nature outside, we suspect some mystery *within* us. What is that mystery? Then your finger turns back towards you. So, one is called *parāk-tattva*, and the other is *pratyak-tattva*—reality *out*, and reality *in*. Reality itself does not know any of these distinctions. For our sake, we use these distinctions. Keeping the body as the measuring rod, we say there is something *out there*, something *in here*. Similarly, *pratyak* and *parāk* are two dimensions of the *same* reality called nature. And, nature, of which Western physical science knows only its *parāk* aspect, Vedanta, with its unifying vision, recognizes nature's *parāk* and *pratyak* dimensions; that is nature in its comprehensive sense. Vedanta says: *Prakṛti*, or nature, has these two dimensions: *aparā prakṛti* and *parā prakṛti*. *Aparā* means ordinary, that is, the *parāk* dimension; *parā* means higher, that is the *pratyak* dimension. So, Vedanta recognizes that nature has two dimensions, *parāk* and *pratyak*, but, there are not two natures. There is only one nature with these two dimensions. In Western science, we study the *parāk* dimension, which includes also politics, economics, and other studies which deal with the *parāk* dimension. But, in those dealings, if you want to achieve real happiness and welfare, you must have a touch of the *pratyak* dimension. The more spiritual you are, the more you are able to handle the world around you, the more you radiate love and peace around you. These are the two great words: *parāk* and *pratyak* dimensions of *prakṛti*. Śrī Kṛṣṇa is telling about this *pratyak* dimension. No sense organ can reveal to you this truth. It is beyond its level. Not even this mind, controlled by the senses, can reveal this truth. How can we realize this truth? That is the teaching of the whole *Gītā*.

While working at home or in an office or factory, and in all inter-human relations, we can slowly realize this profound truth. That is how life has to be lived. A complete philosophy of life will include *parāk* and *pratyak* dimensions of nature. We shall handle the world outside. But we shall, through that handling, also realize our true nature. Now, this orientation through Śrī Kṛṣṇa's own original contribution, will come to you after the 38th verse of this chapter. Here only the first ideas of the *jñana* path are being given, the path of Self-realization. Śrī Kṛṣṇa wanted Arjuna's action to be based on this knowledge, but based on this knowledge, our tendency is 'not to act'. Let us realize this truth. Why should we run about here and there? That is the impression that you get. So, Śrī Kṛṣṇa could not influence Arjuna to face the battle in front, basing upon this teaching. This teaching makes you feel like an ascetic, that is why this *jñāna-mārga,* based on *neti, neti,* 'not this, not this,' 'this world is *Māyā,* I don't want to have anything to do with it, let me realize the immortal, eternal dimension of Atman', acted on the minds of the people. Śrī Kṛṣṇa understood it after some time. Arjuna was not convinced through this philosophy that he should act, that he should face the challenges of life. Much better to go into a quiet corner and discover one's own true nature. But it is being presented here first by Śrī Kṛṣṇa, before he formulates his own more comprehensive spirituality *based on men and women at work*. In Śrī Kṛṣṇa's philosophy, there are two dimensions of spirituality: spirituality of work, and spirituality of meditation: both are combined into a comprehensive spirituality. That message will begin from the middle of this chapter. But before that, he is expounding this path of *jñāna,* which he will refer to in the later verses as *Sāṅkhya* path.

In India, we have seen for the last thousand years, this *jñāna-mārga* could not be digested properly by our people, only its negative aspects were emphasized. That made our people self-centred, quiet, not interested in whatever may be happening in the world outside, a certain amount of callousness developed, because we did not have the spiritual strength to digest this profound philosophy. And very often people become dry. We never understood the next section of the second chapter called *yoga* or *buddhi yoga*. But now a healthy understanding of the *Gītā's* message of practical Vedanta is coming. That is the great contribution of Swami Vivekananda—the presentation of a comprehensive spirituality of the *Gītā*. Nobody needs say: I am a worldly person. Whether you are working, or dealing with the world in various ways, you are never worldly, you are in the world, but you are not worldly; you have some sense of your own spiritual nature, you are strengthening it day by day. So, it is all spirituality throughout. That is why Swami Vivekananda said, 'I do not call a man or a woman a Hindu, if he or she is not spiritual.' Our spirituality is pervasive. One need not go to Uttarakasi or Rishikesh to become spiritual; not at all. You are spiritual at home and at your work place. It is your birthright. 'Each soul is potentially divine,' says Vivekananda: everyone has just to recognize it and try to live it in whatever measure one can. That is what Śrī Kṛṣṇa is going to tell one and all in the middle of the second chapter (2. 40): *svalpam api asya dharmasya trāyate mahato bhayāt,* 'even a little of this *dharma* will save one from great fear.' Śrī Kṛṣṇa continues:

वासांसि जीर्णानि यथा विहाय
नवानि गृह्णाति नरोऽपराणि ।
तथा शरीराणि विहाय जीर्णानि
अन्यानि संयाति नवानि देही ॥२२॥

Vāsāmsi jīrṇāni yathā vihāya
navāni gṛhṇāti naro'parāṇi ;
Tathā śarīrāṇi vihāya jīrṇāni
anyāni samyāti navāni dehī — 2. 22

'As the embodied person throws away a worn out dress and puts on a new one, so does the embodied Self discard worn out bodies and adopt other new ones.'

Whenever the wearing cloth becomes old, 'one quietly throws away the old cloth', *jīrṇāni yathā vihāya. Navāni gṛhṇāti naraḥ aparāṇi,* 'one adopts another fresh cloth'. That is what one normally does with one's clothing. *Tathā,* 'similarly', exactly similarly, *dehī,* 'the embodied person', *śarīrāṇi vihāya jīrṇāni,* 'giving away a body when it has become *jīrṇa,* worn out', unfit for one's life's purposes, 'one quietly sheds it'; and, *anyāni saṃyāti,* 'takes a new body', to work out one's destiny, that is, one enters into another body.

This is the wonderful idea of death and rebirth in Vedanta. I shed my body. We have still the feeling, I was the body, now my body is finished. That attitude is there. So, it is the body point of view we all understand. But those who are very high spiritually, they understand that this body is like an old cloth, which we cast away and put on a new cloth. When Vivekananda passed away on 4 July 1902 at Belur Math, near Calcutta, a little after 9 p.m., Swami Ramakrishnananda, who was in Madras and was known as Sashi, had a dream that very night. He heard Vivekananda telling him: 'Sashi, Sashi, I have spat out my body.' And next day the telegram announcing Vivekananda's passing away came from Calcutta. Men and women like him can say, 'I have spat out the body.' Many don't have spiritual knowledge and experience. They think they are the body. They are sorry to lose it. And so, the idea that they are the eternal Self has not come to them yet. But, a little awareness is there. And that little understanding has spread throughout the Hindu, Buddhist and Jain society. What do we say about death?, 'we threw away the body', *śarīr choḍ diyā.* Even the commonest people's language in India is *śarīr choḍ diyā,* meaning, 'the body has been discarded'. In the West it is different. They have been taught, that the body is everything. So, when they die, the language used in English is, he lost his soul. That is why they preserve the body. We in India don't preserve the body; we burn it away. Sooner the better. All others preserve the body, even put all sorts of good things there. In ancient Egyptian religion, you will find that all the things needed by that person, especially the pharaohs, will be put into the grave. But, we burn it away. *Bhasmāntam śarīram,* as the sage in the *Īśa Upaniṣad* said, 'let this body', which has been a good chemical laboratory for my life's purpose, now that it has become old and useless, 'be reduced to ashes'; let their components go back to their own chemical elements, is the language used in that *Īśa Upaniṣad.* In the 10th *śloka* of chapter 15, Śrī Kṛṣṇa will say later:

> *Utkrāmantam sthitam vāpi bhuñjānam vā guṇānvitam;*
> *Vimūḍhā nānupaśyanti paśyanti jñānacakṣuṣaḥ* —

'Two types of people, *vimūḍhāḥ,* 'foolish, short-sighted, sense-limited people' and *jñānacakṣuṣaḥ,* 'those who have got the eye of *jñāna*', the eye of wisdom, they see things differently. What is that? When you are living in the body, when you are experiencing the various delights of the body, or when you finally leave the body, there is something as the subject experiencing all the objects here; that truth is known only by the *jñānacakṣuṣaḥ,* man of subtle vision. *Utkrāmantam* means 'going out of the body', *sthitam vāpi,* 'when it is functioning in the body', *bhuñjānam vā guṇānvitam,* 'when experiencing through *sattva, rajas, tamas*'. This Self, ever present like this, *vimūḍhā nānupaśyanti,* 'foolish persons never understand this', *paśyanti jñānacakṣuṣaḥ,* 'those who have the eye of knowledge, *jñānacakṣu*, see this truth'. This is a central teaching only in this wonderful land of ours. From here it spread to various countries through the spread of Jainism, Buddhism, and Hinduism. And most of the mystics of other religions in earlier periods also liked this idea. And today, this idea is spreading like wild fire all over the western world, especially in U.S.A., only because the alternative to this idea is the unscientific concept of the devil. All the evil in the world comes from the devil. And modern-minded people don't like the idea of the devil. When you banish the devil, you need some substitute. That substitute is: *karma* and *punarjanma* or rebirth, these together constitute the real substitute to that most unscientific notion of the devil in Western religious thought. That is going away, and this idea is spreading all over the world as being more reasonable, though it is not demonstrable. To the sages of India, it is a most satisfying truth. Sri Ramakrishna's example is so beautiful in this connection: Coconuts belong to two categories; green coconut and ripe coconut. In the green coconut, the kernel is attached to the shell. If you scoop the kernel, a little shell also comes along with it. That is our ordinary state of mind. We are attached to the body. Anything happening to the body will affect the self as well, and vice versa. But take the ripe coconut. We will hear the *kaḍa kaḍa* sound of the copra within when we shake the coconut. The kernel is separated from the shell. That is the example for spiritual realization.

In the West, one person in all history had realized this truth. And that person was Socrates. In the *Dialogues of Plato,* Plato describes Socrates facing death. Without a sense of courage, we cannot generally face death with equanimity. We are frightened, we are depressed, etc., etc. In the case of Socrates, he had such a calm and peaceful and fearless mind, because of this deep knowledge that he was not the body, but the immortal Self. This event is expressed by Plato in his dialogues where, when Socrates is drinking the poison, all his young disciples sitting around him were emotionally upset and the only calm person in that audience was Socrates himself. Then Socrates chided them: 'I asked the ladies to go away, because they were crying a lot, it was not giving me the peace I need at the time of death; but you young people also are crying.' That is the chiding that he gave to the people around. Then one of them, an aged person named Crito, turned to Socrates and asked this question: 'Socrates, how shall we bury you?' The man is not dead yet! He is taking the poison; after a few minutes, the poison will act and he will die. But he is asking the question already: 'Socrates, how shall we bury you?' This question was greeted by Socrates with a gentle smile, saying, 'Crito, you must first catch me, the real me, before you ask this question.' See the language. Pure Vedanta, in every word of it. You must first catch me, the *real* me, before you ask that question, and he added: 'Be of good cheer, Crito. You refer to this body. As to the body, do with it what you do with other people.' There you can see that this particular knowledge of the immortality of the Atman gives absolute peace of mind, great composure, great courage, and the power to pacify people around also. Therefore, it is not a theory. It is an experience; but in the whole of Western history, it is only one such person, that we come across in Western literature. This greatness of that one person could not be understood by the people around, Athenians around, because their philosophy had no understanding of this higher dimension of the human being. Though the oracle of Delphi had told the Greeks, 'man, know thyself', they knew man only from the external point of view: eating, drinking, pleasure, comfort, and then imperialism and war was all that they knew. They were very gifted in all these fields. The only one who knew this truth was Socrates, and therefore the Greeks could not understand this man. And they brought a charge against him of misleading the youth. Imagine such a great soul being charged in the court by the Athenian state as one who misled the youth of Athens and was condemned to death by drinking hemlock or poison! What a tragic situation! The finest citizen has become the object of judgement by the people, because they could not understand this higher spiritual dimension of the human personality. Everything else they could understand.

I used to tell people in Greece or other European countries or America: suppose Socrates was in India, what would have been the reaction? The Indian people would have understood him, and instead of killing him, would have treated him as a great sage. But the Greek culture never understood this spiritual dimension of the human personality. And anybody who teaches people things beyond their understanding, is liable to be persecuted or killed. The same thing happened to Jesus. He spoke something which the priests around him couldn't understand. And he was charged as an agent of the devil! And he was crucified. I remember, the famous remark of late Bertrand Russell: 'if you teach people faster than they can learn, you will be in trouble for yourself'. Socrates taught something which they could not understand, but Plato understood, a few others also understood. The mobs of Athens, democratic Athens, killed Socrates. And that made Plato hate democracy.

We have also the challenge of democracy before us in India today. And if we are guided by the broad and deep ideas of Vedanta, we shall be able to create a progressive humanist society in our country. If the broad Vedantic ideas do not influence our character, we may as well convert our democracy into the worst type of mobocracy. Even now there are such tendencies in our politics, manifested in our mobs going to the airport to receive a leader by breaking all rules and regulations, and violently enforcing a strike programme by a political party. When a little bit of this Vedantic discipline will come to our people, and it is my hope that it is going to come, we shall succeed in building a true democratic state and society in India. Our modern teachers like Vivekananda have asked us to effect a thorough social revolution from feudalism to democracy. We have many blots to wipe away before true democracy comes. That will come when education and culture reach our people. Not only education. Education can make us crude; and today I see a lot of young educated people, crude in their behaviour. But with culture, education will become a redeeming factor. I had said in some of my lectures in the West that this section of Plato's dialogues can be exactly a chapter in any one of our Upaniṣads. As for that, a British intellectual, E.J. Urwick, in his famous book, *The Message of Plato,* has said, that you can never understand Plato and Socrates without studying the Upaniṣads, and, in his book, he gives various illustrations as well.

So, these verses dealing with the immortal nature of the human being are going to be a source of tremendous attraction to people in the modern age, to people in all parts of the world. We know only one part of life, that is life. We don't know the other part of life, that is death. Death and life are two aspects of the same reality. This is an ancient teaching in India's *Ṛg-Veda*, the oldest book of humanity, *yasya chāyā amṛtam yasya mṛtyuḥ,* 'that reality, whose *chāyā* or shadow is immortality and mortality'. So, if you want to understand reality, you must understand life *and* death, not merely life. The Greeks understood only life. Lowes Dickinson, another great British scholar, writing on the life of Greece says: 'the Greeks understood life; they could never reconcile with death. When they were to die, they felt like being snatched by some power; they didn't like it at all.' But, with one exception, as I said; that is Socrates. He understood the meaning of life and death. In today's Western civilization, the same situation obtains in our lives; we don't know the meaning of death, and that the death of the body is not the death of the soul. Man is immortal. When these two are put together, fear of death will become less and less. And our India, particularly, needs this teaching more and more. We are so afraid of death. In fact, in my house, when I was very young, if I ever mentioned death, people used to tell me: 'Oh! no, don't talk of death at all! Why should we die even before death comes? That is the meaning of cowardice. 'Cowards die many times in their life, but the valiant taste of death but once,' said Shakespeare. That is literally true. A nation which fears death, cannot be great. Only if you can face death, you become great. That lesson Swami Vivekananda taught us in this modern period. So, this *śloka* says there:

Vāsāmsi jīrṇāni yathā vihāya
navāni gṛhṇāti naro'parāṇi;
Tathā śarīrāṇi vihāya jīrṇāni
anyāni samyāti navāni dehī—

This is what we do every day with our dress. And the soul does that at the time of death. This cloth is old, this body is old, let me get a new one. But there are occasions, when you throw away even a good cloth. That is why, even when the body is young, we have to face death often. But, normally we discard the cloth when it is torn and old, then get a new one. Similarly, a body which has become useless for our purpose, death comes at that time. Majority of people die only when they are old and decrepit; not when they are young, their number is much less, percentage-wise. Then Śrī Kṛṣṇa continues:

नैनं छिन्दन्ति शस्त्राणि नैनं दहति पावकः ।
न चैनं क्लेदयन्त्यापो न शोषयति मारुतः ॥ २३ ॥

Nainam chindanti śastrāṇi nainam dahati pāvakaḥ;
Na cainam kledayantyāpo na śoṣayati mārutaḥ— 2. 23

'No weapons can cut this Atman, no fire can burn It, no water can wet It, no air can dry It.'

This Self, the Atman, 'no weapons can cut it', etc. That is the nature of the Atman. Take mind, for example. You can't cut your mind, you can't wound your mind, cannot do any such thing. Though as a self, as an ego, I may feel wounded. But a mind has no wound at all. We associate ourselves with these kinds of limitations of the body and we say we are also wounded. But nobody can cut the mind. It is so subtle; it is not a material thing. Still more subtle is the Atman. Naturally, no fire can burn it, no water can wet it, etc. Then He positively says:

अच्छेद्योऽयमदाह्योऽयमक्लेद्योऽशोष्य एव च ।
नित्यः सर्वगतः स्थाणुरचलोऽयं सनातनः ॥ २४ ॥

Acchedyo'yamadāhyo'yamakledyo'śoṣya eva ca;
Nityaḥ sarvagataḥ sthāṇuracalo'yam sanātanaḥ — 2. 24

'This Self cannot be cut, nor can it be burnt, nor wetted, nor dried. Changeless, all-pervading, unmoving, immovable, this Self is eternal.'

That is a repetition of the same idea.

Again and again, the truth is pressed upon us: we are not this body-mind complex. Within this there is something profound. This is like a gem-box. The box looks very beautiful, but the gem inside is more valuable; don't forget that. That idea is repeated again and again even in our mystical literature. The Holy Name of God is like a gem: *Rām-ratan maine pāyo,* in a famous Hindi song by Meera Bai, 'I have received the gem of Rāma's Name'. It is immortal, by which all fear vanishes, etc., etc. So, we have been taught this again and again by great mystics and spiritual teachers. *Gītā* is expressing it here in these verses:

अव्यक्तोऽयमचिन्त्योऽयमविकार्योऽयमुच्यते ।
तस्मादेवं विदित्वैनं नानुशोचितुमर्हसि ॥२५॥

Avyakto'yamacintyo'yamavikāryo'yamucyate;
Tasmādevam viditvainam nānuśocitumarhasi —2. 25

'The Atman is said to be unmanifested, beyond thought, beyond modification; knowing It as such, it is not proper for you to grieve.'

This Atman is said to be unmanifested. We can't feel the touch of the Atman anywhere. *Avyakta* means unmanifested. Similarly, *acintya,* unthinkable. You cannot catch it with a piece of thought. You cannot conceptualize it. Everything in the world we try to catch through two sources: one is thought, the other is speech. Once you give a speech and a thought to enclose something, you say you understand that thing. We can do this with everything in the world. But with regard to the Atman, speech and thought recoil unable to touch it. That is why It is unthinkable. In fact, the *Bṛhadāraṇyaka Upaniṣad* (1. 4. 7) spoke of realizing the Atman in these words: *Ātmā iti eva upāsita.* On this Śankarācarya comments:

> *Yah tu ātmaśabdasya iti paraḥ prayogaḥ, ātmaśabdapratyayoḥ ātmatatvasya paramārthato aviṣayatva jñāpanārtham. Anyathā ātmānam upāsita iti evam avakṣyat*

'The use of the particle *iti* (thus) along with the word *ātman*, or "Self", to which you referred, in the text, only signifies that the truth of the ātman is really beyond the scope of the term and the concept "Self". Otherwise, the *śruti* would only say, one should meditate upon the *ātman.*' We have to use some word; so we use the word Atman. But don't run away, Atman is not a thing. It is eternal Consciousness behind all things. That is stressed again and again. So, *avyakto'yam acintyo'yam.* One beautiful verse demonstrating the profound depth of psychological insight occurs in a verse in the *Aṣṭāvakra-Gītā: Acintyam cintyamāno'pi cintārūpam bhajatyasau,* 'when you think of the unthinkable, you resort to a piece of thought only'. When you think of the unthinkable, you don't catch that unthinkable at all. You formulate a thought, that is all. It is an object. Thought is an object. This is the unthinkable Self, eternal Self.

Now, this kind of subtle knowledge of these deep realities, you get not only in Indian literature but also in Chinese philosophy of Tao, in Zen Buddhism, and in some of the writings of Christian and Muslim mystics; but, not in their official religions, formal religions. There is this truth beyond all conceptualization. That is the Atman, eternal Self, the subject, the seer, and not an object. Similarly, *avikāryo'yam,* this is unchangeable. The whole world is changeable. This is unchangeable. The external world is simply a tissue of change. This Atman never changes, eternally the same. That is the one truth the world is seeking. What is that eternal, changeless reality? Formerly, we used the word God for it. But, the word God has become involved in so many controversies. And ultimately, some people said we don't want God. In fact, it was the German philosopher Nietzsehe, in the last century, who said, god is dead. Well, that kind of god has no status at all. But Vedantic God is quite different. It is the eternal Self. It is always the witness of every event. Every 'yes' and 'no' is watched by the eternal Self. Therefore, this has got a strong foundation in experience, in your own Self.

This was the experience Śrī Ramaṇa Maharṣi had when he was a boy of 16 or 17, the first and last spiritual experience of his, when he felt 'I am going to die', became frightened, came home, lay down in his room on the floor, and said to himself: 'I am dying, I am dying', and he imitated the whole experience of death. 'Yes, I am just dying.' And I am dead. Then he found to his great joy that he was still there to watch his death. 'I' am deathless, the one who watches my death is always there. That is my true Self. That was his first and last spiritual experience according to his own words. Of course, he got it so easily because he had high spiritual development earlier, with good *vāsanas* and *samskāras*. We may not get it so easily. But, even if you get a glimpse of the truth, 'yes, there is some truth in it,' work on it. That much is enough for us to begin with. So, *tasmādevam viditvainam,* 'knowing Him to be like this', *na anuśocitum arhasi.* 'It is not fit for you to experience grief'. Then Śrī Kṛṣṇa changes the line of argument:

अथ चैनं नित्यजातं नित्यं वा मन्यसे मृतम् ।
तथापि त्वं महाबाहो नैवं शोचितुमर्हसि ॥ २६ ॥

Atha cainam nityajātam nityam vā manyase mṛtam;
Tathāpi tvam mahābāho nainam śocitumarhasi — 2. 26

'Even if you think that this Self has constant birth and constant death, even then, O strong-armed one, it is not fit for you to mourn.'

The next verse clarifies this:

जातस्य हि ध्रुवो मृत्युर्ध्रुवं जन्म मृतस्य च ।
तस्मादपरिहार्येऽर्थे न त्वं शोचितुमर्हसि ॥ २७ ॥

Jātasya hi dhruvo mṛtyuḥ dhruvam janma mṛtasya ca;
Tasmādaparihārye'rthe na tvam śocitumarhasi — 2. 27

'Whoever is born, to him or her death is certain; to the dead, birth also is certain; it is not, therefore, fit for you to mourn for this unavoidable fact.'

'Whoever is born will have to die', *jātasya hi dhruvo mṛtyuḥ.* Anybody who is born, must die. One English poet says, 'our hearts are beating funeral marches to the grave'. That is one way of putting the truth, that if you have life, you will have death also. 'Therefore', *tasmāt aparihārye'rthe,* 'in this inescapable situation', *na tvam śocitum arhasi,* 'it does not behove you to experience sorrow and grief'. Then a very profound idea comes in the next verse:

अव्यक्तादीनि भूतानि व्यक्तमध्यानि भारत ।
अव्यक्तनिधनान्येव तत्र का परिदेवना ॥ २८ ॥

Avyaktādīni bhūtāni vyaktamadhyāni bhārata;
Avyaktanidhanānyeva tatra kā paridevanā— 2. 28

'Beings come from the unseen, in between they become the seen, and they return also to the unseen; what is there to be worried about?'

All beings are *avyakta*, 'unmanifest', in the beginning, *vyakta*, 'manifest' in the middle, and *avyakta* again, in the end. That is a very famous utterance.

In the *Mahābhārata*, in its *Sanatsujātiya* section of the *Śānti Parva*, there is a beautiful expression of the same truth: *adarśanāt āpatitaḥ punaśca adarśanam gataḥ*, 'we came from *adarśana*, the unseen, and we go back to *adarśana*, the unseen'. That is our everyday experience. Let the truth be known. There is a past, there is a future, and in between there is the present. Let us do as well as we can in that present state. This is a very difficult subject, but it is also a profound truth. Extreme subtlety of thinking is needed to comprehend even a little bit of it. That is expressed in the next verse:

आश्चर्यवत्पश्यति कश्चिदेनम्
आश्चर्यवद्वदति तथैव चान्यः।
आश्चर्यवच्चैनमन्यः शृणोति
श्रुत्वाप्येनं वेद न चैव कश्चित् ॥२९॥

Āścaryavatpaśyati kaścidenam
āścaryavadvadati tathaiva cānyaḥ;
Āścaryavaccainamanyaḥ śṛṇoti
śrutvāpyenam veda na caiva kaścit — 2. 29

'Some see this (truth) as a wonder; some others speak of It similarly as a wonder; some others hear about It as a wonder; some others even after hearing of It, do not understand it at all.'

Some see this truth as an *āścarya*, a wonder; so also some speak and hear about It as a wonder. But very few understand It. A tremendous mystery is this Atman. It is there, but It doesn't allow you to detect It all the time. That is a hidden truth. In fact, one of the British poets of the last century, Robert

Browning, who was very much influenced by Vedantic ideas, has written a poem called *Paracelsus*. In that poem he speaks of the Atman as the *imprisoned splendour*. There is a profound splendour in every one of us, but It is imprisoned by the body-mind complex. You have to release that imprisoned splendour. That is spiritual life. *Eṣa sarveṣu bhūteṣu gūḍho ātmā na prakāśate,* says the *Kaṭha Upaniṣad*: 'This Atman is present in every being, but *gūḍho,* hidden', very, very mysterious. *Na prakāśate,* 'It does not manifest'. That is the truth, but we can realize It. We can release that splendour from its imprisoned state. That is what we do in our spiritual life. All hatred and violence, all exploitation will go, when a little light of the Atman will light up your day-to-day life and human relationships. So, this concept of the 'imprisoned splendour' is a very beautiful concept.

This Atman remains a mystery all through. But it can be cleared. It can be realized by appropriate methods. That is the Vedantic technique of spiritual life and spiritual realization. In the *Kaṭha Upaniṣad,* this very expression comes (I. ii. 7), *āścaryo vaktā kuśalo'sya labdhā, āścaryo jñātā kuśalānuśiṣṭaḥ.* 'The teacher of the Atman must be an *āścarya,* a wonderful person, the student of the Atman must also be an *āścarya'*; when these two come together, that is, 'when taught by an efficient teacher, the one who realizes the Atman also is wonderful'. So, you stand before this great mystery in wonder, worshipping It. What else can we do with It? We can only silently meditate upon It, worship It. We can't capture It by our mind, by our thought. That is the nature of this supreme truth which is so close to ourselves as our Self, but so far away from us, from our understanding. The Upaniṣads repeat this idea. It is very near to you and It is very far from you. To the ignorant, It is far; to the knowing, It is near. The whole centre of human freedom is in that particular mystery. When you realize It, you become truly free. Other freedoms are necessary; but this freedom is the freedom of all freedoms. You may have all the wealth and power, but you may be absolutely unfree. But with this knowledge of your true nature, even though you may not have many material possessions, you will be really free in the true sense of the term.

So, that is how verse 29 has brought before us this tremendous mystery, this imprisoned splendour, and the challenge to you, to me, and to everyone else, is how to release it from that genetic prison. Let it come out. Let it manifest. So, Vivekananda defines religion in one scientific sentence: 'Religion is the manifestation of the divinity already in man.' It is hidden; let it manifest. What a change will come in human life and in inter-human relations, when a little of this divinity manifests in our life! That is the great teaching that is being expounded in the *Gītā*. We are just at the beginning. Through all the eighteen chapters, we shall be in the midst of this great theme. And the whole world is the audience today for the *Gītā*. Formerly, only some people of India, not even the majority of our people were benefited by its message. Today, the whole world is increasingly eager to get a copy of the *Gītā*. Recently, a seeker from Sofia, the capital of Bulgaria, wrote to me, 'We don't know anything, we have got one or two books. Please send us some other books. We are hungry for these ideas.' That is the situation in the world today.

Even in physical science, when you look at a small living cell, to the scientist it is a marvel. A marvel of construction, a marvel of organic activity within itself, creating, withdrawing, shaping, multiplying—it is a marvel. Even in the science of physics, it is a marvel to see that a tiny piece of matter can contain enormous energy; that is nuclear science. We can say regarding that also, *āścaryavat paśyati*. When you probe deep into nature, the wonder that you see outside becomes less, and greater wonders within nature become revealed to you. Similarly, looking at man, and that study has only just started in the West. As Sir Julian Huxley said: 'The study of the mind has just begun.' Shakespeare has expressed, 'how wonderful a thing is man', in a famous passage. This man can control this world, he can understand it, he can transcend it, what is that something in him which is such a marvel? Earlier, I referred to the term coined by Robert Browning, the British poet, 'the imprisoned splendour'. When modern science, in its psychology and neurology, will probe deeper and deeper into man, this marvel will be revealed increasingly. The study of the brain itself is a tremendous marvel. How the brain operates, how the various cells work together, and then produce a coherent life and reaction to the world, all these are subjects of marvel. But the most marvellous is what the Upaniṣads are dealing with, the infinite Atman. Behind this body-mind complex, which is so tiny, which is so contracted an organism compared to the world outside, yet within that is something tremendous, that is the biggest challenge before modern thought. Indian thought faced it successfully long long ago. That is what you find expressed in these verses: *āścaryavat paśyati kaścit enam.*

Sri Ramakrishna used to say, *Śiva* realizing his own infinite *Śiva*-nature, couldn't control himself and started dancing. Generally, you dance when you overflow in energy. Then only you will dance. If you are weak in energy, you will never dance. An expansion of energy within will make you dance. *Śiva's* dance is a result of that. He Himself is amazed to see the *Śiva*-nature within Himself. He is *Śiva,* the infinite one. So, these are the beautiful ideas coming out of this profound discovery of the Self of man.

Vivekananda says (*Complete Works of Swami Vivekananda,* vol. 2, p. 250): 'No books, no scriptures, no science can ever imagine the glory of the Self that appears as man… .' This is a remarkable reality. Normally, we are creaturely individuals with very limited powers. But we suspect that there is something very profound within every human being. That suspicion turns into a marvel, when he or she tries to understand the truth. And later on, it becomes a matter of realization.

It was in the eighteenth century when the French philosopher and mystic, Pascal, said:

'In space, the universe engulfs me and reduces me to a pinpoint. But, through thought, *I understand that universe.*'

What must be my true dimension then? Am I merely a speck of dust? No, that speck of dust contains a tremendous splendour. That is the Atman, the subject of this marvel. If this experience of the world through the sense organs is wonderful, million, million times more wonderful will be that experience of the Atman 'imprisoned' within. That profound truth has fascinated the Indian mind for centuries. After the Upaniṣads, our people were inspired by this discovery. I must know this truth. That is why so many people went to the forests and caves for meditation, just to realize this profound truth. None of the technologies of physical science can help us there. And so you find rock caves, here, there, all over India. And in history, India produced a Buddha. A man who really penetrated into this 'imprisoned splendour', and realized this immortal truth. He was full of joy for seven days and nights, and was walking up and down under that very tree under which he realized this truth. That tree later came to be called *bodhi-vṛkṣa,* tree of enlightenment. So, this verse 29 is expressing that marvel. The human being is not a speck of dust, is not a creature, but is free. Within him or her there is something wonderful; that is the one truth we must impress upon all our children. That is the first Vedantic teaching for every child, a teaching which the child will realize as true, as it grows up and becomes mature. That is the one truth that is central to all Vedantic teaching. So, verse 30 tells us:

देही नित्यमवध्योऽयं देहे सर्वस्य भारत ।
तस्मात्सर्वाणि भूतानि न त्वं शोचितुमर्हसि ॥३०॥

Dehī nityamavadhyo'yam dehe sarvasya bhārata;
Tasmātsarvāṇi bhūtāni na tvam śocitumarhasi — 2. 30

'The One that all bodies enclose is eternally free from being killed; therefore, you (Arjuna) need not grieve for all beings.'

This *dehī,* 'the Self'; *dehī* means one who lives in the *deha,* or body; *nityam avadhyo'yam,* 'none can destroy the *dehī* at any time'. That is the nature of this infinite truth. *Dehe sarvasya bhārata,* 'in all bodies', this Self or the *dehī* is indestructible, O Arjuna'. *Tasmāt sarvāṇi bhūtāni na tvam śocitum arhasi,* 'you need not, therefore, grieve for any entity, any being, in this world'. You can never touch that real dimension of the human system.

Somebody takes away my shirt, that has not affected me. I can take another shirt. In that way we speak of material things. But those who know the subject, whatever you may do with the body, my Self is untouched. If that is kept intact, then there will be nothing to worry. Stronger the person, the more is the capacity to express this truth in life and action; greater courage, greater endurance will come to him or her. Like that Jewish scientist in Hitler's Nazi prison: they were all subjected to tremendous pressure, all sorts of persecution, torture, suffering; many perished in that kind of treatment. But one survived. And he, Victor Frankil—he now lives in New York—wrote a book, *Man's Search For Meaning*. And there he mentions, that he was subjected to so much of pressure, so much of persecution. He would have broken down, but he detached himself from the body, began to think of himself as a *sākṣi,* as a witness to what was going on, as the Self. He could stand all this pressure on him. His mind was undisturbed at the end of the war; so, he could write this book as a result of those experiences. He calls that method 'attitude control'. You cannot control what others do to you, but you can control your attitude towards those things. That is in your hands. There is a very remarkable statement made by Victor Frankil in his *Man's Search For Meaning*. Somebody abuses me; well, he abused me and went away. I took it in, I nourished it, and it became a serious thing for me. I even went to commit suicide, because I am weak. If I am strong, I will say to myself: 'well, he has said a few words. What indeed did he say?, All the twenty-six alphabets put together in a particular order'. That way you can say to yourself and dismiss the whole thing. That needs lot of strength. So, attitude control is a very great lesson for all of us. Mostly we are our own enemies. We create trouble for ourselves. Others give only a little trouble. We multiply it by ourselves. There, attitude control can save the situation. That it is true, was proved. Victor Frankil further refers to it in American second World War hospitals in Italy. One ward was full of highly wounded personnel, hand is gone, leg is gone, such kinds of people; there was great suffering. In another ward, there were soldiers with minor injuries from the battle. They were also under treatment. An investigation showed that soldiers who had serious injuries, were more peaceful, more co-operative; the less injured people, the investigation found, were full of complaint, stress, and had no peace of mind; that was something strange. How could it be explained? These people (the severely injured) should have been much more in distress, than these people (with minor injuries). Then they found, on investigation, the power of attitude. In the case of these less injured people, they were people who would be soon treated, set right, and they know they will be sent to the front once again. But, in the ward in which the more injured were housed, they knew that the war was over for them, they would go back to their wife and children. They were perfectly at peace. The leg is gone, doesn't matter. We shall live with our people.

Now, here we can see two situations, and two reactions to these two situations. So, it proves the idea of attitude control, and that book gives you this truth, which only brings into prominence the great truths of the *Gītā*. The author who suffered in Nazi prison developed attitude control and could write a book to enlighten other people. So, these are the truths. After reading that book which confirms our super-sensory and spiritual nature, anyone will come closer to that marvel that is our true nature. That is what the *Gītā* tells us. And the *Gītā* specially stresses that this marvel can be realized in the context of human life, work, and inter-human relations. You need not have a separate life for it. 'Life itself is religion,' as Vivekananda said, because spirituality is my true nature. I have not to borrow it from somebody. So, this concept of the inherent divinity of man is at the back of Śrī Kṛṣṇa's teaching throughout this book hereafter. In this first part of the second chapter, he is using these arguments to tell Arjuna, 'why are you afraid of the world, of entering into the battle, you are not an ascetic, you have got so many things to do here'. All this is being argued about to make Arjuna take part in the war in front. Many more worldly arguments will come later, when he found these arguments did not click with Arjuna. Yes, he used worldly arguments also; these are coming in the next few verses.

स्वधर्ममपि चावेक्ष्य न विकम्पितुमर्हसि ।
धर्म्याद्धि युद्धाच्छ्रेयोऽन्यत्क्षत्रियस्य न विद्यते ॥ ३१ ॥

Svadharmam api cāvekṣya na vikampitumarhasi;
Dharmyāddhi yuddhācchreyo'nyatkṣatriyasya na vidyate—2. 31

'From the point of view of your own *dharma*, it is not fit for you to waver; for a *kṣatriya* there is nothing more auspicious than a just war.'

Even from the point of view of your own *dharma*, you should not recoil from this challenge before you, because, for a *kṣatriya*, a war is a producer of glory. It is a very doubtful proposition that a war can be righteous. Two or three weeks ago, I had the occasion to say that the war against the Nazi movement in Germany was a righteous war; the whole world would have been completely distorted, if the Nazi movement had won the war. So, the whole world joined together to fight against that pernicious doctrine of racial superiority and military despotism, which destroyed millions of people. Occasionally, occasions of a righteous war will come. But not every war is righteous; a war of aggression to subdue other people can never be a righteous war. All war for defending a nation's freedom is righteous. On the contrary, if you don't do it, you will pay for it, and your coming generations will pay for it. Therefore, the words, *svadharmamapi cāvekṣya: svadharma,* that is, your *dharma;* the *kṣatriya* has to protect the freedom of the people. So, that is the nature of a *kṣatriya*. Today, we have the old Indian concept in a new situation. The old *kṣatriya* is today a politician, a soldier, and an administrator. What is his work? His work is to protect the people, nourish the people, serve the people. Somebody *has* to do it. It is the political and administrative system that does these things. Even the policeman protects you from being robbed when you are asleep; though often they don't succeed in it, and so many are robbed at night. That shows the inefficiency of our administration and the indiscipline in our society. So, in this way, the politician, the administrator, and all defence services including the civil defence services like the police, they also belong to the *kṣatriya* class. Their work is to serve others with their power, their energy. They handle power. But the power is for the service of the people. That is the nature of that power. So, when Yudhiṣṭhira wanted to renounce the kingdom after the *Mahābhārata* war, Bhiṣma told him—it is a very interesting sentence—in the *Mahābhārata Śānti Parva*: *Daṇḍa eva hi rājendra kṣatra-dharmo na muṇḍanam*, 'Oh! Supreme King, the duty of a *kṣatriya* is *daṇḍa*, meaning exercise of power to serve the people, and not *muṇḍana*, shaving the head and becoming an ascetic.' That is what Śrī Kṛṣṇa is telling Arjuna: *dharmyāddhi yuddhācchreyo'nyat kṣatriyasya na vidyate*, 'a *kṣatriya* is happy to fight a war which has a great cause to inspire it', a human liberation war, for example. But to claim every war as *dharmya*, cannot be accepted. Actually, history will condemn some wars, which were thought to be *dharmya*, but were not *dharmya* in a later kind of study. So also, this one is perfectly *dharmya*, to protect your national freedom. A defensive war is always *dharmya*; offensive wars, some are, some are not. Very few are. Most are not. Just like what India has done in sending, at the request of the U.N., some soldiers and officers to monitor the peace between Iran and Iraq. Similarly, we sent our army to Congo and Korea, all for peacekeeping purposes. These are all very good examples where you are not there for aggression, not for gaining some property or land for yourself, but to establish the peace that was broken earlier. So, all these arguments are included in this particular statement: *Dharmyāddhi yuddhācchreyo'nyatkṣatriyasya na vidyate*, 'there can be no better opportunity for a *kṣatriya* to exercise one's intelligence, ability, and love for humanity, than to take part in a battle to establish human values, freedom, and dignity of the individual person'. Then in this case, the next *śloka* says:

यदृच्छया चोपपन्नं स्वर्गद्वारमपावृतम् ।
सुखिनः क्षत्रियाः पार्थ लभन्ते युद्धमीदृशम् ॥ ३२॥

Yadṛcchayā copapannam svargadvāramapāvṛtam;
Sukhinaḥ kṣatriyāḥ pārtha labhante yuddhamīdṛśam—2. 32

'The *kṣatriya* is happy when he gets this type of war which comes unsought and which opens the doorway to (hero's) heaven.'

This war is, *yadṛcchayā ca upapannam,* you didn't seek it, 'it has come by itself', *yadṛcchayā,* 'by chance'; *svargadvāram-apāvṛtam,* 'the doors of heaven are open'. *Sukhinaḥ kṣatriyāḥ pārtha labhante yuddham-īdṛśam,* 'a *kṣatriya* is happy if he gets such opportunities to exercise his military talent'. Other aspects he won't like. That is why much of the army is dissatisfied when they are employed in stopping civil disturbances, killing one's own people. They are not happy at all. And no nation should do it except in rare emergency circumstances. This war is *yadṛcchayā upapannam,* 'it has come by chance'; the Pāṇḍavas wanted to avoid it. But the Kauravas had no such qualms. Nobody accepts war as a necessity. The *Mahābhārata,* of which the *Gītā* is a part, always stresses the avoidance of war. Try to seek peace always. In this great epic, a war-like attitude is not there; a war-like philosophy is not there. But, war is there, because of the disparity in the human situation; there are occasions for self-protection, and any activity that ensures that self-protection, is to be resorted to. In that sense only war is used in the *Mahābhārata* context. The book is spiritual and the greatest leader of the Pāṇḍavas is Yudhiṣṭhira, a man of peace, with no hatred to anybody; his another name is also very significant, *Ajātaśatru*, one whose enemy is yet to be born. His brothers also were of this nature, and Śrī Kṛṣṇa is also advising them to forsake war, and enter into negotiations with the Kauravas. If you study the totality of the *Mahābhārata,* you will never find that it is a book of war. But war was developing. Human nature has become corrupt in many ways; arrogance, pride and all these things came. So, you can see various incidents leading up to the Kurukṣetra war. There was no possibility of settling it otherwise. When the *Mahābhārata* serial will be screened in the New Delhi Doordarshan, you will see the story developing in small ways, developing into the biggest civil war that we had in ancient times, about 1400 BC., which really destroyed many of our people and our culture. Things took a different turn thereafter. The *Mahābhārata* war is a big turning point in the history of our own country. Then Śrī Kṛṣṇa tells Arjuna:

अथ चेत्त्वमिमं धर्म्यं संग्रामं न करिष्यसि ।
ततः स्वधर्मं कीर्तिं च हित्वा पापमवाप्स्यसि ॥ ३३ ॥

Atha cettvamimam dharmyam samgrāmam na kariṣyasi;
Tataḥ svadharmam kīrtim ca hitvā pāpamavāpsyasi—2. 33

'If you do not fight this righteous war, then, deviating from your righteous duty and fame, you will incur sin.'

If you don't face this battle now, Arjuna, what happens to you? *Tataḥ svadharmam kīrtim ca hitvā*, 'you will destroy your own *dharma* and your own great name', *pāpam avāpsyasi,* and 'incur sin'.

अकीर्तिञ्चापि भूतानि कथयिष्यन्ति तेऽव्ययाम् ।
संभावितस्य चाकीर्तिर्मरणादतिरिच्यते ॥ ३४ ॥

Akīrtiñcāpi bhūtāni kathayiṣyanti te'vyayām;
Sambhāvitasya cākīrtirmaraṇādatiricyate — 2. 34

'People will recount your infamy for long; for a person of honour, infamy is worse than death.'

Other people will also speak ill of you. You will be the butt end of ridicule from other people. They will say that Arjuna was a coward, he ran away from battle. And to one who has already achieved a place of honour, to lose that honour is worse than death itself. That is a wonderful statement. You get it in English, 'death before dishonour'; this is exactly what we had long ago in the *Mahābhārata: Sambhāvitasya cākīrtirmaraṇāt atiricyate,* 'death is better than living in dishonour'. That is the wonderful idea. All heroic people think that way. Many of our people today do not understand this truth. The sense of personal honour and self-respect is going down and down. I am prepared to be dishonoured, but I want only money, nothing else. When money plays a greater part in human life, honour becomes less and less important; decent people want honour, and will not exchange honour for money. Earlier, I had given the example of late Chittaranjan Das of Calcutta, whose father died in debt and insolvency, because of poverty. And Das became a lawyer. In the first case he got some money. What did he do with that money? The first thing he did was to go to the court, take the dead father's name from that dishonour of insolvency. That is an example of personal honour being superior to money. That lesson we have to learn in a new way. We have lost it for the last few decades. Today, some people do not mind at all losing all their honour; still they walk about in society as if they are big people. He becomes the centre. He will write a book and make a million rupees out of that book. That is the current state in our society and elsewhere also.

भयाद्रणादुपरतं मंस्यन्ते त्वां महारथाः ।
येषां च त्वं बहुमतो भूत्वा यास्यसि लाघवम् ॥ ३५ ॥

Bhayādraṇāduparatam mamsyante tvām mahārathāḥ;
Yeṣām ca tvam bahumato bhūtvā yāsyasi lāghavam—2. 35

'Great heroes will consider that you have run away from battle out of fear'; *yeṣām ca tvam bahumato bhūtvā yāsyasi lāghavam,* 'they who honoured you till now, will now belittle you.'

अवाच्यवादांश्च बहून्वदिष्यन्ति तवाहिताः ।
निन्दन्तस्तव सामर्थ्यं ततो दुःखतरं नु किम् ॥ ३६ ॥

Avācyavādāmśca bahūnvadiṣyanti tavāhitāḥ;
Nindantastava sāmarthyam tato duḥkhataram nu kim—2. 36

'Your enemies will speak against you all manner of words, not fit to be spoken; they will be deriding your capacities and talents.' *Tato duḥkhataram nu kim,* 'what can be more unhappy than that?' So, give up this cowardice. Face up to your problems, is Śrī Kṛṣṇa's final advice to Arjuna in verse 37.

हतो वा प्राप्स्यसि स्वर्गं जित्वा वा भोक्ष्यसे महीम् ।
तस्मादुत्तिष्ठ कौन्तेय युद्धाय कृतनिश्चयः ॥ ३७ ॥

Hato vā prāpsyasi svargam jitvā vā bhokṣyase mahīm;
Tasmāduttiṣtha kaunteya yuddhāya kṛtaniścayaḥ —2. 37

Hato vā prāpsyasi svargam, 'if you are killed, you will get *vīra-svargam,* heaven meant for heroes.' 'Or, if you conquer, you will enjoy the earth; therefore, stand up, O Arjuna, with the firm determination to fight.'

Today, how much we remember the Rajput heroes who faced foreign invaders and gave up their lives with honour and dignity! We remember them, we honour them even to-day. So, Śrī Kṛṣṇa is telling Arjuna: *jitvā vā bhokṣyase mahīm,* 'suppose you win the battle, you will enjoy dominion in this world.' So, either way, you are not a loser. That is the appeal to all heroic sentiments in a human being. *Tasmāduttiṣtha kaunteya,* 'therefore, stand up, O! Arjuna.' *Kaunteya* means the son of Kuntī. *Yuddhāya kṛtaniścayaḥ,* 'fully determined to face up to the war situation that has come', 'I shall not run away, I shall face this problem,' with that determination, stand up.

As I said in the beginning, when I was dealing with the first chapter, Arjuna had a real war to face. You and I do not have real wars to face. But the *Gītā* teaching is relevant to all of us, because the nature of war for you and me is day-to-day problems. We have to face them. We have to overcome them, summon enough energy from within to face up to all this. That is the philosophy which also has given to one universal application. Śaṅkarācārya referred to Śrī Kṛṣṇa making Arjuna an instrument, *arjunam nimittī kṛtya,* to teach the rest. Whether you are here in India, or in America, or in Europe, Soviet Russia, China, the philosophy remains the same. It need not be always for a person who has actually to kill somebody in battle. Not at all. So, from now onwards, you are taking a particular instance and putting it in a universal context. A profound philosophy of life and action is being expounded hereafter. Its intention was to make Arjuna face up to the battle situation. But its intention with respect to you and me is to make us courageous and strong, and face up to life's challenges. A human being must show that he or she is the master of the environment. He should not become a creature of the environment. To restore the human being to that dignity, you need a philosophy. That is the philosophy Śrī Kṛṣṇa is going to expound throughout this book. It is a philosophy of life, very practical, that is why, in the next few verses, the Gītā will call it *yoga*. I am teaching you *yoga*. But when I say *yoga* merely, we only recall *prāṇāyāma*, or standing on the head, and all these physical exercises. Nothing of that is meant here. It is a practical philosophy of life, how to handle this wonderful human situation, by which you develop your own spiritual consciousness within, and you become instrumental for the happiness and welfare of the people around you. *That is the philosophy of a comprehensive spirituality that Śrī Kṛṣṇa is expounding, calling it by that short word yoga.* We will come to it a few verses later. *Tasmāt uttiṣṭha,* 'therefore, stand up'. Don't lie down, don't be lazy, don't be cosy. Be alert, be energetic, be active. Buddha also said, be always alert. There is a tendency for us to be cozy and lazy. That should not be. So, in Vedanta you will find this *uttiṣṭhata, jāgrata,* 'arise, awake', a constant refrain. No, life is for the hard-working people, not for the weak, not for the sleepy, not for the lazy; that message comes again and again, like the famous Sanskrit verse, popular verse, coming from ancient times:

Udyamena hi siddhyanti kāryāṇi na manorathaiḥ;
Na hi suptasya simhasya praviśanti mukhe mṛgāḥ—

'It is through *udyama,* hard work, industrious activity, that you achieve things in this world'; *na manorathiaḥ,* 'not by daydreaming', simply by imagining, I shall do this, I shall do that; that is called *manoratha,* carrying your mind as a *ratha,* as a chariot, and flying about in the air. That is not the way. Then an example is given: A *simha* or lion has become a little old. It stopped pursuing its prey; it will just lie down with a wide-open mouth with the belief that some deer will oblige it by entering into its mouth. That way the lion will not get any food. It has to work hard to get its food for the day; that is the example given in that verse. Similarly, Śrī Kṛṣṇa is telling all humanity to work hard to enjoy life.

Now, from verse 38, you will be hearing a new music. *That music is the powerful music of Śrī Kṛṣṇa's original philosophy, a philosophy of life developed from the philosophy of practical Vedanta, from the science of human possibilities developed in the ancient Upaniṣads.* Śrī Kṛṣṇa is expounding the technical application of that science for total human development from verse 38 of this second chapter onwards.

What does Śrī Kṛṣṇa say?

सुखदुःखे समे कृत्वा लाभालाभौ जयाजयौ ।
ततो युद्धाय युज्यस्व नैवं पापमवाप्स्यसि ॥ ३८ ॥

Sukhaduḥkhe same kṛtvā lābhālābhau jayājayau;
Tato yuddhāya yujyasva naivam pāpamavāpsyasi —2. 38

'Having made pain and pleasure, gain and loss, conquest and defeat, the same, engage yourself then in battle. So shall you incur no sin.'

Keep your mind even, *sukhaduhkhe,* 'in happiness and misery', *lābhālābhau*, 'in profit as well as in loss', *jayājayau*, 'in victory or in defeat'. In all these various changing situations, try to keep the mind as calm as possible. *Tato yuddhāya yujyasva,* 'with such a mind enter the battlefield', as well as your life. Then you will never incur sin. *Naivam pāpam avāpsyasi,* 'you will never incur sin, if you have this attitude'. This concept of calmness of mind is a wonderful concept. Whenever you want to achieve great things, it is not through excitement that you achieve. With calm, silent, steady work, you achieve great things. In today's politics it is all excitement. You go and excite the whole people, and the excitement also dies down after some time. But those who are great workers, they are not of that nature. They have tremendous convictions, they are calm and steady, they work, they face problems, they overcome them keeping their mind calm and steady. It is the calm and steady man or woman that works best. The excited man or woman shows that he or she is working well; but, it is noise and show. Dr. Radhakrishnan said in one of his lectures, that the modern man, and the modern woman, do not believe in God; they believe in what they call 'going about doing good'.

But when you watch closely, 'it is more going about than doing good'. So much of excitement, so much of noise, and so little work is turned out. We have plenty of such in our society today. But, calm, silent, steady work is real work. That is the type of work Śrī Kṛṣṇa is telling now; it applies to a housewife, to an administrator; so also, to any professional. Calm, silent, steady work. The mind's tendency is to go up and down. In fact, that is a big psychology in itself. Every experience of the external world, throws the mind into waves, just like dropping a stone in a lake making for waves coming up; the mind is like that. Some experiences make for bigger waves, and some become like Atlantic waves. That is all bad. You are thrown off your ground. You lose your mental balance thereby. Most of us have some measure of balance in the midst of day to day life except when something extraordinary happens to us. But by training we can increase our capacity to keep the mind steady, even when unsteadying influences work on it. That is what Śrī Kṛṣṇa is introducing now, because he is now going to give you a philosophy of life and work. And life and work mean upsetting of the mind often. So, you must learn to handle the mind. You must keep it calm and steady. It is the beginning of the teaching. He will later on define His philosophy itself as *samatvam yoga ucyate, yoga* is *samatvam.* This mind is calm and steady—that is *yoga.* Normally, it is not.

Take any animal. Any impulse arising in an animal throws its mind into a convulsion. Then it must find an immediate expression in an action. Then, that impulse dies away. That is the nature of animal behaviour. But, in the case of a human being, when he or she has not started training the mind, very often this is the behaviour; when we were primitive, we were doing like this. Though even then, a certain calmness had come to the human system, because nature had provided for it, that every sensory input will be observed, then passed on as a motor output. A little gap between input and output, even the most ordinary men have.

That is the beginning of a tremendous development in our human psyche. Śrī Kṛṣṇa is just indicating the beginning of that development. Just put a little stop between input and output. Suppose, somebody abuses me; immediately I abuse back. Don't do so; that means you are an animal, an automaton, as we say. And always we say, action and reaction are equal and opposite. That is the mechanical law. But in the case of human beings, it can be altered. If the action is one unit, reaction can be ten units, or it can be no unit. That shows you are free. When life appears on the horizon of evolution, even in a very elementary form, freedom also appears. There is no other definition of freedom. You are not merely a creature of some external circumstance. You regulate your reaction. As soon as you start regulating your reaction, you have started achieving your humanness. Then the march inward is unique. You are handling your own mind. You are creating a sense of calmness within. Great achievements will come thereby. Human evolution begins with the achievement of this balancing of the mind between a sensory input and a motor output. That must be strengthened more and more. We shall come across this subject again and again, because *the whole subject of the Gītā is the training of this human mind for total human development by handling this world around it, and by handling oneself also in a masterly way.* We don't remain a creature of some masterly process outside. We are the masterly force, handling our life. This must be achieved by every human being, and our neurology and physiology today tell us, that nature has endowed the human being with that organic capacity to handle one's life from this masterly point of view. He or she need not remain a mere creature. He or she can be free and can exercise this freedom; this is the teaching of modern biology, neurology, and the ancient Vedanta. Vedanta takes the experience of freedom to the highest level of development. It calls it *mukti.* This wonderful development of initial human freedom to insert a gap between input and output experience—that is the beginning of the human march to freedom. Out of that will come a wonderful achievement.

Towards the end of this chapter, after expounding his philosophy, Śrī Kṛṣṇa will give you, in about 18 or 19 verses, the nature of that human mind which has achieved perfect equilibrium, perfect steadiness, which the *Gītā* calls *sthitaprajñā*. It is a wonderful word. *Prajñā* means knowledge, or wisdom; *sthita* means steady. Our knowledge is not steady. It comes and goes. But, by training, we can make the mind steady, wisdom steady. Those verses are masterly verses at the end of the second chapter. First the exposition, then an illustration. That is the type of character we must develop in ourselves. So, the whole subject is meant for every citizen, every human being—man, woman and child. How to build up this human equanimity. How to handle this packet of psycho-physical energy which you have got at birth; how to develop it, expand it, bring out the best out of it. Who is to do it? Each one of us; others can help. But the actual work is your own. As the English saying tells us: 'You can take a horse to the water but cannot make it drink.' So, Vedanta repeatedly stresses this point: building up your character and your life is your own work, your own privilege. Don't leave it to others. Take help from anybody, but the work is your own. And when you develop, the world will marvel: yes, here is one who with a given capital of psychic energy, has built up a huge business of intellectual and spiritual life—just like any business man starting with a thousand rupees capital, later on becomes a millionaire, because he invested it properly and worked hard. The same thing in the case of human personality. How are we to build up, on the given capital, a big personality which is a great blessing to oneself and to the world outside? That subject will come up now and continue all through the chapters. Though this is told to Arjuna, Śrī Kṛṣṇa tells it to everyone. Arjuna is only a *nimitta,* an instrument. What shall I do with my packet of psychic energy?

In industry and commerce, we are seeing a new type of entrepreneurship in India. Our people, especially in the business community, were generally lazy and cosy before. They were satisfied with money-lending. But political freedom has brought a sense of one's own importance and a new energy to work hard. So, a few months ago, the weekly *India Today,* published a big despatch: On the New Entrepreneurs in India. I found it to be an inspiring article. A man has only a thousand rupees. He invests it, works hard, builds up; and now he has become a big industrialist. Like that, hundreds of cases; India is showing this initiative, this enterprise; no more are we given to the *kismat* idea: it is my fate to be weak like this. That philosophy is going away. The *Gītā* philosophy is coming; when these hundreds of entrepreneurs study the *Gītā*, they will develop a new type of entrepreneurship, adding to it a strong sense of national responsibility. They will consider that all this that we earn by hard work and development of national resources, I will spend for the good of all, for the good of society. That second blessing will come to those entrepreneurs when they get the *Gītā* message along with their own tremendous energy and enterprise. Enterprise is beautiful.

When I was a student at the High School, I read a small book, a statement from Macaulay, and from his own teacher, John Stuart Mill. He says: 'it is always advisable to be in the forefront of opportunity in matters of enterprise, and in the backyard of opportunity in matters of indulgence.' For pleasure, you are at the back; for enterprise you are at the front. That is the type. Just like when there is food to be cooked, I am there; it is time for eating, bell has rung, I am there. Some people come only when the bell rings. Some people are ready to do the cooking. This one is far better than that other one. In matters of enterprise, be in the forefront. In matters of indulgence, fall far behind. Tell this to your children, then we shall develop this nation to its highest level of character. At present it is not. We are teaching all our children: Be at the forefront at the time of pleasure and profit. Enterprise: if it is personal, you do; if it is for the nation, don't do anything. Keep quiet. That teaching we are giving, ruining the character of our children. So, let us take from this great book that wonderful new orientation we have given to our education, in name only, namely, human resource development, value-oriented education. The *Gītā* is full of these ideas. So, carry this message to the society, to our children, to our students everywhere.

We studied verse 38 in the second chapter. This is the dividing line between the previous verses and the verses that are yet to come. A measure of stabilization within the mind is needed for effective work. Frenzy is not a good accompaniment of efficient work. Calm, silent, steady work is what brings about permanent results. The one lesson we have to learn is that people who jump about and shout about, they are not efficient at all. Those who work silently, they alone know how to work. In the whole teaching of the *Gītā*, this subject is uppermost: how to work? How to work efficiently? This subject immediately brings up the idea of the training of the mind. What is the state of the mind? Unless it is a little calm and quiet, great work cannot be done. Just emotional effervescence is not efficiency; it all disappears in no time. So, Śrī Kṛṣṇa is giving us an initial teaching about developing a measure of stability within the mind. We have the capacity to bring it about. We have to exercise that capacity. So, our mind is always going up and down. That mind has to be stabilized a little, an inner stabilization.

Some weeks ago, I quoted the famous French physiologist who said, *a fixed interior milieu is the condition for a free life*. It is an inner stabilization out of which will come great energy, tremendous response to the human situation. People who make noise and who shout are not efficient workers. Today, in India, there is so much of noise, so much of shouting at the time of work. That only shows we are not good workers. We are not efficient. Simply emotional excitement. The *Gītā* will teach us the distinction between noisy and showy type of work, and calm, silent, steady, and efficient work. Long ago when I was in Delhi, the autorickshaw had been just introduced at that time, a new species of vehicle. Such a noise it used to make, and I thought it must be a powerful conveyance; I got in. And it started in a shaking movement all the time making a big noise; but, I found that the speed was only twelve miles per hour! Later on, when I travelled by a first class motor car, its movement was quiet but the speed was about eighty miles per hour. I have also travelled in Europe at 106 miles per hour, with no shaking or noise. In human beings also you find this difference. When one is not efficient, he or she makes noise, shouts, and is full of frenzy. When one gets tremendous inner strength, he or she becomes calm and steady, and turns out more work than other persons. That is the one lesson we, as a people, have to learn. We can become great workers, changing the world around us in the right direction. That is called creative work. That subject is coming up in the great teachings of the second and third chapters of the *Gītā*. The third chapter is called *karma-yoga,* the great *yoga* of action. So, in this earlier chapter, the warning is given to us: try to keep the mind as calm and balanced as possible. Some great thing is coming out of it. Not only the good work outside, but also a penetration inward, towards your own true nature; that needs that wonderful calmness and balance of mind.

Earlier, we discussed the concept of homeostasis in modern neurology, that the body has got a thermal equilibrium. Nature achieved it in the later mammals for survival. Changes in outside temperature will not affect the body temperature; it remains constant. That is called a homeostatic condition. Out of that only, nature could develop the human higher brain, whose function is to take man to freedom, to emancipation, says a neurologist, Gray Walter in his book: The *Living Brain*. For all mammals, 'homeostasis meant survival. But for man, it means emancipation'. What a wonderful idea! Nature has given us one type of homeostasis, namely, physical. The *body* has got homeostasis. The blood stream has a constancy of oxygen, of various other components. In work you disturb it, and it automatically restores itself. So also, temperature; it automatically restores itself. This automatic stabilization of the inner system is known as homeostasis. So, nature says to man, 'I have given you a physical homeostasis; you achieve a psychic homeostasis for yourself, by your own efforts, for which I am giving you this wonderful cerebral system.' That background must be kept in view when you study this verse:

Sukhaduḥkhe same kṛtvā lābhālābhau jayājayau; Tato yuddhāya yujyasva naivam pāpamavāpsyasi. Enter into work in the battle of life with this calm attitude, balanced attitude, then you will achieve great results. Now we come to the next verse 39.

एषा तेऽभिहिता सांख्ये बुद्धिर्योगे त्विमां शृणु ।
बुद्ध्या युक्तो यया पार्थ कर्मबन्धं प्रहास्यसि ॥ ३९ ॥

Eṣā te'bhihitā sāmkhye buddhiryoge tvimām śṛṇu;
Buddhyā yukto yayā pārtha karmabandham prahāsyasi —2. 39

'The wisdom of Self-realization has been declared unto you. Hear now the wisdom of *yoga,* endued with which, O son of Pṛthā, you shall break through the bonds of *karma.*'

He says, till now I have been conveying to you the *Sāṅkhya,* wisdom, meaning *jñāna-yoga.* This world is unreal. The Atman alone is real. In that transcendental state, you will realize this Atman. This world is a world of passing shadows. That kind of teaching was given in *jñāna-yoga.* And Śrī Kṛṣṇa was telling Arjuna to fight the war on the basis of that teaching of *jñāna-yoga.* Now He says, *eṣā te'bhihitā sāṅkhye,* 'till now I have told you about the approach of the *Sāṅkhya* line of thinking', but now you hear from Me the *yoga* way of thinking and action, the *buddhi-yoga.* I am going to speak to you the *yoga* of action, *yoga* of active endeavour, out of which also you achieve spirituality. So, He said, *buddhiryoge tvimām śṛṇu,* 'now I am going to tell you this new philosophy of yoga, how work can lead us to spiritual realization; and if you have to work, the work you do is real, people with whom you deal are real; if you think the world is unreal, there is no fun in work. In fact, we have been taught this idea of the world being unreal. And yet we have to work there. And our work will show absolute unconcern. Half-minded work. Most of our people now when they work are half-sleepy. They have no interest in the work around, except very special individual persons. But why did that attitude come? Because this 'unreal world' philosophy was spread through various channels to the people. *Sab duniyā jhūṭā hai.* There is nothing in it, you remain your own Self. That teaching was given to our people long ago through various channels. Without looking at all aspects of the teaching, we became distorted in psyche. First of all, self-centredness and unconcern for others. This kind of philosophy had gone deep into our mind with the result that our human relations became weak, unconcerned. In a great teacher, or in a great spiritual *sādhakā*, this human unconcern was not there; but to millions of people, the result was a dried-up heart. No concern for others. That attitude also came in politics. That is why this *yoga* path of Śrī Kṛṣṇa is a strong medicine for most of us. We did not understand or follow it till Vivekananda came in the modern period.

What will be the result of this *yoga buddhi?* Śrī Kṛṣṇa answers: *buddhyā yukto yayā pārtha karmabandham prahāsyasi,* if you develop this *buddhi, yoga buddhi,* one great result will be that through work you will attain that very spiritual freedom which *jñāna* gives. You can continue to work. You can handle the work situation, handle other human beings. In and through all these you would become free from all bondage that work produces otherwise. Action produces bondage, only if you do it ignorantly. But this *yoga buddhi* will help you to perform actions, and yet not to have any bondage at all. Achieve that same spiritual freedom, which the *jñāna-yogī* gets. But, in addition, you will be a warm-hearted person, deeply interested in the people around you. You will be doing great good to the people, to the society.

This new philosophy, which Śrī Kṛṣṇa is expounding to Arjuna and to all of us, has not been expressed in our life and action all these one thousand years. But in the modern age we can do so, and we will do so. Our whole life and work system in India needs a revolutionary transformation. That comes only from hard work, work with dedication, work with a great sense of human urgency. So, that philosophy is very very important for us and for a large part of the world as well. So, Śrī Kṛṣṇa said, *buddhyā yukto yayā pārtha karmabandham prahāsyasi,* 'endowed with this *yoga buddhi,* O Arjuna, you will destroy all bonds of action.' You are afraid of action that it may create bondage, I am assuring you, if you take to *yoga buddhi,* no bondage will come. That is the philosophy which can bless and elevate every human being. Most people cannot give up work; so most of us will be in bondage. Why should it be so? All of us can be in work, as well as kept free from bondage. That is its universal relevance. *Karmabandham, bandham,* 'bondage', arising from *karma,* 'you will destroy it', *prahāsyasi. Karma* will remain, *bandha* will go. This is a great teaching for all people. Then Śrī Kṛṣṇa gives a beautiful characteristic of this path.

नेहाभिक्रमनाशोऽस्ति प्रत्यवायो न विद्यते ।
स्वल्पमप्यस्य धर्मस्य त्रायते महतो भयात् ॥४०॥

Nehābhikramanāśo'sti pratyavāyo na vidyate;
Svalpamapyasya dharmasya trāyate mahato bhayāt—2. 40

'In this, there is no waste of unfinished attempt, nor is there production of contrary results. Even a little of this *dharma* protects (one) from great fear.'

Neha abhikrama nāśo'sti, 'in this great path of *yoga buddhi,* there is no fear of any loss of unfinished attempt'. You do something. You leave it due to some circumstances. When you come next to it, you have to start *a, b, c,* once again. Many things in life belong to that category. This is specially true of all religious rituals. But in this case, there is no such trouble. So, rituals you do. You finish a ritual half; when you return to it, you cannot continue the next half. You have to start from *a, b, c,* once again. But, in this path, everything is cumulative. You do what you can, then leave it, and after some time you can come back again and continue from where you left it off. Continue further, continue further: what can be called cumulative development. In fact, that is the nature of character-building. Character development is always cumulative. You do something, you build up character; then you have other things to do, then you forget all about it, come back again, and restart it. That is the meaning of this wonderful śloka. *Neha abhikrama nāśo'sti* and *pratyavāyo na vidyate,* 'there is no evil resulting from some mistake in the action'. Then comes a tremendous assurance: *svalpamapyasya dharmasya trāyate mahato bhayāt,* 'even a little of this *dharma,* this philosophy, will save us from great fear'. Character development is not just a matter of one day. You go on doing it, slowly build up, build up a great character, a strong character; it takes time. And so, cumulatively you are building up a wonderful character with tremendous humanist resources. So, *nehābhikramanāśo'sti,* in all character development, 'there is no *abhikramanāśa*', 'waste of unfinished attempt', whatever you have done before leaving off, remains yours; you come back and start from where you left off. Just like a man building a house; it has got a hundred thousand rupees as the estimate, he has only ten thousand, so, he lays the foundation, builds up the plinth. Then the money is exhausted. Let it remain, it is good for it. It will be well stabilized. Later on, again he got ten thousand. He builds it up still further. Then further money came. In this way, in so many stages, the building becomes completed. This is what happens in all efforts at character development, and this development of character has one wonderful quality, it makes you strong, it makes you fearless, it makes you compassionate, it makes you feel one with all. Therefore, 'even a little of this *dharma* will save us from great fear', *Svalpamapyasya dharmasya trāyate mahato bhayāt. Gītā's* teaching is, even a little is better than nothing; it is not 'all or nothing'. Śrī Kṛṣṇa says to one and all: As much as you can, take from my teaching, build up your own life and character as much as you can. Don't depress yourself with the thought: 'O! That man has done so much, I don't have that strength. I shall do nothing'. That is not a correct attitude. That man has done according to *his* strength. You do according to *your* strength. Step by step, inch by inch, build up your great character and personality, by handling this psychophysical energy system that is within you. Out of your psychic energy system, you are going to produce a remarkable product, namely, *buddhi. Buddhi yoga, yoga buddhi,* discriminative faculty, a luminous point within the human sensory and psychic system. That is to be developed out of the same psychic energy system. It is a tremendous psychic chemistry we do within the human system. We convert the whole body into a laboratory. There we are slowly evolving this *buddhi. Buddhi* is your intelligence, discriminative faculty, your will, and all emotions mixed with it in a beautiful harmony. It is the greatest instrument of human development: reason, imagination and will are integrated in it. That is what we need. And the *Gītā* is going to tell us again and again, the greatness of *buddhi*. In many places you will find it invoked in the *Gītā: buddhau śaraṇamanviccha,* 'take refuge in *buddhi*'. With that *buddhi* you will achieve everything. *Buddhi* is essentially reason, but not dry intellectual reason. Reason which has been reinforced by emotions, by feeling. All motivation comes from emotion and feeling, not from intellect. And then comes will with its power of impact. And so, when you combine all the three, you get a wonderful instrument of human development. That is called *buddhi*. A student in school and college studies various books, but the ultimate result of all study should be the evolution of that *buddhi*. Then great things will come for oneself as well as for others. A person goes to a doctor, the doctor examines and tells the patient, you must take one litre of milk every day for your health. Doctor, I don't have that much money to take one litre of milk everyday. All right, then take half a litre everyday, he will say. Then, finally, one-fourth litre; take even a little, it is good for you. That is the nature of this teaching. As much as you take, that much is good for you. If I can't take one full litre, I shall not take any milk at all—that is not correct. So, *svalpamapyasya dharmasya trāyate mahato bhayāt*. What is the nature of that *buddhi*? The next verse gives the answer.

व्यवसायात्मिका बुद्धिरेकेह कुरुनन्दन ।
बहुशाखा ह्यनन्ताश्च बुद्धयोऽव्यवसायिनाम् ॥४१॥

Vyavasāyātmikā buddhirekeha kurunandana;
Bahuśākhā hyanantāśca buddhayo'vyavasāyinām—2. 41

'In this, O scion of Kuru, there is but a single *buddhi* with a one-pointed determination. The purposes of the undecided are innumerable and many-branching.'

One is called *vyavasāyī*, the other is called *a-vyavasāyī*. *Vyavasāya* means endeavour, effort, tremendous determination—all that is called *vyavasāya*. The opposite is *avyavasāya*.

Here, in this *buddhi-yoga* philosophy, there is a *vyavasāyātmikā buddhi,* a *buddhi* of tremendous determination. *Vayavasāya* means determination, a tremendous effort. All that is included in that. That is what you get, and that is one, not two or three, or multiple. The whole energy has been organized and unified. Look at the human body. What diversity is there in the human body! From the cell to the biggest organs of the system, everything is so diverse, and yet there is a perfect unification. Everything works for everything else. There has been differentiation and integration, as modern biology says. Evolution proceeded through differentiation and integration. Similarly, when you build up your inner life, the same thing must happen—differentiation and tremendous integration. That integration is what is mentioned here; *ekeha kurunandana,* 'the *vyavasāyātmikā buddhi,* O Arjuna, is only one in this school of *yoga* philosophy'. But, in ordinary life, *bahuśākhā hyanantāśca buddhayo'vyavasāyinām,* 'those who are *avyavasāyīs,* without that kind of determination, their minds function in a scattered way'. There is no energy developed within the system. Everything is scattered.

Mind has two states: one is a scattered state, the other is the gathered state. In all *yoga* teaching, you speak of a gathered state: gather all this energy. In normal life, the mind is scattered in a thousand ways. Therefore, it has not that energy. So, Śrī Kṛṣṇa is telling that, in this *karma yoga,* philosophy of action, we have to develop that type of *buddhi*—unified *buddhi*—it is a wonderful idea, because in the other state, *bahuśākhā hyanantāśca buddhayo'vyavasāyinām.* In the undecided type, the mind is scattered in a thousand directions; no energy is developed out of it. This is what we have to do here. So, this verse brings before us the idea of a human being developing a unified psychic energy within oneself. It is not scattered here and there, and that mind, we have to develop within ourselves. This is the basis of a healthy philosophy of life and human development. *Bahuśākhā hyanantāśca,* 'a mind that is many-branched and scattered', we see people with such minds, with scattered energies. That cannot make an impact on a life situation, because there is no unification of energy. Great minds like Gandhiji's, for example, had a tremendous unification of energy in their minds. One mind only, not two or three. And that mind works in various fields. But the mind is one only. He or she has integrated the entire psychic energy within the individual and the power of impact of such a person is tremendous. So, we also must develop that kind of a capacity that it will not be scattered in a thousand causes and each cause gets only a little psychic energy thereby. Whenever the rays are scattered, they cannot penetrate. When the rays are concentrated, then they can penetrate the body as in the x-ray, for example. Similarly, in the human mind also it is the same. In all education, whether it is institutional or non-institutional, this work of integration of psychic energy must go on. How to unify my psychic energy? How to give it the power of impact, the power of penetration—that should be our concern. Nobody else need to see it even. They will see the result of it in the wonderful way I handle the world around me. So, that is the goal of all human education. Not reading some text book and passing examinations—that is only the outside part of education. The real inner part is this development of the mind; making it of this nature.

The next three verses convey a profound message:

यामिमां पुष्पितां वाचं प्रवदन्त्यविपश्चितः ।
वेदवादरताः पार्थ नान्यदस्तीति वादिनः ॥४२॥

Yāmimām puṣpitām vācam pravadantyavipaścitaḥ;
Vedavādaratāḥ pārtha nānyadastītitivādinaḥ— 2. 42

'They are the unwise who utter flowery speeches, O Arjuna. They delight in the letter of the Vedas and argue that there is nothing else.'

कामात्मानः स्वर्गपरा जन्मकर्मफलप्रदाम् ।
क्रियाविशेषबहुलां भोगैश्वर्यगतिं प्रति ॥४३॥

Kāmātmānaḥ svargaparā janmakarmaphalapradām;
Kriyāviśeṣabahulām bhogaiśvaryagatim prati— 2. 43

'They are full of desires, consider heaven as the highest which yield the fruit of rebirth and actions, and are full of specific rites that yield enjoyment and power.'

भोगैश्वर्यप्रसक्तानां तयापहृतचेतसाम् ।
व्यवसायात्मिका बुद्धिः समाधौ न विधीयते ॥४४॥

Bhogaiśvaryaprasaktānām tayāpahṛtacetasām;
Vyavasāyātmikā buddhiḥ samādhau na vidhīyate—2. 44

'Those who have given themselves to pleasures and power, whose minds have been enslaved by them, there is no chance of developing that *buddhi* or determination which leads to *samādhi*.'

Those who have a scattered mind run after all sorts of pleasures, earthly, and heavenly, and enter into all sorts of rituals and ceremonies, based upon some teachings in the Vedas regarding rituals. Those who are involved in such things, they can never develop this *vyavasāyātmikā buddhi*. In the *śloka* He says, *yāmimām puṣpitām vācam pravadantyavipaścitaḥ*, 'that type of people who are *avipaścitaḥ*, without wisdom, without understanding, they speak *puṣpitām vācam*, flowery language, in the name of religion'.

They always quote the Vedas, discuss about what the Vedas say. Here the Vedas mean the *karma-kāṇḍa*, the ritualistic section of the Vedas, which promises you heaven. Do all these sacrifices and rituals, and you will go to heaven. They are captured by that attitude. *Kāmātmānaḥ*, 'full of sensual desires', I want this, I want that. Similarly, *svargaparā*, 'devoted to going to heaven'. Many religions have this heaven-philosophy. *Janmakarmaphalapradām*, 'the result of which is birth, and rituals'. *Kriyāviśeṣabahulām bhogaiśvaryagatim prati*, 'various rituals are there, only to get sense pleasure in the end'. *Bhogaisvarya prasaktānām tayāpahṛtacetasām*, 'those whose minds are captivated by these *bhogaiśvaryas*, pleasures and power'; what happens to them? *Vyavasāyātmikā buddhiḥ samādhau na vidhīyate*, 'that *buddhi* which can take one to the highest spiritual realization will not come to them at all'. Their *buddhi* is always scattered in thousand streams of desires and ambitions etc.

This is a strong criticism of the enormously ritualistic position of the Vedas. In the Upaniṣads also, we come across this kind of ritualism of the Vedas. Here also the same type of criticism, because it does not help to develop character and spirituality; what is needed is spiritual development and the capacity to love and serve people around you. The policy should be minimum ritual and maximum character development. None of this will come through such hedonistic philosophy of pleasure on earth as well as in heaven through a series of rituals.

Having said this, Śrī Kṛṣṇa is telling us an assessment of the Vedas which you find only in our *Sanātana Dharma* tradition. Every tradition speaks of its own scripture in the highest language. In this *Sanātana Dharma,* however, even though we revere the Vedas, our most sacred books, we do not give it the highest status. It is always secondary. They do not contain Truth. They contain only information regarding Truth. That is how Sri Ramakrishna also has put it in our time: He says, in the Hindu *Pañcāṅgam* or almanac, it is forecast that so many inches of rain will fall this year. But, if you take the almanac and squeeze it, you won't get a drop of water. Similarly, in the Vedas so many beautiful things are said, including realizing God, the Atman, etc. But squeeze the Vedas, you won't get any such thing. Only by squeezing your own experience, will you get Truth, will you experience Truth. So, study what the Vedas say, then leave it aside, and practise and realize Truth for yourself. That attitude was developed very early in our history in our Upaniṣads. *Bṛhadāraṇyaka Upaniṣad,* one of the oldest of the Upaniṣads, contains this revolutionary statement: *vedo avedo bhavati,* 'when one realizes the Truth, the Vedas cease to be of any value'. Vedas become 'no Veda' at the stage of realization. What a beautiful idea! In no other religion will you find this bold statement, go beyond the *Bible* or beyond the *Koran*, nobody will say, though their mystics have done it and sometimes have suffered punishment for it. Only in India, the stress is: use the Vedas, use the scriptures, understand what they say, and then try to realize the truth for yourself. Experience is much higher than what is merely contained in books. Therefore, in spite of the profound respect for the Vedas, we, in India, are taught that we have to go beyond the Vedas. That is the truth that Śrī Kṛṣṇa is now going to convey to us:

त्रैगुण्यविषया वेदा निस्त्रैगुण्यो भवार्जुन ।
निर्द्वन्द्वो नित्यसत्त्वस्थो निर्योगक्षेम आत्मवान् ॥४५॥

Traiguṇyaviṣayā vedā nistraiguṇyo bhavārjuna;
Nirdvandvo nityasattvastho niryogakṣema ātmavān—2. 45

'The Vedas deal with the three *guṇas*. Be you free, O Arjuna, from the triad of the *guṇas*, free from the pairs of opposites, ever-balanced, free from the thought of getting and keeping, and established in the Self.'

What a revolutionary statement! *Traiguṇyaviṣayā vedā*, 'the Vedas deal with the three *guṇas*': *sattva, rajas* and *tamas*. But, you, Arjuna, *nistraiguṇyo bhava!* 'you go beyond the three *guṇas*'. That means you go beyond the Vedas also. *Nirdvandvo*, 'beyond all dualities', like heat and cold, profit and loss, these are called duality; *nityasattvastho*, 'established for ever in the pure *sattva* nature'; *niryogakṣema*, 'without any care for your own *yoga* and *kṣema*, profit and preservation'. Go beyond all survival philosophy, and become *ātmavān*, 'ever established in the Atman'. That kind of achievement, we must get—going beyond the Vedas, beyond the scriptures, by experiencing the truth which they expound for you and me. Every spiritual teacher in India will say, take the scripture, grasp the truth given there, and then try to realize the truth given there. Don't simply hang on to the book all the time. This has been very well expressed by Vidyāraṇya, who was in the Vijayanagar empire in the 14th century, in a famous verse of his Vedantic book *Pañcadasi*. How do we handle a spiritual book? He says:

Granthamabhyasya medhāvi jñāna-vijñāna-tatparaḥ;
Palālamiva dhānyārthī tyajet grantham-aśeṣataḥ —

'Like a person who is in search of rice, he takes paddy, husks it, throws the husk away, and takes the rice to cook and eat', similarly, the *medhāvi*, 'the intelligent person', first studies the books, *grantham-abhyasya,* 'after studying all the books'; what is your aim? Your objective is not to become a scholar. You are a *jñāna-vijñāna-tatparaḥ,* 'desirous of achieving knowledge and realization'. If so, what will you do? After gathering whatever is contained in the books, *tyajet grantham aśeṣatah,* 'you throw away all books'; they are of no further value at all. So, Sri Ramakrishna said, a person wrote a letter to his relative in the town, 'when you come back to the village, please bring so much cloth and so much of sweets, etc.' And he misplaced the letter; started searching the whole house for the letter. With great difficulty he rediscovered the letter. Then the letter was read: 'Bring this, bring that, when you come to the village.' He tore the letter away, went to the shop, and got the things that were mentioned there. What is the use of keeping the letter, or reading it again and again? The main thing is to get the things mentioned there. So, similarly, whatever is contained in the sacred books are to be realized. Then the books are of no further value. Then, *tyajet grantham aśeṣataḥ,* throw away all dependence on books, that has been the attitude in India.

All mystics in all religions have done the same. When they directly experienced the truth, what need can they have for books? When you take to religion as an experiment, you don't need the book. So, in the sixth chapter, Śrī Kṛṣṇa will say, *jijñāsurapi yogasya śabda-brahma-ativartate,* 'even when you become an enquirer into the nature of spiritual life, you go beyond the purview of sacred books.' You don't need them further. Only to understand the problem, you need books. Now you are an experimenter, not merely a student of books. So, when you become an experimenter, the control of books on you will become reduced more and more. So, *nirdvandvo nityasattvastho niryogakṣema ātmavān,* 'free from the dualities of life, completely Self-possessed (poised), you become without any anxiety or worry; you are established in the strength of the Atman within you.' This is what we have to achieve. Books are secondary, realization is primary. This is what Jesus also said (*New Testament*): 'The letter killeth, the spirit giveth life.' This search for the essential and casting away the non-essential is a hoary tradition in Islamic spirituality also, except when the priests dominate. Maulana Jalaluddin Rumi of Persia, in his famous book *Masnavi* which is accepted in the Muslim world generally as next only to *Koran* in holiness says:

Man ze Qurān maghz rā bardāstam;
Ustukhān pese sagāṅ andakhṭam —

'The marrow from the *Koran* have I drawn, and the dry bones unto the dogs have cast,'

That is the constant emphasis in our *Sanātana Dharma* tradition. *Sādhanā* and *anubhava,* 'spiritual practice and realization'—scholarship has no meaning at all. It is only an initial help, nothing more than that. So, when you achieve that state, what type of achievement is it? A very profound verse comes here in this particular context:

यावानर्थ उदपाने सर्वतः संप्लुतोदके ।
तावान्सर्वेषु वेदेषु ब्राह्मणस्य विजानतः ॥४६॥

Yāvānartha udapāne sarvataḥ samplutodake;
Tāvānsarveṣu vedeṣu brāhmaṇasya vijānataḥ— 2. 46

'To the spiritual person who has known the Self, all the Vedas are of so much use as a reservoir is, when there is a flood everywhere.'

That person, that spiritual seeker, who has realized the truth, what do these Vedas mean to him? Then He gives the example: Here is a huge reservoir, with water up to the brim. *Yāvānartha udapāne sarvataḥ samplutodake,* 'everywhere, water, water, up to the very brim in a lake'. You are sitting near by. Now, are you going to dig a well for a little water? Just stretch your hand, so much of water is around you. Similarly, when a person has realized the Atman, the Vedas become of just that much help to him, as much as a well, for a person sitting beside a big lake. That is the example given. *Tāvān sarveṣu vedeṣu brāhmaṇasya vijānataḥ,* 'a person who knows this truth, a spiritual seeker, he or she will deal with the Vedas from that point of view'. Just like there is no need to dig a little well for water, when there is a flood of water all around you! You can just stretch the hand and get it. So, this is how an example is given by Śrī Kṛṣṇa in this context, that the effort towards spiritual realization takes you more and more beyond the control of books; books are good to begin with only. Mere scholarship is not the goal of religion; it is spirituality. Sri Ramakrishna always said: scholars without that spiritual inclination and practice behave like vultures, soaring high up in the sky but their attention is always on the dead bodies on the earth. That is the nature of *mere* scholarship. Without discrimination, without spiritual urge within, mere scholarship is never rated high in our tradition. Similarly, in the next verse, Śrī Kṛṣṇa expounds a beautiful idea, considered to be central to this teaching of *yoga-buddhi,* philosophy of *yoga.*

कर्मण्येवाधिकारस्ते मा फलेषु कदाचन ।
मा कर्मफलहेतुर्भूः मा ते सङ्गोऽस्त्वकर्मणि ॥४७॥

Karmaṇyevādhikāraste mā phaleṣu kadācana;
Mā karmaphalaheturbhūḥ mā te saṅgo'stvakarmaṇi—2. 47

'Your right is to work only; but never to the fruits thereof. May you not be motivated by the fruits of actions; nor let your attachment be towards inaction.'

'To work alone you have the right', *karmaṇyeva adhikāraste. Mā phaleṣu kadācana,* 'not to the fruits of work'. But, if we don't get *phala*, or fruit of action, we may ask, why should we work at all? If you say so, 'no, continue to work', says the *Gītā*. *Mā karmaphalaheturbhūḥ,* 'don't work always looking at the fruit that is going to come out of it'; and in the end, the *Gītā* says, *mā te saṅgo'stu akarmaṇi,* 'don't be attached to inaction'. This is a verse combining four propositions. First, you have the right to work only; not to the fruits; let not the fruits be your motive for work; and don't remain inactive. This is a very important verse, which can also create a lot of misunderstanding in people. How can we work without looking for fruits? We ask that question. It is a profound statement here. I have seen students sometimes, when they hear this kind of *śloka,* they see only the surface statement that is there. So, when gardening work was going on—I was the warden of the hostel—and the students were all working in the garden producing flowers and fruits. Someone said, to work we have the right, the fruits will go to the Swamiji! Making fun, they said like that. One day I gave them a talk about the meaning of the verse. Some deeper meaning they found. So, all of us need a little exposition of this verse, which is considered to be central to the teaching of the *Gītā*. Mahatma Gandhi wrote his book *Anāsakti-yoga,* 'Yoga of non-attachment'—non-attachment to the fruits of work. That is the meaning of *anāsakti*. *Āsakti* means attachment; *anāsakti,* non-attachment. So, when you ask this question, what is the nature of my work? And the fruits coming out of the work, to whom do they belong? You find new light coming on this particular verse.

I am not alone in this world. Whatever work I do, I take the fruit of it and forget everything else. That cannot be done. We belong to a world. There are other people also there, we have to share whatever we have with everybody else. So, a little attitude of detachment is needed from our usual attitude that this is *my* work and everything belongs to *me.* That attitude has to go. The vast world is around us. We cannot do without it. We cannot become human without a human world around us. How much we owe to the world of other human beings around us! If you cut yourself away from society, you become a nobody. Therefore, this idea of work, which keeps in front of us this idea of social welfare, human development—I am only one beneficiary of the fruit of work that comes out of my efforts, other beneficiaries must also be considered. In the words of Sri Ramakrishna: the *kācā* or unripe 'I' must develop into the *pākā* or ripe 'I'. So, detachment from what? From the ego, the little self that is centred in our genetic system. Until this little 'I' is overcome and a larger 'I' manifests in us, we remain a stunted individual. Until we learn to say *you,* we have not developed at all. We remain an unripened ego; when this little 'I' expands, it becomes the ripe ego which alone can experience its oneness with everybody else. Then I will never say everything belongs to me only. We will learn to say *we* in place of *I*. That is a tremendous development, the first stage of spiritual growth.

So, today we shall study this datum of the ego within man. It is a remarkable datum which has been thrown up in evolution only at the stage of man. In animals there is no ego. A chimpanzee has no ego. No other being in the world other than this human being has the ego. If any animal had developed this ego, we would not have been here; it would have dominated the world. This ego is a wonderful new datum. Modern physical science did not worry about this subject till now. It was concerned about the world outside, it probed into it, tried to get the energy hidden there, to make for a better civilization. That is all their developed thinking. Now, as thought has advanced, the centre of study has become the human being, and that profound datum, the ego, or the 'I'. What does it mean? It was not there in any animal, it is not there even in a new-born baby. After about two to two-and-a-half years, you find the child says, 'I', 'I want this, I want that.' Till then it will say, 'This wants it. This wants that.' But a time comes, a little manifestation of this 'I' appears in the child. A profound new datum; that is being realized today by neurology in the West, as we, in India, had realized its profound significance long ago in Vedanta. Vedanta treats it as an initial datum; it is not in its final state; only a small sprout has come; there is plenty of spiritual development ahead. That constitutes the whole subject of the development of *Ātmajñāna*, and all the teaching of practical Vedanta of the *Gītā* coming out of it. Therefore, this subject has to be treated as a profound theme, and I am glad to find that for the last 50 to 70 years, the West has been turning its attention to this wonderful subject of the ego and its possibilities. This subject finds an exposition as a feeble echo of Vedanta in a book called *The Science of Life* written in the 1920s by H.G. Wells, G.P. Wells and Julian Huxley. You find therein a wonderful passage dealing with the status of the ego in evolution (pp. 875–79):

'Alone, in the silence of the night, and on a score of thoughtful occasions, we have demanded, can this self, so vividly central to my universe, so greedily possessive of the world, ever cease to be? Without it surely there is no world at all. And yet this conscious self dies by night when we sleep, and we cannot trace the stages by which in its stages it crept to an awareness of its own existence. Personality (centred in the ego) may be only one of nature's methods, a convenient provisional delusion of considerable strategic value.

'The more intelligent and comprehensive man's picture of the universe has become, the more intolerable has become his concentration upon the individual life with its inevitable final rejection. ...

'He escapes from his ego by this merger (identification with and participation in a greater being) and acquires an impersonal immortality in the association, his identity dissolving into a greater identity. This is the essence of much religious mysticism, and it is remarkable how closely the biological analysis of individuality brings us to the mystics. The individual, according to this second line of thought, saves himself by losing himself. But in mystical teaching he loses himself in the deity, and in the scientific interpretation of life, he forgets himself as Tom, Dick and Harry and discovers himself as man. ... The Western mystic and Eastern sage find a strong effect of endorsement in modern science and the everyday teaching of practical morality; both teach that self must be subordinated, that self is a method and not an end.'

Ego 'has a strategic value in evolution. It is a provisional delusion', don't treat it as a final stage. You have to discover its higher dimensions. That is the work the Upaniṣads did ages ago. How to make it grow into its own true dimension? That approach has to be kept in view when we handle this great *śloka:*

Karmaṇyevādhikāraste mā phaleṣu kadācana;
Mā karmaphalaheturbhūḥ mā te saṅgo'stvakarmaṇi —

If I am satisfied to stay at the level of this little ego, which has just sprouted in me, and I do not at all care to rise to its higher dimensions, then this *śloka* has no meaning to me, but if I want to experience the further reaches of this initial datum, then this *śloka* will be the opening of the gate to the higher dimensions of the human being. And so, we have to ask this question: What is this ego that appears in me? I possess the world through this ego; through it, I am the centre of the world. That is what we all feel, even a child. When the ego develops in it, the child becomes the centre of the world. All others are dancing around the child. But very soon, the child has to change that attitude and find a place for others also. That ego has to expand, has to grow, has to achieve *ātma-vikāsa*. The whole philosophy of this initial datum of the ego, now under the control of the genetic system, has to grow into its infinite dimension; this is the message of Vedanta.

About the relationship of Vivekananda's Vedanta and modern physical science, Romain Rolland says in his *Life of Vivekananda* (15th impression, 1997, pp. 262–63):

'But it is a matter of indifference to the calm pride of him (Vivekananda) who deems himself the stronger whether science accepts free religion in Vivekananda's sense of the term or not, for his religion accepts science. It is vast enough to find a place at its table for all loyal seekers after truth.'

In no other part of the world has this subject been so thoroughly investigated and expounded, and we are glad to find that some neurologists and physicists today are handling this subject almost on identical lines, and slowly going closer and closer to what ancient Vedanta had said about it. A child will say, on seeing a rock jutting out of the ocean, that a little rock is there; but its father will tell that it is an immense rock; much of it is under water, and only a little is seen above the water level. Similarly, to the sensory vision of man, the ego is a tiny entity, but if you know its depth, it will reveal its infinite dimension. That is the teaching the Upaniṣads give. In that light only, you can understand this verse and many other verses coming hereafter.

We have the *Chāndogya Upaniṣad* teaching, *tat tvam asi*, 'you are That,' you are not this tiny ego. You are not this little self which you consider yourself to be. You are that infinite

Consciousness, the Atman. This *tattvamasi* is a profound teaching of the Upaniṣads, which has been and is still attracting the minds of some biologists and nuclear physicists in the Western world like Erwin Schrodinger and J.B.S. Haldane. So, when one keeps in view this background and then studies this verse, a new meaning comes. You don't want to be a child, you want to grow. This ego is like a child; why should it remain always like a child? Some of the egoist's language is like the child's language. You can find it in every society, many big people also talk 'I', 'I', 'I' all the time. They do not understand the higher dimensions of their own self. They know it only as a tiny initial datum. And it creates great tension, great suffering, for oneself as well as for others. So, there is need for probing into the infinite dimension of the ego that appears to us at the age of about 2½ onwards. That is the subject of *Ātma-jñāna, adhyātma-vidyā,* based on which Śrī Kṛṣṇa is expounding a philosophy of life and action for every human being. The whole *Gītā* is dealing with men and women at work, unlike in other spiritual books, which treat of man or woman centred in prayer, meditation, worship, or some ritual or ceremony. But in this great book, the central theme is developed as to how a man or woman at any kind of work can achieve spiritual development and fulfilment, and they form the majority of people in the world. Every person will question, if I do not get the fruits of work, what is the use of work? It is good to ask that question and try to find an answer.

Towards the end of the book, *The Science of Life,* there is a section dealing with the philosophical implications of modern biology. I quoted from that section dealing with the unreality of the ego. Remember those words: this ego in man, that is called the self, *may be one of nature's devices,* 'a convenient provisional delusion of considerable strategic value (in evolution)'. In the whole cosmos you don't find the ego. In the whole animal kingdom you don't find the ego, only in man you find it. In our ignorance we are basing our work on this provisional delusion of the ego. What a powerful 'I' is the ego in the waking state; and when we go to sleep there is no ego; it dies and later comes to an awareness of itself. Sri Ramakrishna says in one of his beautiful sayings: even the most powerful person, when he or she goes to sleep, if a child spits on his or her face, there will be no protest! And then the authors say that this is similar to what you speak of in science as detachment, objectivity. Suppose you want to know the truth of a thing, you have to remove this ego from the investigation. Ego will always wrongly judge the thing. You must detach yourself from it. Then only scientific, i.e., objective, judgement is possible. A judge in the court must banish his or her ego for the time being, to be correct in the judgement. So, on any number of occasions in life, we are asked to set aside this ego, because it is unreal, because that is not our true nature or status. But you can go beyond and penetrate to the root of this ego. That is the infinite Self. That Atman is one with all. The true Self in us is one with all. You and I are one. When Jesus was asked, What is the teaching in the commandment? He said two things: 'Thou shalt love thy God with all thy heart, with all thy soul, with all thy mind'. That is the first and greatest commandment. And the second is like unto the first, and what is that? 'Thou shalt love thy neighbour as thyself'. On these two hang all the laws and all the prophets. This is a beautiful summary of the spiritual and ethical dimensions of human life. Paul Deussen, a German philosopher and a scholar in Vedanta, speaking in Bombay in 1892 after his tour in India, said: Here is a great statement: love thy neighbour as thyself. But why, if you ask, the Bible has not given the answer. The answer is in the Upaniṣads. You *are* your neighbour. You are one. There is only one infinite Self, pulsing in me, in you, in all in this world.

And so, from this genetically limited ego, which considers this whole world as planets moving around the sun, which is itself, we shall have to advance and realize our true dimension. If you want to do so, then this detachment is absolutely essential. Detach from the ego; that is why this whole book is a teaching of detachment. It is a negative concept but with a positive content: by detaching from something lower, you are manifesting something higher. Mahatma Gandhiji's book on the *Gītā* is called *Anāsakti-yoga*, '*yoga* of non-attachment', non-attachment to this tiny ego centred in this organic system. This is not true actually in life; even in families, a man or woman works, for whom? For wife, husband or children, for their welfare, not for one's own. In every department of life we find that people are concerned with the society in which they live. We owe a debt to it. Everything is not our own. There is a social context of human behaviour. That is why we pay taxes. We live in an ordered society, because there is a government; it rightfully takes taxes from us, and we pay. Similarly, many other obligations also are there. When we understand this truth, we expand our concept of self. And that is the first thing we have to do. The self that is contained in the organic system is only a 'convenient provisional delusion'. When you set it aside, you begin to expand your concept of self. You feel spiritual oneness with others. So, whatever work I do, the fruits of it are not for me alone; it will go to all. And a state will come, when there will be nothing of 'I' left; everything will be 'we'. We lose ourselves in the universal. And then, the authors say, this is what mystical teachings have taught us all the time. The little self must be transcended; it is only a means, not an end. Similarly, modern biology teaches us, you forget yourself as Tom, Dick and Harry, and realize yourself as man, that is your real identity, spiritually one with all the other human beings.

Now, this is the correlation between the ancient spiritual current and the modern scientific current—when you penetrate deeper into reality. In this light you can understand a little more this enigmatic proposition—the four-member proposition: to work you have the right; not to the fruits thereof; don't be running after the fruits; and, don't remain inactive. This tendency of claiming exclusive fruits of all work to oneself, and remain inactive otherwise, has become maximum in India. In spite of all the religiosity we have, we are utter failures in the social context. Public property is nobody's property. Public tap is nobody's tap. We are only concerned with our own taps. We allow water to flow and be wasted from the public tap in the street; we don't mind since it is not mine. This kind of littleness of self has overwhelmed and weakened our nation. A little of this *Gītā* teaching will do immense good to our nation—that there is a society around you, that its welfare is also your concern. Even to become a citizen of a free democratic nation, we must go beyond this little self. It is not enough that you live in India, but also that you are *of India* and *for India*. So, Śrī Kṛṣṇa will be telling us in the third chapter (3. 13): 'he or she who cooks only for oneself, eats only so much of sin,'—*bhuñjate te tvagham pāpā ye pacanti ātmakāraṇāt*. All those who cook and eat only for themselves, never thinking of others, they eat only so much of sin.

This little self is only a delusion, said Buddha. There is no separate self. Belief in a separate self, in a separate individuality, is the centre of all evil. All selfishness and corruption, all violence, all exploitation come from that limited attitude. Therefore, when I realize my belongingness to a society, I can't attribute the results of all my actions to myself. The word 'self' becomes wider, wider, wider. That is the criterion of human development. A little baby wants everybody else to look to it as the centre. If he or she says something, you must do that something, because *he* or *she* is the centre. It is harmless for a baby, but not for a grown-up person. We have to respect other people, respond to other people, work for them, help them. There is so much need of intercommunication in a society. All this is based upon this one single teaching of the second chapter: Do work, but don't appropriate the results to yourself. There is a higher point of view from which you can do your work. That higher point of view *must* come to us today. In fact, as I said several times, co-operative societies, state and union governments, will become a great success in India the day we understand this *Gītā* teaching. What is not physically mine, but belongs to all, I must take more care of that. That one lesson can change our social situation. But what obtains now is just the opposite. Because it doesn't belong to me, it doesn't concern me, I am not interested in it. So, public sector of all types will be a failure, will not produce the expected results, so long as this character is not there. But when we learn this lesson, we shall see tremendous developments in all aspects of our national life. No private sector can compare with such a public sector. In India the whole thing is opposite. In any country you go, government schools are the most efficient; in India, it is just the opposite. Private schools are always efficient, government schools are always bad. Why? Nobody cares.

Therefore, this petty selfish attitude to work has ruined the whole nation and retarded our post-independence progress. The English saying is perfectly correct with respect to our history. 'I and mine, and the devil take the hindmost.' And we invited the devil, the devils invaded our nation, and we are seeing now the devil's play in India in the form of exploitation, suffering, corruption from top to bottom, and violence. We want to overcome that situation. So here comes a profound message. The more people go into it, the more they will get meaning out of it. The next *śloka* gives us the positive aspect of this subject of work. If you ask me not to run after the fruits of action, that is merely negative. What shall be the attitude of my mind at the time of my action? That is the theme of the next verse.

योगस्थः कुरु कर्माणि सङ्गं त्यक्त्वा धनञ्जय ।
सिद्ध्यसिद्ध्योः समो भूत्वा समत्वं योग उच्यते ॥४८॥

Yogasthaḥ kuru karmāṇi saṅgam tyaktvā dhanañjaya;
Sidhyasiddhyoḥ samo bhūtvā samatvam yoga ucyate—2. 48

'Being steadfast in *yoga,* O Arjuna, perform actions, abandoning attachment, remaining unconcerned as regards success and failure. This evenness of mind is known as *yoga.'*

Here that word *yoga* comes once again. What is *yoga? Samatvam* is *yoga.* 'Equanimity, mind in perfect balance, that is called *yoga.'* But then what point of view shall I adopt during work and human relation? *Yogasthaḥ kuru karmāṇi,* 'do actions established in *yoga*'. That *buddhi-yoga,* that came earlier, is the attitude from which you can work and achieve most effective results. *Saṅgam tyaktvā,* 'giving up attachment', that comes from this truncated self. All attachments come from that little man. That attachment has to go; but how does it go? When you deny this little 'I', the large 'I' begins to manifest. In Sri Ramakrishna's words, when the unripe 'I' goes, the ripe 'I' will manifest. Therefore, *Sidhyasidhyoḥ samo bhūtvā,* 'becoming even-minded in *siddhi* and in *asiddhi,* success and failure'. Too much depression in failure, too much elation in success, is not proper. Therefore, 'try to keep the mind even', *samo bhūtvā.*

In the *Mahābhārata,* there is the story of a young prince by name Sañjaya (not of the *Gītā* but of the northern Sind region) getting defeated in a battle and becoming very depressed and inactive. If he had succeeded, he would have been very proud. His mother, Vidula, was a heroic woman. That mother told her son, 'don't remain depressed like this. Be manly, be strong. Failures come, successes come; you should not be much affected by them. They are like waves in the sea. You must be above them.' And then comes a famous exhortation of Vidula compressed in a small number of words: *muhūrtam jvalito śreyo na tu dhūmāyitam ciram,* 'it is better you flame forth for one instant than smoke away for ages'! What a tremendous message for every human being! Go on smoking for ages, what fun is there? Flame forth for one instant, instead of smoking away for ages! As the English Poet, Ben Johnson, expresses it: 'In small proportions do we but beauty see, in short measures life may perfect be.' Ādi Śaṅkarācārya who lived only for 32 years, lived a most intense life affecting the thought of a vast country like India. So, in this way, a very purposeful, heroic philosophy of life will contain all these positive elements. All those petty attitudes of 'I' and 'mine', 'I don't care for others', will have no place in such a philosophy.

So, Śrī Kṛṣṇa says: *yogasthaḥ kuru karmāṇi,* 'do actions from the *yoga* level of consciousness'. That is a big subject and it constitutes a complete and comprehensive philosophy of life. In the West today, this is a very very attractive theme. How to raise our consciousness levels? After all, all actions come from a particular level of consciousness. If it comes from another level, the action will also be different in effect. A criminal has one action. His consciousness level is in a particular state. A very generous man also does action. His action comes from another consciousness level. And so, this subject of raising consciousness levels, *bodha unnamana*, is an attractive subject in all countries today. If an officer or a clerk in the Government Secretariat is unconcerned with the people, his or her activity comes from a low level of that little self, controlled by the genetic system. The genes are selfish, says modern biology; they cannot be the source of values. Another clerk or officer, interested in the welfare of the people will respond with an attitude of 'what can I do for you? How can I help you?' This response comes from another consciousness level, above the genetic system. That consciousness level from which positive actions come, positive good to society comes, is called the *yoga* level, or from the *yoga-buddhi* level. So, *yogasthaḥ kuru karmāṇi,* 'do work from that vantage ground of *yoga*'. Then comes one of the two definitions of *yoga: samatvam yoga ucyate,* '*yoga* is equanimity, balance'. Every experience throws the mind into a wave, small wave, big wave. You have the power to control that wave-formation. If you exercise that power, you are a free person, you are really using your higher cerebral system. If you don't, you become like a creature of circumstances. Somebody says, 'you weep', and you weep. Somebody says, 'you smile', and you smile. You have no freedom. That should not be. I shall smile when I want to, not because somebody dictates to me or nature dictates to me. That is called freedom. *The whole of the Gītā teaching is based upon the truth of human freedom*. From freedom we come, in freedom we live, and to freedom we return. That is the Vedantic teaching, said Swami Vivekananda. And so here, the capacity to keep the mind in balance when so many circumstances come to unbalance it, that is the real test of human greatness, human strength. So many examples are available in this connection. From the highest level of a Buddha up to the ordinary levels of greatness in a society, we find many types of this achievement. But every step you take in that direction, to show that you are free from external constraints, is progress, real human progress. That is to be emphasized again and again.

Earlier, I had referred to modern neurology telling us about the achievement of thermostatic equilibrium within the body, from later mammals to human beings, and other similar equilibria within the human system, like the constitution of the blood, etc. Everything is in balance. When it is upset by work, it automatically restores itself to balance. That is called the homeostatic condition of the human body. That is a wonderful achievement, not by you and me, but by nature. And on this subject, Claude Bernard, the famous French physiologist, had said, and I had quoted it earlier: 'a fixed interior milieu is the condition for the free life'. If you want to truly achieve freedom, you must try to establish a fixed interior milieu, not a milieu which is being made to move up and down by external forces. So, to that extent you are progressing towards your life's perfection. So, a fixed interior milieu we have to establish. This is a very difficult subject and so, I quote Gray Walter of England who discusses this subject in a very fascinating passage by quoting the words of his teacher, Sir Joseph Barcroft, in Cambridge (*The Living Brain* p. 17):

'How often have I watched the ripples on the surface of a still lake made by a passing boat, noted their regularity and admired the patterns formed when two such ripple systems meet. ... but the lake must be perfectly calm. ... To look for high intellectual development in a milieu whose properties have not become stabilized is to seek ... ripple patterns on the surface of the stormy Atlantic.'

Similarly, to expect high intellectual development in a mind which has not achieved a measure of inner stability is simply impossible. So, all intellectual growth, creative growth, and spiritual growth, need this prior stabilization of the human psychic system. *Samatvam yoga ucyate*. 'That is *yoga* which is based on *samatva*, calmness, balance'; everything tries to imbalance me, I must develop a system in me which balances it automatically, as the body does it. So, physical homeostasis, which nature has given to you, must be complemented by a psychic homeostasis gained for yourself by your own efforts. This inner homeostasis is what is meant by the two great words of our spiritual tradition, namely, *śama* and *dama*. *Śama* is the discipline of the mind. *Dama* is the discipline of the senses. When *śama* and *dama* operate in me, then this *samatva* becomes well established. *Śama* and *dama* are highly significant words in our spiritual tradition; *dama* is this riotous sensory system getting controlled and calmed. And *śama* is this mind which also is riotous because it is tied to this sensory system, getting calmed. This calmness, *samatvam,* becomes a natural state by constant practice of these two virtues. This is *yoga* in its early stages. There is nothing particularly impossible, nothing magical, nothing mystical about it; any human being can do it, can achieve it, here and now, in the context of daily life and work. It is not exclusively an ascetic's privilege but every one's. And one great lesson, Vivekananda stresses again and again: that it is the calm steady person that turns out the largest quantum of work, not the excited unsteady type of people. They may make noise, but their work will be very poor. This is what everyone has to learn.

This is the great teaching Śrī Kṛṣṇa is giving us. Do work, but the consciousness level from which your work proceeds must be of that nature; stable and steady; that is called *buddhi-yoga,* or *yoga-buddhi, buddhi* established in *yoga.* That state is the best source from which all actions can come. They will always be good, good for oneself and good for all, and, therefore, these two virtues, *śama, dama,* are highly praised in our literature. Great workers, great world-movers, unless they had that *samatvam* within, could not have summoned that tremendous energy to make the world move in that particular direction. And so, for all of us, as much as we can, even one step ahead is good for us, for making our life efficient; and this *yoga* is going to be defined later on in a verse as 'efficiency in life and work'. So, there is nothing magical in it. People must banish all idea of magic and miracle from this philosophy of *yoga*. This is down to earth. Take a person by the hand, slowly lift him or her up, and take him or her to the highest level of life. That is what this philosophy does. Everything is clear, everything can be communicated. It can be practised; it is difficult, all great things are difficult, even climbing a small hill is difficult. But, the more a great achievement is difficult, the more will be the challenge to the human mind. 'I don't want an easy life', that attitude must come. Then only you can have a society of heroic minds. No easy life, 'I am prepared to pay the price and get it', no charity; that is a wonderful idea.

In India, the Sikh gurus, from Guru Nanak to Guru Govind Singh, were the people who taught this wonderful idea of self-reliance. Don't seek for easy life, work hard, don't beg. Work and earn. Nowhere in India will you find the command of that great teaching in the life of the people as you find in Punjab from these gurus. Even at the most difficult times of India's political partition, refugees were coming from Pakistan Punjab to Indian Punjab and Delhi, with absolutely empty pockets, and yet none of them begged; they only asked for work. There you can see the tremendous energy coming out of this little discipline which the gurus gave. So, the whole nation stands to gain by applying to one's life even a little of this *Gītā* teaching. And this *Gītā* will in due course inspire thousands of people in all parts of the world.

Only today, I was reading our famous Professor Fritjof Capra of Berkeley University, author of that famous book *Tao of Physics*, telling a reviewer,

'I first got interest in eastern thought by studying the *Bhagavat Gītā*. That put me on in this direction.'

So many are reading this great Song Celestial all over the world so that, after some decades, the effect of all this study and teaching and practice will be found in the emergence of a better humanity, more pure, more compassionate, more intelligent, more efficient. The *yoga* of the *Gītā* sponsors all these virtues and graces in people in all parts of the world. And so, in this verse 48, Śrī Kṛṣṇa tells all humanity through Arjuna: *yogasthaḥ kuru karmāṇi,* and *samatvam yoga ucyate.* Even at the age of four and five, a child must be taught a little *samatva.* Children are generally excitable, and it is not bad at their age, but they must be slowly initiated into this: 'now, try to calm your mind; don't be excited all the time.' That means, the child is being taught to handle its own mind, and not to continue to be a plaything of the external world. That is the meaning of *śama* and *dama.* From the world outside, somebody says to you that you are a fool, and you become wretched and depressed; that man, who called you a fool, is dead and gone, but you are living a depressed life because somebody said you were a fool. That is what an American writer said: to put your mind in somebody else's pocket is the most unfortunate thing you can do. And so, learn to put it in your own pocket. 'I shall determine how I react to any situation'; that can come only when the mind has that balance. Sir Joseph Barcroft said, if the lake is calm—the lake of the mind—then it will form wonderful ripple patterns in the inner life of human beings; even so, spiritual development cannot be formed in a milieu which has not been calmed and made even. That is why if you want to become great as *a person,* you have to achieve all this by handling your mind.

The first thing you have to do is to handle your mind. We rarely handle our minds. We handle tools, but the biggest tool is the mind itself; we never handle it. We let it go in its own way. So, the *Gītā* is going to give us that other teaching. Handle the tools, but handle the mind also. The tool of all tools is the mind. Then something great will happen to you. So, this is the first definition of *yoga: samatvam yoga ucyate.* And two ślokas later, you will find again in verse 50 another definition which is much more pervasive in meaning and significance. The next verse, verse 49, says:

दूरेण ह्यवरं कर्म बुद्धियोगाद्धनञ्जय ।
बुद्धौ शरणमन्विच्छ कृपणाः फलहेतवः ॥४९॥

Dūreṇa hyavaram karma buddhiyogāddhanañjaya;
Buddhau śaraṇamanviccha kṛpaṇāḥ phalahetavaḥ—2. 49

'Work (with desire) is verily far inferior to that performed with the mind established in *buddhi-yoga.* O Dhanañjaya, seek refuge in this *buddhi*, evenness ot mind; wretched are they who act for (selfish) results.'

These few verses in the heart of the second chapter of the *Gītā* are masterly, conveying a profound philosophy of life for all humanity, and particularly verse 49, which I read out just now, *dūreṇa hyavaram karma buddhiyogāt dhanañjaya*, 'Arjuna, work done with a selfish motive is far inferior to work done from that *buddhi-yoga* point of view'. *Buddhau śaraṇam anviccha*, 'take refuge in *buddhi*'. Develop *buddhi* in yourself. *Kṛpaṇāḥ phalahetavaḥ*, 'those who run after fruits, they are very small-minded', *kṛpaṇāḥ—kañjūs*, as we say in Hindi. They are small-minded. Now, this verse was quoted in a public lecture by the Secretary-General at the United Nations a few years ago. In quoting this verse he said, if people can follow in their life this teaching, the world will be a better place to live in. *Buddhi* is a great word in Vedanta, coming again and again in the *Gītā*. Actually, it is the faculty of reason, judgement, discrimination. It represents the integration of the intellect, emotion and will. It controls, or ought to control, all the psychic and sensory processes in a human being. This cerebral system is the organic instrument of that *buddhi*. The cerebral system is the latest development of the brain in human beings. That is meant to control and regulate the entire human organism other than the organism's automatic functions. By understanding this, and trying to practise this a little, anybody can develop this *buddhi* within oneself as an instrument of achieving the goal of evolution at the human stage. It is manufactured out of the psycho-physical energy system within everybody. We only purify that energy, refine it; then it becomes *buddhi*.

I often refer to this subject of refining psychic energy. All high character is based upon the refining of psychic energies. Raw psychic energy gives you crude character. This is a very important subject. We have refineries in India now, we take crude oil and refine that oil, and out of that refinery we get beautiful petroleum products. Even fine scents you get out of it. Refining is essential so far as crude oil is concerned.

Similarly, nature has given to man a wonderful refinery of experience within this human system. Take crude experience, refine it, and then, send out beautiful products of character—love, compassion, peace, efficiency of work, dedication—out of the crude energy that you get in yourself. This is a subject which every youth must think about and work out in life. How to refine my experience? Today, in the concept and practice of education all over the world, there is very little of this refining of experience. The crudity that has come to our life is appalling. Crudity in ordinary human relations, crudity in politics, crudity everywhere; education is there, but not refinement; psychic energy is there, but no refining; that crudity is a sign that we have not used our body-mind complex as a refinery of experience. All these ideas pertain to the teaching that Śrī Kṛṣṇa is giving us in this second chapter. Where there is no *buddhi,* we live and work from a lower level of life. Then we become a *phalahetavaḥ*—'motivated by fruits for oneself'. There is no place for 'you' or 'we' at all in our thinking then. Compared to that, all thought and action proceeding from the level of *buddhi* will seek the welfare of others along with that of oneself; 'what can I do for you'—that attitude will be always there. That is called *buddhi-yoga* or *yoga-buddhi,* the only source of high character-energy. That *buddhi* in you is nearest to the Atman or Brahman, the one Divine Self in all. Ādi Śaṅkarācārya calls it *nediṣṭham brahma,* 'nearest to Brahman'. *Buddhi* has only to turn back, the Atman is there, the infinite one.

When we study the *Kaṭha Upaniṣad,* we come across a beautiful chariot imagery. Human life is a journey to fulfilment. There are two types of journey: external journey, for which the body is the chariot, sense organs are the horses, mind is the reins, and *buddhi* is the charioteer. Within the chariot is the Self, the master of the chariot. In the context of that very journey, there is also an inward journey. That inward journey is what makes for character, makes for high spiritual and character attainments. This beautiful chariot imagery is given in the third chapter of the *Kaṭha Upaniṣad* (I. iii. 3–9).

In that chariot imagery, the driver of that chariot is *buddhi.* It directs the whole movement of the sense organs or horses of the chariot; all energy of movement is in the horses. And the horses need to be controlled by the reins; and the reins must be held by somebody; that somebody is *buddhi.* And the reins stand for the *manas*, this psychic system. So, *buddhi* is the controller and director of the whole journey. It sets the pace of the journey. It, and not the horses, can see *far* ahead, what they call in English, far-sight and foresight. The sensory system has no far-sight and foresight. Psychic system has a little far-sight, better than the sensory system. But when you come to *buddhi,* you get high foresight and far-sight, *dūradṛṣṭi.* That is called wisdom. Buddhi is a unique instrument for directing human life and for achieving human destiny. So, here Śrī Kṛṣṇa is telling: *buddhau śaraṇam anviccha,* 'take refuge in *buddhi*'; don't allow your journey to be redirected by the chariot or the horses, or the reins. Similarly, in the human system, let not the body decide your life's purpose. Let not the sensory system decide it, not even the psyche, but let the *buddhi* decide the course of our life's journey. The mind is stingy, that is the meaning of *kṛpaṇaḥ.* Here it means you are petty, small, nothing big will come out of you. So, verse 49 conveys a beautiful idea of work and life, of every human being—no distinction of race, caste, nation, sect, or creed; just a human being, young or old. How shall they live and work? That is being answered much more definitely by the next verse, where *yoga* is defined by Śrī Kṛṣṇa in a more concrete and comprehensive form. It is a very important verse, the very heart of the *yoga* teaching, the finest and shortest definition of *yoga.*

The whole of Vedanta can be described by one phrase coined by Sir Julian Huxley. He wants modern science to develop into 'a science of human possibilities' from what it is now; namely, a science of physical nature's possibilities. Tremendous possibilities are there hidden in every one of us. Why should I remain weak and helpless all the time? Parallel development must take place in the body, mind and spiritual fields of life. These ideas are conveyed through these verses in the second chapter. And the whole thing is set in the context of a person at work, not at prayer, meditation, or mystical absorption. The majority of people are working people. As a working person, how can I utilize that work situation to expand my mind and heart and to manifest the tremendous possibilities lying within. That is real education for a human being, and so, in the next verse, verse 50, we have the keynote statement of the *Gītā* teaching given in the briefest possible language. In fact, the whole philosophy of the *Gītā* itself is expressed by the briefest definition of *yoga* in verse 50, which says:

बुद्धियुक्तो जहातीह उभे सुकृतदुष्कृते ।
तस्माद्योगाय युज्यस्व योगः कर्मसु कौशलम् ॥५०॥

Buddhiyukto jahātīha ubhe sukṛtaduṣkṛte;
Tasmādyogāya yujyasva yogaḥ karmasu kauśalam—2. 50

'Endued with this evenness of *buddhi*, one frees oneself in this very life, alike from virtue and vice; devote yourself, therefore, to this *yoga. Yoga is efficiency in action.*'

What a brief definition! *Buddhiyukto jahātīha ubhe sukṛtaduṣkṛte.* 'All these dualities of *sukṛta* and *duṣkṛta;* good deeds and bad deeds, that we do in our lower life are full of these conflicts'. But, 'when you rise to the level of *buddhi,* you go beyond these conflicting dualities'— *buddhiyukto jahāti iha ubhe sukṛtaduṣkṛte. Tasmāt,* 'therefore', *yogāya yujyasva,* 'connect yourself with this philosophy and technique of *yoga*'. Get your whole mind and heart established in *yoga.* Then, what is *yoga?* The last phrase explains it. *Yogaḥ karmasu kauśalam, 'yoga* is efficiency or dexterity in action'. You are working; that is beautiful. It can become not only a means for your worldly welfare but also a school of your own inner development. *That is the unique feature of the Gītā teaching. In no other religious literature, in India or abroad, you find this definition of spirituality. Spirituality is defined here as efficiency in work. What kind of definition is it? It is a combination of productive efficiency without, and spiritual efficiency within.*

Efficiency is a great word and it is a great characteristic of modern Western civilization. Everything must be efficient,

efficient machines, efficient workers, efficient managers, efficient doctors and efficient nurses. Śrī Kṛṣṇa also stresses this concept of productive efficiency: with minimum effort producing maximum results. There you can see efficiency in various departments of modern life and work. Accepting this, the *Gītā* introduces a second and higher dimension of efficiency, which is greatly needed today in our civilization. There are two levels of efficiency in work. When you work, you change the world around you. It is work that changes the world around you. You dig a pit, the world is changed thereby; you build a house, the world is changed. And today, you build so many industries and other things, the world is changed—sometimes for good, sometimes for bad. That is the one result of work; you change the ratio of forces around you by the work that you do. That is one aspect of work that is highly emphasized in modern Western civilization, and that is being accepted by non-Western countries as well. But, Śrī Kṛṣṇa emphasizes a second aspect also which is much neglected in modern civilization. It refers to what has happened to your mind by that productive efficiency? Has that work done any good to your mind; has it made you better, purer, broader? Has it made you realize your own true nature? If that is done, efficiency gets a second dimension.

In normal language we say, productive efficiency is the first type of efficiency. Good workers, strong, efficient farmers, industrial workers, administrators, professional people, everyone must be efficient to discharge one's responsibilities to society. That is one aspect of efficiency. The second aspect is highly neglected, and Śrī Kṛṣṇa stresses it throughout the *Gītā*. See what has happened to you after years of productive efficiency. Have you grown spiritually? Have you realized something of the divine spark that is within you? Have you gone beyond the body-mind complex and its pulls and pressures, and become calm and steady within yourself? All these are profound questions that some people in modern Western civilization are asking. What has happened to the human being? He or she has been a good worker. But he or she has become a broken person after years of productive efficiency. Work has done no good to the worker, except his or her salary and whatever creature comforts could come out of that salary. What about the inner life of the worker? Is he or she rich within, peaceful and fulfilled? In this way, Śrī Kṛṣṇa defines the *yoga* taught in the *Gītā* as a double efficiency: productive work efficiency, and inward personal or character efficiency. These must go side by side. Don't separate these two. By the same work, if one can achieve two great things, how much greater will be our profit thereby?

This second emphasis is highly needed today all over the world, because we find man has become smaller and smaller, more subject to tension, sorrow, unfulfilment, and suicidal tendencies. All these things are there in this most efficient technological civilization. Man has become a creature of the environment, *jantu,* i.e., creature, as we call it in Sanskrit. Because we neglected the second dimension to the concept of efficiency. The *Gītā* gently advises all working people to take care of this also. As you work, you bring blessings to society by your honest, efficient, co-operative labour in whatever fields you are working; see also that your inner life becomes qualitatively richer, full of joy, full of peace, full of love and concern for humanity. That is spiritual growth. Today, we can call it a qualitative enrichment of human life.

And this is the first time, modern science, especially twentieth-century biology, is stressing the importance of quality in human life. Earlier, the stress was all on quantity. But today, evolution, at the human stage, needs this criterion of quality to show that there is progress. What is that quality of your life? Quantity of production, quantity of consumption, we stress again and again. And all work efficiency goes for that. And this consumption goes on, galloping, even beyond the luxuries of life; a mad consumerism has set in. That is civilization today. But the result is the qualitative impoverishment of man. Why? Because modern science has no insight into human nature beyond the sensory level. Therefore, one aspect of efficiency is stressed and the other is neglected. That second aspect is slowly attracting the attention of the modern mind, that there is a science and technology by which you can enrich yourself qualitatively.

This warning is being given now by some of the scientists themselves. I refer to the British biologist, Sir Julian Huxley. In his lecture on *The Evolutionary Vision* at the Chicago Congress of Scientists celebrating Darwin Centenary in 1959, he refers to this subject (*Issues in Evolution, Evolution After Darwin*, vol. 3, p. 259):

'Once we truly believe that man's destiny is to make possible greater fulfilment for human beings and fuller achievement by human societies, utility in the customary sense becomes subordinate. Quantity of material production is, of course, necessary only up to a certain degree. More than a certain number of calories or cocktails or TV sets or washing machines per person, is not merely unnecessary, but bad. Quantity of material production is a means to a further end, and not an end in itself.'

Now, Śrī Kṛṣṇa foresaw this kind of difficulty for humanity. He was a great worker himself. And so, he developed a philosophy, so many thousand years ago, where efficiency gets a double dimension, where quantity *and* quality go together. Are those who work efficiently peaceful? Can they live at peace with each other? Serve each other? These are all important questions. We shall succeed to abolish war, violence, and crime from society by this qualitative enrichment of human life. There is no other way except this. But we in India have been neglecting the work side of our life. We have to develop that side very much today. Our problems like poverty and backwardness cannot be overcome without stress on work, efficient work, and team work; these are all great demands on our national character today. When we become good workers, producing goods and services, we shall solve the problem of mass poverty in India. All the eight hundred million people, well fed, well educated, well housed, what a beautiful development will it be! So, productive efficiency is a profound message for all of us in all these developing countries, especially for India and Africa. But even in the course of doing so, we should not neglect the second dimension. We have already started neglecting it, and we are already reaping its bitter fruits. More of mental tension, more of strain, more of break-down, all these things are also coming to us. And to us, till now, religion means only doing some ritual, or paying some money to the priest to do the ritual. No benefit is going to come to you thereby unless your mind is trained. All happiness and peace come from and in the mind, they don't come from outside. When the mind is properly trained, it becomes peaceful. So, this training of the mind must go on as part of the work that we do, we have to take special care in India if we want to preserve the spiritual quality of our cultural heritage.

So, this concept of personality efficiency, inward efficiency, is very much needed in all parts of the world today. Soviet Russia is feeling the need for this great philosophy. There is nobody to teach these things. It is a profound subject that people are seeking for. And so, the books like the *Gītā* are being sought after and read by increasing numbers of people. I am sure some good will come by one's own reading, and trying to apply the teaching as much as possible in one's own life and work. This special declaration, *yogaḥ karmasu kauśalam,* is a unique type of definition of man's spiritual life, not opposed to man's worldly life, but comprehending both of them. *Yoga* of the *Gītā* comprehends both dimensions of human life, outer life and inner life. Outer life of work, inner life of inward development. *Gītā* doesn't make a gulf between one's secular life and religious life. That gulf has been bridged by Śrī Kṛṣṇa ages ago. So, this definition will appeal to every thinking mind, to every rational mind, to agnostics, even to atheists, who are afraid of the word 'religion'. There is no religion in all this, by way of dogma and ritual in the normal sense of the term. It is a comprehensive philosophy of life, philosophy and spirituality of life, that one gets from the *yoga* of the *Gītā*. It is meant for every human being. Let us, Śrī Kṛṣṇa says, be *yogīs*. Śrī Kṛṣṇa is whispering to everybody, 'be a *yogī*.'

Immediately many of us may come to the wrong conclusion: 'to be a *yogī,* we must be a special kind of people; some magic, some miracles, this and that, must be there to be *yogīs.*' Śrī Kṛṣṇa says, 'no, I don't mean any of that. I mean the most normal life, but with a depth added to it.' What a universal philosophy it is! You are living, you are working, you are dealing with others, and in all this, you are also shaping your mind and heart, trying to manifest the divine spark that is within you. In this way, a parallel development takes place, externally, social welfare and development, inwardly, spiritual growth and fulfilment.

And some of these ideas are coming to us from modern biology, that the goal of evolution at the human stage is not organic satisfaction, numerical increase, or organic survival. These are the words of Sir Julian Huxley and others of the twentieth century biology. At the pre-human phase of evolution, these were the goals. Every animal wants organic satisfaction. It needs numerical increase. It needs organic survival. Everything it does is for organic survival, as far as possible. But, in this twentieth century, evolution has found a new goal at the human level. That Huxley defines as fulfilment; organic satisfaction, organic survival, numerical increase, these are all secondary. The primary objective is fulfilment, what a beautiful term! It is by introducing this concept of fulfilment that Huxley coined that phrase which I quoted earlier: 'If fulfilment is the goal of evolution, we shall need a new science of human possibilities.' What are these possibilities and how to bring them out? At present we don't have it in the West. But when you study India's Vedanta, you come across this very science and the technique of manifesting in life those possibilities. And so, this definition of *yoga* as *karmasu kauśalam* must be meditated upon by everyone to get the best out of it. And Śrī Kṛṣṇa whispers to everyone of us, 'be a *yogī,* be a *yogī.*' I spoke at the Mussorie Lal Bahadur Shastry Academy of Administration on *yogaḥ karmasu kauśalam* because the Indian Administrative Service, the I.A.S., has taken this as its motto. This is not merely for the I.A.S., but for every one; Śrī

Kṛṣṇa whispers to a government official, 'be a *yogī*'; to a teacher or a doctor, and to everyone, 'be a *yogī*'. What type of *yogī?* Not the cheap kind of *yoga* which you get, by change of dress and external forms. Some profound change takes place *in* you. A new ratio of forces comes *within* you. That is the spiritual growth of man; and that takes place in the context of work itself, in the context of human relations. *What can be a more luminous and universal and practical message than this*!

Work hard, bring happiness and welfare to society through your work. This cannot be done by simply praying to God or by performing some rituals. That has been our mistake. We sought for material improvements by rituals and ceremonies. To obtain wealth, one installs a picture of Lakṣmī, goddess of wealth, and goes on doing *ārati* before that picture. That was the foolish thing many people did. Go and work. That is what creates Lakṣmī. Lakṣmī is the product of efficient labour, co-operative labour. In recent centuries, we forgot cleanly this truth: one can worship the picture of the goddess after doing hard work. Not understanding the meaning of Sarasvatī, the goddess of knowledge, by merely worshipping a picture of Sarasvatī, we are not going to achieve knowledge. These are only symbolic worship, just a picture you worship once in a year, and be quite happy, after doing hard and productive work and after study of books and thinking for oneself; that is how knowledge comes. That lesson we forgot. We have to regain and re-learn it today. We shall be true devotees of Sarasvatī and Lakṣmī and we shall learn a new lesson in this modern period, which Swami Vivekananda particularly stressed, that Lakṣmī is the product of Sarasvatī. The more knowledge you have, the more wealth you will be able to create. Ignorance is not able to create wealth. First, therefore, pursue knowledge; that is called the worship of Sarasvatī. Then, apply that knowledge to the nature's forces around you. That becomes wealth, that becomes Lakṣmī. They are two very beautiful loving sisters. The old experience was that they are jealous sisters. Wherever Lakṣmī comes, from there Sarasvatī will run away and vice versa! In our case it was true. Rich people may not have much knowledge, and knowing people will not have much wealth. That has been our condition, not understanding the true meaning of Lakṣmī and Sarasvatī. Today, we have to bring back these two sisters to every home, to the whole of our society. *First* Sarasvatī, *then* Lakṣmī. Apply your knowledge, then wealth comes.

Pure science and applied science, we say. Knowledge transforming into the fruit by way of economic and environmental development. Even today, our rural population, if they had better education up to the 8th class, even if not up to the Matriculation standard, how much development would have taken place all over India! The real worship is study, deep thinking and hard work. That has to come back to India. But, if economic prosperity comes, and if poverty comes in your mind and heart, that will be a tragedy. We shall abolish it from the mind and the heart also by developing the spiritual awareness within ourselves. Those who have become good workers and developed high character, public spirit, spirit of service and dedication, they will be the greatest asset of any nation. To produce such people in abundance in all parts of the world, is the mission of the *Gītā* in the modern age. And the *Gītā* will do it, and people are seeking for such a rational practical religion, without any kind of mystification or dogmatic and credal limitation. So, this brief definition must be studied and thought over and applied according to one's own strength.

Śrī Kṛṣṇa had earlier said: 'Even a little of it is good': *svalpamapyasya dharmasya trāyate mahato bhayāt*. If productive efficiency increases even by five percent in India, we shall be taking leave of all this poverty and backwardness. Śrī Kṛṣṇa asks me to be a *yogī*. I can't be a hundred percent *yogī;* so I will remain what I am; that is not a correct attitude. Become a *yogī* one percent, five percent, as much as you can. All that is going to bring a lot of blessing to you and to your society. That truth we have to keep in view constantly. All laziness must go from our society; in the name of religion, we became lazy; in the name of meditation, in the name of *samādhi,* we became lazy and went to sleep for centuries together. This *Gītā* comes like a clarion call, Śrī Kṛṣṇa's *śaṅkha-dhvani,* to wake us up. He will say that in the eleventh chapter (verse 33): *Tasmāt tvam uttiṣṭha yaśo labhasva jitvā śatrūn bhuṅkṣva rājyam samṛddham,* 'Arjuna, get up', *tasmāt tvam uttiṣṭha yaśo labhasva,* 'acquire the glory that belongs to man'. There is a glory attached to human beings. We have lost this glory; we have to regain it now. *Jitvā śatrūn,* 'overcoming your enemies', in the form of poverty, backwardness, etc. And then, *bhuṅkṣva rājyam samṛddham,* 'enjoy life fully in this beautiful country of ours'. How wonderful will be that state! When today's poverty and backwardness are overcome, in that kind of a country, it is a pleasure to live and to interact with each other. That kind of change will come when this philosophy becomes applied by increasing numbers of our people.

Swami Vivekananda calls it 'Practical Vedanta'. Vedanta has been till now a matter for discussion, what is called tea-table *carcā* or discussion. All over India we had this kind of Vedanta *carcā.* I have seen it actually when I was in Mysore; many *paṇḍits* will gather together after meals at noon. 'Now let us discuss something. What subject shall we take?' Then one of them will say, 'Our cloth is not clean, so, we shall not discuss our own *sampradāya;* we shall discuss the other *sampradāya*!' Such pettiness was there, and the great Vedanta was lost in all this morass of superstition and wordy arguments. Then Swami Vivekananda came bringing with him the lion roar, *simhagarjan,* of Practical Vedanta.

This is the first time we are having a nationwide effort to build a Vedantic society and civilization in our country, which will combine worldly welfare and spiritual development. Both will go side by side. That is the *yoga* of the *Gītā*. You will get its confirmation when we study the last verse of the *Gītā* some months later, where Sañjaya concludes the whole book, 'Wherever there is the spirit of Śrī Kṛṣṇa, wherever there is the spirit of Arjuna, in that society there will be *Śrī,* prosperity, *vijaya,* victory, *bhūti,* general welfare, and *dhruvā nīti,* perennial justice.' This is a beautiful summing up of the *Gītā* with respect to human life and destiny. So, today, our whole stress must be on practical Vedanta. Theory we have in plenty, tons and tons of theory, but one ounce of practice is worth tons of theory. That lesson we have to learn. Let us live this Vedanta as much as we can.

Swami Vivekananda, therefore, stressed practical Vedanta again and again. In his Madras Lecture in 1897, he took up the subject of *Vedanta and Its Application to Indian Life*. In his Lahore lecture, a few months later, he exhorted our people: 'Wipe off this blot, of untouchability and casteism'. Let us learn to treat man as man, not as a creature. When millions of our educated citizens will assimilate the Vedantic spirit, India will experience a thorough revolution in its politics and society. In a military revolution, so many people will be killed, not much gain will be there towards the end. But this type of revolution, the thought revolution, the attitude revolution—that will be permanent. That is what we need. A few do's and don'ts cannot help to bring about that revolution. It is like the code of conduct being discussed for all sorts of people—doctors, lawyers, engineers, politicians, everybody. You can have a whole volume of code of conduct! What does it matter? I won't do wrong when you are looking at me. When you are not looking at me, I will do what I like. That is called your so-called code of conduct. A little good it may do, when I am serious about it. Otherwise, do's and don'ts do not make any difference to me. People have become sufficiently cynical today. So, do's and don'ts will not help you. But, if you can change your mind, be convinced, 'this is a better way, this is a better way,' then high character will come out of that individual. We have to keep in view that it is the thought behind the actions that has to be handled. Then, not only this action, every subsequent action, will be in terms of that new thought. So, thought revolution is what we need.

Vivekananda said: spread healthy ethical, humanistic, spiritual ideas all over India. A great development will come thereby. This is the importance of this *yoga* of the *Gītā*. Always remember, it is entirely practical. It shapes our work and our life in new forms, bringing beauty and qualitative richness to the individual concerned. And so, this definition, *yogaḥ karmasu kauśalam,* is just a brief definition. Two *ślokas* earlier, Śrī Kṛṣṇa had defined *yoga* as, *samatvam yoga ucyate,* 'equanimity, evenness of mind, is *yoga*'. This is a complement to that, and much more pervasive in meaning. *Yogaḥ karmasu kauśalam,* this teaching, has to go round the world, because today we need a philosophy which can bring quality to human life. Stress on quantity alone has almost destroyed the stability of modern civilization.

We can't have religion by paying money to a priest to recite some mantra there. Most of us believe in that kind of religion. To what low level has our concept of religion come! The lowest level is what I noted in places like Hardwar; you go, pay five rupees to a *paṇḍā,* take hold of the tail of a cow, and you will go to heaven. That is called religion to many people. To what a low level it has gone! What has happened to *you* thereby? Nothing, *paṇḍā* got five rupees, and you held the tail of a cow; you are the same, cow is the same, and *paṇḍā* is the same. No difference at all. But this inner growth, spiritual growth, *adhyātmika-vikāsa,* slowly, gently, taking place, there is no big show about it, no flash about it; We thought of becoming saints by show. Showy saints; there is no showy sainthood. A very ordinary looking person may be a tremendous saint. Such saints we need in our society. We have got professional saints. That is too much in India. But sainthood comes to you normally, naturally, as a growth—that is the type of sainthood we need scattered all over India. Otherwise, like a huge banyan tree, and small shrubs all around, that is India. A few great giants of spirituality, and so many small pigmies around.

If an average citizen uses one's work situation properly, he or she will be spiritual. It is this type of life that the *Gītā* expounds throughout these eighteen chapters. We are just at the beginning of the *yoga* message. Starting from now, this concept of *yoga* will become richer and richer just like a Ganga starting from Gangotri, becomes bigger and bigger, when new tributaries enter into it, until, when you come to Allahabad, it becomes a mighty river of holiness and agricultural prosperity. Similarly, the *Gītā* also grows; as the chapters proceed, new ideas, new dimensions of life, new values come in. Specially, the great tide of *bhakti* comes in a little later. *Karma* becomes completely transformed when *bhakti* also enters into the picture. That development will come later. Here we are just at the beginning. That is why this definition has a great part to play to reshape our thinking and outlook. *Yoga-buddhi, buddhi-yoga*—both are used—the *buddhi* which is fixed in *yoga*, or the *yoga* that inspires *buddhi*, that *buddhi* we have to utilize to work and for human relations, that *buddhi* is what takes you to your spiritual dimension.

When Vivekananda returned to India after four years of successful work in the West, he set to organizing his nation-building and man-making work in India, the Ramakrishna-Vivekananda movement. Just like the phrase you have in the *Gītā, yogaḥ karmasu kauśalam,* he gave a similar brief motto. That motto is: *Ātmano mokṣārtham jagaddhitāya ca*, 'for one's own liberation and for the welfare of the world.' Combine work for the world with work for your own spiritual liberation. If the first part of the motto is not emphasized, we become used as a machine, and, when the machine is old, it is thrown into the scrap heap. That will be our condition. That should not be. *Ātmano mokṣārtham,* you must become freer and freer. This cannot come unless you orient your work situation in this inward direction. Not merely a productive individual; a machine also is a productive unit. Some of the machines can do more work than you and I can do. When you cease to work also, you have some value within you, an intrinsic value. Raise the nation, raise the people of the world, to the highest level of human development. That is external work. While doing so, *ātmano mokṣārtham,* be free spiritually. Achieve your own spiritual perfection. That is the message you get in this definition of *yoga* by the *Gītā* and Swamiji's motto for the Ramakrishna-Vivekananda movement. What a wonderful new message is coming out of the old *Gītā,* through new teachers, for the good of all, in this modern age.

Yoga is the theme of the whole *Gītā*. According to Lokamanya Tilak in his famous book *Gītā Rahasya*, the word *yoga* and its associates have come more than eighty times throughout the *Gītā*. And towards the end of the *Gītā*, Sañjaya also tells Dhṛtarāṣṭra that it was 'my' blessed privilege, through Vyāsa's grace, to listen to the exposition of yoga by 'Yogeśvara Kṛṣṇa' himself. Also, at the end of every chapter of the *Gītā*, it is reiterated that it is an exposition of the science of *yoga: Śrīmad bhagavad gītāsu upaniṣadsu brahmavidyāyām yogaśāstre Śrī Kṛṣṇārjuna samvāde*, 'thus in this *Bhagavad Gītā*, it is an Upaniṣad taken out of *Brahma Vidyā* (Science of Brahman) in the science of *yoga*, in the dialogue between Śrī Kṛṣṇa and Arjuna'.

I wish to stress this point that the entire stress in the *Gītā* is on man or woman at work, and how to utilize that work situation for one's own good and for the good of the world. A few verses later, Arjuna is going to ask this very question, what is the nature of that stability, that strength, and Śrī Kṛṣṇa will answer him in very well-known verses, which will close this second chapter. And now, we take up the next verse, verse 51.

कर्मजं बुद्धियुक्ता हि फलं त्यक्त्वा मनीषिणः ।
जन्मबन्धविनिर्मुक्ताः पदं गच्छन्त्यनामयम् ॥५१॥

Karmajam buddhiyuktā hi phalam tyaktvā manīṣiṇaḥ;
Janmabandhavinirmuktāḥ padam gacchantyanāmayam—2. 51

'The wise, possessed of this evenness of mind, abandoning the fruits of their actions, freed for ever from the fetters of births, go to that state which is beyond all evil.'

Karmajam phalam, 'whatever fruits come out of *karma*'; those who have *yoga-buddhi*, they know how to handle those fruits. They never take these fruits for themselves. *Karmajam buddhiyuktā hi, phalam tyaktvā*, 'they renounce these fruits for the good of all'. *Manīṣiṇaḥ*, 'the wise people'; *janmabandha vinirmuktāḥ*, 'they become freed from the bondages of birth and death'. *Padam gacchanti anāmayam*, 'they attain to that state free from all evil'. When? Here, in this very life. That is a great stress in all Vedanta and the *Gītā*—not a promise to be realized in a heaven, a post-mortem heaven, but here itself you will reap the fruit, you will know that this is true. This can be achieved, this has been achieved by people. I can also achieve it. So, I am fashioning my life and work in such a way that, that blessing will come into my life—what I referred to earlier as the main theme of twentieth century biological evolution, namely, quality. This is what is to be achieved in the course of our lives and work. That is the philosophy Śrī Kṛṣṇa is expounding here.

At every place, Śaṅkarācārya will say, *ihaiva, ihaiva,* 'here itself, here itself.' Generally, religion gives us something of a promise in a future life. That is not the philosophy taught in the *Gītā*, or in the Upaniṣads. It is all 'here and now.' That infinite nature of man. When you realize it, you realize it here itself. That is how fulfilment comes in human life in this very world. It is said of Buddha that he achieved *bodhi,* illumination, at Bodh Gaya. And so the concept of spiritual realization in Vedanta and Buddhism is very unique. You get 'it' here and now. And in the case of Śrī Kṛṣṇa and Buddha, you will find the story that Brahma and Indra, even gods in heaven, they came down to be blessed by these two great personalities. Anyone who realizes this truth here, is far superior to all the gods which we or others have. The greatness of the human system is such that the divine is present within him or her with the organic capacity to realize that truth. What heaven can compare with this remarkable achievement of spiritual realization here and now. And so, verse 52 tells us:

यदा ते मोहकलिलं बुद्धिर्व्यतितरिष्यति ।
तदा गन्तासि निर्वेदं श्रोतव्यस्य श्रुतस्य च ॥५२॥

Yadā te mohakalilam buddhirvyatitariṣyati;
Tadā gantāsi nirvedam śrotavyasya śrutasya ca— 2. 52

'When your intellect crosses beyond the taint of illusion, then shall you attain to indifference, regarding things heard and things yet to be heard.'

This reference to Arjuna is also a reference to all of us. Our minds are confused, *yadā te mohakalilam buddhiḥ vyatitariṣyati,* 'when your mind will cross this area of *moha,* delusion'; clear thinking with pure mind helps us to cross the ocean of delusion. And, when you do so, *tadā gantāsi nirvedam śrotavyasya śrutasya ca,* 'then you will get utter dispassion for things heard and things yet to be heard'. 'I want to hear this, I want to know this': mind is constantly flickering all the time. But that will end and stability will come. You don't need to read books, or to hear this and hear that. You have gone beyond it. In Vedanta, this idea that a seeker can go beyond books is very very important. On this subject, the next few verses will tell us much more. The next verse, 53, says:

श्रुतिविप्रतिपन्ना ते यदा स्थास्यति निश्चला ।
समाधावचला बुद्धिस्तदा योगमवाप्स्यसि ॥५३॥

Śrutivipratipannā te yadā sthāsyati niścalā;
Samādhāvacalā buddhistadā yogamavāpsyasi— 2. 53

'When your intellect, tossed about by the conflict of opinions, has become immovable and firmly established in the Self, then you will attain Self-realization.'

When your mind, 'which is disturbed by conflicting ideas coming from hearing this and hearing that, etc.,' *śrutivipratipannā*; some books say this, some books say that, some man says this, some man says that. Here, in the midst of conflicting situations, mind is never peaceful. When that kind of situation changes, *yadā sthāsyati niścalā,* 'when the mind becomes steady', overcoming all this distraction of hearing this, hearing that, reading this, reading that, etc., that mind becomes steady. Where? *Samādhau,* 'in *samādhi*'. What is *samādhi?* Says Śaṅkarācārya: *Asmin samādhīyate iti samādhiḥ,* 'That in which you get established, i.e., in your Self'; that is the Atman, your own infinite Self. *Achalā, buddhiḥ,* 'the *buddhi* becomes *achalā,* immovable, steady'. That is the state you will get by what is called spiritual progress. There is such a thing as *adhyātmika vikāśa,* spiritual growth.

In all the teachings of the *Gītā,* you find this stress on spiritual growth. In ordinary ritualism, that concept of spiritual growth is never emphasized. We pay some five rupees to a priest, he does some ritual, and we are satisfied, but we remain the same. Even at the age of eighty, it is the same mind. No change at all. But, in the science of spirituality, which is the *Gītā*, there is this stress on spiritual growth. Are you growing spiritually? Are you spiritually stronger and stronger? Are you more peaceful? Are you more compassionate? Is the infinite Atman manifesting in your life and work? All that is spiritual growth. Without spiritual growth, religion becomes a mere static piety. It does no good at all. And it can do much harm also. So much of fanaticism and show. All this will come in religion, when that stress on spiritual growth is not there. That is the story of most of the religions of the world. Vivekananda wrote in a letter (*Complete Works,* vol. 7, p. 501),

'Religions of the world have become lifeless mockeries. What we want is character.'

Every religion today has become dead from this point of view. In the name of religion, we can do any amount of wickedness and violence and human discrimination. That religion has no value today. What is to be stressed is the spiritual growth of men and women. As the body grows, as the mind grows, spirituality also grows. Stress that point again and again. *Yoga* is something to be achieved. We have to go step by step. There is nothing external about it, no show. That simple housewife, or a labourer in the fields, everyone can develop spirituality. That is our birthright. So, people developing spiritually in every department of life—that will be the great situation when the *Gītā* is understood by more and more people in the way in which it is meant to be understood. *Yoga* as the spiritual growth and fulfilment of men and women everywhere. We get established in our own infinite Self. That is the most important feeling we must develop by watching one's mind, one's actions, and one's inter-human relations. The word *samādhi,* Śaṅkara interprets as *asmin samādhīyate iti samādhi.* 'That in which the mind is established, that is called *samādhi*'. What is that thing? Atman, your own infinite divine nature.

Through the path of *yoga,* you realize your own true nature. What a beautiful concept! We don't know our own nature. Even when we get mental distortions, when there is a psychic breakdown or nervous breakdown, we lose our own nature. We behave like children at that time. Then psychiatry will come and put us back into our own true nature. We become normal again. So, the greatest thing we can do to ourselves is to *be* ourselves. What is that? I am the Atman. I am that infinite one, ever pure, ever free, ever enlightened, that is my true nature. Let me rise to that level. At this stage, we are now in a hypnotic condition. All sorts of evil things we are doing, not knowing our true nature. That is why Vivekananda presented Vedanta in the West as the philosophy which de-hypnotizes people. People are already hypnotized, I am black, I am white, I am man, woman, I am rich, poor, all these are hypnotism. Vivekananda's Vedanta is to de-hypnotize people by installing them on their own true nature. That is *yoga. Tadā yogam avāpsyasi,* 'then you will really attain *yoga,*' in the true sense of the term. So, when this subject was presented by Śrī Kṛṣṇa, Arjuna got an opportunity to put a question. During all this time, Arjuna has been simply listening. In the beginning of the chapter, he had put some questions. And now he gets an opportunity to put another question, and that question is on behalf of all of us, as you will find. We also want to know that subject which Arjuna is posing before Śrī Kṛṣṇa.

अर्जुन उवाच –
Arjuna uvāca —

'Arjuna said:'

This last section, verses 54 to 72, is devoted to this subject which is that state of absolute stability, strength and infinite compassion. Something great has taken place in the human being. All that is petty and small has been washed away. What is that state? We want to know. So, Arjuna is asking that question on behalf of all of us:

स्थितप्रज्ञस्य का भाषा समाधिस्थस्य केशव ।
स्थितधीः किं प्रभाषेत किमासीत व्रजेत किम् ॥५४॥

Sthitaprajñasya kā bhāṣā samādhisthasya keśava;
Sthitadhīḥ kim prabhāṣeta kimāsīta vrajeta kim— 2. 54

'What, O Keśava, is the description of a person of steady wisdom, merged in *Samādhi*? How does the person of steady wisdom speak, how sit, how walk?'

How does a *sthitaprajña* live, move, talk and behave? That is the basic question Arjuna is asking. Outwardly he looks like me and you. Inwardly, there is a tremendous difference. That is a subject we should all remember. We all look alike outwardly, but inwardly the stuff inside is different. Sri Ramakrishna used to say: just now you had the Gaṇeśa festival; many houses made that *modaka;* beautiful sweet; inside which is coconut and jaggery and very thin rice powder covering it; very tasteful. Now that is coconut and jaggery. Suppose you put only some *ḍāl* powder-mix inside, that will be inferior quality. So, sweets may be very nice from outside; inside may be different stuff. Similarly, all human beings look alike, but, inside the stuff is different. There is one who is so lofty, whose mind is always thinking of the happiness and welfare of all people; outwardly he or she looks ordinary. Here is another person who is petty, small, trying to cheat people. They both look alike, but inwardly they are different. In Bhāsā's *Avimāra,* the great dramatist of about 6th or 7th century AD, there is one verse which says, *prājñasya mūrkhasya ca kārya-yoge samatvam abhyeti tanuḥ na buddhiḥ.* 'When a wise person and a foolish person work, there is similarity at the bodily level, but dissimilarity in their *buddhi* level'. It is there we read the character of a person. We must be able to go beyond the appearance and see what is inside. And so, how does one of steady wisdom, *sthita-prajña, sthita* means steady, *prajñā* means wisdom, 'how does he or she appear, *kā bhāṣā?* What is his or her nature? *Samādhisthasya keśava,* 'who has established oneself in the Atman', *sthitadhīḥ kim prabhāṣeta kimāsīta vrajeta kim?* What does one of steady wisdom say? How does one like that sit or move about? All these questions Arjuna is putting through that one verse. So, Śrī Kṛṣṇa gives the answer, which form the verses of the book up to the end of this second chapter.

श्रीभगवानुवाच –
Śrībhagavān uvāca —

'Śrī Bhagavān said.'

Every one of these verses is so full of meaning. They contain the science of human depth dimension yet unknown to modern physical science. In no part of the world will you find this penetrating study of the human mind—up to the very depths, and then wisdom, not only knowledge, coming out of that investigation. Depth study of the mind started only in the beginning of this century in the West through Freud's analysis of the subconscious levels of mind. That study revealed man in the worst light. And the West today is trying to get rid of that obsession, what you call Freudianism. Freudian study was depth study, but a minimal one, revealing only sex and violence, and irrationality. But from his time, including his disciples like Carl Jung and, later on, Maslow and others in America, they have been trying to see something deeper in the human psyche, apart from sex and violence. That work is going on. That work is getting joined with India's contribution to human depth psychology. And today there is a beautiful meeting of the East and the West in this field of psychology, and, in that context, these verses will be of tremendous significance.

प्रजहाति यदा कामान्सर्वान्पार्थ मनोगतान् ।
आत्मन्येवात्मना तुष्टः स्थितप्रज्ञस्तदोच्यते ॥५५॥

Prajahāti yadā kāmānsarvānpārtha manogatān;
Ātmanyevātmanā tuṣṭaḥ sthitaprajñastadocyate— 2. 55

'When one completely casts away, O Pārtha, all the desires of the mind, satisfied in the Self alone by the Self, then he or she is said to be one of steady wisdom.'

That person is a *sthitaprajña* in that condition, what is that condition? When he or she has overcome all the desires of the heart, 'I want this, I want that.' When the mind and the heart cease to hanker after this and that. A stage will come in life when a person realizes that these petty desires are nothing compared to his or her true nature as the infinite and ever free Atman. Why should I identify myself with them? We thus overcome desires by intelligent understanding that nothing can equal in value my own infinite Self, neither five rupees nor a million rupees, nor any other big gift from outside. How can they compare with the infinite value of the Self which is my true nature? This knowledge comes after a long struggle of inward penetration. As a child, 'I want this, I want that.' A child cannot understand its own true nature. So, always it wants something to eat, something to bite, something to play with; always out, out, out, the child-mind goes. But, when the mature mind comes, it realizes that these things are nothing compared to one's own true stature. That is a tremendous life achievement. Today, however, many people do not have that idea that the Atman within me, my own infinite dimension, is far superior to all the petty things of the external world—lust and gold, name and fame; all these we seek in the external world impelled by desire. And desire is the movement of the mind out. I am not satisfied within me, I want something from the outer world. That is how desire operates. But, by discrimination, by the practice of *yoga,* step by step, we come to a stage which is described here.

Prajahāti yadā kāmān, manogatān, 'when all the *kāmas* or desires of the heart are thrown away', that is one statement; and Śaṅkarācārya tells us in his commentary that that alone cannot make you a *sthitaprajña.* 'I don't desire anything.' It can be a pathological state. There may not be anything spiritual about it. When you go to a mental hospital, you will find some people who fully accord with what is said in the teaching of the first line, 'I don't want anything,' arising from what they call in psychology an apathetic attitude. There are such mental cases in the hospital, they live in a corner, don't want anything. They are immersed in themselves all the time. Are they *sthitaprajñas?* Not at all. So, the first line is not enough. Śaṅkara is going to say that something greater is to be added to it. That is what is said in the second line: *Ātmanyeva ātmanā tuṣṭaḥ*, he or she is fully delighted in the Self by the Self. Because of *that*, I don't want anything. That is the nature of true and positive renunciation. I have got something infinite with me. What can these petty things do for me? They are all tinsel, without any value, like children running after toys, bubbles, etc. 'I am not a child, I don't want these things,' we say when we are grown up. Similarly, the highest maturity of the human mind is that it is not dragged away by desirable objects from outside. Not by any effort, but by an effortless spontaneous process arising from one's knowledge of one's own infinite nature. I am the infinite Atman. What can these things do to me? That is renunciation, natural and spontaneous.

I once read a story of a Catholic Christian saint of the very early centuries. That saint had a friend, a magistrate. The magistrate was telling another friend, 'before I die, I want to give all my property to this saint, my friend.' And that man reported it to the saint. Then the saint asked, 'what did he say?' 'Before I die, I want to give all my property to the saint.' 'Did he say that?' 'Yes, sir.' 'Does he not know that I have already died earlier than himself?' What a beautiful expression! I am already dead to all these things. I don't need any one of these. Now, that is a natural state. There is no need to prod a man to develop that feeling. Because he has achieved something greater, namely, love of God, *bhakti*. What worldly things can compare with that wealth that comes to you through *bhakti*? Therefore, the second line of the verse says, *Ātmanyevātmanā tuṣṭaḥ*, 'oneself is satisfied with one's own infinite Atman'. Then only, *sthitaprajñaḥ tadā ucyate*, 'one can be said to be a *sthitaprajña*'. My heart is not empty. First I emptied it of all these finite external desires, but I did not leave it empty, I filled it with the infinite Atman. Then no more desires can come.

This has been expounded in various ways in the Upaniṣads, especially in the *Bṛhadāraṇyaka Upaniṣad*, which gives three words: *āptakāma, ātmakāma, akāma*. Three statements are there. First is called *āptakāma*, 'all desires have become fulfilled', fully satisfied, that is called *āptakāma*. How?

Ātmakāma. 'When you realize the Atman only', then that state can come. And in that state you become also *akāma*, 'desireless'. This is achievable by every human being, by proper discrimination, by realizing one's own true nature as infinite, immortal, and divine. I am not this tiny body-mind complex. I am not a tiny *creature*. Even in the limited levels of life, this kind of thinking is very very effective. As I often say, a person says: I am a petty school master in a village school, or I am a petty clerk in an office. By this thinking, the person reduces himself or herself to a pettiness, by a wrong attitude. He or she need not do so. He or she can tell that he or she is a citizen of free India, working as a clerk, working as a teacher. There, you put your being first, and function, second. But, normally we put function first, and being, nowhere! The little function you do, you identify with it. Nobody is petty unless one makes oneself petty. You are a citizen of free India. What can be a greater status than that? So, even in socio-political life, this attitude makes a lot of difference to a human being's status. And in spiritual life, it works wonders. I am the infinite Atman, or I am the child of God. It is very difficult to give up desires; it becomes easy when you realize your own true nature more and more. You don't try to drive them away. 'I don't need them'; that attitude will come. I am full. What a wonderful idea! This is the teaching that makes for *sthitaprajña*, steady wisdom. Even if you get five percent of that steadiness, even that will make your life and work very very rich and joyous. We don't expect millions of people to become fully *sthitaprajñas* of this nature. But, here is the ideal towards which we all can move. If one takes one step, that is a blessing. If one takes more steps, all the better.

The late British agnostic thinker Bertrand Russell says in his post second World War book, *Impact of Science on Society* (pp. 120–21):

'We are in the middle of a race between human knowledge as to means and human folly as to ends. Unless men increase in wisdom as much as in knowledge, increase of knowledge will be increase of sorrow.'

That is the goal of human evolution. The human being is greater than his or her possessions. This is a truth which sometimes is driven home to us in crises of life.

And I saw this truth revealed during the Burma to India evacuation during the last war. I was in Rangoon from 1939 to 1942, when the Japanese bombing and invasion of Rangoon took place; life in the city was completely dislocated, and people started evacuating to India. They belonged to Andhra, Uttar Pradesh, Bihar, Bengal and Tamil Nadu; everybody wanted to carry as many of their possessions as possible to India. So, from their households they carried with them big radios, bedding, blankets and many other costly things. But how could they carry all these through the long distance to India? After some distance, one item was left behind on the road, then some other items, till only the person and his or her bare necessities remained as their possessions. And only the person reached India! Such experiences must have occurred in such situations in other parts of the world also.

So in a crisis period, you realize that the ultimate value is the person alone, and not what he or she possesses. I have seen these possessions lying on the road. They knew that they could again gain these possessions if they were alive. How many of us fall down with a desire-wind blowing on us, but if we are well rooted, nothing can blow us away. That rooting is the Atman. My life is rooted in my awareness of the Atman. Then nothing can shake. This is very similar to the famous parable of Jesus in the *New Testament*:

'A foolish man built his house on sand, and the rains descended, and the floods came, and the winds blew, and beat upon that house, and it fell, and great was its fall. But a wise man built his house on rock, and the rains descended, and the floods came, and the winds blew, and beat upon that house, and it fell not, because it was founded on a rock.'

A very beautiful parable: when you raise your whole life on this rock of the Atman, nothing can shake it. That is called a steady character. Like a person who has high character strength arising from spiritual awareness, if somebody comes to bribe him with a hundred thousand rupees, he will say to him, 'please go away.' Wherefrom does that strength come? Only from this spiritual dimension of the human being; he or she has founded one's personality on the rock of one's infinite nature. If he or she had founded it only on the sand, a little breeze of five rupees bribery would have made him or her fall down. That steady state will come when these *Gītā* ideas are understood by the people. They are meant to be lived by the people, so that they can become men in the true sense of the term; and not creatures which can be thrown off their balance by some external force. So, *ātmanyevātmanā tuṣṭaḥ,* 'when one becomes delighted in the Atman alone', *sthitaprajñaḥ tadā ucyate,* 'then is one known to be possessed of steady wisdom'. Those who become ascetics, if they continue to be cheerful, then that asceticism is correct asceticism. Ascetics who are cheerful, who have got compassion, who love people, their asceticism is absolutely normal and high level. An ascetic who is dry, who reacts to other people in a very bad way, there is something wrong with that ascetic. He has lost something precious, the joy of the Atman. Joyous asceticism is the most beautiful thing a human being can ever have. Wherefrom has this smile come? From some infinite divine nature within, and not from outside. This has been expressed in a great verse in Ādi Śaṅkarācārya's *Vivekacūḍāmaṇi:* (Verse 543)

> *Nirdhano'pi sadā tuṣṭo'pyasahāyo mahābalaḥ;*
> *Nityatṛpto'pyabhuñjāno'pyasamaḥ samadarśanaḥ —*

What a beautiful expression!

'That person is an extraordinary person who though he or she has no wealth, no power, no resources, is yet full of joy, full of cheer; though he or she has no helpers, is infinitely strong; ever satisfied though not experiencing sense pleasures; though he or she is incomparable, looks upon all others as his or her equal.'

Asamaḥ samadarśanaḥ, he or she is *asamaḥ,* like Mount Everest; no other peak can be equal to it, but yet he or she treats all as one's equal. In our life, we see one person in the political field who approached the ideal depicted in this particular *śloka* of Śaṅkarācārya. That was Mahatma Gandhi. This kind of greatness is called spiritual greatness. Ordinary greatness cannot produce this quality.

Sri Ramakrishna says, '*Śiva* dances with joy realizing his own infinite nature'. This is the possibility hidden in all of us. We are not an item among items in this world. A table or chair, or a property, or this and that, cannot be equated with our own true nature. When we realize this truth a little, we shall still have property, we shall still have money, but we won't be slaves of these. That is the stress placed in the *Gītā*. Life will continue as it is, but value-systems will be different. I won't cheat a man for the sake of a few rupees. I know the value of money, but I know that the value of man is greater than the value of money. In this way, it can change human life from top to bottom. After all, a little change in our attitude and life can make for more and more happiness. Say, in our families, there is often so much of fight and quarrel for a little money; it is a terrible situation. Brothers, sisters, all fighting and quarrelling. That whole picture will change with a bit of this message influencing the minds.

Our people must learn to think and feel for things and persons in a big way. A sister has become a widow; they are there to help and serve her in her unhappy situation, and not to swindle her. That kind of pettiness will never afflict a society when a little bit of spirituality, a little *sthitaprajñā* attitude, comes to the human mind. So, this first verse of *sthitaprajña* section is the most promising verse: that you give up external attractions in a natural way, because you realize something greater within yourself. A small thing is given up, because a big thing has come to you. You have realized your own bigness, as the finite being underwritten by the infinite Being within you. That knowledge, even a little, can destroy all the pettiness in social life which is afflicting our society just now. It has relevance to all of us in every level of life, because this Atman, infinite and immortal, is our birthright and we have to become aware of it.

During Gandhiji's time, these verses used to be read in his Āśrama every day because it is so elevating. Even to think of it, even to meditate upon these ideas, is a great education in human development, human spiritual growth.

For success in life, we need a bit of steadiness of mind. An unsteady mind cannot achieve anything great. Most people have a measure of steadiness. That shows they have given some training to the mind. That training is elaborated here with a lot of insight so that you can achieve greater and greater stability in your inner life. So, the second verse on this subject follows immediately, verse 56:

दुःखेष्वनुद्विग्नमनाः सुखेषु विगतस्पृहः ।
वीतरागभयक्रोधः स्थितधीर्मुनिरुच्यते ॥५६॥

Duḥkheṣvanudvignamanāḥ sukheṣu vigataspṛhaḥ;
Vītarāgabhayakrodhaḥ sthitadhīrmunirucyate— 2. 56

'One whose mind is not shaken by adversity, who does not hanker after happiness, who has become free from blind attachment, fear, and anger, is indeed the *muni* or sage of steady wisdom.'

That *sthitadhīḥ*, 'that person whose *dhīḥ* or *buddhi* is *sthita*, steady', is called a *muni*. The word *muni* in Sanskrit correctly means, *mananaśīlo muniḥ*, a very thoughtful person. Normally, we associate the word *muni* with one who observes silence. That is only a very external part of that wonderful term. The essential part is 'being deeply thoughtful'. The words *muni* and *ṛṣi* are often used in our literature. The *muni* is a great word. Look at a *muni's* face; you will find a thoughtful face, not a light-hearted one, nor an empty, shallow kind of face. We are having democracy today. The success of any democracy depends upon more and more people developing the capacity for thought, and for love and service. Those who live in uncontrolled emotion and frenzy of action, which now characterize most of our politics, they can destroy our democracy. But, in a very stable democracy, we need more of the *muni* quality in human beings. *Mananaśīlo muniḥ*, 'thinking people are *muniḥ*'. All progress in society comes from the capacity to think. When we use the word *muni* in this context, we may feel, 'O! It is a high ideal! How can we be *munis* like that?' But, we can be *munis* at our own level. There are so many levels of being a *muni*. So that is the line we must always remember. *Duḥkheṣu anudvignamanāḥ*, 'whose mind is not depressed by sorrow'. Similarly, *sukheṣu vigataspṛhaḥ*, 'not carried away by ambition in happiness'.

Then comes a beautiful expression: *vīta rāga bhaya krodhaḥ*, 'who has overcome three emotions which are very harmful to man'; what are they? *Rāga, bhaya, krodha*, 'attachment, fear, anger'. These three, beyond a certain range, are highly destructive of happiness and peace in a society. So, this is expressed again and again in the *Gītā*. When we deal with the 4th chapter, we shall be coming across this teaching more explicitly. Now, fear is considered to be an evil throughout Vedanta. It never encourages fear as a religious virtue. That is the one lesson our society must learn. We train our children by instilling fear in them, fear of this and fear of that. Vedanta says, 'no, let children grow in fearlessness'. 'Fearlessness is virtue. Fear is a sin', Swami Vivekananda said. That is a Vedantic teaching. *Bhaya* or fear has no place in the moral education of any child. Normal fears are there. If there is a tiger, I am not going to embrace that tiger! That is intelligent, rational fear. But irrational fear making for abnormality of behaviour has to be avoided. We instil a lot of abnormal fears in our children. And therefore, they can't have a true moral life. They have to be made moral through fear. That is what people generally understand by morality, fear of policemen, fear of public opinion; we try to behave well by such fears. That kind of fear has no place in the psychology of character development as understood in Vedanta. In no other literature do we find fear being considered as bad for a human being. Fearlessness alone is virtue, not fear. I speak a lie, why? I fear, therefore, I lie. If I have no fear, I shall never speak a lie. I will speak the truth to father or mother. So, children brought up in fearlessness, they will naturally be moral. They will be straightforward. They will be spontaneous in their life. Never instil fear into the minds of children; as grown-ups also, we have to try to overcome fear. This is a running theme in this great book *Bhagavad Gītā*. So, overcome attachment, *rāga, bhaya,* fear, and *krodha,* anger.

It is very difficult to control anger; but, we have to train the mind in controlling anger. First of all, we get angry; we become cool after some time. Then, we must reflect: why did I get angry? I lost control; now I shall try. In this way, by repeated exercise of will-power and dedication to higher causes, we can slowly overcome these evil emotions called fear and hatred. We 'explode' into anger. Harvard University Professor William McDougall's famous book, *Character and the Conduct of Life,* contains a good exposition of this problem of anger, how to control it, and how to make use of it also. It is useful in life. No emotion, including anger, is bad by itself, according to psychology. But, one must know how to handle them. And anger has a place in human life. You see some injustice going on around you; it must rouse your indignation, under control. Unless you have anger, you cannot react properly to it. It will multiply only. So, anger can be channelised into socially useful purposes. That we don't do efficiently in India. We have anger but never channelised to fight evil and seek justice in society. That is where one of the biggest part of education for character comes. McDougall calls that 'righteous indignation'. We see so much injustice around us. We just take our eye away from it, and say, we have nothing to do with it. But useless anger we have in plenty—at home, dealing with dependants. That is why we cannot handle this emotion properly. Educate it, let it be for the good of society. So, that anger has tremendous value in our collective life. Without that anger, evils will multiply. In India; particularly, this is our great drawback. We had no urge for righteous indignation. We let things pass. That kind of attitude has only created a society full of injustice. Some improvements are setting in the modern age. So, though anger is to be removed, it cannot be removed just by plucking and throwing it away. It is an automation to be educated in a proper direction.

Every one of our emotions, can be educated and disciplined. We have to take the energy of the emotion and use it for some good purpose. In this way, we give a constructive orientation to these emotions. That is how we build up character. 'Emotion, controlled and directed to work, *is* character', says Vivekananda. Ordinary anger, just out of pride and arrogance, is absolutely a static type of energy. It has no value; we have to overcome it. How to overcome anger is told in all these books; but what the books say is nothing, unless we try to put into practice: 'I must overcome', 'I shall overcome'. Then you will find slowly that you are winning the battle.

In many parts of the world, I have come across this one question being asked again and again: How to overcome anger? Even in the West, sometimes, men and women are angry with children, with neighbours; they want to overcome anger. So, I tell all this. But, I also tell a radical method. 'Whenever you are angry, put a few coins in the charity box'; it may make you give up anger when the box is getting full! A second method is to apologize to the person after the anger cools. Śrī Kṛṣṇa said, *sthitadhīḥ,* 'whose *dhī* or *buddhi* is *sthita,* steady'. *Munirucyate,* 'is called a *muni*'. Every citizen must possess a bit of these qualities. Then only we can form a healthy society. Never think that it is enough if we have some *munis* and *ṛṣis* in the Himalayas, and we shall all remain small like as now. That is a very wrong attitude. Every one of us will grow one inch taller morally by trying this kind of disciplining of our emotional energies. Be a *muni,* be thoughtful; thought is behind all social progress. Great thinkers initiate new ideas. That is how progress comes.

But, even Bertrand Russell says, every child has a natural capacity for thinking. One of the aims of our education today is to clear him of this quality. What an observation: the thinking power goes away in education! Without education, there have been people who were great thinkers. Education as it is now, doesn't give us that thinking power. It stifles thinking, because of the emphasis on study—memorising. But what is needed is to stimulate thinking. That must come in our education, so that we shall have thoughtful people, *munis* in large numbers. Even amongst professors and students in universities, there is now no question of thinking at all. Everything is excitement, frenzy, and frenzied action. That whole system must change if you want to produce men and women worthy of a great society, capable of creating a greater society. So, that is the importance of this verse and the words specially occurring in this verse. Similarly, the next verse says:

यः सर्वत्रानभिस्नेहस्तत्तत्प्राप्य शुभाशुभम् ।
नाभिनन्दति न द्वेष्टि तस्य प्रज्ञा प्रतिष्ठिता ॥५७॥

Yaḥ sarvatrānabhisnehastattatprāpya śubhāśubham;
Nābhinandati na dveṣṭi tasya prajñā pratiṣṭhitā— 2. 57

'One who is everywhere unattached, not pleased at receiving good, nor vexed at evil, his or her wisdom is steady.'

Tasya prajñā pratiṣṭhitā, 'his or her *prajñā* or wisdom is well established'. Whose? *Yaḥ sarvatra anabhisnehaḥ,* 'who is perfectly detached'. *Tat tat prāpya śubhāśubham, na abhinandati na dveṣṭi,* 'who, whenever favourable things happen, is not elated, and, whenever unfavourable things come, is not depressed'. Such a one has that control of mind. That person's *prajñā* is well established. In life you do need a measure of these qualities and we do find also men and women of this type. We are not like any animal reacting exactly to the stimulus you are getting from outside. We have the capacity to study the situation and discriminate before reacting. When we exercise that quality, we get this kind of stability of our *buddhi,* more and more. And so, the next *śloka* presents an example, one of the famous examples in Vedantic literature:

यदा संहरते चायं कूर्मोऽङ्गानीव सर्वशः ।
इन्द्रियाणि इन्द्रियार्थेभ्यः तस्य प्रज्ञा प्रतिष्ठिता ॥५८॥

yadā samharate cāyam kūrmo'ṅgānīva sarvaśaḥ;
Indriyāṇi indriyārthebhyaḥ tasya prajñā pratiṣṭhitā—2. 58

'When also, like the tortoise drawing its limbs, one can completely withdraw the senses from their sense objects, his or her wisdom becomes steady.'

We have studied the tortoise: whenever it senses some trouble outside, it withdraws itself within its shell. And nothing can harm it there: it knows when to withdraw, it knows when to come out also. So, we have to develop this capacity of the tortoise to withdraw into oneself and, later, come out also: *yadā samharate cāyam kūrmo'ṅgānīva sarvaśaḥ,* 'as a tortoise withdraws all its limbs, and protects itself', similarly, *indriyāṇi indriyārthebhyaḥ,* 'we have to develop the capacity to withdraw our sense organs from the sense objects, and come out later.' This capacity, this freedom, when we develop, then we become a *sthitaprajña. Tasya prajñā pratiṣṭhitā,* 'his or her *prajñā,* wisdom, is well established'. How much observation of animal behaviour you will find in our literature! The *Mahābhārata, Rāmāyaṇa,* are full of observations of animal behaviour, and how we can learn lessons from the behaviour of animals. Animal stories are in plenty in our literature; it has gone to various countries from India—these animal stories which inspire all children all over the world, even grown-ups also. Then comes the next verse which is a verse containing a deep psychological study of the human mind.

विषया विनिवर्तन्ते निराहारस्य देहिनः ।
रसवर्जं रसोऽप्यस्य परं दृष्ट्वा निवर्तते ॥५९॥

Viṣayā vinivartante nirāhārasya dehinaḥ;
Rasavarjam raso'pyasya param dṛṣṭvā nivartate— 2. 59

'Sense objects fall away from the abstinent person, leaving the longing behind. But even that longing ceases when one realizes the supreme.'

Every word is full of meaning. We can study the human being from the surface, but that won't account for his or her activities, successes, and failures. If we can go deep into the human system, and find out and discover what forces are acting there, then we can establish a more stable personality. Just like in modern Western history, there was supposed to be an era of enlightenment up to the beginning of this century, based on rationalism of the human mind. Freudianism challenged this assumption. What is that enlightenment? In one second it can be thrown down by the energy coming from the subconscious and the unconscious. That was a great discovery, a type of depth psychology, revolutionary as far as the West was concerned. Freud found it full of sex and violence.

But a true depth study of the human mind was thoroughly undertaken over 4000 years ago by the sages of the Upaniṣads who discovered the shining truth of the ever-free and immortal Atman, the Self behind the subconscious levels and behind also the sense-bound ego or self. The exposition of human life and destiny in the *Gītā* is entirely based on the science of human possibilities of the Upaniṣads. In the *Gītā*, that depth knowledge of the human psyche is taken to the highest and deepest level. *Viṣayā vinivartante nirāhārasya dehinaḥ. Dehī,* 'an embodied human being', says to oneself: 'I shall not eat today', and observes a fast. But, the person is not truly fasting. Craving for food is very strong in the mind. Thus, with respect to every sensory craving, by taking away the sense object from your front doesn't make you a self-controlled person. The person is described as *ṛasavarjam; rasam* is that craving, *rasam*, it is still there. Can you overcome that craving? Then you are wonderful. That is the great statement in the second line. *Param dṛṣṭvā nivartate,* even that craving goes away *'when the supreme Atman is realized'*. When God, who is the Self of all, is realized, even that craving goes away. *Viṣaya* is a technical term in Sanskrit for sense objects, and, *viṣayī* is the term for the subject, the human being. These two are technical terms in Vedanta. When the cravings go, then only you are fully free. Otherwise, craving can create new situations, new kinds of challenges all the time; new temptations can come. But, when the craving itself is gone, absolutely free you become. This is the highest type of mind, where the craving has been completely uprooted, through the knowledge of one's own nature as the infinite Atman.

We have the story in our mythology of God Śiva doing *tapas.* You get it in Poet Kālidāsa's Sanskrit classic in a Himalayan setting, *Kumāra Sambhavam,* where Pārvati is eager to marry Śiva. She comes to Śiva, who was then an ascetic, practising asceticism, and requests Śiva for permission to serve him. For an ascetic to have a young woman to serve is not a good situation, because it will inflame whatever cravings are there. But Śiva was of a different type. He allowed her, yes, you are free to serve me. I have nothing to worry. This subject is put into a beautiful verse by Kālidāsa (1. 58):

Pratyartha bhūtām api tām samādheḥ
suśrūṣamāṇām giriśo anumene;
Vikārahetau sati vikriyante
yeṣām na cetāmsi ta eva dhīrāḥ —

'When Pārvati entreated Śiva for permission to serve him, Śiva knew that this may be an obstacle to his spiritual practices; even though he knew it, he accepted her service'—*giriśo anumene, Giriṣa,* means Śiva, *anumene* means, gave permission. Then comes Kālidāsa's own commentary on it: 'Those persons alone are *dhīras*, i.e., intelligent and heroic', *ta eva dhīrāḥ,* who are not afraid of these conditions, because, *vikārahetau sati vikriyante yeṣām na cetāmsi,* 'their minds are not agitated when agitating circumstances prevail.'

So, this truth: Even the craving goes away when the Atman is realized. Śiva knows his own Śiva-nature, infinite, immortal; as the *Samudra-Manthan* myth tells us, even drinking the poison rising from the churning of the ocean did him no harm at all. And Sri Ramakrishna says in the modern age that every human being has that Śiva nature and, that service of the *jīvas* or human beings is worship of Śiva.

Kālidāsa mentions that Śiva burnt to ashes the Indian cupid, Kāmadeva, after which only the marriage between Śiva and Pārvatị took place, and after Pārvatī herself had undergone severe penances. This Śiva's acceptance of her is presented by the poet in another great verse (5. 86):

Adya-prabhṛtyavanatāṅgi tavāsmi dāsaḥ
krītaḥ tapobhiriti vādini candramaulau;
Arhāya sa niyamajam klamam utsasarja
kleśaḥ phalena hi punaḥ navatām vidhatte —

Śiva said: 'From now onwards, O blameless one, I am your slave; you have purchased me through your austerity. When Śiva, who has, on his head, the crescent moon, said this, she overcame all stress and strain caused by the rules of austerity; all strain and pain become recreated anew when they yield their fruits.'

Because of this spiritual greatness of both, Kālidāsa had said, at the beginning of his book, 'Śiva and Pārvatī, I salute as the parents of the universe'—*Jagataḥ pitarau vande pārvati-parameśvarau*. What a wonderful pedigree humanity has when the myth says it has such people as parents! This truth is referred to by ancient Vedanta and Sri Ramakrishna in the modern age as the union of, or absolute identity of, Brahman and Śakti; as Śiva and Pārvatī; as God, the Impersonal, and God, the Personal.

Now, this *Gītā śloka,* therefore, is a challenge to everyone:

Viṣayā vinivartante nirāhārasya dehinaḥ;
Rasavarjam rasopyasya param dṛṣṭvā nivartate —

'When the Supreme is realized, even the *rasa* or secret craving of the embodied being, goes away.' Nothing can tempt such a person; he or she is a *dhīraḥ*. That is the language of Vedanta. Then, when we struggle like this, we have to be careful about our sensory system. They are very powerful. That is the theme of the next verse.

यततो ह्यपि कौन्तेय पुरुषस्य विपश्चितः ।
इन्द्रियाणि प्रमाथीनि हरन्ति प्रसभं मनः ॥६०॥

Yatato hyapi kaunteya puruṣasya vipaścitaḥ;
Indriyāṇi pramāthīni haranti prasabham manaḥ— 2. 60

'The turbulent senses, O son of Kuntī, do violently snatch away the mind of even a wise man who is striving after perfection.'

These are all truths which every human being, boy or girl, should know, if character-development is the goal of education. What is the constitution of the human system?

What are their characteristics? We should know them, then we can fare better. Ignorance is no fun. In this whole physical system, this sensory system of the human being is very powerful. Every action comes because of its impulse. So, let us know the nature of that sensory system. *Yatato hyapi kaunteya,* 'even though one is struggling to discipline the sensory system', *puruṣasya vipaścitaḥ,* 'even of a very intelligent wise person', even such a person finds that 'the sense organs are dragging him or her'. *Indriyāṇi pramāthīni haranti prasabham manaḥ,* 'the powerful sense organs drag away the mind of even a wise man.' That is the nature of the sensory energy.

In all our books of the science of spirituality, you will find this subject being expounded. This emphasis on sense restraint has no meaning if the human being's personality ends with the body, sense organs, and the mind. This is the position of all materialistic philosophy now current in modern Western culture. But this becomes irrelevant when the depth study of the human being, as done by Vedanta, reveals a luminous and free reality of the Atman in every human being. In the *Manu Smṛti,* there is this beautiful observation. *Balavān indriyagrāmo,* 'the entire sensory system is very powerful'. *Vidvāmsamapi karṣati,* 'they carry away even a *vidvān* or a learned person'. That is the warning given. Vedanta proclaims that humanity's inner journey takes one to something real and profound; therefore, we need this control and discipline of sensory energy. In any character formation, a measure of discipline of sensory energy is essential; otherwise, there is no character formation at all. This attraction of the senses for the sense objects, implanted in us even from the animal stage onwards, is the world of *Māyā* in which we all live. We have to reckon with that *Māyā*. So, in the *Devī Māhātmyam* (1. 55), one of the mystical books dealing with God as Mother, you find this utterance:

Jñāninām api cetāmsi devī bhagavatī hi sā;
Balādākṛṣya mohāya mahāmāyā prayacchati —

Mahāmāyā, that supreme *Māyā,* which is described by Ādi Śaṅkarācārya in his *Vivekacūḍāmaṇi* (verse 109) as *Mahādbhutā anirvacanīyarūpā,* 'as a great wonder and indeterminable'. It is the echo of this what you get in modern quantum physics as Heisenberg's principle of uncertainty when consciousness is added to it. It is that which drags away even the minds of the *jñānis,* knowledgeable persons. That *Māyā* is the same as the primordial Divine Mother, *Ādyā-śakti,* who exercises, as explained by Sri Ramakrishna, two types of *māyāśakti*—one, *avidyā Śakti,* dragging down power, another, *vidyā Śakti,* power which lifts up. We sometimes hear of very highly developed people committing big blunders, because at that moment they came under the power of the *avidyā śakti* of *Māyā.* Very often you find this happening in society. So, the language is 'beware!' Awakening is necessary, alertness of mind is necessary.

We are dealing with so many forces within us, those forces can consume us; let us control them, discipline them, then continue our journey to the highest level of perfection. You keep the mind in a good situation, the senses will carry it to a bad situation. *Indriyas* have that power. So, reckon with it. The *ślokas* coming later, 64 and 67, are going to tell us what we should do then. Shall we remain helpless? No! You can have all your senses working among the sense objects, no need to fear, provided you are a *master,* provided you develop that discipline of these psychic energies within you. If you don't do so, your life will suffer shipwreck in this world. Two great verses are coming immediately after. We are not asked to leave aside our sensory system or the sense objects, but learn how to handle them. Let it not be that you were trying to catch a sensory object, but the sensory object caught you by the neck. That should not be. You should be the master. There is a saying in Hindi, *kambal choḍtā nahī.* Somebody saw in the flood water a blanket-like thing floating. He thought it was a good blanket. He started towards it to obtain it. The people on the bank were waiting; he is not coming back. They said, leave it! No, it doesn't leave me! Come away! I cannot come! Because it was a bear and it had caught hold of him! So, *kambal choḍtā nahī.* 'That *kambal* does not leave me!' That is the story.

That is all what Vedanta teaches humanity to achieve as the goal of human evolution—spiritual freedom. Vivekananda says again and again: 'Work like a master, and not like a slave.' If horses draw your carriage to wherever the horses want it to go, you become a helpless victim. You are the rider, but you are not free; don't be so. Therefore, the next *śloka*, 61, says:

तानि सर्वाणि संयम्य युक्त आसीत मत्परः ।
वशे हि यस्येन्द्रियाणि तस्य प्रज्ञा प्रतिष्ठिता ॥६१॥

Tāni sarvāṇi saṃyamya yukta āsīta matparaḥ;
Vaśe hi yasyendriyāṇi tasya prajñā pratiṣṭhitā— 2. 61

'The steadfast, having controlled them all, sits focussed on Me as the Supreme; his or her wisdom is steady, whose senses are under control.'

Therefore, *tāni sarvāṇi saṃyamya,* 'discipline all these sensory energies within you'. Don't leave out even one. If there is one out, that is enough to destroy you. *Saṃyama* means 'disciplining, controlling'. They will remain; we don't destroy them. We want a very strong sensory system. But they must be under control. Just like in a journey, you want a powerful set of horses. Then only you can reach your destination. But, they must be under your control. Otherwise, it will be the *horse's* journey, *not yours*! That should not be. So, the verse says, *yukta āsīta matparaḥ*, 'devoted to *Me*', remain in this life controlling the psychic and sensory energies'. *Vaśe hi yasyendriyāṇi,* 'in whose control is the sensory system' and the energies residing there, *tasya prajñā pratiṣṭhitā,* 'his or her wisdom is steady'. What makes for unsteadiness of the mind and the *buddhi,* namely the sensory system, is already overcome. We have to discipline them; that is the beginning of all character training. When children do something wrong, mothers will say, 'don't do that'. Why do they tell these do's and don'ts in the beginning? Because, a certain training is needed of the sensory impulses, when we are young. Till we are able to control them, our parents will help us, must help us. As we grow up, we take up the matter ourselves. We know what to do, what not to do, how far to go; that kind of training we try to give to ourselves. Such a mind which has the power to discipline the enormously powerful sensory system, that mind is certainly going to be very steady.

We start from the sensory system. In fact, take any stone, there is no sensory system there. Only in a living being, there is the sensory system. From the cell onwards up to man, there is this sensory system in simple and complex forms. That sensory system up to the chimpanzee level is controlled by the external world or by the sensory objects. At the human level alone we find a little capacity to say, 'no' to a sensory impulse. That 'no' must be well developed, strong and steady. What is worth while, I shall pursue, not others. That energy comes only from the spiritual dimension. That is the training that makes for high character and spiritual development. And so, this idea, *vaśe hi yasyendriyāṇi,* 'in whose control are the senses', *tasya prajñā pratiṣṭhitā,* 'his or her wisdom is well established'. This human body is a dead body. What makes it alive? The sensory energy; that energy makes the body a centre of immense powers; and I have to handle them myself. Nobody else can handle them for me; if I don't handle them, they will handle me. And we become failures in life. That truth the *Gītā* is going to say in verses 64 and 67—two wonderful verses. So, here in verse 61, He says, this is how we have to deal with the sensory system. If we don't know how to deal with it, there is every chance of our falling down and down, and becoming completely lost. And it doesn't happen quickly. Step by step, slowly, we slide down. This sliding down is an interesting experience in human life. If you keep a car on a slightly inclined road, that car will start moving down gently if you have not applied the brake; later on, it accelerates and develops high speed and gets destroyed. Similarly, in the human system, there is this tendency to go downwards. The *Gītā* is going to handle that subject in the next two verses; they are very famous verses.

ध्यायतो विषयान्पुंसः सङ्गस्तेषूपजायते ।
सङ्गात् संजायते कामः कामात्क्रोधोऽभिजायते ॥६२॥

Dhyāyato viṣayānpumsaḥ saṅgasteṣūpajāyate;
Saṅgāt samjāyate kāmaḥ kāmāt krodho'bhijāyate— 2. 62

'Thinking of sense objects, attachment to them is formed (in a human being); from attachment rises desire to possess; and from longing, anger emerges.'

क्रोधाद्भवति संमोहः संमोहात्स्मृतिविभ्रमः ।
स्मृतिभ्रंशात् बुद्धिनाशो बुद्धिनाशात्प्रणश्यति ॥६३॥

Krodhāt bhavati sammohaḥ sammohātsmṛtivibhramaḥ;
Smṛtibhramśāt buddhināśo buddhināśātpraṇaśyati—2. 63

'From anger comes delusion, and from delusion loss of memory. From loss of memory comes the ruin of discriminative power, and from the ruin of discrimination, the person perishes.'

How do we fall down in life? Suppose you visit a prison; you find a young person there who has been arrested and put into the prison. What had the person done? He or she stole something from a shop; that is all. Now study how the person developed this tendency to steal, how he or she finally landed up in the jail. You will find these verses giving the answer. *Dhyāyato viṣayān pumsaḥ.* 'When you go on thinking, over and over again, about the sensory objects' and finding them very attractive, then what happens? *Saṅgasteṣu upajāyate,* 'mind develops an attachment for them'. 'I like it.' First, I am only seeing it. Then, I have already got glued to it, attached to it. Then what happens? *Saṅgāt samjāyate kāmaḥ,* 'I *must* possess it,' that 'desire begins to come through that attachment'. So, first observing a thing, dwelling on it for long, then *drawn* by it, then the desire to *possess* it. And if people obstruct it, *kāmāt krodho'bhijāyate;* 'anger will come from desire', if anybody obstructs my getting it. Then what happens? *Krodhāt bhavati sammohaḥ,* when *krodha,* or anger, comes, *sammoha,* delusion comes. You forget your surroundings, forget your own individuality, your family background, everything is forgotten in that state. That is why, in psychology it is said, an angry man or woman is mad at the time of his or her anger. Temporary madness is called anger. You lose all bearing at that time. Then what happens? *Krodhāt bhavati sammohaḥ,* 'from that anger you develop delusion', *sammohaḥ.* You have no clear thinking after that. Everything is confused. That is the nature of the mind at that time. Can't see what is what. Then, *sammohāt smṛti vibhramaḥ,* 'through that *sammoha,* you lose your memory', 'who are you?, what are you?', 'what is your background?'. That you are coming from a good family; all that is forgotten. And so, you are now ready to do the evil act at that time. All weakening has taken place; just like when the body is weakened by various diseases, then it can invite all the toxins from outside. It invites them and the body becomes full of evil. Similarly also, the mind. So, this way we finally go down. *Krodhāt bhavati sammohaḥ, sammohāt smṛtivibhramaḥ, smṛtibhramśāt buddhināśo,* when the *smṛti* goes away, memory of our environment, our identity, etc., etc., then *buddhināśa,* 'that discriminative faculty, that reason, which alone can tell you what to do and what not to do, completely goes away'; then what happens? *Buddhināśāt praṇaśyati,* 'you just perish from *buddhināśa*'. Thus, step by step, we go down.

We must know this nature of the mind; then we can fight against it and build up a more healthy and stable personality. So, these two verses tell how even good people do evil things, and suffer various maladies thereafter. In the newspapers I often used to read, while travelling abroad, of thefts in super-bazars. In many countries—in India also we started them now—you can just go in, pick up something, bring it to the counter, pay for it, and go away. Some people also steal in super-bazars. In America, friends told me that about ten percent of things are stolen, but it being more costly to protect this ten percent, they decided to overlook this ten percent loss. Now somebody enters, a decent person, sometimes a diplomat's relative, who finds something very attractive, and quietly puts it in his or her bag. Sometimes they are caught. And then you can imagine the sorrow for the loss of all that high status. All such situations are revealed by these few *ślokas.* It is good to know these evil possibilities so that we take adequate precaution, strengthen our discriminative faculty, and never allow it to be eroded by the energy coming from the sensory system. The sensory system should be controlled by the *buddhi; buddhi* should not be controlled by the sensory system. A charioteer should not be controlled by the horses; horses must be controlled by the charioteer. That is the language of the Upaniṣads and the *Gītā*. And so, after these two verses, you get that verse which I referred to, verse 64. It says:

रागद्वेषवियुक्तैस्तु विषयान् इन्द्रियैश्चरन् ।
आत्मवश्यैः विधेयात्मा प्रसादमधिगच्छति ॥६४॥

Rāgadveṣaviyuktaistu viṣayān indriyaiścaran;
Ātmavaśyaiḥ vidheyātmā prasādam adhigacchati— 2. 64

'But the self-controlled person, moving among sense objects with the senses under one's restraint, and free from attraction and aversion, attains to tranquillity.'

The *Gītā* does not want us to leave the sensory world and go to lead an ascetic life in some corner; not at all. Live in the world, live in the midst of sensory objects. There is no harm, but do something to strengthen yourself against the energies that have the tendency to pull you down. So, *rāgadveṣa viyuktaistu,* 'when you give up *rāga* and *dveṣa,* attachment and aversion', *viṣayān indriyaiḥ caran,* 'with your sensory system moving freely among sensory objects'. *Caran* means moving about freely. But, *ātmavaśyaiḥ,* 'by one who is self-possessed'; *vidheyātmā,* 'a person who has achieved self-mastery', such a person, *prasādam adhigacchati,* 'attains real peace, tranquillity, serenity'. The calm, joyous, free state of mind is called *prasāda.* 'Such a person attains to tranquillity,' *Prasādam adhigacchati.* When you get *prasāda* of the mind, what happens to you? Today we speak of quality of life. That qualitative enrichment of life comes to you at that stage. The next *śloka* refers to it:

प्रसादे सर्वदुःखानां हानिरस्योपजायते ।
प्रसन्नचेतसो ह्याशु बुद्धिः पर्यवतिष्ठते ॥६५॥

Prasāde sarvaduḥkhānām hānirasyopajāyate;
Prasannacetaso hyāśu buddhiḥ paryavatiṣṭhate— 2. 65

'In tranquillity, all sorrows are destroyed. For, the intellect of one who is tranquil-minded is soon established in firmness.'

When *prasāda* or tranquillity comes, 'all sorrows are destroyed', *sarvaduḥkhānām hāni.* I have seen even in ordinary people this steady *buddhi* in the presence of temptation. In the Ramakrishna Mission Institute of Culture in Calcutta, when I was Secretary there in the 1960s, a person living in our International House lost a purse of ten thousand rupees, or rather left it in the room along with his air ticket and passport, and went away to Delhi. Going there, he found everything gone. Then he phoned to me at Calcutta. What happened? The worker who looks after the room found all this lying there—a purse of ten thousand rupees and the tickets. See the greatness of that employee who was getting a small salary of about Rs. 700 a month; yet he quietly brought these to the office, 'this person has suffered, he has left it, and you must restore it to him'. He could have easily taken that money; he also was in need; but, no! He had another way of looking at things. Such a way of looking at things is getting less and less. What is the cause? The sensory system is very very powerful, and the controlling *buddhi* is weak. The capacity to feel and respond to another person's problem as one's own is a spiritual capacity. That capacity can come to all people. But sometimes the high in society may not have it. In India, we have now two types of poor people—the poor and the poverty-stricken, namely, the rich. The latter have much but they always want and seek more and more through corrupt practices; they cannot manifest this *buddhi,* which is a spiritual quality and doesn't depend upon social status. Any human being can achieve this quality. So, *prasanna cetaso hyāśu buddhiḥ paryavatiṣṭhate,* 'the buddhi of a person with tranquil mind soon becomes steady'. This is the important statement in this section; verses 64, 65 go together. When we now go to verse 67, we will find the opposite of it. When this quality of *ātmavaśyaiḥ vidheyātmā* is not there, people collapse morally. In these matters each one must help oneself. These are all human achievements. Instead of striving for going to an unknown heaven in the sky, why not be a decent human being here on earth and realize the infinite Atman hidden within you?

Don't be a creature; be free; is the supreme message of Vedanta to all humanity. In several verses this is stressed again and again. This discipline at the sensory level is what makes for *yoga;* remaining at the stage of sense pleasure makes for *bhoga.* We all begin with *bhoga,* but Vedanta and the science of human possibilities tells us not to continue at the *bhoga* level all the time. It tells humanity to rise slowly to the *yoga* level. Sri Ramakrishna puts the subject in a beautiful way; if you don't rise from *bhoga* to *yoga,* you will be in *roga,* i.e., all sorts of mental and nervous ailments, and social tensions will come to you. He also speaks of three levels of *ānanda* or bliss available to all; *viṣayṣananda,* sensual joy, *bhajanānanda,* joy arising from singing hymns and *bhajans,* and *brahmānanda,* joy arising from realising our infinite and immortal nature as Brahman. So, march on; don't stay at the sensory level. The child lives entirely at the sensory level. But as it grows older, it can get intimations of something higher. 'Let me go towards that'. That means a little discipline of the sensory system. Even to become a law-abiding citizen, you need a little control of the sensory system. Even to be a member of a healthy society, you need a little control over the sensory system. This is what is insisted upon by the *Gītā,* not as an end in itself. In the very first *śloka* in this section, when Śrī Kṛṣṇa started expounding the nature of the *sthitaprajña,* he said that it is not that you drive away all sensory attractions, and make the mind empty. That doesn't make a man a *sthitaprajña.* Mind must also be yoked to the Atman that is within. Realize your own infinite nature, beyond the sensory level. Then, he or she is a *sthitaprajña.* A mere negative ascetic attitude is never respected nor presented in Vedanta literature. It must be something which gives you joy. If the sensory system gives you joy, what lies above the sensory system will give you a million times more joy. That is the language used in the Upaniṣads. In the *Taittirīya Upaniṣad,* while discussing the subject of enquiry into the nature of Bliss, it is said that joys of men on earth, gods in heaven, and every other type of joy are only a fraction of the joy of the Atman, the infinite nature of one and all. And therefore, these two verses give us the freedom to live in this world, to work in this world, and to enjoy bliss in this world at various levels. The *Gītā* stresses that point. The next verse, 66, tells us:

नास्ति बुद्धिरयुक्तस्य न चायुक्तस्य भावना ।
न चाभावयतः शान्तिः अशान्तस्य कुतः सुखम् ॥६६॥

Nāsti buddhirayuktasya na cāyuktasya bhāvanā;
Na cābhāvayataḥ śāntiḥ aśāntasya kutaḥ sukham—2. 66

'No knowledge (of the Self) has the unsteady. Nor has he or she meditation; to the unmeditative there is no peace, and how can one without peace have happiness?'

Step by step. What a profound depth psychology you get here! It is not some dogma or theory which you may just believe and go away; examine for yourself, is it true? Study your own mind, your own reactions. So, the verse says, *nāsti buddhirayuktasya*, 'to the *ayukta*, there is no *buddhi*'. That *buddhi* by which we have to achieve a stable life and realize the true freedom within ourselves, that *buddhi* cannot come without this *yukti*, 'discipline at the sensory level'. The *buddhi* yoked to the Atman, the *buddhi* that can get pulsations of the Atman itself, 'that *buddhi* cannot come without this prior self-discipline at the sensory level'. That is the first statement; *nacāyuktasya bhāvanā*, 'without this sensory discipline, no meditation is possible'. *Bhāvanā* is a word for 'meditation'. It also means spiritual imagination—imagination which is able to catch the radiations from the spiritual dimension of the human personality. That is a wonderful quality—the capacity for imagination. Here it means that type of meditation by which we are able to stabilize our system and get a glimpse of something beyond the sensory level. *Na cābhāvayataḥ śāntiḥ*, 'without that meditative mind there can be no *śānti*, or peace of mind'. Today, we deal with tension and stress in our daily life, in our highly industrialized civilization. And everybody is eager to get rid of this tension because, with that stress and tension, you won't enjoy life or even your work. You are a mere creature of the environment in which you are working. Therefore, that meditative state, where you are perfectly at peace with yourself, that state cannot come without this kind of disciplining of the sensory energy system below. And lastly, *aśāntasya kutaḥ sukham?* What a beautiful expression! 'Without that *śānti,* where is happiness?' Mind is constantly in a disturbed condition. Then where is happiness? Happiness is a wonderful state. You are serene, you are calm, you are fulfilled, then only happiness comes. Therefore, if happiness is the objective, you have to handle this mind; to handle the mind, you have to handle the sensory system which is below the mind; then a disciplined inner life sets in.

An agnostic thinker like Bertrand Russell, in the last chapter of his book on *The Conquest of Happiness,* says that you can get happiness when you have three integrations achieved in your life: 'integration between you and society; integration with the nature outside; integration within your own mind'. *Ātmavaśyaiḥ vidheyātmā,* 'if you are perfectly self-restrained with tremendous discipline within', you can freely move about the sense objects. Otherwise, it will be a tragedy of human life which the next verse, verse 67, expounds. You can study all the various tragedies in literature, from the Greek tragedies to our own *Mahābhārata,* in which you see tragedy from beginning to end. So also in Shakespeare and Goethe. We see tragedy everywhere around us. Now, this tragedy of human life is put into one verse here. Why does this tragedy take place? Some discipline is lacking in the human being or beings concerned. That is put in a beautiful language.

इन्द्रियाणां हि चरतां यन्मनोऽनुविधीयते ।
तदस्य हरति प्रज्ञां वायुर्नावमिवाम्भसि ॥६७॥

Indriyāṇām hi caratām yanmano'nuvidhīyate;
Tadasya harati prajñām vāyurnāvamivāmbhasi— 2. 67

'For, the mind, which follows in the wake of the wandering senses, carries away his or her discrimination, as a wind (carries away from its course) a ship on the waters.'

The sense organs are being carried away by the sense objects. And 'the mind also follows in the wake of the sensory system towards the sensory objects', *indriyāṇām hi caratām yanmano-anuvidhīyate;* when the mind does like that, what happens to the human being? *Tadasya harati prajñām,* 'that destroys whatever little wisdom one has in one's life'. And what is the example? *Vāyurnāvam iva ambhasi,* 'like a ship being carried away by wind in the sea'. That is tragedy, and all types of tragedy have this common characteristic of losing control and being overwhelmed by forces around you. Tragedy is beautiful when depicted on the stage; it is dangerous if depicted in one's own life. What you see as tragedy must purge you of the evil so that you become free from tragic situations; they call this the cathartic theory of tragedy. You see a tragedy, you develop a catharsis—catharsis is the word for purgative. A mental purgative you get, by seeing a tragedy. Then, it is hoped that you don't commit that tragedy again. But, unfortunately, people see a tragedy, and re-enact it in one's own life. That is the bigger tragedy. That tragedy should not be.

In many of world's literature, this human tragedy, which takes place everywhere, every day, has been depicted, and one author has depicted it very beautifully. That is the German dramatist and poet, Goethe, in his book *The Faust*. Faust is the main character in that book. In chapter 14 or so, there is a section called 'Faust's soliloquy in the woods'. Sitting in the forest, he is speaking to himself in a calm quiet way. What has happened to me, he is thinking. Then comes this famous passage:

'Oh, for the broken state of man: I know
Our unfulfilment now! Thou gavest bliss
Which brings me near and nearer to the gods,
And gavest, too, the dark companion whom
I cannot rid me of, though with his scorn
He breaks my pride, and in a single word,
A breath, turns all thy gifts and makes them nothing.
He builds a wildfire in my heart, a blase,
Till from desire I stumble to possession,
And in possession languish from desire.'

That is called the tragedy of human life. 'From desire I stumble to possession, and in possession languish from desire.' This is the broken state of man. Can any philosophy help me not to get into this tragic situation? That is the philosophy that the *Gītā* presents, not to a sect or creed or nation, but to humanity at large. The totality of life must prove to be a success. That needs the guidance from a scientific philosophy of life. Two pictures we must keep before ourselves: do I want my life to be destroyed? Do I want to suffer shipwreck in life? Or, do I want to ride high this life with joy and peace? That is my question to myself, and I must find the answer. This is how the *Gītā* initiates that struggle for a higher life in every individual, giving hints and suggestions how we can be successful, but asking the person to do it oneself. Nobody else can do it for you; there is no proxy that can do it for you. In the *Vivekacūḍāmaṇi*, verse 51, Śaṅkarācārya particularly mentions it. He says:

> *Ṛṇamocana kartāraḥ pituḥ santi sutādayaḥ;*
> *Bandha mocana kartā tu svasmādanyo na kaścana* —

'If a father has debts, a son or others can clear them on his behalf; but, if the father is in bondage, none other than oneself can remove that bondage.' Another verse (52) says: 'if there is a heavy load on my head, *mastaka-nyasta bhāra,* somebody can come and remove it from my head and release me.' *Kṣudhādhikṛta duḥkham tu vinā svena na kenacit,* 'but if one is hungry, one must eat for oneself and not someone else.' Therefore,

> *Vastu svarūpam sphuṭabodha cakṣuṣā*
> *svenaiva vedyam na tu paṇḍitena;*
> *Candra svarūpam nija cakṣuṣāiva*
> *jṇātavyam anyair avagamyate kim*—

What a wonderful verse!

'The nature of truth', *vastu-svarūpam, vastu* is a very rich technical word in Vedanta. Any existing thing is called *vastu.* That table, it is a *vastu,* similarly, the Atman is a *vastu.* Brahman is *vastu;*

they are all existing realities. One is sensory, the other is supersensory. How do you know *vastu-svarūpam*? *Sphuṭabodha cakṣuṣā svenaiva vedyam*, 'you must realize it for yourself by developing the clear eye of reason'. *Bodha-cakṣu*, 'the eye of understanding, the eye of reason'; *sphuṭa* means clear; *svenaiva vedyam*, 'must be known by oneself'; *na tu paṇḍitena*, 'but not by a scholar on your behalf'. Then comes the example: *Candra svarūpam nija cakṣuṣaiva jṇātavyam anyairavagamyate kim?*, 'the beautiful form of the full-moon, you must see with your own eyes; how can somebody else see it on your behalf?' This is the constant stress in Vedanta. Developing awareness in ourselves, higher and higher. That is the way of spiritual development and fulfilment. The *Gītā* is the science and technique of that human development: from creatureliness to freedom, from creatureliness to blessedness. And then, therefore, the next *śloka*, 68, says:

तस्माद्यस्य महाबाहो निगृहीतानि सर्वशः ।
इन्द्रियाणीन्द्रियार्थेभ्यः तस्य प्रज्ञा प्रतिष्ठिता ॥६८॥

Tasmādyasya mahābāho nigṛhītāni sarvaśaḥ;
Indriyāṇīndriyārthebhyaḥ tasya prajñā pratiṣṭhitā—2. 68

'Therefore, O mighty-armed, his or her knowledge is steady, whose senses are completely restrained from their objects.'

Tasmāt, 'therefore,' if this is true, what follows? *Yasya indiryāṇi indriyārthebhyaḥ nigṛhitāni sarvaśaḥ*, 'whose sense organs have been brought perfectly under control from all sides'. To be a citizen of a free country, you need a measure of self-discipline; without that, there cannot be citizenship at all. And ethical values, all higher values, come from this discipline of the sensory energy system. The sense organs and the sense objects have an affinity for each other. But I am here to see that they don't do what *they* want to do. I want them to do what *I* want them to do. That truth will be presented again in the third chapter in a little more detail. *Tasya prajñā pratiṣṭhitā*, 'that person's *prajñā*, wisdom, is steady'. Having said this, the *Gītā* gives you a remarkable idea which you find in many of Tao's teachings in China. Says verse 69:

या निशा सर्वभूतानां तस्यां जागर्ति संयमी ।
यस्यां जाग्रति भूतानि सा निशा पश्यतो मुनेः ॥६९॥

Yā niśā sarvabhūtānām tasyām jāgarti samyami;
Yasyām jāgrati bhūtāni sā niśā paśyato muneḥ—2. 69

'That which is night to all beings, in that the self-controlled wakes. That in which all beings are awake, is night to the Self-seeing *muni*.'

The word *niśā* means in Sanskrit 'sleep', or 'night'. Then *jāgarti,* means 'awake'. So, this *śloka* presents an interesting paradox: *Yā niśā sarvabhūtānām,* 'that aspect of reality which is treated as darkness by all beings', the *yogī* perceives intense light there, and *yasyām jāgrati bhūtāni sā niśā paśyato muneḥ,* 'that aspect of reality where people see plenty of light, the *yogī* sees only darkness there'. This is the comparison between the two. What is *niśā* to one, is not *niśā* to the other; it is *jāgrat* to the other. The reverse also is true. The *yogī* realizes the Atman and does not run after wealth and pleasure and power. However, the worldly person finds no interest in higher things; rather he or she feels happy when one goes and says, 'I will run after money driven by greed, and even cheat people, use violence'. The *yogī* sees nothing but darkness there.

A child plays with toys; it is its intense pleasure. But the parents are not interested in the toys. They have got other 'toys' to play with. When we play as children, we are so absorbed in the play; that is our everything at the time; I remember, as a boy, when we played football, even when night had fallen and we could not see the ball, still every one of us continued the play; it was the most important thing for our life at that stage. This is the nature of human life; we go from one pleasure to another pleasure, and to still higher pleasures. So, Vedanta says that there are various dimensions of joy; we have to seek them one after the other; don't get stuck up at any particular level. No level is condemned; every level has its own value. But, march on, march on, march on; that is the supreme word of Vedanta. *Caraiveti, caraiveti,* 'march on', says the *Yajur-Veda;* don't stagnate at one particular level.

Whenever civilizations stagnate at the sensory level, they decay and die away. Sri Ramakrishna said in a beautiful parable, *egiye jāo, egiye jāo.* In Bengali *egiye jāo* means *āge baḍo* in Hindi, march onward. A woodcutter used to cut wood going to a forest, a small quantity, and sell it in the market, and make his living; he went on thus for a long time; one day a holy man passed that way. He saw the woodcutter doing this. He simply told the woodcutter, 'march on, *egiye jāo*'. At first the woodcutter didn't take it seriously. But, one day the thought came, I am just cutting wood here. That holy man told me to go onward. Why not try it? He went a little deeper into the forest; he got more high quality wood there, and got more money; then he said, why should I stop here? Why not go still deeper? Then he came across a copper mine, then a gold mine, and finally a diamond mine; he became immensely rich. That is Sri Ramakrishna's parable of *egiye jāo*. So, spiritual life also is like this. *Egiye jāo, egiye jāo,* greater experiences are waiting for you; there is a spiritual maturity waiting for all people. Then comes a tremendous statement. What is the nature of that mind, that is undisturbed, that cannot be shaken by all these various pressures going on around? The only way the *Gītā* would express it is through a remarkable illustration given in the next verse:

आपूर्यमाणमचलप्रतिष्ठं
समुद्रमापः प्रविशन्ति यद्वत् ।
तद्वत्कामा यं प्रविशन्ति सर्वे
स शान्तिमाप्नोति न कामकामी ॥७०॥

Āpūryamāṇamacalapratiṣṭham
samudramāpaḥ praviśanti yadvat;
Tadvatkāmā yam praviśanti sarve
sa śāntimāpnoti na kāmakāmī — 2. 70

'As into the ocean, brimful and still, flow the (flood) waters (of various rivers without agitating the ocean), even so is the *muni* into whom enter all desires; he or she attains to peace, and not the desirer of desires.'

A person who runs after various desires and sensory cravings, that is one type; another person is one into whom so many cravings are going, but they do not make any disturbance inside, which is absolutely calm and steady. One's desires, others' desires, all enter into that person creating no agitation at all. What is the nature of that mind? It is like a big ocean, *āpūryamāṇam acalapratiṣṭham samudram; samudra,* 'the ocean'; *āpūryamāṇam,* 'full to the brim'; and *acalapratiṣṭham,* 'unshaken like a mountain'; *āpaḥ praviśanti,* 'enter waters'; *tadvat,* 'similarly'; *kāmā yam praviśanti sarve,* 'into whom enter all desires (without agitating the person)'; *sa śāntim āpnoti,* 'he or she attains peace'; *na kāmakāmī,* 'and not the desirer of desires'. In the Buddhist language they say, *bodhicittam,* the *cittam,* or mind, of a Buddha. *Bodhicitta* is a wonderful *citta.* Anything and everything can enter there without disturbing the peace of that *citta* or mind. So, this *śloka* refers to that human being who has established tremendous strength and stability within oneself, and all these various attractions around do not make any difference to him or her; the person is absolutely calm and steady, 'not agitated, like an immense lake', *mahāhṛdavat akṣo'bhyamānaḥ,* as expressed by Śaṅkarācārya in his *Kaṭha Upaniṣad* commentary. So, this particular *śloka* refers to that fullness one has achieved. And so,

विहाय कामान्यः सर्वान्पुमांश्चरति निःस्पृहः ।
निर्ममो निरहंकारः स शान्तिमधिगच्छति ॥७१॥

Vihāya kāmānyaḥ sarvānpumāṃścarati nispṛhaḥ;
Nirmamo nirahamkāraḥ sa śāntimadhigacchati— 2. 71

'That person who lives devoid of sensual longing, free from all desires, without the sense of "I" and "*mine*", he or she attains peace.'

'I' and 'mine' makes for that craving. If I feel my oneness with you, my craving to that extent becomes less. I then want to satisfy your craving. That is why in a healthy society, we will have a disciplined type of mind. I don't want to get everything at the cost of others. I will work for others also. There, morality comes, ethics comes. *Sa śāntim adhigacchati,* 'he or she attains peace'. In the other case, nothing but greed remains.

Earlier I had referred to the story of *Śrīmad Bhāgavatam* (11. 7. 29), where King Yadu comes across a young wandering ascetic, calm and self-possessed; the king puts a question to that ascetic, how he, in the fullness of youth, could attain this inner peace, 'when others are burnt by various desires', *janeṣu dagdhamāneṣu*. It shows that this is not a theory or dogma but a fact of experience.

Now, comes the last *śloka*, 72, of this chapter of the *Gītā*. That *śloka* proclaims the goal of human evolution attainable in this world, in this very human body:

एषा ब्राह्मी स्थितिः पार्थ नैनां प्राप्य विमुह्यति ।
स्थित्वाऽस्यामन्तकालेऽपि ब्रह्मनिर्वाणमृच्छति ॥७२॥

Eṣā brāhmī sthitiḥ pārtha naināṃ prāpya vimuhyati;
Sthitvā'syāmantakāle'pi brahmanirvāṇamṛcchati—2. 72

'This (*sthitaprajña* state) is having one's being in Brahman, *brāhmī sthitiḥ*, none, O son of Pṛthā, attaining to this, becomes deluded. Being established therein, even at the end of one's life, one attains to oneness with Brahman.'

Eṣā, 'this', showing with the hand, *brāhmīsthitiḥ pārtha*, 'Arjuna, this is called *brāhmī sthitiḥ*, getting established in Brahman', the ultimate and the intimate reality; *naināṃ prāpya vimuhyati*, 'once you achieve this, never again can delusion overpower you'. *Sthitvā asyām antakāle api brahmanirvāṇam ṛcchati*, 'if you achieve this even at the end of your life, even then you achieve *brahmanirvāṇam, nirvāṇa* in Brahman, becoming one with Brahman', in this very earth and not in any heaven; if one couldn't achieve this when young, one can achieve it in old age before the fall of the body by slowly developing enough spiritual strength. *Sthitvā'syāmantakāle'pi*, 'even attaining this just before death', *brahmanirvāṇamṛcchati*, 'you will achieve oneness with Brahman'.

Śaṅkarācārya's comment upon this is very inspiring: 'if you achieve it just before death, it is wonderful; but how much more wonderful will it be if you had got it earlier, as a youth and lived under its inspiration!'

That is the message which the second chapter gives to every one of us. It is a rational message, a practical message, a universal message. We can, all of us, have this attitude developed within ourselves, and this achievement we can have in this very life. That is the teaching of the *Gītā*.

We have completed the second chapter today. We shall next enter the third chapter known as *Karma Yoga*. This chapter expounds some doubts and their clearance; and such doubts are Arjuna's as well as yours and mine. Chapters two and three constitute the exposition of the philosophy and practical spirituality of *yoga*, and the fourth chapter will tell us that this *yoga* expounds the spirituality of the whole of life, not just life during your prayer times. 'You are spiritual' means, you are aware of your spiritual nature in the context of your life and work. In society, most people are householders, who have jobs to do, social responsibilities to bear, and children to look after; they can't be lying on a couch or somewhere in some mystical trance experience; they will be spiritual in the very context of their life and work. Where there is work, you need to pay attention to that work. That is how the *Gītā* puts the message of *yoga* before us to make our working life deeply spiritual, emphasizing that spirituality is everyone's birthright. The infinite and immortal Atman or Brahman is our true nature.

Here is a description of the profound and subtle truths of the Atman discovered by the ancient Upaniṣads whose echoes you will find in modern Quantum and Particle Physics. *Kaṭha Upaniṣad* says (I. ii. 20–21):

Aṇoraṇīyān mahato mahīyān
ātmā'sya jantor nihito guhāyām;
Tam akratuḥ paśyati vītaśoko
dhātuḥprasādāt mahimānam ātmanaḥ —

'The Atman is smaller than an atom and larger than *mahat* or the cosmos; It is present in the cavity of the heart of all beings as their Self; Its glory is realized by the person who has renounced all desires and has gained full control over the mind and sense organs; he or she then becomes free from all sorrow.'

Āsīno dūram vrajati śayāno yāti sarvataḥ;

'Though sitting, this Atman goes far, though lying, It travels everywhere.'

Professor Fritjof Capra, the author of *The Tao of Physics*, in his third book *Uncommon Wisdom*, refers to his conversations with Werner Heisenberg, the great discoverer of the Principle of Uncertainty in Quantum Physics which replaced the strongly-held Newtonian causality principle (pp. 42–43):

'When I asked Heisenberg about his own thoughts on Eastern Philosophy, he told me to my great surprise not only that he had been well aware of the parallels between Quantum Physics and Eastern thought, but also that his own scientific work had been influenced, at least at the sub-conscious level, by Indian Philosophy.

'In 1929, Heisenberg spent some time in India as the guest of the celebrated poet Rabindranath Tagore with whom he had long conversations about science and Indian Philosophy. This introduction to Indian thought brought Heisenberg great comfort, he told me. He began to see that the recognition of relativity, interconnectedness, and impermanence as fundamental aspects of physical reality, which had been so difficult for himself and his fellow physicists, was the very basis of the Indian spiritual traditions. "After these conversations with Tagore", he said, "some of the ideas that had seemed so crazy suddenly made much more sense. That was a great help for me."'

Prajñānam brahma, 'Brahman is Pure Consciousness,' says the *Aitareya Upaniṣad; ayamātmā brahma,* 'this Self (in human beings) is Brahman,' says the *Māṇḍūkya Upaniṣad.* The *Kaṭha Upaniṣad,* says that this Atman is the Light of all lights (II. ii. 15) which is echoed in the *New Testament* as 'the Light that lighteth every soul that cometh into the world':

Na tatra sūryo bhāti na candra tārakam
Nemā vidyuto bhānti kuto'yam agniḥ;
Tam eva bhāntam anubhāti sarvam
Tasya bhāsā sarvam idam vibhāti —

'The sun does not shine there (in the Atman), nor the moon and stars; neither these lightnings shine there, what to speak of the fire (in our households); when It itself shines, all other things shine; by Its light all this manifested universe is lighted.'

This truth of Brahman, as the one source of the many, illumines the whole manifested universe, says the last verse of chapter 2 of the *Muṇḍaka Upaniṣad* in a joyous proclamation (II. ii. 11):

Brahmaivedam amṛtam purastāt brahma
paścāt brahma dakṣiṇataścottareṇa;
Adhaścordhvam ca prasṛtam
brahmaivedam viśvam idam variṣṭham —

'This whole manifested universe is only the immortal Brahman; in front is Brahman, behind is Brahman, right side and left side is Brahman; It is spread below and above; this manifested univese is only this adorable Brahman.'

This great science of *yoga* which is practical Vedanta, and expounded for the first time in the second and third chapters of the *Gītā,* will be strengthened and nourished further by other ideas coming in other chapters hereafter.

I wish to point out two truths here before entering the third chapter. The first is that there is repetition of spiritual truths in the *Gītā* and, naturally, in this exposition also. Repetition is considered as a fault in literature. But, in his commentary on the Upaniṣads, Śaṅkarācārya quotes this statement of India's ancient *Mīmāmsā* philosophers that 'repetition is not a fault in the conveying of spiritual truths', *na mantrāṇām jāmitā asti.* They are difficult to grasp and retain, and hence, repetition helps.

The second is the importance of this last verse, and similar other statements in the *Gītā* and the Upaniṣads, in the context of modern biological view of human evolution, that spiritual realization is the goal of human life and that it can be had *here and now,* and not in an imaginary post-mortem heaven.

Modern biology accepts the uniqueness of the human being, and is facing problems dealing with understanding the goal of human evolution and how to reach it. Let me put it in the late eminent biologist Sir Julian Huxley's own words as given in the last two pages of the main part of his own latest book, *Evolution: The Modern Synthesis,* which I like much for its truthfulness and clarity and boldness. He wrote to me a letter after reading my book, *The Message of the Upaniṣads,* which, and my detailed reply, are now included in the Appendix of *The Message of the Upaniṣads* (pp. 571–72):

'I agree that the Upaniṣads are remarkable achievements considering the date of their composition. …

'In my *Essays of A Humanist* and in my book on *Evolution: The Modern Synthesis,* I have tried to set forth the modes, methods, and main trends of evolution in its various aspects.'

Huxley cites several conditions for determining the process and goal of human evolution in his second book:

One: 'it should not be a standstill or a degeneration.' On this subject, India's Vedanta teaches that life, being a journey to fulfilment, should not be allowed to stagnate at any stage; this is expressed by the clarion call of the *Kaṭha Upaniṣad,* chapter 3, freely rendered by Swami Vivekananda as 'Arise! Awake! and stop not till the goal is reached.'

Again, 'And this human purpose can only be formulated in terms of the new attributes achieved by life in becoming human.'

Vedanta developed the concept of the four *puruṣārthas,* 'purposes sought after by a human being' in response to this demand.

Again, 'Man as we had stressed is, in many respects, unique among animals; his purposes must take account of his unique features as well as those he shares with other life.'

This also is emphasized in the above teaching of the four *puruṣārthas;* it has special reference to the last *puruṣārtha,* namely, *mokṣa* or spiritual liberation, about which modern biology knows nothing. Huxley continues (*ibid.*, p. 577):

'Obviously, the formulation of an agreed purpose for man as a whole will not be easy.'

To this, Vedanta will firmly say that it will make it easy, and it has made it easy, by formulating a science of human possibilities, a science of human being in depth, long long ago. Out of that we can get all the ingredients for a full science of human evolution, the goal of this evolution as well as its stages and steps. Vedanta has already formulated the truth that the *science of values is the link between the physical sciences and the science of spirituality.*

Huxley continues: 'There have been many attempts already. Today we are experiencing the struggle between two opposed ideas, that of subordination of the individual to the community, and that of his intrinsic superiority.'

Vedanta accepts both; at certain levels, the community has a voice; at certain other levels, it has no voice, the individual is supreme.

Then Huxley says: 'Another struggle still in progress is between the idea of a purpose directed to a future life in a supernatural world, and one directed to progress in this existing world. Until such major conflicts are resolved, humanity can have no single major purpose, and progress can be but fitful and slow.'

Huxley, and most Western thinkers, and many modern Indian thinkers as well, do not know that Vedanta blew off the conflict between this world and a supernatural world long long ago in the Upaniṣads and in this *Bhagavad Gītā.* In all of them, spiritual realization and life fulfilment are conveyed in firm language as one profound experience to be attained *here* and *now,* in this very world, in this very body. The *Muṇḍaka Upaniṣad* used strong language against the desire to go to a supernatural heaven (I. ii. 10):

Iṣṭāpūrtam manyamānā variṣṭham
nānyat śreyo vedayante pramūḍhāḥ;
Nākasya pṛṣṭhe te sukṛte'nubhūtva
imam lokam hīnataram vā viśanti —

'Utter fools are they who think that they will do some ritual and attain *puṇya* or merit here and enjoy it in the highest heaven, and they think that there is nothing better; but, having enjoyed pleasure in heaven, when their merit is exhausted, they come back to this human world or even go down to lower levels.'

The same idea is found in the *Gītā* also (5. 19):

Ihaiva tairjitaḥ sargo yeṣām sāmye sthitam manaḥ;
Nirdoṣam hi samam brahma tasmāt brahmaṇi te sthitāḥ —

'Here itself (in this very world) they have conquered relative worldly existence, whose mind is established in *sāmya,* sameness or unity; for, Brahman is verily devoid of all evil and is the same in all; therefore, such persons are established in Brahman.'

Huxley says further: 'Until such major conflicts are resolved, humanity can have no single major purpose.'

I have discussed this subject more elaborately in my book, *Practical Vedanta and the Science of Values,* published by Advaita Ashrama, Calcutta 14.

When Vedantic ideas spread throughout the world in the modern age, thinkers in various parts of the world will understand: Yes, here is a major purpose for all humanity, as given in the last verse of the second chapter, to be pursued according to one's capacity; and thinkers like Huxley *of that period* will say: Yes, now we have discovered a common purpose for human evolution, namely, to realize Brahman or Atman, the infinite and non-dual source of all evolution, for which evolution has fitted the human being with the necessary organic capacity; the human being is, therefore, 'having the capacity to realize Brahman'. *Brahmāvaloka dhiṣaṇām,* as the *Śrīmad Bhāgavatam* expresses it. Śaṅkarācārya refers to this realization by a human being, in a human being's lifetime, to be the *source* of the whole universe, and contrasts it, in his *Bṛhadāraṇyaka Upaniṣad* commentary, to the Indian *paurāṇika* view of the universe merging into Brahman at the time of cosmic dissolution or *pralaya;* modern Western astronomy also holds the same view that eventually, after billions of years, the whole universe will contract and attain the *state of singularity* (since it does not accept yet the principle of intelligence).

It is interesting to find that, in his commentary on the *Viṣṇusahasranāma,* verse 19, of the *Mahābhārata,* Śaṅkarācārya comments on the word *tvaṣṭa,* the fifty-second name of Viṣṇu, as 'the energy that contracts the universe, *tanūkṛtam,* at the time of *pralaya* or cosmic dissolution.'

इति सांख्ययोगो नाम द्वितीयोऽध्यायः ।
Iti sāṅkhyayogo nāma dvitīyo'dhyāyaḥ —

'Thus, the end of the second chapter designated as *Sāṅkhya* and *Yoga.*

BHAGAVAD GĪTĀ

CHAPTER 3

KARMA-YOGA
THE YOGA OF ACTION

We completed the study of the second chapter of the *Gītā*, especially the last few verses dealing with the philosophy of *yoga* and ending with the nature of the *Sthitaprajña*, a person of steady wisdom. And the whole section ended with the statement in the last verse: *Eṣā brāhmī sthitiḥ pārtha*, 'Arjuna, this is the *brāhmī sthitiḥ*, 'the state of being established in Brahman, the ultimate reality', *naināṁ prāpya vimuhyati*, 'if you are established in it, you will never again come into delusion'. *Sthitvāsyām-antakāle'pi*, 'even if you are established in it just before the time of death', *brahmanirvāṇam ṛcchati*, 'you achieve *nirvāṇa* in Brahman, complete absorption in Brahman'.

On several occasions during these weeks I have said that, a steady mind, a strong mind, is the greatest asset that we can have in life. A flimsy mind, shaken by every passing fancy, will not be helpful for a fulfilled life. So, the training of the mind is the greatest work we have to do, whether it is for worldly life or higher life. Make the mind your friend, that is what the *Gītā* will say in the fifth and sixth *ślokas* of the sixth chapter; don't make it your enemy. Very often our mind is our own enemy and we suffer thereby. The whole of education and religion, and all inter-human relationships, have only this objective: how to make this mind strong, steady, and an instrument for the fulfilment of life. So the second chapter ended with that high note, *and it was emphasized that this was a state to be realized here and now,* not in some faraway heaven.

That idea needs to be expressed again and again. And this is the best thing we can do: a thoroughly disciplined life, a mind which is friendly to our own aspirations, and to train that kind of a mind, so that this life will be fulfilled.

In Vedantic thinking, the next life or rebirth comes only when I am unable to fulfil my life's purposes in this very life. Then Vedanta will say, all right, you will get another opportunity. That will find mention in the sixth chapter. But, the best thing is to use this very life to achieve the best in this life itself; *ihaiva, ihaiva,* 'here itself'; *Gītā* will say later on in chapter 5, *śloka* 19. This is a special emphasis. Along with that emphasis comes the emphasis on the training of the mind and developing ethical and moral values by which alone this achievement can be had in this life. A mere life of ritual and ceremony will have no meaning if *this* is the ideal; that what we want to achieve is to be achieved here and now, not at some place or time far away. So, we enter the third chapter where Arjuna gets an opportunity to put a question, and as I said last Sunday, most of these questions, you will find, are our own questions. We also feel like questioning on this particular matter. And so, sometimes Arjuna questions, sometimes Śrī Kṛṣṇa, *assuming a question,* gives the answer. That is how you begin the third chapter with Arjuna's question in two verses.

अर्जुन उवाच –

Arjuna uvāca—

'Arjuna said.'

ज्यायसी चेत् कर्मणस्ते मता बुद्धिः जनार्दन ।
तत् किं कर्मणि घोरे मां नियोजयसि केशव ॥१॥

Jyāyasī cetkarmaṇaste matā buddhiḥ janārdana;
Tat kim karmaṇi ghore mām niyojayasi keśava — 3. 1

'If, O Janārdana (Kṛṣṇa), according to you knowledge is superior to action, why then, O Keśava, do You engage me in this terrible action?'

O Kṛṣṇa, if you think that thought is superior to action, that *yoga-buddhi* which he referred to in the last chapter, verse

49, where Śrī Kṛṣṇa had said, 'develop *yoga-buddhi*'; if You think so, 'why do you ask me to engage myself in this terrible action?' *Tat kim karmaṇi ghore mām niyojayasi keśava?* I shall develop a *yoga-buddhi*. Why ask me to get into this mess of a war? A very relevant question. Then he explains his question further.

व्यामिश्रेणेव वाक्येन बुद्धिं मोहयसीव मे ।
तदेकं वद निश्चित्य येन श्रेयोऽहमाप्नुयाम् ॥ २ ॥

Vyāmiśreṇeva vākyena buddhim mohayasīva me;
Tadekam vada niścitya yena śreyo'hamāpnuyām— 3. 2

'With these seemingly conflicting words, You are, as it were, bewildering my understanding; tell me that one thing for certain, by which I can attain to the Highest.'

'By confusing words as it were', you are deluding my mind. *Vyāmiśreṇeva vākyena,* sentences containing mixed-up ideas. And their effect is to confuse my mind, to delude it. *Tad ekam vada niścitya,* 'tell me for certain that one path', which you consider as good for me, *yena śreyo'ham āpnuyām,* 'by which I can attain my welfare'. This is Arjuna's request. We saw in the 49th verse in the last chapter, *dūreṇa hyavaram karma buddhiyogāt dhanañjaya,* 'these ordinary actions that we do are far inferior to that *buddhi-yoga'*; therefore, *buddhau śaraṇam anviccha,* 'take refuge in *buddhi*.' So, Arjuna is taking it up: I shall develop *buddhi,* I shall develop this attitude; why should I work? Why should I waste my energy in this work, especially, in this terrible work, like a war? That is the question. And Śrī Kṛṣṇa gives the answer in this and the next chapters.

This subject that comes up so often in the *Gītā* is something that has worried our Indian minds for hundreds of years. *Action versus inaction*. This subject comes again and again in our religious literature. Why should I act? Why not keep quiet? After all, the Atman is absolutely inactive. If I want to be the Atman, I should be inactive; so this theory of inaction had a tremendous appeal to the Indian mind. Why should I work? And that developed in such a way that more and more laziness came upon the people! Because of this tradition of thinking, this *naiṣkarmya* or actionlessness dominated the Indian mind for centuries; it was strengthened for sannyasins by an important Vedantic book, *Naiṣkarmyasiddhiḥ, Attainment Through Non-action.* That *naiṣkarmya* attitude slowly invaded the minds of the householders also; and it ruined the nation when its meaning was not correctly understood. Śrī Kṛṣṇa had taken up this subject of 'action versus inaction' in the *Gītā*; but it is only in the modern period that the *Gītā* is being correctly understood through the powerful teachings of practical Vedanta by Swami Vivekananda. The teaching that action becomes inaction by a true spiritual method comes in the *Gītā* in the fourth chapter, *śloka* 18; in this chapter, Śrī Kṛṣṇa is dealing with the subject of action and inaction, and He stresses the importance of action, as you will see in the various verses that we shall be studying.

श्रीभगवान् उवाच –

Śrībhagavān uvāca—

'The Blessed Lord said.'

Śrī Kṛṣṇa is called *Śrī bhagavān* in the *Mahābhārata* and other literature, 'That Supreme Bhagavān' said:

लोकेऽस्मिन् द्विविधा निष्ठा पुरा प्रोक्ता मयानघ ।
ज्ञानयोगेन सांख्यानां कर्मयोगेन योगिनाम् ॥ ३ ॥

Loke'smin dvividhā niṣṭhā purā proktā mayā'nagha;
Jñānayogena sāṅkhyānām karmayogena yoginām —3. 3

'In the beginning (of creation), O sinless one, the twofold path was given by Me to this world—the path of knowledge for the *Sāṅkhyas*, and the path of work for the *yogīs*.' In the middle of the second chapter, Śrī Kṛṣṇa, after speaking about the Atman which is inactive, which is ever free, ever pure, etc., said, '*Eṣā te'bhihitā sāṅkhye buddhiryoge tvimām śṛṇu*, 'till now I spoke to you about the *buddhi* devoted to *sāṅkhya*, that life of inaction and inward meditation. Now listen to me when I speak to you about the path of *yoga* based on *buddhi*'. If the path of *jñāna* takes one to the highest *mokṣa*, the path of *karma* also will take one to the highest *mokṣa*. These are the two paths that are there. And He will be saying in the *Gītā*, that between the two, *karma-yogo viśiṣyate,* 'the path of *karma* is superior'. It yields both the fruits of *abhyudaya* and *niḥśreyasa.* That is the development of thought in the *Gītā,* that, by a certain spiritual technique, you convert action into inaction: you get the fruit of inaction through action itself. That is a tremendous study. And in the Taoist philosophy of China also, it is very much emphasized. In fact, in management techniques today, this is a serious subject of study. While in the U.S.A., I read a book by a Chinese scientist connected with the MIT in America, where he mentions that, in all these management techniques, you are acting all the time, but by a certain spiritual technique you cease to be acting. There is such a state of mind, calm and steady, in which you do a lot of work, yet you don't feel it, you carry so little burden. Now this kind of study is becoming more and more appreciated in modern management techniques. The most heavy responsibility is there, yet you reap the benefit of inaction in the midst of action. That will be expressed in one single verse by Śrī Kṛṣṇa later in the fifth chapter, *śloka* 18, of the *Gītā*. And he gives the reason:

न कर्मणामनारम्भात् नैष्कर्म्यं पुरुषोऽश्नुते ।
न च संन्यसनादेव सिद्धिं समधिगच्छति ॥४॥

Na karmaṇāmanārambhāt naiṣkarmyam puruṣo'śnute;
Na ca saṃnyasanādeva siddhim samadhigacchati—3. 4

'By non-performance of action, none reaches inaction; by merely giving up action, no one attains perfection.'

This is a very clear simple statement. *Na karmaṇām anārambhāt naiṣkarmyam puruṣo'śnute,* 'true *naiṣkarmya,* actionlessness, cannot be attained by non-performance of action'. Let me do nothing, then I shall attain actionlessness—that can never be; *na ca saṃnyasanādeva,* 'not even by renouncing action', *siddhim samadhigacchati,* 'one is going to get spiritual perfection'. First, you begin an action, then you give it up. That is called *saṃnyasana;* the other is, *karmaṇām anārambha,* 'by not beginning any action at all'. It is a very important thought that is contained in this verse, and it has wide ramifications also for society. Now, you enjoy a quiet hour after you spend some time in hard work. The whole day you work, in the evening you get relaxation in meditation or other higher spiritual practices. You enjoy it. The whole day you are lazy, no work to do, you want to enjoy that meditation! Is that possible? It is like a person who is unemployed, and you tell him: 'I give you one month's holiday'! What is the use of a holiday for an unemployed person? An employed person can enjoy a holiday. But, many of our people have not learnt this lesson yet. Real holiday-enjoyment can be experienced only *after* a period of hard work. First, *karma*, then comes *naiṣkarmya.* Śrī Kṛṣṇa's statement has reference to all of us, especially in India, that all enjoyment of actionlessness is possible *after* pursuing action, expressing your energy in action and endeavour. So, he said, *Na ca samnyasanādeva siddhim samadhigacchati,* 'by mere renunciation of action, you are not going to get perfection'. Action is a profound subject. Śrī Kṛṣṇa will tell us later on, in the next chapter, verse 17: *gahanā karmaṇo gatiḥ,* 'the way of action is mysterious,' difficult to understand.

One of the British writers, I think it was L.P. Jacks, who was a very prominent writer about eighty years ago, mentions this truth: if you trace action, at the end of it you will find inaction; if you trace inaction, at the end of it you will find action. In all society, you will find this. Action is a mysterious subject for us to understand. Śrī Kṛṣṇa uses the same word: *gahanā karmaṇo gatiḥ,* 'the way of *karma* is mysterious', not easy to understand. So, he is going to illumine that subject by his own exposition in this and the next chapter. And he continues:

न हि कश्चित्क्षणमपि जातु तिष्ठत्यकर्मकृत् ।
कार्यते ह्यवशः कर्म सर्वः प्रकृतिजैर्गुणैः ॥५॥

Na hi kaścitkṣaṇamapi jātu tiṣṭhatyakarmakṛt;
Kāryate hyavaśaḥ karma sarvaḥ prakṛtijairguṇaiḥ—3. 5

'Verily, none can ever rest for even an instant, without performing action; for all are made to act, helplessly indeed, by the *guṇas* (or forces) born of *prakṛti* (nature).'

No man or woman sits, even for an instant, without doing some work or the other. See the language! Everyone is working; so many things are going on. Where is real actionlessness except in death? A table or a chair, you may say, is inactive. But a man is always active in one form or the other. *Na hi kaścitkṣaṇamapi jātu tiṣṭhatyakarmakṛt,* 'not doing action, nobody remains even for a moment'. *Kāryate hyavaśaḥ karma sarvaḥ prakṛtijaiḥ guṇaiḥ,* 'impelled by the forces of nature all are engaged helplessly in some action'. This is the way of human life. Something pulls us out into action. That is our own nature within. That nature finds expression in making us do this work, that work, something or the other. So, this is the first lesson we must understand. If I go away from Hyderabad and go to Kashmir for a holiday, there also I am active, but I perform a different type of action. That is all. Action is still there. In holiday also there is action, but not the particular type of action which I was doing; a change of action, that is all. All holiday is only a change of action, due to a change of situation. That is all. *Kāryate hyavaśaḥ karma; avaśaḥ,* 'in spite of yourself'. *Rājasik, tāmasik,* and *sāttvik* nature is there within us; *rājasik* nature impels us to do some work or the other. This is why we are told that we cannot escape action. If that is so, how shall I perform action? The next two verses give the answer and are, therefore, very important; they convey a profound philosophy of action.

कर्मेन्द्रियाणि संयम्य य आस्ते मनसा स्मरन् ।
इन्द्रियार्थान् विमूढात्मा मिथ्याचारः स उच्यते ॥६॥

Karmendriyāṇi samyamya ya āste manasā smaran;
Indriyārthān vimūḍhātmā mithyācāraḥ sa ucyate—3. 6

'One who, restraining the organs of actions, sits revolving in the mind thoughts regarding sense objects, he or she, of deluded understanding, is called a hypocrite.'

Here Śrī Kṛṣṇa is giving us a warning! That if you do like 'this', you will be a hypocrite. And in the next *śloka,* verse 7, he gives the other side: *this* is the way to do work by which you get the highest. The first is what makes for hypocrisy; the second is what makes for real spiritual growth and development in the individual. So, he says: 'That person is called a *mithyācāri'*. *Mithyācāra* is the exact word for hypocrite in Sanskrit. Now, Śrī Kṛṣṇa says: 'controlling all organs of action', *karmendriyāṇi samyamya; ya āste manasā smaran,* 'but the mind is constantly thinking of sensory objects', though physically, the person is absolutely quiet. Such a person is a *mithyācāri,* a hypocrite. There is lot of such hypocrisy in the behaviour of people. We thought that 'to be inactive' is a high ideal. But our spiritual development is not very high. Our sensory cravings are very strong. So, we try to do all this in a subversive way by secret methods. That makes for hypocrisy; not straight. The honest way is: do you want this? Yes, I want it. The devious way is: I don't want it, but he or she will be seeking for it by devious means. That kind of hypocrisy has come to us due to not understanding this high ideal of actionlessness, desirelessness, etc. In our present state we can say honestly, yes, I want sense pleasure. There is no hypocrisy in it. I run after a thing, I seek it, I want it, but why be a hypocrite? When the mind develops, I will be able to say, I don't want it because I have achieved something higher within me. Then there will be no hypocrisy. And so, *karmendriyāṇi samyamya ya āste manasā smaran indriyārthān,* 'restraining the organs of action, but with the mind thinking of sense objects.' Such a person is nothing but a *mithyācāri,* a hypocrite. Don't be a hypocrite, Śrī Kṛṣṇa tells every human being. And so the next verse puts it in a positive way.

यस्त्विन्द्रियाणि मनसा नियम्यारभतेऽर्जुन ।
कर्मेन्द्रियैः कर्मयोगमसक्तः स विशिष्यते ॥७॥

Yastvindriyāṇi manasā niyamyārabhate'rjuna;
Karmendriyaiḥ karmayogamasaktaḥ sa viśiṣyate—3. 7

'But, O Arjuna, one who, controlling the senses by the mind, and remaining unattached, directs the organs of action to the yoga of action, excels.'

Sa viśiṣyate, 'he or she excels'. Who? *Indriyāṇi manasā samyamya,* 'who disciplines the sense organs by the mind'. Mind is the master. *Ārabhate arjuna karmendriyaiḥ karmayogam,* 'O Arjuna, he or she is busy in the yoga of action with the sense organs of action'; such a person does it with a special *yoga buddhi;* that *karma* becomes *karma-yoga,* not mere action, but action which can elevate a person spiritually. *Asaktaḥ,* 'unattached'. The mind is not at all attached to these things. It has been detached from these things. Therefore, it can do things better and better. *Asaktaḥ sa viśiṣyate,* 'such an unattached person is excellent'. Here comes human excellence in action. *This particular verse is the best description of excellence in action. Niyamya,* 'disciplining', *indriyāṇi,* 'sense organs', *manasā,* 'by the mind', *ārabhate karma-yogam,* 'does the *yoga* of action with that attitude'; such a person is a *karma-yogī. Sa viśiṣyate,* 'he or she is most excellent'; that is the training everyone has to give to the mind. A sense of masterliness is manifested there. One is not lost in the work, but is always free. Work with freedom, that is the idea. And Vedanta repeatedly says, work freely, give freely, whatever you do to the people, give it with a free mind, not with a sense of that *kanjūs* or miserly attitude with a very very limited mind. That is not correct.

Then Śrī Kṛṣṇa gives advice to all of us:

नियतं कुरु कर्म त्वं कर्म ज्यायो ह्यकर्मणः ।
शरीरयात्रापि च ते न प्रसिद्ध्येत् अकर्मणः ॥८॥

Niyatam kuru karma tvam karma jyāyo hyakarmaṇaḥ;
Śarīrayātrāpi ca te na prasiddhyet akarmaṇaḥ — 3. 8

'Do you perform obligatory action; for action is superior to inaction; and even the bare maintenance of the body will not be possible if you are inactive.'

Niyatam kuru karma tvam, 'whatever actions are to be done, do them well'. *Niyatam* means what is to be done. Suppose you are working in an office, you have got some responsibilities: discharge them properly—let not anybody have to come to supervise or say, do this and that. We need to develop self-respect so that we will do the work allotted to us to the best of our capacity. That attitude is an excellent attitude, a free people's attitude, far different from the attitude of a slave for whom somebody must be there with a stick to see that he or she does the work properly. That is a wrong attitude.

So, *niyatam kuru karma tvam,* 'whatever is apportioned to you as your duty, do it carefully, do it well'. *Karma jyāyo hi akarmaṇaḥ,* '*karma* is superior to *akarma*'. Action is superior to inaction. *Śarīrayātrāpi ca te na prasiddhyet akarmaṇaḥ,* 'if you are inactive, even the care of your body will not be possible for you to do'. You have to do something even for the maintenance of your body. *Śarīra-yātrā, jīvan-yātrā,* these are the words used here. To carry on the body as a living entity, you need to do some work. If you say I will be absolutely inactive, that won't be possible. The stress is on action, but with that *yoga-buddhi* which was described in the second chapter. So, the idea of getting anything by not doing any work is a very peculiar attitude—waiting for some magic or miracle to happen; no miracle is going to happen. The only miracle will be that you will be left behind! A Sanskrit verse, a traditional verse says,

Udyoginam puruṣasimhamupaiti lakṣmī
daivena deyamiti kāpuruṣā vadanti;
Daivam nihatya kuru pauruṣam-ātmaśaktyā
yatne kṛte yadi na sidhyati ko'tra doṣaḥ —

'Lakṣmī or Fortune comes to that lion among human beings who is industrious', *udyoginam, puruṣasimham,* 'that lion among human beings', *upaiti lakṣmī,* 'Lakṣmī runs towards such a person with blessings'. *Daivena deyamiti kāpuruṣā vadanti,* 'the low-level human beings, *kāpuruṣā* says that, he or she depends on one's own destiny'. So, the verse says, *daivam nihatya,* 'throwing away all concept of destiny', *kuru pauruṣam-ātmaśaktyā,* 'through your own inner strength, be industrious, be active'. *Yatne kṛte yadi na sidhyati, ko'tra doṣaḥ?* 'In spite of all your efforts, if you did not get exactly what you wanted, what is wrong with it? That intense struggle, that effort, is the important thing. And most people do get when they undertake the struggle. Sometimes you may not get, that is no reason why you should give up industry and activity. Then he says that the activity we do with and in this body, can be made an instrument of our own spiritual liberation. That is the essential teaching of the *Gītā* that, normally, all the work you do increases the bondage, but because of the spiritual turn you give to it, you find work becomes an instrument of spiritual liberation.

This idea is expounded now from this verse 9 and onwards, from another point of view, using a very ancient word which was so constantly used in Vedic literature, especially the ritualistic portion of the Vedic literature, the concept of *yajña*. *Yajña* means sacrifice, normally ritualistic sacrifice. Every doctrine, every religion, has a chapter on sacrifice: you light a fire, offer things into that fire. That is called Vedic sacrifice. In the old ritualistic section of the Vedas, many types of sacrifices are mentioned. So, the word *yajña* is used for it. Śrī Kṛṣṇa takes this word, but gives it a new meaning, makes it ethically significant. That is what he has done in the third and fourth chapters. *Yajña* or sacrifice: the whole world is based on it, he is going to tell us. What is the meaning of sacrifice? Verse 9 says:

यज्ञार्थात् कर्मणोऽन्यत्र लोकोऽयं कर्मबन्धनः ।
तदर्थं कर्म कौन्तेय मुक्तसङ्गः समाचर ॥९॥

Yajñārthāt karmaṇo'nyatra loko'yam karmabandhanaḥ;
Tadartham karma kaunteya muktasaṅgaḥ samācara—3. 9

'The world is bound by actions other than those performed for the sake of *yajña;* do you, therefore, O son of Kuntī, perform action for *yajña* alone, devoid of attachment.'

The world is bound by such kinds of actions which are not done in the spirit of *yajña*. If you do it in a spirit of *yajña,* there is no bondage at all. So, *tadartham karma kaunteya,* 'do your actions in that spirit of *yajña*', *muktasaṅgaḥ samācara,* 'free from attachment, do that action'; then there will be no bondage. This is based upon the theory of sacrifices mentioned in Vedic literature. This is true of all religions: sacrifice is an essential item in the Jewish religion. The idea is, you give something to the Divine, then what remains is yours. That is the most important concept of *yajña*. So, you live on what remains after *yajña*. First give; then what remains after giving, is good. So, in the *Manu Smṛti,* the *Mahābhārata,* and in many other books also, this idea comes repeatedly. Bondage comes when you cook and eat for yourself. When you eat after working for the good of others, what food remains, is pure and holy. That is the language. 'One who cooks only for oneself, eats only for oneself, eats only so much of sin', Śrī Kṛṣṇa is going to tell us soon. That is the discharge of one's obligation to society, also to nature, and to the whole world. Never forget that we are all interconnected. *That concept of interconnectedness is the central theme of this chapter*. Just like we perform a sacrifice, that goes to the gods, they enjoy it, they send you rain and other valuable things back here for us. That is the old idea. Extend that to the whole of life and to the universe; take it away from its ritualistic mooring. Make it an inter-human and an internature philosophy. Make it ethical and moral. Then we shall be able to understand what Śrī Kṛṣṇa has done with that word *yajña* in this and other chapters. *Yajñārthāt karmaṇo'nyatra loko'yam karmabandhanaḥ,* 'when work is not done in the spirit of *yajña,* this world suffers bondage from actions'; that is the simple teaching. A selfish person works only for oneself. Naturally, it is bondage; this contraction of life to a point; any action done, without the spirit of *yajña* inspiring it, makes for bondage. Therefore, *tadartham karma kaunteya,* 'do action in that spirit (of *yajña*)', *muktasaṅgaḥ,* 'giving up attachment'. And Śrī Kṛṣṇa takes it further in the next verse by saying:

सहयज्ञाः प्रजाः सृष्ट्वा पुरोवाच प्रजापतिः ।
अनेन प्रसविष्यध्वमेष वोऽस्त्विष्टकामधुक् ॥१०॥

Sahayajñāḥ prajāḥ sṛṣṭvā puro'vāca prajāpatiḥ;
Anena prasaviṣyadhvameṣa vo'stviṣṭakāmadhuk— 3. 10

'The Prajāpati (the Lord of creatures), having in the beginning projected mankind (from out of Himself) *together with yajña,* said, "By this shall you multiply; this shall be the milch cow of your desires."'

This *yajña* concept is not merely of the earth; it is not limited to our own human experience. This has a cosmic dimension. The whole cosmos is based upon this concept of *yajña.* That is a wonderful development of thought you will find in Vedanta as well as in the *Gītā,* that everywhere there is give-and-take going on. Before taking, give; then you get the best. There is a unity in this universe. Everything is related to everything else. Nothing is unrelated. This is a wonderful idea in modern physics also, that any event taking place in any part of the world affects the whole world. May be very small, but it is there, this interconnectedness. This is further expounded by modern Western biology. The tremendous connection among all living species is very much emphasized in biology. From Darwin onwards, biology studied nature, and discovered this interconnectedness of things. Some examples are given in his scientific books. A bird flies, goes far away; you catch that bird, and examine its legs. You can detect mud in that leg; in the mud you will see some seeds of plants. That mud and the seeds are planted in the earth and they sprout; the bird does not know it. The bird is an instrument of nature for this great diffusion and for the concept of interconnectedness of things in nature. Similarly, you destroy a species; thereby you destroy agriculture itself. The example taken in biology is of that most humble earthworm; it does immense good to the earth by nourishing it and improving its fertility. But we do not understand its services until a scientist tells us. Earthworms are doing immense work. We destroy nature out of greed and we suffer later on. In ignorance, we destroy the great ecological balance of the world. *That old concept of yajña is today developing into the truths of ecological balance.*

That Prajāpati, the projector of the universe, projected the universe first and in order to maintain this universe, he projected also this *yajña. Sahayajñāḥ prajāḥ sṛṣṭvā purovāca prajāpatiḥ,* 'having projected this universe (out of oneself) along with *yajña, Prajāpatiḥ* said long ago'; what did he say? O Yajña, may you be a great blessing to all these beings; they will be able to live at their best, because of you. *Anena prasaviṣyadhvam,* 'may you prosper with the help of this *yajña*', *eṣa vo'stviṣṭa-kāmadhuk,* 'let this be a *kāmadhenu,* to all of you', the wish-fulfilling cow of our mythology. We are thus asked to strengthen the spirit of *yajña.* There will then be more happiness in society. Today we understand it more and more from an international point of view; international co-operation, international aid, is the language today.

There you can see the concept of *yajña,* as stated in the *Gītā,* finding expression in human relations. Within society you help each other. Today that national society has become international society, including the natural environments of plants and animals of the world. All are included in it in a very comprehensive vision.

On this subject, Swami Vivekananda said in his lecture on 'Vedanta and Its Application to Indian Life' delivered in Madras in 1897 (*Complete Works,* vol. 3, p. 241):

'Our Upaniṣads say that the cause of all misery is ignorance; and that is perfectly true when applied to every state of life, either social or spiritual. It is ignorance that makes us hate each other, it is through ignorance that we do not know, and do not love, each other. As soon as we come to know each other, love comes, must come, for are we not one? Thus we find solidarity coming in spite of itself. Even in politics and sociology, problems that were only national twenty years ago, can no more be solved on national grounds only. They are assuming huge proportions, gigantic shapes. They can only be solved when looked at in the broader light of international grounds. International organizations, international combinations, international laws are the cry of the day. That shows the solidarity.'

In English they use the word creation, because the people believed in duality like a potter turning out pots out of clay. The Creator is different, the material is different, and the product is different. That is creation. But in Vedanta we have no place for such a concept of creation. The word *sṛṣṭi* is wrongly translated as creation, but actually it is to be translated as *projection*. God projected the world out of himself; first the cosmos, then the starry heavens and all living organisms and eventually the human species. Everything comes from that One, and into that One the whole world will go eventually. That is the Indian concept of creation as projection. The Upaniṣads give three examples of creation as projection: first, the spider sending out its web, living in it, and taking it back; second, plants growing from the earth; third, hairs growing from the living human body. In all these, there is spontaneity and no second factor; similarly, from the One, the many has come. *Eko'ham bahusyām,* 'I am One, let Me be many.'

A society is strong, people are progressive, if the *yajña* principle inspires people in society. If there is not the idea of giving and taking in a mutual way, society becomes weaker and weaker and goes down.

देवान् भावयतानेन ते देवा भावयन्तु वः ।
परस्परं भावयन्तः श्रेयः परमवाप्स्यथ ॥११॥

Devān bhāvayatānena te devāḥ bhāvayantu vaḥ;
Parasparam bhāvayantaḥ śreyaḥ paramavāpsyatha—3. 11

'Cherish the *devas* with this, and may those *devas* cherish you; thus cherishing one another, you shall gain the highest good.'

In the book, *The Secret Life of Plants,* written in America, you will find the word *deva* used again and again; it is the personification of Nature's forces. *Devān bhāvayatānena,* 'help the *devas* with this *yajña*'; *te devāḥ bhāvayantu vaḥ,* 'they, the *devas* will help you'. Then he says, *parasparam bhāvayantaḥ,* 'nourishing each other', *śreyaḥ param avāpsyatha,* 'all will rise to the highest level'. Mutuality, interdependence is the way to progress; not by isolation, not by confrontation, not by exploitation. We violate nature and we become violated by nature. This should not happen. Nature is not something to be destroyed. Nature can be used, but it must be replenished also. If you don't replenish it, you will be in trouble. And today the whole world is conscious of this problem. It is in this context that we should see this exposition of *yajña* by Śrī Kṛṣṇa in the third chapter of the *Gītā*. From the Vedic context he takes ideas, but he uses his own philosophy to expound them, and they become perfectly human, of most intense value to all of us here. So, this language, *parasparam bhāvayantaḥ śreyaḥ param avāpsyatha,* 'help each other, then both of you will achieve progress'; go on destroying each other, both will perish.

In one particular field, you can see this truth being recaptured by a group of people. In America we have the Women's Liberation Movement. About twenty years ago, it started in a big way, 'We don't want to be a slave of man, we don't want to be tied down to the kitchen. This is a prison to us, let us get out. It is a joy that we shall be ourselves.' That was the beginning of that liberation movement. Betty Friedan, the famous liberationist, wrote her famous book, *The Feminine Mystique,* which began this liberation movement. Now, after twenty years, families are breaking down, children have no parents, and so many problems are arising in American society, and this very lady goes round America and writes a second book, *The Second Phase (of the Liberation Movement).* There she quotes the remarks of many women, who have been liberated from the household and the kitchen, and are in high employment. But, they complain that they have not achieved real liberation; we are still treated as an item among items in industry; we have not discovered our personality at all. We get high salary, no doubt; but that is no real liberation. This very author, Betty Friedan, therefore, gives one or two beautiful ideas, which are old ideas put in a new context. And the first principle, she says, is, *there is no women's liberation apart from men's liberation.* I liked it very much; it is the echo of the *Gītā* idea: *Parasparam bhāvayantaḥ śreyaḥ param avāpsyatha!* I have quoted her exact words in my booklet, *Women in the Modern Age,* published by the Bharatiya Vidya Bhavan. I am giving this example to say that we think we can do it alone, but we cannot. For some time we can do, then we shall find that it will not be possible. You will have to carry others also with you; nobody will be happy otherwise; women will not be happy, men will not be happy. Of course, children will never be happy in such a situation.

So, *parasparam bhāvayantaḥ śreyaḥ param avāpsyatha,* is a wonderful message Śri Kṛṣṇa is giving to all humanity. Even the relationship between Soviet Union and America today is based upon this principle: *parasparam bhāvayantaḥ.* They were constantly enemies of each other. Iron curtain, and then it became a bamboo curtain, even that curtain is going away now. That is the start of the spirit of a healthy international human order. That is what the Divine Creator gave to the world along with creation: the principle of *yajña*. Strengthen this *yajña* value, and we will all be happy; weaken it, and we shall be in trouble. That *yajña* includes not only our relationship with other human beings, but also with nature. Today there is a tremendous recognition of this mutuality between humanity and its natural and human environment. That is the immense scope of this teaching of the third chapter, the concept of *yajña*. Some more relevant ideas are coming in the next verses.

The principle of a healthy social life is also based on this *parasparam bhāvayantaḥ* principle; not by fighting with each other, but by helping each other, serving each other; that will help all people to rise to the highest level. If you take from nature and not give back to nature, you will suffer. Take and give back, take and give back, that is the nature of a healthy human environmental relation. And as I said earlier, today we are realizing it by experiencing the evils of consumerism, over-technology, increasing industrialization, and all the various steps human beings are taking that cause poisoning of our environment, including the weakening of the far-away ozone layer that protects the earth from the harmful high frequency radiation coming from the sun. So this subject is of vital importance to the human being; and the whole subject comes under one word, *yajña*, originally meaning 'ritual sacrifice'. But in the *Gītā*, it means this ethical sense, this spirit of service, this capacity to give and not merely to take. Therefore, it is *parasparam bhāvayantaḥ śreyaḥ param avāpsyatha*. If nature is exploited too much, it will destroy humanity itself, and that lesson is being driven home to us in the modern experience.

When we come to verse 16, we shall come across the very term *cakram* or wheel or cycle, being used by the *Gītā*, referring to the term 'ecological cycle'. Just like what we see in a seed, then a sprout, then a plant, a flower, fruit, and again back to the seed: there is a *cakram* here. So also, solar energy coming down to the earth, becoming plants, natural energies, animals, and human beings, and the energy goes back again; in this way there is a *cakram*. This is a cosmic principle according to this *Gītā* chapter. We are concerned only with the earth and the nearby environment, but actually *yajña* is a cosmic principle, expressing what modern science has recognized as the interrelatedness of things. So, the next verse says:

इष्टान्भोगान् हि वो देवा दास्यन्ते यज्ञभाविताः ।
तैर्दत्तान् अप्रदायैभ्यो यो भुङ्क्ते स्तेन एव सः ॥१२॥

Iṣṭān bhogān hi vo devā dāsyante yajñabhāvitāḥ;
Tairdattān apradāyaibhyo yo bhuṅkte stena eva saḥ—3. 12

'The *devas,* cherished by *yajña,* will give you desired-for objects, so, one who enjoys objects given by the *devas* without offering back to them (what is due), is verily a thief.'

Whenever you give back to nature, nature also gives you good things. We are seeing already in India that our forests are getting depleted, and our weather is getting into trouble. And weather gets into trouble means you and I also are getting into trouble. So, we are slowly realizing that truth: *Iṣṭān bhogān hi vo devā dāsyante*, 'nature's gods, they will give you back what is good for you'. But, *tairdattān apradāyaibhyo yo bhuṅkte*, 'if you enjoy what they have given to you, without returning to them their share', then what happens: *stena eva saḥ*, 'such a person is only a thief'. He doesn't give back what is due to nature and nature's gods, so the *Gītā* calls such a person a thief. Most of the modern technological civilizations are thieves from that point of view. But, fortunately, we have understood the seriousness of the situation and have decided not to remain a thief hereafter. That is why there are programmes like afforestation and cleaning of river pollution going on all over India. We are giving back to nature something we have increasingly destroyed. Then, we can enjoy what nature gives to us. The word used is *stena,* which means 'a thief'. The human being becomes a thief with respect to the environment, and the thief will be punished. And that punishment is already going on; all the rivers and other water sources are polluted, and, in some cases, the pollution is extreme.

यज्ञशिष्टाशिनः सन्तो मुच्यन्ते सर्वकिल्बिषैः ।
भुञ्जते ते त्वघं पापा ये पचन्त्यात्मकारणात् ॥१३॥

Yajñaśiṣṭāśinaḥ santo mucyante sarva kilbiṣaiḥ;
Bhuñjate te tvagham pāpā ye pacantyātmakāraṇāt—3. 13

'The good people, living on the remnants of *yajña,* are freed from all sins; but those, on the other hand, who cook food (only) for themselves eat only sin.'

Whatever you eat after a sacrifice is called *yajñaśiṣṭa,* the remnant of a *yajña*. It is a technical term. *Yajñaśiṣṭa* is also called *prasāda*. Whatever is a *prasāda* is holy food; what is not *prasāda* has no elevating power for the human system. Even in the social context, you earn, you pay your taxes, what remains is your wealth to enjoy; by trying to avoid paying taxes through all sorts of tricks, society suffers; you also suffer. This idea we have to imprint upon the mind of everyone, that you can't get a peaceful social order without paying for it. Tax is what we pay for making a stable society. Those who avoid paying taxes, and adopt all sorts of tricks for it, they are not citizens, they are only *in* the nation, but not *of* the nation, and not *for* the nation; they are not fit to live in an ordered society. They are fit to have a life of their own separately in some unpopulated island; but, then, without human company, they will not often develop humanness. *Kilbiṣa* means sin or evil.

Then comes the statement: *Bhuñjate te tvagham pāpā ye pacanti ātmakāraṇāt*. This is a very profound idea. 'One who cooks only for oneself (and eats separately without caring for others), eats only that much sin.' That is the language. *Agham* means sin; *pāpa,* also means sin; *ye pacanti,* 'those who cook'; *ātmakāraṇāt,* 'only for oneself'. I am cooking only for myself; I don't care for others. That attitude is extremely bad. Therefore, very often, in our traditional Hindu houses, they follow what is called *bhūta-yajña,* the setting apart of a small portion of food after the cooking is over. That is given to any beggar, or birds, whoever needs it. They keep it separate; only the rest they utilize. The idea behind it is what this verse expresses. In the *Gītā,* the *Mahābhārata,* and the *Manu smṛti* this idea is expressed: *Agham tu kevalam bhuṅkte ye pacanti ātmakāraṇāt,* 'one who cooks for oneself, eats only that much of sin'. That self-centredness is not appreciated at all. So, this is one important idea. Don't eat sin; eat virtue; food becomes virtue when it becomes a *prasāda.* You have given something to other people and you used for yourself what remained; that is beautiful. The *yajña* value is manifested there. This very teaching is given also by the *Īśa Upaniṣad,* first verse: *tena tyaktena bhuñjīthā,* 'enjoy life through renunciation'. Then only you get the best of life. You care only for your own life; by that you will never enjoy the best of life. So, in verses 14 and 15, you find mention of this *cakram* or 'wheel or chain of life'.

अन्नाद् भवन्ति भूतानि पर्जन्यात् अन्नसम्भवः ।
यज्ञात् भवति पर्जन्यो यज्ञः कर्म समुद्भवः ॥१४॥

Annād bhavanti bhūtāni parjanyāt annasambhavaḥ;
Yajñāt bhavati parjanyo yajñaḥ karma samudbhavaḥ—3. 14

'From food come forth beings; from rain, food is produced: from *yajña* arises rain; and *yajña* is born of *karma* or action.'

This is the chain of events. From food come all of us. 'All living beings come from food'. *Annāt bhavanti bhūtāni.* How does food come? *Parjanyāt annasambhavaḥ,* 'from rain food comes'. As soon as rain does not fall, food production also suffers. *Yajñāt bhavati parjanyo,* 'when you keep up that *yajña* spirit with respect to the environment, then rain also will fall in due time'; otherwise, you can spoil the rainfall system by spoiling your environment. What was a ritualistic idea in the *Karma-kāṇḍa,* ritual portion of the Vedas, becomes converted into an ethical idea of renunciation and service in the *Gītā.* Then, *yajñaḥ karmasamudbhavaḥ,* '*yajña* is the product of *karma*'. *Yajña* means an action oriented to the welfare of all around you, including yourself. That is called *yajña*. *Yajña* is an action. So, you find *anna, parjanya, yajña,* and now *karma*. These four items have come. Then the chain still continues:

कर्म ब्रह्मोद्भवं विद्धि ब्रह्माक्षर समुद्भवम् ।
तस्मात्सर्वगतं ब्रह्म नित्यं यज्ञे प्रतिष्ठितम् ॥१५॥

Karma brahmodbhavam viddhi brahmākṣara samudbhavam;
Tasmāt sarvagatam brahma nityam yajñe pratiṣṭhitam—3. 15

'Know *karma* to have risen from the Veda, and the Veda from the Imperishable. Therefore, the all-pervading Veda is ever centred in *yajña*.'

'Consider *karma* as born out of Brahma'; Brahma here means the Vedas. Vedas are often referred to as Brahma. *Karma* is interpreted in the Vedas. There you get this teaching. *Brahma akṣara samudbhavam;* from where did the Vedas come? 'From the Imperishable Reality itself'. From the Imperishable Brahman the Vedas came as a series of truths regarding the cosmos and human life and destiny. *Tasmāt sarvagatam brahma nityam yajñe pratiṣṭhitam,* 'therefore, this all-pervading Brahman is found established always in *yajña*'. Whenever you perform a dedicated action, you are already expressing that infinite Brahman, the Imperishable Reality. Swami Vivekananda said therefore (*Complete Works*, vol. 5, p. 228):

'The national ideals of India are RENUNCIATION and SERVICE. Intensify her in those channels, and the rest will take care of itself.'

What a wonderful teaching! The whole of ethical life is concentrated in two principles: renunciation and service. Renunciation of what? This self-centred ego or self. That has to be renounced. The larger Self must manifest. Then every action becomes service. That is why renunciation is the preceding value. The succeeding value is service. You can't do service without some form of renunciation. If I want to help somebody, to that extent I must give up my own self-interest. And so, renunciation and service are what is meant by this concept of *yajña*.

A ritualistic concept of the Vedas thus becomes transformed into a highly ethical principle, making for integration of human beings with other human beings in society, and of the human being with nature outside. Therefore, Śrī Kṛṣṇa says here that this infinite and imperishable reality of Brahman finds expression in every act of *yajña* that we do. What a wonderful idea it is! That apparently far away Brahman is close to you when you convert your action into *yajña*. Protection of animal species, plant species, and human beings—we have responsibility for all of them, only because we have the brain power to destroy all of them or to protect and nourish all of them. If the human being doesn't discharge this responsibility by expressing one's actions in terms of *yajña,* he or she will ruin everything and will ruin oneself also. That is why it is said here that everything is centred in *yajña,* sacrifice—not ritual, but work with this sense of dedication. A large Self feeling its oneness with all, oneness with nature, oneness with other human beings and expressing it in service. And we enjoy whatever remains after that kind of service and dedication. So, we now deal with verse 16 where this concept of a cosmic cycle is expressed very explicitly:

एवं प्रवर्तितं चक्रं नानुवर्तयतीह यः ।
अघायुः इन्द्रियारामो मोघं पार्थ स जीवति ॥१६॥

Evam pravartitam cakram nānuvartayatīha yaḥ;
Aghāyuḥ indriyārāmo mogham pārtha sa jīvati — 3. 16

'One who, in this world, follows not the wheel thus set revolving, living a life of sin and being delighted in the senses, O son of Pṛthā—he or she lives in vain.'

Śrī Kṛṣṇa is very emphatic about this truth. This *cakra,* this wheel of interconnections, has been established from the very beginning of the universe. When the cosmic evolution started, this *cakra* also started, 'this interconnected cycle'—*evam pravartitam cakram.* 'One who does not follow this in this life', *na anu vartayati iha;* one who neglects this concept of *cakra* and breaks it, makes life one-sided, selfish, self-centred, etc.; what happens to such a one? *Aghāyuḥ,* 'his or her life is a life of sin', a life of evil. *Āyuḥ* means life, and *agha* means sin or evil. Why is he or she *aghāyuḥ?* Because he or she is *indriyārāmo,* 'being delighted only in one's own sensory pleasure'; he or she doesn't care to protect nature—just like poaching in the forest, destroying fine birds, rare animals and trees, though the State has prohibited it; people do all this; but why?, they want to sell all such, make plenty of money, and live a comfortable life; such people are living in sin, because they are *indriyārāmaḥ,* 'their delight is sensual only'. Up to a certain limit it is good to satisfy sensory cravings; but, beyond this limit, it is dangerous.

Today, in all international discussions on the subject, we make a distinction between human needs and human wants. And Gandhiji said, there is enough in this world to meet human needs, but there is not enough to meet human wants. Wants are multiplying all the time. Why do they do so? We yield to our sensory cravings all the time. Mind cannot discriminate, though every human being has that wonderful capacity which no animal has. Therefore, when a whole society becomes *indriyārāmaḥ,* 'devoted only to satisfying sensory cravings', then that society begins to decline. In fact, all civilizations begin to decline when the number of *indriyārāma* people begins to increase in that society. In our own Indian history it has happened several times—this stage of *indriyārāma,* resulting in social stagnation; *mogham pārtha sa jīvati:* 'Pārtha! Such people's life becomes vain, empty, meaningless, uncreative'. *Mogha* means meaningless. The life they live, this *indriyārāma* life, is a meaningless life. All the animals live accordingly. And human beings follow the same! But they forget their uniqueness; he or she can concern oneself with the welfare of others. But the *indriyārāma* state cannot help one to do this. So, these two are combined: *aghāyuḥ indriyārāmo mogham pārtha sa jīvati,* his or her life is in vain—absolutely meaningless, empty. Take for example, our India: three hundred million people are suffering from poverty, backwardness, illiteracy. And a few percentage of people have plenty of wealth; and they indulge in it. Look at that! An empty meaningless life. They have no concern for the world around them.

Referring to this type of people in India's past few centuries, in a letter from America dated 20 August 1893, Swami Vivekananda says (*Letters of Swami Vivekananda,* 1948 edition, p. 69; *Complete Works,* vol 5, p. 16):

'I pity them. It is not their fault. They are children, yea, veritable children, though they be great and high in society. Their eyes see nothing beyond their little horizon of a few yards—the routine work, eating, drinking, earning, and begetting, following each other in mathematical precision. They know nothing beyond—happy little souls! Their sleep is never disturbed. Their nice little brown studies of lives never rudely shocked by the wail of woe, of misery, of degradation and poverty, that has filled the Indian atmosphere—the result of centuries of oppression. They little dream of the ages of tyranny, mental, moral, and physical, that has reduced the image of God (that is man) to a mere beast of burden; the emblem of the Divine Mother (that is woman) to a slave to bear children, and life itself, a curse.'

This is the wonderful statement in verse 16. And in verse 17, you find another type of life placed before all human beings. When a person becomes pure, disciplines the senses, and is on the way to realize one's own infinite Self, the Atman, then he or she becomes a unique type of person who is not bound by any sense of external compulsion of duty, but his or her love and compassion and service flow out naturally, spontaneously. His or her very existence is a blessing to society; that idea is expressed in the next verse 17:

यस्तु आत्मरतिरेव स्यात् आत्मतृप्तश्च मानवः ।
आत्मन्येव च सन्तुष्टः तस्य कार्यं न विद्यते ॥१७॥

Yastu ātmaratireva syāt ātmatṛptaśca mānavaḥ;
Ātmanyeva ca santuṣṭaḥ tasya kāryam na vidyate —3. 17

'But the person who is delighted in the Atman, satisfied in the Atman, and finds joy in the Atman alone, he or she has no obligatory duty to perform.'

That person has no *kāryam,* 'duties', to be done, because he or she has attained fulfilment. Evolution has reached its consummation in the realization of the immortality of the Atman. How is it achieved? *Ātmaratireva syāt,* 'one's joy is entirely in the infinite Self', God hidden within all of us. *Rati* means delight, it signifies also sex delight. All delight is included in this word *rati,* and here the *rati* is *ātmaratıḥ eva syāt,* he or she has found tremendous joy only in the Atman, the infinite Self, the One Self in all beings; *ātmatṛptaśca mānavaḥ,* 'the human being who is also fully contented in the Atman'. Such a one doesn't need anything from outside. That person doesn't want to get any sensory object for his or her joy. He or she is full of joy within oneself. That language, taken from the Upaniṣads, is used here. That comes only at the highest level of evolution. *Rati* or pleasure we want, we want delight. In the beginning we get these in sense objects, but when we evolve, we realize that we are the infinite Self, and far far superior to all the sensory objects in the external world. When that knowledge comes, we come to this realization. *Ātmanyeva ca santuṣṭaḥ,* 'finds delight in the Atman only'. To such a person, *tasya kāryam na vidyate,* 'he or she has no duties to perform'. He or she is absolutely free and becomes a blessing to the rest of humanity. When have we duties to perform? When we are imperfect, unfulfilled. But, when one realizes the infinite Atman, he or she does good to society not as a duty, not out of social compulsion, but as a spontaneous outflow of love and service.

The *Taittirīya Upaniṣad* has a section entitled *ānandasya mīmāmsā,* 'investigation into Bliss'. And the Upaniṣad says that 'all types of human pleasures are only a fraction of *ātmānanda,* the Bliss of Atman', *etasya eva ānandasya mātram upajīvanti.*

When you realize the Atman, your mind doesn't go out at all for sensory satisfaction; because there is no desire, hence there is no action. There is no action without desire. Impelled by desire, we engage ourselves in action. *Tasya kāryam na vidyate.* Why?, the next *śloka* explains it.

नैव तस्य कृतेनार्थो नाकृतेनेह कश्चन ।
न चास्य सर्वभूतेषु कश्चित् अर्थव्यपाश्रयः ॥१८॥

Naiva tasya kṛtenārtho nākṛteneha kaścana;
Na cāsya sarvabhūteṣu kaścit arthavyapāśrayaḥ — 3. 18

'He or she has no object in this world (to gain) by doing (an action), nor (does he or she incur any loss) by non-performance of action—nor has he or she any need of depending on anyone for any desirable object.'

'He or she has nothing to achieve by doing some work,' *naiva tasya kṛtenārtho.* Take a young boy, age of ten or twelve. We must constantly teach him, 'Work hard, work hard. You have to achieve many things.' In fact, the very word achievement is a technical word used by Carl Jung of Zurich in his book, *Modern Man in Search of a Soul* (pp. 118–20). Pleading for an important place in life for the culture of the personality, or the spiritual enrichment of the individual, Carl Jung says (*Modern Man in Search of a Soul,* pp. 125–26):

'The afternoon of human life must also have a significance of its own and cannot be merely a pitiful appendage to life's morning. The significance of the morning undoubtedly lies in the development of the individual, our entrenchment in the outer world, the propagation of our kind, and the care of our children. This is the obvious purpose of nature. But when this purpose has been attained—and even more than attained—shall the earning of money, the extension of conquest, and the expansion of life go steadily beyond the bounds of all reason and sense? Whoever carries over into the afternoon the law of the morning—that is, the aims of nature, must pay for so doing with damage to his soul, just as surely as a growing youth who tries to salvage his childish egoism must pay for his mistake with social failure. Moneymaking, social existence, family, and posterity are nothing but plain nature—not culture. Culture lies beyond the purpose of nature. Could by any chance culture be the meaning and purpose of the second half of life?'

A young person must be asked to work hard. Go into the world; *achieve* something. That is called achievement. That is not the time to keep quiet at all, or remain without any work. Not at all. That will ruin the person concerned. Let the person go out, work, satisfy his or her desires, make achievement the goal of one's life at that stage. The same person, after achievement is over, must begin to think of other higher things. Then he or she slowly withdraws one's mind from action and achievement. There is something I have missed, my own true nature. Let me try to realize this truth. That is the second stage. And Jung calls it, 'culture'.

So, this particular person, whose knowledge and joy and sport are in the Atman, has nothing to gain in this world by running about here and there. He or she is fulfilled. If at all he or she does something, it is for the good of others. He or she has nothing of one's own to gain. Śrī Kṛṣṇa will tell this later on in this very chapter.

Sri Ramakrishna gave a very beautiful example:

'You pour ghee or butter into the fire-pan, and when it is hot, you put some cake material (dough) into it. Then it makes sound. That sound is called sizzling; because it is still unripe, it is not cooked yet; so, sizzling goes on. Once it has become cooked, all sizzling stops. Absolutely calm and quiet.'

We are all in that sizzling stage in the first part of our life; we have got so many things to achieve. Then Ramakrishna added:

'But when you put a second cake again, again the sizzling will start.'

There is somebody else's desire to be fulfilled. It is free and not compelled by nature. That is the second state. Śrī Kṛṣṇa will refer to that later on. When you have nothing of your own to obtain, you serve to help others to gain their interests in life. That is a wonderful quality of human life. These are the two dimensions, both are welcome. Achievement is great, but personality enrichment is greater; we must have both in human life. So, *naiva tasya kṛtenārtho na akṛteneha kaścana,* 'neither by doing nor by non-doing he or she is going to gain anything'. He or she has achieved fulfilment. *Na ca asya sarvabhūteṣu kaścit arthavyapāśrayaḥ*, 'he or she has not to go to any being to achieve anything for oneself'. He or she has gained the highest, the ever pure, ever free Self itself.

This verse tells humanity that there is a state where we go beyond all sensory attractions and desires. Today's Western civilization is making its thinkers aware that there is too much of this tyranny of consumerism that is ruining their civilization. About America it is said that 6 per cent of the people of the world are enjoying 40 per cent of the world's resources. After all, there is a limit to consumable things that are available in this world. So, many protests are coming from various sections of society against this wrong philosophy of consumerism; and only when the world understands that there are dimensions above the sensory level of the human personality, then, only then, will set in a turn of human energy inward: let me see what is my own true nature, I am not this sensory system, there is something higher. That person is described here. *Na cāsya sarvabhūteṣu kaścidarthavyapāśrayaḥ*. 'He or she has not to go before anybody and pray, give me this and give me that', Such a person is full, is fulfilled. That state is also there. Even as this state of insatiable desire is there, that other state of fulfilment is also there. So, Śrī Kṛṣṇa is dealing with that subject here, and he will give his own example in that matter. The next *śloka*, verse 19, says:

तस्मात् असक्तः सततं कार्यं कर्म समाचर ।
असक्तो ह्याचरन् कर्म परमाप्नोति पूरुषः ॥१९॥

Tasmāt asaktaḥ satatam kāryam karma samācara;
Asakto hyācaran karma paramāpnoti pūruṣaḥ — 3. 19

'Therefore, do thou always perform obligatory actions, without attachment; by performing action without attachment, the human being attains to the highest.'

Tasmāt, 'therefore', *asaktaḥ satatam kāryam karma samācara*, 'always perform your duties without attachment'. Any amount of work you can do if there is no impulsion of this craving of sensory desire—I must have this, I must have that, that kind of attitude. *Asakto hyācaran karma param āpnoti pūruṣaḥ*, 'one who performs actions in a spirit of detachment, he or she will achieve the highest realization'. *Param āpnoti,* 'will achieve the Supreme', here, in this very life itself. That is the teaching *Gītā* is going to stress again and again. To be detached is very difficult. But that does not mean we should not start trying. In the beginning it may be difficult, but as you go on doing, you will find more and more areas in which you are able to perform actions in a spirit of non-attachment; by constant struggle, we can enrich our lives with the spirit of non-attachment. Action goes on, attachment is not there; why should it be impossible? In fact, very often, when we hear these teachings, the idea comes, 'O, it is impossible!', meant for only saints and sages. Some people think like that.

Gandhiji was once asked about non-violence. 'O, it is impossible,' people say. Then Gandhiji said, 'In this marvellous scientific age, how many impossible things are becoming possible! Why not this also?' After Gandhiji's time, we have seen many more impossible things becoming possible: man landing on the moon, seeing the other side of the moon. Nobody had earlier seen the other side of the moon. We have been told all these thousands of years, 'nobody has seen the other side of the moon.' But what an impossible thing we have achieved today! We have *seen* the other side of the moon, we have *gone* to the moon. We have got down there. What is impossible then? Similarly, 'O, I can't control attachment, I can't control anger, I can't control this and that. It is impossible.' Don't say it is impossible. There is nothing impossible. Tremendous capacity is there in the human mind. Have faith in yourself, you will achieve it. That spirit must come. Then only, these ideas will be translated into human life and work. So, we can begin with no attachment in certain areas, and extend it later to other areas. But it is a wonderful teaching. Work goes on, attachment goes away. Attachment makes for bondage—bondage for both. Even between wife and husband, love liberates both, attachment binds both. The one who is attached, and the one on whom attachment is placed, both are in bondage there. *Satatam* means always; *kāryam karma samācara,* 'perform whatever duties you have to do in life'; do all those actions with great zest and devotion, but in a spirit of detachment.

Then Śrī Kṛṣṇa gives an example, how by doing one's work, discharging one's social responsibilities, people have achieved the highest realization. And the famous example taken in many of our books is the story of King Janaka of Mithila in Bihar. Janaka was the ruler of a kingdom but he was also a *brahmajñāni,* knower of Brahman. Even the young sage Śuka was sent by his father for his spiritual education to this King Janaka. So, that example Śrī Kṛṣṇa is citing here: 'don't think that only when you are alone or in some forest, you can practise detachment. You can practise it in the midst of all your worldly responsibilities around you, that is heroism; but detachment practised when there is nothing to trouble you is not heroic. That is what Śrī Kṛṣṇa says now in verse 20:

कर्मणैव हि संसिद्धिमास्थिता जनकादयः ।
लोकसंग्रहमेवापि संपश्यन् कर्तुमर्हसि ॥ २० ॥

Karmaṇaiva hi samsiddhimāsthitā janakādayaḥ;
Lokasamgrahamevāpi sampaśyan kartum arhasi —3. 20

'Verily, through action alone, Janaka and others attained perfection; even with the view to ensure *lokasamgraha,* the stability of human society, you should perform action.'

Men like Janaka, who was a great king, they all performed action and attained perfection. *Samsiddhim* means 'perfection'. *Karmaṇaiva hi,* 'by performing actions alone', they achieved *samsiddhi.* They had conquered attachment; sitting on the throne as an absolute monarch, with people honouring him; he was not carried away by all this. That is a wonderful achievement. When a little knowledge of the Atman comes, this energy comes to the human being, incorruptible power comes to the human being. An ordinary person is carried away by a little power, by a *little* temptation from the outside world; how small that person must be! Here is another person, huge temptations come, but no disturbance at all in the mind. That is the example given in the second chapter towards the end describing a person of steady wisdom: *Āpūryamāṇam acalapratiṣṭham samudram āpaḥ praviśanti yadvat,* 'minds unshakeable like a mighty lake, full to the brim, into which so many rivers flow without disturbing that lake, without causing a ripple in that lake'. Our minds must be like that. That is what the *Gītā* said earlier. Strong, stable minds, gigantic minds, heroic minds, and not goody-goody small type of people. Too many small people are there in power in many countries. That should not be and need not be. Some strong people, of heroic attitude, must be there. All that will come only when we start this kind of struggle. Then something great will happen to this nation and every other nation.

Writers often quote Lord Acton's famous dictum—power corrupts; absolute power corrupts absolutely. The *Gītā* gives us a philosophy of life and work which can make power incorruptible. The *Gītā* will deal with this subject in its fourth chapter through its *rājarṣi* concept which we shall deal with in due course.

This will make possible more happy inter-human relationships. Therefore, He said: *Karmaṇaiva hi samsiddhim āsthitā janakādayaḥ,* 'without giving up action (or going to the forest), even as a king, men like Janaka achieved *samsiddhi,* perfection even in the midst of action'. *Lokasamgraham evāpi sampaśyan kartum arhasi,* 'you should work even with the view to ensure the stability of human society'. Suppose you have no desires of your own. You are free. You don't need to work at all. Still you must work, because there are others who are in need; you are there to help. That is called *lokasamgraha,* 'ensuring the stability of the human society'. *It is a wonderful concept in the Gītā, the ethics of lokasamgraha, welfare of the world.* Why should anybody suffer in my society? I am here, as Gandhiji said, to wipe the tears from the last weeping person in my society. There also, again, action continues, but it is not for one's own sake. It is for the good of others. That is a very important concept of ethics in the *Gītā*: this concept of *lokasamgraha.* How to see that not merely our own society, but the international community, the whole world, is made better, happier, more fulfilled? I am here to work for it, I have nothing to gain for myself—there must be that attitude. So, Śrī Kṛṣṇa is adding that: *lokasamgrahamevāpi*, 'even from the point of view of ensuring the stability of human society', one should not remain quiet. Though you have no desires, do work for the good of others. How much more should we, who are in the world with our own problems, sympathise with others. Therefore, continue to work, help each other. *Parasparam bhāvayantaḥ śreyaḥ param avāpsyatha.*

One of the greatest truths that must inspire India today is this concept of parasparam bhāvayantaḥ. What have we achieved during these forty years of freedom? We could have banished illiteracy, even the dismal poverty of our millions. But all the upper class people became so self-centred that they did not care for anybody else. All the colleges, all the schools, would be inside or near about the towns. Rural areas were neglected, about three hundred million people were left in their dismal condition. The result is we have a lopsided development, apparently a powerful nation, but with feet of clay. In spite of having the third greatest scientific manpower state in the world, we have got about three hundred million people in dire poverty. What is the use of that scientific manpower? Now this kind of revolution in our thinking has just begun. It will do immense good.

In that context, the *Gītā* ideal will be a tremendous inspiration to translate all these into national character-strength and bright transformation of our human situation. So, *lokasamgrahamevāpi sampaśyan kartum arhasi:* 'even from the point of view of *lokasamgraha*, we should act vigorously'. *Samgraha* means protection, care, welfare, etc.; *loka* means people, especially common people, keeping in view the happiness and welfare of the millions and millions that are there. Gandhiji told one of the Congress patriots at that time: 'whenever you have a doubt on a particular question, you just keep quiet for a minute, ask this question to yourself: "If I do this, will it bring good to the lowest man in society?" If it will bring good, then you adopt it.' That kind of ideal Gandhiji gave. How to chose an action? We can choose it for our own fattening. No. Ask: 'Does it bring good to the poorest and lowest people?' Then it will be perfectly all right. Lot of such thinking has to come to our nation. We have been too self-centred at the upper level. And whatever good policies are adopted in our Parliament, when it comes to implementation, it is stolen at each level by the staff employees, and very little reaches the people who are far below in society. That has been our experience all this time. That will go when we understand these teachings as given in the *Gītā* and in our man-making and nation-building Vivekananda literature. So, *lokasamgraha* is a tremendous concept of general human welfare, and it must be a constant attitude in our minds. In some of our villages I have seen that the powerful members of the village will appropriate whatever is good for them, and will not care to do what is good for the common people around. How can a nation grow when people behave like this? Therefore, a little of this philosophy of *lokasamgraha* must enter into the mind and heart of our people.

Then, Śrī Kṛṣṇa gives a universal truth. In society, there is such a thing as imitation by ordinary people of other eminent people. Suppose that in a village there is an important person. Whatever he or she does, other people will like to follow. There is this mimetic tendency, imitation tendency, in society. In sociology we study it. Because that is so, the eminent person must set an example so that those who imitate him or her will do good and not bad. So, anybody who is prominent in society has to keep a standard of conduct and behaviour. That subject is coming up now with Śrī Kṛṣṇa taking his own example—it is a very interesting section in this third chapter. He says:

यद्यद् आचरति श्रेष्ठः तत्तदेवेतरो जनः ।
स यत् प्रमाणं कुरुते लोकस्तत् अनुवर्तते ॥२१॥

Yadyad ācarati śreṣṭhaḥ tattadevetaro janaḥ;
Sa yat pramāṇam kurute lokastat anuvartate — 3. 21

'Whatever the superior person does, that is also followed by others; what standard he or she demonstrates by action, people follow that.'

Śreṣṭhaḥ means one holding a high position; money, intellect, political power, whoever has more of any of these, that person is a *śreṣṭhaḥ* in that particular society; 'whatever he does, other people try to follow'. That is the nature of human society: *yadyad ācarati śreṣṭhaḥ tat tat eva itaro janaḥ; Sa yat pramāṇam kurute lokaḥ tat anuvartate,* 'whatever standard he or she keeps up, all others follow that very standard'. What a beautiful concept! Yet, it can also be in the wrong way. That is why today, with corruption at the top, corruption has reached down from top to very bottom. So, the people at the top must be of high standard of conduct. In our concept of human society, we had in earlier centuries till now a wonderful idea and practice; the highest person in society, namely the *brāhmaṇa,* was also the poorest person. He or she kept a very high standard of conduct and behaviour for centuries together till the whole society fell down in its decadent period. I have dealt with this in detail in the Introduction.

In the beginning of the nineteenth century, Sri Ramakrishna's father, Kshudhiram Chatterjee, was asked by a zamindar to give false evidence in the court in his favour. He replied, 'Sorry, I cannot. I know it is not true, I cannot give false witness'. That zamindar was a wicked man, who told him: 'Then you will have to suffer.' 'I don't mind. I shall speak the truth only. I am not going to give any false witness.' Because of that, Sri Ramakrishna's father was sent out of that village by the Zamindar. He took his small bundle of possessions and, with his two children and their mother, started to walk out. After some distance, another zamindar, a good man, in another village saw him. He told Kshudiram: 'you come and stay in my village, Kamarpukur. I will give you a piece of land.' In that village Sri Ramakrishna was born. See that quality of life, that high standard of moral conduct; money is not everything; there is honour, there is truth. Year by year, after national independence, we are losing that capacity. For example, we wanted to get political freedom. We had to suffer, we had to get police beating. And yet many came forward and paid the price of freedom by suffering. We had that capacity then, but that is almost gone now. That is our misfortune today.

Yadyad ācarati śreṣṭhaḥ tattadevetaro janaḥ. 'Other people follow the way that the *śreṣṭhaḥ* takes'; *sa yat pramāṇam kurute lokastat anuvartate,* 'whatever *pramāṇa* or standard he or she keeps up, other people follow that standard'.

A father at home keeps a high standard of conduct; the mother also keeps a high standard, children will follow the ways of the father and the mother. People very often forget that, around them, are little children *very* critical and observant of what the father or mother is doing. And if they do bad things, the children will say to themselves: 'alright, we will do double of that bad thing'. It is natural. So, Śrī Kṛṣṇa is telling here that to be at the top of society is not easy. You have to set high standards. That is not what is happening. In fact, more and more evil people are getting all the honour in human society. In Australia, or America, or England, the media gives most space to evil people; somebody robs a bank or passengers in a running train, involving millions of dollars; the media makes that robber a hero, books are written about him and he becomes a millionaire in no time. An honest person has no place at all. This is an inverted type of social value system. Here Śrī Kṛṣṇa is giving this teaching for the good of society. Beware! If you are a leader, set a good example for the rest of the community. To be a leader is not very easy. You have to be very strict about yourself—a *sardār*, leader, must be a *sirdār,* i.e., one who gives his head for a cause. That is the teaching which he is giving us in the third chapter in the name of *karma-yoga,* Yoga of Action. Living and working in society, how careful we have to be to see the increase of only the good in the society and not of the bad. That is leadership in the true sense of the term. So, having said this, Śrī Kṛṣṇa is going to tell us his own example. That is a fine way in which he has put it. 'I have nothing to gain in the whole world, but see how active I am.' That is the subject that is coming up in the next three verses.

What a great responsibility it is for one to be a senior, the junior looks up to the senior. Both senior students and junior students, we have in our schools. Junior students look up to the senior students. However the seniors behave, the juniors like to follow. Śrī Kṛṣṇa expressed this idea as a sociological truth and as a truth which involves a sense of social responsibility on the part of people who are called leaders. In the next verse, verse 22, Śrī Kṛṣṇa is referring to himself as an example. 'Look at me, Arjuna,' he is telling in the next two beautiful verses:

न मे पार्थास्ति कर्तव्यं त्रिषु लोकेषु किंचन ।
नानवाप्तमवाप्तव्यं वर्त एव च कर्मणि ॥२२॥

Na me pārthāsti kartavyam triṣu lokeṣu kimcana;
Nānavāptamavāptavyam varta eva ca karmaṇi — 3. 22

'I have, O Pārtha, no duty, nothing that I have not gained, and nothing that I have yet to gain, in the three worlds; yet, I do continue in action.'

As an incarnation of the Divine, Śrī Kṛṣṇa is speaking: 'Look at me, Arjuna, I have nothing to attain in the three worlds, and yet I am constantly engaging myself in action.' The sense of duty comes from a certain need in you to obtain something from society, and you return that to society through a sense of duty. This is an important statement. Though a divine incarnation, Śrī Kṛṣṇa played various roles such as a political leader, spiritual teacher, a philosopher, as depicted in the *Mahābhārata*. Everybody looked up to him, he could have easily lived a lazy life. He need not have acted at all. Everything would be found for him. But he says, 'no, I am always active, though I have nothing to gain for myself.' He was extremely busy. He was constantly going from Dvāraka on the Gujarat sea coast area to Delhi near the present capital of India. How many times he has gone up and down through the Rajasthan desert, also going to faraway Magadha in Bihar! And, as beautifully expounded in the *Udyoga Parva* of the *Mahābhārata*, going as an ambassador of the Pāṇḍavas to the court of Kauravas to plead for peace between the two and avoid war and requesting the Kauravas to give half the kingdom to their Pāṇḍava cousins, and even reducing that demand to just five villages! I wish that some scholar will write a book on the political and diplomatic speeches of the *Mahābhārata.* Readers will find echoes of those speeches in our contemporary United Nations!

Why was Śrī Kṛṣṇa so active? He gives the explanation in the next verse:

यदि ह्यहं न वर्तेयं जातु कर्मण्यतन्द्रितः ।
मम वर्त्मानुवर्तन्ते मनुष्याः पार्थ सर्वशः ॥२३॥

Yadi hyaham na varteyam jātu karmaṇyatandritaḥ;
Mama vartmānuvartante manuṣyāḥ pārtha sarvaśaḥ—3. 23

'If ever I did not continue to work without any relaxation, O Pārtha, men and women would, in every way follow my example.'

'If I remain idle and do not do any work, other people looking up to me will think within themselves: "that is a good idea, let me also not do any work."' The language is *yadi hi aham na varteyam,* 'if I do not work', *jātu karmaṇi atandritaḥ,* 'constantly and with great energy'; if I do not work like this, *mama vartma anuvartante,* 'people will follow *my* way', *manuṣyāḥ pārtha sarvaśaḥ,* 'all people, O Arjuna, in every way.' What is wrong in that? They will suffer. They need to work, they need to earn, they need to do many things, but they won't, following Śrī Kṛṣṇa's example. Śrī Kṛṣṇa will then become the enemy of the people by setting a bad example before them and ruining their life.

Just like a father at home, he does not need to play with toys; but children need to. So, father also joins with his children to play with toys, just to encourage them. That kind of communication between children and parents is very necessary for the growth of the children. So, a man like Śrī Kṛṣṇa, who doesn't need all this, says, 'look at my example. I am working very hard, if I remain idle, people will suffer.' That is expressed in the next *śloka:*

उत्सीदेयुरिमे लोका न कुर्यां कर्म चेदहम् ।
सङ्करस्य च कर्ता स्यामुपहन्यामिमाः प्रजाः ॥ २४ ॥

Utsīdeyurime lokā na kuryām karma cedaham;
Saṅkarasya ca kartā syāmupahanyāmimāḥ prajāḥ —3. 24

'If I did not do work, these worlds would perish, I would be the cause of social disruption and I would also be ruining these people.'

If I keep quiet, become lazy, and do not do any work, 'I will be destroying these people', *utsīdeyuḥ ime lokā. Saṅkarasya ca kartā syām upahanyāmimāḥ prajāḥ*, 'I shall create utter social confusion and destroy the chances for fulfilment of many many people.' There is a profound truth in this, and our own social history is illustrative of this truth. We had the philosophy of 'non-action', *naiṣkarmya,* in the name of high mystical attitudes. We could digest it and spiritually benefit from it. After some centuries, most of our common people also followed that example: Laziness, no interest in work, minimum work, avoiding work, incapacity for team work, this kind of trait you find today in the character of many of our people. This is the result of our people's indigestion while trying to follow their great spiritual leaders who kept quiet because they had nothing to gain through exertion. And our people followed them. We are now trying to get rid of that 'holy laziness', that want of energy in work in our people. Take our rural people as an example. They are not interested in any improvement. They cannot work together to improve the village, its economic condition, its sanitation; except in a few villages, this is true of most of them. That indigestion came to them from centuries of experience of a wrong type. We have to change all this. We need the philosophy of Śrī Kṛṣṇa and his *Gītā*. In that way, Śrī Kṛṣṇa is telling something of great relevance to all of us in our society here, and so these three verses give us Śrī Kṛṣṇa as an example and as a teacher. He says next: if so, what shall be our attitude to work?

Śrī Kṛṣṇa says in the next two verses that there are two types of people: the enlightened people, and the un-enlightened.

सक्ताः कर्मण्यविद्वांसो यथा कुर्वन्ति भारत ।
कुर्यात् विद्वान् तथा असक्तः चिकीर्षुः लोकसंग्रहम् ॥२५॥

Saktāḥ karmaṇyavidvāṁso yathā kurvanti bharata;
Kuryāt vidvān tathā asaktaḥ cikīrṣuḥ lokasaṁgraham —3. 25

'As the unenlightened, attached to work, acts, so should the enlightened act, O descendent of Bharata, but without attachment, desirous of the well-being of the world.'

Vidvān is a Sanskrit word to indicate the enlightened one, the knowing person. *A-vidvān* means the un-enlightened one. These two have two different approaches to life. This is what Śrī Kṛṣṇa is telling in this verse. Very important verses are these, especially when we deal with citizenship responsibilities in our democratic society. These verses contain a profound message to all of us. If I am un-enlightened, how do I perform work? I work hard, but only to fatten myself. I don't care for others at all. That is called the un-enlightened type. The other is the enlightened type. Work hard for the good of all, to develop the nation, to develop the whole world. Work hard with that attitude. That attitude is expressed in one profound word in this verse: *loka saṁgraham, the welfare of the whole world*. Unless you work hard, you can't ensure the welfare of the whole world. And when you work hard, keep that motivation 'I must serve the people; I must help them to achieve fulfilment along with my own personal fulfilment.' In this way, with a sense of social responsibility I must work. Then only I do work in the right spirit. So, this *śloka* says, *saktāḥ*, 'attached'. *Āsakti* means attachment, attachment to oneself, one's pleasures, comforts, etc. Such people are called *saktāḥ. Karmaṇi*, 'in or to work'. Because through this work, I shall fatten myself: earn more money, enjoy more pleasures. That is called *saktāḥ karmaṇi.* Who are they?, *avidvāṁsaḥ,* 'the un-enlightened people'. All the work that they do is only to fatten themselves. Therefore, they are called un-enlightened people. *Avidvāṁso yathā kurvanti bhārata,* 'as the un-enlightened perform work', similarly, *kuryāt vidvān,* 'the enlightened person will also work'. What is their objective?, their motivation is different. 'This motivation is for bringing happiness and welfare to the whole world', *cikīrṣuḥ lokasaṃgraham. Loka-saṃgraha; loka* means 'people of the world', *saṃgraha* means their welfare, their stability, their strength; all this is included in that word *saṃgraha. Lokasaṃgraha* is the wonderful motivation for work of a highly spiritual type that, in this world of work, we can become deeply spiritual if the motivation is *lokasaṃgraha.*

Throughout the *Gītā*, the *karma-yoga* expounded in it keeps up the *lokasaṃgraha* ideal in front always. We are all interdependent. That concept of interdependence we heard in a previous verse in this very chapter: *parasparaṃ bhāvayantaḥ śreyaḥ param avāpsyatha.* How can I be happy when millions are unhappy? Even today we can see two worlds within the same country: one, extremely poor, buried in dismal poverty; the other, very wealthy, living high life, and consumerism-oriented. How can one be in such a situation, unless one is dead as far as the soul is concerned? So, work hard that that disparity should not remain. So, Śrī Kṛṣṇa says, *kuryāt vidvān,* 'the *vidvān* should do work like that', *cikīrṣuḥ lokasaṃgraham,* 'in order to bring about happiness and welfare of the whole world'. This is a wonderful idea. When we deal with citizenship responsibilities in a democracy, we get this idea. A citizen is not merely one living *in* a nation, but one who is *of* the nation and *for* the nation. He or she feels one with the people of the country. Then only he or she will be a true citizen. That citizenship implies an enlightened attitude. This attitude is the correct one for everyone to adopt in every country. Then comes the next verse:

न बुद्धिभेदं जनयेत् अज्ञानां कर्मसङ्गिनाम् ।
जोषयेत् सर्वकर्माणि विद्वान् युक्तः समाचरन् ॥२६॥

Na buddhibhedam janayet ajñānām karmasaṅginām;
Joṣayet sarvakarmāṇi vidvān yuktaḥ samācaran — 3. 26

'One should not unsettle the understanding of the ignorant, who are attached to action; the enlightened one, oneself steadily acting in the *yoga* spirit, should engage the ignorant also in all work.'

If there are ignorant people around you, you should not disturb their minds and their attitudes. You have to help them to improve themselves. But, in doing so, you should not unsettle their minds and make them bewildered as it were. You can make men and women bewildered by speaking to them something for which they are not prepared; that is not correct. Make them understand, slowly lead them step by step. That is the teaching. But, simply telling something to bewilder somebody is not correct. Because they are not so intellectual, not so educated, we should not bewilder the minds of people by telling all sorts of fantastic things to them. So, Śrī Kṛṣṇa says, *na buddhibhedam janayet*, 'don't create *buddhibhedam,* confusion of mind', in the minds of people 'who are not so enlightened but are attached to action', *ajnānām karmasaṅginām. Joṣayet sarvakarmāṇi vidvān,* 'the *vidvān,* the enlightened one, will do the work that others are doing, and become an example to them in that very line', and thus make them go forward to higher levels. We have to go *with* them.

Long ago, I read a book by one Bruce Barton, an American. There he had said, 'a good teacher is one who will come to the level of the student, and then slowly lift him or her up'. If you want to get into a moving car, you must run *with the car* and then get into the car; otherwise, you will suffer. That is the way great teachers do. Go with the people, then educate them. So, men like Jesus and Buddha, they belong to that category. All good teachers belong to that category. Sri Ramakrishna was of that nature. Vivekananda said in his two lectures on 'My Master' delivered in New York and London in 1896 (*Complete Works of Swami Vivekananda,* vol. 4, p. 183):

'Do not try to disturb the faith of any man. If you can, give him something better; if you can, get hold of a man where he stands and give him a push upwards; do so, but do not destroy what he has. The only true teacher is he who can convert himself, as it were, into a thousand persons at a moment's notice. The only true teacher is he who immediately comes down to the level of the student and transfers his soul to the student's soul and see through the student's eyes and hear through his ears and understand through his mind. Such a teacher can really teach and no one else. All these negative, breaking-down destructive teachers that are in the world can never do any good.'

So, in the case of people who are not so highly educated or enlightened, we should just not disturb their minds by giving them some abstract ideas. Education is lifting a person step by step to a higher position. So, Śrī Kṛṣṇa says: *joṣayet sarvakarmāṇi*, 'he or she is working, you also work similarly'; set an example to him or her. Because he or she needs it, you are educating him or her in that particular direction. A true *yogī* is one who can come to the level of the other people and slowly lift them up even without their knowledge. His or her very contact is enough to lift that person up from the level in which he or she is now living. So, this is an example which enlightened people have to set in society.

Then comes a section dealing with nature and the forces that are operating in nature, and the same forces operating in human beings also. It is a wonderful scientific idea developed in Indian philosophy, that the whole of nature consists of three *guṇas*, three forces, *sattva, rajas* and *tamas*. They are there in you and in me. Nature is there in us and also outside. This is the great philosophical truth propounded by ancient Sāṅkhya philosophy and adopted by Vedanta and others as well. *Sattva, rajas, tamas*: One is inertia, *tamas;* the other is tremendous energy, *rajas;* and balance, calmness, that is *sattva.* Now, when these are in equilibrium, there is no creation; then these three forces are in equilibrium; that equilibrium state is similar to the state of singularity in Western astrophysics. When that equilibrium is broken, cosmic evolution starts. Then only diversification becomes possible. So, nature in its original state was a perfect equilibrium of the three *guṇas, sattva, rajas* and *tamas.* Then at the time of creation what happened? A small disequilibrium started. That went on expanding, and that made for the evolution of the universe, the One becoming the many. *Prakṛti* is the word for nature; everything is a play of these three forces, *sattva, rajas, tamas*. You are feeling absolutely lazy, you sit quiet. Then *tamas* predominates in you. Very active, full of energy, *rajas* predominates in you. But, when you are perfectly serene and calm—occasionally we get into that mood also—*sattva* predominates in you. Now, this subject of *sattva, rajas* and *tamas,* and how to go beyond them in this very life will be the main topic in chapters 13, 14, and 15 of the *Gītā.*

In the context of work, what is it that works in you and in me? Śrī Kṛṣṇa says that *Prakṛti* or nature is working in you and me through these three *guṇas.* So, verse 27 says:

प्रकृतेः क्रियमाणानि गुणैः कर्माणि सर्वशः ।
अहङ्कारविमूढात्मा कर्ताहमिति मन्यते ॥ २७ ॥

Prakṛteḥ kriyamāṇāni guṇaiḥ karmāṇi sarvaśaḥ;
Ahaṅkāravimūḍhātmā kartāhamiti manyate — 3. 27

'The *guṇas* of *prakṛti* perform all actions; with the understanding deluded by egotism, the human being thinks, "I am the doer."'

Prakṛteḥ kriyamāṇāni guṇaiḥ, all these *karmas,* all these activities, 'are actually done by the three *guṇas* or energies of *prakṛti, sattva, rajas* and *tamas*'. Their permutation and combination create the whole cosmos. And that very nature has created us also, has evolved us in the course of cosmic and organic evolution. In due course, the human being also appears on the scene. Nature's activities are everywhere. That is the language; but actually the human being arrogates all these activities to oneself, to one's ego. *Ahaṅkāravimūḍhātmā,* 'the foolish person full of egoistic tendency', what does he or she say?, *kartā aham iti manyate,* 'he or she thinks "I am the doer."' Nature has given that little ego into all of us and that ego arrogates all actions to oneself. Actually, it is nature that is doing all this within us as well as outside us. So, nature is a predominant force, and, unlike in modern Western scientific thought where nature means only external nature, Vedanta includes human nature also; in Vedanta nature in the human being is both external nature as well as a higher dimension of nature which finds expression as intelligence; this distinction between lower dull external nature, *aparā prakṛti,* and higher inner nature, *parā prakṛti,* will be discussed by the *Gītā* in its 4th, 5th, and 6th verses of the seventh chapter. The chemistry and physics of the world appear in you and me as the biochemistry and biophysics of the body. So, the body has its own logic of action. So also, the sensory system. But we think, 'we are doing everything'. Actually, it is not we. Nature impels us to do all these things. That is a profound truth we must realize today. You want to eat. You think you are *choosing* to eat. Nature *compels* you to eat. So also many things you do. Nature is impelling you to do these things. We had seen earlier Carl Jung's statement that we are only instruments of external nature, when we marry and produce offspring.

This truth must be realized: how nature is a powerful force, both cosmically and in the human system. And Śrī Kṛṣṇa will say later on, 'you cannot resist these energy impulsions of nature'. Very often you have to submit, very often you have to say 'yes' to them. *But at the same time, let Western scientific thought realize that there is a higher dimension of nature in human beings, which is intelligence, that is the focus of human freedom.* When that becomes manifest, we are able to go beyond the constraints of this external physical nature. Both are *prakṛti,* both are nature. One is called lower nature, *aparā prakṛti,* the other is called higher nature, *parā prakṛti.* Both together constitute the totality of the universe.

Here Śrī Kṛṣṇa says, *prakṛteḥ kriyamāṇāni guṇaiḥ karmāṇi sarvaśaḥ,* 'various *guṇas* of nature, *sattva, rajas, tamas,* they do all these actions'. But, the human being, full of ego and with pride and arrogance, *kartā aham iti manyate,* says, 'I am doing everything'. Human freedom is limited by several factors dictated by nature. Take, for example, our genetic constitution; it operates in its own way; it limits the freedom of the ego. The human being has to submit to these energies that are present in nature.

It is good to recognize the forces of nature that are operating within us. Take for example modern studies of the psyche of the human being. The conscious mind, with the ego presiding, is mostly at the service of the subconscious and the unconscious. And that is all nature. That nature dictates to the conscious ego, but the ego thinks 'I am free'. It is good to recognize this, so that, if at all there is a hope of freedom, we can achieve it after knowing this truth and taking appropriate steps to achieve freedom from external nature, and realize our own higher nature or *parā prakṛti. There the subject of spirituality comes in.* Spiritual knowledge (*jnāna*) and realization (*vijñāna*) come in at that stage.

As we have seen earlier, take, for example, we eat, we drink, we develop our bodies; even we go to school, study and obtain marks, and get a job. Then we marry, then we rear families; most of this you will find is the play of nature only. Nature impels you to do this, impels you to do that. That is all what is happening. But when you become spiritually awakened, you are able to regulate these nature's functions and make them moral and ethical and value-oriented. *All values, says Vedanta, have their source in the Atman.* That is what you can do by developing your own spiritual awareness. Until then, it is merely all nature. In animals, nature completely predominates. When in any human being such a condition arises, he or she is an animal. In men and women, this little ego, a little focus of freedom, has come. But, it is extremely weak; much of it is nature itself. *The whole subject of the science of religion and spirituality, which is Vedanta, is how to strengthen that little focus of freedom and make the human being truly free from thraldom to nature.* Only human beings can do it. But it cannot be done by merely arrogating everything to this ego. Ego is not really free. The waking ego dies in sleep and a dream ego appears in dream; and both egos disappear in deep sleep. It is under constraints of nature's forces. *Behind the ego is the Atman, our own infinite divine nature, which is the only source of all freedom and of all values.* When you realize that truth, you go beyond the constraints of nature. So, throughout the *Gītā,* both are mentioned. Ordinarily, we are subject to the forces of lower nature. But you *can* go beyond them. Go beyond them slowly, steadily; not with a sense of ego and arrogance, but by understanding the truth which is beyond this ego, your own infinite Self, the Atman. *That truth will be constantly dealt with in the Gītā as the message of spiritual freedom of every human being. That is our birthright.* At present we are subject to the forces of nature. Nature compels. So, don't try to fight nature frontally, you will never succeed thereby; fight nature in a diplomatic way. Śrī Kṛṣṇa is going to tell us that this egoistic approach is the foolish person's attitude. A wise person who knows the truth, how does he or she think? The next *śloka* explains it.

तत्त्ववित्तु महाबाहो गुणकर्मविभागयोः ।
गुणा गुणेषु वर्तन्त इति मत्वा न सज्जते ॥ २८ ॥

Tattvavittu mahābāho guṇakarmavibhāgayoḥ;
Guṇā guṇeṣu vartanta iti matvā na sajjate — 3. 28

'But one who has true insight into the domains of *guṇa* and *karma,* knowing that *guṇas* as sense organs merely rest on *guṇas* as sense objects, does not become attached.'

To one who knows the *tattva,* the truth about things—*tattva* means the truth; Śaṅkarācārya explains it as *tasya bhāvaḥ tattvam,* 'the truth about a thing is called *tattvam'*; and *tattvavit,* 'one who knows the truth': how does he or she think? *Guṇakarmavibhāgayoḥ,* those who know the truth, 'about the division into *guṇa* and *karma'; guṇa* means the forces of nature, *karma* means activity—the one is dictated by the other. Those who know the truth of the relationship between *guṇa* and *karma,* how do they think? *Guṇā guṇeṣu vartante, 'guṇas* are working amongst *guṇas', guṇas* are interacting with the *guṇas. Iti matva,* 'knowing this truth', *na sajjate,* 'are not attached'. The ego becomes detached and rises in the spiritual level. When one gets caught up in the force of the *guṇas* of nature, one becomes a slave. When the person becomes detached, he or she becomes free. So, in this case, *guṇā guṇeṣu vartante, 'guṇas* work among *guṇas'; sattva, rajas, tamas guṇas* in the form of nature outside, as well as *guṇas* inside in the form of the sensory and psychic system; they are nothing but *guṇas* working among *guṇas.* Knowing this truth, *na sajjate,* 'he or she doesn't get attached'. *A wonderful attitude of detachment from all ego assessments comes and the Gītā specially emphasizes this idea of detachment. Modern scientific temper also emphasizes this idea of detachment*. The flow of the current of life is going on, I am also in it, but I am detached from it. This is how Śrī Kṛṣṇa is developing this great idea.

This concept of the *guṇas* is expressed in many places in the *Mahābhārata:* The whole universe is the play of the *guṇas*. Today's physics speaks of three or four forces in nature. We are trying to understand them. One is gravitation, then electromagnetism, then the weak force, and then the strong force, within the atom. Now, these are the energies that constitute the whole of nature. Physics has not unified them yet. But it is trying to unify them; but in the state of singularity, astrophysics takes them as unified. The concept of the *guṇas* is a profound subject which deals with nature's energies in terms of the human being and the cosmos and which thinkers are trying to understand in terms of modern scientific terminology. Śrī Krāṇa continues:

प्रकृतेः गुणसंमूढाः सज्जन्ते गुणकर्मसु ।
तानकृत्स्नविदो मन्दान् कृत्स्नवित् न विचालयेत् ॥ २९ ॥

Prakṛteḥ guṇasammūḍhāḥ sajjante guṇakarmasu;
Tānakṛtsnavido mandān kṛtsnavit na vicālayet — 3. 29

'Persons of perfect knowledge should not unsettle the understanding of people of dull wit and imperfect knowledge who, deluded by the *guṇas* of *prakṛti,* attach themselves to the functions of the *guṇas.*'

Those who are dull-witted don't understand this truth. They are part of the flow of the *guṇas;* such people have to be educated gently. Don't unsettle their minds. But, slowly educate them. Otherwise, you will do harm to them. *Prakṛteḥ guṇasammūḍhāḥ*, 'those who are deluded by the *guṇas* of *prakṛti*', *sajjante guṇakarmasu*, 'they are attached to the activities dictated by the *guṇas*'. 'Such people of small understanding', *tān akṛtsnavido mandān; kṛtsnavit na vicālayet,* 'a person of full understanding should not disturb'. If you can, help them to understand better. But don't leave them in that disturbed condition. *Tānakṛtsnavido mandān kṛtsnavit na vicālayet*, 'the one who knows the whole truth, should not disturb one who knows only partial truth'. Then, for the first time, Śrī Kṛṣṇa is making a passing reference to his own divine nature as the inner Self of all; it will be more and more in focus as you proceed into the chapters ahead.

मयि सर्वाणि कर्माणि संन्यस्याध्यात्मचेतसा ।
निराशीः निर्ममो भूत्वा युध्यस्व विगतज्वरः ॥३०॥

Mayi sarvāṇi karmāṇi sannyasyādhyātmacetasā;
Nirāśīḥ nirmamo bhūtvā yudhyasva vigatajvaraḥ —3. 30

'Renouncing all actions to Me, with mind centred on the Self, getting rid of hope and selfishness, fight on, free from mental fever.'

A beautiful verse! *Yuddha* means battle. *Yudhyasva*, 'fight on', carry on the battle of life! How?, *vigatajvaraḥ*, 'without fever, i.e., inner tension', in a calm and serene way; *Mayi sarvāṇi karmāṇi sannyasya*, 'renouncing all actions in Me'. There is a divine infinite Consciousness behind and beyond all nature which is only its manifested energy. As the *Svetāsvatara Upaniṣad* says, *Māyām tu prakṛtim vidyāt, māyinam tu maheśvaram*, 'the whole of nature is called *Māyā*, and the Supreme Divine is the Master of this *Māyā*'.

Sri Ramakrishna used to say: Magic and the magician; magic is not true, magician alone is true. Don't concentrate only on the magic. Remember, to have the magic, you need the magician. And so Śrī Kṛṣṇa said, *Mayi sarvāṇi karmāṇi sannyasya*, 'renouncing all your actions in Me', who is beyond *Māyā* and is the master of *Māyā*, *adhyātmacetasā*, 'developing a spiritual attitude', a spiritual frame of mind, *nirāśīḥ*, 'without craving', *bhūtvā nirmamo*, 'becoming free from the "I" and "mine"', *yudhyasva*, 'engage yourself in the battle (of life)', *vigatajvaraḥ*, 'without fever or tension'.

That is the profound message of this *karma-yoga* chapter of the *Gītā*. Do work without tension. Work without fuss. It is a very profound message. Generally, we haven't got the strength to work with calmness. Therefore, we make a lot of noise, a lot of fuss. A machine makes a lot of noise when it is not efficient, when it is not properly oiled. But if it is a good machine, it is silent and quiet. Formerly, our water pumps used to make lot of noise. Today, silent pumps are there. More efficiency is coming to our machines. Even our old auto-rickshaws, what noise they used to make! Only twelve miles per hour, but such a noise! Whereas a first class car runs at 80 miles an hour without any noise. So, in the human system also, there is such a thing as efficiency in life and action. That efficiency is measured by the high quantity of work turned out, but in calmness. Any kind of fussy work is inefficient work. We have seen people, even in households, making much noise and fuss, but with little actual turn out of work. Why not do work with a calm and quiet demeanour? Carry the burden with a smile as if there is no burden at all. This kind of spiritual strength must be behind all efficient work. That is why Śrī Kṛṣṇa says, *vigatajvaraḥ. Jvaraḥ* means 'fever' in Sanskrit; *vigata* means 'without'. Fever means here, tension, excitement, fussiness. Specially fussy work, there are people who go on shouting all the time in the midst of work. That is inefficient work. The *Gītā* wants us to be absolutely calm and steady while at work. When we fly at high speed of about 600 miles per hour in a jet plane, we don't feel that it is moving at all; that is the mark of efficiency of a machine. Similarly, the human system must be trained to perform: *Yudhyasva vigatajvaraḥ*. It is the most urgent message we in India have to understand and apply today.

All our national problems we can solve, when we become efficient and honest workers, calm, silent, and steady. People who think that much passion is needed, much noise must be made, in the midst of work, don't know the science and art of work. It is the silent man that does the best of work. *Samatvam yoga ucyate;* Śrī Kṛṣṇa has defined his message of *yoga* in the second chapter as 'equanimity', *samatvam*, and *yogaḥ karmasu kauśalam*, '*yoga* is efficiency in action'. Nothing is off your control when you work efficiently; and if you have a controlled anger, it will be perfectly relevant then; but, if anger takes control of you, then something goes wrong with you. So, in this matter, this particular teaching is very very significant. Śrī Kṛṣṇa is telling in the next verse, verse 31, how one becomes freed from the bad effects of work thereby:

ये मे मतमिदं नित्यमनुतिष्ठन्ति मानवाः ।
श्रद्धावन्तोऽनसूयन्तो मुच्यन्ते तेऽपि कर्मभिः ॥३१॥

Ye me matam idam nityamanutiṣṭhanti mānavāḥ;
Śraddāvanto'nasūyanto mucyante te'pi karmabhiḥ —3. 31

'Those persons who constantly practise this teaching of mine, full of *śraddhā* or faith and conviction, and without cavilling, they too, are freed from (the evil effects of) all work.'

Those who listen to my teaching as given here, with faith and devotion, and implement it in their lives, they also will become free from all relativity and bondage, and achieve perfect spiritual freedom. The *jñāni* attains it, and the *karma-yogī* also will attain it. Action creates bondage; but, there is a method by which you can remove the bondage aspect of action, so that action takes you to freedom. *That is a great message for the benefit of all human beings*. That is why Śrī Kṛṣṇa's message is declared to be a *Gītā*, a music for the human soul, a *Song Celestial*, as Sir Edwin Arnold terms it. Millions and millions of people, though caught up in the battlefield of work, will also grow spiritually when they follow this philosophy. That is the great assurance given by Śrī Kṛṣṇa to all the working people of this world. And almost everybody is a worker, whether you are rich or poor, or high or low, in society. *So, it is a universal philosophy for all humanity*. Then Śrī Kṛṣṇa says, 'those who do not care to listen to this teaching and even pooh pooh it, they will have a very low level of life':

ये त्वेतदभ्यसूयन्तो नानुतिष्ठन्ति मे मतम् ।
सर्वज्ञानविमूढांस्तान्विद्धि नष्टानचेतसः ॥३२॥

Ye tvetadabhyasūyanto nānutiṣṭhanti me matam;
Sarvajñānavimūḍhānstān viddhi naṣṭānacetasaḥ —3. 32

'But those who, decrying this teaching of mine, do not practise it, thoroughly devoid of all knowledge and discrimination, know them to be mindless and ruined.'

Those who, *etat abhyasūyanto,* 'decrying this teaching of mine'; *na anutiṣṭhanti me matam,* 'do not practise this teaching of mine'; *sarvajñāna vimūḍhān tān,* 'they are deluded in all spheres of knowledge'; what happens to them?, *viddhi naṣṭān,* 'know them to be ruined'; *acetasaḥ,* 'who are mindless'. It is just like a *rat* entering a trap, it can also come out by the way it got in; but it does not know it, it is deluded, and only runs about in the trap. Says Śrī Kṛṣṇa: there is a *method* by which all can be free and I am giving that.

So, a great teacher comes and tells us, we have entered into this bondage, and we shall get out of it. There is a way to get out of this bondage. So, the *yoga* philosophy of the *Gītā* is a philosophy for one and all: we have to face the challenges of the world, challenge of work, challenge of all this *prakṛti,* physical nature, around and in us, and we take up that challenge, follow this teaching, and become free in this very life. That is the profound message Śrī Kṛṣṇa is giving to the whole of humanity. That is why the *Gītā* is attracting the attention of working people. Lazy people cannot appreciate this teaching, only working people can. Those who work, work with zest and with joy, and, *in* work, learn calmness and the serenity of the human mind and heart; what a wonderful joy it is to work in such a way! It is like gliding. When we glide, we don't find any pressure or friction. The wind carries us this way, that way. Life becomes a gliding as it were; or, we can also call it the hang-gliding of today. Life moves on just like that, absolutely spontaneous, natural; how?, because of the change within your system. A new element has come in, the higher nature, *adhyātma cetasā,* 'with a spiritual attitude'. So, the whole work becomes different. Anyone can *actually* demonstrate it in one's life. When we are untrained in mind, we work, we get tired, we get depressed, we get so many ups and downs in our mental state during the whole day. But, when you have this *adhyātma cetas,* 'spiritual orientation of mind', you are able to face all these difficulties better and better. Not that in one day you can achieve it, but by applying it in various situations, you grow in spiritual strength and become able to carry more heavy burdens with a smile. This is the possibility opened up by the *Gītā* to the whole of humanity.

So, though a very ancient book, yet how modern and how thoroughly relevant it is to the times in which we live! Only truth can be relevant like that for all times, not dogmas. Great books are eternal books, immortal literature. About five thousand years ago, the *Mahābhārata* war took place. Śrī Kṛṣṇa gave this message to Arjuna. After all these thousands of years, you find it is so relevant to everyone in the amazing modern age, not only in India but also outside India. The message given to human beings: how to make him or her free; that freedom is one's birthright, it is built into each person, only he or she doesn't know how to manifest it. Śrī Kṛṣṇa is helping us to manifest that ever-present freedom that is within ourselves. That is his great message in this third chapter, known as the chapter on *karma-yoga*. Further teachings come, some more verses are there. And towards the end there is a wonderful seven-verse section dealing with the origin of crime in society and how to overcome it.

Śrī Kṛṣṇa says here:

सदृशं चेष्टते स्वस्याः प्रकृतेः ज्ञानवानपि ।
प्रकृतिं यान्ति भूतानि निग्रहः किं करिष्यति ॥३३॥

Sadṛśam ceṣṭate svasyāḥ prakṛteḥ jñānavānapi;
Prakṛtim yānti bhūtāni nigrahaḥ kim kariṣyati — 3. 33

'Even a wise person acts in accordance with his or her own nature; beings follow nature; what can suppression do?'

The word *prakṛti* has been used in several of these verses. We call it nature. The whole of nature outside, and the same nature within us also. This body-sense-mind complex is an evolution of the same material out of which the external nature has also evolved. That is the Vedantic teaching, and that is also modern scientific teaching. So, nature is also within us, not merely outside. Our body, our sensory system, even our psyche, are all outposts of external nature in you and me. That nature exerts a great force within us. We are pulled down by that nature to live like an ordinary animal or beast; we must reckon with this nature. Śrī Kṛṣṇa says here, even a man of knowledge is impelled by nature within to act in particular ways: *Sadṛśam ceṣṭate svasyāḥ*, 'one's own nature dictates how one shall act', what conduct one shall adopt; *prakṛti* or nature within us will dictate what we shall do, what we shall not do. Now that *prakṛti* consists of the impulses of the sensory system to go out to the external world all the time, and the mind follows the senses and also goes after the sensory pleasures outside. And by doing so, we create another type of nature within us, namely, innate tendencies, what we call *samskāras* or *vāsanas,* a beautiful scientific term in Vedantic psychology. We have these within the mind, below the conscious level, in the subconscious and unconscious mind of man, which is innate nature in its raw state. Everything is there and they try to come out, try to express themselves through our conscious mind; and, not only you and I, *jñānavān api,* 'even a person of knowledge', is dragged by these forces within. In spite of possessing knowledge, he or she is being pulled in a particular direction by these forces.

Vedanta wants people to understand what are these forces operating upon them? And Vedanta answers: there are two forces: external forces and internal forces. People neglect these internal forces. That is why they are in trouble. If we don't neglect this, and if we know how to handle these internal forces, then we can live a better and fuller life. That will be taught in the verses to follow. So, *prakṛter jñānavān api,* 'even a *jñāni,* one of knowledge, is carried away by the forces of nature' implanted within oneself. *Prakṛtim yānti bhūtāni,* 'beings follow the impulsions of nature', *nigrahaḥ kim kariṣyati,* 'what can *mere suppression* do?' You can't suppress these forces of nature. That is not the way. We have to educate them. As Sri Ramakrishna would say, 'give them a new direction', *moḍe phiriye dāo,* that is his Bengali expression. A new direction, ethical, moral, spiritual, you have to give to such impulses, and not suppress them. That is your own responsibility. When you try to do so, you need help. Then you turn to books like the *Gītā* and other spiritual books. They give you guidance in this matter. And so, it is a problem everybody has to face, human beings in particular. Animals are all controlled by nature; they don't protest against nature. You can see nature in its fullest expression in the animal. But in a human being, that nature in its outer and inner forms, is there; but, something else is also there, the highest form of nature, the Atman. That something is the human source of freedom, the Atman manifesting through the body-mind complex as an urge for freedom: 'I want to take my life in my own hands and shape it, I don't want nature to shape it.' In this way, there is an element of freedom in every human child, which you won't find in any animal. *Vedanta therefore calls this human system as cit-jaḍa-granthi, a combination of cit and jaḍa,* that means consciousness and inert matter. These two are combined in the human system. What is inert matter, is what nature has implanted in us. What is consciousness, is also present within us in our 'higher nature', *parā prakṛti*; in evolution, it has found a higher manifestation in this human system. We are in a difficult situation. We would have no struggle in life, if that consciousness and its urge for freedom were not there, if *only* ordinary nature was there; we would then say 'yes' to every impulse. But, because that consciousness is there and it is tied to this nature, you revolt against it. All moral life, all culture, all civilization, comes out of that struggle. I want to assert my own true nature which is of the nature of pure consciousness. We are, says Vedanta, *cit-jaḍa-granthi,* the knot of *cit* and *jaḍa, cit* means 'consciousness', and *jaḍa* means 'unconsciousness or inertness'. Nature is inert outside. That nature has implanted itself within us; when that is strong, we are carried away. *Prakṛter jñānavānapi,* 'even a *jñāni* is subject to this pressure'.

In the *Devī Māhātmyam,* that great book of *bhakti* to the Divine Mother, there is this *śloka* (1. 55):

Jñāninām api cetāmsi devī bhagavatī hi sā;
Balād ākṛṣya mohāya mahāmāyā prayacchati —

'That Divine Mother manifesting as *Mahāmāyā,* that great delusion which is functioning in this world of manifestation, drags away even the mind of a *jñāni,* person of knowledge, towards delusive life, delusive action.'

And so we have to be careful. Everything is not easy within us. Human life is a struggle. The concept of human life as a struggle is a wonderful concept. Animals do not struggle to manifest themselves on a higher plane. We struggle. Their struggle is for mere survival, eating, drinking, and mating; ours is not for mere survival; something within us is seeking expression and to dominate this body-mind complex. That is how we develop culture, we develop civilization: saying 'no' to nature, going beyond nature to some extent. Nature says: remain in sun and rain; the human being says, 'no', and builds a house. But even then, even a person of culture and civilization is subject to the pressures of nature. And we can see it in civilization everywhere. There is a deeper dimension to human life, not merely civilization. Civilization is only more of comfort, more of conveniences, more of gadgets. I sometimes quote a sentence from Disraeli, the British Prime Minister about a hundred years ago, who was a great scholar. There he says, 'the European talks of progress because by the aid of a few scientific discoveries, he has constructed a society which mistakes comfort for civilization.' Because we are more comfortable, we are more civilized! That is not correct. There is something higher which we have to manifest. Comfortable life is not a truly civilized life. So, the verse says: *Prakṛtim yānti bhūtāni,* 'beings follow impulsions of nature'. Most of what we are doing, are nothing but impulsions of nature, as I have said earlier quoting Carl Jung of Switzerland. In all these matters, what functions is just plain nature. But that is not the whole thing. There is such a thing as culture or personality development. There you are on your own ground. You are trying to manifest some dimension within you beyond the nature level. Out of that comes ethics, morality, and higher spiritual life.

Indian thought divides human life into four stages: *brahmacarya,* student life, *gārhastya,* married state, *vānaprastha,* retired life, *sannyāsa,* life of renunciation. The last two deal with the higher dimension in a more concentrated way. During the first two also, we shall be having something to do with the higher dimension, but the struggle of life is so strong that we cannot divert our major attention to it. But now that you have *achieved* something in life, you have got a family, you have got name, fame, everything has come to you, now it is time to develop a new philosophy for yourself. That is the philosophy of the 'afternoon' of human life. Have I *enriched myself qualitatively?* What a beautiful concept! More of peace, more of joy, more of compassion—that spiritual development must become the main activity in the afternoon of one's life. If you carry over the forenoon activities to the afternoon, what will be the result? Diminution of personality, as quoted from Carl Jung earlier. We will become smaller and smaller day by day, because the world rejects us; nature rejects us.

Take, for example, the concept of genetics. Any organism is valuable for nature only so long as it can reproduce. As soon as it ceases to reproduce, nature has no interest in that organism. Nature may reject you, but why do *you* reject yourself? You have the capacity to take life to a higher level, higher than nature. Don't live at the nature's level all the time. This is a profound truth. In these verses, the *Gītā* is stressing this idea that much of our life is at the level of nature. We accept it, but it need not always be so. We can rescue ourselves from the bonds of nature. There is something within us, which is free. We can manifest that freedom. There comes a higher philosophy of life, and both these should not contradict each other. They follow one after the other. First is *achievement,* certainly as Jung says, a young person of twenty, instead of sitting quiet 'looking into the navel', sitting in meditation, let him or her work hard, earn money, and do other things.

Otherwise, he or she will be a failure. In these verses, you get that truth expressed by Śrī Kṛṣṇa: *Sadṛśam ceṣṭate svasyāḥ prakṛteḥ; svasyāḥ prakṛteḥ sadṛśam ceṣṭate,* 'according to one's own *prakṛti* or nature, one acts'. Even the *jñāni* is forced to act accordingly. *Nigrahaḥ kim kariṣyati?*, 'what can mere suppression do? 'You suppress it here, it will come out there in another form.

You cannot destroy nature. It is there. But you must know how to handle it. A depth psychology has been used to develop the spiritual message of Vedanta. Without doing violence to human nature, we *educate nature* and go higher and higher and still higher. No direct confrontation, no suppression. Suppression has no meaning at all, because suppressed energies find a way to come out. In fact, they come out in a disguised form. That is one of the big contributions of Freud to Western human psychology: Whatever is unpleasant to you, whatever your conscience doesn't like, you just suppress it into the mind. It goes into the subconscious or unconscious. From there it comes out in a disguised form, in various forms of psychic distortions and complexes manifesting as this distorted behaviour and that distorted behaviour. You don't know what they are. A psychologist or psycho-analyst may be able to know better, and so he or she analyses and traces it to the suppressed energy which has created this distortion. So, Śrī Kṛṣṇa says, that suppression is not the way, educate these energies; *they can be educated.*

Sri Ramakrishna puts it in a simple statement, *moḍ phiriye dāo,* 'turn the direction of these energies'. They are all centres of energy; every emotion is a centre of energy, every psychic experience is a centre of energy. That energy has to be refined and given a direction. That capacity we have. Only we must do it carefully, judiciously, not through a direct confrontation. Those who have enormous spiritual strength, they can do it with a direct confrontation. But most people cannot and should not. They will lose in the battle. That is the meaning of the statement: *nigrahaḥ kim kariṣyati,* 'merely suppressing, what can it do?' Better to work out these various tendencies, impulses, with a discriminating mind, so that you can climb higher and higher. The word discrimination, *viveka,* comes here again and again. So, this is the teaching regarding nature implanted in human beings, the same nature that is outside. That is why, Śrī Kṛṣṇa will say later on that there is a similarity between the two, attraction between the two: nature outside, and my sensory and psychic system. He says in the next *śloka* 34:

इन्द्रियस्येन्द्रियस्यार्थे रागद्वेषौ व्यवस्थितौ ।
तयोर्न वशमागच्छेत् तौ ह्यस्य परिपन्थिनौ ॥ ३४॥

Indriyasyendriyasyārthe rāgadveṣau vyavasthitau;
Tayorna vaśamāgacchet tau hyasya paripanthinau —3. 34

'Attachment and aversion of the sense organs for their respective sense objects are natural; let none come under their sway; they are one's highway robbers.'

Indriya and *indriyasyārtha* are two words. *Indriya* means sense organ. *Indriyasyārtha* means sense object. 'These two are related to each other', *indriyasya indriyasya arthe.* How do they get related? Through two emotions: one is called *rāga,* attachment, the other is called *dveṣa,* aversion. If it is favourable, I am attached to it; if it is unfavourable, I am averse to it. These are the ways we react to all external sensory experiences. A pleasant experience is welcome. We try to run away from the unpleasant. That is how we behave with regard to the external sensory world. *Rāgadveṣau vyavasthitau,* '*rāga* and *dveṣa* are well established'. Our human system is well established in the sensory world through these two emotions, *rāga* and *dveṣa.* Then Śrī Kṛṣṇa says, *tayoḥ na vaśamāgacchet,* 'don't get into their clutches'. Why?, *tau hi asya paripanthinau,* 'they are well known as one's highway robbers'. See the language: *paripanthinau.* You are going along a road, a highway robber comes and loots away all that you have. We have plenty of highway robbers today, in buses and trains, everywhere. But, everyday, in our very life, we are having this kind of highway robbers. What do they rob from us?, our discrimination, our knowledge, our wisdom.

Therefore, be careful. Be alert, is the language. So, this is a warning that is given to all wayfarers' lives. We are all wayfarers. We started our lives as babies, going on in this world as a pilgrim to achieve this and that. To all of us this warning is given. You want your lives to be successful, be careful. These robbers are there. You cannot afford to be careless in your journey. Then:

श्रेयान् स्वधर्मो विगुणः परधर्मात् स्वनुष्ठितात् ।
स्वधर्मे निधनं श्रेयः परधर्मो भयावहः ॥ ३५ ॥

Śreyān svadharmo viguṇaḥ paradharmāt svanuṣṭhitāt;
Svadharme nidhanam śreyaḥ paradharmo bhayāvahaḥ—3. 35

'Better is one's own *dharma*, though imperfect, than the *dharma* of another well performed; better is death in one's own *dharma;* another person's *dharma* is fraught with fear.'

Everyone has his or her own *dharma*, or way of life and work and human relations. According to one's psychological disposition, a person has a particular bent of mind and work capacities. That is one's *dharma*. Śrī Kṛṣṇa says, better to die in one's own *dharma,* than to live in somebody else's *dharma*. That *dharma* is good for that person, this is good for you. Find out your own *dharma* based on your own mental disposition. *Śreyān svadharmo viguṇaḥ*, 'even though one's own *dharma* is not of high quality, still it is the best for oneself'. This is a teaching based on the individual identity of every human being, like the individuality of one's thumb impression. Similarly, there is a psychic individuality. That is based on a certain bent of life, attitudes, reactions, likes and dislikes. All these constitute one's individuality; let one respect it and not imitate somebody else; don't be ashamed of yourself. This *śloka* refers to this need on our part to have faith in ourselves, confidence in ourselves, in one's own psychological disposition. One can *change* it for the better but should not *exchange* it, should not cast yourself in the mould of somebody else. Then comes the question, 'how do we commit blunders and crimes in life?' What is the etiology of crime? This very important subject comes at the end of this third chapter. Arjuna is putting a very pertinent question on this subject:

अर्जुन उवाच –
Arjuna uvāca—
'Arjuna said.'

अथ केन प्रयुक्तोऽयं पापं चरति पूरुषः ।
अनिच्छन्नपि वार्ष्णेय बलादिव नियोजितः ॥ ३६ ॥

Atha kena prayukto'yam pāpam carati pūruṣaḥ;
Anicchannapi vārṣṇeya balādiva niyojitaḥ — 3. 36

'Then, impelled by what does a person commit sin or crime, though against one's wishes, O Kṛṣṇa, carried away, as it were, by a force?'

This is a question which everyone must be asking every now and then silently in one's mind. Arjuna is only a sample of what humanity is. Arjuna asks, 'by what impulsion does a human being commit crime?' *Atha kena prayukto'yam*. *Kena* means by what or by whom; *prayuktaḥ* means impelled by. *Pāpam carati*, 'commit sin or crime'. *Pūruṣaḥ*, 'a human being'. *Pāpam* is generally translated as sin in theology. In sociopolitical thought, *pāpam* means crime. Crime against society, crime against other human beings or other living beings. In Vedanta, we don't make much distinction between sin and crime. The question, therefore, is: why does man commit a crime or an evil deed?, bloodshed, murder, robbery; in fact we have a plentiful variety of crimes today, multiplying day by day. So, it is good to know the origin of this crime and how to eliminate it from society. In fact, in sociology and in criminology we study this subject. The *Gītā* is giving us an insight into it based on Vedantic study of the depth dimension of the human personality through its *science of human possibilities*. *Anicchannapi*, 'even though (the person) is unwilling', says Arjuna's question; this is true of many criminals but not of all; this is reiterated by Arjuna by saying *balādiva niyojitaḥ*, 'as if impelled by some force'. These last seven verses are a depth study of the subject of crime, its etiology, and how to overcome it.

श्रीभगवान् उवाच–
Śrībhagavān uvāca—
'The Blessed Lord said.'

काम एष क्रोध एष रजोगुण समुद्भवः ।
महाशनो महापाप्मा विद्ध्येनमिह वैरिणम् ॥ ३७॥

Kāma eṣa krodha eṣa rajoguṇa samudbhavaḥ;
Mahāśano mahāpāpmā viddhyenamiha vairiṇam —3. 37

'It is sensual desire, it is anger, born of the *rajo-guṇa*; of great craving and of great sin; know this as the enemy here (in human life).'

Śri Kṛṣṇa is giving the reply: *Kāma eṣa krodha eṣa,* 'it is *kāma*, insatiate desire, and it is *krodha,* anger'; *rajoguṇa samudbhavaḥ,* 'they are born out of the *rajo-guṇa* in human beings'; *mahāśano mahāpāpmā,* 'great consumer and great sinner'; *viddhi enam iha vairiṇam,* 'know this as the enemy here'.

Kāma is a great word. It has been treated from two points of view. In *Manu Smṛti,* there is a great praise of *kāma*. *Akāmasya kriyā nāsti,* 'without having *kāma* or desire within, one can't act at all'. All action is impelled by *kāma.* So, *kāma* is praised here. Take our own rural population, millions of them have no desire for a better life; so they live in insanitary conditions, satisfied in their illiteracy, even though there is a school nearby. They have absolutely no desire. Can we say that they have become great sages? Not at all. The first lesson, so far as they are concerned, is to stimulate desire. There is a young child; you stimulate desire in it to gain knowledge; and it goes to school and, later on, works hard to live a comparatively decent life. So, the first stage of life is *kāma.*

Similarly, *krodha,* anger; sometimes you need *krodha.* I had occasion to say earlier, how human life will be very dull without this emotion called *krodha,* as righteous indignation against social misbehaviour. *Kāma* and *krodha* have a place; but, they need discipline, regulation. They are blind forces. Then comes human education, including value awareness through ethical and moral awareness. At that stage, you are called upon to regulate *kāma* and *krodha;* you have to say 'no' to *kāma,* you have to say 'no' to *krodha,* when they overstep the limits. Then only can we live in a peaceful society of millions of people. If I am alone on an island, I don't need to control and restrain my *kāma* and *krodha.* I can go on all over the island, run about wherever I like, and take whatever I like, get angry with everything that is there. That I can do. There is no worry at all. But, in a society, because there are other human beings on whom your *kāma* and *krodha* will have effect, therefore, there is a need for restraining these two forces. And when we do not check them, they become evil forces. If you check them, they are not evil. Remember the meaning of the word *kāma.* In this very *Gītā,* in verse 11 of chapter 7, Śrī Kṛṣṇa will tell us, 'I am the *kāma* in the heart of all beings, but a *kāma* unopposed to *dharma* or ethical sense', *dharmāviruddho bhūteṣu kāmo'smi bharatarṣabha.* So, *kāma* is not condemned right through. But, unrestricted *kāma,* unrestrained *kāma,* also *krodha,* and also other evils coming along with them, are our primary enemies.

Vedanta speaks of six enemies of every human being. They are all inside the human being: *Kāma, krodha, lobha,* greed; *moha,* delusion; *mada,* pride and arrogance; and *mātsarya,* jealousy. These things are known as *ṣaḍ-ripu,* 'six enemies' of every human being. The human being alone can tackle them and defeat them with spiritual strength. Of these, *kāma* and *krodha* are the most important and dangerous. Once these are controlled, the other four are easy to control. So, Śrī Kṛṣṇa answers Arjuna by saying: they are two: *kāma* and *krodha.* What is their origin? A beautiful psychological study: *rajo-guṇa samudbhavaḥ,* 'they are born from the excessive *rajo-guṇa* that is within the human being. First is *tamas,* inertia. When you are in *tamas,* you neither do good nor evil. Just like this table or chair, all *tamas;* but, as soon as *rajas* manifests, it can be either good or bad; when good predominates, the human being becomes active to serve other people; when bad predominates, excessive *kāma* and *krodha* manifest and make for harmful activities. So, we need to educate a child from *tamas* to *rajas* and to create *kāma* in that child: 'I want this, I want that, if there is an obstruction, I shall try to remove it with all my energy'. So, *kāma* and *krodha* thus become utilized for human development. The child also must be taught to restrain these two in order to make them harmless to society.

This *rajo-guṇa* and its offspring, *kāma* and *krodha,* if not properly disciplined by the person concerned, will land one in trouble. These two are *mahāśano mahāpāpmā*, 'big consumers and big sinners'. *Aśana* means eating; *mahā* means big; big eaters. That means like fire, you add fuel and it will consume more and more of fuel, never becoming satisfied; *kāma* and *krodha* are like that. You go on satisfying desire, it will always say, more, more. That is the nature of desire in human beings. Earlier I had quoted the beautiful passage from Goethe's drama, *Faust,* his soliloquy in the woods:

> 'Oh, for the broken state of man: I know
> Our unfulfilment now! …
> He builds a wildfire in my heart, a blase,
> Till from desire I stumble to possession,
> And in possession languish from desire.'

There you can see the meaning of *mahāśanaḥ*, desires are endless. As soon as you satisfy one, ten will rise in its place. Today, we refer to this in the economic language as need and greed. Human needs we can satisfy; human greed we cannot satisfy. In this world there are enough resources to satisfy the needs of all the four billion human beings, but not their greed; if greed operates in society, millions of people will have to go without elementary needs. That is one of the problems of the modern age. Economists, philosophers, and thinkers are stressing this point today that we should contain this greed, what is called consumerism-mania. Many writers criticise America, for example. Six percent people of the world consume forty percent of world's resources. That is America today. Americans themselves make this criticism. These are good signs. We are trying to understand the human situation better and better: that there is enough to meet the needs of the people, not enough to meet the greed of even a small number of people; nature becomes destroyed, ecological balance becomes disturbed because of greed.

Take, for example, birds. How many birds have become extinct, because people go on hunting them, and take their feathers to make dress for men, and more especially for women. There was a bird in Mauritius called dodo. Up to two hundred years ago, it was there. Colonial people went there, went on shooting and killing them. It is a very heavy bird and cannot fly quickly to safety. So, it is extinct today. That is why in English we say, 'dead as dodo'. Whales are getting reduced and also many other species of animals. In this way, ecological balance which is needed for human survival becomes disturbed by greed. So, the word *mahāśana,* 'great consumer', is a wonderful word; it has relevance to what we think of the human situation today.

Mahāpāpmā, the second word, is what impels you to do much evil, much destruction. All sin, evil, and crime, come from these two forces: *kāma* and *kròdha,* which arise from *rajoguṇa.* Just think deeply how we can handle the *rajas* in us. Śrī Kṛṣṇa will give the method later: Moderate this *rajas* with a touch of *sattva,* give it a higher dimension. Refine it, then something great will happen. The same energy will bring blessings to hundreds of people through you. That is what doesn't happen when *kāma* and *krodha* become connected only with one's own self-interest. So, Śrī Kṛṣṇa says: *Viddhi enam iha vairiṇam. Iha,* 'in this human world'; *enam,* 'this'; *viddhi,* 'know'; *vairiṇam,* 'as your enemy'. That is the first answer.

Next *śloka* gives an illustration: Vedanta has discovered a divine spark in all beings, because the universe has evolved out of the infinite divine Reality. By our ignorance and delusion, we hide that 'imprisoned splendour', as the British poet Robert Browning puts it; knowledge is hidden by something; *āvriyate* is the word for 'hiding'.

धूमेनाव्रियते वह्निः यथाऽदर्शो मलेन च ।
यथोल्बेनावृतो गर्भः तथा तेनेदमावृतम् ॥३८॥

Dhūmenāvriyate vahniḥ yathā'darśo malena ca;
Yatholbenāvṛto garbhaḥ tathā tenedamāvṛtam — 3. 38

'As fire is covered by smoke, as a mirror by dust, as an embryo by the amniotic sac, so this (Reality) is covered by that (*rajas*).'

Three examples are given. This spiritual knowledge in a human being, this discriminatory capacity, is hidden in human beings. How? Just like this: *Dhūmena āvriyate vahniḥ*, 'as fire is covered with smoke'. Similarly, *yathā ādarśo malena ca*, 'as a mirror is covered with dirt'. And thirdly, *yatholbena āvṛto garbhaḥ*, 'as the baby inside the womb is hidden by the amniotic sac'; *tathā tena idam āvṛtam*, 'similarly, this (knowledge) is hidden by that (*rajo-guṇa* expressing as *kāma* and *krodha*). Having said this, the next *śloka* expressly states that the *jñāna* that is within every human being is covered by *kāma*.

आवृतं ज्ञानमेतेन ज्ञानिनो नित्यवैरिणा ।
कामरूपेण कौन्तेय दुष्पूरेण अनलेन च ॥ ३९ ॥

Āvṛtam jñānametena jñānino nityavairiṇā;
Kāmarūpeṇa kaunteya duṣpūreṇa analena ca — 3. 39

'Knowledge is covered by this, the constant foe of the wise, O son of Kuntī, the unappeasable fire in the form of (unrestrained sensual) desire.'

This *jñāna* in human beings is hidden, is covered over, by this. By what?, by this *kāma* and *krodha* arising from *rajas* which is the human being's *nityavairī*, 'eternal enemy'. Unrestrained *kāma* and *krodha* are all human being's eternal enemies. *Nityavairī* is the word used here, 'eternal enemy', not only once or twice but throughout life. *Jñānino*, 'of a person of knowledge', they hide this *jñāna,* and when the *jñāna* is hidden, the person does all sorts of blunder. *Kāmarūpeṇa kaunteya*, 'in the form of *kāma* O Arjuna'; *duṣpūreṇa analena ca*, 'like an unquenchable fire'. This is the teaching of the *Gītā* on the origin of crime; but we want to know how to get out of it. How can we be free from this crime and the tendency to commit crime?

In the human being, when *rajas* and *tamas* predominate, crime and similar problems arise, but as soon as the mind rises to the level of *sattva,* the whole aspect changes. The human being becomes calm, steady, peaceful, compassionate. No crime can come from that state of mind. How do we achieve it? By each one training one's mind. Everything is in the mind; if you have a healthy mind, all that you do will be healthy. If you have an unhealthy mind, whatever you do will create tension in yourself and tension in society. *Āvṛtam jñānam etena,* 'knowledge is covered by this'. Suppose I am a fine person; when I commit a crime, at that moment my knowledge of my identity, my status, all that is hidden from me for the time being. *Kāma* and *krodha* hiding the knowledge that is within me, of my own nature, of my own status. Vedanta always emphasizes this point that the human being is essentially divine. These forces hide the divine. The sun is always luminous. But a patch of cloud can cover the sun. And the sun becomes dark. Similarly, this divine nature, the knowledge of it, becomes hidden by the overwhelming nature of this *kāma* and *krodha* born of *rajas.* It is out of this that every other evil will come. We have to handle this particular problem.

We have seen that problems arise from *unchecked* desire, unchecked craving, what we call today the evil of consumerism. How much of destruction of nature is going on by that kind of consumerist philosophy! And crime in society, violence in society, we can trace them to their source, and we shall find these coming from this want of discipline of the mind. We have to train the mind to overcome the force of *kāma* that impel us to do things which in our normal mood we will never do. Hence, this particular expression, *jñānino nityavairiṇā,* these are 'the eternal enemies of one who seeks knowledge'. What impels me to act is desire. So, that desire under restraint is essential. All culture and civilization are the products of human desire. But that desire becomes disciplined when you become a cultured individual. In all culture and civilization, there is both the presence of desire and the disciplining of that desire. Society itself is a field for the discipline of desire. I can't do what causes harm to somebody else. There is civil law, there is criminal law. There is the political state and my moral conscience. All these are there to discipline this powerful force within the human being; but that desire becomes an eternal enemy of the human being, when it is not checked and disciplined properly. Your whole life becomes a waste because of this.

In the *Śrīmad Bhāgavatam,* there is the story of Yayāti, an emperor. He had a tremendous desire to live a pleasant life, a happy life, a worldly life. He did it; he became old. He wanted to become young once again; he asked his son for his youth. One of the sons gave to him his youth and took his old age to himself. Again the emperor continued to enjoy pleasures, and again he became old. Then he began to think a little: the body has become old for a second time. Desire is still fresh like that of a young boy. Desire has not become old. It is always fresh. So, a little thoughtful mood came upon him and he pronounced a great piece of wisdom in a beautiful verse:

Na jātu kāmaḥ kāmānām upabhogena śāmyati;
Haviṣā kṛṣṇavartmeva bhūya eva abhivardhate —

'Desire is not quenched by the satisfying of desire; it only gets inflamed like fire into which butter is poured (to put it out).'

This is a profound wisdom that came to India very early in her history.

Today the world is seeking for that wisdom. Today's civilization is suffering from the same problem: simply craving for new things, new gadgets, and an efficient technology provides them, destroying the resources of nature, creating ecological problems and difficulties. In a materialistic philosophy there is nothing higher than these sensory cravings and their satisfaction. A more comprehensive philosophy of human life and destiny is needed and that is what the *Gītā* gives. It does not merely say to the human being 'control your desire'. It says, 'divert your desire to something higher'. The sensory craving and satisfaction is not the highest state of a human being. There is human growth beyond and above the sensory level. The *Gītā* does not leave a human being as a dry ascetic person. But it says, 'there are other heights to conquer. Don't get stuck up at this particular level.' Today's civilization is silently seeking for that wisdom. So, this Yayāti's wisdom is echoed in much of modern writing on the subject of the problems of modern civilization. *Na jātu kāmaḥ kāmānām. Jātu* means 'never'. Never is *kāma* satisfied through enjoyment of *kāma.* It only multiplies just as fire inflames when you try to put it out by butter. That is the wisdom that finds expression in some modern writings.

I like to quote a sentence from a commission's report in the United States. Just after the Second World War, a *Hoover Committee commission* was appointed to study the 'recent' economic trends in the United States. In the report of that Commission occurs this sentence which echoes what Yayāti said ages ago in India, minus the spirit in which Yayāti said it: 'This study has revealed that human desires are endless.' That is the first sentence. And the second sentence is that 'there are no new desires which will not give way to newer desires as soon as they are satisfied.' That is the nature of the human mind. So, what shall I do? Shall I go on flowing with the current of desire in the world of desire? No. But that wisdom has yet to come to modern thinking. Modern thinking has no inkling about the super-sensory level of experience. That second part, a positive part, is given in this *Bhagavad Gītā* as well as in the Upaniṣads. This kind of teaching about the spiritual dimensions of human life is slowly coming into modern scientific thought, especially in neurology and biology. Modern biology will tell you that organic satisfaction is not the goal of evolution at the human stage. That is the goal of the pre-human phase of evolution. That one sentence is enough to tell us that modern biology is going in the right direction: that, in a pre-human phase, evolution emphasized three things—organic satisfaction, numerical increase, and organic survival. Today's biology says that these are secondary at the human level; something else is primary. And what is that? *Fulfilment.*

Are you fulfilled? If you are to achieve that fulfilment, you will have to do many things which earlier biology never understood at all. We have to achieve a new type of evolution beyond the organic dimension—such is the language. Organic evolution has brought us up to this level. It has given us the most versatile organ, the cerebral system. With the help of this you can create any gadgets you like: just like creating the aeroplane, instead of developing two wings on your body. So, if organic evolution has no relevance at the human level, what exactly is the trend of human evolution?

To that question British biologist Sir Julian Huxley gave a reply in his address to the Chicago Congress of Scientists in 1959, celebrating Darwin's Centenary. He said, '*evolution has risen from the organic to the psychosocial level*'. This psyche must be able to expand beyond this organic system and dig affections in other psyches in society. That is love. That is compassion. That is humanist concern. You grow spiritually thereby. This is a wonderful idea. So, today's biology is slowly giving us a positive direction to human energy, not merely negative; and that is the central theme of Vedanta. How to raise this human being to the highest possibility, he or she is capable of. We in India, ages ago, developed in the Upaniṣads a *science of human possibilities*. And this is a phrase coined by that very Sir Julian Huxley. 'Today we need a new science,' other than the current physical science, he had said, and he called it: 'A science of human possibilities'. To take the human being to that highest level of evolution, the guidance of that science is needed. When you study Vedanta, when you study the *Gītā*, you find that they are exactly that science of human possibilities.

Take, for example, hatred. We can overcome hatred. That is a *human* possibility. Hatred also is a human possibility; and controlling hatred is again a human possibility. Similarly, desire, craving, that is a human possibility; controlling it and transforming its energies to a higher level, also is a human possibility. So, Vedanta developed a science of human possibilities ages ago. These few verses are the offshoots of that science.

What does that science say on this particular question of crime in society? How shall we reduce crime? One method we all have: increase the police force! Pass laws and regulations in the Parliament. That is what we do all the time. But today we realize that it is absolutely incapable of achieving the result. The human being cannot be made moral by an Act of Parliament. That is a great lesson we have to learn. *There is such a thing as human spiritual growth.* Education is meant to help us to start that spiritual growth and become decent citizens who can live at peace with other citizens in society. That doesn't come from an Act of Parliament. It comes from education. Education actually means, in the language of Vivekananda, 'manifestation of the perfection already in the human being'. We are to unfold those beautiful possibilities hidden within ourselves, so that peacefulness, humanist concern, a spirit of dedication and service, all these can come from within ourselves, if only we know how to handle this wonderful thing called the human mind. All education is, therefore, the training of the mind and not stuffing of the brain. Nowhere in the world today is education of this kind; of training of the mind. Mostly, it is stuffing of the brain. And ours in India is the worst from that point of view. These lessons from the *Gītā*, from this great master-teacher, Śrī Kṛṣṇa, we need very much today. We have got the most untrained minds in India. A little self-discipline will transform our people.

From now onwards, as Swami Vivekananda has taught us, we in India have to place the first emphasis on the training of the mind. You go to the temple, did you train your mind there? Could you compose yourself and remain calm and steady? In this way, the whole of life becomes the training of the mind. When you train the mind, you are the master. If you don't train the mind, you become a slave. And when you become a criminal, you become a slave to your own natural instincts or *vāsanas*. This subject of training the mind is not meant merely for school and college students. Every citizen in every field of life, whether alone or in the field of work, must be busy with this one work: to train this mind so that efficiency may increase and self-restraint gained. When I begin to understand the mind and its functioning, I come across these forces of *kāma* and *krodha* acting in me. There is no devil coming from outside to trouble me. The 'devil' is inside me only. That is why, in our literature, there is no place for the devil. You are the 'devil' within. You must be able to control him, direct him. This is why training the mind is most important for everyone.

Śaṅkarācārya's statement in the *Vivekacūḍāmaṇi,* verse 181, says: *Tanmanaḥ śodhanam kāryam prayatnena mumukṣuṇā,* 'those who seek to have freedom of spirit, must train the mind with great effort'; *viśuddhe sati caitasmin muktiḥ karaphalāyate,* 'when the mind becomes pure, then *mukti,* liberation, becomes palpable like a fruit in the palm of one's hand'. You can feel it: 'Yes, I am free, I am free'. How?, the mind is trained. The mind is pure. Freedom, which is my birthright, I have got it today. Till now it was not experienced by me. So, this energy of *rajas* and *tamas* which motivate the mind towards *kāma* and *krodha,* that energy has to be transformed into *sattva.* I have to do it myself. Nobody else can do it for me. A boy or girl of twelve can be given advice by his or her parents; but, the work of training the mind has to be done by himself or herself. Nobody can train another's mind. That is expressed in the English saying: you can take a horse to the water, but cannot make it drink. So, this is how parents must tell children, 'I can help you, but the training of the mind you have to do yourself'. This is a *constant* process, this training of the mind—in work, in leisure, in human association, everywhere we are training the mind, silently, quietly, provided we know the *science and technique* of it, and the *need* for it. That is what is lacking today. *We don't know the need for it*. We just go headlong propelled by our inner nature; whatever the mind says, I do that; and the mind follows whatever the sense organs say. Mind is a servant of the sense organs. So, the ultimate dictate comes from the sense organs; that is unnatural and must be reversed; the mind must regulate the sense organs. The head of the dog must wag the tail, not the tail the head! And in verse 40, Śrī

Kṛṣṇa tells us where these evil forces are functioning within the human system. *Where* is your enemy? If you want to attack your enemy, you must know his location. That is the language. Just like a general, pointing with his finger and giving the order to his army: 'Go and capture that fort, a very strategic fort!, then you will be able to win the war.' Similarly, Śrī Kṛṣṇa is telling Arjuna, and you and me, that here are the centres where the enemy is functioning; you can attack the enemy there. What are those centres? In verse 40 Śrī Kṛṣṇa gives you the direction:

इन्द्रियाणि मनो बुद्धिः अस्याधिष्ठानमुच्यते ।
एतैः विमोहयत्येष ज्ञानमावृत्य देहिनम् ॥४०॥

Indriyāṇi mano buddhiḥ asyādhiṣṭhānamucyate;
Etaiḥ vimohayatyeṣa jñānamāvṛtya dehinam — 3. 40

'The sense organs, the mind and the intellect are said to be its abodes; through these it deludes the embodied soul by veiling its wisdom.'

Indriya, manas, buddhi—these three factors in the human personality are the centres where this infection takes place. Just like in medical science we ask, what is the focus of infection? Then we can apply the remedy to remove that toxin and restore the body to health. So, within the human system, crime and many other evils affecting society proceed from the sense organs, the mind and the intellect. The human body is animated by the sensory system; actually the nervous system behind the sensory organs. That is the first focus of infection from which all other evils come. Second is the mind, *manas.* That also catches the infection in course of time, if you don't take care. And lastly the *buddhi,* the intellect, the discriminative faculty, that which distinguishes between what is right and what is wrong. That *buddhi* also becomes infected destroying its discriminative capacity. It is *buddhi* that ultimately destroys our life when it is thoroughly infected. If it is not infected, then it can save us also. So, we have to find the location of our enemy in these three areas of the human personality. *Etaiḥ vimohayatyeṣa jñānam āvṛtya dehinam,* 'evil deludes these three focal points in the human system—senses, mind and intellect—and covers *jñānam,* spiritual knowledge, of the embodied being.' *Etaiḥ vimohayati,* 'these are deluded'; without delusion, you don't do anything wrong. When you are in clear thinking, you never do anything wrong. When you do any wrong, there is a delusion behind it. The outermost is the *indriyas,* innermost is *buddhi,* and in between is *manas.*

In the *Kaṭha Upaniṣad,* Yama had told Naciketa: 'Life is a journey to fulfilment, every human being has been properly equipped for this journey. What do you want for a journey? You want a chariot, you want horses, you want reins, you want a driver. Then you can have a beautiful journey.' Nature has given you all these equipments. Body is the chariot, sensory system are the horses; motive power of the journey is in the horses—not in the chariot. So, here is the sensory system, full of energy. Then, to control the sensory system is the *manas,* like the reins to control the horses. And the reins are held by the charioteer, the driver; that is *buddhi. Buddhim tu sārathim viddhi,* 'know *buddhi* to be the driver of the chariot', Yama said there. And Yama warns us that if this journey is to take us to the destination, we must take one particular wisdom with us: Let not the journey be controlled by the sensory system, namely, the horses; nor by the reins, the *manas.* The journey must be controlled by the *buddhi,* the driver, the charioteer. These are all energies to be controlled and directed by the *buddhi.* But if each one of them becomes infected, *buddhi* also becomes infected, then you never reach the end of the journey. You will suffer 'shipwreck' in your journey. Yama had said this in the *Kaṭha Upaniṣad.* That idea must be kept in view here.

Here is the beautiful equipment in our human system, the sensory system with the nervous system and the brain. It converts this human body into a centre of the most dynamic activity in the whole of nature. What tremendous energy is functioning there! But we have to guide that energy, discipline that energy, and direct it to higher purposes. That is where your free individual effort comes in. If you don't do so, these energies will be lost in self-cancelling activities. *A* cancels *B, B* cancels *A,* you remain where you are, or you go down! Therefore, there is need for masterly handling of the whole energy system within yourself. Energy, controlled, disciplined, directed, increases in quantity and quality. We can see it in ordinary physical energy also. A disciplined energy is greater in quality and quantity. The waterfall shows the tremendous energy of water. And it goes away and is dissipated. But as soon as you discipline that energy and produce electricity and divert its waters along irrigation channels, you get power and increased agricultural production. Therefore, in this human system, this system of five sense organs is the centre of tremendous energy, but energy *without* direction. There comes the *manas.* The first instrument holding together all these energies and co-ordinating all the five senses is the *manas.* It also is like a sensory system, the sixth sense and slightly more subtle. It has the capacity, like the reins, to control this energy of the 'horses'. A tough rein is needed to control a very reckless horse. So, let the senses be dynamic, as in young people. But don't let it function independently; then it will be the horse's journey and not your journey. So, tie the reins to the horses. Then only you can carry that energy in a direction which *you* consider to be worthy. Otherwise, it will be horse's own journey with you as a helpless victim. *Manas* is what helps us to co-ordinate the sensory system, and *buddhi* is the one that regulates and directs all this energy. *Buddhi* must be sound, discriminative. You don't entrust your journey to a drunken driver of a carriage. You are sure to lose your life on the way. *Buddhi* must be perfectly calm and steady. That is the greatest purpose of education: to make this *buddhi*, balanced, discriminative, and with a capacity for clear thinking; then life gets the best guidance. Such a *Buddhi* is the safest guide of human life. Śrī Kṛṣṇa has already told us in chapter 2, *śloka* 49: *buddhau śaraṇam anviccha,* 'take refuge in *buddhi*'. If not, all energy with us will run helter skelter, ruin our life, and ruin society as well. We see this in increasing violence, increasing crime, all over India today, all over the world today, because we have not done anything particular in this field. And many of those who commit violence and crime are educated people! We don't even like to restrain any energy in us. Let us live at our impulse level, at our sensory level. Let us give it free rein. That is the fruit of the materialistic philosophy by which most people live today.

When I was on an 18-month cultural lecture tour of U.S.A. in 1968–69, I had the occasion to speak about this need for discipline of the energies within the human system. I was speaking over the Portland Radio at night 10 o'clock. A twenty minute radio programme, originally fixed, became a two-hour programme, because Mr. Fenwick, the radio broadcaster, deeply affected by the current Hippy movement, found the subject very interesting. I had referred to the need for disciplining of the energies within the human being; immediately, the broadcaster shouted into the radio: 'We don't want discipline; we want a spontaneous natural life.' I told him: 'You were praising Pandit Ravi Shankar's music, how natural, how spontaneous! Did you ever consider the years of discipline Ravi Shankar had to undergo to become such a great musician? Don't we give a little toilet discipline to our children? We don't give any such toilet discipline to a calf or a goat.' Extremely happy to hear these words of mine, he literally shouted into the radio: 'Listen to this great person from India,' and asked me: 'Are you tired? Can we continue?' By that time the announced twenty minutes were over. I agreed to continue, and it continued till midnight. And he and his wife came to hear my public lecture at the Portland Vedanta Society the very next Sunday!

Vedanta accepts that a natural, spontaneous life is the best for human beings; but you won't get this without passing through the hell of discipline. Otherwise, it will be animal nature and nothing else. Then, I had quoted a relevant verse from the *Śrīmad Bhāgavatam* (3. 7. 17):

Yaśca mūḍhatamo loke yaśca buddeḥ param gataḥ;
Tāvubhau sukhamedhete kliśyatyantarito janaḥ —

'Two types of people in the world enjoy happiness (and spontaneous living)—the utter foolish person and the one who has gone beyond *buddhi* (and realized the Atman); all people in between are in varying stages of struggle and tension.'

We first pass through the struggle, we discipline the energies of the sensory system through the help of the *manas* and *buddhi*. Then we come to a second type of naturalness. That is a real naturalness, a naturalness of a Ramaṇa Maharṣi, for example. A Sri Ramakrishna was natural and spontaneous. The American youth at that time, at the time of the hippie movement, were eager to have naturalness. No more of tension, no more of discipline. They didn't like all this. Perfectly right; but if the youth want to get the true type of naturalness, they would have to pass through a life of discipline of the inner energies. Without getting this guidance, the hippy movement in U.S.A. slowly gravitated towards crime, drug, and sheer laziness, and finally died away. What they told me in America about that movement was this: 'we like to follow an impulse-release philosophy.' They did not want to control any impulse; just release impulses as they come. Such a philosophy will eventually convert human society into an animal farm', I said. All impulses are not meant to be released. You have to discriminate which is worth releasing and which is not. When you become truly 'spiritually strong', then you can release all impulses because they will always be pure, coming from the depth of the human spirit, not from the lower sensory level, not from the toxic level.

That is the background of these beautiful ideas Śrī Kṛṣṇa is conveying to us on this most important problem of civil peace in society. Unless there is peace, how can we enjoy human life? Unless I trust you, how can I enjoy my life?, and how can you enjoy your life? That comes from this disciplining and training of the raw energies that are within us. Chasten them, purify them, transform them into something better and better. Socialization is a great word in sociology. A human child is to be socialized, fit to be a member of a community, with a capacity to dig affections in each other. That comes from discipline of this raw human energy system. If you don't do so, you will have a society with increasing numbers of criminals and disjointed people, mentally distorted people. Nobody wants that kind of society. But, today it is going in that direction. We have to change it. It is in this context that these verses become of supreme significance to modern humanity. Śrī Kṛṣṇa says, *etaiḥ vimohayatyeṣa jñānam āvṛtya dehinam*, '*Jñāna* is hidden by these forces controlling *manas, buddhi* and *indriyas*, and delusion sets in.' These three locations have been shown here to us. The next three verses convey great insight into the human depth psychology. Nowhere else you will find this kind of a deep study of the human system and light being thrown on man's life progressing in the direction of the fullest manifestation of spiritual possibilities lying within. Therefore, Śrī Kṛṣṇa says:

तस्मात् त्वमिन्द्रियाण्यादौ नियम्य भरतर्षभ ।
पाप्मानं प्रजहि ह्येनं ज्ञानविज्ञाननाशनम् ॥४१॥

Tasmāt tvamindriyāṇyādau niyamya bharatarṣabha;
Pāpmānam prajahi hyenam jñānavijñāna nāśanam —3. 41

'Therefore, O Bull of the Bharata race, controlling the senses as the first step, kill this sinful factor, the destroyer of knowledge and realization.'

'Therefore, Arjuna, first discipline your sensory system.' That is the doorway through which all infection comes in. Wonderful idea! Wherefrom has this infection entered my body? You must find out. A medical doctor will ask that. Then try to stop that source of infection. So here, psychically, infection doesn't come from *buddhi*. It comes first from the sensory system. Therefore, regulate the sensory energy system, discipline them. *Tasmāt tvam indriyāṇyādau niyamya*, 'therefore you first regulate and discipline the sensory energies'. *Ādau* means 'first'. Then, *pāpmānam prajahi hyenam*, 'this *pāpmānam*, this sinner, this criminal that is within you, overcome it'. I won't allow any infection to enter into me through the doorway of the sensory system. I shall regulate them; I shall discipline them. What is that evil or infection that enters through the sensory system? *Jñāna vijñāna nāśanam,* 'the destroyer of spiritual knowledge and wisdom'. If you don't take care of it in the beginning itself, it will go on increasing like cancer. A few cancer cells get in and develop until it becomes incurable. *Prajahi,* 'conquer' is the word. *Enam,* 'this', pointing it out, it is so palpable. Just like in the physical body, we have infection: we can isolate that infection, examine the blood, examine the stool and urine, and discover the focus of infection and apply treatment. In the psychic system also it is the same method: *enam,* 'this', this well-known evil that is there. Your sensory system has become infected. Take care! From there every evil starts. This is the warning that is given by Śrī Kṛṣṇa. *Jñāna-vijñāna-nāśanam,* 'destroyer of *jñāna* and *vijñāna*'.

Then comes a beautiful study of the depth dimensions of the human personality. You must know what are the dimensions of this human individual system. This is a wonderful study in the Upaniṣads, and also here in this chapter of the *Gītā*. This *śloka* is only one here, it will be two in the *Kaṭha Upaniṣad*. But this one is a beautiful summary of the whole description of the dimensions of the human personality.

Take, for example, our body. Skin itself has so many layers. Then below the skin you begin to see the flesh. Then the veins and the arteries. Then you have the nerves and the bony system. Within the bone you have the marrow. So, you can see within the physical system various layers: one inside the other. Similarly, taking human being as a whole, our Upaniṣads made a study. The *Taittirīya Upaniṣad* is a special study of this subject. They call it the Science of five *kośas, pañca kośa vidyā*. Five *kośas* are there. *Kośa* means a sheath; place a sword in its sheath. Here is the Self, ever pure, ever free, and ever illumined; that Self is covered by five sheaths. Not just one. Begin with the body, *annamaya kośa*. Then *prāṇamaya kośa, Prāṇa,* 'vital energy'; *Manomaya kośa,* 'psychic energy'; then, *'buddhi', Vijñānamaya kośa*. And lastly, 'bliss', *ānandamaya kośa*. These are the five *kośas* inside which is your true Self, the Atman, hidden in all of them. It is good to know this truth.

So, here we are referring to three of these *kośas*. First, the *indriyas*, the sensory system, bio-energy system. *Indriyāṇi parāṇyāhuḥ*, 'these *indriyas* are very high in quality', compared to the body which is a dead dull piece of matter; what makes the body alive are these sensory energies. They are certainly superior, *parā*, compared to the body or the matter that constitutes the world outside. The word *parā* is used here. *Parā* means higher, superior. *Indriyebhyaḥ param manaḥ*, '*manas* is superior to the sensory energy system'. And then, *manasastu parā buddhiḥ*, 'superior to, higher than the *manas* is the *buddhi*'. So you can see the gradation: ordinary, higher, still higher. So, these are the words used regarding the three. Then, what is beyond the *buddhi?* Only one truth is beyond the *buddhi*. What is that?, the Atman, the infinite Self. *Yo buddheḥ paratastu saḥ*, 'the one who is beyond the *buddhi*, higher than the *buddhi*, is He, the infinite Atman, which is beyond all gender distinctions, your true Self, hidden by all these three sheaths.

This is a great subject of utmost significance to the human being in this marvellous age of scientific civilization. We know so much about the world, we know much about things that are *there*, but we know so little of what is hidden in the human being. Even Sir Julian Huxley had said, 'the study of the mind has just begun', whereas Vedanta had penetrated deep into this subject a few thousand years ago. So, what we know of matter from surface to depth from physical science, we shall retain; that is a wonderful knowledge. But it must be complemented, sustained, and strengthened by this other knowledge: what is the depth dimension of the human personality? If that knowledge also is achieved, we shall have a wonderfully stable and rich civilization. Where quantity is the criterion today in civilization, quality will become the criterion when this knowledge comes to us. And that is the direction of today's science and even of the process of civilization itself. That is why Vedanta is so relevant to human beings today in both East and West. It is a subject of tremendous significance. I have seen people in Western countries sitting with utmost interest to listen to and understand this subject. 'We know so little about it. We want to know more about it.' What Sir Julian Huxley said is true. We have only scratched the surface of this subject so far. But here is a philosophy that has gone deep into it. The insight and wisdom of that philosophy is highly necessary today for humanity to face and overcome problems in this twentieth and the following centuries.

'Discipline the sensory energies', *niyamya*. The text doesn't say 'suppress', or 'destroy'; it says 'regulate'. *Niyama* means regulation. Without it you cannot build up your character, your personality, or achieve life's fulfilment. Animals never discipline the sensory system. They have got a natural discipline, as I said earlier, built into their genetic constitution. Man alone can consciously discipline sensory energies. When the mind becomes infected, it is very difficult to handle that infection, and still further, when the *buddhi* becomes infected, the only instrument we have for *viveka* discrimination or handling that infection becomes still more difficult. We see not only intelligence at the level of *buddhi,* but also the will. A combination of intelligence and will is what makes for *buddhi.* So, the *buddhi* decides finally according to the infection that has come to it. Then it becomes extremely difficult to handle the problems. Better to do it in the early stage at the sensory level.

When I was in Tokyo in 1986, they had arranged for me a lecture along with a luncheon. And the subject there was *Children, Humanity's Greatest Asset*. That lecture was published by the Bharatiya Vidya Bhavan, Bombay. The most important asset is our children, not the house, nor the bank account; these are all secondary. The primary asset is our children. If they are healthy, if they are in a well-balanced disposition, we are happy, they are happy, and the world is happy. If they go wrong, all are unhappy. So we have to protect the health of our children, physical as well as psychic. And today there is a great need for psychic health of children and to protect that psychic health. In advanced countries, physically children are well-fed, well looked after, they get all the calories they need in food; but their greatest problem is infection of the senses and the mind; distortion of the mind starts very early in life.

Earlier, I referred to my Portland radio lecture. I give below a little background of the theme discussed there. I saw young people following a particular philosophy in America. They called it *impulse release* philosophy. Whatever impulses arise in the mind, give a quick release for it. Don't check it, don't control it. That is the impulse release philosophy, against which I was arguing in that radio talk. Several youths in the U.S.A. accept this impulse release philosophy. Parents also accept it. Teachers accept it. Psychologists accept it. And they tell children, if you are deprived of the free expression of your impulses, it will be dangerous for your personality. You will get a traumatic condition. The word trauma is used there. If you check your impulses, you will have a trauma. And a series of traumas will be bad for the child. That is a strange new doctrine that has come in modern civilization, against which I was trying to argue: that some impulses are worth releasing, but not all impulses. Some ought to be checked. Why do you get trauma?, because of some spiritual weakness within. We are mentally very delicate today. Our spiritual strength is nil. A little scolding will make a man go and commit suicide. That kind of weakness you find in people today, even in India. Extremely sensitive; that is inner spiritual weakness. So, certain impulses need checking. Otherwise, you won't be a human being. You will be an animal. That idea I put forth in that discussion. And the interviewer was very happy. He had not heard these things. So, I said: 'Here is an impulse. I check it. I verify it. It has come as a result of a sensory system coming in contact with sensory objects. The impulses come. But discriminate them, that is absolutely essential. Otherwise, a worse distortion will come to the human psyche, which will, later on, be beyond your control. You must be able to withstand a little bit of this trauma. You must have inner strength, knowing that it is needed at the human level. Human life is a struggle; animals have no struggle.

The human being is a combination of necessity and freedom. We are partly determined by nature, partly we are free.

A little bit of that freedom in us makes us restless. The human being is the only restless being in God's creation: that little freedom in me wants to find expression. So many things are thwarting me all the time. So, a combination of freedom and necessity makes a human being a unique creature in the whole of nature. We are asked to take charge of this little freedom and let it not become a slave to the senses, which is no freedom at all. That we were already as an animal. When we have risen to the human level, we want to be free, to be unlike an animal which only says 'yes' to whatever the sensory system tells it. We are asked to discipline the sensory energies without which no higher development is possible. The human being alone can have that higher development. And so this 40th *śloka* tells us: *Tasmāt tvamindiryāṇyādau niyamya bharatarṣabha,* 'therefore, O Arjuna, you discipline the sensory system first', you can overcome all the unhealthy developments that may come later. Then only you will be free from that infection 'which otherwise will destroy your *jñāna* and *vijñāna*', *jñānavijñānanāśanam.*

In any study of crime and criminal behaviour, we can see the operation of these truths mentioned here clearly. When I commit a crime, that crime has behind it a series of changes taking place in my system. That is being studied in this chapter. And here is the advice given by Śrī Kṛṣṇa. First handle the sensory system. As a human being, if you want to develop character, if you want to realize your higher potentialities, you must discipline this tremendous energy system known as the senses. It is like controlling the horse to ensure a safe journey. Then what happens? When the sensory system is free from infection, mind remains healthy, and *buddhi* remains healthy. Your pursuit of human excellence becomes a success. Human excellence is the goal. There are profound possibilities lying hidden within us. We have to unveil them. All that is needed is this initial discipline of the sensory system.

Now we take up verse 42. That is a wonderful verse. It gives you an idea of various layers of the human personality. We look like simple individuals; we are not! So many layers are there. Just like the skin, as I said earlier, which has many layers. We see only one skin. But an anatomist can see various layers of the skin.

इन्द्रियाणि पराण्याहुः इन्द्रियेभ्यः परं मनः ।
मनसस्तु परा बुद्धिः यो बुद्धेः परतस्तु सः ॥४२॥

Indriyāṇi parāṇyāhuḥ indriyebhyaḥ param manaḥ;
Manasastu parā buddhiḥ yo buddheḥ paratastu saḥ —3. 42

'The sense organs are said to be superior (to the body); the mind is superior to the sense organs; the buddhi or intellect is superior to the mind; and that which is superior to the intellect is He (the ever-free Self, the Atman).'

In one simple verse the *Gītā* gives you the entire knowledge, as referred to earlier, contained in the *Taittirīya Upaniṣad,* which is a special study of these various layers of the human individuality.

There is one key word coming in this enumeration, the word *parā. Parā* always means superior, greater, better, higher. So, *indriyāṇi parāṇyāhuḥ,* 'the sense organs are superior, it is said'. *Indriyebhyaḥ param manaḥ,* '*manas* is superior to the sensory system'. *Manas* is meant to control and regulate the sensory system. That is certainly higher and superior in value. *Manasastu parā buddhiḥ,* '*buddhi* is superior to *manas*', because it is meant to control the *manas* and the sense organs also. What lies beyond the *buddhi, yo buddheḥ parataḥ tu saḥ,* 'what is superior to the *buddhi* is He (the Atman)'. The word *saḥ* literally means 'He' (not in gender sense).

Śaṅkarācārya in his *Bṛhadāraṇyaka Upaniṣad* (1. 4. 7) commentary says that 'the Ultimate Reality, of the nature of pure Consciousness, infinite and non-dual, cannot be limited by any name, even by the words Atman and Brahman'.

Just behind the *buddhi* is the Atman. This truth of Atman or Brahman is referred to in Vedanta in various ways. *Om tat sat,* 'Om That Truth'. Similarly, *Tat tvam asi,* 'You are That'. A special feature of that Truth is: It is ever pure, ever free, ever luminous. That is the supreme teaching of Vedanta. No sin can affect the Atman. No infection can touch the Atman. That is why it is called ever free. It is only in Vedanta, and in all the teachings of mystics of the world religions, you will get this teaching: Sufi, Christian, Buddhist, Hindu. The mystics have experienced the truth, and will always say that the Self in the human being is always pure, ever free, ever illumined. All infections come from lower levels. They never reach there. That is a profound truth and also the most inspiring truth for humanity. If everything is dirty, how can you remove dirt? Suppose there is so much of dirt around you, and you go to take water to wash it; that water is also dirty. How can you then remove dirt? There must be some clean water to remove the dirt. So, in this Vedantic thinking, as a result of penetration to the innermost Self of all, the sages discovered the pure, infinite Self behind the body-mind-*buddhi* complex.

In his *Brahma-Sutra* Commentary, Śaṅkarācārya refers to it as, *nityaśuddha, nityamukta, nityabuddha svabhāva paramātman,* 'that supreme Self which is *nityaśuddha,* ever pure, *nityamukta,* ever free, *nityabuddha,* ever illumined'. It is only the ego, which is the Atman tied to the body-mind complex, that is subject to evils like crime, sin, etc. Within us both these dimensions are there. The one that is subject to joys, sorrows, crime—that is the little ego controlled by the genetic system. The other is the ever pure, ever free, ever illumined Atman. How beautifully the Upaniṣads describe this remarkable phenomenon in the human being by giving the example of two birds on the self same tree (*Muṇḍaka Upaniṣad,* 3. 1. 2):

Dvā suparṇā sayujā sakhāyā
samānam vṛkṣam pariṣasvajāte;
Tayoranyaḥ pippalam svādvatti
anaśnan anyo abhicākaśīti —

'On the self-same tree are two beautiful birds, intimate friends, with fine plumage. Among the two, one bird tastes the fruits of the tree, while the other sits in its own glory without eating the fruits.'

That is the *jīva* or individual soul and Atman within the same tree of the body. It is the first bird, the *jīva,* that suffers and enjoys, that does crime, that does good, etc. We feel that we are that, but our true nature is that of the other bird. The teaching given therefore to this lower self is: 'you are really That'. This you are because you are tied down to the body-mind complex. In Vedanta therefore, this penetrating investigation into what may be called the science of human possibilities, revealed this truth before the luminous mind of the sages: *there is the possibility of our redemption built into each one of us;* that is the Vedantic teaching. We never say, therefore, that any human being is a sinner. Nowhere in the Vedantic teaching will you find the idea that the human being is a sinner. He or she commits sin, no doubt. But he or she is not a sinner. Because, not knowing one's true nature, one commits sin; but our redemption is also built into each one of us. That is what Śrī Kṛṣṇa is going to tell us in the last verse of this chapter.

Swami Vivekananda referred to this great truth while addressing the Chicago World Parliament of Religions in 1893 (*Complete Works*, vol. 1, p. 10):

Is man a tiny boat in a tempest, raised one moment on the foamy crest of a billow and dashed down into a yawning chasm the next, rolling to and fro at the mercy of good and bad actions. ... The heart sinks at the idea, yet this is the law of Nature. Is there no hope? Is there no escape?—was the cry that went up from the bottom of the heart of despair. It reached the throne of mercy, and words of hope and consolation came down and inspired a Vedic sage, and he stood up before the world and in trumpet voice proclaimed the glad tidings:

"Hear, ye children of immortal bliss! Even ye that reside in higher spheres! I have found the Ancient One who is beyond all darkness, all delusion: knowing Him alone you shall be saved from death over again."

"Children of immortal bliss"—what a sweet, what a hopeful name! Allow me to call you, brethren, by that sweet name—heirs of immortal bliss—yea, the Hindu refuses to call you sinners. Ye are the Children of God, the sharers of immortal bliss, holy and perfect beings. Ye divinities on earth—sinners! It is a sin to call a man so; it is a standing libel on human nature. Come up, O lions, and shake off the delusion that you are sheep; you are souls immortal, spirits free, blest and eternal; ye are not matter, ye are not bodies; matter is your servant, not you the servant of matter.'

This Vedic sage of the *Śvetāsvatara Upaniṣad* could say like the Greek Archimedes 'Eureka! Eureka!'. 'I have discovered a wonderful Truth.' And when Swami Vivekananda pronounced the meaning of that verse before that American audience as quoted before, he carried the force of that tremendous discovery on to the people. 'Please listen', *śṛṇvantu*. *Viśve* means 'of the universe', everywhere. And the sage addressed humanity from *his* point of view: *amṛtasya putrāḥ*, 'children of immortality!' O Ye!, Children of Immortality! Listen to me, I have good news to tell you. Not only that, see the audacity arising from the all-comprehensive vision of the sage; he sends up his message 'to gods and angels in heaven if there are any', *āye dhāmāni divyāni tastuḥ*. What is that message? Did you get it from some books, or you built it up by your fertile imagination? No! *Veda aham etam*. 'I *know* this Truth'. I have realized, experienced this Truth. This *Vedāhametam* idea is the wonderful truth that has inspired all subsequent developments of religion in India, but we do not understand it today, we have made religion a dead letter. It is not 'I believe', but, '*I have realized It*'. I have experienced It. He is going to tell later on: 'You too can realize It'. What is That? *Puruṣam mahāntam*, 'the infinite human being behind the finite human being'. *Alpa* and *mahā*, two Sanskrit words meaning small and big. The ego is *alpa*, and the Atman is *mahā*. When we are *alpa*, we are prone to crime; when we are *mahā*, that cannot happen. And all crime, all delinquency come from this self which is *alpa*, not knowing one's *mahān* or immense nature. Gandhiji was called *mahātmā*. Everyone can be a *mahātmā*. That is our birthright. So, the sage says: 'I have realized that infinite Self behind this finite self.' *Vedāhametam puruṣam mahāntam. Āditya varṇam*, 'glorious or luminous like the sun', *tamasaḥ parastāt*, 'beyond all darkness and delusion'. That is the Truth I have realized. But he did not then say, 'you only believe me to be saved'. He said: *tam eva viditvā atimṛtyumeti,* 'you also realize this Truth to become immortal', because It is your own birthright. You have not to beg and borrow this Truth from somebody else.

Never will you find in the world's literature such authentic utterance of human greatness and glory as in the Upaniṣads. It is said with such conviction which carries conviction to the listener. Having said this, the sage added: *nānyaḥ panthā vidyate ayanāya,* 'there is no other way, there is no other way to freedom'. See the language: *nānyaḥ panthā vidyate,* 'there is no other way'. Realizing this truth even a little, even a glimpse of it, can change your life. Today, I am a corrupt individual. I get a glimpse of this truth through some person or other; my life becomes changed into an honest person inspired with an attitude of service to humanity.

About five hundred years ago, there lived in Karnataka a miserly jewel-merchant whose later name is Purandara Dāsa, 'servant of the Lord Viṣṇu of Paṇḍarpur'. He will not give any money to help anyone in need. That person, by one divine touch, became completely transformed. He called the people around, distributed all his wealth, all the ornaments that were there, and taking out a small bundle, started out as a *dāsa,* a servant of the divine, servant of man, singing gloriously divine songs with philosophical and spiritual ideas to awaken humanity; that Purandara Dāsa inspires people even today. What happened to him? He had found the pearl of great price within himself; all these worldly things became utterly meaningless to him, that very message he conveyed to uncommon and common people in such beautiful Kannada language, and in high music. Purandara Dāsa is one among hundreds of such people. That will make modern civilization healthy and stable.

In a Buddha, a Śrī Kṛṣṇa, a Jesus, we can see how sinners become saints by one touch, one word, one look of a great soul; it awakens that divine dimension in such people. 'Go and sin no more,' Jesus said, and the sinner becomes a saint. This possibility is because we are *essentially sinless.* If we are really sinners, nobody can change us! A thing cannot change its character. *Svabhāvam na jahāti sā,* 'an object which has a particular character cannot give up that character'. But if it is only an external appearance, behind which is the true character, then it can change. It realizes its own true nature. Fire cannot give up its heat. Water cannot give up its wetness. That is their nature, *prakṛti,* as we call it. So, Śaṅkarācārya quotes this *svabhāvam na jahāti sā*. No object can give up its true nature. Temporarily it can give up, as it were. A piece of iron is cold to touch. You put it on fire, it glows; when taken out, it becomes again that original cold stuff.

Vedanta proclaims a great truth for all humanity. That is why the world today is eager to know it and live by it. This is just like the truths of the physical sciences; they proclaim a universal message, and the whole world is after physical science: we have not to thrust it on people. Truths are always universal. Opinions and dogmas are limited in scope. Here a profound Truth is uttered: *śṛṇvantu visve amṛtāsya putrāḥ,* 'Hear me, O children of immortality!' Every child is a child of immortality. Convey these blessed ideas to your children when they are young, says Vivekananda. Like that Queen Madālasā whose story appears in our spiritual literature. When a child was born she used to place it in the cradle and sing to it this truth in a song: *nityo'si, śuddho'si, nirañjano'si samsāra māyāmala varjito'si,* 'Child, why are you weeping? You are that pure one, you are that ever free one, free from all the taints of *samsāra*'. That is how Madālasā educated her children and this is highly commended by Swamiji also (*Complete Works,* vol. 3, p. 243). You respect the child as a person; some profound dimension is in it, and the most profound dimension is this Truth, *amṛtasya putrāḥ.* That is education *and* religion, for religion so understood is continued education: experience rising from the sensory level to the super-sensory level.

That is the basis of this particular *Gītā* verse which you heard, *śloka 42: Indriyāṇi parāṇyāhuḥ indriyebhyaḥ param manaḥ; Manasastu parā buddhiḥ yo buddheḥ paratastu saḥ.* Just above and behind the *buddhi* is the Atman, your own infinite Self.

Śaṅkarācārya calls the *buddhi,* therefore, as *nediṣṭham brahma,* 'nearest to Brahman or Atman'. Only look behind, it is there. But that looking behind takes ages of struggle; it is not easy; that is why all this teaching is given. But one single truth that comes out of this teaching is: whatever part of your physical system might have become corrupted, there is one dimension which is ever free from all such corruption. That is your own true Self. Otherwise, sinners would have no hope. Dr. S. Radhakrishnan said in one lecture: 'every sinner has a future as every saint had a past'. That Truth about the human being has been expounded in the clearest and most rational language only in one literature, the Upaniṣads. It is found nowhere else in the world. It is, therefore, called in the Upaniṣads *aupaniṣadam puruṣam.* A disciple goes to a teacher in the Upaniṣads and asks: *aupaniṣadam puruṣam pṛcchāmi,* 'tell me about that Puruṣa which is taught only in the Upaniṣads'. *Upaniṣatsu eva vijñāyate, na anyatra,* Śaṅkara comments upon it: 'taught only in the Upaniṣads, not elsewhere'.

When our people went to Benares on pilgrimage in those days, they often placed their ten thousand rupees into the hands of a friend in the village before going away. After about one and a half years, the person was likely to return; if I die during the pilgrimage, give the money to so-and-so, he would have said to the friend while departing. After a long time the pilgrim returns and the friend gives him back the ten thousand rupees; there was no cheating. The friend knew that money was an object and that he was not the servant of money. That is the one great lesson we have now almost forgotten. We are the servants of a few rupees. People can do any evil just for getting some money—not poor people, even well-to-do people. So, when we speak of the problem of poverty and beggary in India, I always say that there are two types of beggars in India. One is the beggar in the street, the other is the beggarly person living in high mansions. All that has come about because this truth was completely overlooked. Vedanta will teach human beings this profound truth for which India produced this *Vedānta keśari,* Lion of Vedanta, namely Swami

Vivekananda. Earlier, it was Śaṅkarācārya, earlier still it was Buddha. Still earlier it was Śrī Kṛṣṇa: the Lion of Vedanta. That roaring of the lion of Vedanta we need today. And Swamiji did it in the modern period. That is what Swamiji said (*Complete Works*, vol. 4, p. 351): 'Let the lion of Vedanta roar; the foxes will fly to their holes.' And so, this *Vedāntakeśari* is a wonderful instrument for taking us out of this crime, delinquency, and other evil forces afflicting society, and restoring the human being to his or her own worth and dignity.

In this verse, the word *parā,* as I said earlier, has a deep meaning. While dealing with the three dimensions of the human personality, namely, *indriyāṇi, manas, buddhi,* I referred to the word *parā* used in the verse: *Indriyāṇi parāṇyāhuḥ, 'sense organs* are superior to the sensory objects, etc. I shall now discuss it in the light of what Śaṅkarācārya has said in his commentary on similar verses in the *Kaṭha Upaniṣad* (1. iii. 10).

Śaṅkarācārya says that whatever is subtle compared to the gross is *parā.* The gross is ordinary; the subtle is higher, superior, to the gross. The sense objects are gross, you can touch them, you can handle them, but the sense organs are not gross; they are comparatively more subtle and we have always understood that energy in gross form is inferior to energy in subtle form. So, *parā* has this meaning of being subtle, *sūkṣmā*.

Then the second attribute comes in; *mahāntaśca,* more in range and power. Energy is there in quantity; but, the subtle has more energy. The word *mahāntaśca* means big, expansive. So, *sūkṣmā* and *mahāntaśca.*

And then comes the third and the last. *Pratyagātmabhūtāśca,* 'nearer to one's own inner Self'. This body is external to you, and the nervous system and sensory system are internal to you, nearer to your own Self; the mind is still nearer to the Self. *Buddhi* is nearest to the Self. These are all scientific terms developed by Vedanta: *Sūkṣmā mahāntaśca pratyagātmabhūtāśca.* When you use the word *pratyagātmā,* it means the Atman, the inner Self. The external world is also Atman, but in its outer expression—*parāk svarūpa;* when the word *parāk* is used, you point your finger out to point to an objective reality. But, whenever you turn the finger towards yourself, that is to indicate the *pratyak* dimension of reality, the observer, the subject, the Self. That yonder is *parāk,* and this within is *pratyak.*

Nature has these two dimensions: *parāk* dimension, and *pratyak* dimension. The *parāk* dimension we study in the physical sciences, because that dimension is the object, in Sanskrit the *viṣaya,* revealed by the five senses. All sense data form the basis of all physical sciences. But, when you finish that study, the finger begins to turn inwards, towards yourself, man's consciousness, man as the observer, as the *viṣayi* in Sanskrit, as the subject, as the knower, as the Self; a more profound mystery is lurking there. Till now modern physical science did not understand nor care for this truth. But now, in this twentieth century, with all the revolutionary advances made, especially in nuclear physics, the observer, the subject, is slowly appearing on the horizon of modern science. That consciousness has a part to play in understanding quantum phenomena—a scientist will put it that way. Therefore, a new dimension of awareness, a new dimension of reality, is opening up before physical science. Vedanta anticipated this four thousand years ago and said that after the *parāk tattva* is studied, we have to study also the *pratyak tattva. Tattva* means truth or reality. *Parāk tattva* is truth, i.e., nature, outside; *pratyak tattva* is truth, nature, within all. That is a large field of study by itself. And today, the study of consciousness is an important study in western psychology. Till now it was not there. Now that subject is becoming more and more important from various points of view. When you study physics and biology from the *theoretical point of view,* you come across this truth of something profound in the human being; from the *practical point of view* you come across the human situation; very distorted has become the human psyche because of the high technological developments. Physical science can't ignore this problem for long. If you want peace, if you want a fulfilled life, study your own mind and consciousness. It is in that *pratyak tattva* you will get the answer and the remedy. Not by adding more gadgets, more of consumer goods, are you going to get it. This kind of a compelling reason from both theoretical and practical considerations reveals the importance of this subject.

So, mark the importance of these two words, *parāk* and *pratyak*. Don't study only one dimension. Our Indian sages studied first the *parāk* dimension, the world outside, and developed many departments of physical sciences. Then only they studied the *pratyak* dimension. And, therefore, they got a unifying vision of reality, of the total reality, that Advaitic vision of one and non-dual Reality which appears as nature outside and as human consciousness within. This is what has made Vedanta to heartily accept modern Western science which had to fight with European religion and theology every inch of the way. This Advaitic vision came only because India investigated both the *parāk* aspect and the *pratyak* aspect. So, Vedanta calls the Atman *pratyagātmā, pratyak svarūpa, pratyak tattva.* All these words occur in Vedantic literature: what is the truth that is pulsing within you? Look at the eyes of a newborn baby. Some depth dimension is revealed through those eyes. What is that dimension? Take a doll baby. Look at its eyes. There is no depth at all; only the surface. In any living baby, its eyes will reveal a profound depth. It is this investigation that revealed to the sages these three coverings *indriya, manas,* and *buddhi* of that real *pratyak tattva* that is within you as the Atman.

In 1981, there was a special public meeting in Chicago to celebrate the Golden Jubilee of the Chicago Vivekananda Vedanta Society; there this subject was discussed by two of us: Dr. S. Chandrasekhar, the famous astro-physicist of the Chicago University, on *Approach to Truth in Science,* and myself who spoke on *Approach to Truth in Vedanta.* Both are search for truth. So, the word *pratyak* and *parāk* are significant words. Modern physical science has studied only the *parāk* aspect of nature. Now the *pratyak* aspect is slowly looming on the horizon of physical sciences. So, *parāṇyāhuḥ* signifies more *sūkṣma,* more *mahāntaḥ,* more *pratyagātmabhūtaḥ.* These are the three words: subtle, immense in range and power, and more near your own true Self, inner Self in the context of what the word *parā* means. *Pratyagātmā* means inner Self.

We have so far discussed the first category among the three, namely, the sensory system. When we go to the *manas,* we find that it is much more *sūkṣmā,* 'subtle', than the sensory system, *mahāntaśca,* 'more immense in range and power', and, *pratyagātma-bhūtāśca,* 'more inward as the inner Self of man'.

The *manas* is not palpable, you can't touch it, you can't handle it. The nervous system, you can handle. The sensory system, you can handle: eyes, ears, everything. But the *manas* cannot be handled. And yet the mind is there. It contains much more energy than the sensory system. If the *manas* is weak, the sensory system goes down. In this way, they found *manas* is 'subtler', *sūkṣmā,* 'more immense in range and power', *mahāntaśca,* and *pratyagātma-bhūtāśca,* 'being more near to one's inner Self'.

Then you come to *buddhi,* the third item in the human system. *Buddhi* is far more subtle, far more immense in range and power, far more truly your own self than either the sensory system or the psychic system, *sūkṣmā mahāntaśca pratyagātmbhūtāśca.* These three we can study; and the one truth that comes out of it, as I said earlier, is that the more inward you go, the more energy resources you find in yourself.

Buddhi is considered to be 'the nearest to the Atman', *nediṣṭham brahma.* Brahman, also called Atman, is your Self. When the *buddhi* develops the purity to be able to look back, it realizes the infinite Atman or Brahman, and the person who experiences this becomes a Buddha, the enlightened one. Śaṅkarācārya says that this *sūkṣmatva, mahāntatva, pratyagātmabhūtatva* achieve their infinite value in the ever-free Self, the Atman. Every human psychophysical system possesses a small quantum of explicit energy, and an infinite quantum of implicit energy. What is explicit is found in the body, muscle, nerve, mind, *buddhi;* what is implicit is lying behind in the Atman. So, every one of us is handling only a small packet of energy, though behind it there is an infinite packet of energy and we do not know it.

Vedanta wants to tell every human being that there is such a fund of energy of the Atman within you. Earlier, I said that this Atman is always free. No sin or crime can tarnish It; no evil can touch It. That is our true nature. That is the supreme truth conveyed by Vedanta to all humanity. That announcement in the Chicago Parliament of Religions by Vivekananda from the *Śvetāsvatara Upaniṣad,* I have referred to earlier. Anyone can protest that he or she does not know it; but not knowing doesn't abolish a truth. Centuries ago, people did not know that the earth is round. Later science only *discovered* this truth, not created it. Similarly, here is that profound truth of the Atman discovered by the great sages on behalf of the whole of humanity. The *Gītā* said in the previous verse that sin and crime can infect the sensory system, the psychic system and the *buddhi.* It can never infect the Atman. One focus in everyone is absolutely ever pure, ever free. Therefore, I said then, that *our redemption is built into ourselves.* We have only to discover this truth. None can destroy that truth. Śaṅkarācārya says in his *Gītā* commentary that not even God can destroy the real Self of human beings. That is the language. So, these three ideas, *sūkṣmā, mahāntaśca, pratyag-ātmabhūtāśca,* reach their infinite dimension in the Atman. What a beautiful conception!

When the human being becomes aware of this truth, this *buddhi,* this *manas,* this sensory system become invested with a new purity, a new quality of love and compassion. What a welcome change comes to human life and inter-human relations when this truth is realized even a little; Śrī Kṛṣṇa had said this in the second chapter of the *Gītā, svalpamapyasya dharmasya trāyate mahato bhayāt.*

The Atman as pure Consciousness cannot be divided. The *Gītā* will tell us in the chapter 13, *śloka* 16: *avibhaktam ca bhūteṣu vibhaktam iva ca sthitam,* 'this Atman exists undivided in all beings which appear to be divided'; also as *avibhaktam vibhakteṣu,* (chapter 18, *śloka* 20) 'undivided in these apparently divided things'. That is the most profound discovery based on which the *Gītā* is giving us a profound philosophy of life and action. The *Gītā* brings out the practical implications of that truth in human life and destiny, including the overcoming of criminal tendency in human beings and how to reduce crime in society. In a very corrupt society nobody will be happy. In a healthy society, all will be happy. It is man's privilege to work for a crime-free society, a society of equals, with a sense of belongingness and co-operation. It is for this purpose that great spiritual teachers come again and again: to take humanity to this path of mutuality, interdependence, co-operation, and away from conflict, violence, and crime.

In the *Mahābhārata*, which you see in the Delhi's television broadcast every week, you will find the King Drupada of the Pāñcālas became proud and arrogant when his classmate, Droṇa, went to him for help. Droṇa was very poor. They were classmates and the King had promised Droṇa, 'any time you want any help I am ready to give you'. But as soon as Drupada ascended the throne, the man changed! Power has come. Mind has become arrogant and proud. And he insulted Droṇa. The whole later tragedy of the *Mahābhārata* and the Kurukṣetra war began from there.

There is a very meaningful story told in a fascinating language in the *Śānti Parva* of the *Mahābhārata*. There was a sage doing *tapas* in the forest. One dog had somehow come into the Āśrama, and the sage took care of it. Whatever little food the dog got, it ate and remained a good dog. After some time, the dog felt, 'I am frightened by a little ordinary tiger that comes near the Āśrama. I want to be stronger than that tiger.' So, it appealed to the sage, 'I am your faithful servant here. Can you make me unafraid of that tiger?' 'Okay,' he said. He took some Ganges water, sprinkled it on the dog. The dog became powerful. Then the tiger began to run away; no more coming to the Āśrama, because the dog had become strong. After some time another big animal, a lion, was coming and troubling the dog. Again it told its master. The master also said, 'okay, I will make you strong'. And it became stronger;

no lion dared to come near. In this way, three or four types of animals, more fierce than the previous one, all of them became afraid of this dog through the blessing of this sage. Now that situation is interesting—increase in power. Then what happened? The dog became very powerful. So many animals used to come to the Āśrama; but, now no animal comes, because they are afraid of this dog. One day, the sage was in meditation, and this dog felt, 'I am now all powerful. Only one person is more powerful than me. It is this sage. Let me get rid of him, and then I will be supreme!' Thinking so, it rushed towards that sage to kill him. The sage opened his eyes, took a little water, sprinkled it on the dog; immediately it became that old dog once again; all its power vanished. When a person misbehaves with power in his or her hands, the only power to make that power constructive is discrimination; that comes to the *buddhi* only by alignment with the Atman.

So, Śrī Kṛṣṇa is telling all humanity, *yo buddheḥ paratastu saḥ,* 'He who is beyond *buddhi* is the Atman', *where this subtlety, immensity, inwardness reach their infinite dimension.* That is humanity's nature. *Tat tvam asi,* 'you are That', as the *Chāndogya Upaniṣad* proclaims. The more people realize this truth, better shall human society be. There is no dogma, there is no creed. It is a science of human being in depth, discovered by sages, rediscovered by other sages, and placed before all for our own rediscovery. It is not a dogma to be swallowed, nor a theory to be believed. In this way, *Bhagavān* Śrī Kṛṣṇa is giving to humanity this philosophy of the human being in depth by which we shall enjoy a life of fulfilment, make others also live a life of fulfilment. That is the goal of human evolution. International peace, international welfare, these are all possible, because these values are present in every human being; only, he or she must carry human evolution beyond the organic level to higher ethical, moral, and spiritual levels.

And so this word *parā* is very important. Usually we translate it as 'higher'. But what does this 'higher' mean? Higher can mean spatially higher. Put a thing upstairs, it becomes higher. That is not the sense. So, in one sentence you can give the whole of this subject, and that is—*human energy resources are organized on an ascending scale of subtlety, immensity, and inwardness.*

That is a beautiful sentence coming from the hands of Śrī Śaṅkarācārya in the *Kaṭha Upaniṣad*. That ascending scale rises to its fullest when we come to *yo buddheḥ paratastu saḥ*; 'that infinite Self, the Atman, beyond and superior to *buddhi*'. Crime is a serious problem in our society today; also in all international societies. How can you lead a peaceful and happy life when there is crime and violence around you? How can you sleep soundly when you know that a robber may come and rob you or even kill you any day? It is good that people know this science more and more. This land of India, known for its peace and harmony, about which three hundred years ago foreign ambassadors had spoken of as people not locking their homes, has become a land of crime and violence. It is because we were engaged in understanding only the *parāk* nature of the world. The *pratyak* nature we ignored in recent centuries. Now the time has come to turn a little attention to the *pratyak* dimension and discover the *tattvam* that is there. *Parāk* and *pratyak*, both are *tattvam*, truth. There is only one infinite truth appearing as external or internal. That is the language of Vedanta.

That is expounded in a great verse in the *Māṇḍūkya Upaniṣad Kārikā* of Gauḍapāda. It is a wonderful verse (2. 38).

> *Tattvamadhyātmikam dṛṣṭvā tattvam dṛṣṭvā tu bāhyataḥ;*
> *Tattvībhūtaḥ tadārāmaḥ tattvādapracyuto bhavet* —

'Having realized the *tattvam* that is residing within your own self', *tattvam adhyātmikam dṛṣṭvā*, and 'realizing the *tattvam* residing in external nature', *tattvam dṛṣṭvā tu bāhyataḥ; tattvībhūtaḥ*, 'becoming one with truth', *tadārāmaḥ*, 'taking delight in that truth', *tattvād apracyuto bhavet*, 'you never fall down from the truth'.

You become absolutely insured against all evil once for all. Mark the word *tattvam* coming in that verse—*tasya bhāvaḥ tattvam,* 'the truth of a thing is *tattvam*', says Śaṅkarācārya. There is such a thing as a search for *tattvam.* That may be in the external world; it also can be in the internal world. Ultimately *tattvam* is one. External or internal have no meaning so far as *tattvam* is concerned. Just like saying that the earth is surrounded by only one ocean. But for convenience sake, we call it the Indian Ocean, the Pacific Ocean, the Atlantic Ocean. But the ocean is one, and not many. And so, external *tattvam,* internal *tattvam*—these are purely for the purpose of study and research. *Tattvam* itself is one, infinite, non-dual. Its realization is the goal of human evolution, says Vedanta. Are you going towards *tattvam?* What a beautiful idea! Vedanta has proclaimed this as the goal of human life. Jesus said, 'Thou shalt know the truth, and the Truth shall make you free'. Our Indian nation was dedicated to Truth, by our national Constitution-makers forty years ago. That is why they took the motto from the *Muṇḍaka Upaniṣad: Satyameva jayate,* 'Truth alone triumphs'. Today, unfortunately, it has mostly disappeared from our nation; only untruth triumphs. Out of this hell we have to convert India into a land where more and more people seek Truth and a truthful life, not a false life. Only then can we 'dance freely, spontaneously', as given in a parable of Sri Ramakrishna:

And Śrī Kṛṣṇa concludes this third chapter and this topic of crime and its prevention with this exhortation:

एवं बुद्धेः परं बुद्ध्वा संस्तभ्यात्मानमात्मना ।
जहि शत्रुं महाबाहो कामरूपं दुरासदम् ॥४३॥

Evam buddheḥ paraṁ buddhvā saṁstabhyātmānamātmanā;
Jahi śatrum mahābāho kāmarūpam durāsadam — 3. 43

'Thus, knowing that Reality which is superior to the *buddhi,* and restraining the self by the Self, destroy, O mighty-armed, that unseizable enemy in the form of *kāma* or unrestrained sensual desire.'

You will find military language here. Śrī Kṛṣṇa was a warrior, and Arjuna was also a warrior. *Evam,* 'thus', *buddheḥ param buddhvā,* 'realizing that Truth which is beyond *buddhi*', *samstabhyātmānamātmanā,* 'disciplining the little self by the infinite Self', *jahi śatrum,* 'conquer the enemy'. Which is that enemy?, *kāmarūpam durāsadam* 'in the form of *kāma* which is difficult to capture' and which is the source of the tendency to crime and other evils. They are difficult to conquer, you have to marshal all your energies for that purpose. Don't take it easy, don't take it lying down. Nobody can become moral by simply sauntering into morality. It needs hard struggle. That struggle gives you energy and strength. So, this last sentence is the message to all people, especially to our people in India, today. Like a General in battle pointing out to his soldiers the citadel of the enemy and issuing orders: 'go and conquer it,' Śrī Kṛṣṇa is telling all people, through Arjuna, to attack and conquer the source of all crime and delinquency. Then alone you are free. Unlike the battle of Kurukṣetra which ended after 18 days, this is a continuous battle for all humanity to carry human evolution to its highest goal, namely, spiritual freedom and fulfilment. That inner war will remove also the tendency to wage external wars in the world.

The title of a book which I once read in America is *Success Through a Positive Mental Attitude,* published in 1894. Positive Mental Attitude is also called P.M.A. as against the negative mental attitude, N.M.A. When one has that confidence, that faith, more energy comes to him or her to build up a character with peace within and love and service without.

In the whole of world's literature, the *Gītā* and the Upaniṣads are the only two great books where you find this subject constantly emphasized, namely, faith in oneself—*ātmaśraddhā.* Strength and fearlessness. In the words of Swami Vivekananda, in his lecture given in Madras in 1897 on *Vedanta in Its Application to Indian Life* (*Complete Works,* vol. 3, p. 238):

'And the Upaniṣads are the great mine of strength. Therein lies strength enough to invigorate the whole world; the whole world can be vivified, made strong, energised through them. They will call with trumpet voice upon the weak, the miserable, and the downtrodden of all races, all creeds, and all sects to stand on their feet and be free. Freedom, physical freedom, mental freedom, and spiritual freedom are the watchwords of the Upaniṣads.'

It is fearlessness inspiring fearlessness in others; this will come in the twelfth chapter of the *Gītā*.

इति कर्मयोगो नाम तृतीयोऽध्यायः –

Iti karma-yogo nāma tṛtīyo'dhyāyaḥ—

Thus ends the third chapter designated *The Yoga of Action*.

BHAGAVAD GĪTĀ

CHAPTER 4

KARMA-SANNYASA-YOGA
YOGA OF RENUNCIATION OF ACTION

We concluded the study of the third chapter of the *Bhagavad Gītā.* The last seven verses dealt with the very important topic of crime in society and how to overcome it. Now we begin the fourth chapter. The main philosophy that Śrī Kṛṣṇa is expounding has been already presented in the second and third chapters. Now he is only adding new ideas, new streams of spiritual life, in the remaining chapters, to make it richer and richer. This becomes relevant when we study the first few verses of the fourth chapter. The chapter begins:

श्रीभगवान् उवाच।
Śrībhagavān uvāca —

'Śri Kṛṣṇa said.'

इमं विवस्वते योगं प्रोक्तवान् अहमव्ययम् ।
विवस्वान् मनवे प्राह मनुरिक्ष्वाकवेऽब्रवीत् ॥१॥

Imam vivasvate yogam proktavān ahamavyayam;
Vivasvān manave prāha manurikṣvākave'bravīt— 4. 1

'I told this imperishable *yoga* to Vivasvān; Vivasvān told it to Manu; (and) Manu told it to Ikṣvāku.'

Imam yogam, 'this *yoga*'; that means the philosophy he has expounded in the second and third chapters; *vivasvate proktavān aham avyayam,* 'this imperishable *yoga* I imparted to

Vivasvān'. *Vivasvān manave prāha,* 'Vivasvān taught it to Manu'; *Manurikṣvākave abravīt,* 'Manu taught it to Ikṣvāku'. Ikṣvāku can be treated as a historical person; in his family succession Śrī Rāma came in a later age. *Vivasvān* means 'the sun'. Manu and Vivasvān belong to our ancient mythology. Therefore, Śrī Kṛṣṇa says I taught it to these people in the past ages. And the next *śloka* speaks of how it was passed on from teacher to student in a spiritual succession.

एवं परम्पराप्राप्तमिमं राजर्षयो विदुः ।
स कालेनेह महता योगो नष्टः परन्तप ॥२॥

Evam paramparāprāptamimam rājarṣayo viduḥ;
Sa kāleneha mahatā yogo naṣṭaḥ parantapa — 4. 2

'Thus handed down in regular succession, the royal sages knew this *yoga;* this *yoga*, by long lapse of time, declined in this world, O scorcher of foes.'

This philosophy, what is called by the simple word *yoga,* and is treated as Practical Vedanta, was thus communicated by a succession of teachers and students. *Evam,* 'thus'; *paramparā* means succession, *prāptam,* 'attained by', a *guru-siṣya paramparā,* 'teacher-student succession'; *rājarṣayo viduḥ,* 'the *rājarṣis* knew it'. *Rajānaśca te ṛṣayaśca iti rājarṣiḥ,* says Śaṅkarācārya; 'those who are *rājās* and *ṛṣis* in one, are called *rājarṣis'*, a very important word for us and for all else. When we study the *Gītā* and deal with the importance of this philosophy for our country today, and for other countries as well, in the fields of administration, politics, and management, in all these various fields in which we are trying to work out the destiny of human beings, their happiness and welfare, we need a philosophy to guide us. Therefore, Śrī Kṛṣṇa presents this kind of philosophy to all persons who are in possession of power and responsibility. He calls them *rājās* because they handle power; he calls them *ṛṣis* because they follow this philosophy of *yoga* and possess spiritual motivation. So, he calls them royal sages.

All our energy comes from the sun. We have, in India, idealized the concept of the sun. In fact, *The National Geographic*

Magazine of U.S.A (Sept. 1948) in its article on 'The Smithsonian Institution' by Thomas R. Henry, says:

'The sun is the great Mother. All life on earth may be considered as transient materialization of the *exhaustless* floods of radiance which she pours on the planet's surface. This enables green plants to synthesize sugars and starches from water in the soil and from carbon-di-oxide gas in the atmosphere, thus making possible all other essential foods. We eat sunshine in sugar, bread, and meat, burn sunshine of millions of years ago in coal and oil, wear sunshine in wool and cotton; sunshine makes the winds and the rain, the summers and winters of years and of ages.

'Particularly interwoven are the threads of life and light.'

Ancient India had understood the significance of the sun for human life and destiny. It became an object of adoration in the *Ṛg-Veda,* of which the most important *mantra* is the famous *Gāyatrī:*

'Om tat savitur vareṇyam,
bhargo devasya dhīmahi,
dhiyo yo naḥ pracodayāt.'

'Om. We meditate on the glory of that divine Savita; may He endow us with (pure) intelligence.'

The physical sun is an external part of the spiritual reality behind the sun. That is the principle of life and light. Now, this is the mythical side of this teaching. But, when you come down, you come to the human level. *Vivasvān manave prāha,* 'Vivasvān taught it to Manu'. Manu is considered to be the first human being, from whom all humanity has come. So, human beings are called *mānavas,* the word *mānava* coming from the word Manu.

Manu taught it to Ikṣvāku. Ikṣvāku is the one who founded the *Sūrya vaṁśa,* 'solar dynasty' lineage of beings, in which Śrī Rāma came later. So, here are three people who were men of tremendous responsibility; they wanted a philosophy to guide them, and 'I taught it to them', Śrī Kṛṣṇa says here.

Then 'this philosophy has been coming down', *paramparā prāptam imam rājarṣayo viduḥ;* 'a succession of *rājarṣis* knew this philosophy'. *Kālena mahatā,* 'but after a long lapse of time', *sa yogo naṣṭaḥ parantapa,* 'this *yoga* was lost in society, O Arjuna'. When we studied Śaṅkarācārya's Introduction to his commentary on the *Gītā,* we had occasion to refer to Śaṅkarācārya's statement that *Dharma* declines when men and women become too much avaricious, too much lustful, sensory-oriented; then higher faculties disappear from society; what you see in India today is the same: higher values are disappearing. We are in that condition. So, Śrī Kṛṣṇa says, after long ages, this dilution took place: *Dharma* became reduced, and naturally *adharma* increased. That caused a crisis in human history. *Yogo naṣṭaḥ parantapa, 'yoga* was lost, O Arjuna'. Śaṅkarācārya comments on that statement in his commentary on this verse to explain how the *yoga* was lost. A beautiful expression: *durbalān ajitendriyān prāpya yogo naṣṭaḥ parantapa,* 'when this *yoga* fell into the hands of 'weaklings', *durbalān,* physically weak, mentally weak, *ajitendriyān,* 'without any discipline of the sensory energies', *yoga* becoming diluted day by day was lost'.

Anyone can understand this statement when he or she studies our own history and the history of other countries like Babylonia and Rome. People sometimes understood life and religion in a heroic sense. They did wonderful work, creative work, built up a rich culture and civilization. Later on, a tiredness of mind came, physical weakness came; people began to dilute religion also, making it cheaper and cheaper. So far as India is concerned, in this declining process, what we inherited in the modern period as religion was of the cheapest type. Perform a few rituals, and that too through a priest for a payment, and nothing else; no high character energy, no creative impulse, no humanist concern, these higher things disappeared. How much diluted it had become! Then we have had various do's and don'ts from morning till evening. Whether we should drink water with the right hand or with the left hand was a big problem, and *paṇḍits* will assemble to discuss which is the correct one! Thus developed any number of discussions on these petty subjects, besides marrying away of girls at the early age of eight or ten; even today you will find all sorts of puerile discussions in the name of religion. All the broad aspects of religion were completely forgotten, and all concern for the weaker human beings dried up. Therefore, we can see what Śaṅkarācārya says: when people lost their physical strength, their mental vigour, and also their control over the sensory system—high character cannot come without a measure of control of the sensory system—when such a situation came, this *yoga* became diluted and lost. That is what he tells us here in the second verse: *Sa kāleneha mahatā yogo naṣṭaḥ parantapa*, '*yoga* was lost, O Arjuna'. Then Śrī Kṛṣṇa continues:

स एवायं मया तेऽद्य योगः प्रोक्तः पुरातनः ।
भक्तोऽसि मे सखा चेति रहस्यं ह्येतद् उत्तमम् ॥ ३ ॥

Sa evāyam mayā te'dya yogaḥ proktaḥ purātanaḥ;
Bhakto'si me sakhā ceti rahasyam hyetad uttamam—4. 3

'I have this day told you that same supremely profound ancient *yoga* considering you as my devotee and my friend.'

Śrī Kṛṣṇa says: *Sa evāyam mayā te'dya yogaḥ proktaḥ purātanaḥ*, 'that same ancient *yoga* I am now communicating to you, ' Arjuna'. But, why? *Bhakto'si*, 'you are my devotee'; not only so, *sakhā ceti*, 'you are also my friend'. Śrī Kṛṣṇa and Arjuna were of the same age. They were friends; *sakhā*, 'friend', that is the word Śrī Kṛṣṇa himself uses. In the eleventh chapter you will find (*ślokas* 41–42), when Arjuna saw Śrī Kṛṣṇa's *viśvarūpa* or Universal Form, Arjuna saw himself also in that Universal Form. Then he became frightened and asked pardon of Śrī Kṛṣṇa: 'So many times while eating, drinking, playing, making merry with you, I treated you as my friend. Excuse me for all this. Now, I understand what a tremendous dimension your personality has!' But, otherwise, they were great friends.

In fact, just before the *Mahābhārata* war, King Dhṛtarāṣṭra sent Sañjaya to the tents of the Pāṇḍavas in the Kurukṣetra battlefield to find out what was going on there: how Śrī Kṛṣṇa, Arjuna, Bhīma, Yudhiṣṭhira, and others were behaving there.

Dhṛtarāṣṭra wanted this information. When Sañjaya entered Śrī Kṛṣṇa's tent, he saw Arjuna placing his leg on the lap of Śrī Kṛṣṇa, and a free conversation was going on between them. Sañjaya, after some time, returned to Dhṛtarāṣṭra, and said, 'When I saw that picture, that Arjuna had put his leg on the lap of Śrī Kṛṣṇa, and that this great personality called Śrī Kṛṣṇa was fully behind the Pāṇḍavas, I concluded that this war is lost for you, you will never win this war.' That report, however, did not impress Dhṛtarāṣṭra's son, Duryodhana. 'We shall win, we shall win,' that feeling remained strong in him. But see the intimate relationship between Śrī Kṛṣṇa and Arjuna! So, *bhakto'si me sakhā ceti rahasyam hyetad uttamam; rahasyam* may mean 'a secret', it may also mean 'something very profound'. Here it means 'something very profound'. There is no secret in religion, but there is something very profound about it. This *uttamam rahasyam,* 'this best *rahasyam*', this profound Truth by which human beings can be lifted from creatureliness to freedom. What can be a greater message than that! So, 'I communicated it in the past to Vivasvān; I am now communicating it to you, O Arjuna.'

As I said earlier from Śaṅkarācārya's commentary, *durbalān ajitendriyān prāpya yogo naṣṭaḥ parantapa,* '*yoga* was lost when it fell into the hands of weaklings and people without that discipline of the psychophysical energy system', which is the basis of all character. Without a little discipline of this energy system, you can't have character. Animals do not have discipline of the sensory energy system. They *live* at the sensory level. The human being alone can rise above that sensory level by a measure of discipline of the sensory system. More of the discipline and a high character is developed, but even a little of it is needed if you want to be a decent citizen in a free society. So, Śrī Kṛṣṇa said, 'I communicated this message to *rājarṣis*.'

It is good for us to understand what is the significance of this *rājarṣi* concept in the *Gītā*. You will find that word occurring in the *Mahābhārata* in several places. We in India were for a thousand years, till recently, an unfree nation; we never exercised political power, except whatever feudal power we had within our feudal social system. The main political power was not in our hands. But once independence was gained, power came to our hands. People who were 'nobody', are now 'somebody', holding tremendous power in their hands. That is a big change that has come in the past forty years. But, one subject we have failed to discuss in that context: it is easy to hold power, but it is difficult to handle it properly. So, how to handle power? This is a big subject in every free society. Western societies have discussed this subject; so many books have been written. One of the books by agnostic Bertrand Russell is on this subject of *Power*.

In his book on '*Power*', Bertrand Russell says in Chapter 17, *Ethics of Power*, 1938 edition:

'Love of power, if it is to be beneficent, must be bound up with some end other than power.'

'It is not enough that there should be a purpose other than power; it is necessary that the purpose should be one which, if achieved, will help to satisfy the desires of others. … This is the second condition that love of power must fulfil if it is to be beneficent; it must be linked to some purpose which is, broadly speaking, in harmony with the desires of the other people who will be affected if the purpose is realized.'

This orientation of power, mentioned by Russell, is what Vedanta calls the fruit of spiritual growth, the *ṛṣi* aspect of the *rājarṣi* concept of the *Gītā*.

Power in the hands of a politician, an administrator, an industrialist, an intellectual—everywhere there is the problem of power. Somebody has *more* power, somebody *less*. And, generally, an ordinary citizen has very little power except to cast his or her vote at the elections. But any ordinary clerk or constable, or any other political or administrative functionary, has more power compared to the ordinary citizen.

But we have not learnt to ask this question to ourselves: 'What shall I do with this power? How to handle it? We are a democracy; our Constitution promises great things to our people. I am an instrument of that Constitution. How shall I therefore function with the power that is in my hands?'

Because we did not discuss this subject and educate ourselves on this question, we have, during these forty years, plenty of instances of the misuse of power to the detriment of the people. Everyday you come across instances of misuse of power, self-aggrandizement, corruption, and all sorts of other evils, coming from the not handling of power in a way which can bring strength to the people. In a democracy, the state is meant to give strength to the people, not to keep them weak. Imperialistic governments keep the people weak. Feudal governments keep the people weak. But democracy is meant to strengthen the people. We have not kept these ideals clearly before us all these forty years. There have been exceptional individuals who had some moral and human sensitiveness in them. They did it. But by and large we have ignored this very important subject and have paid a heavy price for it, namely, remain a low developing nation even after forty years of independence!

We studied in this campus in Hyderabad, three years ago, Bhīṣma's discourses on *Rāja-dharma,* the Politics of the State, or Ethics of the State, in the *Śānti Parva* of the *Mahābhārata.* That is a wonderful subject. In that connection, we discussed this subject of 'handling of power to bring good to the people'. This is a universal problem. Every country has some people who have extra power, and some people who have less power. How do the 'extra-power' people behave?, that problem obtains in every country, in every society. The answer that Śrī Kṛṣṇa gives in the *Gītā,* and generally in the *Mahābhārata,* and some of the teachings of the Chinese sages, have tremendous relevance to all people today, particularly for us in India. It is in that context that you must understand this concept of *rājarṣi* that Śrī Kṛṣṇa has introduced at the beginning of this chapter: *rājarṣayo viduḥ,* '*rājarṣis* knew it'.

Whenever you handle power, you are called a *rājā. Rājā* need not be a crowned-head. Anybody who handles power is a *rājā.* In a very limited sense only *rājā* means a crowned-head. But handling power is what makes one a *rājā.* He or she may be crowned, but, suppose he or she has no power, then what kind of a *rājā* is he or she? *Sa rājate, virājate,* he or she shines in the power, in the political power, that is in his or her hands. That is how the word *rājā* was used. So, that political power, intellectual power, all types of power, is power *over* others. That is the meaning of power. In any society, we need somebody to handle power. So, politics is essential in a society. The ancient Greek concept of a state is called a polity. A 'polis' means a city, and there you have a polity, a group of people living together. 'How do they live together? How do they negotiate with each other? How are they governed and how is their polity defended against foreign encroachments?', these are the questions the Greeks discussed very thoroughly in ancient times. Modern Western nations also have developed this concept of power from the Greek city-state to the modern nation-state. And today we are reaching out to the international community. Recently, we are finding that the United Nations is getting more and more power to handle human affairs all over the world. So, this is the development of the power concept. Where there is more than one person, the idea of power comes in, the idea of management comes in, administration comes in. Where there is only one person, there is no problem at all. When somebody lives on an island all alone, there is no problem, there is no second person. He can do whatever he likes there. But whenever other people are there, negotiation between the different peoples becomes necessary. We have to regulate that kind of a relationship. That means power. So, law, regulation, acts, assemblies and parliaments, all these come into the picture.

So, having come to this situation that we are a vast democracy, tremendous power is there in the hands of the Village Pañcāyats, the Zilla-Pariṣads, Assemblies, and finally, the Union Parliament, and, above all, the vast and ever-increasing administrative machinery. So, the fact of power we can all recognize today. But the question, how shall this power be used, is the most important question.

Even a father or mother at home has power over their children. They can't misuse that power. There are cases where parental power has been misused. That is why the United Nations developed this concept of prevention, by state action, of cruelty to children. So, father has power, mother has power, a teacher has power, everybody has some power over somebody who is below him or her.

However, in political and administrative power, we have the most important aspect of power over many segments of people. It is there that we need a philosophy to guide the holders of power. If that philosophy doesn't inspire the holders of power, he or she runs amuck, becoming inebriated by power. You can easily see how a human being becomes *inebriated* by getting a little power in one's hands. Today, the person is very simple and nice; tomorrow he or she is elevated to a position of power. His or her whole aspect changes: 'Don't you know who I am now?', power comes out in that burst! That shows that that person has not been able to *digest* that power. When you don't digest power, it inebriates you. Just like taking a little extra wine inebriates the mind. Power is called something that inebriates the human mind. That power can be political power, intellectual power, money power, or feudal pedigree power.

In the *Mahābhārata,* there is an important verse dealing with this subject (V. 34, 42):

Vidyāmado dhana madaḥ tṛitīyo'bhijanomadaḥ;
Ete mada avaliptānām eta eva satām damāḥ —

In a few words what a beautiful message comes out of this verse. The first *mada* or inebriation is from *vidyā,* knowledge. 'I have knowledge, I am an intellectual, don't you know?' That is called *vidyā-mada.* The second is *dhana-mada.* Till now I was poor; suddenly I came across lot of money. And that makes for *mada.* And the third is *abhijano-mada,* inebriation from family pedigree. The second line says, *Madā ete,* 'these are *madas,* inebriations', *avaliptānām,* 'only for the *avaliptas,* unrefined people, uncultured people'. But, *ta eva satām damāḥ,* 'to the great-minded people these very *madas* become *damas*'. In

Sanskrit alone you can find the beauty and significance of that word *mada* becoming *dama*. The word *mada* is reversed. If *mada* means inebriation, *dama* means perfect self-control. Perfect self-discipline is called *dama*. He or she has digested all power; there is nothing to inebriate.

You have seen in our *Rāmāyaṇa* epic, how Rāma had digested power, how Bharata had digested power. *Ta eva satām damāḥ*, 'all *mada* becomes *dama* in all truly great people'. When one takes more wine, the person becomes inebriated; then he or she won't feel the gravitational pull of the earth. The person will be staggering all the time, and with some misbehaviour coming in between. So, many people in poetry and drama compare power to a drink, that which inebriates. In this *śloka* or verse you will find that special mention; but there are people who can digest even heavy drinks. Similarly here; some can digest all this power. It is a spiritual digestion. That comes from this *yoga*. The *yoga*-power helps one to digest all this power, and all *madas* become *damas* for that person.

Sri Ramakrishna said one day about an old brāhmaṇa who used to come to him and talk with him freely. One day he came and accosted Śri Ramakrishna in a very sarcastic and supercilious way: 'Hello! O Priest! How are you?'. Hearing this, Sri Ramakrishna told his companion, 'He seems to have come across some money. That is why I find this change in him today!' There is also a very important parable of Sri Ramakrishna on this subject:

'One day, a frog, jumping about in the garden, came across a rupee, a *shining* rupee. The frog took that rupee, looked at it, felt it very fine, took it to its hole, and kept it there; but from that day it became a different frog. "I have *one rupee* with me! I am that much rich." So, another day, an elephant passed by the hole of that frog; and this frog came out angrily; "What business has this elephant to pass by *my* hole?" Saying so, it went and gave a few kicks to that elephant, went back, and gazed at the rupee in its hole. The elephant never knew that that frog existed in the world at all; but, the frog was satisfied: "I have expressed my sense of power and dominance."'

This is undigested power. And in world's literature, there is quite a bit of reference to this kind of indigestion of power. I use the word 'digestion', because you can understand it. If you eat food, if you digest it, it becomes strength to you. If you don't digest it, it becomes a toxin. It becomes a poison. Similarly, all experiences are to be digested. And there is only one energy that can digest them; that is the spiritual energy within you. The fire of spirituality can digest all kinds of power. Later in this chapter, we shall be coming across the expression, *jñānatapaḥ,* 'fire of knowledge'. That is the meaning of *yoga* here.

This subject comes in English literature in a famous passage in Shakespeare's drama, *Measure for Measure* (Act II, Sc. ii):

'But man, proud man,
Drest in a little brief authority,
Most ignorant of what he's most assured,
His own glassy essence, like an angry ape,
Plays such fantastic tricks before high heaven
As make the angels weep; ...'

What is this man? He could have done wonderful things; but he is behaving like a monkey. Angels weep seeing the man's condition. Why? He has been dressed in a little *brief* authority. Not for too long. Long ago, one of my friends, a deputy commissioner, said to me in Mysore: 'Swamiji, as soon as the order of my transfer comes to the office, when I go there, nobody stands up. Till then they all used to stand up. Now they have stopped standing up.' That is called 'brief' power. So limited it is. Shakespeare understood this great subject: 'man dressed in a little brief authority, most ignorant of what he is most assured, his own glassy essence,' his own Atman, the infinite Self. If he had known It, he could have digested the power. He doesn't know It, so he 'plays such fantastic tricks before high heaven, as make the angels weep'.

How much injustice is going on in our society today by the misuse of power by those who wield power. I give one example; we can multiply it million-fold. In Delhi, a citizen asked a telephone officer to replace his bad telephone; he demanded a large bribe; he could not afford it. The citizen approached none other than the Prime Minister, and he received his phone. A few days later, that very officer took away his phone! How helpless the citizen is! These smaller level bribes are the most distressing to the citizens at large.

We come across hundreds and hundreds of instances of injustice. A democratic state becomes weakened day by day by the increase of injustice in society. There may be poverty, there may be ignorance, that won't weaken it. But if there is injustice, and it increases, that will weaken the fabric of a democratic society. This injustice comes because those who hold power misuse it. There is no spiritual strength in the person to digest that power and to make it useful to the people. To help the democratic processes so as to strengthen our infant democratic state, and solve the problems of the millions, we need a philosophy. That philosophy is what Śrī Kṛṣṇa is giving here. Have power. We do need power, but we must know how to handle it for the good of the state and the people; that digestive power will come to the holders of power from a deeper source in them, namely, the spiritual nature of the human being. When you manifest that power, everything becomes simple. No injustice, no oppression, no exploitation: only the spirit of humanism, the spirit of service, will inspire you throughout your career. If we can educate at least 10 or 15 per cent of our administration in this philosophy, even then there will be a tremendous change in the human situation. But it is not happening yet, though we have the remedy with us; because we have the remedy with us, we need not be afraid of the malady. Malady is bad; malady without remedy is worse. But if it is a case of 'malady with remedy available', we can always overcome the malady one day or the other. And my hope is that our people will understand this great philosophy of the *Gītā* and its concept of *rājarṣi,* and become imbued with love for the nation and the people and the spirit of service.

During my Introduction to this book, I had referred to my talk with General J.N. Choudhary, Military Governor of Hyderabad in 1949, when he asked, 'Does this *Gītā* have any message for me as a Governor?' I had said: 'Yes, a tremendous message for you.' He thought it was only 'to give me a little peace of mind, I read a few verses from the *Gītā*.' 'No, that is absolutely wrong. This philosophy will teach you how to handle your power for the good of all,' I replied. *Kṣatriyāṇām balādhānāya,* Śaṅkarācārya comments in this section: 'in order to give strength to the holders of power, the *kṣatriya*'. Till now it was a caste, *kṣatriya* caste, only in India. But the quality of *kṣatriyahood* is a universal phenomenon. President Reagan of U.S.A. is a *kṣatriya.* So also Gorbachov of Soviet Union is a *kṣatriya.* Our Indian Prime Minister is a *kṣatriya.* So, all of them are *kṣatriyas,* because they are holders of power; no need to be crowned heads. Power they have; but they all need a new kind of strength by which they will digest that power, and use it for the good of all. So, Śaṅkarācārya calls it: *kṣatriyāṇām balādhānāya,* 'in order to give strength to the holders of power'. By this power they may be 'capable of serving humanity around them'. *Janān paripipālayitum,* to govern people in such a way as to make them feel big—that is called a democratic government. People must feel big by the touch of political and administrative power, and not become small. That latter is feudal. In a feudal society, feudal power touches man and woman to make him or her small. In a democratic society, political power touches people to make them big with self-respect and a sense of freedom. When they get this power of *yoga* philosophy, they become capable of working for the happiness and welfare of the people. What is *that* power that can digest all these political and administrative powers which are distracting the human situation and creating injustice and exploitation? That is called *yoga* power, inherent in every human being.

The great epic, *Mahābhārata,* speaks of three sources of power in every human being. I referred to it earlier also. First is *bāhu balam,* muscular energy. If you are weak physically, a strong person can push you to the wall; that is called muscular power. But that is a very ordinary power. The second power is *buddhi balam,* intellectual power. You can harm people and also exploit people with your superior intellectual power. But with it you can also do good to the people. But doing good to the people comes to the intellect not from itself, but from another source. That third source is called *yoga balam* or *ātma balam.* So, *bāhu balam, buddhi balam, yoga balam* or *ātma balam.* Three *balams,* strengths, are there in you and me. And the *Gītā* says that those who are invested with political and other powers, must also develop a little bit of this *yoga balam.* Not much is necessary; even a little will make the person a source of fearlessness and blessing. They need not become big *ṛṣis,* but they must become people on the road to *ṛṣihood,* become a little spiritual, by which they will utilize the situation of power to serve the people and to make them better and happier. This is the importance of *ātma balam* or *yoga balam.*

Śrī Kṛṣṇa has already told in the second chapter: *svalpamapyasya dharmasya trāyate mahato bhayāt,* 'even a little of this *Dharma,* this philosophy, can save one from great fear'. Imagine, therefore, a collector of a district with a little spiritual strength in him or her: how much good will come to the people around! So also a teacher in a village primary school: a little spiritual power will make him or her the servant of the children, looking after them, educating them, making them good citizens of the nation. All these higher motivations come only from this particular source: *ātma balam* or *yoga balam* inspiring the *buddhi balam. Buddhi* becomes chastened by the spiritual energy coming from the deeper level of the human personality. And this is a universal feature of humanity, according to Vedanta. *Yoga balam* is present in every human being. Only one must try to bring it out, unfold it, manifest it. So, when a teacher goes to a class, he or she must ask himself or herself: 'What am I here for? These are children coming from faraway places; they never had education for ages. Our country is now free; as a citizen of India, I am an instrument of our nation to give them education, to give them knowledge.' That very moment that teacher will become a big person, no more that tiny school master. He or she becomes an instrument of the nation for human purposes. Whenever he or she speaks, it will be only to educate the children, make them good citizens of the nation. So also a clerk in the Secretariat, or a constable on the roads, and every other state functionary. A bit of spiritual strength can make a big change in our society.

Therefore, Śrī Kṛṣṇa stresses this point that all power must be a union of *rājā* and *ṛṣi* in one. Don't be only a *rāja,* don't be only a *ṛṣi,* combine *rāja* and *ṛṣi* in one. You have the power, chasten that power by a bit of spiritual strength. Chastened power is what we need. 'Taming of power' is what they call it today. We have to 'tame' power. Usually, in every Constitution, power is tamed by *external* means. What is that?, what you call 'balancing of power'. The President has one power, the Prime Minister has another power, and the judiciary has its own power; one will check the other, and in this way there is a constitutional balancing of power given by the Constitution. But we can always upset it, as we are seeing it every now and then; but when this spiritual power comes in to chasten the power of the power-holder, then the administration will flow smoothly; no kind of harmful confrontation will take place.

So, what we want is to see a happy society, peaceful and co-operative, and everybody trying to help everybody else. The spirit of service comes only from that higher level of *ātma balam*. Whenever you have power without that chastening of power, you use your power to exploit people and to aggrandize yourself by corrupt practices. A chastening is what we need. So, the word *rājarṣi* is used by the *Gītā*. Be a *rājā,* but also be a *ṛṣi.* How?, by a bit of spiritual strength coming to you, manifesting a bit of the spiritual energy which is your essential nature. This is what we need, says *Bhagavān* Śrī Kṛṣṇa here.

I have dealt with this subject of people-oriented Government, through the Rājarṣi concept, in more detail, in my book titled *Democratic Administration in the Light of Practical*

Vedanta, published by the Ramakrishna Math, Mylapore, Chennai-4. It contains six lectures delivered to the following audiences:

1) Staff of the Mysore (now Karnataka) State Secretariat in the *Vidhan Soudha* Conference Hall, Bangalore, under the auspices of the Indian Institute of Public Administration, Mysore Regional Branch, on 19th February, 1979, on *The Philosophy of Democratic Administration.* 2) Lecture at the Indian Institute of Public Administration, New Delhi, on 2nd August, 1979, on *Social Responsibilities of Public Administrators* 3) A Lecture at the Indian Institute of Public Administration, Maharashtra Branch, Mantralaya, Bombay, on 6th February, 1979, on *The Science of Human Energy Resources.* 4) Lecture delivered at the Institute of Management in Government, Barton Hill, Tiruvanantapuram, Kerala, on 15th December, 1983, on *Human Values in Administration.* 5) Lecture delivered at the Delhi Municipal Corporation in its Town Hall, on 5th December, 1984, on *The Role of Local Self Government Institutions in our Democracy.* 6) Lecture delivered to the Andhra Pradesh Secretariat Employees, assembled in the open grounds of the Hyderabad Secretariat, on 24th March, 1986, on *Administrative Efficiency and Human Resource Development.*

It will contain, in the next edition, a similar seventh lecture, delivered at the special meeting of the Uttar Pradesh Government Secretariat Staff held at the Tilak Hall, Vidhan Bhavan, Lucknow Secretariat, on 2nd April, 1968, on *The Philosophy of Service*, now included in the third volume of *Eternal Values for a Changing Society*, published by the Bharatiya Vidya Bhavan, Bombay-7.

The whole teaching of the *Gītā* goes to the people all over the world with this message of *ātma vikāsa*, 'spiritual growth'; this is a type of greatness, before which all others also will feel great. What a beautiful idea! Before a mother's greatness, a child feels very elevated. Before a Gandhiji, everyone felt elevated. Our dignity is enhanced thereby. Before a Mussolini or a Hitler, all felt smaller and smaller. They gained greatness by destroying other people's greatness. To impart greatness to the people, to the most common people, you need the type of personality involved in the union of the *rājā* and the *ṛṣi*. Without the touch of the spiritual, that personality can never come. Wherever such personalities have come, their spiritual qualities have drawn people to them. They may not have gone to temples or churches or any gurudwaras; they may be atheists and agnostics. But they have grown spiritually. U.S. President Abraham Lincoln is especially an instance in American history before whom even the humblest person became elevated in dignity. That is real human greatness. In a feudal society, we had such greatness, occasionally only. Before a feudal lord, everybody else became slaves. In a feudal society, before parents, children become small. That is the old society. But the new society is going to be otherwise. Before the parents, children feel dignified. They get faith in themselves. What a beautiful idea! This is the type of human growth that comes when a bit of this *Gītā* message of *yoga* enters into the mind and heart of the people. It is an intensely practical philosophy. It has nothing to do with theory, nothing to do with ritual or ceremony, much less with anything magical or mysterious. *It is a transformation, a human spiritual growth, unfolding one's infinite possibilities, step by step.*

Our Indian society till now stifled human development in recent centuries. Somebody wants to get up; some blow comes and lands on his or her head; wherefrom we do not know! That was our society. Now our society says to every one: 'Get up! I am here to help you. I shall make you stand on your own feet.' What a change! That is the change Swami Vivekananda wanted to bring about in India today through his message of practical Vedanta of which he considered the *Gītā* to be the best exposition. Every child must feel, every labourer must feel, that he or she has a place in society, must feel elevated, and know that free India is there to help him or her. What beautiful ideas these are! These are all Vedanta, intensely practical Vedanta. We didn't know anything about them till Swami Vivekananda came. Our priests and even *sādhus* will discuss Vedanta only theoretically, but live and act most un-Vedantically, and misguide society also accordingly. Vedanta teaches the innate divinity of every human being, while the Indian society trampled on the poor and the low of the same society. After Swami Vivekananda's arrival and exposition of the enormous possibilities of Vedanta to transform the human situation, the condition of the masses is changing for the better. That is what we are trying to achieve today in our society. Everyone feeling a sense of dignity, a sense of worth. 'Stand erect before me', that is the call of our democracy today to the common people, Hindu, Muslim, or Christian.

I have found it difficult to make our common people understand this. People have been told for centuries, 'you are nobody, you are nobody.' If I tell them that they are somebody, they don't understand at all. It is a new philosophy for them. When I was in the Ramakrishna Mission in Rangoon in 1939–42, I remember peons coming to deliver letters to me from the Government Secretariat or from other offices. The weather was hot, the man was perspiring. I am to sign the receipt; till then the peon will be standing there. So, I said, 'there is a chair, please sit down.' He said, 'no, I won't sit down. I am not allowed to sit down.' 'No, I am telling you, please sit down.' He won't; he has been hypnotized. I argued, 'a chair is meant to be sat upon, not to be carried on the head; so sit down please.' Finally I will say, 'You are not *my* servant. You are the servant of somebody else. Therefore, you can sit down here; please sit.' So, I somehow made him sit for a minute. I was in Karachi from 1942 to 1948. One day, the postman delivered me a letter; he was perspiring heavily. It took time for me to sign the papers, and he was standing there. I said, 'Please sit down. There are sofas there.' He quietly sat on the floor. He won't sit on the sofa. 'Please sit on the sofa. It is meant for you all.' 'No.' Then I had to gently lift him and put him on the sofa! These common people have been told again and again, 'You are nobody. You are nobody.' They also believed they were nobody. You have to take the other side and say, 'You are somebody. You are somebody.' There should be none of these types of treatment of human beings which destroy their human dignity. These ideas were entirely foreign to our people two or three generations ago. They would say, these are all strange ideas, revolutionary ideas. But Vivekananda said that we need these revolutionary ideas.

Our society has become very stagnant, very antihuman. But, the modern age will witness a peaceful thorough social revolution with the inspiration of practical Vedanta and modern Western thought. The arrested development of our society, from north to south, from east to west, will give way to the full development of India's one-sixth of the world population. Inspiring ideas and movements for the unprecedented national development are already gently percolating in Indian society. Swami Vivekananda expounded in powerful language all these ideas in 1897 in his *Lectures from Colombo to Almora* and *Letters of Swami Vivekananda.* One sentence I wish to share with you. This comes in a letter of Swami Vivekananda from America to a disciple in India. He is dealing with the low dismal human situation in India during the last two centuries. Today things have changed a lot. But remember, he wrote it on 20 August 1893 to Alasinga Perumal of Madras (*Complete Works of Swami Vivekananda,* vol. 5, p. 16):

'They little dream of the ages of tyranny, mental, moral, and physical, that has reduced the image of God [that is man] to a mere beast of burden; the emblem of the Divine Mother [which is woman], to a slave to bear children; and life itself, a curse.'

That was India's social consciousness about a hundred years ago. We are changing it. That is the direction of progress. Here the best of modern Western thought and the best of Vedanta, have joined together to lift men and women to the highest pinnacle of dignity and glory. And on his return to India in 1897 after four years of intense spiritual and cultural work in U.S.A. and England, he began his public lectures in India in Ramnad, near Rameswaram, before a large and enthusiastic audience with these prophetic words (*Complete Works of Swami Vivekananda*, Vol. 3, pp. 145-146):

'The longest night seems to be passing away, the sorest trouble seems to be coming to an end at last, the seeming corpse appears to be awaking...India, this motherland of ours....from her deep long sleep. None can resist her any more; never is she going to sleep any more; no outward powers can hold her back any more; for the infinite giant is rising to her feet.'

That is the importance for us in today's India, of this reference in the fourth chapter to the *rājarṣi* concept—*rājarṣayo viduḥ*, '*rājarṣis* knew this subject' They will treat a human being as a human being, and increase human dignity with the power they handle. We need that transformation today in a big way. From primary schools to the highest educational institutions, from our Pañchāyats to the national Parliament, and in all administrative spheres, these ideas must inspire the concerned people. Then only will a thorough human transformation come in India. We are having industrial transformation, plenty of technology, improvement of export and import, but if the human mind in India does not get transformed by the freedom and national responsibility of democratic citizenship, it will be a national tragedy. A tragedy which was referred to two centuries ago by the British writer Oliver Goldsmith: 'Ill fares the land, to hastening ills a prey, where wealth accumulates, and men decay.' That will be the fate of our society if human development doesn't keep pace side by side with economic and technological development. It is that human development that Vedanta advocates through the teaching of the *Gītā*: the fullest human development, through man-making and nation-building education, as Vivekananda repeatedly said.

I would like to present one incident to contrast the way government staff treats citizens in India and in Britain. When I was the Secretary of the Ramakrishna Mission Institute of Culture in Calcutta in the 1960s, we had a Dutch lady, but British Citizen, as the Manager of our International House. One day she came to me with a smiling face and said that from the British Government in London, she has received a communication saying that she was now eligible for old-age pension and, as the first instalment, a cheque had been enclosed. What wonderful human concern; she herself had not thought about it; but the faraway British Government had given her what was her due! When will such a situation, such a humanist concern invade our State and Union Government employees! The spread of this *Gītā* message is the only solution to this problem. It contains remedies for the maladies which our nation and several other nation are suffering from.

We have studied the first three verses of this chapter, and in the last verse there was a hint which made Arjuna confused. In the first verse and up to the third verse Śrī Kṛṣṇa had said: 'I taught it to Vivasvān, etc., etc.', and 'I am teaching it to you.' 'What kind of teaching is this? Śrī Kṛṣṇa, You are my contemporary, how could you teach them?' On this subject, therefore, Arjuna puts a question. A very important subject comes up there. This message of *yoga*, or practical Vedanta, has come in a succession of teachers and students; but through a long course of time, this message became diluted and lost. In the context of the first three verses, Śrī Kṛṣṇa had referred to the importance of this concept of *rājarṣi*; a man or a woman who handles political, social, economic and other powers, and yet uses them only for the good of the people. Such a person has combined power, on the one side, and inward spiritual growth on the other. The concept is *spiritual growth*, not just religion. We can have any amount of religion as usually understood—some ceremony, ritual, creed, dogma. That doesn't give us that capacity to handle power for the good of the people. But a little spiritual growth makes all the change, *adhyātmika vikāśa*, as we say in Sanskrit or Hindi, to mean 'spiritual expansion'. The concept of 'I' becomes expanded to include 'you', and to include 'all others'. That is spiritual growth out of which will come all value-oriented attitudes and actions—human concern, the spirit of service, the spirit of dedication. Vedanta holds that all values are spiritual and their source is the divinity in every human being.

A big, but sad change has to come to our government staff at all levels. They should stop harassing the citizens for bribes when they come for a legitimate government sanction for starting a project or building a house. Their response to all such requests must be: 'What can I do to help you?' When such people multiply in a government, the state becomes well governed and the people fearless and happy. The great Indian epic, the *Mahābhārata,* conveys to us today, after about four thousand years, one criterion of social health and of a well-governed political state. In the *Rāja Dharma* or *Ethics of the State,* section of the *Śānti Parva,* Bhīṣma tells Yudhiṣṭhira (12. 68. 32, Bhandarkar Edition):

Striyaśca āpuruṣā mārgam sarvālamkāra bhūṣitāḥ;
Nirbhayāḥ pratipadyante yadā rakṣati bhūmipaḥ —

'If women having decorated themselves fully with ornaments, and without any men accompanying them, can move about freely and fearlessly through the streets and lanes (unmolested by anybody), that state is well-governed.'

And here the word *ṛṣi* is used to indicate this spiritual growth which Vedanta considers to be the birthright of every human being. Usually, when we hear the word *ṛṣi* or 'sage', we think of Visvāmitra, Vasiṣṭhā, or some other mythical sages. But why? Anybody can be a *ṛṣi* or sage by a little or more of that spiritual growth.

That possibility comes from the Vedantic teaching of the inherent divinity of every human being and his or her organic capacity to manifest it in life, action, and human relations. Swami Vivekananda expresses this truth of Vedanta in a brief utterance (*Complete Works of Swami Vivekananda,* vol. 1, p. 124):

'Each soul is potentially divine. The goal is to manifest this divinity within by controlling nature, external and internal.'

In a letter to Sister Nivedita, Swamiji had written (*Complete Works of Swami Vivekananda,* vol. 7, p. 501):

'Religions of the world have become lifeless mockeries. What the world wants is character.'

That character is the fruit of spiritual growth, *adhyātmika vikāsa.* It is not dogmatic religion but this spiritual growth that results in a value-oriented life. That alone can resist easily all temptations, including all bribery, big or small. This is what I earlier referred to from the *Mahābhārata* as *ātma balam* over and above *bāhu balam* and *buddhi balam.* Those who have *buddhi balam,* intellectual strength, have no capacity to resist even small temptations; actually, they succumb to temptations more easily than others.

We are on the road of developing into an age when we start growing spiritually and live a value-oriented life. Our tiny ego, caught up in the meshes of our genetic system, can detach itself from this system and expand in love and concern. That is what is called spiritual growth. That is what is called *psychosocial evolution* in modern biology. Your psyche is able to detach from its genetic limitation and control and expand in sympathy, love and concern. Modern biology affirms that genes are selfish and cannot be the source of values. That expansion is an important development in education capable of achievement by every human being; and that is the goal of evolution at the human stage. The whole world is waiting to get the message of that evolutionary advance. Religions, we have plenty, but spiritual growth we have so little. Spiritual growth is what makes for character; or, wherever there is character, value-oriented activities, there is spiritual growth, says Vedanta. When you are on that road, even if you advance only a few steps, that is a great gain. So, in India we have to learn this one great lesson that, in the field of spiritual growth, it is not *all or nothing*; even a little is important. Unfortunately, our whole thinking is otherwise. 'If I can't become a sage Vasiṣṭha, I shall become a selfish worldly fellow.' We have to learn that even a little is better than nothing. So, why not take the next step? Go one step further. Have love and concern; do work in a spirit of service. When you do that, you are already on the road of spiritual growth. It is such spiritually grown people, that must handle power, political power, administrative power, money power. When they do so, they do it for the good of all. Society becomes happy, human development takes place, there is peace and harmony. So, this concept of *rājarṣi* is very important for us and for other nations; it will make our democracy healthy and strong. Śrī Kṛṣṇa considers his philosophy of *yoga* as practical Vedanta, as a teaching to produce *rājarṣis;* that is indicated by the opening words of the fourth chapter: *imam vivasvate yogam proktavān* and *rājarṣayo viduḥ.*

And in this context, I wish to refer to the ancient Chinese thinkers who had also developed this idea. The *rājarṣi* concept appears in Chinese thought as *sagely within and kingly without*. Outwardly you are a king, inwardly you are a sage. That is a wonderful expression—exact translation of the word *rājarṣi.* So, this is the transformation that the whole world, both undeveloped and developed nations, needs. That such growth is possible is guaranteed by the Vedantic truth of the innate divinity of every human being. If there is corruption, if there are social malpractices, if there is more and more crime, it all comes from an absence of that spiritual growth. 'Even a little of that spiritual growth will suffice', *svalpamapyasya dharmasya trāyate mahato bhayāt,* the second chapter had assured us. There is no other remedy; no legislation, no Act of Parliament, can make a person grow spiritually. It comes from handling the energies hidden within oneself by one's own effort. This kind of growth in the spiritual dimension, beyond the genetic dimension, makes a person big inwardly to be able to embrace others in love and service. The word *mahātmā* in Sanskrit means that. Great soul, *mahā ātmā;* why was Gandhiji called a *mahātmā?*, because his soul was not a prisoner of his tiny organic system. It had detached itself from it, and expanded in love and human concern. So, we called him a *mahātmā.*

The opposite of *mahātmā* is *alpātmā,* small soul; in this there are several levels as in the *mahātmā* concept. It is relevant to know what is the lowest level of *alpātmā.* In our national and state level politics and administration, there are these two types at various levels. We can consider the lowest of the *alpātmā* as the well-paid government officer who gets his wife burnt after taking an 'insufficient' dowry from her parents, and marrying another for a larger dowry! In all such cases, we can mark that the *small* soul of the person is entirely under the control of his genetic system. The genes are selfish, says modern biology. In his book, *The Selfish Gene,* the British biologist, Richard Dawkins, says (pp. 2–3):

'The argument of this book is that we, and all other animals, are machines created by our genes. ... I shall argue that a prominent quality to be expected in a successful gene is ruthless selfishness. This gene selfishness will usually give rise to selfishness in individual behaviour. ...

'My own feeling is that a human society based simply on gene's law of universal ruthless selfishness would be a very nasty society in which to live. ... Be warned that, if you wish, as I do, to build a society in which individuals cooperate generously and unselfishly towards good, you can get little help from "biological nature". Little help means no help!'

Let education put every child on this road to being a *mahātmā;* little by little so that by the time the child reaches the age of retirement, he or she would have achieved a good deal of spiritual development. That is real scientific education, making for spiritual growth, development, fulfilment, and carrying the world also with oneself by that inner growth. It is that concept that Śrī Kṛṣṇa is referring to in the first few verses, and the teaching of *yoga* in the second and third chapters of the *Gītā* is meant for putting all humanity on the road of its spiritual growth; that is the march to evolutionary fulfilment; if such an onward movement does not occur, biologists like Sir Julian Huxley affirm that human evolution will stagnate at the sensory level and decay and die.

This kind of spiritual growth is the birthright of every human being, says Vedanta. This is the central theme of the *Gītā*. It is not an ascetic philosophy; it is not a world-rejecting philosophy; it is life in action, but life in action motivated by humanistic considerations of love and service. The statement of Śrī Kṛṣṇa raised a question from Arjuna; and we shall deal with that question now.

अर्जुन उवाच –
Arjuna uvāca —

'Arjuna said.'

अपरं भवतो जन्म परं जन्म विवस्वतः ।
कथमेतद् विजानीयां त्वमादौ प्रोक्तवान् इति ॥४॥

Aparam bhavato janma param janma vivasvataḥ;
Kathametad vijānīyām tvamādau proktavān iti— 4. 4

'Later was your birth, and that of Vivasvat prior; how then should I understand that you spoke about this earlier?'

'Your birth is recent', *aparam bhavato janma.* Arjuna and Śri Kṛṣṇa were of the same age. Arjuna knew it; *param janma vivasvataḥ,* 'Vivasvān, (Manu and Ikṣvāku) were born long, long ago'. How can this 'poor Arjuna' understand that you taught it to them? This is a very relevant question. Any one of us would have put this question. *Katham etad vijānīyām tvam ādau proktavān iti,* 'that you taught it in very ancient times', *ādau,* 'in the very beginning of the process of creation' you taught it to such powerful persons, 'how can I understand this?'

To this question of Arjuna, Śrī Kṛṣṇa gives the answer; and in this answer you have that wonderful teaching of the *Sanātana Dharma* about Divine Incarnation: *sambhavāmi yuge yuge,* 'I come again and again'; that is what Śrī Kṛṣṇa will tell in the eighth verse. This teaching is found only in the *Sanātana Dharma,* and also in Christianity, with the only difference that in Christianity the incarnation comes only once; no second time, except to wind up the whole show. But here it is, *yuge yuge sambhavāmi,* 'I come in every *yuga:* whenever there is a need'. That is the famous teaching about the *avatāra* in the *Gītā* and all the *Purāṇas*: the concept of Divine Incarnation.

श्रीभगवान् उवाच –
Śrībhagavān uvāca —

'The Blessed Lord said.'

बहूनि मे व्यतीतानि जन्मानि तव चार्जुन ।
तान्यहं वेद सर्वाणि न त्वं वेत्थ परन्तप ॥५॥

Bahūni me vyatītāni janmāni tava cārjuna;
Tānyaham veda sarvāṇi na tvam vettha parantapa—4. 5

'Many are the births that have been passed through by me and by you, O Arjuna; I know them all, while you do not know, O scorcher of foes.'

Many are the births that you and I have undergone, *bahūni me vyatītāni*, 'I have gone through many (births)';, *tava ca*, 'and of you also'; *tāni aham veda sarvāṇi*, 'I know all of them'; *na tvam vettha parantapa*, 'you do not know that, O scorcher of foes'; you are only a *jīva* or soul, you understand only the present birth, but I know that you and I have lived several times before. I know all of them. That is the first statement. How did Śrī Kṛṣṇa take birth again and again? And what was the purpose? That he says in the next two verses:

अजोऽपि सन् अव्ययात्मा भूतानामीश्वरोऽपि सन् ।
प्रकृतिं स्वामधिष्ठाय सम्भवाम्यात्ममायया ॥६॥

Ajo'pi san avyayātmā bhūtānāmīśvaro'pi san;
Prakṛtim svāmadhiṣṭhāya sambhavāmyātmamāyayā—4. 6

'Though I am unborn, of changeless nature, and Lord of all beings, yet subjugating my *prakṛti* or divine nature, I am born by my own *māyā*.'

Even though I am *aja*, 'unborn or birthless'. From this negative Sanskrit word *aja* and positive word *janma* comes the positive English words like gene, genetic, etc. Even though I am *aja*, and *avyaya*, 'birthless and imperishable', and *bhūtānām īśvaro'pi san*, 'even though I am the Lord of all creatures', *sambhavāmi ātma māyayā*, 'yet I assume a body by taking recourse to my own power of *māyā*'. I am the infinite divine, but using my power of *māyā*, I become a finite human individual; that is the nature of an incarnation. Outwardly very ordinary, inwardly possessed of some tremendous dimension, which ordinary people cannot easily see. Śrī Kṛṣṇa will say that later on. *Prakṛtim svām adhiṣṭhāya sambhavāmi*, 'taking recourse to my *prakṛti* or *māyā,* I am born.' This *prakṛti* or nature itself is *māyā.* That power is there in the hands of the divine. How could the One become the many? It is through *māyā.* Though *māyā* plays a great part in all aspects of religion in India, whether it is *Bhakti* or *Jñāna,* in the *Gītā* (7. 14) you later on get a wonderful statement by Śrī Kṛṣṇa that 'this *māyā* is difficult to overcome; those who take refuge in me alone, they alone will overcome this *māyā*'.

A magician does magic, and you are carried away by this magic. You think it is all true. Not at all. Look at the magician. Then you will understand the magic. If you are caught up in the magic, you become completely caught in an illusion. So, you go from *māyā* to the master of *māyā, māyāvi.* This is understood through a statement in the *Svetāsvatara Upaniṣad* (4. 10): *Māyām tu prakṛtim vidyāt, māyinam tu maheśvaram,* 'know *māya* to be this *prakṛti* or nature, and that supreme Divine is the master of this *māyā*'. The difference between God and all of us is: we are subject to *māyā,* but all *māyā* is subject to the Divine. He is free, we are not free. We are the same divine, but we are subject to this *māyā,* therefore we are finite, human individuals. But our true nature is that infinite One, as Vedanta will say again and again.

Sri Ramakrishna puts it in a simple Bengali saying: *Pañcabhūter phānde brahma paḍe kānde,* 'Brahman weeps when He is caught up in the net of the five elements.' The body and mind are made of five elements: earth, water, fire, air and space, the *pañcabhūtas.* In that net, Brahman is caught. Then Brahman behaves like a bird, an insect, a human being, etc., etc. Brahman weeps in you and in me. That is the language. So, Sri Ramakrishna also said: God *enchained* is man, man *unchained* is God. Whenever this *māyā* moves away, you and I know our true nature. But so long as *māyā* is there, we weep, forgetting our true nature.

So, this is the difference between all of us and the divine. He himself has become the universe; he entered into each one of these things. That is the language of the *Taittirīya Upaniṣad* (II. vi. 1): *Tad anuprāviśat,* 'He entered into it'; *tad anupraviśya,* 'and having entered', he is functioning. He has forgotten his true form. This is a wonderful teaching: *Māyā* is what all of us are experiencing in our life.

As Vivekananda said in his famous 'Maya' lectures in England (*Complete Works of Swami Vivekananda,* vol. 2, p. 89):

'Māyā is not a theory but a simple statement of facts; what we are and what we see around us.'

So, this *māyā* is under the control of the Divine, who takes recourse to that *māyā* and uses it to become a tiny human child. And you have seen in the *Mahābhārata* T.V. serial, how Śrī Kṛṣṇa was born as a tiny child in Kamsa's prison, but revealed to his parents his divine form. The words 'small' or 'big' have no meaning, so far as the infinite Divine is concerned: *aṇoraṇīyān mahato mahīyān,* 'smaller than an atom, bigger than the universe'; that is the Atman, says the *Kaṭha Upaniṣad* in the second canto of the first chapter.

And so, Śrī Kṛṣṇa says, *prakṛtim svām adhiṣṭhāya sambhavāmi,* 'I take birth taking recourse to my *prakṛti*'. What is that?, *ātma māyayā,* 'by my own *māyā*', by my own power: 'Let me become an ordinary human being. Let me function there. Some great good has to be done for humanity. God alone can do this work.'

So, when God incarnates, a new energy appears in the world—a world-transforming energy. In fact, consider the word '*avatāra*', the Sanskrit word for 'Incarnation': how do we give this particular status of an '*avatāra*' to a human being? Ordinary individuals are subject to all the limitations of life, and an *avatāra* is also subject to bodily limitations. He has hunger, he has thirst, like others. But he is also infinite within. And he knows it, and that slowly manifests and works to uplift humanity. A tremendous energy flows out of him—a world-transforming and epoch-making energy. When you see such energy in any person, remember that the divine is manifested there. It is only in course of time that we realize that a divine manifestation was there. Time is a great factor. Ordinary greatness cannot stand the test of time. Today, you hear so many people are great, even a road is named after somebody. After two generations, nobody knows who he or she was. Nobody will know. That is called ordinary greatness.

As against it, there is another type of greatness, which goes on expanding more and more, century after century, after the death of the person, after the body has been burnt away. Such people we characterize as divine incarnations, who defeat the flow of time itself, or make time flow in the reverse direction. When he was alive, very few people knew him. After his death, many people come to know him. Many people begin to honour him, worship him. Even after two thousand years, people still continue to honour and worship him. What does that show?, an enormous power was manifested there. It is not ordinary human power. That greatness we have seen in a few people. This is something unique. Therefore, India calls that person a divine Incarnation, an *avatāra*.

So, Śrī Kṛṣṇa is expounding this subject for the first time in our spiritual and cultural tradition. *Sambhavāmi ātmamāyayā*, 'by my own *māyā*, I am born', as a divine Incarnation. Śrī Kṛṣṇa's birth was extraordinary, all divine birth is extraordinary. The birth of Jesus was extraordinary. So also of Śrī Rāma. Every one of these is a 'world-moving force' as Vivekananda calls them. An ordinary saint cannot make the world move. A few people may benefit. But when an incarnation comes, he or she makes the world move. And he or she can produce many saints by one's own spiritual energy. In the name of *Bhagavān* Buddha, how many saints came! In the name of Śrī Kṛṣṇa, how many saints came! Through Jesus, how many saints have come! This is the special quality of an incarnation.

To all such people we give divine status. They are not ordinary human beings. We worship them. And a whole religion is centred in the worship of the divine incarnation. Most intense spirituality comes through the worship of a divine Incarnation. Find out for yourself. In your history you will find that, wherever there is that devotion to a divine Incarnation, high character, tremendous energy, all these qualities will flow from that kind of a devotion. We can say that almost the whole of Hindu religion is centred in Śrī Rāma and Śrī Kṛṣṇa. Centred in Jesus, you have the same in the Western world.

So, He said, 'I body forth through control of my *māyā* power. Though infinite and imperishable, I become a finite human being.' And that story is very beautifully expressed in the *Śrīmad Bhāgavatam* dealing with Śrī Kṛṣṇa's birth. If you read the tenth Book of the *Śrīmad Bhāgavatam*, in the first few chapters, you will find the story of the birth of a tiny child in the prison of king Kamsa. And there, Devakī and Vasudeva, father and mother, salute the newborn child! A divine Child with a glow around Him. 'We know that You are not an ordinary human child. We know that You are the divine Person. You have come into this world in this Form.' In that way, Devakī and Vasudeva are praising Śrī Kṛṣṇa and they are some of the most beautiful and highly philosophical hymns in the *Śrīmad Bhāgavatam*. And then the Incarnation's purpose must go on. If father and mother understand that this child is a divine Incarnation, and not a human being, they will not be able to do service to him, and he won't be able to fulfil his own life's mission. So, the *Śrīmad Bhāgavatam* says, after the hymn of praise was over, Śrī Kṛṣṇa withdrew his *māyā*, withdrew his divine form, became an ordinary child, and started crying like any ordinary child. *Babhūvaḥ prākṛtaḥ śiśuḥ*, a *prākṛta śiśu*, 'became a *prākṛta śiśu*, a normal child'. And mother and father forgot his divine dimension. Then only could they *look after* the child. After that only, you come across the fascinating Kṛṣṇa Līlā, the Līlā or play of Śri Kṛṣṇa as a child, which has enthralled India for ages. And today it is enthralling many people in other countries also. And, later, as a grownup person, he performs a great *līlā*, namely, the teaching of this *Gītā* to Arjuna and through him to millions of people throughout the world. That is the charm and power of this Śrī Kṛṣṇa Incarnation.

Now, you find this kind of understanding of a divine Incarnation in modern writers on Sri Ramakrishna. I like one sentence from the French thinker, M. Romain Rolland, in his *Life of Ramakrishna*, where he presents Ramakrishna and Vivekananda as 'the splendid symphony of the universal soul'. In the section, *To My Western Readers*, p. 13, Romain Rolland says:

'The man whose image I here evoke was the consummation of two thousand years of the spiritual life of three hundred million people. Although he has been dead for forty years, his soul animates modern India. He was no hero of action like Gandhi, no genius in art or thought like Goethe or Tagore. He was a little village Brahmin of Bengal, whose outer life was set in a limited frame without striking incident, outside the political and social activities of his time. But, his inner life embraced the whole multiplicity of men and Gods.'

Earlier, in the Preface *To My Eastern Readers*, he had said (pp. 2-3):

'And it is because Ramakrishna more fully than any other man, not only conceived, but realized in himself the total Unity of this river of God, open to all rivers and all streams, that I have given him my love; and I have drawn a little of his sacred water to slake the great thirst of the world.'

This extraordinary dimension was revealed only to a very few persons in the beginning. Narendra, i.e., later Vivekananda, could understand; a few others also could understand. Just like in Jesus, one or two could understand; not others: one of whom remarked: 'is he not the carpenter's son?'

So, the inner dimension of an incarnation and its immense range become understood only as centuries roll on. And today, without difficulty we can see the greatness of Śrī Kṛṣṇa. But when he was alive, how many people could understand his greatness? Some accused him for stealing that garland called Syāmantaka, and he himself had to justify that he had not stolen it. Contemporary rulers like Śiśupāla also accused him. So, like any other human being, an incarnation also has to pass through the ups and downs of life. But that doesn't detract him from his tremendous divine energy resources within. Those energies begin to flow slowly and silently.

Śrī Kṛṣṇa imparted the *Gītā* to Arjuna on the battlefield of Kurukṣetra. It may be over three thousand years ago.

Only Arjuna was there, and Sañjaya was also observing it from the capital through sage Vyāsa's boon. But today, millions of people are listening to what Śrī Kṛṣṇa said on that Kurukṣetra battlefield. Similarly, Buddha spoke to five disciples at Sarnath in Varanasi in the sixth century B.C. Within five hundred years, what he uttered then spread throughout Asia, changing human life. Jesus spoke to eleven disciples. And that voice reached millions of people in the next thousand years. So, here you can see that one who is called a divine incarnation is not a mere ordinary individual. There is something extraordinary about him; but, ordinary people cannot understand him. Unless we have spiritual development in ourselves, we cannot understand the greatness of an incarnation. Śrī Kṛṣṇa will say later on that 'many people do not know my true dimension. Those who are spiritually sensitive will be able to understand.' He tells Arjuna: 'I come on earth as an incarnation, *sambhavāmi,*' but when? The next verse answers it:

यदा यदा हि धर्मस्य ग्लानिर्भवति भारत ।
अभ्युत्थानमधर्मस्य तदात्मानं सृजाम्यहम् ॥७॥

Yadā yadā hi dharmasya glānirbhavati bhārata;
Abhyutthānamadharmasya tadātmānam sṛjāmyaham—4. 7

'Whenever, O descendant of Bharata, there is decline of *Dharma,* and rise of *Adharma,* then I body myself forth.'

That is the purpose of the Divine advent. No other power can do it. This is a famous verse quoted thousands of times by our spiritual seekers: *Yadā yadā hi dharmasya glānirbhavati bhārata,* 'whenever there is a *dharmaglāni,* a decline of *dharma*', and *abhyutthānam adharmasya,* 'increase of *adharma*', *tadātmānam sṛjāmyaham,* 'I body forth myself at that time.' The purpose is:

परित्राणाय साधूनां विनाशाय च दुष्कृताम् ।
धर्मसंस्थापनार्थाय संभवामि युगे युगे ॥८॥

Paritrāṇāya sādhūnām vināśāya ca duṣkṛtām;
Dharmasamsthāpanārthāya sambhavāmi yuge yuge—4. 8

'For the protection of the virtuous, for the destruction of the wicked, and for the establishment of *dharma*, I come into being in every age.'

In order to protect what is *dharma*, what is virtue, what is good and pure, in order to destroy what is evil and what is wicked, I come, not once, but in *yuga* after *yuga*, 'age after age'. Whenever there is a need, I come for that purpose. The maintenance of the world in good condition is an important objective of the divine. We studied in the beginning Śrī Śaṅkarācārya's introduction to his *Gītā* commentary, where he refers to this situation that the social fabric is getting broken up because there is no 'cement' to unite one human being with another. Therefore, there is disruption in society; there is violence, there is crime, there is unfulfilment all through. That situation has to be retrieved; no scholars or politicians can do it; no bishops or priests can do it; no parliaments can do it. Only a divine power can do it. Moral and spiritual progress in a given human situation can come only from highly spiritual personalities, not through any other means. Therefore, Śrī Kṛṣṇa said, *sambhavāmi yuge yuge*, whenever such a situation comes, 'I body forth myself age after age'. India having a 5000-year history, such situations have come up again and again. During short historical periods you may not see many incarnations. Over long historical periods, there are many such examples of a divine manifestation and life becomes fresh once again, moral values come, humanistic values come, this continues for some time, again there is a decline, again there is a process of regeneration. What began with high moral values becomes low in course of time due to passing through human experience, needing a new inspiration. That is why, 'I come again and again', *sambhavāmi yuge yuge*, and the purpose is *paritrāṇāya sādhūnām*, 'for the protection of the good'.

In many of our government departments, we see today that good and honest staff suffer at the hands of powerful dishonest ones; in an office, if there are one or two honest officers, they are in trouble. All the others will try to pull them down, and bring even false cases against them. You can actually see this happening in our society, so that a straightforward honest person finds it difficult, because the ratio of forces is against him or her. So, the person finds it difficult, and after some struggle he or she may also say, 'I will be one with you.'

At the time of our political independence in 1947, what an elevating atmosphere we had! But after that, every year, there was this sliding down, and it continues even now. When you study Vivekananda literature, you find a new energy coming: Let us go upwards; no more going downwards! Let us develop love for the nation, for the millions of our weaker sections and energetically serve them. When that message reaches more and more of our people, that kind of change will come. Today, that tremendous power that manifested through Sri Ramakrishna, Swami Vivekananda, and that divine personality, Sri Sarada Devi, the Holy Mother, will generate a widespread revival of the moral and humanistic awareness and energy. Vivekananda had said (*Complete Works of Swami Vivekananda*, vol. 5, p. 228):

'The national ideals of India are *renunciation* and *service*. Intensify her in those channels, and the rest will take care of itself. The banner of spirituality cannot be raised too high in this country. In it alone is salvation.'

It takes time for great ideas to spread in society. It took about three hundred years to make Buddha's message current coin in Indian society during Mauryan Emperor Ashoka's time. And Vivekananda says that the greatest period of Indian history was when Buddha's message inspired Indian society and many nations in Asia also, with the spirit of compassion, purity, and the spirit of service, including service to animals with even hospitals for animals; all these started in many parts of India at that time. But after some five hundred years, slowly decline set in. By the seventh-eighth century A.D., the essential energy of that message had become diluted. *Huen Tsang*, the Chinese pilgrim who visited India in the seventh century A.D. and who has left an account of that seven-year Indian visit, saw that decline. It was at that time, *from the spiritual and philosophical points of view*, a Śaṅkarācārya came, a personality of immense power, purity and compassion, and did his marvellous work at the philosophical and mental levels of the people including establishing the cultural unity of India. It is Swami Vivekananda who conveyed the Vedantic harmony between the message of Buddha and Śaṅkarācārya to the common people, to lift up our whole nation. That is the work that is now set in motion through the divine manifestation of Sri Ramakrishna, the messenger of harmony, in our own time. Swami Vivekananda expressed this harmony of Sri Ramakrishna in a beautiful hymn in praise to Sri Ramakrishna, while he was installing Sri Ramakrishna's picture in a devotee's house in Howrah:

Sthāpakāya ca dharmasya sarvadharmasvarūpiṇe;
Avatāravariṣṭhāya rāmakṛṣṇāya te namaḥ —

'Salutations to you, Ramakrishna, who came to establish *Dharma*', *sthāpakāya ca dharmasya:* the same promise of Śrī Kṛṣṇa. *Sarvadharmasvarūpiṇe,* not to establish any particular sect, or a particular creed bearing a special label or his name, but 'the embodiment of every religion', and *avatāravariṣṭhāya,* 'the supreme divine manifestation', *rāmakṛṣṇāya te namaḥ,* 'to you, Ramakrishna, we offer our salutations'. You will find, therefore, that this divine *avataraṇa* is happening again and again in the Indian context. In other countries, this happened only once—in Christianity—and even then people there didn't accept him; they crucified him. It is not enough that God comes into the world, but the people must be prepared to accept him. That is something unique in India. India has a philosophy and a culture, which can appreciate a divine manifestation and welcome him. We don't crucify our great teachers! Other nations kill even religious reformers; but that also never happens in India. We always try to understand an incarnation or a reformer, first a few people, then more and more people; in this way the *avatāra* begins to function for the good of society, and in this modern age, not only in India and for India, but also in and for all countries abroad. That is the great work that is going on now, silently and quietly. This was initiated by Śrī Kṛṣṇa a few thousand years ago, may be three or four thousand. That is the wonderful teaching that we are now studying in the fourth chapter.

These verses, 7 and 8, deal with the concept of the divine Incarnation. I have referred to this concept of divine Incarnation in two articles in volume one of my 4-volume book on *Eternal Values for a Changing Society* published by the Bharatiya Vidya Bhavan, Bombay-7. These articles were entitled *Avatāra as History-maker*, and *Avatāra as Divinity*. These two values, of history-making and of divinity, together coalesce in certain types of great people. And they command the reverence of humanity. They set in motion a current of love and compassion, tolerance and understanding. They continue to command that reverence even after hundreds and hundreds of years. To such a category, a small number in world history, we could give no better name than *avatāra* or 'Divine Incarnation', and to them humanity offers divine honour and divine worship. Such people are not many in world history. Lesser personalities, influencing human life in various directions, have been in plenty. Sometimes a great author can inspire great sociopolitical movements, like Voltaire and Rousseau and Karl Marx. So also, other writers, artists, and great intellectuals in many countries. But this type of greatness, namely, a Divine Incarnation, is unique. That is what is being expressed here: that the divine spark in all of us, which shines only a little bit, in a twinkle, shines in brilliance in that divine personality. So, he is described as the divine embodiment, and he comes to lift us up to our own inherent divine stature. That is the significance of the *avatāra* in the Indian cultural context.

Śrī Kṛṣṇa accepts in the eighth verse that, in order to increase *dharma* or ethical and humanistic values in society, he comes again and again to the world as a human being and plays his part. In the earlier Incarnations, like Śrī Kṛṣṇa and Śrī Rāma, we see them actually destroying evil people, being born as *kṣatriyas,* like Śrī Kṛṣṇa destroying a Kamsa or a Śiśupāla and Śrī Rāma destroying Rāvaṇa. But in Buddha, we don't find any killing of evil people physically; only absolute love and compassion and the lifting of people morally and spiritually. In Jesus also you find the same. A spiritual energy flows from them touching all sorts of people including the sinners. Today, in Sri Ramakrishna, you find that same power working, just to influence people gently, silently, even without their knowing it. That is the divine power manifesting through a human body in various ways. Śrī Kṛṣṇa referred to it once, and he will refer to this divine birth and action of an Incarnation in verse 9. If one knows it as it truly is, that there is a divine power playing in this person, not an ordinary human power, then he or she will achieve one's spiritual development. In our *bhakti* movement in India, *bhakti* centred in a divine Incarnation is the source of great power to stimulate human spiritual progress. That *bhakti* is something dynamic, because it has a divine personality as an example to inspire it. Therefore, most of our *bhakti* movements are centred in these divine Incarnations; *bhakti* can be centred also in the divine personality of myth and legend, like Śiva, Viṣṇu, Devī, which also will help to develop human spiritual life. But it is most intense when that divine manifests as a human incarnation. So, Śrī Kṛṣṇa says:

जन्म कर्म च मे दिव्यमेवं यो वेत्ति तत्त्वतः ।
त्यक्त्वा देहं पुनर्जन्म नैति मामेति सोऽर्जुन ॥९॥

Janma karma ca me divyamevam yo vetti tattvataḥ;
Tyaktvā deham punarjanma naiti māmeti so'rjuna—4. 9

'One who thus knows, in true light, my divine birth and action, after leaving the body, is not born again; and he or she attains to me, O Arjuna.'

My *janma* and *karma*, 'my birth and actions', are *divyam*, 'divine'; they are not of the ordinary type. We have got our own *janma* and *karma*. We are *jīvas*, ordinary human souls. We are hungry for so many things, we are after this or that. That is our *janma* and *karma*. The case of an Incarnation is different. They have nothing to run after. They are full. But from the beginning, they are there to give, to give out of the plenty within. That is their *janma* and *karma*. From very young days they know that they have come for a great work. *Janma karma ca me divyam. Evam yo vetti tattvatah,* 'those who understand'—*vetti* means understand; *tattvataḥ* means in reality, the exact truth: 'this is something divine, I recognize it'. When you do so, you must have attained some spiritual development. Otherwise, you cannot appreciate a divine personality. So, *tyaktvā deham punarjanma naiti,* 'after leaving the body at death that person never takes rebirth'. He or she becomes perfect, centred in the love of the divine Personality, knowing him to be a divine Incarnation. He or she will no more have rebirth. *Saḥ mām eti Arjuna,* 'he or she comes unto me only, O Arjuna'. He achieves oneness with me. That is the highest spiritual development. A devotee seeks to be with God, living in his presence just like fish living in water always. Water is its life, it cannot live outside water. So, we live in God all the time. Such a person is a very great spiritual *sādhaka* or seeker. Śrī Kṛṣṇa is telling us that this capacity to understand the greatness of a divine Incarnation doesn't come to everyone.

Sri Ramakrishna says, even many sages, like Bharadwāja and others, at the time of Śrī Rāma's Incarnation, couldn't understand that he was a divine Incarnation. 'He is a great soul', that is how they evaluated him and respected him. A few others could immediately recognize the divine character of Śrī Rāma's personality. So, this you can see in the case of Jesus also who was treated as a carpenter's son by many. Some could not understand at all Śrī Kṛṣṇa's divine greatness. But those who could understand, they got tremendous spiritual nourishment through that understanding. The next *śloka* is number 10; it is very famous and full of divine meaning:

वीतरागभयक्रोधा मन्मया मामुपाश्रिताः ।
बहवो ज्ञानतपसा पूता मद्भावमागताः ॥१०॥

Vītarāgabhayakrodhā manmayā māmupāśritāḥ;
Bahavo jñānatapasā pūtā madbhāvamāgatāḥ — 4. 10

'Freed from attachment, fear, and anger, absorbed in me, taking refuge in me, purified by the fire of knowledge, many have attained to my being.'

Here is very simple Sanskrit, with profound meaning, compressed in a few words. The last line says: *bahavo madbhāvam āgatāḥ*, 'many have achieved oneness with me'. Earlier he had said, 'those who realize me truly as the divine Incarnation, they come unto me'. Now he repeats it: Many have achieved this spiritual realization. It is not something new. All through the ages, 'many people have striven and achieved this spiritual realization.' *Bahavo madbhāvam āgatāḥ*. That is the main framework of the verse. Many have come unto me and become one with me. Not one, not two, but many. It is a tremendous tradition of spiritual growth, development, and realization. How did they achieve it? That is the statement in the rest of the verse. And that statement has a profound meaning in our everyday life all over the world.

Three things they overcame. What are they? *Rāga, bhaya, krodha. Vita* means without. Without *rāga, bhaya, krodha; rāga* is sensory attachment; *bhaya* is fear; *krodha* is anger. Three emotions, unrestrained, which are against the moral and spiritual life of humanity. Mind you, Vedanta does not consider even fear as a friend of moral and spiritual life. Fear is an inhibitor of high action. To survive as a human being we need ordinary small fears. But beyond that, fear is a negative force, though many religions put stress on 'fear of God', trembling due to the fear of God; it has no moral value, according to Vedanta; fear makes you moral because of external pressure. Just like the policeman's baton makes you behave the right way on the road. You are not moral thereby. You are made moral by external force. So, fear has nothing to do with moral and spiritual life. Vedanta is insistent on it. Overcome fear. A true person does not need fear at all. So, that emotion is added to what we have to overcome. Attachment, fear and anger: three emotions which contain enormous energy. We are not to destroy that energy; we have to transform that energy. How to do so?

That is the significance of the next famous phrase: *jñānatapasā pūtā*, 'purified through the *tapas* of *jñāna*'. What a beautiful expression! *Jñāna*, spiritual knowledge, is given the characteristic of *tapas,* which literally means austerity: austerity of knowledge. What a beautiful idea! We often perform physical austerity, fasting and all that. That is very very ordinary. The greatest *tapas* is mental: mind doing *tapas,* purifying the personality through that *tapas.* That is called *jñānatapas* or knowledge-*tapas.* Suppose a child goes to school. He or she starts *jñānatapas;* he or she has to study a book, try to understand it, try to reproduce it in an essay. All this is *jñānatapas.* It is a hard job. You are training the mind thereby; so, that is one aspect of *jñānatapas.* The whole of secular education was treated in India as a *jñānatapas.* Knowledge doesn't come straight for you. You cannot just swallow knowledge. You have to work hard for it. When *tapas* goes away from education, education becomes cheap, very cheap. And much of education all over the world today is treated as cheap by great thinkers. In our country it is the worst. Education has become so cheap. No need to think at all. The mind doesn't play any part. *Jñānatapas* has been taken away completely from education.

Thinkers in India, and in many other countries including the U.S.A., have expressed dissatisfaction with and criticized the current educational programmes. The *Gītā* will say that this criticism is due to the search for knowledge being separated from the concept of *tapas.* The human mind must be raised to the level of knowledge-seeking. And what is learned must be digested, must be assimilated. All that is *tapas.* A very hard job, as I told you. You hear a lecture from a teacher, then reproduce it in an essay. And then the teacher examines it and finds that you have done well. How much of mental *tapas* you had to go through to do this! That *tapas* is now almost gone.

Another aspect of *jñānatapas* is still more important. Emotions of anger, lustful tendencies, hatred, fear—all these have to be burnt in the fire of knowledge. That is the real *tapas;* that *tapas* is supreme; that is what makes for high character. And therefore, this *śloka* says: *Vita rāga bhaya krodhā,* 'those who have overcome *rāga, bhaya* and *krodha,* attachment, fear and anger', *manmayā,* 'and have become filled with me', *mām upāśritāḥ,* 'have become devoted to me'. They have known that this Divine Reality is their own inner Self, he is the Self of all. Their mind is drawn to that great reality. *Bahavo,* 'many such', *jñānatapasā pūtā,* 'purified in this fire of knowledge', transforming the energies of the three emotions of attachment, anger and fear into constructive, creative forms to strengthen personality and character: that is *tapas.* Without *tapas,* none of these can happen.

I often mention that we take crude oil from the earth, refine it, and produce beautiful and useful petroleum products. So, this human mind and body have to become a refinery, a psychological refinery. Take all these emotions, and just refine them. Out of this refining process, what comes out? All ethical and humanistic values—love, compassion, fearlessness, spirit of service. Vedanta proclaims that the source of all values is the infinite and ever-pure and ever-free Atman in the depth of the body-mind complex. *Vedanta also holds that the science of values is the link between physical sciences and the science of spirituality.* What a beautiful conception of *jñānatapas!* We have never thought about it in modern civilization. We are thinking of external things all the time. What is happening to people? They become egoistic, petty-minded, quarrelsome, and also violent and criminal. All this is happening to educated people. We never handled education from this new point of view; that was wrong. Handle your mind and refine its thoughts and emotions! Your mind, your emotions, these are the nearest to you. Handle them; purify them; refine them. What a high character energy will come out of this! And how happy human life will be! How peaceful inter-human relationships will become; how loving and peaceful husband-wife relationships will become! What a fulfilled life humanity will have! And modern biology considers *fulfilment* as the goal of human evolution.

So, the emphasis in *śloka* 10 on this concept of *jñānatapas* is highly relevant today. Have you done *jñānatapas? Jñāna* is knowledge, any knowledge, but in this context it means spiritual knowledge; have you treated it as a *tapas?* The greatest *tapas* is *jñānatapas.* Physical *tapas* is very ordinary: some endurance record, that is all. But this is something that makes for high character, and tremendous energy comes out of the individual concerned. We have to create that refinery in ourselves. Nobody else can do it for you and for me. If I want an oil refinery, I am sure any foreign country can advance lot of money for the refinery. But in this field, nobody is going to help you. You have to do it yourself, though you can get guidance from others. In the sixth chapter of the *Gītā* which we shall be studying later, verses five and six give us this message:

Uddharet ātmanātmānam nātmānam avasādayet;
Ātmaiva hyātmano bandhuḥ ātmaiva ripurātmanaḥ —

'Raise yourself by yourself, do not weaken yourself; you are your own friend, you are your own enemy.'

Bandhurātmātmanaḥ tasya yena ātmaivātmanā jitaḥ;
Anātmanastu śatrutve vartetātmaiva śatruvat —

'One is one's own friend when he or she conquers oneself; if unsubdued by oneself, one operates as one's own enemy.'

This is a beautiful idea which must be given to every child. By the time it is five or six, it must be made aware of how to make its body and mind a refinery; it must start to refine impressions coming from outside and responses going out of itself. If one gets something bad from outside, one must refine it, and send out what is only good. That is the nature of the human psychological system when it is aware of the Divine behind it. *Therefore, all can do this in varying measures*. So, this *śloka* has tremendous reference to human development, fulfilment, happy inter-human relationships, including international relationships. Any politician can create tremendous problems for interstate relationship, if he or she hasn't got even a little of this refinement within. But, if they are well refined, they will be a source of national strength and tremendous international understanding and peace. Similarly, also in a family, between parents and children. So, we have to initiate this process, little by little, when people are young, from the age of five or six onwards. Then it becomes more intensive from ages twelve to fourteen, and by the time one is 25, one must feel, 'yes, I have converted my body-mind complex into a laboratory for refining experience.' What a beautiful idea of education! Along with it, get whatever knowledge you can get from books and teachers, through schools and colleges. But without this, that knowledge will not be fruitful . *Pūtā jñānatapasā; pūtā* 'purified or refined', *jñānatapasā,* 'by the *tapas* of *jñāna*'; *madbhāvam āgatāḥ,* 'they have become one with me'. *Bahavo,* 'many'. If many have achieved this, why not I? So many people all over the world, through various spiritual practices, through various ethical and moral disciplines, have come to this wonderful state. Even atheists and agnostics can come to this state, because they may deny a God 'there', but they can't deny their own inner Self. So, atheism, agnosticism, and all types of religious beliefs are all one in this particular process. We can overcome fear, anger, as well as unrestrained sensory attachment. Convert every experience into the pure form by this *jñānatapas,* or the refining capacity of the human mind. The great word *tapas* has been interpreted by Śaṅkarācārya, quoting from *Yājñavalkya Smṛti* as: *manasaśca indriyāṇām ca aikāgryam tapa ucyate*—'the concentration of the mind and the sense organs is called *tapas*'. I may not believe in a God, but I can become deeply spiritual, deeply ethical, deeply human. There are many people among the agnostics who have high character. We never speak ill of agnosticism and atheism from the Vedantic point of view. Ordinary religions may be afraid of these people, but not Vedanta. There is a significant verse in the *Vivekacūḍāmaṇi* which explains how Vedanta achieved this broad vision (verse 573):

Astīti pratyayo yaśca yaśca nāstīti vastuni;
Buddhereva vikāretau na tu nityasya vastunaḥ —

'The affirmation of the theist that ultimate Truth is, and the negation of the atheist that the ultimate Truth is not, are only modifications of the mind and do not affect the Eternal Truth (of the Atman).'

Vedanta welcomes everybody; you are a human being, you have a tremendous centre within you though you may not know it. But it is there. That is manifesting when you become moral, kind, and compassionate; you are manifesting the divine within you. Vivekananda's definition of religion given earlier becomes relevant in this context: 'Religion is the manifestation of the divinity already in man'. When my ego manifests, I repel people, but when the Atman manifests even a little, I attract people. That is the meaning of manifestation of the divine as the science of religion, as the science of human possibilities. Everyone who has manifested this divine within even a little becomes a beautiful person; he or she will have happy relationships with other people. So, this is the most important thing for human beings to remember and implement.

This *śloka* or verse occurs not only here in this *Gītā*, but also in that great book, *Māṇḍūkya Upaniṣad Kārikā* of Gauḍapāda, Śaṅkarācārya's teacher's teacher, who lived on the banks of the Narmada river about seventh century AD. There it is slightly different, dealing with the transcendental experience of *samādhi,* beyond the world of relativity, beyond the world of name and form, the state when the mind rises and realizes the infinite, the Absolute. How does it happen? Describing that, that *śloka* says (II. 35):

Vītarāgabhayakrodhaiḥ munibhiḥ vedapāragaiḥ;
Nirvikalpo hyayam dṛṣṭaḥ prapañcopaśamo'dvayaḥ —

'The *munis* or sages, freed from attachment, fear, and anger, who have gone beyond the Vedas, have realized this non-dual *nirvikalpa* or 'no-mind' state, where this ever-changing universe of relativity ceases to be.'

From the Advaita level of experience, this *śloka* says the same thing as the *Gītā śloka* said about going beyond *rāga, bhaya, krodha.* Those who are *munis,* 'thoughtful people'; *mananaśīlo muniḥ,* thus Śaṅkara defines it. Ordinarily, by *muni* we mean a man of silence; *maunam* means silence; but, the real meaning is, not silence of speech, but that the mind is under great discipline, thinking is under discipline, and the person is thoughtful. That kind of a person is called a *muni;* whatever he or she says, behind that there is tremendous thinking, not mere blurting out. A *muni* cannot blurt out. There is weight in what he or she says. In most of the talk by men and women, there is no weight. Whereas when *munis* talk, there is weight in it; half a sentence is enough to carry tremendous meaning for you. That kind of '*speaking less and thinking more*' is called *muni.* Such *munis* overcome *rāga, bhaya* and *krodha.* Further, they have achieved one more thing: *veda pāragaiḥ,* 'they have gone beyond the Vedas'. *Nowhere in the world's religious literature, except in India's Sanātana Dharma, will you find an expression like this, of a devotee going beyond the Vedas or any other scripture.* Go beyond the Vedas, beyond the Koran, beyond the Bible, means: don't be satisfied with belief but experience the truth for yourself. Words do not give you the truth. Truth comes only through experience. So, such people, who begin to experiment in spiritual life and want to experience the highest, they go beyond the Vedas. They go beyond all these sacred books. What a beautiful revolutionary idea! Throughout India's history, we have *always* emphasized this point. That a mystic who experiences truth goes beyond all these holy books. Volumes are needed for you and me to learn some elements of spiritual life, but these people have *lived* it, *experienced* it. In one passage in the Vedas themselves—in the *Bṛhadāraṇyaka Upaniṣad*—it is actually said that for one who knows Brahman, the ultimate Reality, the Veda has no meaning: *vedo avedo bhavati,* 'Veda becomes no-Veda'. Mark the firm language: *vedo avedo bhavati.* And Śaṅkarācārya also comments on it by saying in a passage that, 'like a servant who carries a lamp in front of you to find your way, and you have found it, so becomes the Veda to that person'. What is the Veda?, utterances of those who have known the Truth. Here is one who has known the Truth; why should he or she depend upon the

Veda further? Actual experience takes you beyond books. At a certain stage, books become a botheration. The Upaniṣad itself says that: *vāco viglāpanam hi tat*, 'words are only so much of distraction for such minds'.

So, in many passages of India's religious books, you will find this emphasis that the human being can take recourse to books in the beginning, but, later on, he or she has to discard them and try to realize the Truth that is mentioned there. So, the real stress of true religion is on experience, not reading, not scholarship, on 'being and becoming' as Vivekananda has put it. Sri Ramakrishna says in one of his parables: 'Great scholars, who do not practise moral and spiritual life, are like vultures flying high up in the sky, but their attention is fixed on the dead bodies on the earth below! High scholarship and small mind! What is the use of that? Develop a high mind. That is more important. So, *munibhiḥ vedapāragaiḥ*, 'thinking people who have gone beyond the Vedas'. You have already heard from the second chapter, Śrī Kṛṣṇa telling Arjuna, 'Vedas deal with the three *guṇas;* go beyond the three *guṇas,* O Arjuna', *Traiguṇya viṣayā vedā nistraiguṇyo bhavārjuna.* So, in this way, Gauḍapāda says, there have been many people who have overcome lust, fear and anger, become very thoughtful, and then had gone beyond the Vedas. *Bahavo,* 'many such', *jñānatapasā pūtā,* 'purified by the *tapas* of *jñāna*'; we saw this expression in the *Gītā*. But here in the *Māṇḍūkya Kārikā* it is, *vīta rāga bhaya krodhaiḥ munibhiḥ vedapāragaiḥ nirvikalpo hyayam dṛṣṭaḥ,* 'this *nirvikalpa* state has been realized'. *Vikalpa* means mental modification; *nirvikalpa,* no mental modification, absolute stillness. The ocean full of waves is one state, all the waves have subsided and the ocean is perfectly calm, that is another state. So, *nirvikalpo hi ayam*, 'this *nirvikalpa* state', it is spoken of with such definiteness, 'this *nirvikalpa* state has been realized' by such people. What is the nature of that state? *Prapañcopaśamo,* 'in which this world of duality, this world of change, the world of relativity, is completely dissolved'. Imagine what a beautiful statement this is! Why do I see duality? We get duality through the five senses. If I can look at reality as it is, it will be quite different. You will see everything as Brahman, everything as pure consciousness. So, *nirvikalpo hyayam dṛṣṭaḥ prapañcopaśamo,* the whole *prapañca* or the manifested world becomes completely dissolved in that ultimate reality. Everything is Brahman.

When Albert Einstein was asked about the highest understanding of reality in physics, he said that there are two realities in physics today: one is matter, the other is the field. Both cannot be true, he said, for, the field alone is true. The field is that in which matter is a bubble. The whole universe is like a few bubbles, that is all. That infinite energy field, that is the physical truth. *That knowledge, which is purely intellectual knowledge, becomes an experiential knowledge through this kind of tapas, which Vedanta describes as nirvikalpo hi ayam dṛṣṭaḥ prapañcopaśamo.* Not only so, *advayaḥ*, 'non-dual'. There is no multiplicity in this ultimate Reality; there is no duality there. One infinite consciousness is there, in which all this universe appears with all its diversity; we see this diversity now with our senses, and when we realize this truth, diversity goes. Only one Atman in every being. That is the highest spiritual realization.

In the Upaniṣads this is highly commended. Here is a wonderful passage from the *Bṛhadāraṇyaka Upaniṣad* dealing with creation as self projection of Brahman, the ultimate Reality (II. i. 20):

Sa yathā ūrṇanābhiḥ tantunā uccaret,
yathā agneḥ kṣudrā visphuliṅgā vyuccaranti;
Evam eva asmāt ātmanaḥ sarve prāṇāḥ
sarve lokāḥ, sarve devāḥ, sarvāṇi bhūtāni vyuccaranti;
Tasyopaniṣad—satyasya satyam iti;
prāṇā vai satyam, teṣām eṣa satyam —

'Just as a spider (produces out of itself and) moves about in its own web, just as from a fire minute sparks fly about, exactly so, verily, from this Atman have come forth all (physical, biophysical, and psychophysical) energies, all worlds, all gods, all beings.

'Its mystic name (Upaniṣad) is *Truth of truth.* The energies, verily, are truth; this Atman is the Truth of those energies.'

In the *Muṇḍaka Upaniṣad,* which we studied here before we took up this *Gītā*, we read that in one of its verses it is said, *brahmaivedam amṛtam,* 'this whole universe is the immortal Brahman'. *Idam* is the technical term for *this manifested universe.* 'It is the immortal Brahman', *brahmaivedam amṛtam.* Then it is explained further in the same *śloka: purastāt brahma,* 'Brahman is in front'; *paścāt brahma,* 'Brahman is behind'; *dakṣiṇataścottareṇa,* 'on the right as well as the left'; *brahmaivedam viśvamidam variṣṭham,* 'the whole manifested universe is that worshipful Brahman'. That is the summit of spiritual realization, where all duality has been overcome, and you find absolute unity of pure consciousness.

So, *Māṇḍūkya Kārikā* says the same thing which *Gītā* is telling from another point of view, that this is something *which many have realized*, and many *can* realize, because we have the organic capacity. Only, we must turn in that direction. We have to learn how to discipline this psychophysical energy system and make it move in the direction of this supreme truth, and not be satisfied with sensory comfort and pleasure. Most people use this body-mind complex only for comfort and pleasure. Today that is maximum in our civilization. That is why we call it a consumerist civilization. We want only consumerist goods to pamper our physical system. And a very efficient technology pampers our sensory cravings. We are stuck up at the sensory level. But at some time human beings will begin to feel this as irksome as it doesn't express the best in us; there is something missing, let us try to understand that. At some time, every human being will begin to ask this question: what next?, what next? I have money, I have power, I have pleasure, but something is missing. That hunger for something higher, not exactly clear yet, is a tremendous experience. Out of that hunger comes this scientific and spiritual search for the Infinite and the Eternal. Several people in some of today's advanced nations are experiencing this hunger, a hunger which Śaṅkarācārya expressed in the last line of his famous hymn: *tataḥ kim, tataḥ kim, tataḥ kim, tataḥ kim?* You have health, you have wealth, you have power, you have pleasure, still the mind will ask, what next?, what next?, what next?, what next? We may stifle it in the beginning, but at some time it will become very insistent. Then you begin to think seriously. Something is missing, let me find out that something.

And so, this spiritual striving is a real fact. Many have gone through it; that spiritual road has been walked by several people: like a pilgrim road. You can also walk over it, in this life itself, not in a future life, says Vedanta. When you are young and vigorous, develop this refinery within yourself, so that your life will be really richer. That is why it is meant to be adopted gently by all young people. From the age of 16, it must be pursued with more seriousness along with other pursuits of *achievement*. Day-to-day work goes on, moneymaking goes on, human relations go on, but the mind is experiencing a new stir—a stir which, if pursued, will make the mind a better instrument for human relationships. This is what modern civilization has forgotten; this is what Vedanta holds all the time before humanity as the road for it to travel. Physical pleasure is not meant to be the ultimate aim for man. It is only the beginning; a baby can have physical pleasure. For, what else does the baby seek except comfort and pleasure. The safety and security of the mother's body and the milk the mother gives, that is what the baby wants and nothing else. That is the first stage. But after 2 to 2½ years, the baby wants knowledge. If mother gives milk again, 'No, I don't want, I want something better', mental food: knowledge, it wants. That is the line of creative, not stagnant, human evolution. It is when we proceed on that line of human evolution towards higher knowledge, that we will finally find that we are in the world of Brahman, the world of spiritual evolution. That is where knowledge matures into wisdom. That is what is to be done today, so that all this knowledge-seeking becomes meaningful. Today, it is meaningful only to fatten oneself more at the physical level. Your knowledge gives you more money, more pleasure, more comfort, that is all. Has it made you better as a person? Not at all, except in a few cases, more knowledge and more money become allied with more wickedness and more petty-mindedness. Therefore, our ancient teachers said: 'March on! Develop your spiritual strength. That is your evolutionary path and goal.' And, in the present age, Swami Vivekananda has given this *Upaniṣadic* clarion call: 'Arise, Awake, and stop not till the goal is reached.'

Nature has given us this cerebral system. It has a tremendous capacity to discriminate, to fix goals and to proceed in that direction. No animal has got it. Animals have only pleasure and comfort, reproduction, and effort for survival. Man alone has the capacity to seek knowledge: knowledge physical, knowledge spiritual. Both are knowledge for us, and so let humanity take that road, not this road which we have already traversed as animals. This idea comes again and again in the *Mahābhārata* and in our other books. Swami Vivekananda asked this question in his lectures in England and America, 'which human being can enjoy a meal with more gusto than a pig?' A pig's life is entirely in the body. It can enjoy a meal much better than you and I. Our experience in the sensory realm becomes interfered by our capacity for knowledge, by our thinking, by our logical faculty. So, we cannot have that much sensory enjoyment as an animal has. An animal body is meant for more and more of physical comfort and pleasures. A human body also can have it, but that is not its goal; it has to transcend it. That is what our spiritual teachers have said. The search for higher things will be emphasized again and again in the case of human beings. That is the line of human evolution; otherwise, it will be absolute stagnation at the physical level. This human being, with an extraordinary instrument called the cerebral system, has become stagnant at the sensory level, at the level of *samsāra,* worldliness; what a tragedy! That is what Vedanta says. Such a person is called a *samsāri,* a man or a woman getting stagnant at the sensory level. Living in the world does not make one a *samsāri;* but getting stagnant at the sensory level makes one so; a whole civilization also can become stagnant as a *samsāri*.

So, we begin to think about it; then we find that nature has placed this cerebral system at the top level of the human body. Nature could have put it in the hip or somewhere else. In fact, today's neurology tells us that some huge mammals had a second relay brain in the hip, so that, as British neurologist Gray Walter humorously puts it, 'that mammal could argue a-priori and a-posteriori!' Later, that second one was abolished by nature and the brain at the crest was slowly developed and became the instrument of human evolution for one who knew how to use this remarkable instrument. According to physiology, all the ordinary functions of the body, so far as self-preservation is concerned, are done by the lower brain, which we share with the animals. Only this higher brain has got a different function: how to think and develop far-sight and foresight, how to take this life to higher levels? It has to achieve not only knowledge but also insight and inward penetrating power. The word *insight*, in the psychological context is defined by Geraldine Coster of England (*Yoga and Western Psychology*, p. 92):

'It is defined as the capacity for being able to call up a greater variety and number of correlates to any given idea or stimulus, and enables the fortunate possessor to react with "originality" to given situations.'

However, if we make this cerebral system the servant of the sensory system, what a tragedy it will be! Just for survival, just for pleasure, this brain is not to be used only for that! Unfortunately, the more educated a person, the more he or she uses this brain for only that and not for lifting life to higher levels. From the Vedantic point of view this is a great tragedy of the educated in the modern age. Nature has intended this higher brain to be the instrument of man's emancipation. I am quoting a neurologist in this connection: Gray Walter, referred to above, from his book, *The Living Brain*. He said, evolution sees that various capacities have been developed in the animal body, like automatic temperature control, for the purpose of survival; when evolution rises to the level of the human body, many new capacities have also come. Now what do all these mean? The human body has inherited that temperature control in the body. That was achieved in the later mammals first, not the earlier mammals. Early mammals did not have this kind of thermostatic equilibrium in the body. But nature found that they could not survive; so, in order to help the species to survive, nature evolved this thermostatic equilibrium within the later mammals and in the human body which also belongs to the mammalian species.

Dealing with the evolutionary significance of this mechanism, British neurologist Gray Walter says (*The Livine Brain*, p. 16):

'The acquisition of internal temperature control, thermostasis, was a supreme event in neural, indeed, in all natural history. It made possible the survival of mammals on a cooling globe. That was its general importance in evolution. Its particular importance was that it completed in one section of the brain, an automatic system of stabilization for the vital functions of the organism—a condition known as homeostasis. *With this arrangement, other parts of the brain are left free for functions not immediately related to the vital engine or the senses, for functions surpassing the wonders of homeostasis itself.*' (italics not by the author).

And relating this physical homeostasis of organic evolution to the mental and spiritual homeostasis of *yoga*, Gray Walter concludes (p. 19):

'And once again, as new horizons open, we become aware of old landmarks. The experience of homeostasis, the perfect mechanical calm which it allows the brain, has been known for two or three thousand years under various appellations. It is the physiological aspect of all the perfectionist faiths—*nirvāṇa*, the abstraction of the *yogī*, the peace that passeth understanding, the derided "happiness that lies within"; *it is a state of grace in which disorder and disease are mechanical slips and errors.*' (italics not by the author).

He had said earlier that for all mammals, homeostasis meant only survival; but for man, emancipation.

So, in these *Gītā ślokas* you find humanity is asked to take this truth seriously. This brain is not meant to be a mere instrument for personal survival. It is meant to take us to the highest level of freedom, and take others also to that high level of freedom—for spiritual growth, development and fulfilment of oneself and others. This is the great lesson that even the subject like physiology will teach us; and yet, today's materialistic oriented physical science does not know this truth. To make the higher brain the servant of the lower brain is the worst thing that a human being can do. The lower brain is meant only for survival, not for any higher purpose. Śrī Kṛṣṇa had earlier referred to *buddhi-yoga: Buddhau śaraṇam anviccha,* 'take refuge in *buddhi*'. *Buddhi* represents the capacity of this higher brain, the luminous organ. The lower brain has no luminosity. It has only energy, and it knows the survival purpose, nothing more. But luminous, with the capacity to see far ahead and take you in that direction, only *buddhi* can do. Therefore, develop *buddhi, Gītā* had said. *Buddhi* alone can take one to the highest level; it is enlightened reason and will combined.

And Śrī Kṛṣṇa is going to tell us later on (*Gītā*, 10. 10): 'When I want to bless anybody, I only help him or her to resort to this *buddhi*,' *dadāmi buddhi-yogam tam,* 'I give them *buddhi-yoga*', *yena mām upayānti te,* 'by which they will themselves find their way towards me'. That *buddhi-yoga* means detaching this higher brain from the control of the lower brain and making it function independently and freely by aligning with the Atman just behind. That will help to take you to higher and higher levels. What is the use of giving me money?, what is the use of giving me something luxurious? Give me *buddhi-yoga.* I will get all these things by myself. I get all the energy thereby. To this urge in a human being, Śrī Kṛṣṇa says that the best blessing that one can get is this *buddhi-yoga,* and the worst curse one can have is to lose one's *buddhi.* You heard about it in the second chapter, *buddhināśāt praṇaśyati,* 'when the *buddhi* is lost, one perishes'. A person who does a terrible crime had *buddhināśa* when he or she committed that crime.

So also, *buddhināśa* is behind any other evil that we do. But, if the *buddhi* is alert, none of this will happen. So, take recourse to *buddhi.* Develop your *buddhi* is the message of the *Gītā* to all. That comes through, what I said earlier, developing the psychophysical system as a refinery of experience. When you refine experience, you take all that energy, transform it into high creative energy, and that becomes *buddhi*-energy. The same psychic energy can be either at the sensory level, or at the psychic level, or at the *buddhi* level. These levels are there for the same energy. Whatever functions through your eye, ear, etc., that is also psychic energy. But it functions at the sensory level. Very low level it is. When you go to the mental level it is higher. A little more subtle, and more pervasive. But when it comes to the *buddhi*-level, it becomes pure, and transparent and of wide range and scope.

I had referred to Mahatma Gandhi. What was special about him? He had converted his body-mind complex into a high class refinery. So, when so much hatred came to him—he was even beaten by the police in South Africa—he took all that into that refinery and quietly transformed it into love and compassion. He told, don't do anything to that policeman, he did it out of ignorance. Now, what is that attitude of Gandhiji due to? There is no miracle in it. He has tried it and succeeded; we don't try it even. When we try, we also can achieve it. Why not convert hatred into love in this refinery?, you ask that question to yourself. When you begin to think about it—suppose that man hates me, I begin to *think* about that hatred—even then that hatred becomes less. When you *think* of a subject, it becomes different. When you don't think about it, it rules over you. You are subject to it. Therefore, human refinery means that *jñānatapas,* converting the mind into a *tapas* of *jñāna.* These are all intensely practical propositions. Many have done it, why not I? I can understand, some people don't know all this. But they can know today; these books like the *Gītā* are there. Having known, we have to put it into practise and say, 'Yes, this is meant to develop character. All the knowledge I gain is meant to put it into life, experience, and character.' That second step is important for all people. There is nothing impossible. Impossible things are happening today: landing on the moon, one of the space vehicles, the Voyager, is going beyond the solar system into outer space! If technology-physical can achieve this, cannot technology-mental achieve similar things in the sphere of life?

This discipline of the mind, making a refinery of it, where all experience gets refined, and the pure products come out of it—what a beautiful idea! Today, nothing can inspire children more than these ideas. Nobody has told them. If you tell them that your body-mind is a beautiful laboratory; you go to physics and chemistry laboratory to do so many things, continue to do that, but don't ever forget that your own body-mind is a big laboratory. You have to refine all the experiences coming there. Father scolded you one day, you become depressed, convert that depression into cheerfulness once again by putting it through that refinery process. Soon it will become a very simple matter. Children become stronger and stronger as days go by. This is the meaning and wide significance of this wonderful verse 10: *Vītarāgabhayakrodhā manmayā mām upāśritāḥ; Bahavo jñānatapasā pūtā madbhāvam āgatāḥ*. Remember that word *bahavo* meaning many. It is not a new thing. It is an ancient road.

In Buddha's time 2600 years ago, he himself said, I am not teaching anything new. I am only cleaning up a road that has been there, it has been overgrown with weeds. I am cleaning it up so that people can walk over that road. This is the language he has used, and he added twice: *Eṣa dharma sanātanaḥ, eṣa dharma sanātanaḥ,* 'this is an eternal *dharma,* this is an eternal *dharma'*. Teachers like Buddha extend this invitation to all humanity, with full knowledge that humanity has the organic capacity to undertake this journey and succeed in it. Suppose we had not the needed organic capacity. What is the use of telling people all this? But, no!, even today's neurology will tell you that human beings have tremendous capacity through this versatile cerebral system, to achieve both knowledge of the external world and knowledge of the Inner

Self. This is the invitation Vedanta sends to all humanity, not any dogmas or sectarian doctrines. This is a human problem, and there is a human solution. That universality in language and tone, we can find in all these statements. And that is why the modern world is seeking a touch with this great and ancient wisdom. This is not knowledge, but wisdom; knowledge maturing into wisdom, and knowledge *must* mature into wisdom. Otherwise, knowledge will be dangerous. This is not the view of a religious teacher, but of a confirmed agnostic, namely, Bertrand Russell, who said (*Impact of Science on Society*):

'We are in the middle of a race between human knowledge as to means and human folly as to ends.'

And he ends that statement by saying, 'Unless men increase in wisdom as much as in knowledge, increase of knowledge will be increase of sorrow.'

What a beautiful language! When you had no knowledge, you had less sorrow. When you have more knowledge, you have more sorrow! Convert knowledge into wisdom, again you will become free. This is the line of advance for modern humanity. This subject of *jñāna,* knowledge, physical and spiritual, is coming throughout this *Gītā*.

Here comes the significance of the words, *tapas* of knowledge, *jñāna tapas.* Everyday we are confronted with so many problems. We have to face them, solve them. We need strength for it. We have to develop that *jñāna* within. Both the knowledge of the external physical world and of our own inner world is *jñāna,* in which the latter becomes more significant.

We shall now deal with the eleventh verse. This verse is another important milestone on the road of harmony. India has one uniqueness, and that is harmony between one religion and another religion, harmony between religion and science, harmony between religion and atheism and agnosticism. India did not experience any conflict in their best days between these various groups. That attitude was inculcated in India from the time of the ancient *Ṛg-Veda* up to Sri Ramakrishna in our own times: *Ekam sat viprā bahudhā vadanti,*

'Truth is one; sages call it by various names'. This is a precious asset which no other society in the world has. It is based upon India's high philosophical and spiritual vision of unity in diversity, the Advaitic vision; diverse expressions, behind all of which there is unity. That was a great teaching given to us by the Vedic sages first. Then the various political states in India, as well as the prevailing provincial states also followed this policy. Particularly, you will find Ashoka, the Mauryan emperor of third century BC, proclaiming this truth in his edicts on rocks and pillars:

'If you love your own religion and hate other religions, you harm your own religion, for, in religion *samavāya eva sādhuḥ*, "concord alone is correct".'

In that context comes Śrī Kṛṣṇa's great message in the *Gītā* in verse 11.

ये यथा मां प्रपद्यन्ते तां तथैव भजाम्यहम् ।
मम वर्त्मानुवर्तन्ते मनुष्याः पार्थ सर्वशः ॥११॥

Ye yathā mām prapadyante tām tathaiva bhajāmyaham;
Mama vartmānuvartante manuṣyāḥ pārtha sarvaśaḥ—4. 11

'In whatever way men and women worship me, in the same way do I fulfil their desires; (it is) my path, O son of Pṛthā, (that) people tread, in all ways.

Ye yathā mām prapadyante, 'whatever paths men and women take in the world of religion': You take a path, another person takes another path. The paths are various. But they all come to Me. There is a very strong emphasis on this. 'You come by this road, I accept you. If you come by another road, I won't say, "I won't accept you unless you come by this road only." You can come by any road. I take you by whatever road you come.' All these religions are so many paths, so many roads as it were. Paths are many, but the goal is one. In all other religions, it is always one standard road. On that standard road, there are a few dogmas. Through that you come, and I will accept you. That is the teaching. Just the opposite of what India holds and practises. What a beautiful idea!

We have in Greek mythology the story of Procrustes's bed. Procrustes had a bed. Whenever people passed by, he will invite them: come and lie on my bed. If the man is too long, beyond the bed, he will cut the leg and make it equal to the bed! When he is too short, he will pull the leg and make it equal to the bed! My bed is the standard. All people must be according to my standard bed. This is called in English Procrustean bed of dogmas and creeds. We never had this concept of Procrustean bed in India in religion. Never. We give a person a shirt which he needs for his body size. Not one standard shirt for all.

That is the tremendous contribution of Indian culture, coming not from any kind of expediency or policy, but out of a comprehensive spiritual vision, philosophical understanding: *Ye yathā mām prapadyante tāmstathaiva bhajāmyaham; Mama vartmānuvartante manuṣyāḥ pārtha sarvaśaḥ*. Men and women always adopt a path which is leading to Me only. There is no 'standard path'. You must go by this path, not by that path. There is no such dogmatic standard like that. And so, this idea started from the *Ṛg-Veda* with the utterance: *Ekam sat viprā bahudhā vadanti*, 'Truth is one; sages call it by various names', then through the *Gītā*, through the *Śrīmad Bhāgavatam*, and today, reconfirmed through Sri Ramakrishna's life and teachings: *Yato mat, tato path*, 'as many religions, so many pathways to God'. Practise harmony, practise concord. Don't quarrel in the name of religion. This blessed country is the only country, where this idea is highly appreciated, expounded, and practised by people and the state. If we are losing it today, it is because of our non-understanding of our own heritage. But India will always stick to this great ideal. Today, Sri Ramakrishna and Swami Vivekananda have come to strengthen this great ideal of mutual understanding and harmony among the various religions.

In the Roman Empire there were many religions. People could practise whatever religion they liked. That was the idea. There was a cynical attitude towards religions by the Roman political state and the intellectuals. That is expressed by Edward Gibbon in his famous book, *Decline and Fall of the Roman Empire*. The following remark comes there:

'The various cults and religions of the Roman Empire were believed to be equally true by the multitudes, equally false by the philosophers, and equally useful by the magistrates.'

The political state liked it: be busy with your religion, don't disturb the political system. So, they allowed religions to go on. That is a very cynical attitude, just the opposite of what you have in India. We appreciate these religions; our political or spiritual leaders, our intellectuals, they appreciate and encourage them, 'Go your own way; but don't quarrel and fight, for the goal is one and the paths are many.' By this teaching we established a positive approach towards inter-religious relations known as acceptance. We accept you. You are a Christian, we accept you. You are a Sikh, we accept you. You are a Muslim, we accept you. You are a Vaiṣṇava, we accept you.

This great perennial message of India was communicated to the modern world by Swami Vivekananda through his *Response to Welcome* at the 1893 World Parliament of Religions at Chicago on 11 September (*Complete Works of Swami Vivekananda*, vol. 1, p. 3):

'Sisters and Brothers of America,

'It fills my heart with joy unspeakable to rise in response to the warm and cordial welcome which you have given us. ...

'I am proud to belong to a religion which has taught the world both tolerance and universal acceptance. We believe not only in universal toleration, but we accept all religions as true. I am proud to belong to a nation which has sheltered the persecuted and the refugees of all religions and all nations of the earth. I am proud to tell you that we have gathered in our bosom the purest remnant of the Israelites, who came to Southern India and took refuge with us in the very year in which their holy temple was shattered to pieces by Roman tyranny. I am proud to belong to the religion which has sheltered and is still fostering the remnant of the grand Zoroastrian nation. I will quote to you, brethren, a few lines from a hymn which I remember to have repeated from my earliest boyhood, which is every day repeated by millions of human beings:

"As the different streams having their sources in different places all mingle their water in the sea, so, O Lord, the different paths which men take through different tendencies, various though they appear, crooked or straight, all lead to Thee."'

Śrī Kṛṣṇa is giving prominence to that central theme of our culture: harmony in the world of religion. If religion doesn't help us to establish harmony, what else can help us? The greatest peace is in the heart of religion. But because this attitude was not cultivated, religion became a centre of strife, intolerance, persecution, violence, and war. It is least in Indian history because of this teaching not only by the sages but also by various political states. That is why we could welcome foreign religions like Judaism and Zoroastrianism in India: 'You are welcome, continue to practise your religion. We shall give all help to you.' That is what happened to the Parsis, the Zoroastrians when they were severely persecuted in Persia (now Iran) by the rising tide of Islam, and came to India in the 8th or 9th century AD; the king of a state in Gujarat welcomed them, gave them full freedom to practise their culture and their religion. This fascinating story, which has no parallel in any other country, is well narrated by Piloo Nanavarthy, a Parsi lady, in her book: *The Parsees.* Now this attitude is universal in India. We are not to be taught this thing, whereas in every other country one has to *teach* it, because that is not their way and attitude. 'If I am very religious, I am fanatical. If I cease to be religious, I become liberal. As a religious man, I cannot be liberal.' That was the Western and West Asian attitude.

British historian late Arnold Toynbee refers to an incident in the history of early Christianity in the Roman empire. Bishop Ambrose of Rome told Senator Symmachus of Rome that there is only one path to the Divine and that is Catholic Christianity. Symmachus, who followed the Pagan religion, refuted this exclusive claim and affirmed that there are several paths in religion. But soon Symmachus' voice, and of all paganism, were silenced by the Catholic Church. Narrating this, Toynbee remarks: the voice of Symmachus was silenced; but not the truth he upheld, because millions of Hindus have been and are upholding that voice!

This was followed by a century of violent Christian crusades against Islam in West Asia, and centuries of persecutions by Catholic missionaries and burning of many women at the stake.

Catholic Christianity became stronger and stronger century after century until the Protestant schism broke the Roman Catholic Church in the sixteenth century involving thirty years of fierce civil war between both in Germany.

In the modern age, the problem of peaceful inter-religious relations still remains; but the Indian approach is slowly gaining ground. Bishop Ambrose's remark in the fourth century AD contrasts with Pope Paul VI's ideas about the impression of his visit to India in 1964. The following report of the statement of Pope Paul, after his return to Rome from his visit to India in 1964, appeared in the *Indian News*, Washington D.C., on 1st January 1965:

'Pope Paul VI, on December 22nd, described his visit to Bombay early this month as "full of incomparable human value for us." The Pontiff in his Christmas message to the world said:

"We might have stayed there (in Bombay) like a stranger, isolated, and surrounded only by our brothers in faith … but, on the contrary we met an entire people." He added: "It represented, it seemed to us, immense crowds of the vast Indian territory and those also of all Asia."

"This country is not Catholic", Pope Paul said, "but what courtesy, what opening of spirit, what an avid desire to get a glance, or a word, from this strange traveller from Rome!" The Pontiff said: "That was a moment of understanding, of community of mind. We do not know what these rejoicing crowds saw in us, but we saw in the crowds a humanity of great nobility, identified with its millenial cultural traditions. These crowds were not all Christians, but they were profoundly spiritual, and in so many ways so good and winning."'

Ours is different in India: because of my religion, I am liberal, I accept your religion, I practise harmony. From religion itself comes this impulse to respect every other religion. That is the significance of this statement of Śrī Kṛṣṇa: *Ye yathā mām prapadyante tāmstathaiva bhajāmyaham; Mama vartmānuvartante manuṣyāḥ pārtha sarvaśaḥ*. All people follow various religious paths, crooked or straight, but ultimately leading to the divine. That is the nature of true religion. There are two dimensions to every religion. One is what makes it separate from the other religions; these are their ritual, dogma, creed; these belong to one side. The other side is meant for spiritual development, spiritual growth; that is the higher side. The mystics represent the second part of religion, and mystics generally speak the same language in every religion: Islamic Sufi mystic, Hindu mystic, Buddhist mystic, and Jewish mystic, they all speak the same language, because they realized the One behind the many. Generally, they are more tolerant, and of more understanding attitudes, except when they are controlled by their rigid church or by a rigid orthodoxy of society. But in India we did not have any central church to control. We were free to experiment in the world of religion. New sects rise, new teachers come, followers come, we respect them. Not one of them was persecuted or killed. In religion, variety is essential. The more the types of religion, the more people will get satisfied. A standard religion cannot satisfy everybody. Just like food: you must have a variety of food. My taste is different from yours, but food is food. That will nourish you, whatever be the food you take. So, in this way, India has been taught this great lesson throughout the ages and it is not going to be otherwise in the modern period.

Don't you have communal conflicts and all that?, some one may ask. You will find that almost all of them are based not on religion but on political factors in India today. Religiously there is no quarrel between people and people. But some religions are narrow. They don't believe that any other religion can be true. That has to change. That will change in the Indian context in the coming decades. So, the history of religion has been partly good, partly bad. Hereafter, it will be only good, when this Indian influence comes to influence all the religions of the world. Actually, it is happening. Christianity is changing fast. Christian writers are opening themselves to inspiration from non-Christian sources. That centuries-old rigid mind is not there. So, a big change is coming over Christianity. Dr. Ishananda Vempany sent me his book, *Krishna and Christ,* which he wrote recently. A very serious book of about 300 pages. I wrote a Foreword also to that book at the author's request. He is a Jesuit Father from Ahmedabad, and had stayed with me in this Math. I read through the book; it breathed respect and reverence to non-Christian religions. Such books are coming out more and more now. Formerly, it was not so, only twisting other people's ideas, presenting them in a bad way. Take the best of your religion, compare it with the worst of another religion, that is how books were written till now. Now, you are finding books written differently: respect for every religion, respect for the ideas that are there. 'That' is one approach, 'this' is another approach.

So, Śrī Kṛṣṇa's teaching of harmony is going to influence more and more people in all parts of the world. In this age, we are coming closer and closer, and therefore, this is the only attitude that can work; attitude of respect and reverence to your own belief cannot go along with the attitude that the other persons are on the wrong path, and that you are trying to make him or her to come to the 'right' path. In every religion there are such fanatics. But that has no future. Future is on the lines of harmony, concord, tolerance, understanding. So, this teaching of Śrī Kṛṣṇa will inspire more and more people in all parts of the world, with the *Gītā* itself being translated into all languages and with millions of people reading this great book. So, here is that eleventh verse conveying this important teaching of Śrī Kṛṣṇa. He himself was possessed of a universal mind, embracing every type of worship, every type of religion. That he has also shown in his life. The next *śloka* says:

काङ्क्षन्तः कर्मणां सिद्धिं यजन्त इह देवताः ।
क्षिप्रं हि मानुषे लोके सिद्धिर्भवति कर्मजा ॥ १२ ॥

Kāṅkṣantaḥ karmaṇām siddhim yajanta iha devatāḥ;
Kṣipram hi mānuṣe loke siddhirbhavati karmajā — 4. 12

'Longing for success in action, in this world, (people) worship the gods; because success resulting from action is quickly attained in the human world.'

There is one supreme divine Being, who is the Self of all, and who is also the Self of the universe. That is the central core of Vedanta. But many sects are based on devotion to particular gods or goddesses, deities, and some supernatural powers; such religions are also there. *Kāṅkṣantaḥ karmaṇām siddhim yajanta iha devatāḥ*, 'people worship various *devatas*, deities, expecting some favour'. I am doing some work, I want your favour. So, they worship various gods and goddesses. And this is okay. In this earth, such actions produce their good results. *Kṣipram hi mānuṣe loke siddhirbhavati karmajā*, 'actions produce their results quickly in this human world'. You can do so, but real religion will come only when you understand the truth that these various deities are expressions of the one and the same divine truth as expressed in the *Ṛg-Veda: Ekam sat viprā bahudhā vadanti*. That knowledge must come. Then only, pure religion will come. Here we are trying to exploit gods for our own purposes. We don't love God. Some people want to squeeze gods to get some advantage to themselves. That is not correct religion. But Vedanta does not condemn this; it respects this also.

During his speech in the 1893 Chicago World Parliament of Religions, Swami Vivekananda emphasized this comprehensive approach of *Sanātana Dharma* or Hinduism (*Complete Works of Swami Vivekananda*, vol. 1, p. 6):

'From the high spiritual flights of the Vedanta philosophy, of which the latest discoveries of science seem like echoes, to the low ideas of idolatry with its multifarious mythology, the agnosticism of the Buddhists, and the atheism of the Jains, each and all have a place in the Hindu's religion.'

In the *Gītā* you will find that even the most ordinary idea of religion is respected. Nothing is condemned. 'That person' understands religion that much; he or she is observing religion in that light. When the understanding changes, he or she also will change. A child writes a lesson in the English language, very wrongly, pronouncing wrongly, but we don't condemn him. At that stage, that is all what he can do. But, when he grows up he will be a first-class scholar. Similarly in religion, we can be in its kindergarten, or primary, or high school, or university. Various levels of understanding religion are there. So, we always respect the religion of the people. Wherever one turns to worship the divine through some deities, it is really the worship of the One divine. And Śrī Kṛṣṇa will say later on in the seventh chapter, 'all such worship of deities ultimately becomes worship of me; they are seeking me through these various expressions of gods and goddesses.'

Now, we come to a statement in verse 13; it is a verse which many people have misunderstood, and is a centre of controversy, because it refers to a social problem. So far as the *Gītā* is concerned, the wordings are very, very clear. Here is that *śloka*. The main purpose of the *śloka* is to tell that '*I do things, yet I am unattached*.' So, it gives an example of non-attachment, that is all. The statement is this:

चातुर्वर्ण्यं मया सृष्टं गुणकर्मविभागशः ।
तस्य कर्तारमपि मां विद्ध्यकर्तारमव्ययम् ॥ १३ ॥

Cāturvarṇyam mayā sṛṣṭam guṇa-karma-vibhāgaśaḥ;
Tasya kartāramapi mām viddhyakartāramavyayam—4. 13

'The fourfold *varṇa* system was created by me, based on the differentiation of *guṇa* and *karma*. Though I am the author thereof, know me to be the non-doer, and changeless.'

This social organization based on the four *varṇas*, the four types of people—*brāhmaṇa, kṣtriya, vaiśya, sūdra*—exists in any and every society, according to their inclination and capacity: *guṇa, karma*, 'according to their quality and action'. That will determine whether one is a *brāhmaṇa,* or a *kṣatriya,* or a *vaiśya,* or a *sūdra.* Any family can have offsprings belonging to any one of these types. One will take to military, another will take to business, a third will take to agriculture, and another will take to labour. In this way you will find various people taking to various *karmas* or actions, professions according to the inclinations of their minds, their *guṇas*. That shows the freedom of the individual. Whatever you want to take up as your job, you are free to do so. That is the original meaning of Śrī Kṛṣṇa's statement on this particular subject. Society needs organization—organization into groups— and these organizations we did in India as first labour; then business, agriculture, industry; then we come to administration, defence, political affairs, etc.; then we come to high intellectual and spiritual guidance by a small group of people. Every society has all the four groups. *But what became wrong in India is that, in later ages, it became hereditary*. That is evil number one. By hereditary means we cramped the system as it were. Secondly, we gave more privileges for some and less privileges for others. These two aspects ruined the whole system. So, remove those two evils and we shall find this is what is happening, and what is good, everywhere.

In America you can find this expression very well. In any family you will find, a student says, 'I shall join the military'; 'you are free to do so'. He is a *kṣatriya,* he does the duty of a *kṣatriya.*', or 'I will take to business', *vaiśya;* 'I shall be a labourer', *sūdra;* 'I shall be a priest or spiritual seeker, I will be a *brāhmaṇa* then.' It is up to you. You are perfectly free. When that freedom to chose what you like according to your *guṇa* and *karma* is there, then a society becomes healthy. But when you stop that free choice, people become tied down to their hereditary profession. Then it becomes narrowed down more and more. *And it becomes an evil when special privileges are claimed by one group over the others*. That is what happened to Indian *jāti-vyavasthā,* or caste-system. The *brāhmaṇa* and *kṣatriya* commanded more prestige, more privilege, more power; others had very little power and status; even human status was not allowed to some of them. That kind of distortion took place later on, and today we are trying to break away from this distortion. But, groups will remain. Somebody will be highly spiritually inclined, somebody will be exercising power in the political field, somebody will be busy with business and industry, somebody will be labourers working here and there, according to the situation, according to one's capacity, etc. But no special privilege will be allowed to anybody. Swami Vivekananda said therefore in a lecture in England on 'Vedanta and Privilege', a famous lecture, that differences will be there in every society. Different functions are performed by different people. That is natural. But 'whenever special privileges raise their heads, knock them on the head', said Swami Vivekananda. Perfect equality, that is democracy. So, in a democracy also you can have the *cātur varṇyam* minus its evil features. Every society has it. That will not change. This is the original conception.

You find today so many groups. Small industry becomes one group. People engaged in it have got their own Merchants' Chamber, or Industrial Association. Teachers have their own group. We all make groups. We have hundreds of groups in every society. But India classified them broadly into four types beginning with the *brāhmaṇa* type. When we dealt with the introduction to the *Gītā* by Śaṅkarācārya at the beginning of these discourses on the *Gītā*, we referred to this subject that the goal of human life and evolution is for everyone to achieve *brāhmaṇahood, brāhmaṇatva;* what does it mean?, absolutely moral, self-restrained, full of compassion, never needing a policeman to make him or her behave, because he or she is well restrained within oneself. That enlightened person is the *brāhmaṇa* type. Every society has this *brāhmaṇa* type. How many beautiful *brāhmaṇas,* Vivekananda said, he had seen in America! And he writes in the letter, 'what a beautiful type I have seen here!' So also, you can see them in Japan, or in China, everywhere. In Soviet Russia, you will find them. Then the *kṣatriya* type: ever ready to help people, even though it may cause trouble to oneself. He is ever ready, with that kind of chivalrous attitude. They are the *kṣatriya* type. And then there are those very good in business, industry, agriculture: the *vaiśya* type. And good labourers, the world will always have plenty of labour class. But they will not be deprived of privileges: food, shelter, clothing, everything will be there. And they will also earn well. And you will find one profound truth that, from the point of view of money earnings, in the original Indian social organization, the higher you go, the less becomes your remuneration. Up to *vaiśya,* you have got remuneration. *Vaiśyas* earn plenty. A *kṣatriya* will always care for honour, over and above money. And the *brāhmaṇa* cares neither for honour nor for money. His is the simplest life. That is why the Indian *brāhmaṇa* was the poorest and simplest priesthood in the world. I have seen *brāhmaṇas* living a beautiful life—very contended and happy—on fifteen rupees a month. And yet what brilliant intellects they had.

So, in this way, *brāhmaṇa* is a type; *kṣatriya* also is a type; so also, *vaiśya* and *śūdra*. So, what is the goal of all these social divisions? India said: the *brāhmaṇa* type. Ultimately, all must evolve into the *brāhmaṇa* type. He or she is a *brāhmaṇa* who is not selfish, who feels oneness with all, who has realized God in this very life. When I referred to this subject in the Introduction, I read out from Buddha's teachings from *Dhammapada,* the chapter called *Brāhmaṇa Vaggo,* the chapter on *brāhmaṇa* whom Buddha honours. A man of the untouchable group, like Dr. B.R. Ambedkar, who ably piloted the Indian Constitution Bill in the Constituent Assembly, could easily become not only a Law Minister but also a prime minister; he was a *kṣatriya,* though coming from the scheduled caste. What a glorious life he led, what an intellect he had! I had spent one hour with him in his house in Bombay just before the commencement of the Indian Constituent Assembly Sessions. So, that is the new India taking shape, removing all the evils from that ossified caste system, which have ruined our national life for centuries together.

Śrī Kṛṣṇa is primarily emphasizing in this verse the truth that, even though he created this social organization, he himself is perfectly detached and is not the doer at all. The stress is on this second line. 'Even though I work, I am detached'. Detachment is a great word. I was reading a latest book on the new type of thinking we need in the modern age for stabilizing international situations, where this subject of 'non-attachment' is introduced. Detachment is absolutely necessary for the higher development of the human being. *Gītā's* central teaching is this concept of detachment. Interest is there, zest is there, but detachment also is there. A wonderful idea! You work hard, work with great energy, but the mind is detached. That is the central teaching. So, Śrī Kṛṣṇa says, 'I am working very hard for the welfare of the world, but I am perfectly unattached.' That is a lesson to all of us, and even for management executives. In the book which I read, this idea is given: develop detachment. You can do better work, more creative work, when the mind is detached. That is the language used there. Creativity cannot come from the attached state of mind. From a detached state of mind only it can come. Such books are coming out in good numbers in modern times. So, this is the emphasis in this particular section. Now comes verse 14, to elaborate this idea of detachment.

न मां कर्माणि लिम्पन्ति न मे कर्मफले स्पृहा ।
इति मां योऽभिजानाति कर्मभिर्न स बध्यते ॥१४॥

Na mām karmāṇi limpanti na me karmaphale spṛhā;
Iti mām yo'bhijānāti karmabhirna sa badhyate — 4. 14

'Actions do not taint me, nor have I any thirst for the result of action. He who knows me thus is not fettered by action.'

'No action can ever taint me', *na mām karmāṇi limpanti;* similarly, *na me karmaphale spṛhā,* 'nor do I have any attachment for the fruits of actions'. *Iti mām yo'bhijānāti,* 'those who understand me in this way', *karmabhirna sa badhyate,* 'will also be free from the bondage of action'. He or she can do all actions, but those actions will not bind him or her. If one understands my status like this, and tries to practise it in one's own life, he or she also will not be bound by actions. So, the stress is on action, but with a particular attitude. That attitude is detachment. In the beginning it will be very difficult to practise; there is no harm in that, attachment will be there, one will fumble, but let him or her continue, and by such effort such a person will come to that state of detachment when one's spiritual strength becomes more and more. None expects us to be highly detached people on the first effort. As you begin your life, as Swami Vivekananda says in his famous book *Karma-yoga,* you will find that your mind is fully attached; it doesn't matter. You continue; keep the teaching before you; practise a little detachment in one or another situation; slowly you will gain strength. Then a time will come when you can say, 'Yes, I now feel I am detached.' When I separate my self from the body, I separate the contained from the container. Now they are mixed up. I begin to understand that I am the infinite Self, this body-mind complex is only an instrument. It comes and goes, I remain. A spirit of detachment comes at this stage.

Sri Ramakrishna compares the two situations to a green coconut and a ripe coconut. Take a green coconut, break it open, you will find the kernel; scoop the kernel, you will scoop a little bit of the shell also along with it, because the kernel is attached to the shell. Now take a dry coconut, the shell and the kernel or copra are separate. A *kaḍa, kaḍa* sound you will hear when you shake it. Similarly, the human mind can become unattached. That is the challenge given by the *Gītā* with respect to all work. Especially in this highly industrial age, when work creates tension, blood pressure, and bad moods, the only way is to practise detachment. Then any amount of work will not trouble you. So, detachment, non-attachment, these words are used in the *Gītā* again and again.

Mahatma Gandhi wrote his *Gītā* with the title, *Anāsakti-yoga,* 'the *yoga* of non-attachment'. *Āsakti* means attachment. *Anāsakti* means non-attachment. That is the *Gītā* message of *yoga.*

एवं ज्ञात्वा कृतं कर्म पूर्वैरपि मुमुक्षुभिः ।
कुरु कर्मैव तस्मात् त्वं पूर्वैः पूर्वतरं कृतम् ॥१५॥

Evam jñātvā kṛtam karma pūrvairapi mumukṣubhiḥ;
Kuru karmaiva tasmāt tvam pūrvaiḥ pūrvataram kṛtam —4. 15

'Knowing thus, the ancient seekers after spiritual freedom also performed action. Do thou, therefore, perform action alone as did the ancients in olden times.'

What a beautiful idea! 'It is with this attitude that many seekers of spiritual freedom in ancient times performed action,' *evam jñātvā kṛtam karma pūrvairapi mumukṣubhiḥ.* And in this attitude they could also attain *mokṣa* or spiritual liberation, though they were engaged in the thick of work itself. Since that is so, *kuru karmaiva tasmāt tvam,* 'you also perform action'; *pūrvaiḥ pūrvataram kṛtam,* 'as the ancients did in the ancient way'; you also do it in your own way, in the modern period. Work will continue but nature of work may change; detachment will come and along with it spiritual freedom.

In one *śloka* or verse this idea is expressed. It is quoted by Lokamānya Bāl Gangādhar Tilak in his *Gītā Rahasya:*

Vivekī sarvathā mukto kurvato nāsti kartṛtā;
Alepavādam āśritya śrī kṛṣṇa janakau yathā —

Vivekī, 'a person of discrimination'; *sarvathā mukto,* 'with the mind ever-free'; *kurvato nāsti kartṛtā,* 'though he or she is doing action, he or she does not feel oneself as an agent of action'. How?, *alepavādam āśritya,* 'by accepting the philosophy of non-attachment'. *Alepa* means 'nothing sticking on me'. *Lepa* means sticking; just put some sandalwood paste on your body, it is called *lepana. Alepavādam,* 'the theory of non-attachment, non-sticking; *āśritya,* 'depending on that truth'. Then two examples are given: *Śrī Kṛṣṇa-Janakau yathā,* like Śrī Kṛṣṇa and Janaka; they are famous examples of very hard working people, endowed with the spirit of detachment; you also do similarly.

We have no possibility of renouncing work; our life cannot go on without work. So, work is essential: *kuru karamaiva tasmāt tvam,* 'therefore, you do work all the time', but with this attitude. That is Śrī Kṛṣṇa's advice: *pūrvaiḥ pūrvataram kṛtam,* 'as the ancients did in ancient times'. Work or action is a very difficult subject; the next *śloka* refers to it:

किं कर्म किमकर्मेति कवयोऽप्यत्र मोहिताः ।
तत्ते कर्म प्रवक्ष्यामि यत् ज्ञात्वा मोक्ष्यसेऽशुभात् ॥१६॥

Kim karma kimakarmeti kavayo'pyatra mohitāḥ;
Tatte karma pravakṣyāmi yat jñātvā mokṣyase'śubhāt —4. 16

'Even sages are bewildered as to what is action and what is inaction. I shall, therefore, tell you what action is, by knowing which you will be freed from evil.'

Kim karma, 'what is action?' *Kim akarmeti,* 'and what is inaction?' On this subject, *kavayo'pyatra mohitāḥ,* 'even the sages are deluded on this subject'. It is not easy to understand. *Tatte karma pravakṣyāmi,* 'therefore, I shall speak to you about *karma*'; *yat jñātvā,* 'knowing which'; *mokṣyase aśubhāt,* 'you will be freed from all evil' arising from action'. I will give you a philosophy by which you can do all action, but you will not be bound; like the lotus leaf which is not wetted by water, you will remain free. That is the nature of the mind when it is trained in this spirit of detachment. This is the first *śloka* on the subject. And the second one is the Mount Everest of thought on the subject. It is a very crisp statement with deep meaning. And the language used is almost a language of self-contradiction: *karmaṇi akarma yaḥ paśyet, akarmaṇi ca karma yaḥ,*'one who sees inaction in action and action in inaction'. Before we take up that subject, we shall listen to Śrī Kṛṣṇa's prefatory remarks:

कर्मणो ह्यपि बोद्धव्यं बोद्धव्यं च विकर्मणः ।
अकर्मणश्च बोद्धव्यं गहना कर्मणो गतिः ॥१७॥

Karmaṇo hyapi boddhavyam boddhavyam ca vikarmaṇaḥ;
Akarmaṇaśca boddhavyam gahanā karmaṇo gatiḥ —4. 17

'For verily, (the true nature) even of *karma* or action should be known, as also, that of *vikarma* or forbidden action, and of *akarma* or inaction: the nature of *karma* is deep and impenetrable.'

'You must know what is *karma*', *karmaṇo hyapi boddhavyam; boddhavyam ca vikarmaṇaḥ,* 'you must also know what is *vikarma* or wrong action; *akarmaṇaśca boddhavyam,* 'you must also know what is *akarma* or inaction'. 'The way of *karma* is extremely mysterious', *gahanā karmaṇo gatiḥ.*

The late eminent British educationist, L.P. Jacks, discusses this subject in his book, *Education of the Whole Man.* It echoes the *yoga* philosophy of the *Gītā:-*

'Labour turns into leisure when art is applied to it. Leisure turns into labour when science traces it to its roots. For no two men, are the meaning and value of leisure the same. They vary according to the man who has the leisure and according to the labour which has preceded it. Idle rich versus idle poor.

'Today, to have leisure is to be at the mercy of other people. A man is no longer master of his leisure "in his own interest", as they put it. Today, the more leisure a man has, the more active he is in destroying others' leisure and they his leisure. Leisure is the time we spend in mutual botheration.

'Thus the use we make of our leisure depends upon the use others make of their leisure. ...

'When labour merely tires the body without interesting the mind, man utilises leisure largely in search of external excitements. Industries spring up for catering to these excitements. This means labour of an increasing section of the population. Thus, leisure involves labour. ... Thus every increase in the leisure of a community does not bring a corresponding decrease in its labour. It would have been a decrease if leisure were invariably spent in sleep or silent meditation. But that is not the way modern civilization teaches man to spend his leisure. Except for sleep, the amount of which, I suppose, does not vary from age to age, the leisure of a modern man is the time when his demand for the labour of others is most exacting, and his consumption of commodities most active (p. 122).

'As civilization advances, leisure will increase and the centre of gravity of social problems will shift from the labour end to the leisure end of life. The acid test of a civilization lies in the use that is made of its leisure. A civilization can stand this test only when it makes spirituality the ground and goal of its life.'

I remember friends in Delhi telling me in the 1950's that they were eager to attend my Sunday evening discourses on the *Gītā* in the Ramakrishna Mission. When they are about to start for the Mission, a friendly family turns up as guests. Seeing this happen often, they told me that they began to leave home after lunch and go to any park and turn up in time at the Mission for the lecture. This is one illustration of the above remark of Dr. L.P. Jacks: 'Leisure is the time we spend in mutual botheration.'

In this context, it is interesting to mention that among the more than one thousand audience, sitting cross-legged on the lawn, there were men and women and students, members of the Union Secretariat and the Defence Services, and some ambassadors of foreign countries including Mr. Elsworth Bunker, U.S. Ambassador in Delhi, and Mrs. Bunker. Some officers also told me that when they go out on official tours, they made it a point to return by Sunday noon in order not to miss the elevating and refreshing ideas of the *Gītā*.

'The way of *karma* is deeply mysterious', *gahanā karmaṇo gatiḥ,* says Śrī Kṛṣṇa in verse 17. And now, in the next verse, Śrī Kṛṣṇa gives that famous dictum:

कर्मण्यकर्म यः पश्येद् अकर्मणि च कर्म यः ।
स बुद्धिमान् मनुष्येषु स युक्तः कृत्स्नकर्मकृत् ॥१८॥

Karmaṇyakarma yaḥ paśyed akarmaṇi ca karma yaḥ;
Sa buddhimān manuṣyeṣu sa yuktaḥ kṛtsnakarmakṛt—4. 18

'One who sees inaction in action, and action in inaction, is intelligent among human beings, he or she is a *yogi* and a doer of all action.'

This is a very high level of thought in the whole *Gītā*. 'One who sees inaction in action, and action in inaction, he or she is a real *yogi* and the most intelligent person, and the doer of all action.' *Karmaṇi akarma yaḥ paśyet,* 'seeing inaction in action'. How can we see that? Looks contradictory, but it is not so; in human experience this can be perfectly realized to see inaction in action, and action in inaction. *Sa buddhimān manuṣyeṣu,* 'he or she is the most intelligent of persons', *sa yuktaḥ,* 'he or she is a *yogī*', that is, the state we have to achieve eventually, when we realize our true nature.

This idea is echoed very beautifully in Chinese thought, in Taoism and partly in Confucian thought. There they call it 'no work'. 'No work' is real work. Work is no work at all. It is a question of agency and attachment. When these two are not there, work ceases to be work, it becomes a play, it becomes spontaneous, it becomes natural. So, that is how the idea of work comes when there is effort, struggle, tension. When you become thoroughly detached, then all that tension goes away. You are working, but you don't feel that you are working. What a beautiful idea! Even in normal life, you can see a baby is sick at night and the mother is keeping awake to tend the baby's body. She doesn't feel the strain of that work at all. When there is such love, none will feel that strain. But a paid person will not have the same experience, because there is no spontaneous love there. With a little spiritual development, work ceases to be a burden, ceases to be a *drudgery*. I have used a word which is very current in this modern context. Increasingly, today's industrial civilization is teaching people that work is a drudgery. Joy must be found outside work. That is why too many holidays. As soon as Friday evening comes, millions of people are running out for a holiday. These five days were all drudgery. Let us have joy outside the five days. That seems to be the modern theory. In fact, so many Western writers have written on the subject. I once read an English writer writing thus in a paper:

People leave London on Friday afternoon, go by car, on the way there are so many cars to negotiate, you become angry, you create trouble, then go to the seaside, so many people are there, you don't have vacant place there, you get angry there also, and when you finally return on Monday morning or Sunday night, you are more tired than you were when you left on Friday evening. This is happening all over the advanced part of the world. You can see plenty of it on the Mediterranean coast.

It will happen here in India also, because we separate joy from work. Work as a drudgery, Śrī Kṛṣṇa will not allow that attitude. There is joy in work also. From one joy to another joy is alright. But from drudgery to joy is not at all alright. Work can be full of joy, provided there is love in the heart. Then everything becomes fine. You can carry a heavier burden if there is love in the heart. That is one lesson that we must learn. People who are posted to defend the country in the Himalayan frontier, if they have the spirit of love for the nation, they will do their work happily and efficiently. Similarly, our administrative officers do devoted service when posted to faraway districts. By attachment you rarely do very great work and remain sane.

While working, you are not only working but also expressing your personality in work. In work when you express your personality, it is a wonderful spiritual experience. The *Gītā* is trying to explain that idea, that work itself is a spiritual education. If you want joy on a holiday, you can do so, not because work is a drudgery, but because I want an extra holiday, an extra day of quiet life: there is no harm in that. Never treat work as drudgery. *Gītā* will not allow it. Find joy in work. What a beautiful idea! Even the simplest work, you can find joy in it, because you have put spiritual value into the work. Work itself is just an external action. But it is my mind that gives value to the work that I do. I inject that value into work; then I find it is fine and quite pleasant. No tension. So, 'work on, without tension', Śrī Kṛṣṇa had said in 3. 30, *yuddhyasva vigatajvaraḥ*, 'carry on the battle of life without inner tension, inner fever'; *jvara* means 'fever or tension'; *vigata* means 'without'. Work on, work hard, for the good of all, said Śrī Kṛṣṇa in the third chapter. So, he says,

Karmaṇyakarma yaḥ paśyed akarmaṇi ca karma yaḥ;
Sa buddhimān manuṣyeṣu sa yuktaḥ kṛtsnakarmakṛt —

In some books on management published in America, there are Chinese writers also amongst them, they quote from these Chinese authors and show that with this tremendous detachment, you can carry heavy burden and do much work without feeling that you are working at all. I give here a part of my lecture on 'Divine Grace', which appears in the first volume of *The Eternal Values for a Changing Society* published by the Bharatiya Vidya Bhavan, Bombay 7. There you will find that the thinking is similar.

Says R.G.H. Siu, Chinese scientist at the M.I.T., U.S.A., in his *Tao of Science*, p. 76:

'To be intimately versed in the knowledge of decentralization, the executive must have a sense of the Taoist doctrine of inaction. Accomplishment is attained through the art of doing nothing. This is a somewhat difficult idea to put across, because so many people are quick to confuse it with loafing. But we may get a glimpse of the notion from Chuang-Tse:

"The student of knowledge (aims at) learning day by day;
A student of Tao (aims at) losing day by day.
By continual losing,
One reaches doing nothing;
By doing nothing, everything is done.
He who conquers the world often does so by doing nothing.
When one is compelled to do something,
The world is already beyond his conquering."'

Further, (ibid., pp. 157–58):

'In essence, the action of the philosopher executive is guided by the proper pace of knowledge. Inwardly, he cultivates spiritual enduring; outwardly, he performs social beneficence. He develops, in the phraseology of the old Chinese, "sageness within and kingliness without".'

If even a small percentage of India's legislators and administrators, from the village pañcayat level to the Union Government level, develop themselves in this way, our democratic state will become strong, steady, and peaceful in an unprecedented way.

Detachment is detachment from the ego or the lower self which is under the control of the ever-selfish genetic system. Detachment is not possible until one recognizes the Truth proclaimed by Vedanta or the science of human possibilities, that, in every human being, there is the ever pure, ever free higher Self which is the true nature of all.

There is the famous *Aṣṭāvakra Gītā,* which is a small book of very high Advaita Vedanta thought. There it is mentioned (18. 61):

Nivṛttirapi mūḍhasya pravṛttirupajāyate;
Pravṛttirapi dhīrasya nivṛtti phala bhāgini —

A wonderful *śloka*. 'Inactivity of a foolish man transforms itself into activity; the activity of a wise man enjoys the fruits of inactivity or inaction.'

If I am an intelligent person, even though I am working, I will feel I am having leisure. If I am thoughtless, I may have taken leave and gone on a holiday, yet I will often be in tension; the holiday has done no good to me, because the training of the mind has not taken place. So, that *śloka* is very very important. *Nivṛttirapi mūḍhasya pravṛttir-upajāyate*, 'the *nivṛtti* or inaction of a fool becomes *pravṛtti* or action.' *Nivṛtti* means 'withdrawal from action'; *pravṛtti* means 'entering into action'. This subject of *pravṛtti* versus *nivṛtti,* introduced by Śaṅkarācārya in his introduction to the *Gītā* commentary, we had discussed in the Introduction of this book. So, *nivṛtti* becomes *pravṛtti* for a foolish person. For a wise person, *pravṛtti* becomes *nivṛtti;* even while acting, he or she is perfectly detached, and, as if not acting at all. That is the idea expressed in several books of the Vedanta literature as well as in Chinese thought. So, this is the idea we must keep in view when we work. From morning till evening, a housewife endowed with this attitude can go on working, attending to family members and others; and yet she can feel fresh in the evening. If that is possible, it will be wonderful. *Gītā* says it is possible. Many have attained that state. That comes from the spirit of detachment, the spirit of love and concern for others. *All these things together constitute the spiritual attitude to life.* Otherwise, one can be a complaining mind all the time. There are people who will work hard from morning till evening, always grumbling and complaining. What fun is there in that? Just like a bull driving a cart. Simply going on under this heavy load. What is the use of such a life? There must be joy, there must be satisfaction. I have to get it myself. Nobody else is going to give it to me as a donation. That is a challenge before everyone. Nothing is great in work itself. It is the attitude of the worker that evaluates a work as good or bad. That lesson, the *Gītā* teaches again and again. If the attitude is good, the work is good. If the attitude is wrong, your work is wrong. So, control your attitude. It is in your power.

Thus, Śrī Kṛṣṇa speaks of detachment, which is the central theme of the *Gītā* teaching on work. That this little ego centred in my organic system is not my true Self. I am something infinite, spiritually one with all. That knowledge must come slowly. Then you get a tremendous sense of detachment. So much of cushioning effect of the pressures from the world you get that way. Just like two railway coaches, when they touch each other, there is a cushioning effect, by the bumper that is provided at the back of the coaches, which has a spring action. You don't feel a jerk thereby. So, in the mind, we have plenty of space behind. We can always find space so that no shock will reach us. The deepest is the Atman. So, a little closer towards it, you feel you can do work better. More work, less tiresomeness, less tension. That is a great teaching for all people, because all of us have to work to earn our living and to discharge our social responsibilities. So, this philosophy is meant for all, especially today when work has become such an important factor of human development and welfare.

Verse 18 contains a paradoxical statement; but many logical paradoxes are resolved by the logic of daily life; actual life breaks through all these paradoxes. So, this particular statement affirms: 'One who sees inaction in action and action in inaction, he or she is the most intelligent of human beings, is a true *yogi,* and the doer of all action.'

We can understand the *Gītā* better after studying Vivekananda literature once. That is what I did, and that is what I saw how effective it is.

Having spoken about this truth that, when the mind is properly disciplined, and if there is perfect detachment of mind, then working will be as good as non-working, it will mean relaxation. In work itself you find relaxation. This is a profound message to men and women in the modern age. We had learnt in the twentieth century to associate all work with drudgery, and to seek for pleasure outside work; that is an evil attitude. We should overcome it. There is a joy in work also. When you put your soul in your work and feel a sense of detachment, so far as the lower ego is concerned, you discover the truth of it. But because of this wrong attitude that work is a drudgery, today there is an experience of boredom among people while working. This word 'boredom' does not appear in the eighteenth century Dr. Johnson's English Dictionary! In the United States I found the currency of this new word. Even children telling parents, 'Mummy, I am bored', though there is so much excitement around. How can one be bored in this most exciting age? Something is wrong with the mind. This word 'boring, boredom' is a new word in English. When I read it in Gerald Heard's article, I wanted to make sure that it is correct. So, in Chicago, I sent for Dr. Johnson's English Dictionary from the Chicago Public Library. And I searched under 'B' for boredom. No such word at all. People were not 'bored' at that time! Now, it is there everywhere. Boredom, boredom, I am bored, bored. The spiritual emptiness of man cannot be better demonstrated except through this experience of boredom—not by old people who get jostled in life and experience boredom; that we can understand; but by children of 8 to 12 years of age. If *they* get bored, something is wrong in the whole civilization. That is why in this *Gītā* teaching, work is made to become relaxation. You can try it in your own life, test the truth of it, because these are all not dogmas but truths about the human being by those who had experienced them: work, heavy work and yet you feel relaxed. How can it happen?, because of a trained mind. If the mind is left to itself, it will play all these tricks; during work you will feel a sense of drudgery; and you feel pleasure outside work, constantly running about here and there on holidays. Now this is an extremely wrong attitude. If you trace work to its roots, you will find inaction there. If you trace holiday and inaction to the root, you will find work at the other end. This is Dr. L.P. Jack's remark quoted earlier. So, in this way, *gahanā karmaṇo gatiḥ*, Śrī Kṛṣṇa had said, 'the way of *karma* is mysterious'. Don't think it is easy to understand what is *karma* and what is *akarma,* and what is *vikarma.* This is what is explained in that one single verse 18, by saying that there is a state of mind where heavy work doesn't make you feel a sense of heaviness. You feel relaxed, because you have touched some deeper reality within yourself. You are not the ego, constantly in tension. As Śaṅkarācārya says in the *Vivekacūḍāmaṇi* (142):

Bhānu-prabhā samjanitābhrapaṅktiḥ
bhānum tirodhāya vijṛmbhate yathā;
Ātmoditāhamkṛtiḥ ātma-tattvam
tathā tirodhāya vijṛmbhate svayam —

'As the mass of clouds born out of the sun hides the sun and proclaims itself, so the ego born out of the infinite Atman hides the Atman and proclaims itself as the self.'

Work from the ego point of view is all tension. But behind the ego, there is an infinite spiritual dimension. When that is realized even a little, then extra work won't make one feel that it is heavy. Even ordinary experiences will tell you: whenever there is love in the heart, the worker doesn't feel heavy. When there is no love in the heart, even a little work makes one feel very heavy. As soon as you have love for a particular cause, you can do anything; a man carries a heavy load for his beloved. That load is not heavy for him, because love for the beloved takes away the heaviness of the load, though the heaviness is actually a fact. But, he does not feel it, because his mind has transformed the situation. Hundreds of instances are there in human life where this truth has been verified by many people. Others can also verify it; and so the teaching is here: do hard work, but have a spirit of detachment based on a larger love. You don't even need a separate holiday. So, Śrī Kṛṣṇa is giving a profound message to humanity in modern civilization: Do work, do go for leisure also, not by treating work as a drudgery and seeking for some relaxation outside the world of work. It will be a passage not from boredom to joy, but from joy to joy; that should be the way of human life. And so, in verse 18, and in a few verses thereafter also, these ideas are expressed. Some of them relate to highly developed spiritual minds. Ordinary people have to take as much of it as they can digest. But the teaching is there. So, some of the verses, you may feel, do not relate to you; quite correct. They relate to you fractionally, but they relate fully to somebody else who has got more spiritual strength.

यस्य सर्वे समारम्भाः कामसङ्कल्पवर्जिताः ।
ज्ञानाग्नि दग्ध कर्माणं तमाहुः पण्डितं बुधाः ॥१९॥

Yasya sarve samārambhāḥ kāmasaṅkalpavarjitāḥ;
Jñānāgni dagdha karmāṇam tamāhuḥ paṇḍitam budhāḥ—4. 19

'Whose undertakings are all devoid of *kāma*, sensual desire, and *saṅkalpa*, desire for results, and whose actions are burnt by the fire of knowledge, him or her, the sages call wise.'

Tam āhuḥ paṇḍitam budhāḥ, 'wise people say that such people are *paṇḍitas*', they are really spiritual. What kind of people? *Yasya sarve samārambhāḥ kāma saṅkalpa varjitāḥ*, 'all those whose undertakings are without the stimulus of *kāma* and *saṅkalpa*'; the attitude, 'this I must get', is *kāma saṅkalpa*. That is not there behind their undertakings. And what has happened in their case? *Jñānāgni dagdha karmāṇam*, 'all their actions and undertakings have been burnt away in the fire of *jñāna*', fire of *ātmajñāna*, 'I am the Atman, I am the pure Self'. In that fire, he or she has burnt away all these actions. Here *jñāna* is compared to fire. Such a person, wise people say, is a *paṇḍita*. *Paṇḍita* is a great word in Sanskrit, though today it has got a very ordinary meaning. A cook is called *paṇḍit*, in north India. That is the nature of *paṇḍita* today. Here *paṇḍā* means *ātmaviṣayā buddhiḥ* says Śaṅkarācārya, 'the *buddhi* which is turned towards the Atman, that type of *buddhi* is called *paṇḍā*'. One who has that *paṇḍā* or *buddhi* is a *paṇḍita.* Two or three definitions of a *paṇḍita* are given in this *Gītā;* one is here. The other is: 'one who sees the same Atman in a holy person, in an ordinary human being, in a cow, in a dog, in everyone, that person is a *paṇḍita.' Paṇḍitā samadarśinaḥ,* it is said in that *śloka* 5. 18. A *paṇḍita* is a *samadarśī.* He doesn't look up and down: that man is high, this man is low. No such attitude, he sees only the same Atman in every being. That is also the definition of the word *paṇḍita.* Then comes the next verse, verse 20.

त्यक्त्वा कर्मफलासङ्गं नित्यतृप्तो निराश्रयः ।
कर्मण्यभिप्रवृत्तोऽपि नैव किञ्चित् करोति सः ॥२०॥

Tyaktvā karmaphalāsaṅgam nityatṛpto nirāśrayaḥ;
Karmaṇyabhiprvṛtto'pi naiva kiñcit karoti saḥ — 4. 20

'Forsaking the clinging to fruits of action, ever satisfied, depending on nothing, even though engaged in action, he or she does not really do anything.'

Tyaktvā karmaphalāsaṅgam, 'by renouncing attachment to the fruits of action'; *karma, phala, āsaṅga: āsaṅga* is attachment, *phala* is fruit, and *karma* is action. *Nityatṛpto,* 'mind remaining fully satisfied constantly'. *Nirāśrayaḥ,* 'absolutely free', no dependence on anything; *āśraya* means dependence. *Karmaṇi abhiprvṛtto api,* 'even though he or she is engaged in action'; *abhi* means constantly, day after day, from morning till evening; *pravṛtto api,* 'though engaged in action'. *Naiva kiñcit karoti saḥ,* 'he or she doesn't do anything at all'. That person is enjoying it almost like on a holiday. Heavy work, yet enjoying a holiday. *Holiday in work*. That is a great idea. A bit of it we have to realize in our life. The highest level of it we can reach only when we realize the infinite Self. But a little bit of it is good for all of us in every field of life. The other person, without the trained mind, full of fussy ideas, jumping about, shouting all the time, making the whole world feel that he or she is doing a world-shaking work; actually that person is only expending one's own psychic energy. The result of work is very little. That is a big lesson our people must learn. Silent work is effective work. Noisy work is not effective work. Full of expenditure of emotional energy and shouting this and that; in Bengali we call it '*sarvanāś* attitude' of work; if anything goes wrong in the midst of work, you make a big show of it: *sarva nāś*, 'everything is destroyed'—like Cassandra in Greek mythology, 'we are all destroyed, we are all destroyed', going about in the battle of Troy, that is the story of Cassandra. So we have Cassandra type of people. They make small mistakes appear big. A spiritually trained mind will do much work with no noise, no fuss. Fussy work is really very inefficient work. We have to realize this truth. When you work in society, you can find some people shouting all the time as if they are doing some big work. They are only creating a nuisance. That is all. Calm, silent, steady work, no talking and shouting at all; that is what we must realize today.

I like to quote the words of our ex-President, Dr. S. Radhakrishnan. In Delhi we have so many busy-look-bodies in social life. They want to organize something here, something there, always looking busy. That is all, they do very little work. They want only to achieve a little prominence to themselves, to be photographed with the Prime Minister! In that connection, Dr. Radhakrishnan said at that time, 'the modern men, and more especially the modern women, do not believe in religion or god. They believe in what they call going about doing good. But when you closely observe it, *it is more going about than doing good*.' Such people are there all over the world. More going about than doing good! More shouting, making their presence felt, such people are there in social life, institutions, political parties, everywhere.

In this context, these teachings are seen to be very high, the whole nation can be transformed into great workers, heroic workers.

I chanced to read in an advertisement in a Souvenir, a sentence from Swami Vivekananda. Then I referred to the original text in the *Complete Works of Swami Vivekananda,* vol. 7, p. 168. That is a reference to one of the disciples of Sri Ramakrishna, by name Swami Trigunatitananda. I am talking of the period 1899–1900. He was conducting the Bengali journal, *Udbodhan,* and also serving the Holy Mother; he had also to do the printing of the journal and even delivering it to the people, doing even the press work. Later, he worked as the head of the Vedanta Society of San Francisco for several years and died there. One day, a disciple came to Vivekananda and praised Trigunatitananda:

'A disciple: sir, it is impossible for any other man to labour for this magazine (*Udbodhan*) in the way Swami Trigunatita does.

'Swamiji: Do you think these Sannyasin children of Sri Ramakrishna are born simply to sit under trees lighting *dhuni*-fires? Whenever any of them will take up some work, people will be astonished to see their energy. Learn from them how to work.'

That is a great inspiring utterance, speaking about what this country will be in time to come. Today we are not so. We are very inefficient in our work, we spend more energy in talking than in working. But that will change. A new philosophy is coming. So, this exposition on *Karma-yoga* as well as this new teaching about seeing action in inaction and inaction in action, is going to be implemented this time. More heroic workers will come out of Indian society. Other countries do have good workers, though they need a certain philosophical and spiritual depth. But our country needs to learn how to work *well,* how to work *together,* how to produce tremendous results from the smallest of causes.

When I spoke in Delhi Municipal Corporation Public Meeting about *The Role of Local Self-government institutions in our Democracy* on request of the Corporation Commissioner saying that very few of his staff of 125,000 people were working, I had occasion to refer to this: why all these village pañcāyats and town municipalities are failing; because nobody among the staff works, and the members only talk during municipal committee meetings; nobody cares to deal with the problems of the citizen. There is not that practical orientation. Our pañcāyats could have achieved much progress, but not by talking this or that, and getting a few selfish things accomplished; and the pañcāyat becomes ineffective. How can you run a public institution efficiently with this kind of attitude? Members must be humanly oriented, take out the problems in the agenda one by one—all dealing with human welfare: discuss how to achieve it? Here is a road needed, there is a water tap needed, here is a street light needed, a public toilet needed. Try to implement it, not by talking, but by getting things done; by discussion with each other. Finish the discussion and start doing the work. Instead of that, we go on lecturing. One Vice-Chancellor of a big university in India told me: 'We have ten or twelve agenda; after four hours of one Senate meeting, even half an agenda is not over! Everybody is lecturing all the time.' He told me this literally. So all this is national trait, which we developed during our thousand-year slave period. Now we are free. Why continue in this way? Our pañcāyats will become the most dynamic centres of national life when the members develop character, this capacity to work, and love for the nation. In one hour a pañcāyat can deal with many problems, and then go and execute them. This is how we have to change our whole attitude to work. Whatever we had till now, was quite alright for a slave people, not for a free people. Free people's ways are different; they have the capacity to work, to do teamwork. No great things can be done without teamwork. Ten people must put their heads and hands together; then only we can get things done.

So, I am hoping that with this orientation towards Pañcāyat Rāj, which is just now influencing the Indian thought atmosphere, combined with this character development that must come to our people, our nation can achieve great results in a short time. That is why these *Gītā* teachings are all meant to be applied, meant to be really verified in daily life and work. So, *karmaṇi abhipravṛtto api naiva kiñcit karoti saḥ,* 'even if well engaged in work, he or she is enjoying leisure.' What a joy it is to work for the people! That will solve problems one by one. Villages become bright, with good roads, street lighting, sanitation, health, and education; people have become co-operative, not going to court for litigation against each other, every now and then, which is what they are indulging in now. What a change it will be! The whole country will become a heaven. This is the heaven we have to create in India, instead of waiting to get a ticket from a priest to that post-mortem heaven!, which is all what we understood by much of religion in India till now. Śrī Kṛṣṇa will summon the whole of humanity in India and elsewhere in the eleventh chapter (*śloka* 33) to this great work:

Tasmāt tvam uttiṣṭha yaśo labhasva;
Jitvā śatrūn bhuṅkṣva rājyam samṛddham —

'Therefore, Arjuna, stand up and enjoy the prosperity of the nation after overcoming your enemies!'

Addressing the whole nation, Śrī Kṛṣṇa says, 'stand up, all of you'. *Uttiṣṭha, yaśo labhasva,* 'achieve the glory that belongs to human beings'. Only when you solve your problems, you get your glory; otherwise, you have no glory at all. How?, *jitvā śatrūn,* 'overcoming your enemies': laziness, human unconcern, poverty, insanitation, backwardness, illiteracy, all these are your enemies. Overcome them! Arjuna had a war in front, but our people have this kind of war! And then, *bhuṅkṣva rājyam samṛddham,* 'enjoy life in this prosperous well-developed country'. Then only can you understand the meaning of true physical science and true science of religion. This message we shall come across in the eleventh chapter after Śrī Kṛṣṇa showed his *visva rūpa* or universal form to Arjuna.

These are great ideas. If only these ideas inspire the upper and middle classes and also percolate to the people in the rural areas, what a revolutionary change will come! After all, the human being is teachable. New ideas can change the character of the human beings from bad to good. Our people need new ideas. They live on old, feudal, inherited ideas. First of all, they have lost all faith in themselves. 'What can we do? We are ordinary people.' Who is ordinary? Everybody is ordinary or extraordinary, as he or she thinks of oneself. That is what Vedanta teaches and our people must learn. Have faith in yourself. You can do wonders. This, our people must learn, slowly, steadily, if the nation is to progress. Every word in this *Gītā* is meant to make people better and better, civilization richer and purer, whether it is East or West. And so, Śrī Kṛṣṇa continues in the same strain:

निराशीः यतचित्तात्मा त्यक्तसर्वपरिग्रहः ।
शारीरं केवलं कर्म कुर्वन्नाप्नोति किल्बिषम् ॥ २१ ॥

Nirāśīḥ yatacittātmā tyaktasarvaparigrahaḥ;
Śārīram kevalam karma kurvannāpnoti kilbiṣam— 4. 21

'Without too many ambitions, the body and mind controlled, and all personal possessiveness relinquished, he or she does not suffer any evil consequences, by doing mere bodily action.'

Nirāśīḥ, 'without too much expectations', 'I want this, I want that', the mind building up castles all the time; with that attitude removed, the mind is more steady; *yatacittātmā,* 'the one with a well-disciplined mind', *tyakta sarva parigrahaḥ,* 'with the idea of possessing this and that gone from the mind'. Today, there is too much of this idea of possession, that is why there is so much of theft in the form of corrupt practices and robbery. Self-respect is so little. So, *tyaktasarvaparigrahaḥ,* 'having given up the attitude of "I must have this, I must have that"'. It is not literally giving up one's things but only that 'sense of possessing it', that pride that comes out of that sense of possession. *Śārīram kevalam karma kurvan,* 'even though he or she does work with the body'; *na āpnoti kilbiṣam,* 'he or she doesn't incur any evil'. Then comes the state of a still higher spiritual achievement.

यदृच्छा लाभ सन्तुष्टो द्वन्द्वातीतो विमत्सरः ।
समः सिद्धावसिद्धौ च कृत्वापि न निबध्यते ॥ २२ ॥

Yadṛcchā lābha santuṣṭo dvandvātīto vimatsaraḥ;
Samaḥ siddhāvasiddhau ca kṛtvāpi na nibadhyate—4. 22

'Personally content with what comes without effort, unaffected by the pairs of opposites, free from envy, even-minded in success and failure, though acting, he or she is not bound.'

Yadṛcchālābhasantuṣṭo, 'personally satisfied with what comes by chance', never running after a thing. This is a very high level of spiritual development. We can't do it in the beginning, but we can keep it in view. That stage is there. A young boy or girl of 18 or 20, cannot understand, need not worry about this teaching. There is a possibility in every one to come to that state. I may not have it now. But, I shall keep it in view. That is all what we have to do at this stage. *Yadṛcchā*, 'by chance'; *lābha*, 'achievement of profit or gain'; *santuṣṭo*, 'being pleased with it'. I never ran after it, it came to me—that situation. I have seen people who do not strive for promotion in their office. What is due to me will come to me, that is their attitude. Such people are very few in number; and they have got also what is their due, though things are not so good in our society now. In a just society, one will get what is one's due. But today our society is not just. It is very very unjust; even by struggling you are not going to get your due. I shall do my work well, what is due to me will come. This is a high spiritual attitude. When you are in a very unjust society, there will be no peace. Constant tension will be there. But this unjust society *we* have created. *We* have to change it; it is our national responsibility. Nobody else is going to change this society. How to make it more just? That is the great work in India. In our society today, law and justice do not often go together. Law goes one way, justice goes another way. That society is the healthiest, where law and justice go together. What a beautiful idea! If there is detachment in the law-enforcing agencies, then that will become true. If there is no detachment, if there is worldliness, selfishness, then everything will be unjust. Nobody will be happy in that society. We are passing through a very hard creative period, where so much of evil is there; some good is also there. Increase the good, reduce the evil. You and I have to do it. That kind of commitment to the social good must come out from millions of our people.

There is a *śloka* from Bhartṛhari's *Nītiśataka,* which Swami Vivekananda loved to quote:

Nindantu nītinipuṇāḥ yadi vā stuvantu
lakṣmī samāviśatu gacchatu vā yatheṣṭam;
Adyaiva vā maraṇamastu yugāntare vā
nyāyyāt pathāt pravicalanti padam na dhīrāḥ —

He asks, what is the quality of a *dhīra? Dhira* means an intelligent and heroic type of mind. That is why *dhīra* is a great word in Sanskrit. What is the nature of that *dhīra? Nindantu nītinipuṇāḥ yadi vā stuvantu,* 'let law experts praise or let them blame'; *lakṣmī samāviśatu gacchatu vā yatheṣṭam,* 'let Fortune come now or go wherever She likes'; *Adyaiva vā maraṇamastu yugāntare vā,* 'let death come now, or let it come many years later'; *nyāyyāt pathāt pravicalanti padam na dhīrāḥ,* 'the *dhīra* will not move one inch from the path of *nyāya,* rectitude, justice'. That type of mind must increase in society. *Dhīra* means that. What a wonderful change it will make! Nothing can shake the mind from the path of righteousness, from the path of justice.

And so, *dvandvātīto,* 'free from these dualities, of good and bad, happiness and misery'; these are called *dvandvas;* they always go together. If you have one, you will have the other also. *Vimatsaraḥ,* 'free from all hatred', all kinds of violent thinking; *sama siddhāvasiddhau ca,* 'calm in *siddhi* and in *asiddhi,* in success and in failure'; *kṛtvāpi na nibadhyate,* 'even though acting, he or she is not bound at all'. This is a very high state of human development. Then comes one of the greatest verses of the chapter, verse 23.

गतसङ्गस्य मुक्तस्य ज्ञानावस्थित चेतसः ।
यज्ञायाचरतः कर्म समग्रं प्रविलीयते ॥ २३ ॥

Gatasaṅgasya muktasya jñānāvasthita cetasaḥ;
Yajñāyācarataḥ karma samagram pravilīyate — 4. 23

'Devoid of attachment, liberated, with mind centred in spiritual knowledge, performing work for *yajña* alone, his or her entire *karma* dissolves away.'

Gatasaṅgasya, 'whose *saṅga* or attachment, is *gata*, gone'. The spirit of attachment has vanished. Therefore, *muktasya*, 'he or she is free'. It is freedom here and now in the midst of work. *Jñānāvasthita cetasaḥ*, 'whose *manas*, or *cetas*, or *buddhi* is established in spiritual *jñāna*'. What a beautiful conception!—the mind established in *jñāna*. Then, *yajñāyācarataḥ karma*, 'whatever *karma* is done, is done in a spirit of *yajña*, in a spirit of sacrifice, in a spirit of dedication'. *Samagram pravilīyate*, 'becomes completely dissolved'. It is not that one should achieve the whole of it or nothing of it; no, but one should try to get even a bit of it. *Pravilīyate*, 'become dissolved', *samagram*, 'completely'. There is no *karma* at all; and yet that person has been doing *karma* all the time. This is verse 23. And the next verse, verse 24, is very well known, especially in the Ramakrishna Mission circle, all over the world. Before taking food we recite this *śloka*.

ब्रह्मार्पणं ब्रह्म हविः ब्रह्माग्नौ ब्रह्मणा हुतम् ।
ब्रह्मैव तेन गन्तव्यं ब्रह्म कर्म समाधिना ॥२४॥

Brahmārpaṇam brahma haviḥ brahmāgnau brahmaṇā hutam;
Brahmaiva tena gantavyam brahma karma samādhinā—4. 24

'The offering process is Brahman, the offered clarified butter is Brahman, offered by Brahman, in the fire of Brahman; by that, Brahman alone is to be reached by one who is in the *samādhi* of Brahma-action.'

Wonderful *śloka*. *Brahma arpaṇam*, the process of offering is Brahman; then *brahma haviḥ*, this *havis*, ghee and other things that you offer into the fire, is called *havis*; 'that *havis* is also Brahman'. *Brahmāgnau*, 'in the fire in which you offer'; that is also Brahman'; *brahmaṇā hutam*, 'the one who offers is also Brahman'. And then, *brahmaiva tena gantavyam*, 'Brahman alone is the goal of the one who offers'. As a result of this sacrifice, what does one achieve? *Brahmaiva tena gantavyam*, 'one achieves Brahman only through this'. By whom?, *brahma karma samādhinā,* 'whose *samādhi* is *brahma-karma* action as Brahman'. Such a person knows that whatever he or she does is nothing but the divine. This is a profound Vedantic truth that there is only Brahman in this universe, infinite non-dual pure Consciousness. That has manifested as this universe; objects, actions, subjects, everything is only one infinite Brahman; that is the Truth that is expressed through this verse. This wonderful Truth is given in physiology and other modern scientific thought, and, as I have expressed earlier in dealing with verse 2, the writer of the article *The Sun is the Great Mother* in the *National Geographic Magazine* says, we eat the sun in our food and its digestion, we wear the sun in our cloth, we use sun in our coal and oil and so on, and ending with the sentence: 'Particularly interwoven are the threads of life and light.'

That universal oneness behind this multiplicity is what our ancients in India, from the *Ṛg-Veda* onwards, understood and expressed. This sun is also called the *pūṣan,* 'one who nourishes'. The sun is a physical visible entity. But our sages discovered the spiritual consciousness of Brahman behind the sun, behind the starry system, behind everything. That is Brahman, the ultimate reality, infinite pure Consciousness, one and non-dual. That is the truth behind this universe. That is affirmed during meal time. A beautiful idea: the *jaṭharāgni* or digestive juice inside my stomach and intestines, which digests the food, is also a form of the divine. That the *Gītā* will say some chapters later (15. 14): 'I exist in the stomach of all beings as the fire of digestion, *jaṭharāgni.* I digest all food that is put into the digestive system.' One and non-dual, the whole universe is the expression of that Brahman. Just as in the solar system, everything is solar radiation in condensed form as water, as ice, as stone, as plant, as this or that. Everything is solar radiation. So, this is a great *śloka*:

> *Brahmārpaṇam brahma havirbrahmāgnau brahmaṇā hutam;*
> *Brahmaiva tena gantavyam brahmakarmasamādhinā* —

That is a Truth, not a dogma.

How can this and that be the same?, one may ask. How can the food I take, and the digestive energy in the stomach be the same? Yes, they are! Go to the root, you find that it is from one source that all these have come. Take the human body. The same genetic material has become the hard bone structure, and the same genetic material has become the beautiful visibility through the eye. It is translucent as it were. Some are hard, some soft, some fluid, some as the skin and nail and hair. All these have come from the same genetic material. So, this is the truth that we are taught again and again in physical science. Everything within the body is built up, then repaired, corrected, and made to grow by the same genetic material that is inside. This is a big truth, the Advaita truth, which India discovered ages ago regarding the universe also as a whole. We called it Atman or Brahman, the infinite Consciousness, the one without a second, says the *Bṛhadāraṇyaka Upaniṣad* (II. i. 20) given earlier.

दैवमेवापरे यज्ञं योगिनः पर्युपासते ।
ब्रह्माग्नावपरे यज्ञं यज्ञेनैव उपजुह्वति ॥ २५ ॥

Daivamevāpare yajñam yoginaḥ paryupāsate;
Brahmāgnāvapare yajñam yajñenaiva upajuhvati —4. 25

'Some *yogis* perform sacrifices to *devas* alone, while others offer Brahman as the self, as sacrifice in the fire of Brahman alone.'

Now, several types of *yajñas* are being referred to here. We have studied the subject of *yajña* in the third chapter, *śloka* 9. Here again it is taken and put in a different way. Some *yogis* perform sacrifices to gods, *devas,* the bright ones. Others offer the self as sacrifice by the self in the fire of Brahman as the Self of all. That is high spiritual sacrifice. This little ego is put into the fire of knowledge of Brahman; it is burnt away. Only Brahman remains; that is another type of sacrifice. One is externally oriented, the other is spiritual and inward, which is high-class, resulting in high character and high spiritual awareness and a spirit of service. Similarly,

श्रोत्रादीनीन्द्रियाण्यन्ये संयमाग्निषु जुह्वति ।
शब्दादीन् विषयान् अन्य इन्द्रियाग्निषु जुह्वति ॥ २६ ॥

Śrotrādīnindriyāṇyanye saṃyamāgniṣu juhvati;
Śabdādīn viṣayān anya indriyāgniṣu juhvati — 4. 26

'Some again offer hearing and other senses as sacrifice in the fire of self-control, while others offer sound and other sense objects as sacrifice in the fire of the sense organs.'

Very practical ideas. Everyday you are doing a lot of sacrifice within the body. And one such is mentioned here. Some again offer this wonderful act of hearing, and other senses, as sacrifice in the fire of self-control. You control the sensory system. What do you do thereby? You light a fire. That is called *ātma-saṃyama-yogāgni*, 'the fire of self-control'. You put all the senses into that. You burn them. You find, after that, nothing but pure mind guiding the senses. So, this is also sacrifice. Every development of character is a result of some such sacrifice. That you must remember. Everyday we are doing it, some less, some more; without that there cannot be a human society. Only we don't know that we are doing it as a sacrifice. Similarly, others offer all the other organs of sense. Where do they offer these?, to the fire of the *yoga* of self-control. Suppose you hear something. Sound is being offered to the organ of hearing. In any higher life, it has to be offered to the *yoga* of self-control which is like a fire. It is actually a sacrifice. In this way, in the process of character development, when the sensory system is dealing with the sensory objects, you are already performing various sacrifices. We sacrifice the food into the fire in the stomach, and that becomes our energy of movement, of strength, our physical stamina. So, sacrifice is going on all the time. Only we must know that this is the way that it is being done. Then you will find much more ability to handle the forces working within the human body. Similarly,

सर्वाणीन्द्रियकर्माणि प्राणकर्माणि चापरे ।
आत्मसंयमयोगाग्नौ जुह्वति ज्ञानदीपिते ॥ २७ ॥

Sarvāṇīndriyakarmāṇi prāṇakarmāṇi cāpare;
Ātmasamyamayogāgnau juhvati jñānadīpite — 4.27

'Some again offer all the actions of sense organs and the functions of *prāṇā,* the vital energy, in the *yoga* fire of self-control, kindled by spiritual knowledge.'

In this verse, verse 27, Śrī Kṛṣṇa says, 'some people again offer all the actions of the sense organs and the functions of the vital energy, namely, the *prāṇa,* into the fire of self-control as a sacrifice. We are asked to discipline the whole internal system thoroughly. How do we do that? Lighting the fire of self-control, put all of them into that. That is called this inner sacrifice. These are all symbolic ideas. And, *jñānadīpite,* it is kindled by knowledge. We are doing it knowingly, deliberately. No animal can do it. Automatically you can never do it. You have to do it deliberately. That is why we are asked to light up the fire of knowledge first and then sacrifice everything there. High character comes out of that action. So, you need not do sacrifices only outside. Our people are so fond of such rituals outside, but the *Gītā* advises all people to convert them into this inner sacrifice which will help them to manifest the ever-present divine within.

There are two levels in *pūja,* ritualistic worship, in the path of *bhakti;* One is 'mental worship', *mānasa pūja,* the other is called *bāhya pūja,* external worship. So, when one sits in front of an image and starts worship, first he or she will close the eyes and do worship within. Place the Lord in your heart, offer water to wash his feet, and bathe him; then offer food, and other items. And there you will find one very interesting *mantra* or holy utterance; we want to entertain the Lord in our heart. How do we entertain Him? We consider the restlessness of the mind and the senses as our dancing before the Lord to entertain the Lord. Imagine, therefore, even though we do not like our restless mind to continue, we are now giving it a higher turn. 'This restless mind is conceived as giving entertainment to the divine within', *nṛtyam indriyakarmāṇi cāñcalyam manasaḥ tathā,* that is the *mantra. Indriyakarmāṇi,* 'activities of the sense organs', *cāñcalyam* 'restlessness'; *manasaḥ tathā,* 'similarly, of the mind'. Now, what can be a sacrifice greater than this?, everything going on within the body is given a spiritual direction! Then we open our eyes, bring out the Lord from the heart, place him in front on a flower pedestal, and do the external *pūja.* First is internal *pūja,* second is external *pūja.*

So, here in this *śloka, Sarvāṇīndriyakarmāṇi prāṇakarmāṇi cāpare; Ātmasamyamayogāgnau juhvati; yogāgni,* is the fire of *yoga;* what kind of *yoga?, ātmasamyama,* perfect self-control. The *yoga* of perfect self-control is compared to a fire. Into that fire you are offering all these things. That is beautiful worship, a better ritual than merely the external ritual that we perform. The external ritual must be reinforced by this internal ritual. That does not happen in the case of most of our religious people. They do plenty of external ritual; internally, no ritual at all. No kind of sacrifice there. No lighting of fire of *yoga* within. The result is we remain what we were; if we were wicked, petty-minded, quarrelling, litigating, and with a showy devotion to God also, we remain the same. That should not be. So, the *Gītā* is giving you very many alternatives of *yajña,* by which the whole life becomes a *yajña.* Śrī Kṛṣṇa will say later on in 4. 33 that *Jñāna-yajña,* the *yajña* of knowledge, is the highest.

Professor F. Capra in his *Tao of Physics* says that the *background material* of the cosmos given by modern astrophysics is less pervasive a concept compared to *Brahman* of the Upaniṣads. Brahman includes all physical and non-physical realities in this world. That is the Brahman which is referred to here. Everything is a manifestation of Brahman. Having said that, the succeeding verses also referred to several types of *yajñas,* sacrifices. The earlier Vedic teachings contain many types of sacrifices. But, as I have said earlier, the *Gītā* took up this word *yajña,* gave it an ethical and spiritual content and direction. That we have seen in the third chapter also. Here Śrī Kṛṣṇa is referring to various types of *yajñas* that we do in our everyday life. Every movement of life is a part of *yajña.* That is how *yajña* has been transformed here. And then, finally

Śrī Kṛṣṇa will say that none of these sacrifices can compare with that one type of *yajña* known as *jñāna-yajña, yajña* of spiritual knowledge. That is the greatest *yajña.* Those who control the sense organs, they are also performing *yajña.* They light the fire of self-control. Into that fire they put the sensory stimuli and they are burnt away and transformed. In this way, all inner discipline and outer behaviour are a type of *yajña.* I have a tendency to steal; I control that tendency; how?, I light a little fire of knowledge in me, put that tendency inside it and burn it away. In this way, a pervasive meaning is given to this concept of *yajña.* Fire is essential for *yajña.* That fire is of different types.

Two types of fire we have to reckon with. One, we all know, is the digestive fire in the body, *jaṭharāgni,* the acid and various secretions, which digest the food and assimilate it; by the essence of the food taken, the body is nourished, and the waste matter is thrown away. A big *yajña* like this is going on in the body every day. It is good to have a good *jaṭharāgni.* But, so far as the human being is concerned, that is not enough. So, our teachers said, another fire must be there within the system. That is called *jñānāgni,* 'the fire of knowledge'. No animal can develop the fire of knowledge. Fire of digestion, they have. Fire of knowledge, only humans can have. So, from childhood onwards, we are asked to develop the fire of knowledge, so that experiences come to us, some of them unpleasant, we must be able to digest them. That digestion is done in the fire of knowledge, *jñānāgni.* As I referred to earlier, this is like the oil refinery which refines crude oil and produces beautiful and useful petroleum products. This is how character is formed. This is how we develop compassion, dedication, a spirit of service, and largeness of mind and heart. All this is *yajña.* The character building work itself is *yajña.* We have to put more stress on that hereafter.

When I was speaking in the Universities in the United States, I used to tell the young people there that youth have plenty of digestion, they can digest, what they call in America, Kentucky Fried Chicken and Hamburger! These are common things there. Very strong digestion is needed. Well, that is beautiful. But, remember, you must develop the other fire also, the fire of knowledge, to digest difficult experiences, so that no trauma will come to you. When a wrong experience can create a trauma, a psychic distortion, that should not come. That will not come if you have lit up this fire of spiritual knowledge, *jñānāgni.* Try to build up that *jñānāgni* from childhood onwards.

In this connection, I wish to refer to one or two events during my 1968–69 cultural lecture tour of north and south America from 18 July 1968 to 31 December 1969. One event I have already referred to in the earlier part of this book. That refers to my Portland Radio talk in 1969 which, originally scheduled for twenty minutes, continued for full two hours, from 10 pm. to midnight, including also answering questions conveyed by phone by the listeners.

This book is entitled *Universal Message of the Bhagavadgītā.* It contains the practical expression of Vedanta as a science of human possibilities which is a continuation of the science of physical nature's possibilities developed highly by the modern West, especially in U.S.A., as modern science. During this tour, I found reconfirmed the universality of the message of Vedanta. That tour consisted of 934 lectures and question-answer sessions, of which 90 were television, radio and newspaper interviews, 30 were in churches and temples, 141 were in Vedanta Societies and Ramakrishna Ashramas, 156 were in private parlours, 197 were in public forums, and 320 were in 115 universities and colleges—as reported by the publisher of my book *A Pilgrim Looks at the World,* vol. 2, opening page. Every one hour extempore lecture was followed by a stimulating one-hour question-answer session. 'Please come again' was the remark by the audience on many occasions.

On 19 February 1969 was my announced lecture at the Harvard University. I arrived at the University with Swami Sarvagatananda of the Ramakrishna Vedanta Society of Boston at 8:10 pm. On arrival at the University, the hall meant for the lecture was found overcrowded; the audience moved, through about 200 yards of rain and snow, to a larger hall in another block, on the announcement of a change of venue by the organizers. I spoke, standing, for an hour on the subject of *Self-Knowledge and Human Fulfilment*, chosen by the organizers from a list supplied to them by the Boston Ramakrishna Vedanta Society. Then came a one-hour question-answer session for which I sat on the table, cross-legged, to be able to see the faces of the listeners.

One particular question evoked a mild reprimand from me when I found that, when the chairs in the hall became insufficient for the incoming audience, the old professor would go and bring the chair from the next room; I found no student getting up to do that service. So, while answering that particular question, I said: 'I mark something atrocious. Why does not some student get up and help the professor? Is it not worthwhile to make service an essential part of education? But it is not your fault. Only, your parents and teachers never asked you to do this and that in the fear of any trauma developing in you. That makes the youth fail to develop their individuality into personality. Biologist Sir Julian Huxley defines persons as "individuals who transcend their organic individuality in conscious social participation." I also said that I marked this in other universities also in U.S.A. The audience consisting of students, some professors, and some citizens, accepted this remark without any resentment. My second lecture at the Harvard University was some 14 years later, on the subject of *Vivekananda and Human Excellence,* which has been published as a booklet by the Advaita Ashrama, Calcutta 700014.

I have referred earlier, in the introduction to this book, to the remark of Silvano Ariety, in the book, *The Handbook of American Psychiatry,* vol. 3, by several writers, about the deterioration of creativity in American youth and how to remedy it.

As a boy of 12 years, I had an experience, narrated earlier in this book, which is relevant to refer to in this context. While going to school, I threw a stone at a youth, not expecting that it would go that far; but it did hurt him. His parents complained to my mother; she was naturally upset. When I returned from the school in the evening, I found my mother sullen and grave. 'You have to receive ten canings', she said. I said, 'Yes, I shall, for I have harmed that youth.' Then the elder brother, in mother's presence, gave me ten canings on my palms. I received it and came and sat peacefully by my mother's side and soon forgot all about it. No trauma!

I have found American people, and youth in particular, both boys and girls, open-minded and intensely human, unless controlled by any church group.

The American Reporter, published by the U.S. Embassy, New Delhi, reported in its 26 February 1969 issue, which appears in the Appendix-D of *A Pilgrim Looks at the World*, vol. 2. p. 737, about this despatch, entitled *Vedantic Leader Impressed by U.S. Response:*

'His impact on American audience is evident in this comment by Ann Curtis, a student of Carleton College in Minnesota:

"On the one hand, his incredibly vast knowledge not only fascinated me but thrilled and excited me intellectually. On the other hand, his words reached a depth within me which literally caused me to tingle inside with the realization that each of us, there, was *really* alive and *really* dynamic."

'David Milofsky, Chairman of the Wisconsin Union Literary Committee of the University of Wisconsin, said:

"Your visit helped to broaden our horizons and to see that, although we are separated by great distances physically, there is a universal spiritual kinship between all peoples. I feel that the distances between India and the United States and between Vedanta and Western thought were decreased because of your lecture."'

In India, various practises were developed by way of religious training; some of them left to themselves, being very, very sterile; nothing good will come out of them. For example, people do plenty of *prāṇāyāma*. Here also Śrī Kṛṣṇa will make a passing reference to it later. We can do *prāṇāyāma*. The air is taken in through the nose, and it is held within the body for some time, and then it is thrown out. These are three steps known as *pūraka, kumbhaka,* and *recaka.* But, without the *jñāna* touch, these become merely mechanical. They do not develop high character. During the year 1939, some persons brought to me a person who was an employee in Pune Meteorological office. They told me that everyday this person does *prāṇāyāma.* Also, regularly, and everyday he beats his wife! And his friends told him, stop this *prāṇāyāma.* But, he said, no, I can't stop *prāṇāyāma.* That is essential. So, they all came to me. And I said, what is the use of this *prāṇāyāma,* if you can't love your wife, you can't treat her with respect? It is a mere mechanical action; stop it and develop love. But he said, 'I can't give up *prāṇāyāma.' Prāṇāyāma* had got hold of him. That is one type of people. So, you can see in all these matters, that mere physical activity, mere ritual activity, without the *jñāna* behind it, has absolutely no value for human development, for character development. Śrī Kṛṣṇa is going to tell us that after detailing the various types of *yajñas* that are there.

Sarvāṇīndriyakarmāṇi prāṇakarmāṇi cāpare. 'All the *indriya* activities, all the *prāṇa* activities, all these you can throw into the fire of *ātma-samyama'*, self-control, self-discipline; take all these energies and put them into that fire, then they become high character. *Ātma-samyama,* inner discipline, is compared to a fire. What a beautiful idea! But, *juhvati jñānadīpite,* 'that fire is to be lit up by the fire of *jñāna*'; then only it is worthwhile. Mere dry ascetic practice has no meaning. What is the use of being a dry ascetic? What does one gain thereby? But, if there is *jñāna* along with that asceticism, then it is wonderful; then there will not be need for too much asceticism also. So this emphasis is on *jñāna;* here it is *jñāna,* elsewhere it will be *bhakti,* and pure *bhakti* and pure *jñāna* are one and the same, says Sri Ramakrishna. So many times you will find the word *jñāna* is used, and so many times you will find the word *bhakti* is used. 'Love of God', 'Knowledge of God'—both have the power to transform human character. Therefore, without either love or knowledge, mere physical practice has absolutely no meaning; they are sterile. They don't produce any good at all. Often they produce vanity, pride, arrogance. Then comes several types of *yajñas* put together in one verse:

द्रव्ययज्ञाः तपोयज्ञा योगयज्ञाः तथाऽपरे ।
स्वाध्याय-ज्ञानयज्ञाश्च यतयः संशितव्रताः ॥२८॥

Dravyayajñāḥ tapoyajñā yogayajñāḥ tathā'pare;
Svādhyāya-jñānayajñāśca yatayaḥ samśitavratāḥ —4. 28

'Others again offer material things, austerity, and *yoga*, as sacrifice, while still others, endowed with self-restraint and rigid vows, offer study of the scriptures and knowledge, as sacrifice.'

Yati means one who works hard; who struggles, they are called *yatayaḥ*, those who are interested in working hard to achieve their goal. What kind of *yajñas* do they do? *Dravya-yajña:* take ghee, pour into fire. That is *dravyayajña.* A material entity is called *dravya.* Very often people end up with only *dravyayajña;* but that is only the beginning. *Tapo-yajña,* certain types of 'ascetic practices', self-control, self-discipline, all this is part of this practice. *Yoga-yajña,* 'practising *yoga*', either *prāṇāyāma* or this type of *karma-yoga. Svādhyāya,* 'the *yajña* of self-study'. It is a wonderful *yajña.* How much knowledge we gain by study, and, through that knowledge we develop strength and a measure of fearlessness. Knowledge is strength. In this chapter, there are several verses coming hereafter in praise of knowledge. 'Knowledge is a supreme wealth; develop it,' Śrī Kṛṣṇa is going to tell us. After finishing our university education, we should not give up study. Study and search for knowledge must continue. As long as we live, so long should we continue to study. Sri Ramakrishna has said this in Bengali: '*yāvat bāmchi, tāvat śikhi.*' Study, try to understand what you study, try to apply it, all that is *svādhyāya jñānayajñāśca. Yatayaḥ samśitavratāḥ,* 'those who are well disciplined', whose minds are very sharp, *samśita* means sharp, they practise all these types of *yajñas.* But the first one is *dravyayajña,* sacrifice of material things into fire. Anybody can do that. Sometimes, you don't do it yourself, you appoint a priest, pay him ten rupees, he will do it for you. That is called *dravyayajña.* But, real *yajña* comes in only when *jñāna* comes in. When you develop understanding, develop a little illumination, and its reflection on character, a better person comes out of that. Then is given a few details of the *prāṇāyāma* which some people do:

अपाने जुह्वति प्राणं प्राणेऽपानं तथाऽपरे ।
प्राणापानगती रुद्ध्वा प्राणायामपरायणाः ॥ २९ ॥

Apāne juhvati prāṇam prāṇe'pānam tathā'pare;
Prāṇāpānagati ruddhvā prāṇāyāmaparāyaṇāḥ — 4. 29

'Some offer, as sacrifice, the outgoing into the incoming breath, and some others offer the incoming into the outgoing; stopping the courses of the incoming and outgoing breaths, constantly practising the regulation of *prāṇa,* the vital energy.'

Those who are experts in *prāṇāyāma,* they offer as sacrifice *prāṇa* in *apāna, apāna* in *prāṇa.* When you close one of your nostrils and take in air that is called *pūraka,* filling in the lungs. The breath is held within for some time. That is called *kumbhaka.* Then finally throwing out the air through the other nostril; that is *recaka.* So, some people do like this, says Śrī Kṛṣṇa. *Prāṇāpānagatī ruddhvā,* 'by controlling the movement of *prāṇa* and *apāna*'; *prāṇāyāmaparāyaṇāḥ,* 'they who know the subject of *prāṇāyāma*'.

अपरे नियताहाराः प्राणान्प्राणेषु जुह्वति ।
सर्वेऽप्येते यज्ञविदो यज्ञक्षपितकल्मषाः ॥ ३० ॥

Apare niyatāhārāḥ prāṇānprāṇeṣu juhvati ;
Sarve'pyete yajñavido yajñakṣapitakalmaṣāḥ — 4. 30

यज्ञशिष्टामृतभुजो यान्ति ब्रह्म सनातनम् ।
नायं लोकोऽस्त्ययज्ञस्य कुतोऽन्यः कुरुसत्तम ॥ ३१ ॥

Yajñaśiṣṭāmṛtabhujo yānti brahma sanātanam;
Nāyam loko'styayajñasya kuto'nyaḥ kurusattama —4. 31

'Others, with disciplined dieting, sacrifice *prāṇas* into *prāṇas.* All of these are knowers of *yajña,* having their sins consumed by *yajña.* Those who eat the remnant of *yajña,* go to the Eternal Brahman. (Even) this world is not for the nonperformer of *yajña,* how then another, O best of the Kurus?'

Apare, 'others'; *niyatāhārāḥ*, 'with disciplined dieting', *prāṇān prāṇeṣu juhvati*, 'offer *prāṇas* into *prāṇas*.' All these people are knowers of *yajña*. So what a wide meaning the word *yajña* has got now. In the early Vedic period, *yajña* merely meant lighting a fire, pouring some ghee or some other kinds of grains into that fire. But in the *Gītā*, it has got such a wide meaning. All aspects of life, in fact as I said, even the food that you take, those who are really spiritually inclined, they treat it as offering *yajña* into the fire of Brahman that is in your stomach. That is also *yajña;* eating is not for mere sense satisfaction, you get life energy.

In the *Taittirīya Upaniṣad*, 'enquiry into the nature of Brahman' begins with the statement: *Annam brahmeti vyajānāt*. '(The disciple) understood *annam*, i.e., food, as Brahman.' When you put food in the stomach, out of that food comes energy for you. All your energy comes from there. If you don't have it, you won't get that energy at all. Then the Upaniṣad continues to say that *prāṇa, manas, vijñāna,* etc., were taken to be Brahman. Ultimately, the true Brahman, of the nature of infinite, non-dual, pure Consciousness, was realized as the true Brahman. These others are all the same Brahman at various levels of experience. That is how the *Taittirīya Upaniṣad* discusses this subject. *Sarve'pyete yajñavido*, 'all of these examples are all knowers of *yajña*'. *Yajñakṣapita-kalmaṣāḥ*, 'through those *yajñas* they overcome the evils that are in their mind and heart'. *Yajñaśiṣṭāmṛtabhujo*, 'eating the nectar of the remnant of *yajña*', what was later called *prasāda*, what remains after the *yajña*, that is holy. The idea is: self-centredness means you are only living on poison. That should not be. So, *yānti brahma sanātanam*, 'such people reach the eternal Brahman', evolving slowly. In spiritual life, people slowly achieve the eternal Brahman in this very life. *Yajña* is the means, and that *yajña* is *jñānadīpite*, 'lit up by the fire of *jñāna*, spiritual knowledge'. With that attitude, whatever we do, becomes spiritually beneficial. You serve a guest, you show him or her great regard, you do it with the light of knowledge in you. That is called 'guest service'. They call such a guest, an *atithi,* 'one who comes uninvited on any day.' India has done this service in plenty throughout history. In no other country are guests looked after with so much care as in this country.

In fact, I got this certificate for India from an American professor. When I was in the States, and we were having dinner in the University, he said, 'I was Fulbright Scholar teaching in Meerut University, I and my wife.' 'And three months we were there. Not a single day we were allowed to eat in our own house. Everyday somebody or the other will invite, "please come to my house, please come to my house." I have never seen it anywhere in this world. I saw it only in India.' I said you are right. Our people have practised fully this idea of service of the guest. A person can travel the whole of India without a pie in the pocket. Everywhere he will be looked after. Those who go to faraway Benares, or to Kedar-Badri and other great pilgrim centres, used to be cared for in each place by householders at their homes. That is something extraordinary. So, that teaching of the *Taittirīya Upaniṣad*: 'let your guest be your god', is a beautiful teaching Indians have practised.

So, this concept of *yajña* is being expounded here in the wider sense of the term: that whatever we do, do it in a spirit of *yajña.* A teacher is teaching a student; actually, he is doing a *yajña.* He is communicating knowledge into a mind which is ready to receive that knowledge. So, in all these matters, the concept of *yajña* has become universal in significance, through the touch of the *Gītā.* Here Śrī Kṛṣṇa says therefore, *sarve'pyete yajñavido,* 'all these people are knowers of *yajña*'. The whole life is *yajña,* 'giving'; what a beautiful idea! The work that one does in politics is really *yajña.* It has now lost all its *yajña* character, because search for power is the only thing you find in politics. Spirit of service, how to educate the people in their own political rights, that has almost gone away. Politics is meant to give to millions of people the education that you are citizens of this great democracy, this whole government is meant for you; it depends upon you, derives strength from you. To raise the people's dignity is the purpose of a democratic polity. We rarely do it in India. We search only for our own power, either individual or party. So, you can see, when *yajña* is taken away from any field of life, it becomes very very ordinary, or less than ordinary. It becomes harmful to the human system. But, introduce a bit of *yajña,* everything becomes bright. Administration is *yajña,* politics is *yajña,* education is *yajña.* That is how Śrī Kṛṣṇa is using that word, in the widest sense. *Yānti brahma sanātanam,* such people 'attain the eternal Brahman', by slowly evolving their spiritual strength, their spiritual qualities, etc. 'Those who do not adopt this *yajña* attitude cannot win (even this manifested world), then what to speak of the other (the spiritual world), O best of Kurus?'

एवं बहुविधा यज्ञा वितता ब्रह्मणो मुखे ।
कर्मजान् विद्धि तान् सर्वान् एवं ज्ञात्वा विमोक्ष्यसे ॥ ३ २॥

Evam bahuvidhā yajñā vitatā brahmaṇo mukhe;
Karmajān viddhi tān sarvān evam jñātvā vimokṣyase—4. 32

'Thus, various *yajñas,* like the above, are strewn in the storehouse of the Veda. Know them all to be born of action; and thus knowing, thou shalt be free.'

Many *yajñas* of this type lie scattered in the Vedas. But, *karmajān viddhi tān sarvān,* 'know them all as born of *karma*'. All *yajña* is a type of *karma; evam jñātvā vimokṣyase,* 'you will be free when you understand this truth': through all this *karma* you are developing this *jñāna* within you. Keep that concept constantly within you. Otherwise, mere physical activity or ritualistic activity doesn't help one at all. But, if as a result of all this activity, you light up the fire of knowledge, then you advance spiritually. And you become free in this very life. Even in the midst of the work that we do, the work is positively helpful to us when it is associated with this truth of *jñāna.* Then, in the next *śloka,* Śrī Kṛṣṇa finally speaks of the supremacy of *jñāna-yajña,* 'knowledge-sacrifice'.

श्रेयान् द्रव्यमयात् यज्ञात् ज्ञानयज्ञः परन्तप ।
सर्वं कर्माखिलं पार्थ ज्ञाने परिसमाप्यते ॥३३॥

Śreyān dravyamayāt yajñāt jñānayajñaḥ parantapa;
Sarvam karmākhilam pārtha jñāne parisamāpyate —4. 33

'Knowledge-sacrifice, O scorcher of foes, is superior to sacrifice (performed) with (material) objects; all action, in its entirety, O Pārtha, attains its consummation in knowledge.'

From this verse onwards, you are in the presence of a beautiful hymn of praise to *jñāna,* 'spiritual knowledge'. One of the wonderful passages you find here, like in English poetry, 'In Praise of Wisdom', 'In Praise of Knowledge'. *Parantapa,* 'O Arjuna; *jñānayajñaḥ,* 'the sacrifice of knowledge'; *śreyān,* 'is better'; *dravyamayāt yajñāt,* 'than the sacrifice of material articles'. Those *yajñas* are inferior. This *yajña, jñāna-yajña,* is superior: this is what the first line says; then Śrī Kṛṣṇa concludes by saying, *sarvam karmākhilam pārtha jñāne parisamāpyate,* 'O Pārtha, (if you know the truth), all *karma* will eventually get dissolved into *jñāna'*. Everything becomes *jñāna,* 'spiritual knowledge'. All actions done in the human body, if one knows how to handle them, will reach up to *jñāna* finally. Though you begin with action, you reach up high to *jñāna* finally. That is a very important verse in this section. Therefore, if that is true, do search for knowledge. That is the next *śloka.*

तद् विद्धि प्रणिपातेन परिप्रश्नेन सेवया ।
उपदेक्ष्यन्ति ते ज्ञानं ज्ञानिनः तत्त्वदर्शिनः ॥३४॥

Tad viddhi praṇipātena paripraśnena sevayā;
Upadekṣyanti te jñānam jñāninaḥ tattvadarśinaḥ —4. 34

'Know That (supreme Brahman), by prostrating yourself, by repeated questioning, and by service; the *jñānis,* those who have realized the Truth, will instruct you in that knowledge.'

If that *jñāna* or spiritual knowledge and realization is the ideal, if all the actions are finally going to dissolve into that *jñāna,* and we are asked to develop that *jñāna,* how shall we develop it? Try to understand this truth of *jñāna* by going to a teacher, *tad viddhi,* 'know That'; *praṇipātena,* 'by saluting the teacher'; *praṇipāta* means *namaskār* or salutation; and, *paripraśnena* means 'by constant questioning of the teacher and one's own mind.' Questioning is needed for developing knowledge. It is not a dogma or a creed which dissolves away by questioning; only truth can stand questioning; and it encourages it. It is actual experience. So, knowledge of this type needs constant questioning, *paripraśna,* not mere *praśna* or questioning, but *paripraśna, constant* questioning: what is this?, why should it be so?, how to achieve it?, questioning like that, showing that you are serious about it. Questions can be very ordinary, questions can be serious. Here Śrī Kṛṣṇa means only serious questioning. There are several people who ask lazy questions for nothing. Sometimes when I walk by the road, I have seen people from the neighbouring house ask, 'Sir, what is God?' By the time you answer, he has gone away. He is not interested. Just an idle question. That is all. So, such people are there. But, here it is different. I am serious about it. I must have it.

Sevayā, 'through the service of the teacher'. Service is a tremendous source of spiritual development, character development. In the *Mahābhārata* in several places, you will find even Śrī Kṛṣṇa scolding Duryodhana, the wicked Kuru family prince, 'you don't seem to have served old people, senior people, that is why your character is so bad.' Learn to serve, that is how you develop high character. Otherwise, arrogance alone will remain, nothing else. So, here, service of the elders, service of those who know more than you, service of the holy, is always considered to be a spiritual *sādhanā.*

Upadekṣyanti te jñānam, 'they will instruct you in this *jñāna*'; who?, *jñāninaḥ tattvadarśinaḥ,* 'those who are *jñānis,* who have realized the Truth'. *Tattva* is the word for Truth, meaning 'the thing as it is'. They will communicate to you this *jñāna.* This step is needed to achieve *jñāna.* You have to receive it from somebody who *has* it. A student goes to school; he doesn't know anything about physiology or other subjects; the teacher teaches the subjects and the student learns; somebody gives and somebody receives. In this way when we go to higher levels of knowledge-seeking, we need much more help from a teacher, but mostly by hints and suggestions, not through loud expositions. At lower level, you need detailed knowledge communication. At higher levels, your mind is capable of understanding things. So, a hint or suggestion is enough here and there, and the student begins to understand things better. The difference between a primary school class and a post-graduate class is that, in the latter, you don't have, you don't need, detailed teaching, you only receive hints and suggestions, 'look into that book in the library and find it out for yourself', is the way of teaching. In that way you make the student depend upon himself or herself, because it is a mature mind. But in the earlier stages it is not so. You have to teach every little thing, from a, b, c, d, onwards. So, in this case, in the case of the highest knowledge, the knowledge of Brahman, the infinite, immortal and non-dual Reality, it is taught with very brief utterances: the briefer the better. Even silence is far better than speech in this particular field.

So, Śrī Kṛṣṇa mentions three methods: first is *tad viddhi praṇipātena,* 'know that by salutation'. If the student goes in an arrogant manner, that cannot be a fit mind for receiving knowledge. When one joins the university with a very arrogant mind, what will he or she gain there? Nothing. I want something, there is a vacuum within me, so I go there. So, I respect the teacher who teaches me. He knows more than I do. So, we need that spirit of humility, to be able to receive what is given, and to digest what is received. That attitude of mind is absolutely essential for true knowledge. Knowledge will then flower into character and wisdom. Here *jñāna* means that knowledge which is ripe enough to flower into wisdom and becomes capable of giving spiritual freedom to the seeker. That is the type of *jñāna* that is mentioned here. So, *upadekṣyanti te jñānam*, 'they will communicate to you that *jñāna*'; who?, *jñāninaḥ,* 'those who have that *jñāna*', *tattvadarśinaḥ,* 'those who have realized the *tattvam*'. *Tattvam* is different from *matam* or opinion. What is the truth of a thing? That is called *tattvam.*

And the supreme *tattvam* is Brahman. Behind the whole universe is that one infinite truth, that is called by the Upaniṣads *satyasya satyam,* the Truth of truth, or supreme *tattvam,* or *param tattvam,* etc. These are the words used in Vedantic literature.

So, we can achieve, through the help of spiritually competent teachers, this knowledge, just as we get other types of knowledge from other teachers. They are all knowledge, may be physical, may be psychological, may be spiritual. But, for Vedanta, all knowledge is sacred. And we are in search of knowledge. That is why we are advised to light that fire of knowledge in the heart of the child. He or she wants to read books, to go to school, and doesn't want merely to play with dolls any more. That is how the child starts to light the fire of knowledge in his or her mind. And the teacher in the school helps him or her to make this fire flame forth into a big fire, so that he or she can digest all that one has learnt, assimilate them, make them part of one's character, and become a very good citizen and a very good person on the way to the highest spiritual realization. By knowing this highest truth, what do we gain? No more delusion, no more doubts, no more weakness, that comes in the next *śloka*.

यज्ज्ञात्वा न पुनर्मोहमेवं यास्यसि पाण्डव ।
येन भूतान्यशेषेण द्रक्ष्यस्यात्मन्यथो मयि ॥३५॥

Yajjñātvā na punarmohamevam yāsyasi pāṇḍava;
Yena bhūtānyaśeṣeṇa drakṣyasyātmanyatho mayi—4. 35

'Knowing which, you shall not, O Pāṇḍava, again get deluded like this, and by which you shall see the whole of creation in (your) Self and in Me.'

By realizing 'this truth', *tattvam, na punarmoham evam yāsyasi pāṇḍava,* 'this kind of delusion which has come upon you will never come again'. You will be going beyond all possibility of delusion. Not only actuality, but also the possibility of delusion. Knowledge of Truth destroys even the possibility of delusion. That is the nature of that Truth. *Yena bhūtānyaśeṣeṇa drakṣyasyātmani,* 'by that knowledge, you will see the whole world in yourself, in the infinite Atman'; *atho mayi,* 'as also in

Me', in Śrī Kṛṣṇa, in the Divine Incarnation. That is how, in spiritual development, we take away all sense of separateness between all beings. Normally, we feel separate from each other. As you grow spiritually, separateness becomes removed. We are essentially one. That is the highest knowledge. What a great change is coming over the whole world today! Even one hundred years ago, there were much of racial differences, caste differences and all sorts of other differences. We are overcoming all these differences, slowly and steadily. We are one, humanity is one. What a beautiful concept!

Nearly ninety years ago, Swami Vivekananda referred to this growing international context of human relations in his lecture in Madras on *Vedanta in Its Application to Indian Life* (*Complete Works of Swami Vivekananda,* vol. 3, pp. 240–41):

'The second great idea which the world is waiting to receive from our Upaniṣads is the solidarity of the universe. The old lines of demarcation and differentiation are vanishing rapidly. … Our Upaniṣads say that the cause of all misery is ignorance; and that is perfectly true when applied to every state of life, either social or spiritual. It is ignorance that makes us hate each other, it is through ignorance that we do not know and do not love each other. As soon as we come to know each other, love comes, must come, for are we not one? Thus we find solidarity coming in spite of itself.

'Even in politics and sociology, problems that were only national twenty years ago can no more be solved on national grounds only. They are assuming huge proportions, gigantic shapes. They can only be solved when looked at in the broader light of international grounds. International organisations, international combinations, international laws are the cry of the day. That shows the solidarity.'

And we are also extending our knowledge of oneness with the non-human species also, like birds and other animals. We are looking to extend compassion to them. This kind of teaching is also coming to human beings. So, this is human evolution: separateness being broken down and our essential oneness we realize more and more.

This is the great achievement since the end of the Second World War in 1945. Up to the Second World War, there was so much stress on these differences. But, the Second World War gave a tremendous shake to the human mind, and a new wisdom began to invade the human hearts. After that you will find the slow and steady evolution of a 'humankind awareness'. All the United Nations Organizations are centred in this concept of a humankind awareness. We in India do not say that people in other countries are *mlecchas.* We were telling it till about seventy years ago. Today, we will not say so at all. So also, Western people used to say of non-whites as something below human dignity. Even in Australia, the first time I visited it in 1958, there was the scourge of racial awareness, of separateness; but, during the last few years, I find that racial awareness is almost gone, leaving a small white group to hold on to it. The concept of human oneness is getting realized slowly. And this is the teaching of the *Kaṭha Upaniṣad* (II. i. 11):

Manasaivedam āptavyam neha nānāsti kiñcana;
Mṛtyoḥ sa mṛtyum gacchati ya iha nāneva paśyati —

'Mind must be educated to grasp this truth', *manasaivedam āptavyam.* What is the truth? *Neha nānāsti kiñcana,* 'there is no *nānā* or many or separateness in this world'. Difference is merely on the surface. Deep down there is unity. And then, *mṛtyoḥ sa mṛtyum gacchati ya iha nāneva paśyati,* 'one who sees separateness and lives according to that understanding, he or she goes from death to death'. Against this teaching of her great sages, India has been emphasizing separateness. All India became so many separate pieces, congeries of little states, all separate from each other, fighting with each other, and falling a prey to foreign invasions. So, we experienced the truth of this *mṛtyoḥ sa mṛtyum gacchati ya iha nānā iva paśyati.* In spite of this teaching of Vedanta, we sought differences everywhere. How many differences we created between one human being and another! Untouchability, unapproachability, un-see-ability, all sorts of evils. And, when foreigners come, we won't touch them. We will not share with them what we know, or learn from them.

Al Beruni, who came to India in the 11th century AD, says in his travel book on India: 'What has happened to these people? They have become so narrow, so exclusive, they won't share their knowledge with anybody else. Their ancestors were not like this. They learnt from others, they gave to others. But these people have become so narrow.' What he said a thousand years ago became true for many centuries. And about ninety years ago, Swami Vivekananda also referred to this national folly (*Complete Works of Swami Vivekananda*, vol. 5, p. 52):

'India's doom was sealed the very day they invented the word mleccha and stopped from communion with others.'

We are passing from that to a broader attitude today. We want to mix with other people. We want to see the same human being everywhere, the same compassion, the same capacity to help others. What a beautiful idea! People who go to America often get immense help from somebody there, though they never knew each other. Then they realize, humanity is one.

There is a story told of Swami Rama Tirtha of Punjab, one of the great intellectuals and spiritual teachers of India in the first part of this century. He was very much inspired by Swami Vivekananda. He organized Swamiji's lectures in Lahore in 1897. And very soon, he took to sannyasa. He was a professor of mathematics, a very brilliant mind. Then he went to Japan; from there he went to America. Without money he went; thus, he landed in America; it is told in a story: An American met him. 'Well, you have come from where? From India?' 'Yes, I come from India.' 'So, where are you going to stay? With whom are you going to stay?' Rama Tirtha immediately said, 'I am going to stay with you!' That American was taken aback. He said it with such naturalness, and he became his host and looked after him.

So, you can see, when our minds become free from this idea of separateness, we can *enter* into the heart of other people. Otherwise, you cannot enter into the hearts of others. That is the teaching very much emphasized in Vedanta: *mṛtyoḥ sa mṛtyum gacchati ya iha nāneva paśyati,* 'even if you see a slight difference, that difference will destroy you'. Difference is a fact, but it is not the truth; the truth is, we are one. Physically, we see things are different. Everything is different from everything else. But behind it there is truth, there is unity, *ekam eva advitīyam,* 'the one Brahman without a second' behind the many that is the universe. So, that is *jñāna*. With that *jñāna* we shall be able to achieve great strength, no more of weakness, no more of dying again and again due to cowardice, due to a sense of separateness; such states will never come if this is realized in human life. Today's India is growing in that dimension. Though the old pull is there, to stress human separateness, caste separateness, the overall tendency is to overcome all this and realize our basic humanity, not only within India but also outside.

What a beautiful situation it is for human development in a big way, all over the world; anybody who has gone abroad will be able to vouch for the truth that humanity is the same everywhere. They have the same heart, the same compassion, the same strong hand to help when you are in a difficulty. I myself have experienced plenty of such events in my many foreign cultural lecture tours to about fifty countries. I got down from the railway train in the London station, Paddington or Liverpool station. I got into a taxi, I was to go to some place. So, after I reached the place, when I gave the taxi fare to the Englishman driver, he said, 'No, I won't take any money from you. You are yourself doing good work, I won't take the fare!' I was surprised. Then I said, 'No, that gentleman near us is going to give you, not I. He earns very well, please take.' We gently forced the money on him. Otherwise, he would not have accepted it at all. I never knew him, he never knew me. But, something between us, psychologically speaking, made that sense of separateness vanish. I went to the pilgrim centre of St. Francis of Assissi in Italy. When I went there, I found that somebody from Rome had reserved a room for me in a hotel; the hotel man said: 'This is the room, Swamiji, for you for which he has paid the money.' That is all. I didn't know who that person was. Like that, in many places, people come out to help you because they feel we are all one. That must be strengthened. So, the Upaniṣad said, *Manasaivedam āptavyam,* 'this truth must be grasped by the mind'; teach your children from childhood this truth, *neha nānāsti kiñcana,* 'there is no separateness at all here'; we are essentially one. This sense of separateness must be removed from the minds of children. Then a better world will come. *Mṛtyoḥ sa mṛtyum āpnoti ya iha nāneva paśyati,* 'one who sees differences here, they go from death to death,' and not from life to life. Life to life will only come by realizing our oneness with each other.

That is going to be the development of India in the next century. Tremendous harmony will come between one human being and another, between one group and another; these present troubles are but passing phases. Eventually they will be overcome when the message of Vedanta spreads among the people. The philosophy that stands sponsor to our national development and international relations is the philosophy of Vedanta. And many people are studying Vivekananda's presentation of Vedanta, his great teaching of oneness, non-separateness and the spirit of *tyāga* and *seva,* renunciation and service. As Sri Ramakrishna said, 'tie the knowledge of Advaita in the fold of your cloth, and then live whatever way you like'. That Advaitic *jñāna* must be there within you. Then you will always be successful in dealing with each other. So, *yena bhūtāni aśeṣeṇa drakṣyasi ātmani atho mayi,* 'by this knowledge, you will see all beings in you, and also in Me', in your own infinite Atman and in Me, the Divine Personality, *Puruṣottama,* that is Śrī Kṛṣṇa. And millions of people are attracted to him because of his universal dimension. Anything universal will attract everybody. And Śrī Kṛṣṇa has that tremendous charm and fascination to attract people. He is the 'Pied Piper' of the Indian heart. As soon as his music is sounded on the flute, the whole world will come to him. That is the nature of that attraction. The whole of India is devoted to Śrī Kṛṣṇa because of that. He is our own *antaryāmin,* the inner Self. Having said this, the next *śloka* 36 says:

अपि चेदसि पापेभ्यः सर्वेभ्यः पापकृत्तमः ।
सर्वं ज्ञानप्लवेनैव वृजिनं सन्तरिष्यसि ॥ ३६ ॥

Api cedasi pāpebhyaḥ sarvebhyaḥ pāpakṛttamaḥ;
Sarvam jñānaplavenaiva vṛjinam santariṣyasi — 4. 36

'Even if you are the most sinful among all the sinful, yet, by the raft of knowledge alone, you will go across all sin.'

Even if one is the worst amongst sinners, even then, he or she can cross this ocean of sin by taking recourse to that 'ship of knowledge', *jñānaplava;* knowledge is compared to a ship here. *Api cedasi pāpebhyaḥ sarvebhyaḥ pāpakṛttamaḥ,* 'even if you are the worst sinner among all sinners', even then, *jñānaplavenaiva,* 'through the boat of spiritual knowledge alone', you will cross this ocean of, *vṛjinam,* 'sin' or evil; *santariṣyasi,* 'you shall cross'; all knowledge, especially spiritual knowledge, is powerful; 'knowledge destroys fear', is the English saying. So, don't despair. There is hope for everyone. This *jñāna* is a great blessing to everyone. *Sarvam vṛjinam,* 'all sin', *santariṣyasi,* 'you shall cross'. Then Śrī Kṛṣṇa gives a telling example in the next verse, verse 37:

यथैधांसि समिद्धोऽग्निः भस्मसात् कुरुतेऽर्जुन ।
ज्ञानाग्निः सर्वकर्माणि भस्मसात् कुरुते तथा ॥ ३७ ॥

Yathaidhāmsi samiddho'gniḥ bhasmasāt kurute'rjuna;
Jñānāgniḥ sarvakarmāṇi bhasmasāt kurute tathā—4. 37

'As a blazing fire reduces all fuel into ashes, so, O Arjuna, does the fire of spiritual knowledge reduce all actions to ashes.'

Just as fire reduces to ashes a huge pile of wood, *edhāmsi* is fuel, *yathaidhāmsi samiddho'gniḥ,* 'as fire that has been lit up', *bhasmasāt kurute, arjuna,* 'reduces to ashes, O Arjuna'; *jñānāgniḥ sarva karmāṇi bhasmasāt kurute tathā,* 'similarly, the fire of *jñāna* thus burns to ashes all actions', and only *jñāna* remains. *Jñāna-svarūpa, 'jñāna* is our true nature', that alone remains out of this process. That is how *jñāna* is being praised here in a series of verses. As referred to earlier, *Jñānāgniḥ,* 'the fire of spiritual knowledge' is a beautiful concept! Just like the *jaṭharāgni,* 'digestive fire', which also I had referred to earlier. That knowledge fire will burn all unwelcome experiences, leaving no trauma behind, as I had referred to earlier. This is what all people need to develop as the consummation of their character. High character means a tremendous blazing fire of spiritual knowledge within. A Gandhiji had a tremendous blazing fire of *jñāna* within. So, also all great spiritual teachers. Ordinary human beings, those who are exceptionally good, also manifest this fire of *jñāna*. So, this is not a theory, not a dogma, but a truth to be realized by everyone. When you light the fire of *jñāna*, you are able to handle all your mental troubles and tensions. Today there is so little of *jñāna*-fire in modern humanity. Therefore, so much of trouble, psychic trouble, nervous trouble, and tendency to violence and suicide. But when this *jñāna*-fire is lit up, then we shall achieve that stability. Nothing evil can remain because fire destroys everything. Even the *kacaḍā* or rubbish you put into the fire is burnt down. So this is how the idea of *jñāna* as fire is very much expounded and praised in this section of the *Gītā*. And the next *śloka* adds one more dimension to this praise of *jñāna*.

न हि ज्ञानेन सदृशं पवित्रमिह विद्यते ।
तत्स्वयं योगसंसिद्धः कालेनात्मनि विन्दति ॥ ३८ ॥

Na hi jñānena sadṛśam pavitramiha vidyate;
Tatsvayam yogasamsiddhaḥ kālenātmani vindati — 4. 38

'Verily, there exists nothing in this world as purifying as *jñāna* or spiritual knowledge. In good time, having reached perfection in *yoga*, one realizes that in oneself.'

Na hi jñānena sadṛśam pavitram iha vidyate, 'there is nothing so purifying in this world as *jñāna*'. *Pavitram* means purifying. You wash your clothes with water, your body also with water and soap, all that is good for the body. But for the rest of the human system, the only purifying agent is knowledge. Nothing is so purifying as *jñāna* in this world, *iha* means in this world, in this human life. *Tatsvayam yogasamsiddhaḥ kālenātmani vindati*, 'when you get perfection in *yoga* in course of time, you realize it in yourself', not second hand. It may be a small fire to begin with, but it will become a mighty fire. That will come to you, because that is your true nature, says Vedanta; you need not beg for it or borrow it. *Kālenātmani vindati,* 'you achieve in course of time'; you cannot be hurrying it through; it takes time to build up this fire and to get that blessing from the fire of knowledge. *Ātmani vindati,* 'you will enjoy it in yourself'. You will experience: 'yes, there is that fire within me. Minor troubles will not trouble me now.' Suppose you are able to tell that, what does it mean? That means that you have already lit up that fire of knowledge. When you are able to overcome major troubles, then you can say, 'yes, that fire has now become stronger, much more powerful.'

In this way, there are people, who can stand a good deal of stress and strain, because they have this fire within. Others who have very little of this fire, get upset over little things. Just like what we say in neurology: the threshold of pain is different in different people. Some people can stand a little pain; some people cannot stand even a little bit of pain. In 1933, we had young students in my hostel in our Mysore Ashrama; we got a doctor to inoculate them against malaria. Most of the students could stand the injection. But one or two students, as soon as they saw the needle, they fell unconscious. Seeing the needle, they became unconscious! You can imagine, therefore, how little fire of *jñāna* is there in such a person. But, even he can change. He can build up strength later on. So, in this way you will find that the capacity to handle life successfully depends upon the *jñāna*-fire you light up in your heart, the fire of spiritual knowledge. If that fire is fine, burning bright, you can stand any nonsense, you will not be disturbed at all. That is a steady mind. Śrī Kṛṣṇa has already spoken about it at the end of the second chapter dealing with the *sthitaprajña,* 'the man or woman of steady wisdom'. Here, in this chapter, he is expounding this subject in some more detail.

'Lighting the fire of knowledge', is a beautiful conception. All knowledge is meant for that. The knowledge that you get in education is not meant to be merely book knowledge, but knowledge manifesting as integrated character. That is how you realize you have lit the fire of knowledge in your heart. *Na hi jñānena sadṛśam,* 'there is nothing equal to *jñāna*'. When the Mysore University was started over seventy years ago, they took this *śloka* as the motto: *na hi jñānena sadṛśam,* 'nothing equal to *jñāna*'. What a beautiful conception! Our mottoes are wonderful. But universities rarely try to come up to the motto. Just like our democratic state's national motto: *satyameva jayate,* 'truth alone triumphs', and our nation now follows the opposite: *asatyameva jayate.* That is why mottoes do not play a very big part, unless there is a will to translate motto into lived experience. Who will get *jñāna?* The next two or three verses deal with this subject. You must have *śraddhā,* 'positive faith'. Without *śraddhā,* there is no knowledge. That is the next verse.

Last Sunday, about three hundred students attended the Youth Convention here. Among them some four had inscribed their names on the chairs in this hall. They never asked the question: 'Should I spoil this chair?' That shows that discriminative fire, that *jñānāgni,* had not been lit up in themselves yet. ' Is it worthwhile? Is it proper?'—that is how one will light the fire of discriminative knowledge. In small instances you can experience in life this presence of the fire of knowledge. The whole conduct then becomes transformed. These are all instances where, in our whole education, there is not that sufficient lighting of the fire of *jñāna*. There is reading of books, hearing lectures, memorizing something, and passing examinations. But have you lit the fire of knowledge in yourself? That is what is said here:

Yathaidhāmsi samiddho'gniḥ bhasmasāt kurute'rjuna;
Jñānāgniḥ sarva karmāṇi bhasmasāt kurute tathā —

'As the fire lit with wood reduces the wood to ashes, O Arjuna, so also the fire of knowledge reduces to ashes all actions.'

'Actions will be reduced to ashes by the fire of knowledge'. That is the supreme uniqueness of the human being. He or she acts, but the prompting must come from a deeper source, namely, that fire of spiritual knowledge by which the whole of life becomes well organized, well disciplined, and fruitful from every point of view.

In the language of today's astrophysics we can say, 'In the beginning there was nothing except the Background Material in its immovable condition.' *Ānīd avātam*, in the way the ancient *Ṛg-Veda* puts it, 'It existed without any movement', without any action, without any *karma* or what they call in modern philosophical language 'any process'; processes had not begun. The universe is a product of process. Behind the process is pure Being; then comes this process. Reality and process. And later, at the end of a cosmic cycle, the whole process is transformed back into reality. What we are now experiencing is the acceleration of the process. When that Big Bang took place starting the process, every fraction of a second the world started passing through processes. More and more the concrete world was coming into existence. In the beginning it was not a concrete world. In that state of singularity, electrons, protons, gravitation, etc., never existed during the first few moments of cosmic evolution. Slowly, they began to differentiate and manifest. Then this substantial universe in which we all live and function came into being later. These are all called processes only, up to the human level. Process cannot do anything by itself; it has no freedom. But when evolution reaches the human level, the human being has the power to return the process back into being. This comes from *jñāna*. This *karma* becomes transformed into *jñāna*. So, human beings can understand the source from which we and the universe have come. *We* can become one with it. No object or non-human species of living beings in the world can do so. That is because in the Vedantic conception, that background material is not a mere material entity. It is pure consciousness, infinite and non-dual: *satyam jñānam anantam brahma*, 'Brahman is Truth, Consciousness, and Infinitude', says the *Taittirīya Upaniṣad*.

Śrī Saṅkarācārya says in his commentary on the *Bṛhadāraṇyaka Upaniṣad* (prelude to 2. 4. 12):

'The *Paurāṇikas* hold that this dissolution (of the universe) or *pralaya* is natural. While that which is consciously effected by the knowers of Brahman through their knowledge of Brahman is called extreme dissolution through their knowledge of Brahman, which happens through the cessation of ignorance.'

Paurāṇikas mean the writers of the several *Purāṇas;* they expound both the manifestation of the universe from the non-dual Brahman as its source and its final dissolution in Brahman after several millions of years; this is also what modern Western cosmology says, except that, that source is not consciousness but a highly dense background material; therefore, no human being can *experience* that background material. That truth alone makes a great difference between Vedanta and Western cosmology.

That is what humanity has been endowed with, the capacity for *jñāna*. It is through *jñāna* you go back to your own source which is also the source of the universe. 'What is this universe? Where has it come from? What is its true nature? What is my true nature?'—This kind of understanding, the whole process of it, is known as *jñāna*. So, *jñāna* is able to take us back to the original state, to understand what is that ultimate reality, that Brahman. All cosmic matter is subject to processes. We human beings are also partly being processed by nature. But, we can also process ourselves. We can stop the process of nature. We have that freedom. This is what takes us to the higher levels of *jñāna*. No non-human species in the world has *jñāna* except of the most elementary kind: they can understand this little material world. *Jñānamasti samastasya jantor viṣaya gocare.* In the *Devī Māhātmyam,* a very great book, 'the Glory of the Divine Mother', occurs this *śloka* (1. 47). 'For all these creatures, their knowledge exists only in their sensory apparatus.' That is all. Nothing higher than the sensory knowledge. Some sensation comes, and some reaction takes place. That action-reaction process is the knowledge they have, all limited by the sensory system. It is only in the human being that we find the capacity to go beyond the sensory level of knowledge into the intellectual level of knowledge. That knowledge can be further developed into the knowledge of the ultimate reality, the Brahman; that reality's name itself is knowledge; it is *jñāna svarūpa* or *cit svarūpa.*

The process, called by mistake creation, starts with: 'I am one, let me become the many.' In the process of cosmic evolution, that Consciousness remains latent and becomes patent when cosmic evolution rises to the level of organic evolution. When that organic evolution proceeds further and further, that truth of consciousness manifests more and more, developing into self-consciousness in the human being from being only consciousness of the objective world in the pre-human species. The human being evolves to realize the eternal purity, freedom, and universality of that infinite Consciousness or Brahman or Atman. That ultimate Reality is beyond name and form; but some tentative name has to be given to understand it, hence the words Atman or Brahman. In his commentary on the *Bṛhadāraṇyaka Upaniṣad* (1. 4. 7), Śaṅkarācārya utters this caution, explaining the use of *iti* in *Ātmā iti; iti* means thus: *yaḥ tu ātma-śabdasya iti paraḥ prayogaḥ, ātmaśabda pratyayayoḥ ātma-tattvasya paramārthato aviṣayatvam jñāpanārtham*—'the use of the particle *iti,* along with the word "Atman" ... only signifies that the truth of Atman (the Self) is really beyond the scope of the term and the concept of "Atman" (or "Self").'

It is this evolution that results in the development of what the *Gītā* has referred to as *jñāna* and *jñānāgniḥ.* It cannot be produced from the dull dead material background of the current modern Western astronomy. How childish it looks to trace Einstein's theory of relativity or the infinite compassion of a Jesus or a Buddha to that background material! The *Gītā* will tell more about this and give a wider definition of nature than what modern Western science understands, in verses 4 to 7 in the seventh chapter.

Therefore, here is a great challenge before the human mind. Let us be part of the cosmic process, but let us be also the observer of that process. That is a wonderful word, 'observer', in Sanskrit, *sākṣi.* You are outside of it. You are watching it, you are seeing it. You are trying to know it. You can control it. Then you turn to yourself. Try to understand the body, its various sensory systems, psychic system, and what lies beyond it. What is my true nature? That infinite Atman, our original source, that pure consciousness, is pulsing in me. I can realize that truth. This is something wonderful. That is the supreme uniqueness of the human being. The famous mathematician-mystic, I think Blaise Pascal, made a beautiful statement: 'In space, the universe engulfs me and reduces me to a pinpoint.' That is the first sentence. Physically speaking, spatially speaking, what are we?, a small speck of dust in the immensity of the universe! That is called part of the cosmic process. Is it all? Having said this, in the next sentence Pascal says: 'But *through thought we understand that universe.*' That infinite universe that is engulfing me, we are able to comprehend it with this power of thought when *jñāna* appears in us! That is the greatest mystery of the human being. If you don't accept this mystery, you have not understood even a bit of the science of human possibilities. This is slowly dawning on Western physical science, especially its nuclear science, today, where the observer is becoming an important datum for investigation. By the *act* of observation, we change the nuclear phenomenon. Therefore, it is a big datum to be investigated. Let us try to investigate it. That is the situation in physical science.

So, the *jñānam* which is mentioned in this 37th verse is that infinite pure consciousness, pulsing in you and me, and in all. We neglect it. We don't take care of it. In our day-to-day life when we go to school and try to gain knowledge, we are actually engaged in seeking the pulsing of knowledge ever within us. Says Swami Vivekananda: 'education is the manifestation of the perfection already within the human being.' But we mostly neglect it. We only stuff the brain with some facts and formulae, and live an indifferent life, just like a part of the processes of nature. What about your uniqueness? That is what you have to discover. When you do so, this *śloka* becomes meaningful. *Sarvam karmākhilam pārtha jñāne parisamāpyate,* 'all *karma* in its entirety, O Pārtha, finds its consummation in *jñāna.*' All these processes came from the infinite consciousness, the infinite reality behind this universe, from Brahman. In our *Sanātana Dharma's* theological language we say, Brahman as Viṣṇu, the infinite reality, prompted Brahmā, the Reservoir of all knowledge, who came from the navel lotus of Viṣṇu, to evolve the universe. The entire process of the universe began from Brahmā in the masculine. The other is Brahman, in the neuter gender. So, that is how, in theological language as well as artistic language, we describe the nature of the reality and the process. Brahmā knew that within himself is the infinite Brahman. He projected this universe out of Himself. It started with a *sphoṭa,* i.e., explosion, through the mental activity of Brahmā. Brahmā heard a sound. Looked around, nobody was there. Wherefrom has this sound come? And what was this sound? It was *tapaḥ, tapaḥ,* do *tapas,* do *tapas.* What kind of *tapas? Jñāna-tapas, yasya jñānamayam tapaḥ.* 'His *tapas* is *jñānamaya*'. We are also dealing with *jñānamaya tapas* in the *Gītā.* Through this *jñānamaya tapas* Brahmā projected this universe. *Tapas* transformed itself into a cosmic process, and it is still going on. Śrī Kṛṣṇa will tell further about this subject in verses 16 to 20 of chapter 8.

This Indian truth of consciousness being the source of the universe and not a dense background material is being propounded by the erstwhile materialistic astronomer, Fred Hoyle, in his new book: *The Intelligent Universe,* as I have mentioned earlier.

When we spiritually dissolve the universe in Brahman, we achieve something wonderful. Process will still be going on, but we know that the whole process is nothing but *jñāna* of Brahman. God in Vedanta means that infinite consciousness, *satyam jñānam anantam brahma.* Where is It?, *yo veda nihitam guhāyām,* 'who realizes It hidden in one's own heart'. That infinite one is present in the smallest particle in the universe. That is how we have to realize this truth. That is a great thought occurring in the *Taittirīya Upaniṣad*. *Gītā* is taking from the Upaniṣads the essential teachings, giving it in a form which will be very practical. So, Śrī Kṛṣṇa says: try to convert all action into *jñāna*. That is its own source. That is what is meant by *sarvam karmākhilam pārtha jñāne parisamāpyate*.

Then, try to know this *jñāna* from people who can teach it to you; then comes a high praise of *jñāna*. *Na hi jñānena sadṛśam pavitram iha vidyate*, 'there is nothing so purifying as knowledge, in this world'. All our children would benefit from going to school, if only they know they are in search of *jñāna*. What great change will then come in the educational system and the product of that system! But there is absolutely no understanding of this subject at all, neither from the teachers nor from the students. *Tat svayam yoga samsiddhaḥ kālenātmani vindati*, 'when you are established in it, slowly you will achieve the highest realization of your own true nature'. That supreme knowledge you will experience *in yourself* once you are established in this pursuit of *jñāna*, even as a primary school student. Continue that pursuit of *jñāna*, eventually you will get the highest *jñāna*, undifferentiated, free from all limitations. That is God in Vedanta.

Brahman is described by Vedanta as *jñānasvarūpa*, 'of the nature of *jñāna*', *anubhavasvarūpa*, 'of the nature of experience', *satsvarūpa*, 'of the nature of Truth'. Śaṅkarācārya writes in his Introduction to his *Brahma Sūtras* commentary: *Ātma ekatva vidyā pratipattaye sarve vedāntā ārabhyante*, 'all the Upaniṣads are working to expound the realization of the science of the unity of the Self', and then continues: *anubhava avasānam brahma vijñānam*, 'knowledge of Brahman consummates in the *experience* of Brahman.' By the knowledge of a chair we do not get transformed into a chair. But, when we *know* Brahman, we realize that we are Brahman. In the inner life, all knowing tends to being.

So, all such knowledge is *assimilation*. Swami Vivekananda called education as 'assimilation of ideas'. Whatever knowledge I take in, I become transformed into it. That is how character develops. That is where knowledge progresses smoothly from the secular to the spiritual.

Take a village boy or girl, put him or her to school. Already a purifying agent has come to them. He or she starts to understand oneself and to understand the world. Otherwise, he or she was just a creature. But a little education puts him or her on the road of shedding creatureliness. I am not an item among items, I am an individual.' That is the beginning of *Ātmajñāna*. You continue it, beyond the school and all institutional education, and enter into spiritual education. This is what Śrī Kṛṣṇa is telling here, that you transform your whole life of activity into *jñāna,* into pulsations of knowledge.

When one is established in this *yogasamsiddhi,* 'being established in the *yoga* of *jñāna*', he or she will achieve this knowledge of the Atman, *kālena,* 'in course of time'. We are already in the world process, namely, the evolutionary process; now know that another process is taking you *back to the source.* Sitting in meditation is also a process. You are developing a new type of process, which takes you *back* to your own source, the infinite, the immortal and the divine. From Brahman we came, in Brahman we live, unto Brahman we return, says the *Taittirīya Upaniṣad.* The second process is therefore significant so far as the human being is concerned. He or she alone can find out one's own origin. No other creature in the world can understand its origin. That knowledge comes through the second process known as *nivṛtti,* well explained in the Introduction. The other is *pravṛtti,* mind going out. Here, it is the mind going *in,* the whole of action being transformed from material to spiritual nature. The whole action becoming spiritual.

There is nothing unspiritual in human life. In Vedantic vision, everything is spirituality. That infinite Brahman is in you, in me, in all, pulsing; we neglect it. Don't neglect it, says Śrī Kṛṣṇa. It is that which gives meaning to what you are and what you do. Otherwise, you remain a creature in the hands of the forces of physical nature, of those processes of nature. Don't be so, don't be so, says Vedanta. Try to understand this truth.

Sages have seen the same Atman in every being. That Brahman which is transcendental is also present in all of us. This is the living philosophy expounded by the sages. In the *Svetāsvatara Upaniṣad,* a sage, having discovered this truth by this inward process of *nivṛtti,* discovered his own infinite Atman. And then when he looked out, he found the same Atman in everyone. Then he burst out into a beautiful song:

Tvam strī tvam pumān asi tvam kumāra utavā kumārī;
Tvam jīrṇo daṇḍena vañcasi tvam jāto bhavasi viśvato mukhaḥ —

'Thou art the man, thou art the woman, thou art the boy, *kumāra,* thou art also the girl, the *kumārī,* thou art the old man tottering on the sticks, thou art born in these multiform ways in this world.'

So, when one realizes the Atman in oneself, and looks out, he or she sees the same Atman everywhere. There you have undertaken and succeeded in turning that cosmic process from a 'going out' into a 'coming in': *pravṛtti* to *nivṛtti.* And *nivṛtti* is the source of all values—moral, ethical, spiritual. Blending of *pravṛtti* and *nivṛtti* is what makes for the stability of a civilization. This is what Śaṅkarācārya told us in the Introduction to his *Gītā* commentary which I referred to more fully in the beginning of this book. *Gītā* is the supreme book which combines *pravṛtti* and *nivṛtti* as a totality of human life and human activity. So, both are processes: one is outgoing, the other is incoming. When you begin to think: Is what I am doing correct?, you are already in *nivṛtti;* if you don't think at all, simply do, it is called *pravṛtti.*

In today's politics and other areas of life, we can see so little thinking, so little *nivṛtti* and plenty of *pravṛtti,* full of noise, full of emotion and frenzy. That is why there is so much of violence and crime. There is no *nivṛtti* at all. It is *nivṛtti* that brings morality, ethics, and other high values into society. Human society has to combine these two. That is what is called 'a complete philosophy of life', where all aspects of life are taken into account. That is the Vedanta that is being expounded in the *Gītā.*, based upon the Upaniṣads, according to the statement given in Śaṅkarācārya's Introduction. Creatureliness and freedom are the choices before human beings. If I behave like this, I will remain a creature. If I behave like that, I become free.

Having spoken about the greatness of *jñāna*, Śrī Kṛṣṇa says who will get this *jñāna*.

श्रद्धावान् लभते ज्ञानं तत्परः संयतेन्द्रियः ।
ज्ञानं लब्ध्वा परां शान्तिमचिरेणाधिगच्छति ॥ ३९ ॥

Śraddhāvān labhate jñānam tatparaḥ samyatendriyaḥ;
Jñānam labdhvā parām śāntimacireṇādhigacchati —4. 39

'The person with *śraddhā* or faith and devotion, the master of one's senses, attains (this) knowledge. Having attained knowledge, one attains at once the supreme Peace.'

'If you have *śraddhā*, you will get *jñāna*,' *śraddhāvān labhate jñānam*. *Śraddhā* means faith in oneself, faith in the meaningfulness of this universe. *Śraddhā* is a great virtue, which mere intellectual education can easily destroy. And modern civilization contains so many people who have lost this *śraddhā*. Every third mind is negative. All positive mind is gone. Śaṅkarācārya defines *śraddhā* in a beautiful phrase: *śraddhā* is *āstikya-buddhi*, 'the positive frame of mind is called *śraddhā*'. The other is negative frame of mind. What a beautiful idea! A mind which is positive. When you are jostled in life, you are put into a difficulty, your mind becomes so defeated, you develop a negative state of mind. And the extreme form of negative state of mind, as I have explained before in the introduction, is called the cynical attitude. Absolutely no faith in truth, no faith in human beings, no faith in values. That is called cynicism. *Śraddhā* is the opposite of cynicism. The next *śloka* will deal with the cynical mind. The cynical mind cannot achieve any value, because it scorns all values. When you go to a school or a college, you go with *śraddhā*, 'There is *jñāna* to be achieved, I am going to achieve it here': with this positive attitude. Otherwise, what will you get by going to school and college? *Tatparaḥ*, 'devoted to That', devoted to Truth. *Tat* is the supreme word in Sanskrit for the highest reality. The *Gītā* will tell us in a later chapter: '*Om tat sat,*' 'Om That Truth, as the description of the ultimate Reality; *samyata indriyaḥ,* 'with tremendous discipline of the sensory energies'. You can't rise to knowledge until you discipline the sensory energies. Animals do not discipline sensory energies. But a human being has to discipline them. And today, many in modern civilization do not like the word discipline or even self-discipline. That is short-sighted and unfortunate.

A scientist is doing an experiment regarding a certain aspect of nature. Why does he do so? He has *śraddhā.* He knows there is something hiding in nature; I am here to discover that truth. Suppose he knew in advance that there is no truth at all. Will he ever enter into a scientific inquiry? So, *śraddhā* means the meaningfulness of the world. I have accepted it, I am going in that direction. And I have a faith in myself, that I have the organic capacity to pierce the veil that covers the truth. This is the nature of *śraddhā.* Without *śraddhā* there is no physical science. Without *śraddhā,* there is no spiritual development. I have developed this subject fully in my two lectures in the first volume of the Bharatiya Vidya Bhavan's publication: *Eternal Values for a Changing Society* on 'Science and Religion' and 'Faith and Reason'.

Śrī Kṛṣṇa says, *tatparaḥ,* you are 'in search of truth'. What is the scientist after? He is also after truth. Many appearances are there. But when he penetrates, he finds these are not correct. Keep that as the goal. *Tatparaḥ,* 'devoted to That'. I am in search of Truth. And this human mind alone has 'the capacity to seek Truth', and not to live on mere appearances, or mere physical data. *Tatparaḥ. Samyatendriyaḥ,* 'he or she has disciplined one's sensory energy'. That is why when somebody abuses you, you can immediately abuse him back, but you will restrain yourself. 'No, let me wait and see. Why did he abuse me like this?' If you are a psychiatrist dealing with a psychiatric patient, the patient will abuse the doctor, but the doctor does not return the abuse. He has to understand why the patient has done it. He has to help the patient. Then only is he a doctor. So, *samyatendriyaḥ,* 'having control and discipline over the sensory system'. Then you develop a new mastery of life through a new energy. Then life becomes a pleasure to live. You don't remain a creature of circumstances. *Jñānam labdhvā parām śāntim acireṇādhigacchati,* 'when you get this *jñāna,* in no distant time you will achieve supreme peace', that peace coming from the centre of all peace, namely, the Atman: *Śānto'yam ātmā,* 'this Atman is all peace', says the Upaniṣad. What is the Atman? *Śanti* or peace. Peace, where all tensions have been resolved, that is called the Atman and that is our true nature.

I was asked to speak in the Deaking's University in Australia, near Melbourne, in 1986. They had also given me a cassette. There the subject was 'Religion and International Peace'. There this subject came up. That peace that comes from the deepest level of the human personality alone is peace. At the sensory level, there is tension. At the psychic level, there is tension. A touch of the Atman can bring peace into both the levels. If you realize the Atman fully, then you become a centre of infinite peace. This is the truth of the human being from the physical to the spiritual dimension. The university students attended the talk calmly, they were taking notes, they were very happy, they had not heard this kind of presentation before. Vedanta gives you a new insight into this subject. So, *jñānam labdhvā parām śāntim acireṇādhigacchati. Cireṇa* means long after. *Acireṇa,* not at all long after, but very soon. On the contrary,

अज्ञश्चाश्रद्दधानश्च संशयात्मा विनश्यति ।
नायं लोकोऽस्ति न परो न सुखं संशयात्मनः ॥४०॥

Ajñaśca aśraddadhānaśca saṃśayātmā vinaśyati;
Nāyam loko'sti na paro na sukham saṃśayātmanaḥ —4. 40

'The ignorant person, the person without *śraddhā,* the doubting self, goes to destruction. The doubting self has neither this world nor the next nor happiness.'

Ajña, 'the ignorant person', *aśraddadhānaśca,* 'the person without *śraddhā*', the cynical mind, *saṃśayātmā,* 'constantly doubting person', *vinaśyati,* 'perishes'. He or she won't proceed higher, but will remain as he or she is, a creature. *Samśayātmā vinaśyati,* 'one full of doubts perishes'. In the Introduction to this book, I have referred to the discussion of this subject by Sylvano Ariety in the third volume of *Handbook of American Psychiatry,* where he says that American children must soon be rescued from this evil of too much doubting and the steps needed to correct it. Any one-sided intellectual development makes for cynicism. That capacity to love, to understand, and to become one with others, it is that capacity that makes one creative. He or she is touching some deeper core in one's own being. So, Śrī Kṛṣṇa is saying here: *Ajñaśca aśraddadhānaśca samśayātmā vinaśyati.* Three types: *ajña, aśraddadhāna, samśayātmā,* they all go together, 'the ignorant, the faithless, and the one who is full of doubts'. Here *ajña* is used in a wider sense, not a villager who has not gone to school; he is not the real *ajña;* he knows much more than you and I do about higher values. But *ajña* refers to the intellectual who is *ajña* of the higher levels of life, higher values of life. They have no sense of values. That is *ajña. Samśayātmā,* 'the doubting self', *vinaśyati,* 'is destroyed'.

In every society you can find bundles of people of this nature, spiritually dead, uncreative. Something has happened to them. They have become stagnant. That is the most dangerous thing. It is spiritual death. Physical death is not so serious as spiritual death for the human being who is so high in evolution. Don't die spiritually. Be alive, be full of joy, full of zest in life, take interest in the welfare of other people. In this way, live. That is called a *śraddhāvān,* if that is not there, *aśraddadhāna.* Such a person *vinaśyati,* 'is destroyed'. With this kind of destruction, all creativity goes, he or she gets stuck up at the sensory level and remains there. *Nāyam loko'sti na paro na sukham samśayātmanaḥ. Samśayātmā,* 'the doubting person' can win neither this world, nor the next, nor happiness. They can't make good friends, they can't behave with other people in a happy way, nothing is possible because they are spiritually dead. So, this world they lose, and what lies beyond this, the ultimate reality, that also they lose. Now, the fourth chapter ends with two great wonderful and powerful verses, 41 and 42.

योगसंन्यस्त कर्माणं ज्ञानसंछिन्न संशयम् ।
आत्मवन्तं न कर्माणि निबध्नन्ति धनञ्जय ॥४१॥

Yogasamnyasta karmāṇam jñānasamchinna samśayam;
Ātmavantam na karmāṇi nibadhnanti dhanañjaya —4. 41

'With work renounced by *yoga* and doubts rent asunder by spiritual knowledge, O Dhanañjaya, actions do not bind one who is poised in the Self.'

O Arjuna, that person who is of such-and-such nature, no action can bind him or her. Such a person is free, even in this body, even while living and working in this world. What are those conditions? *Yogasamnyasta karmāṇam*, 'one who has renounced all actions in *yoga*'. Spiritually he or she has transformed actions into knowledge, burnt them in the fire of knowledge. *Yogasamnyasta karmāṇam* means not merely giving up actions, leave the town or village, go to the jungle, and say to yourself: 'I have given up all action'. Not that type of people, but one who is acting, is busy, and yet he or she has renounced all of them through *yoga*. Such a person, *jñāna samchinna samśayam*, 'who has destroyed all doubts through *jñāna*'. *Jñāna* has come, doubts have completely been destroyed. Such a person, *ātmavantam*, 'who is fully established in the Self', 'O Arjuna, no *karma* can ever bind', *na karmāṇi nibadhnanti dhanañjaya*. That is the wonderful verse here. *Samchinna* means 'destroying', knowledge destroying all doubts, *ātmavantam*, 'self-possessed', established in his or her own infinite Self, *na karmāṇi nibadhnanti*, 'no *karmas* can bind that person'. The last verse is similar. Therefore, if that is the truth, Śrī Kṛṣṇa is exhorting Arjuna, and through him all of us, in this modern age:

तस्माद् अज्ञानसंभूतं हृत्स्थं ज्ञानासिनात्मनः ।
छित्त्वैनं संशयं योगमातिष्ठ उत्तिष्ठ भारत ॥४२॥

Tasmād ajñānasambhūtam hṛtstham jñānāsinātmanaḥ;
Chitvainam samśayam yogamātiṣṭha uttiṣṭha bhārata—4. 42

'Therefore, cutting with the sword of knowledge, this doubt about the Self, born of ignorance residing in your heart, resort to *yoga*, and arise, O Bhārata!'

Therefore, Śrī Kṛṣṇa says, this doubt, *hṛtstham*, 'that is creeping into your heart', crippling your life and action, destroy that doubt. *Ājñānasambhūtam*, 'born out of *ajñāna*, ignorance or spiritual blindness'. That is creating doubts and uncertainties in your mind. Therefore, destroy it. How to destroy it?, *jñānāsinā*, 'by making *jñāna* into a sword', cut across the jungle of doubts and confusion in you. Here *jñāna* is compared to a sword; *asi* means sword. *Chittvā*, 'by destroying', these doubts and confusions; *enam*, 'this', this particular trouble that is on us now, our doubts, difficulties, confusions within, because there is not the fire of *jñāna* within. Take *jñāna* as a sword and cut across this jungle of doubts and uncertainties. Then, *yogam ātiṣṭha*, 'rise up to the level of *yoga*', and *uttiṣṭha bhārata*, 'stand up! O Arjuna!' Arjuna was depressed at that time. The Upaniṣad says this again and again, *uttiṣṭha, uttiṣṭha.* Śrī Kṛṣṇa also says so in the *Gītā:* verse 37 of chapter 2 and verse 33 of chapter 11. *Yogam ātiṣṭha, uttiṣṭha bhārata*, 'rise up to *yoga*, and *stand up!*' Stand up to break down this kind of doubt and these weaknesses within, cut them off. You can achieve it. Nature has given you the capacity. Utilize all those capacities and achieve freedom, freedom from doubt, freedom from fear. What a beautiful and powerful message is going to humanity from this great teacher, Śrī Kṛṣṇa! The *Kaṭha Upaniṣad* also sends out this summons to all humanity in its third canto of the first chapter: *Uttiṣṭhata jāgrata, prāpya varān nibodhata*—'Arise, Awake, and approaching noble people enlighten yourself!' Swami Vivekananda gives a free rendering of this verse thus: 'Arise, awake, and stop not till the goal is reached.' This is the last verse of this fourth chapter. The third chapter, we have seen, also ended with a similar clarion call: 'Thus, knowing the Atman that is superior to and beyond *buddhi*, or reason and will combined, and restraining the sense organs through the Self, O mighty armed, conquer the enemy, in the form of *kāma* or unrestrained lust, so hard to conquer!'

इति ज्ञान कर्म संन्यास योगो नाम चतुर्थोऽध्यायः।

Iti jñāna karma sannyāsa yogo nāma caturtho'dhyāyaḥ —

'The end of chapter four, designated, *The Way of Renunciation of Action in Knowledge.*'

Index

A Week on the Concord and Merrimack Rivers, 55.
Abhīḥ, 94, 95.
Abhyudaya, 27, 28–30. *See also* Society: welfare of.
Acropolis, 54.
Acton, Lord, 285.
Acyuta, 76. *See also* Govinda.
Adharma, 65; causes of its increase, 50–51, 56–57, 358.
Adhyātma vidya, 182.
Adhyātmika vikāsa, importance of, 210–211. *See also* Spiritual: growth.
Advaita, 16, 34. *See also* Non-dual; Sri Ramakrishna on, 471.
Advaitic: *jñāna*, 471; vision, 346, 413.
Aitareya Upaniṣad, 249.
Ajāta śatru, 153; highest state of human development, 103.
Al Beruni: on India of 11th century, 469.
Alexander (Greek Emperor), 63.
Ambedkar, Dr. B, R, 424.
Ambrose (Bishop of Rome), 64, 417; statement of, contrasted with Pope Paul VI, 417.
America, 30, 40, 42, 44, 48, 54, 55, 56, 64, 90, 92, 127, 137, 156, 271; a national song of the people of, 117; consumerism in, 282, 317. *See also* Consumerism; impulse release philosophy of, 335; transcendentalist movement in, 54–55. *See also* Transcendentalist movement; withdraws from Vietnam war, 105; women's liberation movement in, 270.
American: civil war, 77; civilization, 54. *See also* Civilization; civilization on decline, 53–54; culture, 31. *See also* Culture; war against Hitler's Nazi ideology justified, 105.
American Handbook of Psychiatry, 30, 455, 487.
Ānanda (bliss): three levels of, 238. *See also* Happiness.
Anantavijaya, 74.
Anāsakti-yoga, 178, 184, 426.
Anger, 35, 50, 400; cause & effect of, 234–235; control of, 223, 394–399; uncontrolled, & desire causes crime, 315–327.
Animals, 34, 120; behaviour of, 159; cannot control feelings, 97; cannot control nature, 308; cannot oppose thumb to the forefinger, 18; cannot seek knowledge, 17, 126, 129, 406; have no ego, 179; observation of behaviour of, in our literature, 226.
Anuśāsana Parva, 25-26.
Anuṣṭup, 15.
Archimedes, 340.
Ariety, Sylvano, 455, 487; on creativity & its cultivation, 31–32.
Arjuna, 12, 18, 22, 97, 106. *See also* Dhanañjaya; conch of, 74; could not be persuaded by Kṛṣṇa to act on the basis of metaphysical vision, 112; dilemma of, regarding action & inaction, 256–257; in grief, 66, 77–78, 85, 110–111; Kṛṣṇa's reaction to the emotional breakdown of, 85–89, 93, 109; nervous breakdown of, 78–83;

Mind (contd.)
chological refinery, 397–399, 410–411; role of, in control of psychophysical energy, 328; *śama* & *dama*, 190, 192; spiritualizing a restless, 451–452; state of Kṛṣṇa's, 111; states of, 170–171; strength of, 116–117; study of, in western psychology, 214; subtler than sensory system, 347; training of, 158–165, 221–225, 255–256, 320, 324–325; tranquillity of, & its result, 236–238; unshakeable nature of the, established in Self, 245–246, 285; *vāsanas*, 324; when does, become free from all cravings, 226–229.
Mobocracy, 138.
Modern, 27, 30, 34; biology, 120; concept of evolution in, biology, 42, 201; man reduced to machine, 29; physics, 120; science moving towards Vedanta, 122, 123; science purging out materialism from itself, 121; western civilization will not die, 63–64.
Modern Man in Search of a Soul, 280.
Mokṣa, 252; *See also* Freedom; two paths for attaining, 258–259.
Mudra. *See Jñāna mudra*.
Mukti, 160. *See also Mokṣa*.
Muṇḍaka Upaniṣad, 122, 352; denounces post-mortem attainment of fulfillment, 252–253; imagery of two birds, 338–339; universe is brahman, 250, 404.
Muni: awareness of a, compared to that of an ordinary person, 244; definition of, 400.
Muslim, 63, 124, 142.
Mussolini, 371.
My Master (the lecture), 44–47, 64, 295.
Mysticism, 180.
Mystics: experiences of, of all religions, 338, 418.

Naciketa, 327.
Naiṣkarma See Work.
Naiṣkarmyasiddhiḥ, 258.
Nakula: conch of, 74.
Nanak, Guru, 191.
Nanavarthy, Piloo, 416.
Nārada, 21.
Nārāyaṇa, Lord, 16; beyond nature, 24–25; incarnates as Śri Kṛṣṇa, 36, 41, 65; who is, 26.
National Geographic Magazine: on sun the great mother, 356, 448.
Nature, 21, 29. *See also Prakṛti;* concept of interconnectedness of things in, 266–277; ecological cycle, *274–275*; is the manifestation of divine consciousness, 302; Occidental concept of, 46; spell of, over us and how to get out of it, 296–301, 306–312; those who break the law of interconnectedness of, *276–277*; two dimensions of, 25, 131, 345–346; undifferentiated, 24.
Nazi ideology: war against Hitler's, justified, 105, 151.
Nehru, Jawaharlal: on Swami Vivekananda, 95.
Nehru, Motilal, 60.
Neurology, 18, 97, 147, 160, 179, 189, 322; control of sense organs, 334, 450; meaning of homeostasis for man, 164, 189–190, 408; physical & psychical homeostasis, 164; role of cerebral